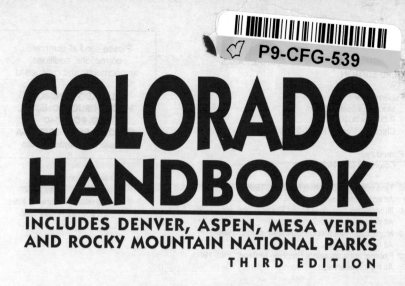

COLORADO HANDBOOK

INCLUDES DENVER, ASPEN, MESA VERDE AND ROCKY MOUNTAIN NATIONAL PARKS

THIRD EDITION

STEPHEN METZGER

MOON
PUBLICATIONS INC.

COLORADO HANDBOOK
INCLUDING DENVER, ASPEN, MESA VERDE AND ROCKY MOUNTAIN NATIONAL PARKS
THIRD EDITION

Published by
Moon Publications, Inc.
P.O. Box 3040
Chico, California 95927-3040, USA

Printed by
Colorcraft Ltd., Hong Kong

ISBN: 1-56691-044-7
ISSN: 1085-2697

Editor: Pauli Galin
Editorial Assistant: Lisa Stowell
Copy Editor: Nicole Revere
Production & Design: Karen McKinley, Carey Wilson
Cartographer: Brian Bardwell
Index: Deana Corbitt Shields

Front cover photo: Breckenridge, CO: Peaks Ten, Nine, and Eight
by Todd Powell courtesy of Photo Network
All photos by Stephen Metzger unless otherwise noted.

Distributed in the U.S.A. by Publishers Group West
Printed in Hong Kong

Please send all comments,
corrections, additions,
amendments, and critiques to:

**COLORADO HANDBOOK
MOON PUBLICATIONS, INC.
P.O. BOX 3040
CHICO, CA 95927-3040, USA
e-mail: travel@moon.com**

Printing History
1st edition — May 1992
2nd edition — January 1994
3rd edition — May 1996

For Betsy and Gina

IS THIS BOOK OUT OF DATE?

In the 1930s, Scribners' editor Maxwell Perkins visited Ernest Hemingway in the Florida Keys. One day they went fishing together, and Perkins, taken by the beauty of the landscape, asked Hemingway why he had never written about it. "Because I haven't been away from it for ten years," he answered.

That's the novelist's luxury—to visit a place, reflect on it, and then later describe it, embellishing where necessary. Unfortunately, travel writers can't do that. Readers want to know *exactly* what to expect when they're traveling. So the writer's got to get to work immediately, recording precisely what he saw, and the publisher's got to get the book in the stores as soon as possible. And though ostensibly the result is a general accuracy that makes the reader's trip more enjoyable, there's a trade-off: Because restaurants come and go, motels raise their prices, and new roads get built, some specific details may be irrelevant or just plain wrong by the time you're reading about them.

If that's the case, we want to hear about it. We're continually working to revise and update these pages, so if you come across an error or omission in the *Colorado Handbook*, write and let us know. We particularly welcome letters from Coloradans who want to share an insider's view and from travelers who've run into problems other visitors should know about. Also, if you find a map or maps difficult to read, or have a suggestion for a map you think would be helpful, please contact us. Be as specific as you can, and document your sources when possible.

Because observations made in the field are usually the most reliable, feel free to jot down notes in the margins of your *Colorado Handbook*. Send it to us, and all contributions will be acknowledged. (Of course we also love to hear from readers who found the book, or sections of it, accurate and useful.)

Address all correspondence to:

Colorado Handbook
c/o Moon Publications, Inc.
P.O. Box 3040
Chico, CA 95927-3040
e-mail: travel@moon.com

CONTENTS

MAPS

MAP SYMBOLS

	INTERSTATE		WATER		FREEWAY
	U. S. HIGHWAY	o	TOWN		MAIN HIGHWAY
	STATE HIGHWAY	o	CITY		OTHER ROADS
	SKI AREA	▲	MOUNTAIN		UNPAVED ROAD
	POINT OF INTEREST		BRIDGE		STATE BORDER
	ACCOMMODATION	△	CAMPGROUND		COUNTY BORDER
					OTHER BORDER

SPECIAL TOPICS

ABBREVIATIONS

BLM—Bureau of Land Management
CO—Colorado, also Colorado State
    Highway
d—double
DIA—Denver International Airport
elev.—elevation
F—Fahrenheit
I—Interstate

km—kilometers
pop.—population
RV—recreational vehicle
s—single
tel.—telephone
US—US Highway
USGS—United States Geological Survey
WPA—Work Projects Administration

COLORADO
HANDBOOK
SECTION
DIVISIONS

NORTHWEST

Walden
Steamboat Springs
Craig
Glenwood Springs

NORTH CENTRAL

Fort Collins
Greeley
Loveland
Longmont
Estes Park
Lyons
Boulder
Nederland
Central City
Kremmling

DENVER AREA

Denver
Black Hawk
Idaho Springs
Castle Rock

SUMMIT COUNTY

Vail
Frisco
Dillon
Breckenridge

Leadville
Aspen
Fairplay
Buena Vista
Gunnison
Salida

SOUTHWEST

Grand Junction
Delta
Montrose
Ouray
Telluride
Silverton
Del Norte
Pagosa Springs
Durango
Cortez

NORTHEAST

Julesburg
Wray
Sterling
Fort Morgan
Burlington
Cheyenne Wells
Limon

SOUTHEAST

Lamar
Las Animas
Springfield
La Junta

SOUTH CENTRAL

Colorado Springs
Cañon City
Pueblo
Walsenburg
Trinidad
Alamosa

© MOON PUBLICATIONS, INC.

PREFACE

I didn't realize it at the time, but I actually began work on this book nearly 25 years ago, the first time the Rockies loomed in front of me as I barrelled westward from California in an attempt to shake free from what I then perceived of as the shackles of adolescence.

January, 1973. I am 18 years old and speeding east across Utah on US 40 in my Mustang convertible. It is sometime between midnight and dawn, and my radio is picking up a megawatt AM rock station out of Oklahoma City or Fort Worth. Between bursts of static, Don McLean is singing about Chevys, levees, American pie, and the day the music died.

I have just graduated from high school, having taken an accelerated course of study in order to finish early. Behind me on the seat is nearly everything I own—a suitcase full of long underwear, flannel shirts, and ragged sweaters; my ski boots; a rolled-up poster of Jean-Claude Killy; a dog-eared copy of *On the Road;* and my notebook. The trunk rack, which I can see through the rear-view mirror and the rip in the plastic back window, holds my skis and poles, which angle into the dark. The heater blasts, does little good.

Before me stretches a Colorado I have never seen, although my mind carries a vague image, drawn from years of magazine articles and "Ski the High Country" ads: big blue sky, cold dry snow, miles and miles of great skiing, Aspen, Vail, Steamboat, and Telluride. My excitement is fueled by a strange love-fear of the unknown that works across my shoulders, down into my chest, and manifests itself in my hand, which trembles slightly when I lift it from the steering wheel.

As the sky grows pink in the east, I stop in Craig for breakfast and coffee, take a seat at the counter of a small diner. A couple of the ranchers and truckers glare at me as though my long hair threatens the existence of free enterprise itself. I eat my hashbrowns and wish I'd had the sense not to put Stevie Wonder on the jukebox.

February. I am sitting inside a lift shack at the top of the Continental Divide. It is my first day of work as a ski-lift operator at Arapahoe Basin. The sky is bluer than I have ever seen it—except where a silvery jet and its trail of vapor slice across it—and the mountains are whiter and more rugged. I am well above the timberline. I watch the skiers ride by on the chairs, unload, tighten their boots, slip their pole straps over their wrists, and take off—some timid, some defiant, all awestruck, as am I, by the peaks and the white and the granite and the sheer majesty of the Rockies at 13,000 feet. At 4 p.m., I stash my notebook in my parka pocket, shut the lift down, lock the door to the shack, and head down with the ski patrol, our skis chattering through the shadows of the closing day.

March. I am standing on the highway just outside Breckenridge, trying to thumb a ride up to Arapahoe. A light snow is falling, but the clouds are growing darker and promise a storm. My Mustang has broken down—two months of neglect in sub-teen temperatures has left it badly in need of a tune-up. But I can't afford that: I have just spent all but a couple of bucks of a two-week paycheck on a brand new pair of skis.

I hoist them onto my shoulder and begin walking, my thumb in the air. A sharp wind blows through the valley. I turn my coat collar up against the cold. Finally, an old Indian in a Rambler station wagon stops and picks me up. We hardly speak, but the sad wisdom of ages clouds his eyes, forming, with the sparkling innocence of my own, a strange and fearless symmetry.

February, 1982. I am sitting at an outdoor café on the Mediterranean coast of Spain in a tiny town north of Barcelona. I have just finished my third cup of espresso, and the novel I am writing—about a young man who comes of age in the Colorado Rockies—is feverishly coming into focus. I don't know if it's any good; that doesn't matter. What matters is that I am beginning to realize what the mountains mean to me, and how being devoted to skiing during such an impressionable period has affected me. From that far away—both in years and miles—I am seeing that skiing can form the perfect metaphor for how we live our lives, or should. When we ski, we are always testing the limits of our abilities; there is a thrill and a passion to skiing only when we push ourselves, because only when we risk falling do we grow. And, too, skiing is largely about friends and family. Though our turns are finally no one's but our own, the experience is far more meaningful when shared—with friends, with family, or even with strangers who become friends for small spots of time during the course of a chairlift ride or a single run. Even falling can be a source of laughter and joy when there are people nearby to help you up.

January, 1995. A gorgeous, cloudless morning at Arapahoe Basin. I am riding the very lift at the top of which, 22 years earlier, I had spent long cold days behind a window in a tiny shack watching skiers unload, trying to imagine the ways my life would unfold. I am excited about being on the road again, about being in the mountains, about skiing. But I am missing my wife and my young daughters, both of whom have already shown promise on the slopes and a natural and unabashed love of the sport.

My Great American Skiing Novel sits in a drawer in California, unpublished; it turned out not to be very good at all. But that doesn't matter. What matters is that I'm back in Colorado. The mountains are breathtaking, the morning air crisp and invigorating. The skiing will be wonderful.

Next fall, I will begin shopping for two very short pairs of skis.

INTRODUCTION
THE LAND

Laws change; people die; the land remains.

—Abraham Lincoln

Comprising over 100,000 square miles, Colorado is the country's eighth-largest state—twice the size of New York and 10 times as big as New Hampshire. Its landscapes remarkably diverse, the state stretches from the vast eastern plains to the gently sloping western plateau, the majestic Rocky Mountains running north to south just west of center. The state's topographical relief is nearly 11,000 feet: from the 3,350-foot-high bed of the lower Arkansas River to 14,433-foot Mt. Elbert. And to the observant traveler, the state is a living, breathing geology lesson, with deep canyons carved by ancient waterways exposing hundreds of thousands of years of the land's settling, uplifting, shifting, and erosion.

A Long, Long Time Ago . . .
During the first part of the Paleozoic era (240 to 750 million years ago), Colorado was largely flat and entirely submerged beneath the waters of a shallow sea. Toward the end of that era, during the Permian period, mountains began to rise up, waters receded, and muddy, sediment-filled rivers wandered about the plains. The remains of the first uplifts can be seen in the bizarre redrock formations at Garden of the Gods in Colorado Springs and at Red Rocks Amphitheater near Denver.

During the Mesozoic era (70 to 230 million years ago), more mountains rose up, and much of the land was lush and marshy. Dinosaurs sloshed through jungles teeming with primitive life-forms. By the end of the era, however, the dinosaurs were gone. In addition, the Gulf of Mexico had crept north to meet the western shores of the Atlantic Ocean, and Colorado was again entirely submerged; the mountains were now underwater reefs.

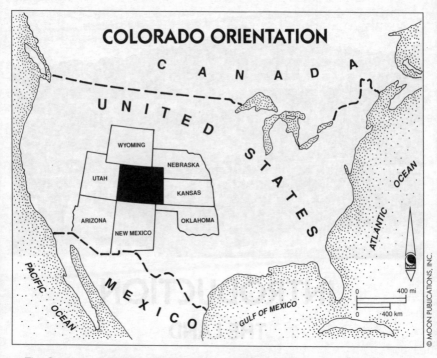

COLORADO ORIENTATION

CANADA

UNITED STATES

WYOMING

NEBRASKA

UTAH

KANSAS

ARIZONA

OKLAHOMA

NEW MEXICO

MEXICO

PACIFIC OCEAN

ATLANTIC OCEAN

GULF OF MEXICO

0 400 mi
0 400 km

© MOON PUBLICATIONS, INC.

The Cenozoic era (beginning 70 million years ago) brought the beginnings of the landscape we see today. Inland seas had receded, though much of the area remained swampy, and mountains were beginning to take forms we might recognize today. During the Pleistocene epoch, starting less than two million years ago, great glaciers advanced and receded over much of North America. During the most recent ice age, however, between 25,000 and 60,000 years ago, the great continental ice sheet did not creep into Colorado, although smaller glaciers continued to carve away at the Rocky Mountains.

By around 20,000 years ago, the climate had begun to warm, and about that time the first humans probably appeared in Colorado. Nomadic hunters, most likely still en route south after having crossed over the Bering Land Bridge, tracked mastodons, mammoths, ground sloths, and antelope across the Eastern Plains and the western plateau area.

The Eastern Plains
The Eastern Plains of Colorado actually begin as far east as the Dakotas and eastern Kansas and Nebraska—then come to a screeching halt just west of Denver, where the Rockies' Front Range looms sharp and massive. Comprising roughly 40% of the state, the plains are marked by vast expanses of low rolling hills and yellow-brown fields of prairie grasses.

Thanks to the development of irrigation systems, these otherwise dry lands are the sites of huge ranches and farms. Herds of cattle graze on sprawling spreads that have been in the same families for a century. Sugar beets, wheat, alfalfa, watermelons, honeydew, and other crops are harvested by hardy farmers who do age-old work with high-tech equipment—cellular phones, computers, and thoroughly modern, air-conditioned tractors.

The Rocky Mountains
The backbone not only of Colorado but of the United States, the Rocky Mountains—and the

Continental Divide, which snakes through them—mark the division point of the sources of all North American waterways. Even those who have seen the Rockies before—even those who live in the Rockies and see and feel them daily—cannot help but be awed by their immenseness and majesty.

Consider: 54 peaks top 14,000 feet (though none tops 15,000), several roadways wind over 11,000-foot passes, and many towns and communities are nestled in valleys 9,000 feet above sea level. Leadville's elevation is 10,188 feet.

The Western Slope and Plateau Country

The western side of the Rocky Mountains slopes much more gradually than does the steep eastern face, and the area from the Continental Divide west to the Utah border is known generally as the Western Slope. For over a hundred years ranchers have taken advantage of these high-elevation flatlands, and hundreds of thousands of cattle graze in these fields from Craig south to Durango. Make no mistake, though: not all of the Western Slope slopes gently, particularly the towering peaks of the San Juan Mountains around Telluride.

In the northwestern corner of the state, the great plateau is largely shale and underlain with vast fields of coal, oil, and natural gas. Remote river canyons slice deep into the earth. The southwestern corner, meanwhile, particularly the Four Corners area, is a land of redrock canyons and mesas, the dry brown land punctuated by clusters of juniper and piñon.

CLIMATE

In Colorado the joke goes, "If you don't like the weather, just wait 15 minutes." And there's some truth to that, to which anyone who's seen a sunny summer day turn suddenly to rain and thunder can testify. In addition, given the state's dramatic range in geography—from the arid plains to the lush mountain meadows of the Rockies to their windswept peaks—it's difficult to make generalizations.

The Rockies

This is where the weather's the least predictable. Keep in mind that it can get *cold* in the winter.

Though it's a dry cold, not nearly as piercing as that damp cold of the coasts, it can still be awfully nasty, especially when the wind blows. Zero-degree temperatures are not at all uncommon in the Colorado Rockies from December to March, and the mercury often drops even lower. Out on the Western Slope, around Gunnison for example, the wind can whip cold and arctic-like across that high plateau. Sub-zero temperatures are not all that rare.

Anyone traveling in the Rocky Mountains in winter should have plenty of warm clothing. Layering is best: Wear a good pair of long underwear (preferably 100% polypropylene), a turtleneck, a wool sweater, and a heavy, water-resistent coat, as well as gloves or mittens and a hat. Also, make sure your footwear keeps you not only warm but *dry*. (See "Hypothermia," under "Health and Safety" following.)

Summer days in the Rockies are often pleasant, into the 80s and even 90s, with the high-elevation sun almost mandating shorts. Remember, though, that afternoon storms are very common, and you should always have warmer clothes and rain gear handy. Also keep in mind that though summer days are warm, night temperatures drop significantly, down into the mid-50s and lower, and if you plan to be outside at night—especially if you're camping—you should have plenty of warm clothing.

The Plains

The climate's not as dramatic out on Colorado's eastern plains as it is in the Rockies. But there are some things to know. First of all, it gets hot, and air-conditioning in your car is more than just awfully nice. Also, summer storms are common; the temperature might be pushing 90° F or even 100° F in mid-afternoon, when all of a sudden thunderheads start building, leaves and dust start swirling, and shadows fall across wheatfields. In fact, the storms on the plains can be even more threatening than those in the mountains, as they often bring with them high winds and even cyclones. In the summer of 1990, a dark twister twirled through the little town of Limon, east of Denver, upending cars and mobile homes and flattening office buildings.

Ordinarily, of course, summer storms on the plains aren't that bad. Still it would be wise to keep rain gear on hand, as well as a coat and a spare pair of shoes. Also, drive especially carefully when that wind whips up and when water pools on the roadways.

Winter on the plains can be harsh. Temperatures dip into the 30s, and biting winds whip across the vast expanses of open fields. Though snow doesn't fall in the amounts it does in the Rockies, it can still pile up in drifts, and sometimes the wind and snow combine in near whiteouts. On the other hand, when the skies are clear and the winds gentle, daytime temperatures can lift into the 60s. In fact, some winter days on the plains are absolutely gorgeous, with views seeming to stretch forever and a cold but tolerable air invigorating you as you draw deep breaths.

Denver

At the western terminus of the Great Plains, Denver, the "Mile-High City," sits snug up against the Front Range of the Rocky Mountains. Summer days are warm but not hot—though occasional heat waves drive temperatures over 100° F—and they're mostly dry; the city receives less than 15 inches of precipitation a year.

During the winter it can get cold, though it's still quite tolerable. Daytime temperatures are generally in the 40s, though they drop considerably at night, often into the 20s and teens. If you plan to explore Denver between October and April, bring warm clothes. Again, layering is best, starting with wicking long underwear and working out to a good wind- and waterproof coat or jacket.

FLORA AND FAUNA

Colorado's widely varied geography and climate make the state home to a huge range of plant and animal life—from the prairie grasses, yucca, fence lizards, spadefoot toads, and pronghorn antelope of the eastern plains to the aspen, spruce, black bears, bighorn sheep, mountain goats, elk, and moose of the Rocky Mountains. In addition, Colorado is home, either part- or full-time, to many different species of birds—owls, pheasants, grouse, geese, ducks, eagles, turkeys, and hundreds of varieties of small birds. Recent field research also indicates the San Juan Mountains of southern Colorado might be home to a handful of grizzly bears, a species whose remaining numbers are so small that the animals had eluded human contact since the 1930s and were thought to be long gone from the area.

Colorado's waters—from the low-lying reservoirs of the eastern plains to the tumbling snow-fed streams of the high mountains—hold many different species of warm- and cold-water fish. Bass, walleye, catfish, bluegill, crappie, and other sunfish are found in the lower lakes, notably John Martin Reservoir near Las Animas and Horsetooth Reservoir near Fort Collins. Trout and kokanee salmon are found in the higher lakes and streams; the most common trout are rainbow and brown, while Mackinaw (lake) trout roam some of the larger, deeper lakes (Grand Lake and Blue Mesa Reservoir, for example).

One of the great joys of visiting Colorado, particularly in the spring and early summer, is seeing the abundant wildflowers that blanket meadows and mountain hillsides. Sheets of bright yellow, blue, and purple contrast dramat-

bighorn sheep

BOB RACE

ically with the backdrops of aspen, fir, and spruce, as well as the great granite snowcapped peaks looming in the distance. Especially beautiful is Colorado's state flower, the columbine, a delicate, commonly light blue to purplish flower that grows in damp meadows either singly or in clusters.

Aspen Trees

Colorado's aspens have become almost mythical. During the winter, these beautiful white-barked trees lose their leaves and stand stoically in groves, skinny and dormant contrasting with the evergreens often found in the same forests. In the spring, the trees begin to bud, and the distinctly shaped "quaking" leaves—pale green at first—reappear. In summer, the leaves begin to yellow, and by fall have turned to stunning electric gold and orange. This is the best time to hike, or drive, into Colorado's aspen forests, though you will not be alone: The vibrant colors attract not only Colorado's color aficionados, but folks from outside the state as well. Tour groups and local boosters have even organized several "color tours" to the various aspen forests.

Bighorn Sheep

One of the other virtual symbols of Colorado is the bighorn sheep. These magnificent beasts, which can weigh up to 350 pounds (and whose horns alone can weigh 35 pounds), are scattered about the state in several specific herds. An article in *Colorado Outdoors* (Nov.-Dec., 1991) lists 13 specific "hot spots" where the animals can best be viewed, including: the Georgetown Wildlife Viewing Area in Georgetown; Rocky Mountain National Park; Poudre Canyon, west of Fort Collins; three spots in the Salida-Buena Vista area; and an area on the east side of US 550 between Ridgway and Ouray.

Elk

One of the highlights of a trip to Rocky Mountain National Park is seeing a big bull elk up close, its huge rack seeming to hold up the sky. Though elk, too, are scattered about the state, and there are many places where you can see them, the park is the best. Here, large herds of elk graze in meadows, huge-antlered bulls wander to within yards of the roadway, and during certain times of the year, the crisp darkness is pierced by their bugling—the music of the night.

HISTORY

THE FIRST COLORADANS

Although recent finds in Central and South America have contributed to contemporary theories of the New World's first human inhabitants, the discoveries in the North American southwest turned anthropology on its ear by proving humans had come across from Asia at least 10,000 years ago, or 8,000 years earlier than previously thought. In the early 1930s, scientists from the University of Denver determined bones found in northeastern New Mexico were from a post-glacial species of bison, long extinct, and embedded in them were spear points used to kill the animal. Since then, Folsom points, as they have come to be called, have been found throughout the southeastern Colorado plains, as well as on the Western Slope near Montrose—proof humans wandered in relatively large numbers in the more temperate regions of Colorado some 10,000 years ago, hunting giant ground sloths, woolly mammoths, and mastodons.

The Anasazi

The first people to settle in what is now Colorado were the Anasazi (the word is Navajo and probably best translated as "Enemies of Our Ancestors"). As early as A.D. 550, Anasazi of the Basketmaker period had begun migrating north from the Rio Grande area of central New Mexico and were building pit houses in the Four Corners area, particularly around Mesa Verde. Between A.D. 750 and 1100, the Developmental Pueblo period, Anasazi architecture changed from primitive pit houses to above-ground shelters, which were often built in clusters to provide homes and storage for several families. In addition, stone towers 10-15 feet tall were built near these early pueblos, suggesting a need for lookouts. At the same time, they were developing a distinct pottery style, characterized by intricate black designs on a white background, as well as sophisticated water-storage and irrigation systems.

During the Classic Pueblo period, A.D. 1100-1300, the Anasazi further developed their architecture. Some single pueblos contained over 400 rooms and were four stories tall; some of these pueblo "cities" were home to 5,000 or more people. Around A.D. 1150, many of the Anasazi of southwestern Colorado began to move into cliff-side alcoves. Although no one knows the real reason for the move, anthropologists suspect it might have been to secure themselves from enemy attack (although no real evidence of enemies or violence has been found) or to protect themselves from the elements. These cliff dwellings are best seen at Mesa Verde National Park, near Durango.

By 1300, the cliff dwellings, as well as the free-standing pueblos scattered about the Four Corners area, had all been abandoned. And again, no one knows why. At one time it was thought the Navajos and Apaches arrived from the north and drove them out, although modern thinking is these tribes didn't show up until around 1450. The most commonly accepted theory today is the Anasazi overfarmed the little valleys in which they grew their corn, beans, and squash; then they simply headed for greener pastures, most likely filtering southwest back toward the Rio Grande area. It's generally assumed that today's Zuni, Acoma, Taos, Sandia, and other Pueblo peoples are descendants of the Anasazi.

The Shoshone and Algonquin Tribes

Between the time the Anasazi disappeared and the white man arrived, Colorado was home to several tribes, most of whom were from the Shoshone and Algonquin linguistic stocks. The most widely spread and the largest in terms of numbers were the Utes, a Shoshonean mountain-dwelling people who roamed from the eastern mountain passes, which they guarded against the Plains tribes, to the lower reaches of the Western Slope.

The Plains tribes, primarily Cheyenne, Comanche, Arapahoe, and Kiowa, hunted the great flatlands east of the Rockies. Often at war with each other, they arrived some time after the

Utes, probably having been pushed west by other groups. Other tribes of Colorado included Pawnee, Sioux, and Navajo; Blackfoot and Crow hunting parties probably ventured south into the north central part of the state.

THE ARRIVAL OF THE WHITE MAN

Early Exploration

Most likely the first explorers in Colorado were members of the Francisco Vásquez de Coronado expedition, who might have drifted north from New Mexico in 1541 in their search for the fabled Seven Gold Cities of Cíbola. Unlike in New Mexico, where records indicate Coronado was responsible for the widespread rape and murder of native people, the expedition apparently didn't do much damage in Colorado.

During the early 18th century, Spain and France both sought title to the western plains, and the Spanish, pushing up from New Mexico, began to explore the San Luis Valley area of south central Colorado. French trappers and traders, meanwhile, pushed west into the mountains. Spain, however, had a stronger hold on the region, and by 1762, France had ceded to Spain all land west of the Mississippi.

In 1776, friars Francisco Antanasio Dominguez and Silvestre Velez de Escalante traveled through southwestern Colorado in search of an overland route that would connect the missions of New Mexico with those of California. The expedition not only provided the first written record of Colorado exploration but also gave the area many of its place names, including the San Juan and Sangre de Cristo mountains and El Rio de las Animas Perdidos en Purgatorio ("The River of the Lost Souls in Purgatory").

The Louisiana Purchase

In 1803, two years after Spain had been forced to turn over its hold on northern Colorado to the French, President Thomas Jefferson bought the Louisiana Territory from Napoléon. Though he was ridiculed at the time for squandering $15 million on real estate that was almost wholly unexplored, the Louisiana Purchase doubled the size of the United States and, as every schoolchild knows, turned out to be a pretty decent deal in the long run.

The First American Explorations

The first American to explore the Colorado area was Zebulon Pike, who pushed into the mountains west of Pueblo and Colorado Springs in 1806. In his journal, Pike described the peak that was named for him as "unscalable."

In 1820, President James Monroe dispatched Major Stephen H. Long to explore the new territory's northern boundary, which had been established a year earlier along the Arkansas River and into the mountains along the Continental Divide. Long's party followed the South Platte River west, then dropped south along the Arkansas, ultimately veering west again near Colorado Springs and venturing as far as Royal Gorge. (One of Long's men, Dr. Edwin James, led the first recorded ascent of Pikes "unscalable" Peak.)

Trappers, Traders, and Colorado Territory

In September 1821, Mexico won its independence from Spain, and almost immediately the United States and Mexico began vigorous trading, with pack trains departing regularly from Missouri for Santa Fe. The Santa Fe Trail, as the route was known, cut across southeastern Colorado and helped further develop this otherwise hostile land. Forts and trading posts were established along the trail, most notably Bent's Fort near Las Animas, providing gathering places for trappers, traders, and mountain men, Americans, French, and Native Americans.

The United States declared war on Mexico on May 13, 1846, and two years later, the Treaty of Guadalupe Hidalgo was signed, which ceded to the U.S. a large chunk of land running from Texas west to California, including some of southern Colorado. Now, all of what is now Colorado belonged to the U.S., although a Colorado Territory was still 15 years down the road.

SILVER THREADS AND GOLDEN NEEDLES

"Pikes Peak or Bust"

Gold was discovered in September 1858 on several waterways near what is now Denver, and within weeks a number of buildings had sprung up along area riverbanks, forming the first traces of what would soon develop into the

state's largest city. Word of the strike quickly spread to the East Coast, and a flood of prospectors began their way west. Their motto, after the prominent landmark just to the south, was "Pikes Peak or Bust."

With the onset of winter, little mining could be done, and while the little settlements grew, so did their inhabitants' anticipation of growing rich. With the thaw, though, came the discovery that the strikes weren't nearly as rich as reported. The summer of 1859 saw thousands of disgruntled fortune seekers heading back the way they'd come, often encountering along the way other Pikes Peak or Busters, many of whom were convinced to turn back long before even reaching the mining camps.

That spring, however, gold was also discovered along Clear Creek in the mountains west of Denver. This time, the strike was for real. Within a matter of days, several mining camps, including Central City, Black Hawk, and Idaho Springs, were teeming with miners. Horace Greeley wrote that at one point 500 men were arriving each day. Over the next few years, dozens of small towns were founded in the nearby mountains, and in 1861, Colorado Territory was officially established.

Early Ranching and Agriculture

During the early days of Colorado Territory, ranchers and farmers began to see the potential of the area's fertile river valleys and vast expanses of grazing lands. The eastern plains and much of the Western Slope were seen as ideal places to raise wheat, corn, and other crops, and to let cattle and sheep roam.

But Wait, Didn't the Land Still Belong to the Indians?

Absolutely, insofar as Native American philosophy allowed for "ownership" at all. And even though the United States now owned this land on paper, the Indians still considered it theirs.

The 1860s and '70s, then, were years of conflict, and often these conflicts were violent and bloody. In 1864, about 30 miles west of the Kansas border, U.S. soldiers under Colonel John Chivington wiped out a Cheyenne village of as many as 500 people, the majority of whom were women and children. Chivington, who claimed he thought the camped Cheyenne were hostile, was court-martialed for the Sand Creek Massacre but never convicted.

Battles also raged in the northwestern part of Colorado, where ranchers and farmers were intruding upon Northern Utes. In 1879, Indian agent Nathan Meeker, known for his lack of diplomacy, tried to convince the Utes to give up their hunting lifestyles and turn to farming. Meeker was killed after he sent for troops to support his position. The Utes were subsequently vanquished to a reservation in Utah. Ranchers, farmers, and other settlers now had Colorado all to themselves.

Makin' Tracks
One of the biggest influences on the development and settling of Colorado was the railroad. In the 1870s, railroad tracks began to be laid across the land, linking isolated towns and communities, mining camps, and supply centers. Almost overnight, the wagon trains and stage coaches were replaced by locomotives, though by foot and burro was still the only way to get over some of the high mountain passes. For the first time, people, cattle, food products, ore,

a Ute family

COLORADO HISTORICAL SOCIETY

and other items could be transported quickly and reliably across the vast expanses of Colorado Territory. In addition, the new industry brought thousands of jobs to the area, with stations needing to be built about every 100 miles. From Burlington to Grand Junction, from Durango to Julesburg, the railroad significantly changed the landscape of Colorado and the lifestyles of its people.

In 1876, Colorado achieved statehood.

More Gold and Silver
Between 1880 and the turn of the century, the Colorado mountains were swarming with mining camps. From Aspen to Cripple Creek, from Leadville to Telluride, dozens of tiny communities were bursting at the seams with miners, real estate tycoons, newspapermen (sometimes a town of 5,000 would support 10 newspapers), various bunko artists, and women working to service them. Grand hotels were constructed and lavish parties thrown; elaborate opera houses attracted the biggest names of the day.

After the Gold Rush
And then it all came crashing down. In 1893, silver was devalued, and Colorado's mining camps went into the skids. Mines closed, smelters shut down, and miners hit the road—many of them ending up in Denver where unemployment rates soared. Towns that had once thronged with the newly prosperous were all but deserted. The great hotels and opera houses were boarded up, and banks closed faster than you can say "S and L scandal." Though a handful of towns continued to prosper—Crested Butte, for example, where coal was discovered—Colorado for the most part was in sad shape as the 20th century approached.

THE TWENTIETH CENTURY

The first years of the new century saw great strife between Colorado's mine workers and owners. In Cripple Creek, Victor, and Telluride, particularly, the conflicts were often violent, and on several occasions the National Guard was called in to try to "keep the peace." In 1903 and 1904 miners in Colorado City and Cripple Creek struck to protest a drop in wages, and when

COLORADO HISTORICAL SOCIETY

*early railroad
passengers on
Marshall Pass*

"mysterious" explosions in several mine shafts killed a number of workers, labor blamed management and management blamed labor.

In 1914, the United Mine Workers union organized Trinidad-area coal workers, who struck for better wages and working conditions, and in April, after reports of violence in the camps, the Colorado National Guard was sent in. The conflict came to a bloody head on April 20, when several strikers were killed and tent fires killed 13 women and children.

A Short-Lived Prosperity

During WW I, silver prices rose, and many Colorado mines reopened. Though the mining towns saw a general caution instead of the wild abandon of the late 19th century, at least some of the little towns could again keep their heads above water. In addition, prices of farm produce, particularly wheat, skyrocketed, and Colorado farmers enjoyed a new prosperity and status.

Which didn't last long.

The Depression hit Colorado hard. Farmers, ranchers, miners, and businessmen found themselves without work and, oftentimes, without homes. Fortunately, the federal government stepped in where it could, and several major projects, including the development of schools and national forests, as well as highway and irrigation systems, provided workers with jobs

and the state with a semblance of stability. In 1935 and '36, Colorado revamped its tax systems, with special sales and service taxes set aside for relief.

Another boon to Colorado's economy was the arrival of the military, which largely came about with the advent of WW II. In addition to the United States Air Force Academy just north of Colorado Springs, several other bases were established in the Denver and Colorado Springs areas.

The Ski Industry

As early as the mid-1930s, downhill skiing was already starting to take hold in some of Colorado's tiny mountain communities. Originally just something to keep locals from getting bored during the long winter months, the sport soon caught on, and folks in the lower-lying areas were making weekend treks to the handful of primitive rope tows.

By the late 1960s and early '70s, skiing had grown up, and Colorado was recognized as one of the best places on earth to strap boards afoot, climb aboard a chairlift, and take off through easy wind and downy flake. In fact, not only had the sport grown up, but it had caught on big time, and new resorts were opening each year, while established resorts were cutting new trails and adding new lifts. In the spring of 1973, the first bore of a tunnel through Loveland Pass was completed, providing Denver-area skiers much easier access to the resorts of Summit County, as well as Vail, just over the next pass. By the late 1980s, Eisenhower Tunnel's four lanes already seemed too few, and on winter weekends traffic bottlenecked horribly as skiers descended in increasing numbers on the ski towns of Dillon, Breckenridge, and Vail.

And the numbers just keep growing. The winter of 1990-91 saw 9.79 million skier-visits in Colorado, with the Forest Service estimating a three percent increase over the next 10 years. So of course, new resorts are being planned, with opposition groups already rightfully positioned—can the forests *handle* more lifts, clear-cut trails, condo complexes, parking lots, and *people?* In the early 1990s, at least three new resorts were in the planning stages, though as of late 1995, development was on hold, pending permits and investment revenue. The ski areas of Lake Catamount, seven miles south of Steamboat Springs, Adam's Rib, 35 miles west of Vail, and East Fork, 20 miles southwest of Wolf Creek, all hover in Colorado's future.

What will happen as more and more skiers demand more and more trails in Colorado's decreasing forest areas? Will the state be able to balance the growth of the ski industry with the undeniable need to preserve forests and delicate ecosystems? Will the cost of skiing ($45 a day for a lift ticket, $600 for a pair of skis and boots) naturally curb the sport's growth? Or will the tiny pockets of backwoods Colorado be nothing more than condos and upscale boutiques by the early 21st century? We can only hope common sense, intelligence, and environmental awareness are the guiding factors.

Recent Developments

In the summer of 1990, Colorado voters approved two measures that will effect significant change, in varying ways, upon the state. The first is legalized gambling. Though limited in scope, gambling was legal in parts of Colorado as of October, 1991. Black Hawk, Central City, and Cripple Creek bettors can now play poker, blackjack, and slots ($5 maximum).

On a more positive note, in the same election, voters also approved major-league baseball for Denver. The first two seasons, the Colorado Rockies played in Mile High Stadium (the Denver Bronco's field), but by the 1995 season they had moved into the gorgeous new Coors Field, the building of which has completely transformed the western end of Denver, known as LoDo (Lower Downtown). The empty warehouses and abandoned storefronts dominating the area until as late as 1993 have been replaced, remodeled, and renovated, and now the area is one of brew pubs, bookstores, restaurants, antique shops, and espresso bars, and a general sense of vitality and good, safe fun. Evenings before and after games the area around the stadium is teeming with folks taking pride not only in the team and stadium but in a rejuvenated part of Denver as well. Live music wafts from rooftop restaurants and bars, and vendors hawk peanuts to the steady stream of fans passing through en route to the stadium.

The only downside to the upscaling of LoDo has been the skyrocketing of rents in the area; some office workers, tenants, and even homeless people who had found shelter in abandoned warehouses have been displaced, either unable to afford to stick around, or hustled along by developers.

ECONOMY

Colorado's economy developed in the 19th century on the backs of the mining, agriculture, and railroad industries, and century-old patterns and outcomes can still be seen. One hundred and ten years after mine owners hauled silver down out of Cripple Creek, building luxurious homes with the proceeds from their booty, parts of Colorado Springs, for example, still maintain a monied and upper-class feel about them. Lives

and lifestyles on the eastern plains and Western Slope of the Rockies still hinge on cattle, alfalfa, melon, corn, and barley crops, and folks watch the skies for rain—while they get the latest stock reports on their computers. Oil, silver, gold, molybdenum, and natural gas means paychecks for miners in Summit County, the Four Corners area, and the plains. And trains still chug between mountain towns—carrying camera-toting tourists from around the world, while railroad museums throughout Colorado document the contributions of the iron horse.

These days, however, the state's economy is more dependent on manufacturing, the defense industry, and tourism. With land remaining relatively inexpensive in Colorado, many companies have moved east from California and built plants for the production of computers and other electronic instruments. In addition, military bases around the state, though threatened by post-Cold War budget cuts, employ tens of thousands, and indirectly keep many times that off the dole.

And nearly 10% of the population is involved in some aspect of the tourism industry. Colorado's ski industry is huge: Tiny Summit County alone saw more ski days in 1995 than the entire state of Utah, whose motto is "Ski Utah" and where the 2002 Winter Olympics will be held. And skiing keeps growing, with new ski resorts in the planning stages and new lifts going in every summer at the existing resorts. Plus, summer continues to attract more and more visitors, as the resorts court mountain bikers, golfers, and sightseers, offering cheap lodging and package deals to keep the rooms full.

Responding to Colorado's growth, Denver International Airport was built in the early 1990s, finally opening in February of 1995 and replacing Stapleton Jurassic. A major mid-continental hub, it is expected to be among the nation's three busiest airports by early in the next millennium, providing access to the city's convention centers and the resorts in the mountains just an hour and a half west.

ON THE ROAD

SIGHTSEEING HIGHLIGHTS

The phrase "No visit to Colorado is complete without . . ." probably pops up more than it should in this book. Likewise, when friends ask for help planning itineraries, my list of things I tell them they've *gotta* see and do is probably way too long. But please understand. Not only do I have a passionate love affair with Colorado, but my travels have taken me to so many parts of the state it's difficult even to come up with a Top-10-type list. So ultimately, I suppose, I defer, dear Reader, to you, as you need to make some decisions about what *kind* of trip yours will be: Will you primarily be sightseeing, or will you be enjoying Colorado's myriad recreational activities? Are you more interested in the state's history than in food, wine, and music festivals? Do you want to explore ancient ruins or modern shopping centers? Do you want to see vast meadows blanketed in white, or mountain hillsides ablaze with brilliant golds and deep, fiery reds?

Once you've answered those questions, you can begin looking at what the state has to offer more clearly. And though you certainly can't "do" all of Colorado in a two-week trip, you can tailor your trip to make it as rewarding and fulfilling as possible. Herewith, then, are some of what I think are Colorado's highlights. Prioritize them as you will.

THINGS TO SEE

Rocky Mountain National Park probably best encapsulates the beauty and intensity of the rest of the state and the Rocky Mountains. Drive through on the above-timberline Trail Ridge Road, or take off with your backpack or cross-country skis into the backcountry. A word of warning: Because the park is so accessible, it gets crowded. On long weekends during the summer, traffic on Trail Ridge Road can be virtually bumper to bumper, and if you drive in from the east, through Estes Park, you'll be flagged through town by traffic controllers, doing their best to keep the steady stream of autos, motor homes, and motorcycles moving. At **Mesa Verde National Park** you can explore thousand-year-old Anasazi cliff dwellings, and just outside of Colorado Springs you can drive to the top of 14,110-foot Pikes Peak, the "purple mountain" to which Katherine Lee Bates referred in *America the Beautiful.* If you're interested in the state's mining history, don't miss **Cripple Creek, Central City, Black Hawk,** and **Leadville,** where you can take mine tours and visit museums displaying the tools and equipment of the 1880s, when these towns were bustling with entrepreneurs and entertainers, prospectors and prostitutes.

If you want to see urban Colorado, you need of course to see **Denver.** From its museums and restaurants to its upscale shopping centers, high-rise hotels, and brand new airport, Denver is at once thoroughly modern and at the same time a town with a palpable link to its past. If you're around during the baseball season, try to take in a **Colorado Rockies** game. Even if you're not a rabid baseball fan, an evening at the park, with the sun setting behind the scoreboard and the Rocky Mountains, is one of the best ways to get a sense of Denver's personality. While in Denver, allow yourself a day to drive up to **Boulder,** an outdoor-oriented university town that seems part Berkeley, part Chamonix, France. Check out the bookstores and street performers on the **Pearl Street Mall** and the coffee shops on **The Hill.**

Another wonderful Colorado town is **Telluride,** though its box-canyon location makes it the kind of town you have to go out of your way to get to (which is part of its charm). Here, Victorian homes cling to hillsides, ski lifts rise just blocks from the main drag through town, and just-passing-through Deadheads share bar space with CEOs.

You might have already formed an opinion about **Aspen,** given its reputation for excellent skiing, expensive lifestyles, and big-bucks resident celebrities. It's a great town, though, and you need neither ski nor be rich to enjoy a visit there—public parks and bike paths allow you to soak in the mountain sunshine, and you can

wander the town's little sidestreets, poke your nose into gift shops, and, weather permitting, grab lunch at any of several outdoor cafes.

Just east of Aspen, CO 82 lifts up above the treeline to **Independence Pass** (12,095 feet), providing spectacular views before dropping back down again into the gorgeous **Arkansas River Valley.** Several other Colorado mountain passes offer stunning scenery, including **Loveland Pass** and **Berthoud Pass** (both over 11,000 feet), **Wolf Creek Pass** (10,850 feet), **Lizard Head Pass** (10,222 feet), and **Rabbit Ears Pass** (9,426 feet). And the entire stretch of **US 550** from **Durango** to **Ouray** seems to take your breath at every turn (and there are lots of them).

THINGS TO DO

Though it's natural to want to relax on vacation, you might not want to do too much of that in Colorado—it'd be a shame not to take advantage of the nearly unlimited recreational opportunities the state affords. Colorado's **skiing** is some of the best in the world, with resorts such as **Aspen, Vail, Crested Butte, Winter Park, Steamboat Springs,** and **Telluride** drawing visitors from as far away as Europe and Asia. Some of the state's lesser-known resorts, though, also offer skiing that locals will tell you rivals that at the big resorts. Not to let the cat out of the bag here, but **A-Basin, Wolf Creek,** and **Purgatory** offer some of the best snow in the Rockies, as well as generally shorter lift lines and an overall more personal and friendly atmosphere than you'll find at some of the larger resorts.

In addition to excellent snow skiing, Colorado also offers first-rate **whitewater rafting, mountain biking, fishing, horseback riding, and hiking,** for just about every level of participant—first-timer to expert. Plus, visitors to Colorado can take **four-wheel-drive tours** of remote mountain passes and ghost towns, or rent vehicles and head out on their own. You can also take **narrow-gauge-train rides** along steep cliffsides and over harrowing bridges crossing deep gorges.

Finally, there are the festivals, scores around the state. To name but a few of the best known: Telluride's **bluegrass** and **film** festivals, Boulder's **Shakespeare** and **music** festivals, Aspen's **food-and-wine** and **music** festivals, Winter Park's **American Music** festival, and Vail's **Winterfaire,** as well as golf tournaments, mountain-bike races, and every other imaginable gathering and celebration. (See "Calendar" in specific chapters for dates and other information.)

A lot to see and do? You bet. And I've only skimmed the surface. My advice: Don't try to do it all; you'll only frustrate yourself. Instead, take time to enjoy what you do decide on, and then, as they say in the shoe business, Just do it. Besides, perhaps no visit to Colorado, even a life-long one, is ever complete.

RECREATION

Colorado offers a huge array of outdoor activities. Skiing, biking, fishing, golf, camping, rock climbing, whitewater rafting, and kayaking—all are immensely popular. In fact, many folks who've chosen to live here will tell you it's because of the wealth of outdoor recreation. No matter where you are, a lake, stream, golf course, ski slope, hiking trail, or trout stream is nearby.

Skiing

To many people, of course, skiing and Colorado are virtually synonymous. After all, the state is home to some of the world's best, biggest, and most well-known resorts: Vail, Aspen, Winter Park, Steamboat Springs, Crested Butte, Telluride, Copper Mountain, Breckenridge, and Keystone. In addition, more than a dozen other smaller and lesser-known but equally fine resorts lie within Colorado's borders; among them are Arapahoe Basin, Purgatory, and Wolf Creek, favorites of local powderhounds and bumpshredders.

If you're thinking about a ski vacation, you couldn't do much better than Colorado. Fly into Denver, take a shuttle to Vail, Winter Park, or any one of the other resorts within an hour and a half of the airport, and then just spend your time mastering the one mountain; or take a road trip—spread your trip over half a dozen or more resorts. Start at Winter Park, head west to Summit County, then over the pass and on to Vail. Even if you end up as far away as Telluride, you're still less than a day's drive from the airport.

Colorado is also a haven for Nordic skiers. With its thousands of square miles of national forests, as well as many privately run Nordic centers, Colorado welcomes those who'd rather ski quietly off into the woods or crank Telemark turns on a backcountry hillside than stand in lift lines

after spending $40 for a ticket. Cross-country skiers will find excellent terrain and Nordic centers near most of the major downhill resorts, including Vail, Aspen, and Telluride, while San Juan, Gunnison, San Isabel, and White River national forests offer exceptional trails, as well as opportunities to explore unmarked backcountry.

For more information on skiing in Colorado, write **Colorado Ski Country USA,** 1560 Broadway, Suite 1440, Denver, CO 80202, or phone (303) 837-0793 or 831-7669 (snow report).

Ski rental prices will vary from resort to resort, as will the degree of hassle of getting equipped. Generally, the cost is approximately $15 a day, but will often be paired with discounted lift tickets or as part of an accommodations package. It is recommended you rent your equipment before you arrive at the ski area, even though most of the resorts' rental shops are efficient and their employees highly qualified and personable—having your skis when you get there means one fewer obstacle between your car and the chair lift. Also, local ski shops offer discounts on rentals, and having your own equipment makes it easier to ski several different resorts on the same visit. On the other hand, most ski areas offer packages, particularly to beginning skiers, which include equipment rental, lessons, and lift tickets. Call the individual resorts for information and prices. Rental shops will also often store your ski equipment in the evenings (and your street shoes during the day), minimizing the amount of lugging around you'll have to do, and at the end of your stay, you can simply drop your stuff off and head back to your car.

Prices of lessons vary depending on whether you want to be part of a group or prefer a private lesson; lessons are also more expensive at the higher-end resorts (Aspen, Vail) than at the smaller, family-oriented areas (Purgatory, Ski Cooper). Group lesson usually run $15-40 for an hour and a half or two (there's generally both a morning and afternoon session). Privates can run $60-90 a hour. Note: Though private lessons offer the advantage of one-on-one instruction, and the money can be well spent, groups are often smaller than you'd think—sometimes just two or three students, guaranteeing a lot of individual instruction. The two main factors determining group size are how crowded the resort is and how advanced the group. Generally, if it's a weekday, and the resort's not too crowded, the groups will be small. Also, the more advanced the group, the more likely it is that it will be small. Beginners will want to look into packages that include lessons, lift tickets, and equipment rental, offered by most of the resorts.

Child care is frequently provided, though it is never free of charge. For example, at Vail, all-day, non-ski daycare for children two months to six years old can run in the neighborhood of $55, and does include lunch. Information has been included on the places where the child care or children's ski school have the best reputations or where folks are most likely to be visiting with kids.

Snowmobiling

Now, I'll admit up front to having mixed feelings about this sport. Although I can see the thrill of blasting through new-fallen snow at 40-plus mph, the crisp air stinging your face while the sunshine shimmers on distant meadows, it also seems like a loud and obtrusive way to get into the backcountry. Of course, the sport is well regulated, nearly guaranteeing minimal environmental havoc, yet the screaming engines still pierce the sanctity of the forests' natural silences, and exhaust fumes still waft into the air. I recommend cross-country skiing or snowshoeing instead. Sorry.

For information on snowmobiling in Colorado, including safety training and organized tours around the state, plus maps of the state's major snowmobiling areas, write **Colorado Snowmobile Association,** Box 1260 Grand Lake, CO 80447. For questions regarding snowmobile registration write the Colorado Division of Parks and Outdoor Recreation, Recreation Unit, 13878 S. US 85, Littleton, CO 80125, or phone (303) 791-1920.

Cycling

While touring is enjoying the same renaissance in Colorado that it is in the rest of the country, mountain biking has taken the state by storm. In fact, Crested Butte and Durango are two of the half dozen or so of the sport's true capitals, and both towns not only offer miles and miles of trails and terrain for all levels of ability but also sponsor races, workshops, and various special events throughout the season (generally May through

waist-deep powder at Vail

JACK AFFLECK

ALPINE SKI AREAS

STATEWIDE ROAD CONDITIONS (303) 639 - 1234
DENVER - AREA ROAD CONDITIONS (303) 639 - 1111

© MOON PUBLICATIONS, INC.

October). In addition, many of Colorado's ski resorts have taken to promoting mountain biking during the summer. At several resorts, including Aspen, Purgatory, Winter Park, and Vail, you can take your bike to the top of the mountain on a ski lift and ride the ski trails back down.

Hiking, Backpacking, and Camping
With the Rocky Mountains as its centerpiece, Colorado claims some of the best hiking, back-

packing, and camping in the United States. From the San Juan Mountains to Rocky Mountain National Park north of Boulder, from Colorado National Monument to Great Sand Dunes National Monument, the state offers wide ranging types of trail hiking with a variety of lengths and degrees of difficulty. You can take short, naturalist-led day-hikes, or you can hike solo into remote backcountry wilderness areas; you can even organize a group and hike hut-to-hut through one of Colorado's "hut systems." Usually sightseeing rides run $10-12, with an additional charge of $5 or $6 for transporting mountain bikes up.

For information on the 10th Mountain Trail Association's hut-to-hut skiing, phone (970) 925-5775.

In the late 1980s, the Colorado Trail was completed. This 469-mile trail, which stretches

WHY SKI COLORADO?

Why do I ski Colorado? You can always duck a "why" question like that by going back to George Leigh-Mallory's answer about climbing Everest: "because it's there." Or be facetious and answer: why not? Or be honest, and say: I ski Colorado because that's where I live, high in the San Juan Mountains in the southwestern corner of the state. But even that was a choice, wasn't it? I moved to Colorado because of a certain tangible magic in these mountains that touches skiing and life in about equal measures. The more interesting question is not why do I ski Colorado, but why do I (and so many others) love skiing here so much?

Start the way skiing itself starts, with snow—great snow. Rocky Mountain snow isn't the whole story, but it's a small miracle. Lighter, drier, more consistent than any snow in the maritime zones of New England or California and other far-west states, Rocky Mountain snow is the stuff skiers' dreams are made of. The small miracle I mentioned is the fact that you, I, all of us, ski better out here than we do at home—if home happens to be anywhere else.

Why is our snow so soft and light? The secret is the continental climate, far from the moist influence of either seacoast, combined with the generally higher elevations of ski areas in Colorado. Not only does Colorado snow fall from the sky as fluff, but often, lowering temperatures after a storm will dry it out even further. Snow here sometimes gets lighter a day after it's fallen. In skiers' terms, this translates into less resistance, less friction, less work to turn and slide. It's as though your skis were always better waxed on Colorado slopes. Powder snow in Colorado is for play not penance, an invitation with no strings attached; and when groomed and packed down into pistes, this stuff becomes a sort of teflon velvet where skis can perform to 110% of their design potential.

Is that all? Hardly. I'd say that on balance Colorado ski resorts are just as special as the snow. Not all perhaps, but most of the resorts here on the backbone of the continent benefit from a special relation to winter, a kind of "skiing culture," a tradition of ski-town hospitality that makes Colorado ski sites more than just overgrown parking lots at the base of

lifts. None of the Rocky Mountain states—Colorado, Utah, Wyoming, Montana, Idaho, New Mexico—is exactly experiencing a demographic explosion. These mountains are wild, beautiful, and lonely. And Colorado, although as wild as any of these Rocky Mountain states, is also the most sophisticated of the lot. Take away Denver, and the Rockies look positively empty. No sprawling, tightly packed urban zones to flood the slopes with their clockwork weekend tides. For this reason, most of Colorado's ski spots have become vacation destinations, not weekend rendezvous as is the case with so many eastern and far-western ski areas. In Colorado, necessity and history have transformed the classic base lodge into an even more classic base village.

Here a high percentage of skiers comes from out of state; these folks come from all directions. This means that often the skiers you meet in Colorado lift lines are a more diverse and interesting bunch than you'll find elsewhere. And for that matter, lift lines themselves are on the way out here. The intense competition between Colorado destination resorts for vacationing skiers has fueled a revolution in ski lifts. High-speed detachable quad chairs are fast becoming the norm not the exception at major Colorado resorts. There's no going back, and no nostalgia for the old days of the slow double chair. This is a sweet, almost painless revolution. Higher lift-ticket prices are more than offset by the increased vertical these new lifts deliver. The cost of skiing per thousand feet is actually declining. And for the first time, hard-core skiers are sometimes quitting before the last lift closes, because they have literally skied themselves to exhaustion. A very nice feeling indeed, and a new one in American skiing.

So why do I ski Colorado? And love it so? Because I'm spoiled. Because we're all spoiled.
—Lito Tejada-Flores

Lito Tejada-Flores is an internationally known ski writer and publisher. He has written scores of articles for major magazines, including Ski, Skiing, *and* Powder, *and he is the author of* Breakthrough on Skis.

from Durango to Denver, offers rich hiking opportunities with specific sections designed for day, overnight, and multi-day hikes. Access points and trailheads are scattered along the trail. One of the best sources for information on hiking in Colorado is the **Colorado Mountain Club**, 2530 W. Alameda Ave., Denver, CO 80219, tel. (303) 922-8315. In addition to publishing a monthly newsletter with articles on climbing and hiking in the state (and beyond), the club sponsors numerous hikes and cross-country ski outings throughout the year.

Colorado's camping opportunities, too, are numerous and varied. Hundreds of public campgrounds are scattered throughout the state in the beautiful San Juan, San Isabel, White River, Pike, Roosevelt, Rio Grande, Grand Mesa, Gunnison, and Arapaho national forests. In addition, Rocky Mountain National Park offers camping in one of most scenic wonderlands in the country, while a handful of national monuments and recreation areas, particularly Curecanti, as well as state parks, also offer good camping.

Overnight camping fees at Colorado's National Forest Service campgrounds range $6-13 a night, depending on facilities (running water, showers, etc.), with most of the campgrounds $6-8. Maximum stay is 14 days. For more information on camping in Colorado's national forests, write **U.S. Forest Service**, Box 25127, Lakewood, CO 80225, or phone (303) 275-5350 in Englewood.

Camping in Colorado's 40 state parks will run you $6-7 a night, or $10 for an RV site with an electrical hook-up. Note: Frequent visitors to the state parks will want to invest $30 in an annual pass, without which you'll be charged an additional $3 entrance fee per day (per vehicle)—10 visits and it's paid off. Phone the **Colorado Division of Parks and Recreation** at (303) 866-3437 for a free camping guide and information on purchasing an annual pass. Fees at the private campgrounds in Colorado (Good Sam, KOA, etc.) generally run $8-10 a night for tent sites and $12-18 for full hookups; many offer weekly and monthly rates.

Rafting and Kayaking
Colorado is a river rat's paradise. Whether your idea of river running is to float lazily down a wide meandering stream in a rubber raft or to shoot Class IV rapids in a tiny kayak, whether you prefer organized trips and camaraderie or solo excursions and soul searching, Colorado's waterways will satisfy.

Although rivers throughout the state offer good rafting and kayaking, most of the state's river running is concentrated in the Buena Vista-Salida area (Arkansas River), the Four Corners area (Animas and Dolores rivers), and the northwestern area (Green and Yampa rivers).

For more information on rafting on Colorado rivers, write **Colorado River Outfitters Association,** Box 502, Westminster, CO 80030; tel. (303) 220-8640.

Fishing
While many of Colorado's waterways are tailor-made for rafting, others are trout streams right out of Izaak Walton's *The Compleat Angler* (and some of the rivers are good for both). Unfortunately, mining has destroyed fish habitat in several rivers once rife with trout, though others have been reclaimed, and the Colorado Division of Wildlife, U.S. Fish and Game, and local organizations have successfully reintroduced fish to nearly lost streams.

In addition, sections of several of the state's rivers have special restrictions. Some stretches allow catch-and-release fishing only and/or permit only the use of artificial lures and single barbless hooks. Among the state's most popular streams are the Blue, Roaring Fork, Eagle, Animas, and Gunnison rivers.

Lake fishermen, too, enjoy Colorado angling. Grand Lake and Blue Mesa Reservoir are stocked regularly with decent-size fish, and patient and knowledgeable anglers have taken huge Mackinaw from their waters. Reservoirs on the eastern plains offer good warm-water fishing for bass, walleye, catfish, bluegill, and crappie.

Remember, a valid Colorado fishing license is required to fish in all waters except private lakes and a handful of small municipal ponds (usually designated for kids only). Fishing licenses are available at most Colorado sporting-goods stores, as well as directly through the Division of Wildlife. Resident fishing licenses are $20.25. Nonresidents can buy one-day ($5.25), five-day ($18.25), or season licenses ($40.25). For more information on fishing in Colorado, write the **Colorado Division of Wildlife,** 6060 N. Broadway, Denver, CO 80216, or phone (303) 297-1192.

Hunting

Hunting licenses are available at sporting-goods stores in Colorado, as well as directly through the Colorado Division of Wildlife. All hunters born in or later than 1949 must have proof of having taken a hunter's-safety course. License fees are significantly higher for nonresidents than for residents (1995 license fees for deer were $20.25 for residents, $150.25 for out-of-staters). For more information on hunting in Colorado, phone the Colorado Division of Wildlife at (303) 297-1192, or, for a recorded message specifically about hunting seasons and licenses, 291-7529.

Golf

Golf has really taken off in Colorado in the last few years, with large numbers of courses not only in the metro Denver area but scattered throughout the state as well, particularly at the ski areas, where some of the state's best courses unveil themselves when the snow melts. In fact, between 1990 and 1994, 27 new courses were built, and by summer 1995 there were 206 courses in the state. These range from nine-hole municipality-run courses to high-profile, nationally known courses, such as the **Broadmoor** in Colorado Springs and **Fox Hollow** in Lakewood (just west of Denver), which in January 1995 *Golf Digest* named the second-best new course in the country. In addition, 12.4 % of Coloradans golf, with more and more women and minority members (particularly at municipal courses) taking up the sport, providing a welcome change from the typically white-male-dominated arena.

For travelers, golf can either be something to add to your intinerary or around which to plan your whole trip. Many of the ski resorts, in efforts to keep drawing visitors after the lifts shut down, offer excellent golf-and-lodging packages in the summertime. Even if you're just passing through, a round of golf can offer a chance to be outdoors under that wonderful Colorado sky and in some areas to see foxes, deer, and other wildlife.

ACCOMMODATIONS

Colorado's travelers' accommodations run the full gamut from backcountry campgrounds to plush bed and breakfasts, from youth hostels to lavish hotels with valet parking and dining rooms with dress codes. Even the most remote towns usually have a motel or two, and you're rarely far from a national forest campground, where sites run about $7 a night. Colorado's main tourist areas—Denver, Colorado Springs, Summit County, Vail, Aspen, and Durango—

have wide ranges of lodging possibilities, including RV campgrounds, luxury hotels, and inexpensive motels. Generally, it's cheaper to stay on the outskirts of town, although you'll sacrifice the convenience of central-location lodging.

Campgrounds

Camping is the least-expensive way to stay in your travels through Colorado, though of course

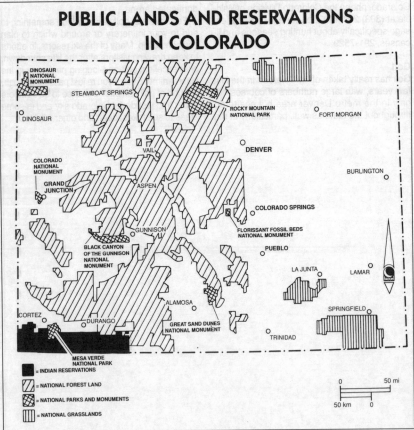

PUBLIC LANDS AND RESERVATIONS IN COLORADO

this is recommended for summer travel only (most mountain campgrounds close Oct.-May). With nightly fees ranging from free to around $18 (for some of the more costly RV sites), the state's campgrounds are generally safe, comfortable, and well maintained. Forest Service campgrounds are not generally equipped with flush toilets or showers, though they usually have running water.

Bed and Breakfasts

Although generally more expensive than staying in a motel ($50-125 a night), this is one of the best ways to see Colorado. Many of the state's bed and breakfasts are situated in turn-of-the-century (and older) homes and decorated with authentic Victorian furnishings. In addition, most innkeepers go out of their way to provide personal and intimate service. The only disadvantage of bed and breakfasts is you often must sacrifice a bit of your privacy. Though rooms are usually perfectly private, you may have to share a bath, and often will be eating breakfast in close quarters with—and sometimes at the same table as—the inn's other guests.

For more information on Colorado bed and breakfasts, contact **Bed and Breakfast Colorado, Ltd.,** Box 6061, Boulder, CO 80306, tel. (303) 494-4994; **Bed and Breakfasts of the Rocky Mountains,** Box 804, Colorado Springs, CO 80901, tel. (800) 825-0225; or **Small Bed and Breakfast Inns of Colorado,** 1102 Pikes

Peak Ave., Colorado Springs, CO 80904 (for a brochure, send $1 and an SASE).

Dude Ranches

Ranch-style accommodations have been a tradition in Colorado since England's Lord Dunraven brought guests from the British Isles to his retreat near Estes Park in the 1870s. Today, there are dude ranches throughout the state, from Durango to Aspen to Steamboat Springs. In addition to offering the proverbial horseback riding, most of the ranches offer a variety of other recreational pursuits as well, including snowmobiling, cross-country skiing, fishing, mountain biking, rafting, and tennis; you can even take part in real ranchhand chores.

For complete information on Colorado dude ranches, write **Colorado Dude/Guest Ranch Association,** Box 300, Tabernash, CO 80478, or phone (303) 887-3128 or (800) 441-6060 (outside Colorado).

Four Distinctive Colorado Hotels

Though there are many excellent hotels in Colorado, particularly in the downtown Denver area, four stand out as places that would make a Colorado vacation especially memorable. **The Broadmoor Hotel** in Colorado Springs was built in the early part of the century and is a sprawling complex actually consisting of three separate hotels, as well as several upscale restaurants, three golf courses, a museum, bou-

COLORADO HISTORICAL SOCIETY

19th century digs and diggers

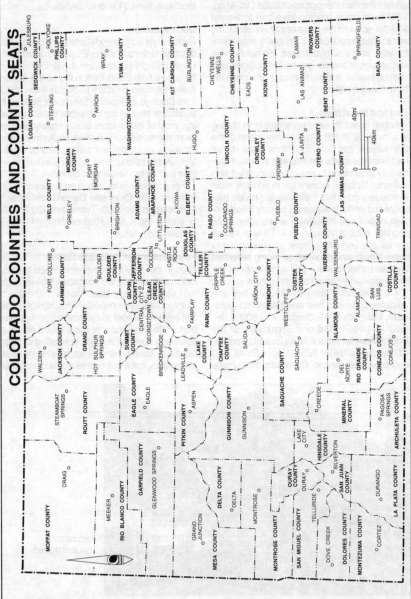

COLORADO COUNTIES AND COUNTY SEATS

© MOON PUBLICATIONS, INC.

tiques, a lake, and an ice-skating arena. One of the classiest and most luxurious hotels in the country, the Broadmoor will take your breath away even if you're prepared to be impressed. Rooms start at about $120, and suites go for over $1000.

Downtown Denver's **Brown Palace Hotel** first opened in 1892 and ever since has been accommodating Denver's most discriminating and well-to-do visitors, from Teddy Roosevelt to the Beatles. Rooms start at about $140.

The **Far View Lodge** is located atop Mesa Verde within a couple of miles of some of the Southwest's most fascinating cliff dwellings. Balconies at each room provide the perfect places to listen to the godly silence and to imagine the juniper- and piñon-studded plateau 1,000 years ago, when the Anasazi were developing their mysterious civilization. Rooms start at around $70.

Estes Park's **Stanley Hotel** stands large, white, and sentinel-like on a hillside above town, squaring off with Rocky Mountain National Park. Built in 1909 by F.O. Stanley, who invented the Stanley Steamer, the rustically luxurious Stanley Hotel has hosted many luminaries over the years, including Stephen King, whom the hotel inspired to write *The Shining* (Kubrick and Nicholson hoped to film the movie here but there wasn't enough snow, so the crew moved to the Timberline Lodge on Oregon's Mount Hood).

Though the Stanley ran into trouble in the 1980s and early 1990s, eventually going into bankruptcy, the hotel was purchased in the summer of 1995 by the Grand Heritage Hotel chain, which has luxury properties around the world—in Milan, London, and the French countryside—and the integrity and class for which the Stanley was formerly known should return. Rooms at the Stanley Hotel start at about $60.

For more information on these hotels, see the "Accommodations" sections in the corresponding chapters.

A Word about Hotel Rates

The more I travel the more I realize how capricious hotel rates are, how the rate you get depends on so many variables—whether you phone in your reservation or walked in off the street, whether it's two in the afternoon or 10 at night, whether you asked for a "discount" or not. Keep in mind hotels, and to some degree motels, have widely fluctuating rates, and that above all they don't want empty rooms. True story: I pulled into Fort Collins one afternoon and walked into the lobby of a major hotel chain. Since it was packed with tour groupers, and waiting 10 minutes at the counter got me no closer to a clerk, I walked outside to a pay phone and called the front desk. "Rates are $79 a night," I was told, "but sorry, no rooms available tonight." So I walked next door, where I was told there was one room available, a smoking room. Nope, wouldn't do. So I walked back to the lobby of the first hotel, worked my way to the counter, and asked for a room.

"Yes, we do have a room, Sir. For $69."

"Do you offer any corporate discounts?" I asked.

"Let's see . . . Yes, we can give you a room for $59."

Now, this is backwards from how it usually works (though it does go to show how arbitrary it can all be). Often you can get a better rate by phone, even if you're calling from just outside the door, as they figure you're not committed yet, and they *want* you. Once you're in the door they figure you're less likely to go somewhere else.

Another true story: One night in Raton, New Mexico, I stopped for the night at dusk at a small independent motel. A man in front of me was talking with the desk clerk.

"How much for a room?"

"Do you qualify for any discounts?" the woman asked.

Shrugging and giving her a blank look, he said, "What do you mean?"

"Triple A, corporate, AARP, you know . . . "

"Uh, I guess not . . . "

"Sixty-four dollars for a single."

He said he'd take it, filled out the registration form, and left with his key.

My turn: "Do you have a nonsmoking single available for this evening?"

"Do you qualify for any discounts?"

"Yes, I do."

"Fifty-four dollars for a single."

"I'll take it."

Is there a lesson here? If there is it's that, like I said, rates are not as fixed as you might think. Some things to keep in mind: The later in the day the better your chance of getting a cut rate. The owners want their rooms full, and, if it looks like they might not be, they'll offer incentives, in the form of a few bucks off the "standard" rate. (Of course, you also risk not finding a vacancy, and that risk might not be worth it to you.) Also, *ask* about discounts. Most hotels offer at least American Automobile Association, American Association of Retired Persons, and corporate discounts, and you might qualify. Finally, in the case of chain and franchise lodging, I've had better luck phoning the hotel directly than calling the 800 number and talking to an operator who might be booking a room in a town 3,000 miles away from where she's sitting.

Bottom line: Phone around, and talk like you do it all the time. You might be surprised at the results.

Hosteling

Although hosteling isn't as popular in Colorado as it is other parts of the country (and world), there are a handful of hostels that have been around for a long time, have excellent reputations and loyal followings, and are located near some of the state's main attractions. Among them are the hostels in Durango, Boulder, Glenwood Springs, and Nederland (outside Boulder). In addition, offices of **American Youth Hostels, Inc.** are in Boulder, and you can get information on other hostels in the area by phoning them at (303) 442-1166. AYH's main number in Washington, D.C., is (202) 783-6161, and the toll-free number is (800) 444-6111. **Internet users** can contact **Hostelling International-American Youth Hostels** at **http://gnn.com/gnn/bus/ayh/usa/colorado.html.**

HEALTH AND SAFETY

Traveling in Colorado is generally very safe, although you should be aware of several specific diseases and climate-caused maladies that could make your visit far less enjoyable and comfortable than it should be. Understanding these problems, and taking the appropriate precautions, will greatly increase the chances of staying healthy while exploring the state. Much of the following information was taken from the American Medical Association's *Encyclopedia of Medicine.*

Altitude Sickness

Also known as mountain sickness, altitude sickness most commonly affects mountain climbers, hikers, and skiers who ascend too rapidly to heights above 8,000 feet. Caused by a reduction in atmospheric pressure, and a corresponding decrease in oxygen, altitude sickness alters the blood chemistry and affects the nervous system, muscles, heart, and lungs.

Symptoms of altitude sickness include headache, nausea, dizziness, and impaired mental abilities. In severe cases, fluid buildup in the lungs leads to breathlessness, coughing, and a heavy phlegm. Untreated, these symptoms can lead to seizures, hallucinations, and coma. Delays in treatment can even lead to brain damage and death.

The best way to prevent altitude sickness is to ascend *gradually* to elevations above 8,000 feet. Take a day or two for each 2,000-3,000 feet. Victims of altitude sickness should return to lower elevations immediately, if necessary carry them. If available, pure oxygen can be administered (ski patrol usually keeps oxygen tanks handy).

Dehydration

Dehydration is the result of a drop in the body's water level and oftentimes a subsequent drop in the level of salt. Being at higher altitudes can cause an increase in dehydration; symptoms include severe thirst, dry lips, increased heart and breath rate, dizziness, and confusion. Often the skin is dry and stiff; what little urine is passed is dark. When salt loss is heavy, there will also be headaches, cramps, lethargy, and pallor. Severe cases of dehydration can result in coma.

To prevent dehydration, you must replace the three (or more) quarts of water your body loses every 24 hours to perspiration and urination. Even in moderate temperatures and climates, you should be cautious and drink more than you probably think you need; a good rule of thumb is to drink enough water to keep the urine pale. Treatment for dehydration includes fluid and salt replacement—in severe cases intravenously.

Giardia

Giardia, or giardiasis, is an infection of the small intestine caused by the single-celled parasite *Giardia lamblia*. Giardia is spread by direct personal contact with another's stool or by contaminated food or water; the latter should be of particular concern to hikers and backpackers. In remote high-country areas clear-running stream water can be contaminated as even wild animals are known to carry the parasite.

Symptoms of giardia usually begin one to three days after the parasite has entered the system and include violent diarrhea, gas, cramps, loss of appetite, and nausea. To avoid contracting giardia, always wash your hands before handling food, and *do not* drink stream or lake water without first boiling or purifying it. Purifying with either iodine (in liquid, tablet, or crystal form) or with 0.1 Micron Water filter is sufficient. If using a powdered drink mix to cover the taste of iodine, wait to add it until after the allotted treatment time, as the asorbic acid (vitamin C) can interfere with the purification process. Check sporting goods stores and mountaineering shops for water-purification kits.

Hypothermia

Hypothermia occurs when the body temperature drops below 95° F and is caused by prolonged exposure to cold. Most common among elderly and young people, whose bodies are unable to generate enough warmth, hypothermia is characterized by a slowed heart rate, puffiness, pale skin, lethargy, and confusion. In severe cases, breathing is also slow. Taking the proper precautions can go a long way toward prevention; wear warm clothing including gloves and a hat, eat high-carbohydrate foods often, and drink plenty of fluids.

Hypothermia requires immediate medical attention, and victims are often treated in intensive-care units of hospitals and warmed under controlled conditions. While awaiting medical assistance, move the victim to a warm place, remove wet clothing, and replace it with a warm blanket; have another person join and hold the victim beneath the blanket and, if possible, give the victim something warm (not hot) to drink. *Do not* let the victim walk, do not rub the skin or apply direct heat, and do not give the victim alcohol.

Sunburn

Sunburn is most common in fair-skinned people and most likely to occur *at high elevations*, where fewer ultraviolet rays are naturally blocked. Skiers and other winter-sports enthusiasts should be especially careful, as the sun's reflection off the snow doubles the effect of harmful rays, while even a cloudy day allows many of the sun's ultraviolet rays to penetrate.

The two best ways to prevent sunburn are by gradual exposure (increasing each day) and by application of a sunscreen with a high sun-protection factor (SPF). Available at pharmacies, sporting-goods stores, and even grocery stores, sunscreens with a high SPF (15 or higher) should be applied liberally and often. Treatment for sunburn includes the application of any of several available lotions and ointments; particularly effective are those with aloe. Severe cases may require medical treatment.

Crime and Public Safety

In previous editions of this book, as well as in *New Mexico Handbook* (Moon Publications, 1993), I've felt a responsibility to include information on crime and public safety. I've talked at length with police officers in major cities, asking them to recommend ways travelers can avoid being victims of crime.

Their answers are pretty standard and shouldn't surprise veterans of the road: don't leave valuables in motel or hotel rooms or in plain sight on car seats, etc.; park and walk in well-lighted areas; travel with companions (especially if you're a woman); ask local hotel and motel employees for the safest route to your restaurant; report suspicious activity—in short use common sense.

Pretty decent advice, I always thought. And pretty responsible of me to have my readers' safety in mind and to try to help them navigate sometimes-seedy urban areas.

But recently, while exploring the stark beauty of Colorado's Four Corners area, alone on a gorgeous summer-stormy day on a remote bluff overlooking McPhee Reservoir near Cortez, I was assaulted myself. Fortunately, it wasn't as bad as it could have been, and though rattled, I was really none the worse for wear.

It was, however, a heck of a wake-up call, and it got me wondering to what degree the rise in the national crime rate was reflected in the country's wilderness areas. So when I got back to California, I phoned a half dozen or so Forest Service representatives, trying to get a feel for the rise in crime, if any, on public lands. Most agreed that it was, but were understandably vague in their answers. "Lots of theft from parked cars," one told me. "Don't leave valuables inside." Another told me boaters at McPhee should make sure to lock up their boats, and to keep an eye on them at night; boats have been stolen from their moorings, only to turn up several days later in another arm of the lake.

But is crime on public lands actually increasing? Yes, according to Debra Shore in a recent Outside Magazine. In fact, Shore says crime on public property has doubled in the last five years. Why the increase? In part, of course, it's due to the larger numbers visiting these areas. But it's also a result of federal-level budget cuts, which in turn means less law enforcement. According to Shore, the country's national parks alone attracted more than 273 million visitors in 1994, up nearly 70 million from the mid-1980s. Yet there are 39 fewer law-enforcement officers: A total of 541 million acres (national park and forest, plus BLM land) is patrolled by 3,600 officers, or, as Shore points out, "about one officer for every 150,000 acres."

In the article, Shore singled out 16 national parks, forests, monuments, and recreation areas where crime was high enough to merit extraordinary caution. Among them: Joshua Tree National Monument (CA), Lake Mead National Recreation Area (NV), Daniel Boone National Forest (KY), and Big Bend National Park (TX). The crimes? Murder, drug growing and trafficking, sexual assault, and theft, as well as less-serious offenses, such as fighting (over the harvesting of extremely valuable mushrooms in Deschutes National Forest in Oregon, for example) and the general mischief (bottle throwing, destruction of public property) of rowdy drunks who are all of 16.

And what about assault, particularly sexual assault? How often does it happen, and nearly happen? How many assaults are not reported and thus can't be factored into the equations? I'm not sure. And I don't think there's any way to find out. I do know this, though: My own private wilderness is no longer what it once was. I will be more cautious on public land, less likely to travel alone. And, sadly, I will not raise my two daughters to think that the wilderness is a refuge from the dark side of humanity, that instead it might sometimes be a refuge for it.

The price, as William Blake would say, of experience.

INFORMATION

Your Colorado vacation will be far more enjoyable if you come prepared. In addition to purchasing a thorough and entertaining guidebook (which you apparently have already done or are about to do), it's a good idea to send away for any and all information you can get your hands on. One of the best sources for general information is the **Colorado Tourism Board**. Write them at 1625 Broadway, Suite 1700, Denver, CO 80202, or phone (800) 433-2656 (for a vacation kit) or (303) 592-5410 (to speak with someone in the business office). Write the **Denver Metro Convention and Visitors Bureau** at 225 W. Colfax, Denver, CO 80202, or phone (303) 892-1112. Their office, at the same address, is an excellent place to stop in when you first get to town; pick up maps, brochures, and other information, and talk with staff members

AREA CODES

about everything from where to park to where to find a good sushi bar.

Virtual Colorado

The Colorado Tourism Board and Colorado Online has lodging, activities, dining, weather, and other information available through the Internet. The web address is: http://www.colorado.com/. You can also get information on Colorado's summertime events at http://www.aescon.com/summer/.

Colorado Welcome Centers

The Colorado Tourism Board has established official Welcome Centers at most ports of entry. These are good places to stop in for information on local, regional, and statewide attractions. Colorado Welcome Centers are located in **Burlington** (48265 I-70), **Trinidad** (309 N. Nevada Ave.), **Cortez** (928 E. Main St.), **Fruita** (340 US 40), and **Dinosaur** (in the center of town on US 40).

Companion Guides

As you'd expect, there are scores of guides to Colorado. Some are thematic; some are regional. Several of these books are excellent and would make ideal companion guides to *Colorado Handbook*. Among these are Lee Gregory's *Colorado Scenic Guide* (Johnson Books, Boulder)—two volumes, northern and southern regions. Of particular value here are the dozens of reprinted U.S. Geologic Survey topo maps, with hiking trails and 4WD routes, as well as the wealth of statistics and facts (including best time of day to take photos). Another good book is Warren Ohlrich's *Aspen-Snowmass Guide to Out-*

USEFUL ADDRESSES AND PHONE NUMBERS

Emergencies: 9-1-1. **Note:** When teaching kids, authorities stress memorization as nine-one-one, as opposed to nine-eleven, to keep them from looking for the "11" on the dial.

Aspen Chamber Resort Association, 425 Rio Grande Pl., Aspen, CO 81611, tel. (970) 925-1940 or (800) 262-7736, fax (970) 925-9008

Boulder Chamber of Commerce, 2440 Pearl St., Boulder, CO 80302, tel. (303) 442-2911 or (800) 444-0447, fax (303) 938-8837

Colorado Division of Parks and Recreation, 1313 Sherman St. no. 618, Denver, CO 80203, tel. (303) 866-3437 (Also with offices in Grand Junction, Colorado Springs, Littleton, and Fort Collins.)

Colorado Division of Wildlife, 6060 N. Broadway, Denver, CO 80216, tel. (303) 297-1192

Colorado Historical Society, 1300 Broadway, Denver, CO 80203, tel. (303) 866-3682

Colorado Springs Convention and Visitors Bureau, Suite 104 S. Cascade, Colorado Springs, CO 80903, tel. (719) 635-7506 or (800) 888-4748, fax (719) 635-4968

Colorado Tourism Board, 1625 Broadway, Suite 1700, Denver, CO 80202, tel. (303) 592-5410, (800) 433-2656, or (800) 558-7829, fax (303) 591-7068

Denver Metro Convention and Visitors Bureau, 225 W. Colfax, Denver, CO 80202, tel. (303) 892-1112, (303) fax 892-1636

Durango Chamber Resort Association, Box 2587, Durango, CO 81302, tel. (970) 247-0312 or (800) 525-8855, fax (970) 385-7884

National Park Service, 12795 W. Alameda Pkwy., Lakewood, CO 80225, tel. (303) 969-2000

Summit County Chamber of Commerce, Box 214, (with offices at 011 S. Summit Blvd.) Frisco, CO 80443, tel. (970) 668-5800, 668-2051, or (800) 530-3099, fax (970) 668-1515

United States Bureau of Land Management, 2850 Youngfield St., Lakewood, CO 80215, tel. (303) 239-3600

United States Fish and Wildlife Service, 134 Union Blvd., Denver, CO 80228, tel. (303) 236-7904

United States Forest Service, Box 25127, Lakewood, CO 80225, tel. (303) 275-5350

Vail Valley Tourism and Covention Bureau, 100 E. Meadow Dr., Vail, CO 81657, tel. (970) 476-1000, 476-5677, 525-3875, or (800) 775-8245, fax (970) 467-6008 *door Activities* (Warren Ohlrich, Aspen). With over two dozen activities, from Telemark skiing to tennis, from dogsledding to kayaking, this book provides lots of useful firsthand information and tips, as well as listings of shops and agencies specializing in each activity.

For general guides, you'd be hard-pressed to find a book more intriguing than the Work Projects Administration's *Colorado: A Guide to the Highest State.* First published in 1941, this fascinating book is part of the famous series that put some of the country's best writers to work during the lean times of the Depression. The book, available now in used and rare-book stores (and re-issued in 1987 as *The WPA Guide to 1930s Colorado* [University Press of Kansas]) includes minutely detailed tours of main routes and back roads, in addition to thorough discussions of the state's history, economy, geography, and population.

For a comprehensive list of other books about Colorado, see the Booklist.

TRANSPORTATION

Although several companies offer tours of Colorado—from cliff dwellings to Pikes Peak—and most of the major tourist areas provide excellent public transportation, you're better off with your own rig. Unless you plan to stay in one specific area for your entire visit (which can work very well, especially if all you plan to do is ski), you're probably going to want to get out and do a little exploring. Remember that it's a long way between places you'll want to see, and you'll enjoy

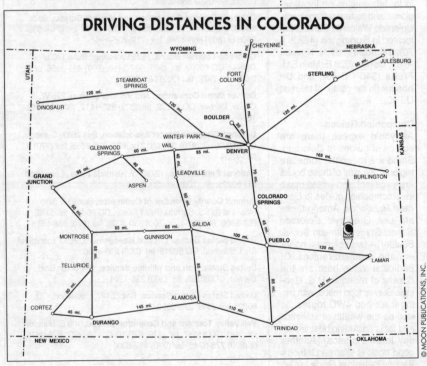

DRIVING DISTANCES IN COLORADO

the luxury of capricious stops—whether for rest, water, or to explore a mining town or recreation area not on your itinerary.

Colorado by Air

The brand new Denver International Airport (DIA), the first major U.S. airport built in 20 years, opened in the winter of 1995, nearly two years after it was scheduled to. The project, ambitious by any standard, was fraught with problems from early in the planning stages to well after planes were coming and going—from engineering glitches that led to luggage leaping from carousels to lawsuits among contractors; embarrassing to both Coloradans and the airline industry, these problems got world-wide press as international travelers waited to see how the new airport would turn out.

Chief complaints consisted of noise restrictions being violated, and take-off and landing patterns sprawling over far more airspace than had been promised in contracts. Indeed, residents of the Front Range, from as far away as Ward and Boulder, complained that planes were flying directly over their homes and decible levels were not only unbearable but in violation of ordinances. In addition, United Airlines, as virtually the only carrier servicing DIA, had jacked prices so high travelers were simply not using the airport in the numbers expected. By midsummer, Denver air traffic was down six percent, yet that at Colorado Springs was up a whopping 67%; Denverites were driving the hour and a half to Colorado Springs to save themselves bucks on airfare.

But things are expected to smooth themselves out. For example, once more airlines begin servicing DIA, fares will come down, and the engineering problems all seem to be history. In fact, you'll probably be impressed with DIA's, "user friendliness," from the design of the terminals to the light railroad whisking you underground from one end to the other. Plus, DIA has made access to other parts of Colorado—particularly the resorts—much easier, with regular connecting flights to smaller Colorado towns, including Aspen, Telluride, Montrose, Durango, and Fort Collins.

And, if you want to forgo DIA altogether, some of the resorts, including Aspen, Telluride, Crested Butte, and Steamboat Springs, offer direct

---

WINTER DRIVING TIPS

- Pay attention to highway rules and regulations, including closures and chain requirements; they're meant for your safety.

- Make sure your brakes are in good working order and your tires have plenty of tread.

- Make sure your cooling system has been properly winterized.

- Check your windshield wipers and wiper fluid—wiper fluid with antifreeze in it is available at auto-parts stores and gas stations.

- Always carry chains.

- Do not brake or turn the steering wheel suddenly.

- If you rent a car, request front-wheel-drive, which offers far greater traction than rear-wheel-drive—4WD vehicles, of course, are best but significantly more expensive.

- Drive slowly, and always stay in control; remember that your car's stopping distance is greater when the road is wet, snowy, and/or icy.

- Stop if you begin to lose control or confidence.

- Keep seatbelts fastened at all times (common sense as well as Colorado state law).

---

flights from several U.S. cities, such as Phoenix, Chicago, Los Angeles, and Dallas-Fort Worth. There are also large jet airports in Grand Junction and Colorado Springs. Contact your travel agent for specific information about flight schedules and rates.

Although you might be able to step off your plane and arrange a rental car, you're much better off making reservations, not only to guarantee you'll get the vehicle you want but to make your airport getaway smoother and quicker. You'll find rental cars available at Colorado's airports. In addition to the standard chains (Avis, Hertz, etc.), several "rent-a-wreck" companies offer discount rates, and a handful of outfits specialize in "snow-ready" vehicles (four-wheel- and front-wheel-drive with ski racks).

NOTE: WINTER STORMS WILL TEMPORARILY CLOSE
SOME OF THESE ROUTES; SOME ROUTES,
PARTICULARLY COLORADO 82 BETWEEN ASPEN
AND LEADVILLE AND U S 34 THROUGH ROCKY
MOUNTAIN NATIONAL PARK, ARE CLOSED ALL WINTER.
DENVER - AREA ROAD CONDITIONS (303) 639 - 1111
STATEWIDE ROAD CONDITIONS (303) 639 - 1234

MAIN ROUTES IN COLORADO

RESPONSIBLE TRAVELING

With each passing day, the world becomes more and more what Marshall McLuhan called a "global village." Television has opened up remote corners of the planet to the eyes of folks sitting in the comfort of their own living rooms in Des Moines and Baton Rouge. Likewise, improved travel technology has opened up the world to tourism. In fact, the recent boom in "adventure travel" has meant package tours to such previously out-of-the-way destinations as Antarctica, the Amazon, and central Africa.

And while all this is generally good (as my colleague Carl Parkes says, "travel spreads prosperity, dissolves political barriers, promotes international peace, and brings about excitement and change"), and host countries do for the most part welcome tourism, there is a dark side to it: Some people who visit native villages forget that people are trying to live their lives there, and the results of such insensitivity can be disastrous. Nor are domestic travelers duty-free of such concerns. Especially in the western states, where native peoples lived for centuries before the first white travelers arrived (in the mid-1500s in some parts of the Southwest, the 18th century in Colorado) and where they are now eking out modest livings on reservations, travelers have immense responsibilities.

The bottom line, of course, is respect and understanding. One organization that has gone to great lengths to encourage this sensitivity is the **North America Center for Responsible Tourism,** whose offices are located in San Anselmo, California. Founded in 1984, the center publishes a newsletter and arranges consultations with groups of travelers. In addition, the center has outlined a "Code of Ethics," which was adapted from a credo written in 1975 by the Asian Council of Churches. The following rules, though originally intended for travelers embarking on trips to remote locations, also apply to American tourists heading out to explore their own backyards.

1) Travel in the spirit of humility and with a genuine desire to meet and talk with local people.
2) Be aware of the feelings of local people; prevent what might be offensive behavior. Photography, particularly, must respect the locals.
3) Cultivate the habit of listening and observing, rather than merely hearing and seeing or knowing all the answers.
4) Realize that other people may have concepts of time and thought patterns that are very different from—not inferior to, just different from—your own.

By Rail

Colorado's history is defined in large part by the development of the railroad, and by rail is still an excellent way to get here and to see the state. One of **Amtrak**'s major east-west routes cuts across the northern part of Colorado, with stops in Glenwood Springs, Fraser (near Winter Park), and Denver.

The **Ski Train** runs weekends during the ski season between Denver's Union Station and Winter Park. Roundtrip tickets start at $25, and the two-hour trip, which dives under the Continental Divide through Moffat Tunnel, guarantees passengers won't have to fight the oftentimes thick I-70 and Berthoud Pass traffic. For information, phone (303) 296-I-SKI. Also, see "Transportation" under "Winter Park" following.

In addition, several of Colorado's historic towns have begun tourist-oriented train tours. The best-known of these is the **Durango and Silverton Narrow Gauge Railroad,** which hauls over 200,000 passengers a year between the two mountain towns. Rates start at about $40 for the eight-hour trip. For more information, phone (303) 247-2733. Also, see "Durango and Silverton Narrow Gauge Railroad" under "Silverton" in the Southwestern Colorado chapter.

Driving in Colorado

Driving in Colorado can be tricky. Even in the summer, when the roads are generally dry and free of snow, you should be very careful. Some of the mountain passes are extremely high and steep, with dramatic switchbacks requiring greatly reduced speed. Make sure your brakes are in good working order.

In the winter, snow drifts across roadways, making visibility difficult, and even when the roads are dry, extreme caution must be taken. When the roads get snowy and wet, it's even more dangerous, and drivers without experience in snow driving should consider waiting

5) Instead of seeing the "beach paradise" only, seek to discover the richness of another culture and way of life.
6) Get acquainted with local customs; respect them.
7) Remember, you are only one among many visitors; do not expect special privileges.
8) When shopping through bargaining, remember, the poorest merchant will give up a profit rather than give up his personal dignity.
9) Make no promises to local people or to new friends, you cannot implement.
10) Spend time each day reflecting on your experiences in order to deepen your understanding. And remember, what enriches you may be robbing others.
11) If you want a "home away from home," why travel?

In addition to these rules for independent travelers, the center has guidelines for those planning package tours. Asking the following questions will help you decide whether the company allows for responsible travel.

1) Does the tour organizer or travel agent demonstrate a cultural and environmental sensitivity to your destination? How are the local people, and the culture you are to visit, portrayed in advertising brochures and advertising materials?

2) Who benefits from the costs of your trip? Which sectors of the host country benefit? What percentage of your money stays in the country you visit rather than leaking out to transnational industry, the hotel chains, or the airlines?
3) Is a realistic picture of your host country (area) presented, or a version packaged for tourists?
4) Will you use accommodations and modes of travel used by members of the local society?
5) Does your travel plan allow for adequate opportunities for meeting with local people? Does its pacing provide time for you to create and accept opportunities for interacting with local people?
6) Are you committed to engaging in a pre-trip orientation program? Have you thought through ways to share your experiences when you return home, to maintain contact with people and keep informed about the country (area) you visited?
7) Are you allowing sufficient lead time when opting for alternative/local travel services?
8) Do you inform your travel agent/tour organizer about your concerns for justice in travel?

For more information about the Center, send a self-addressed envelope with postage (appropriate for two ounces) to North American Center for Responsible Tourism, 2 Kensington Rd., San Anselmo, CA 94960; you can also phone the Center at (415) 258-6594.

---

until the routes have been cleared. Snowplows usually begin clearing interstates and other major arteries as soon as the snow starts to pile up, and these routes are rarely closed very long. Lesser-traveled routes, lower on the priority list, take longer to get cleared. In the spring, melted snow from warm daytime temperatures often trickles across roadways. During the night, this water freezes, resulting in hard-to-see sheets of ice on the road; these spots are even more slick and dangerous than patches of snow.

For recorded information on road conditions, phone (303) 639-1111 (Denver and surrounding area) or 639-1234 (statewide).

NORTHWESTERN COLORADO

The huge northwestern corner of Colorado—comprising Moffat, Routt, Eagle, Rio Blanco, and Garfield counties—is a relatively sparsely populated section of the state, where the highways stretch for miles and miles between tiny little towns. About two-thirds high plateau (the west side) and one-third Rockies' Front Range, northwestern Colorado offers a remarkable variation in scenery. From the barren brown oil shale of the Dinosaur National Monument area to the lush green mountains of White River and Routt national forests, this area is a startling study in contrasts.

Two of the three main east-west routes into the state pass through northwestern Colorado: I-70, which snakes along the Colorado River from the Utah border, then rises up over Vail and Loveland passes; and US 40, which barrels out of northern Utah making a beeline for Steamboat Springs before being turned south by the Rockies' spine, the Continental Divide. Eventually, just east of Loveland Pass, the two routes join forces and assault Denver in tandem.

Northwestern Colorado is best known today for two things: oil and recreation. The western plateau is thick with fossil fuel, and the world's sixth-largest oil field is just outside Rangely. The eastern side of the plateau area—especially around Craig, Meeker, and (appropriately) Rifle—is very popular with hunters, and the mountains, from Steamboat down to Vail, are world famous for their skiing. In addition, the huge expanses of the forest draw campers, backpackers, rafters, mountain bikers, and anglers to the high mountains when the snow melts.

EAST ALONG INTERSTATE 70

Interstate 70 veers north from Grand Junction, follows the Colorado River, and gradually yet persistently rises up into the heart of Colorado and the Rocky Mountains. En route it passes through or provides access to some of the state's most popular attractions: Aspen, Vail, Summit County, Georgetown and Idaho Springs, and Denver.

Between the Utah border and Glenwood Springs, the largest town between Grand Junction and Vail, the freeway is mostly wide open and flat, passing occasionally through deep canyons carved by the Colorado River. In Glenwood Springs, the valley grows narrow, the canyons often pinching tightly together (see

"Glenwood Canyon" under "Glenwood Springs and Vicinity" following). You can find plenty of inexpensive lodging in Glenwood; this is also where you'll turn south to catch US 82 to Aspen or US 133 to Telluride.

Between Glenwood Springs and Vail, the interstate bypasses a number of small towns— Eagle, Edwards, Avon—which also offer lodging and services. At Avon you enter the Vail Valley, a resort region devoted largely to skiing. Three ski areas, Arrowhead, Beaver Creek, and Vail, attract skiers by the thousands (Vail's uphill capacity is 36,000 per hour), not only from Denver, a hundred miles to the east, but from the east coast and around the world. Because of

NORTHWESTERN COLORADO HIGHLIGHTS

Dinosaur National Monument: sightseeing, camping, museums

Steamboat Springs: snow skiing, fishing, rafting, hiking, Winter Carnival, Cowboy Roundup Days

Vail: skiing, shopping, cycling, sightseeing, Arrowhead Ski Area, 10th Mountain Hut and Trail System

Glenwood Springs: Frontier Historical Museum, Doc Holliday's Grave, hot springs, Vapor Caves, skiing, fishing

White River and Routt national forests: camping and cross-country skiing

the area's popularity, as well as I-70's importance to cross-country traffic, the road is kept plowed, and even during the severest of storms delays will be few and short-lived (but carry chains anyway!).

PARACHUTE

About an hour northeast of Grand Junction, Parachute is a little bitty town where you can rest up, gas up, and pick up road pops and other supplies for the cooler. A small picnic area at the turnoff offers a welcome respite for the road weary, who'll also find a booth with tourist information (maps, brochures, etc.) and the Thunder River Trading Post, where you can buy souvenirs, gifts, postcards, T-shirts, and other knickknacks. In addition to the minimarts and other small businesses you can see from the road, a City Market (no salad bar or deli) is located up on the hill in the Battlement Mesa development (follow the signs).

If you're too tired to drive on, Parachute also offers a couple of places to pull off the road to catch some shut-eye, the better to face the road that lies ahead. A **Super 8 Motel,** tel. (970) 285-7936, is located just north of the freeway exit (you can see it from the interstate), and a **Good Sam RV Park** is just over four miles east (stay on the freeway and watch for the sign).

RIFLE

Rifle is located about 63 miles northeast of Grand Junction at the junction of I-70 and CO 13 north, which shoots straight up to Meeker (40 miles) along the base of the White River Plateau. Long a shopping center and meeting place for area ranchers, Rifle is also a base for folks heading up into the mountains of White River National Forest, just north of town; in the late summer and fall, the area is particularly popular among deer and elk hunters.

According to legend, the town's name came about inadvertently when a mapmaker from an early surveying party left his rifle leaning against a tree, headed back to camp, then suddenly realized his mistake. He grabbed the map he was working on and scribbled the word "rifle" to indicate where the tree was. Later, "rifle" being a prominent word on the only map of the area, folks naturally took to calling the town Rifle. And if you believe that . . .

Rifle Creek Museum

This small museum displays frontier gear (saddles, snowshoes, traps, etc.) as well as early farming and medical equipment and domestic utensils. Located downtown at 337 East Ave., the museum is open Mon.-Fri. 10 a.m.-4 p.m. For further information, phone (970) 625-5862.

Rifle Gap Falls and Lake State Recreation Area

This is where locals go to cool off during the hot summer months, for fishing, swimming, sailing, windsurfing, waterskiing, and even spelunking. Camp beside the Rifle Gap Reservoir, and fish for brown and rainbow trout and smallmouth bass, as well as walleye and other panfish.

Rifle Falls is a broad 50-foot-high waterfall on East Rifle Creek, at the base of which are lush foliage and a series of caves. The caves are large, save for a few narrow crawlways, and perfect for novice explorers.

The lake and falls are about 15 miles north of Rifle. Take CO 13 north about five miles, and turn right on CO 325. Cost to get into Rifle Falls is $3 per vehicle; additional cost for camping. For further information, phone (970) 625-1607.

Accommodations

Rifle offers several clean, inexpensive, and easy-to-get-to places to bed down for the night; one of the best is the **Rusty Cannon Motel,** tel. (970) 625-4004, where singles start at about $35—located just off the interstate. Across the street, the **Red River Inn,** tel. (970) 625-3050, also has inexpensive rooms, starting at about $25 for singles. You'll also find budget rooms across the freeway on the frontage road at the **LaDonna Motel,** tel. (970) 625-1741, an older place that's either nicely shaded or quite overgrown, depending on your perspective. You can also get inexpensive rooms (doubles start at about $35) downtown at the **Winchester Motel,** 520 Railroad Ave., tel. (970) 625-1777.

Food and Drink

If you're heading out of (or through) Rifle in the early morning, stop in at **Country Doughnuts** on E. 3rd St., where you can get doughnuts singly or by the dozen, or, if you're looking for something that'll stick to your ribs a bit longer, big diner-style breakfasts for $2-4. This little cafe, full of locals talking weather and small-town politics, has a huge map of the United States at the counter, and customers are invited to put pins up marking their hometowns. Country Doughnuts is also open for lunch, serving sandwiches, burgers, and salads for $2-5, and dinner, with burgers, chicken, and chimichangas for $3-6.

Village Pizza Factory, 160 Railroad Ave., tel. (970) 625-0835, serves pizzas, sandwiches, salads, and spaghetti dishes for lunch and dinner ($5-12).

The **Red Lion Pub** downtown on Railroad Ave., tel. (970) 625-3491, much less the British-style pub its name implies than the local mountain bar the location suggests, plays loud jukebox music and serves domestic and imported beer in *tall* glasses. The place has a reputation for getting downright rowdy, especially on Friday and Saturday nights, when workers come down out of the mountains to blow off steam.

Services

The offices of the **Rifle Police Department** are at 202 Railroad Ave., tel. (970) 625-2331. Phone the **Garfield County Sheriff** at (970) 625-1899. Rifle's small **Clagett Memorial Hospital** is at 701 E. 5th Ave., tel. (970) 625-1510. Larger medical facilities are in Glenwood Springs, about 25 miles west, at **Valley View Hospital,** tel. (970) 945-6535. Rifle's **post office** is at 330 Railroad Ave., tel. (970) 625-1070. Get **maps** and **Forest Service information** at the White River National Forest—District Office, 94 County Rd. 244, tel. (970) 625-2371.

Recycling

Drop off most recyclables at **Blackmore Metals** on the west end of town. Recycle aluminum at the **City Market** at 1320 Railroad Avenue.

Rifle:
a high-caliber town

Information

The **Rifle Visitor Information Center** is located at the rest area at the I-70 exit (200 Lions Park Circle). You'll find information here not only about local attractions, accommodations, and recreation opportunities, but also about much of the White River National Forest and Glenwood Springs-Aspen areas. You can also write Box 809, Rifle, CO 81650, or phone (970) 625-2085.

GLENWOOD SPRINGS AND VICINITY

One of Colorado's most historically and geologically fascinating towns, Glenwood Springs is the site of what it claims is the world's largest natural hot springs pool. Actually comprising two pools—the larger 405 by 100 feet and containing over a million gallons of water—Glenwood Hot Springs has been attracting travelers for centuries, from nomadic Ute, Comanche, Cheyenne, and Arapahoe peoples who believed in the waters' spiritual healing powers to modern-day après-skiers who believe simply in its powers to ease aching muscles.

A gateway to the best ski areas in the state, Glenwood Springs (pop. 6,000; elev. 5,750 feet) has a small ski resort (Ski Sunlight) right in its backyard and is the last decent-sized town you pass through heading east on I-70 before you get into the heart of the Rockies and Colorado's real winter sports arenas: Vail and the ski mecca of Summit County. In addition, Glenwood Springs is at the junction with US 82, the only road into Aspen in the winter (when the highway southeast of Aspen is closed over Independence Pass). In fact, not only do a large number of Aspen-area workers live in Glenwood Springs (where housing's much less expensive) and commute the 40 miles every day to the ski town, but many people who live in Aspen drive regularly into Glenwood Springs to do their shopping; from razor blades to dog food to fresh produce, everyday necessities are far cheaper in Glenwood Springs than in Aspen.

All of which should tell the savvy winter tourist something: If you want to ski Aspen, and you want to save some money, think about staying in Glenwood Springs. Though you'd be hard pressed to find a room in Aspen for much under $80 or $90 a night, Glenwood has several motels where clean rooms start at around $25, as well as a hostel where you can get a bed for about $12. That's a savings of close to $400 a week—which could almost buy you and a date a nice dinner out in Aspen.

HISTORY

Known for centuries to Utes, who, protective of their sacred waters, fought to keep the Cheyenne and Comanche away, Glenwood Springs was first discovered by whites in 1860, when Captain Richard Sopris took sick while exploring the Eagle River Valley and was brought to the waters by the Utes. In the 1870s, the discovery of silver in Leadville brought about a population boom and a flurry of mining-camp construction in the mountains east of Glenwood. Leadville's John Landis arrived at Yampah springs in 1880 and, in true colonial fashion, claimed it for his own.

By the mid-1880s, the Native Americans had been mostly displaced, and white settlers had taken control of much of the fertile Roaring Fork River Valley. In 1885, Walter Devereux, an Aspen miner and engineer, bought the hot springs, incorporated Glenwood Springs, and began to solicit tourism and investment. By the latter part of the 1880s, Glenwood Springs was a rip-roaring town whose nearly two dozen saloons were well known to many of the hard-living miners, ranchers, cowboys, merchants, and lawmen who opened up the West.

The Denver and Rio Grande Railroad pushed through Glenwood Springs in 1887. A year later, thanks largely to the labor of local prison inmates who worked to break up the rock-hard ground and divert water from the Colorado River, old Yampah springs had been converted into a concrete pool, with an adjacent bathhouse, hotel, and casino.

In 1893, the Hotel Colorado was completed, and the area soon became a popular resort destination for some of the more monied eastern families, including Vanderbilts and Astors. Due in part to the influence of this upscale clientele, as well as to the importance of the horse to Glenwood's development, polo became a celebrated local pas-

GLENWOOD SPRINGS

TO VAIL AND DENVER →

GLENWOOD SPRINGS GOLF CLUB

COLORADO RIVER

TO GRAND JUNCTION

HOTEL COLORADO

HOT SPRINGS POOL

AMTRAK STATION

POST OFFICE

9th ST.

GLENWOOD SPRINGS HOSTEL

10th ST.

FRONTIER HISTORICAL MUSEUM

11th ST.

COOPER AVE.

CHAMBER OF COMMERCE INFORMATION

COLORADO AVE.

13th ST.

BENNET AVE.

CEMETERY RD.

GRAND AVE.

19th ST.

VALLEY VIEW HOSPITAL

BLAKE AVE.

ROARING FORK RIVER

27th ST.

TO SKI SUNLIGHT

AIRPORT

82

TO ASPEN

NOT TO SCALE

© MOON PUBLICATIONS, INC.

---

time, and Glenwood teams won national championships in the early part of the century (trophies are on display in the Frontier Historical Museum).

The mid-20th-century was essentially a slow time for Glenwood Springs, as other mountain towns began to draw crowds; however, with the boom in the ski industry (as well as in the health and fitness industries), in addition to an increased interest in local history and heritage, things in Glenwood Springs began to pick up. By the 1970s and '80s, the public was rediscovering the hot springs, realizing the important part this little town played in the development of the state, and taking advantage of its proximity to Aspen and the other nearby ski resorts.

ATTRACTIONS AND PARKS

Frontier Historical Museum

Founded in 1963 by the Glenwood Springs Historical Society, this small museum—originally a home built in 1905 by a local doctor—features a replica of a coal mine, a collection of pioneer-era toys, dolls, and clothing, as well as Native American artifacts and historical maps and photos of Glenwood Springs and the surrounding areas.

Hours are Mon.-Sat. 11 a.m.-4 p.m. (Monday, Thursday, Friday only, 1-4 p.m., in winter). Admission is $2 (no charge for kids under 11).

Hot Springs Lodge at Glenwood Hot Springs

Guided group tours are available by appointment. For more information, write Glenwood Springs Historical Museum, 1001 Colorado Ave., Glenwood Springs, CO 81601, or phone (970) 945-4448.

Doc Holliday's Grave, Linwood Cemetery
An easy half-mile trail leads from Cemetery Rd. (off Bennett Ave.) to Linwood Cemetery, where Doc Holliday—the famous wild-west gambler and roustabout—is reportedly buried: Although a gravestone with his name and the inscription "died in bed" stands in the cemetery, some claim he was buried in an unmarked grave in town. Kid Curry, a member of Butch Cassidy's Hole-in-the-Wall gang, is also buried at Linwood.

In the winter, the trail is perfect for a short Nordic ski excursion.

Glenwood Hot Springs Pool
Advertising itself in the early part of the century as a "Health and Pleasure Resort," serving both "invalids and tourists," this gigantic hot springs has actually been serving travelers for hundreds of years. Utes, who called them Yampah (or "Big Medicine") springs, used the pools, as did early white settlers and several U.S. presidents, including Teddy Roosevelt.

The pools are completely refilled about every eight hours by the three and a half million gallons of 124-degree water that flows from the springs daily—perfect for basking in after a day on the slopes or an afternoon chasing trout in the Colorado or Roaring Fork River. A daily pass is $6 for adults ($3.75 for kids three to 12). There's also a weight and exercise room, and a water slide. Suits and towels can be rented for a nominal fee. For information, write Hot Springs Lodge and Pool, Box 308, Glenwood Springs, CO 81602, or phone (970) 945-6571, (800) 623-3400 (toll free from Denver), (800) 537-SWIM (toll free from the rest of Colorado).

Yampa Spa and Vapor Caves
Three caves, heated by mineral hot springs to 115 degrees and approximately 100% humidity, are open to the public seven days a week. At one time part of the Utes' Yampah springs (along with the hot springs pools), the caves are now privately owned. In addition to a cleansing sweat in the caves, you can get a variety of health ministrations: massages, facials, cranial-sacral therapy, Reiki therapy, reflexology, and earwax removal. Afterward, you can relax in the solarium or on the sundeck with a glass of natural juice. Prices start at $7.75 (for a cave visit) and run to $108 (for the full treatment—massage, foot reflex, facial).

The Vapor Caves are open seven days a week 9 a.m.-9 p.m. For more information, phone (970) 945-0667, or write 709 E. 6th St., Glenwood Springs, CO 81601.

City Park
Glenwood Spring's Sayre's Park is right on the main drag through town (US 82/Grand Ave.) and has picnic facilities, tennis and basketball courts, and spacious lawns.

RECREATION

Skiing

One of Colorado's smaller ski resorts, but a favorite among locals who want to avoid the crowds and pretentiousness of the larger areas, **Ski Sunlight** offers both downhill and cross-country skiing about 10 miles from Glenwood Springs (free shuttles run regularly between town and the resort). With a 2,000-foot vertical drop, Sunlight's 440 acres of trails and runs, serviced by four lists, are 20% novice, 55% intermediate, and 25% advanced.

Lodging, equipment rental, lessons (downhill, cross-country, and Telemark), and day care are all available at Sunlight, as are package deals with local hotels and motels. For more information, write Ski Sunlight, 10901 County Rd. 117, Glenwood Springs, CO 81601, or phone (970) 945-7491 or (800) 445-7931.

Southwest of Glenwood Springs off CO 82, **Spring Gulch** is a Nordic area with 10 miles of trails operated by the Mount Sopris Nordic Council. Skiing is free. For maps and information, check ski shops in the Glenwood Springs-Carbondale-Aspen area. You can also get information on cross-country skiing in the Glenwood Springs area by calling the Glenwood Group of the Colorado Mountain Club at (970) 945-1238; the club has regular cross-country outings and encourages the public to come along.

Golf

Glenwood Springs Golf Course is a nine-hole public course located north of the frontage road in west Glenwood Springs. For tee times or further information, phone (970) 945-7086.

Hiking

Virtually surrounded by mountains and national forest lands, Glenwood Springs offers the hiker and backpacker hundreds of miles of trails to explore. Just a few miles east of town, **No Name** and **Hanging Lake** trails are good day hikes. In town, the **Boy Scout Trail** takes hikers from the top of 8th St. to the base of Lookout Mountain—3.5 miles, approximately two hours. Bring water. **Red Mountain Trail** will take you from the end of W. 9th St. to the site of Glenwood's first ski area, where the lift towers are still standing. The hikes from Cemetery Rd. to Linwood Cemetery and from the Vapor Caves to the Colorado River are both easy, scenic, and enjoyable.

For maps and more information, contact the Glenwood Springs Chamber of Commerce (1102 Grand Ave., tel. 970-945-6589) or the White River National Forest headquarters (900 Grand Ave., P.O. Box 948, tel. 970-945-2521). You can also get USGS maps and tips on hiking and backpacking in the area at **Summit Canyon Mountaineering,** 1001 Grand Ave., tel. (970) 945-6994.

Hunting and Fishing

Come winter, you'll likely hear longtime Glenwoodians talking about how full their freezers are. "Didn't think I was gonna get my elk this year, but I finally did, just before the season closed." Deer, too, are popular prey of local (as well as visiting) hunters, though they know the 150 pounds of meat a decent-sized mulie provides is nothing next to what a big bull elk can—upwards of 400 pounds. Good fishing abounds in the Glenwood Springs area, too—rainbows and brown trout in the Colorado River west of town, and brookies and rainbows in the small lakes in the surrounding mountains. For tips on local fishing, stop by **Roaring Fork Anglers,** 2022 Grand Ave., or phone (970) 945-0180.

Rafting

On the confluence of the Roaring Fork and Colorado rivers, Glenwood Springs is a rafter's paradise, and companies based throughout the area offer a variety of trips, from short, two-hour jaunts to three-day excursions. **Rock Gardens Rafting,** tel. (970) 945-6737, offers short tours ($13), half-day ($20), and full-day trips ($35, including lunch); they also have a campground with RV and tent sites. Located off I-70 two miles east of Glenwood Springs, Exit 119. **Blue Sky Adventurers,** 319 6th St., tel. (970) 945-6605, and **Whitewater Rafting,** 51100 Highways 6 and 24, tel. (970) 945-8477, can also arrange trips.

TOURS

The Glenwood Springs Chamber of Commerce (see "Information" following) has outlined a historic walking tour of downtown Glenwood Springs. Included are the stone bathhouse at the hot springs pool, the vapor caves, the Hotel Colorado, the Glenwood Barber Shop (the only remaining portion of the Hotel Glenwood, built before the turn of the century and mostly destroyed by fire in 1945), and over three dozen other buildings of historical significance—homes, banks, and retail stores. The chamber can provide you with a map.

For snowmobile tours of the area (from two-hour trips to overnight excursions that include meals and lodging), contact **Rocky Mountain Sports, Inc.,** 0412 Sun King Dr., Glenwood Springs, CO 81601, tel. (970) 945-8498. In warmer weather, **Crystal River Jeep Tours,** 116 E. Main St., Marble, CO 81623, tel. (970) 963-1991, offers trips to the Yule Marble Quarry, Crystal City, and Lead King Basin.

ACCOMMODATIONS

Hotels and Motels

Glenwood Springs offers a wide range of comfortable rooms, from dorm-style digs at the hostel to rustic rooms at the historic Hotel Colorado, with quite a bit in between. At the **Glenwood Springs Hostel,** 1021 Grand Ave., tel. (970) 945-8545, you can get a bed for about $12, or $70 a week (students and AYH members slightly less). Walking distance from the hot springs, the hostel offers discounts on ski tickets and rental, free pick-up from the bus and train depots (with advance notice), as well as laundry and kitchen facilities and a record library for use by guests.

The **Glenwood Hot Springs Lodge,** tel. (970) 945-6571 or (800) 537-SWIM (in Colorado only), has doubles starting at about $55, with entry discounts offered for the pool, while rooms at the historic **Hotel Colorado,** tel. (970) 945-6511 or, toll-free from Denver, (800) 623-3400, start at about $50. Also just across from the hot springs is the **Hotel Denver,** tel. (970) 945-6565, one of the nicest places in town. Though like the Hotel Colorado, this is a historic hotel, dating from just before the turn of the century, the place has been better maintained and its restorations are actually quite classy. Doubles range $60-120.

The **Ponderosa Motel and Cottages** in West Glenwood at 51793 US Highways 6 and 24, tel.

(970) 945-5058, has rooms and cabins (efficiency to large A-frames) running $50-100. The **Super 8 Motel,** tel. (970) 945-8888, the **Ramada Inn,** tel. (970) 945-2500, and the **Holiday Inn,** tel. (970) 945-8551, have rooms starting at under $50.

If you're going to be skiing at Ski Sunlight, you'd be hard-pressed to do better than the **Brettelberg Condominiums,** tel. (970) 945-7421 or (800) 634-0481. More a 1940s-style ski lodge than a modern-day condo complex, the Brettelberg is right on the slopes, actually uphill from the base lodge—the ultimate in "ski in and ski out." Rates start at about $80 a night for four people (studio); weekly rates max at about $600 for four. For more information, write Brettleberg Condominiums, 11101 Rd. 117, Glenwood Springs, CO 81601.

Bed and Breakfasts

Glenwood Springs offers a couple of good bed-and-breakfast lodging options. **Adduccie's Inn,** 1023 Grand Ave., tel. (970) 945-9341, in an old Victorian (most rooms share a shower; one has a private bath) has rooms for $35-65. **The Bed and Breakfast on Mitchell Creek,** 1686 Mitchell Creek Rd., tel. (970) 945-4002, is in the mountains outside town and offers one large suite for $90 for two.

Camping and RVing

Campgrounds are scattered throughout the White River National Forest, large units of which surround the Glenwood Springs area. **Deep Lake** and **Coffee Pot Spring** have free camping at moderately improved sites (pit toilets, no showers—drinking water at Coffee Pot Spring only). For more information, phone the Eagle District Office of the Forest Service at (970) 328-6388; for maps of White River National Forest, stop by forest headquarters at 900 Grand Avenue.

RV and tent camping are available at **Hideout RV Park,** tel. (970) 945-5621, about a mile up the road toward Ski Sunlight, and at **Ami's Acres Campground,** tel. (970) 945-5340, off I-70 at Exit 114. A **KOA** campground, tel. (970) 984-2240, in New Castle, 11 miles west of Glenwood Springs on I-70, has tent sites, full-hookup RV sites, and cabins, as well as hot showers, laundry facilities, and a small store. Take Exit

105 from I-70, and follow the signs to East Elk Creek Road. Two miles east of Glenwood Springs, **Rock Gardens Camping and Rafting,** tel. (970) 945-6737, offers tent and RV sites as well as half- and full-day raft trips.

FOOD

The Devereux Room at the **Hotel Colorado,** tel. (970) 945-6511, serves breakfast (pancakes, omelettes, etc.), lunch (fish and chips, sandwiches, salads), and dinner (veal, chicken, beef, and Southwestern food) at moderate prices. For an inexpensive and delicious lunch, try **The Loft,** 720 Grand Ave., tel. (970) 945-6808. Sandwiches, salads (dynamite Caesars!), and burritos run $5-8. For Italian food, try **Florindo's,** 721 Grand, tel. (970) 945-1245, with a focus on homemade food from the south of Italy. Check out **Buffalo Valley Restaurant,** a mile and a half south of Glenwood on US 82, tel. (970) 945-5297, for down-home western grub—buffalo steaks, ribs, barbecue chicken, plus pastas and a salad bar. Live dance music on weekends. **Springs Sports Bar and Grill,** 722 Grand, tel. (970) 945-2388, serves burgers, salads, pizzas—and offers nine TV screens for Broncos and Rockies. Families will enjoy **Andre's Restaurant,** tel. (970) 945-5367, where dolls, puppets, and stuffed animals decorate the walls and an electric train circles overhead in the dining room. Italian entrees and pizzas run $6-10. Located just off I-70 in West Glenwood.

For "Food so good you'll slap yo mama," served by a "well trained . . . and slightly warped staff," try **The Bayou,** on the frontage road in West Glenwood, tel. (970) 945-1047. During ski season, get a free cup of gumbo by showing your lift ticket or ski rental receipt, and a free cocktail if you've got a cast from a ski injury.

About eight miles south of town on CO 82 (to Aspen) is the **Sopris Restaurant and Lounge,** tel. (970) 945-7771. One of the nicer eateries in the area, the Sopris is popular with everyone from local ranchers and outfitters to Aspen luminaries, who rave about the eclectic menu—from American-standard beef dishes to daily continental specials.

ENTERTAINMENT AND EVENTS

Though there's undoubtedly more going on up the road in Aspen, Glenwood Springs does offer its share of nightlife. **Mother O'Leary's,** 914 Grand Ave., tel. (970) 945-4078, features live rock 'n' roll and country-and-western depending on the night of the week—call ahead. **Buffalo Valley,** a mile and a half up the road toward Aspen, tel. (970) 945-5297, has a large dance floor, with live music on weekends. In addition, the lounges at the **Sopris Restaurant,** 7215 US 82, tel. (970) 945-7771, and the **Holiday Inn,** tel. (970) 945-8551, regularly feature live listening and dancing music. For current information on what's going on where, pick up a free copy of *Mountain Leisure,* published every Friday by the *Glenwood Post* and distributed in racks around town. You'll find listings of art, recreation, and nightlife happenings, as well as reviews and theater schedules.

Calendar

Glenwood's biggest annual event is the popular **Strawberry Days** in mid-June. Dating from 1863, this is the oldest town festival in Colorado (canceled only during the food and gasoline rationing of WW II) and features foot and bicycle races, Pony Express rides, a parade, arts-and-crafts fair, beauty pageant (de gustibus non est disputandum . . .), live country-and-western music, and free strawberries and ice cream.

The **International Folk Festival and Oktoberfest** in the fall in downtown's Sayre Park offers food, drink, and entertainment from around the world. And every summer for ten weeks, the city offers **Summer of Jazz** in Two Rivers Park on Wednesday nights. Concerts are by big-name acts and are free, though donations are solicited during intermissions.

For exact dates, times, and locations, as well as for more information on other Glenwood Springs events, contact the chamber of commerce (see "Information" following).

SHOPPING

In downtown Glenwood Springs you'll find a handful of souvenir and curio shops, as well as some stores carrying quality arts and crafts. The **Watersweeper and the Dwarf,** 717 Grand Ave., tel. (970) 945-2000, carries handcrafted pieces carved, sculpted, assembled, and molded from silver, gold, clay, glass, and other odds and ends. **Sioux Villa Curio,** tel. (970) 945-6134, one block west of the hot springs pool on 6th St., sells souvenirs and knickknacks, including moccasins, "authentic" Black Hills gold jewelry, and postcards. The Glenwood Springs Mall in west Glenwood has a **JCPenney, Kmart,** and over two dozen smaller stores selling everything from hats and shoes to jewelry and pets.

SERVICES

The **Glenwood Springs Police Department** is located at 823 Blake Ave., tel. (970) 945-8566. Phone the **State Patrol** at (970) 945-6198 (24-hour emergency line). Glenwood's **Valley View Hospital** is at 6535 Blake Ave., tel. (970) 945-6535. The main **post office** is at 113 9th St., tel. (970) 945-5611.

Recycling

Glenwood Springs operates two recycling centers, both of which will take aluminum and glass. Locations are 1600 Grand Ave. and the **Wal-Mart** at 3010 Blake. Recycle aluminum only at the **City Market,** 1410 Grand Ave., and **Safeway,** 2001 Grand Avenue.

INFORMATION

Stop by or write the **Glenwood Springs Chamber of Commerce** at 1102 Grand Ave., Glenwood Springs, CO 81601, tel. (970) 945-6589. You'll find plenty of information on area history, recreation, dining, and lodging, as well as maps.

For information on the **White River National Forest,** contact either the forest headquarters, 900 Grand Ave., P.O. Box 948, Glenwood Springs, CO 81602, tel. (970) 945-2521; or the Eagle District Office, 125 W. 5th St., P.O. Box 720, Eagle, CO 81631, tel. (970) 328-6388.

The **Book Train** magazine and bookstore, 723 Grand Ave., tel. (970) 945-7045, has an excellent selection of books on Colorado and the Southwest, as well as other travel books,

including those Cadillacs of travel guides, Moon Publications' handbooks. The Glenwood Springs branch of the **Garfield County Library** is located at 413 9th St., tel. (970) 945-5958. The Colorado **Mountain College Library** is at the college at 3000 County Rd. 114, tel. (970) 945-7481.

The **Frontier Historical Museum** has a gift shop with books on the area's history, as well as videos for rent. In addition, the museum's archives are available (by appointment only) for more extensive research. Phone (970) 945-4448 or 945-8465.

For **road and weather information,** phone (970) 945-2221.

TRANSPORTATION

Glenwood Springs' **Amtrak** station, tel. (970) 945-9563, is directly across the freeway from the hot springs pool (accessible via footbridge). The **Greyhound-Trailways** bus depot is at 118 W. 6th St., tel. (970) 945-8501. To rent a car, phone **Defiance Rent-a-Wreck** at (970) 945-7101, located at 1810 Grand Avenue.

Aspen's airport, 40 miles southeast of Glenwood Springs, is serviced by **Continental Express,** tel. (970) 925-3350, and **United Express,** tel. (970) 925-3400. You can rent cars at the Aspen airport (see "Aspen" under "Southwestern Colorado").

GLENWOOD SPRINGS TO VAIL

It'd be tough to find a stretch of American interstate prettier than that running east from Glenwood Springs to Vail, up over Vail Pass, through Summit County, over (or under, via tunnel) Loveland Pass, and into Denver. From Glenwood to Vail, it's about 75 miles and when the road is clear takes less than an hour and a half. Allow more time during winter storms (a main east-west artery, this is one of the first roads to be plowed, yet snow can still pile up, making it slick and dangerous).

A half-hour out of Glenwood Springs, you're approaching the soul of Colorado ski country. The Rockies' sharp peaks loom in front of you; the road grows steeper, the air thinner; condominium complexes begin to proliferate and sprawl at freeway exits. Lift towers, chairs and clearcuts punctuate the hillsides. Finally, you roll into the Vail valley, site of one of the world's premier ski resorts and summer vacation areas.

Glenwood Canyon

Just a few miles east of Glenwood Springs, you enter Glenwood Canyon, the most scenic stretch of the Utah-to-Kansas freeway. Here, I-70 snakes through a 15-mile-long crevice carved by the Colorado River, bridging it and flirting with its steep, rocky banks. In some places, the canyon walls are 2,000 feet high.

An important artery for travelers since 1887, when the Denver and Rio Grande Railroad first laid tracks along the river, Glenwood Canyon has seen several generations of roadways. The recently completed Glenwood Canyon Highway, in planning since the mid-1970s and under

construction throughout the '80s and early '90s, makes every attempt to wed modern transportation needs with the environmental considerations dire to such a sensitive area. While the road was being built, workers had to conform to strict ecological guidelines and were under the constant scrutiny of environmentalists.

The completed stretch of highway, which includes over 40 bridges (totaling over six miles), used 30 million pounds of structural steel, 30 million pounds of reinforcing steel, and 400,000 cubic yards of concrete.

Four rest areas along this short stretch of road offer access to hiking trails into White River National Forest, as well as to the recreation/bike path (wheelchair accessible) that follows the entire course of the highway through the canyon. One of them, Grizzly Creek Rest Area, also has a launch for kayaks, rafts, and other small boats.

VAIL AND BEAVER CREEK

Located in the Gore Creek Valley between the Gore and Sawatch mountain ranges, Vail has earned a reputation as one of the finest ski areas in the world. Just 100 miles west of Denver via I-70, Vail attracts not only hundreds of thousands of skiers each year, but also more and more summer visitors, who descend on the little community of Vail Village (permanent pop. 5,000; elev. 8,150) to take part in the virtually limitless recreational opportunities—golfing, tennis, cycling, fishing, horseback riding, and rafting—as well as to wander through the town's cobblestone streets and Tyrolean-style buildings.

Vail, like Aspen, is almost always associated with money. This is one of the playgrounds of the East Coast rich, and hotel rooms can run $300 a night; you can't very well vacation here if you've got to keep a close eye on finances.

Then there's Beaver Creek, Vail's even richer neighbor, where summer homes run into the millions and a suite in a luxury hotel can cost up to $600. People who can afford to stay here don't even blink at the thought of spending $40 for a ski lift ticket (prices are the same at both Vail and Beaver Creek, both of which are owned and operated by Vail Associates).

But don't let it intimidate you. Even though, as F. Scott Fitzgerald once said to Ernest Hemingway, "The rich aren't like you and me," and they do own much of the Vail area, they don't own all of it. And there are ways for a working person to enjoy a visit without going hopelessly into debt. In fact, one of the best parts of visiting Vail is simply wandering around, browsing in the wide range of specialty shops, and strolling along the bike and walking path between the town and the base of the lifts.

History

Compared to Telluride, Breckenridge, Aspen, and many other Colorado ski towns, Vail is a relative newcomer, barely a quarter century old. The area was probably explored to some degree as early as 1850, when Irishman Sir George Gore (whose surname is unfortunately fitting) and a huge hunting party went on a blood-lusty trophy tour of Colorado and southern Wyoming. In 1873, the Hayden Survey Party passed through the valley, with photographer William Henry Jackson lugging 100 pounds of equipment up Notch Mountain to take his now-famous photo of Mount of the Holy Cross. The near-perfect cross in the photo, first displayed at the Philadelphia Centennial Exhibition of 1876, has inspired thousands of pilgrims to the area.

It wasn't until the middle of the next century, though, that the Vail Valley saw any real settlement. In 1942, some 15,000 troops from the Army's 10th Mountain Division were stationed in the mountains south of Vail. Many of these men—trained in backcountry winter survival, including getting around on skis—saw action in Italy's Po River Valley and Apennine Mountains. After the war, a handful of them, led by Peter Seibert, who had been wounded in Italy, returned to the area and began developing their own ski area. Vail saw its first lift-borne skiers on December 15, 1962. By the winter of 1965, a small village had begun to develop, with several restaurants, saloons, hotels, and a medical clinic. The town was incorporated that year.

In the mid-1970s, Vail began to make itself known as one of Colorado's best ski areas, its "Back Bowls" earning the respect of the most discriminating skiers in the country. In 1974, Gerald Ford, who had owned a home in Vail since the mid-1960s, became president of the United States following Richard Nixon's resignation. Photos of Ford at his "Western White House" graced the pages of newspapers throughout the world.

Work on Vail's sister resort, Beaver Creek, was begun by Vail Associates in the late 1970s; it had originally been part of a plan to bid for the 1976 Winter Olympics (defeated by Colorado voters). By the early '80s the two ski areas had developed a reputation not only for some of the best snow in the Rockies, but for some of the best "show." Vail and big money became almost synonymous, and the perception, not wholly inaccurate if obviously stereotypical, of the Vail visitor was one of furs, fancy German cars, expensive state-of-the-art ski equipment, and a foreign accent, either European or Texan.

Also during the early '80s, Vail and Beaver Creek began to expand from primarily winter playgrounds to year-round resorts. More golf courses were built, gondolas and chairlifts were made available to sightseers and mountain bikers, and the village began to sponsor hot-air balloon rallies, tennis tournaments, and concerts, from chamber music to rock 'n' roll. During the summer of 1988, Vail Ski Area's Back Bowls were further developed, more than doubling the amount of skiable terrain on the mountain.

Colorado Ski Museum

Offering an overview of the history of skiing around the world, with an emphasis on Colorado, this small museum features excellent exhibits, including lots of wonderful historical photos and examples of century-old equipment. Check out skis used by early Colorado miners in the 1880s, early "beartrap" bindings, the first buckle boots and metal-edged skis, the infa-

skiing the Back Bowls at Vail

JACK AFFLECK

mous K2 Cheeseburger Deluxes, and skis used by recent Olympic-medal winners, as well as equipment once belonging to Gerald Ford. You can also learn more about the Army's 10th Mountain Division and view some of their equipment—tents, skis, white camouflage parkas, etc.

The Colorado Ski Museum is located in Vail Village at the corner of Vail Rd. and E. Meadow Drive. Hours are Tues.-Sun. 10 a.m.-5 p.m. Admission is $1. For further information, phone (970) 476-1876.

PARKS AND RECREATION

Recreation is what Vail's all about. Folks come from all over the world to vacation here, to ski the vast expanses of the Back Bowls, to hit golf balls into the 8,000-foot-high, thin mountain air, to toss caddis flies at native rainbow trout. Or just to relax. What better place to hide behind a pair of Foster Grants and a Stephen King novel than beside a pool or at a sidewalk cafe in Vail Village?

The **Vail/Beaver Creek Activities Desk** can arrange a wide array of recreational vacations, from kayaking to jeep tours. Phone (970) 949-9090.

WINTER SPORTS

Vail was founded on downhill skiing, and even as the resort has diversified, downhill skiing remains its primary draw. From mid-November through April, weather permitting, Vail's parking lots are packed with ski-racked 4WD rigs, its streets bustling with ski-booted shoppers, its restaurants and hotels packed to the gills with skiers of all abilities, from complete novices to certified powderhounds and bump bashers. In the winter, just about everything in the Vail valley revolves around snow skiing.

Vail

In a recent *Skiing* magazine article, former Vail ski instructor Lito Tejada-Flores (who has since relocated to Telluride) wrote that Vail's Back Bowls are the "quintessential skiing invitation." In addition, readers' polls sponsored by both *Ski* and *Snow Country* magazines listed Vail as the number one ski area in the country.

Indeed, the resort offers nearly 4,014 acres of wide open skiing terrain divided up fairly evenly for beginner, intermediate, and advanced skiers. The largest single-mountain ski area in the U.S., Vail has a 3,330-foot vertical drop, 25 lifts (including nine high-speed detachable quads), and 120 runs, some of which are over four miles long. Its total uphill capacity is over 42,000 skiers per hour.

Of course as one of Colorado's premier ski resorts, and certainly its most accessible, the place can get crowded, especially on weekends. Only 100 miles from Denver, Vail is close enough even for day-trippers. Still, though, thanks particularly to the new Back Bowls and high-speed chairs, the mobs are handled relatively gracefully, and you should be able to find a fairly uncrowded slope to crank some turns (though if you'd rather strut your stuff for the masses, there's plenty of opportunity for that too).

Like a luxury hotel, Vail is exclusive in both feel and actual cost, and folks on budgets will have a tough time here: A single day's lift ticket will set you back about $48 (though seniors 70 and older ski free). Still, it's a great splurge, and every serious skier owes it to himself to hit Vail at least once in his lifetime.

Vail has a full-service ski school, including programs for kids (three and older; non-ski programs for kids two months to six years), racers, snowboarders, Telemarkers, and cross-country skiers. Vail also offers NASTAR recreational racing.

For more information on skiing Vail, write Vail Associates, Box 7, Vail, CO 81658, tel. (970) 476-5601. For information about children's ski programs, phone (970) 479-2040; adult ski school, (970) 476-3239; cross-country and Telemark, (970) 476-5601, ext. 4390. For information on **snow conditions,** phone (970) 476-4888 or 476-4889. For information on NASTAR racing, phone (970) 476-5601, ext. 4050.

Complimentary "Meet the Mountain" tours are offered Sun.-Tues. at 1 p.m. beginning at Wildwood Shelter.

Beaver Creek

Vail's little sister, Beaver Creek first opened in the winter of 1980-81. Located 10 miles west of Vail, Beaver Creek's almost 1,125 acres are serviced by 10 lifts providing access to 61 trails. Total vertical drop is a respectable 3,340 feet; uphill capacity is 17,540 skiers per hour.

Beaver Creek was originally designed with the 1976 Olympics in mind. It offers a wide range of skiing for all ability levels, with about 40% of the mountain designated intermediate. The resort offers a children's ski school (for kids three and older), a non-ski program for

kids two months to six years, as well as a full range of adult instructional programs, including snowboarding, cross-country skiing, and Telemarking.

For further information about skiing Beaver Creek, write Vail Associates, Box 7, Vail, CO 81658, tel. (970) 476-5601. For information about the nursery and children's ski school, phone (970) 949-2304; adult ski school, (970) 949-5750, ext. 5300; cross-country ski school, (970) 949-5750, ext. 5313. For information on **snow conditions,** phone 476-4888.

Free "Meet the Mountain" tours are offered Monday and Wednesday at 1 p.m. from Spruce Saddle.

Arrowhead Ski Area

Bordering Beaver Creek Ski Area in the west end of Vail Valley, Arrowhead is a young resort (first opened in 1988) offering a break from Vail's high-end prices and attitude—though it's also correspondingly smaller, its facilities less developed.

Arrowhead is the brainchild of Pete Seibert, Jr., son of one of Vail's principle founders. The resort has one high-speed quad chair and a surface lift, a vertical drop of 1,700 feet, rental facilities, and a ski school; lift tickets are about half the cost of Vail's (and sightseers can ride the chair for free).

For further information on Arrowhead Ski Area, phone (970) 926-3029.

bobsledding at Vail

JACK AFFLECK

Cross-Country Skiing

In addition to the designated cross-country trails systems operated by Vail Associates (Golden Peak Center in Vail and McCoy Park at Beaver Creek), the Vail Valley and surrounding area offers some exceptional opportunities for Nordic skiers of all abilities. You can get out and cruise groomed trails for an hour, or you can head out into serious backcountry, staying in designated huts for a week or longer.

For information on cross-country skiing in the Vail Valley, contact one of the offices of **White River National Forest.** The Holy Cross Ranger District Office is at 401 Main St. in Minturn, tel. (970) 827-5715. The national forest's headquarters is at 900 Grand Ave., P.O. Box 948, Glenwood Springs, CO 81602, tel. (970) 945-2521.

You can also get information from most of the retail cross-country ski shops in the area, including **Vail Mountaineering** in Lionshead, tel. (970) 476-4223; **Cascade Sports,** 1300 Westhaven Dr., tel. (970) 476-0186; and **Christy Sports,** 293 Bridge St., tel. (970) 476-2244.

Vail Nature Center

Located in East Vail, this is a popular Nordic center and an excellent place to set out for some low-key touring—an eight-mile track snakes along next to Gore Creek. The center also features natural-history exhibits and offers equipment rental. Open daily 9 a.m.-4 p.m. Take Vail Valley Dr. (Frontage Rd.) east from Vail Village.

For information on special programs, phone (970) 479-2261.

10th Mountain Hut and Trail System

Named for the 15,000 U.S. Army troops who trained in the 1940s at Camp Hale in the mountains south of Vail, this network of backcountry trails and huts offers the ultimate Nordic skiing experience. The trail system itself is immense, 300 miles long and linking the towns of Aspen, Leadville, Copper Mountain, and Vail. It would take most of a season to bag the whole thing. And the "huts"? Well, they're not huts as *I* would use the word. Chalets, maybe. Chateaus.

10th Mountain System skiers can either head out on their own or go with guides. The huts, most of which sleep 16, run about $25 per person per night (bring your own food). Guides

offer three- to eight-day trips, with rates starting at about $60 a day (food and other necessities provided). Though not for the first-timer, most parts of the trail system are suitable for low-intermediate skiers. For further information or reservations (the huts are always booked up in advance), contact the 10th Mountain Trail Association, 1280 Ute Ave., Aspen, CO 81611, tel. (970) 925-5775.

Guided trips can be arranged through **Elk Mountain Guides,** Box 10327, Aspen, CO 81612, tel. (970) 927-9377; **Paragon Guides,** Box 130, Vail, CO 81658, tel. (970) 949-4272; and **Vail/Beaver Creek Cross Country Ski Centers,** Vail Associates, Box 7, Vail, CO 81657, tel. (970) 476-5601, ext. 4390.

Other Winter Activities

Don't think skiing is the only winter activity for Vail Valley visitors. If you're not into strapping boards afoot, there's still plenty to do. The **John Dobson Ice Arena,** 321 Lionshead Circle, tel. (970) 479-2270, is open to the public daily. Skate rentals available.

If you want to get into the backcountry but don't feel like huffing and puffing your way through drifts of snow, you can take a **Snowcat Tour.** You can arrange tours through the **Vail/Beaver Creek Activities Desk,** tel. (970) 476-9090, or through **Nova Guides,** tel. (970) 949-4232.

Those hankering for something a bit more thrilling might want to take a ride on the 3,200-foot-long **bobsled course.** The four-person sleds reach speeds of 40 mph; helmets and instructions provided. Riders 18 and younger must have parents or guardians sign liability releases, and riders must be at least four feet tall. For further information, phone Vail Associates at (970) 949-5750.

Another popular winter activity is **snowmobiling.** Tours and rentals are offered by several companies, including **Nova Guides,** tel. (970) 949-4232, and **Piney River Ranch,** tel. (970) 476-9090.

WHEN THE SNOW MELTS

Cycling

One of the first things a summer visitor to Vail will notice is the proliferation of bicyclists. And why not? Not only is this a community where health and fitness are paramount, but cycling is an excellent way to stay in shape for skiing. In addition, the area is ideally suited to cycling, with excellent paved bike paths and hundreds of miles of backcountry trails beckoning mountain bikers. Also, many of the ski shops change their tune in the summer, renting out bikes instead of skis.

From Gore Creek Campground five miles east of Vail to West Vail Village, this is a perfect valley to explore by bike. Try the mostly flat "recreation path" that winds between the shopping area and the base of the lifts. For something a bit more demanding, head east from the village to the Vail Pass bike path, which you can take all the way into Frisco. Not for the weak of heart, the path tops out at 10,600 feet. If you're up to it, though, you'll find the scenery well worth the effort.

Mountain bikers have most of White River National Forest at their disposal. Maps and information are available from the Forest Service. For tips and advice stop by **Pedal Power,** 555 E. Lionshead Circle, tel. (970) 476-6633.

For the truly ambitious, the **10th Mountain Hut and Trail System** has recently expanded its winter operations to include backcountry bicycle tours. All told, the trail network is 300 miles long, linking Aspen, Leadville, Vail, and several other mountain resort communities. Rent a bunk in one of the 10 huts, which sleep up to 16, for about $22 a night. For information and reservations, contact the 10th Mountain Trail Association, 1280 Ute Ave., Aspen, CO 81611, tel. (970) 925-5775.

Many Vail sporting goods stores and ski shops rent bikes. Hourly rates usually run $6-7, half day $10-15, and full day $15-20. One of the best shops in town is Vail Bike Tech at the base of the gondola, tel. (970) 476-5995.

Golf

The popularity of golfing in Vail shouldn't surprise anyone. After all, this is a town built on a foundation of skiing, and the two sports share some significant similarities, not the least of which are the costs to participate and the resulting generally upscale, monied participants. Also, just as Vail is a premier ski area in anyone's view, the golf courses here are some of the finest in the West, offering challenges, great scenery, and stimulating mountain air.

Vail Golf Course is an 18-hole course and the oldest in the valley. Located at 1778 Vail Valley Dr., the course sponsors several tournaments throughout the season, including the Jerry Ford Invitational (helmets optional). Phone (970) 476-1330 for information and tee times. The fanciest course in the area is the Robert Trent Jones-designed **Beaver Creek Golf Course,** tel. (970) 949-7123. Greens fees for the 6,400-yard par-70 course are $95 (including cart), with discounts offered in May. In contrast, **Eagle-Vail Golf Course,** tel. (970) 949-5267, is a relatively modest course with considerably lower greens fees ($37 after 4 p.m., cart included). The course is about 10 miles west of Vail in Avon. **Singletree Golf Course,** tel. (970) 926-3533, is located about 15 miles west of Vail at Edwards. Rated by *Golf Digest* one of the top 50 courses in the country, the course is one of the first in the area to open each year, with early season greens fees (until May 1) a mere $20 (as opposed to $90 when the season's in full swing).

The most recent additions to the Vail-area golf scene are the 18-hole **Cordillera,** which opened in 1994 and is a private club for members and guests of the **Lodge at Cordillera,** tel. (970) 926-3500, and **Willow Creek Golf Course,** a nine-hole, beginner-oriented course west of Vail near Battle Mountain, tel. (970) 845-PAR3.

You'll also find several fine golf courses just over Vail Pass in Summit County.

Hiking and Backpacking
Surrounded by national forest lands, the Vail Valley offers nearly unlimited hiking and backpacking opportunities, from short day-hikes to serious backcountry excursions. For maps, information, and advice, stop by the **Holy Cross Ranger District Office,** 401 Main St., Minturn, or phone (970) 827-5715. You can also get information from **White River National Forest Headquarters,** 900 Grand Ave., Box 948, Glenwood Springs, CO 81602, tel. (970) 945-2521. Local bookstores and mountaineering shops carry books and hiking guides that discuss specific routes in detail. The following descriptions provide an idea of the range of hikes available.

BOB RACE

Mount of the Holy Cross near Vail

One of the shortest but still visually rewarding hikes is the two-miler to **Booth Falls,** a 60-foot waterfall that's the highlight of a series of cascades on Booth Creek. The hike is only moderately demanding. From Vail Village, go east, crossing over to the frontage road on the north side of I-70, and continue to Booth Falls Road.

At the other end of the spectrum is the climb to the top of **Mount of the Holy Cross**—about 12 miles roundtrip. At just over 14,000 feet, the peak offers excellent views of the surrounding mountains.

Camping
White River National Forest also offers superb camping, with scores of campgrounds scattered throughout the forest's two million-plus acres. In addition, backcountry camping is available in the Holy Cross and Eagles Nest wilderness areas.

Forest Service campgrounds in or near the Vail Valley include **Gore Creek Campground,** five miles east of Vail (take Exit 180 from I-70), as well as **Tigiwon, Half Moon,** and **Gold Park** campgrounds, all south of Vail via US 24 to Leadville. Contact the Forest Service (see "Hiking and Backpacking" above) for information and reservations.

Fishing
Along with biking and golfing, fishing is one of the sports that truly characterizes summer in Vail. In the very center of Vail Village you'll probably see anglers practicing their casts by tossing fly lines out over the pools of **Gore Creek.** Though fishing can actually be respectable right in town, if you'd rather not fish near boutiques, head upstream to Gore Creek Campground and beyond.

Another popular stream is the **Eagle River,** the South Fork of which parallels US 24 south of town. When fishing in streams, particularly, be sure to be aware of local restrictions; many stretches of trouty water are designated artificial bait and/or single barbless hooks only.

Local lakes that regularly offer good fishing include **Homestake Reservoir** (take US 24 south three miles south of Redcliff, and turn west on Homestake Rd.), and **Black Lakes** at Vail Pass (lots of traffic, but regularly stocked).

For information and gear, stop in at **Vail Fishing Guides,** 183 E. Gore Creek Dr., tel. (970) 476-3296, where you can also arrange guided tours.

Rafting
One of the best ways to stay cool when the summer sun pierces that thin mountain air, rafting is growing more and more popular in the Vail Valley. Several outfitters offer trips on local waters (the Eagle River), as well as rivers in other parts of the state (the Arkansas and Colorado). Among the local companies offering half- and full-day tours are **Adventures in Rafting,** 1000 Lions Ridge Loop, tel. (970) 476-7645; **Nova Guides,** tel. (970) 949-4232; and **Timberline Tours,** (970) 476-1414.

Ballooning
Though not as popular as in Aspen, where the wider valley is more conducive to expansive views and meandering flights, hot-air ballooning is still a way to see Vail from a unique vantage point. For information and reservations, contact **Camelot Balloons, Inc.,** Box 1896, Vail, CO 81658, tel. (970) 476-4743.

Horseback Riding
For those who want to see the backcountry without having to tax the ol' heart and soles, horseback is a great alternative. Local outfitters offer a range of rides—from easy, one-hour trips on virtually catatonic critters to more demanding,

multi-day adventures on properly spirited steeds. Try **Piney River Ranch,** tel. (970) 476-3941.

Tennis

Many of Vail's condominium complexes have their own tennis courts. Public courts are available at **Booth Creek, Gold Peak, Ford Park,** and **Lionshead.** For more information, phone the **Vail Metropolitan Recreation District** at (970) 479-2296. You can also play at the **Avon Municipal Courts** in Avon, 10 miles west of Vail, tel. (970) 949-4280.

Chairlift Rides

Vail Associates offers both chairlift and gondola rides from shortly after ski season ends into the early fall. For non-skiers, especially, who aren't used to this kind of transportation and the scenery it affords, this can be a wonderful way to see a different side of Vail. The 15-minute gondola ride from Vail's Lionshead to Eagles Nest guarantees stunning panoramas. At the top you can grab a barbecue lunch, take some photos, and climb back in the gondola for the ride back down, or you can hike back to the base on marked trails. Tickets cost about $14 for adults, $7 for kids under seven (seniors 70 and older ride free). Rates at Piney River Ranch as of 1995 were: $21/hour; $42/two hours; $63/three hours; $72/half day with lunch; $104 all day; $199 all day with fly-fishing; $295 overnight pack ride. Beaver Creek also offers chairlift rides, somewhat scaled down but more reasonably priced; rates are adult $6, kids under 12 $4. For more information, phone Vail Associates at (970) 476-5601, ext. 3071.

Llama Trekking

Paragon Guides offers three- and four-day llama treks into the Holy Cross Wilderness. Costs are about $200 a day for adults, $100 a day for kids under 10. Phone (970) 926-5299.

Take Me out to the Ball Game

In a town where it seems you're constantly forking out dough to buy, rent, reserve, and tip, it's nice to know there are still some things to do that are absolutely free. Watching a local softball game is one of the most relaxing ways to spend a couple of hours on a weekend afternoon or weekday evening. Grab a lawn chair and set up on the bank above the fields, which are located just off the south frontage road in Vail—you can't miss 'em.

Parks

You'll find several parks throughout the Vail Valley, most of them perfect for a picnic or to park the bike and take a snooze in the shade of a poplar. There's a **children's playground** in Vail directly behind the softball fields and adjacent to Gore Creek.

ACCOMMODATIONS

Vail is a decidedly upscale ski area, defined in large part by its luxury accommodations—most of which are within a ski pole's toss of the slopes. Keep in mind this is the playground of the rich and famous, and you won't have much luck finding bargain-rate lodging. But if you're talking Vail, you're already talking major financial commitment, and if you're gonna pamper yourself, why not go whole hog? Especially if it's for a honeymoon, a special week away from the kids, or that once-in-a-lifetime vacation you've always dreamed about.

On the other hand, if you strictly want the ski experience, and want to cut corners everywhere else, there are possibilities. You'll find less expensive lodging in Eagle (see below) about 30 miles west of Vail, and there are still a handful of relatively inexpensive motels in Frisco and Dillon (see Summit County), over Vail Pass about 25 miles east.

Remember, too, rates are significantly lower in the off-season (late spring, summer, and fall). Though Vail is growing rapidly as a year-round resort area, winter is still high season. Many of the high-end lodges offer relatively attractive low-season rates with special incentives, such as golf, biking, tennis, and sightseeing packages. Keep in mind the prices given below should be used for comparison only, and that the *huge* range accounts for seasonal adjustments. The low prices will generally be effective mid-April through mid-November, high prices during the ski season's peak times (Christmas and Easter holidays). Remember, too, most visitors do opt for multi-day stays (most often a "ski week," Mon.-Sun.), when the price *per night* isn't quite so unnerving.

For further information on lodging in Vail, contact the Vail Associates-affiliated **Vail Beaver/ Creek Reservations,** Box 7, Vail, CO 81658, tel. (800) 622-3131. You can also get information on lodging from the **Vail Valley Tourism and Convention Bureau,** tel. (970) 476-1000, 476-5677, 525-3875, or (800) 775-8245, who can also provide information on air and ground transportation, packages (skiing, golf, etc.), and convention and group facilities.

Hotels

The most "Vaily" Vail lodge is probably the **Westin Resort,** at 1300 Westhaven Dr. in Vail Village, tel. (970) 476-7111 or (800) 228-3000. Offering every imaginable amenity—ski and golf packages, exercise facilities, luxury dining rooms, and kitchens, not to mention its convenient location—the Westin is without doubt among the creamiest of a very creamy crop. Doubles range from about $150 to $335. The largest hotel at Vail is the **Radisson Resort,** tel. (970) 476-4444 or (800) 333-3333, which recently underwent a $5-million renovation; rooms go for $85-290. Other classic Vail hotels, all centrally located and offering full amenities, include **The Lodge at Vail,** 174 E. Gore Creek Dr., tel. (970) 476-5011, where doubles run $110-450; **Lodge Tower,** 200 Vail Rd., tel. (970) 476-9530, $80-350; and the **Westwind,** 548 S. Frontage Rd., tel. (970) 476-5031, $50-250.

For Vail tradition, try the **Gasthof Gramshammer,** 231 E. Gore Creek Dr., tel. (970) 476-5626, one of the oldest and most respected lodges in the village. A classic Tyrolean-style inn, the Gramshammer has been Old-World-charming returning visitors for years.

In Beaver Creek, **St. James Place,** on Village Rd., tel. (970) 949-5750, is unquestionably one of the most luxurious hotels in the state. Doubles here *start* at about $130 and go to about $600. The **Hyatt-Regency,** also on Village Rd., tel. (970) 949-1234, has rooms for two running $90-350, and you can stay at the **Inn at Beaver Creek,** tel. (970) 845-7800, for about $90-400 a night.

Motels

You'll find somewhat lower rates at the scattering of motels in Vail, including the **Best Western Vailglo Lodge,** 701 W. Lionshead Circle, tel. (970) 476-5506 or (800) 541-9423, where doubles run $70-200. The **Sitzmark Lodge,** 183 Gore Creek Dr., tel. (970) 476-5001, has rooms for two starting at about $50 and maxing out at $200. The **Comfort Inn** to the west in Avon, Exit 167 from I-70, tel. (970) 949-5511, also has doubles running $80-225. You'll find a handful of other motels in Avon as well. Contact the **Avon Chamber of Commerce,** 400 Benchmark Rd., Avon, CO 81620, tel. (970) 949-5189.

Bed and Breakfasts

Due to the fact Vail Valley is narrow and development within it therefore concentrated, and all of the buildings are relatively new, you won't find small back-street bed and breakfasts in old Victorians like you do in Breckenridge and Aspen. Still, some of the inns are moving in that direction, offering either continental or full breakfasts with a night's stay. Two miles west of Lionshead, the **Black Bear Inn,** tel. (970) 476-1304, offers 12 rooms with private baths, ranging from $95-195, including full breakfast. The **Eagle River Inn,** 145 Main St., Minturn, tel. (970) 827-5761, is an adobe Southwestern-style lodge offering a healthful breakfast of yogurt, granola, and fruit. Built in 1894, the Eagle River is decorated with Indian rugs and pottery; each room has a private bath. Rooms go for $95-200.

For a Real Splurge

If you're looking for totally distinctive deluxe digs, **Trapper's Cabin** may be the answer. Operated by Vail Associates, this 3,000-square-foot inn, at 9,500 feet between Beaver Creek and Arrowhead, can indulge most every whim—its solitude enhanced by the lack of telephones, televisions, and radios. Use the cabin as a base to explore the mountains by foot, horseback, or cross-country skis. In the evenings dine on elk steak, pheasant breast, duck, or salmon.

Rates: $2200 a night for up to four people, one night's stay; $2000 per night, two or four people, two or more nights. For information and reservations, phone Vail Associates' Hospitality Corporation at (970) 949-5750, ext. 6206.

Camping and RVing

The Vail Valley is in the thick of the White River National Forest, and most of the campgrounds in the area are small, Forest Service-administered areas. Some private RV campgrounds can be found nearby though, including **Eagle River Village** in Edwards (about 16 miles west of Vail), tel. (970) 926-3754, and **Best Western Eagle Lodge and RV Park** in Eagle, tel. (970) 328-6316. For information on national forest campgrounds contact the Forest Service (see "Hiking and Backpacking" above).

FOOD

Dining is a big part of the Vail experience. The valley has a number of first-class continental-style restaurants, and Vail Village seems to consist of about one-third eateries, serving everything from pastries to chimichangas to stir-fry. The socializing at many of them is as crucial as the actual eating.

Thankfully, many of the restaurants in Vail post their menus outside, so you can scope out the offerings and prices. Indeed, one of the best parts about a morning's shopping stroll through the village is scanning the various menus and deciding where to have lunch. If the basil-chicken special doesn't grab you, see what's cooking next door.

Start Me Up

Offering a wide range of imported and gourmet coffees, the **Daily Grind**, 288 Bridge St., tel. (970)

476-5856, also serves freshly baked croissants, muffins, bagels, and other pastries daily from 6:30 a.m. For something a little heartier, try an omelette or breakfast burrito at **D.J. McCadam's,** 616 Lionshead Circle, tel. (970) 476-2336.

Restaurants

The dining room in the **Gasthof Gramshammer,** 231 E. Gore Creek Dr., tel. (970) 476-5626, is a high-end Vail favorite. Specializing in wild game, the restaurant also serves beef, seafood, and salads in a comfortably rustic Austrian setting. The **Tyrolean Inn,** 400 E. Meadow Dr., tel. (970) 476-2204, is another favorite for wild game, as well as pasta, seafood, and lamb; entrees run $20-30. For a romantic rendezvous, try **Sweet Basil,** 193 E. Gore Creek, tel. (970) 476-0125, also in the $20-30 range. The Westin's **Alfredo's,** 1300 Westhaven Dr., tel. (970) 476-7111, is another of the valley's first-class restaurants, specializing in northern Italian cuisine; also serves Sunday brunch.

For more moderately priced meals, try the **Ore House,** 228 Bridge St., tel. (970) 476-5100, for steaks, chicken, seafood, salad bar, or Vail's entry in the microbrewery market, the **Hubcap Brewery and Kitchen,** in Vail Village, tel. (970) 476-5757, where trad brew-pub fare (burgers, pot pies, fish and chips) runs $8-12.

For Mexican food, try **Los Amigos,** 476 Bridge St., tel. (970) 476-5847, or **The Saloon** in Minturn, tel. 827-5954.

summertime in Vail Village

ENTERTAINMENT

You shouldn't have too much trouble finding something to do in Vail once the lifts shut down (or it's too dark to find your errant golf ball). Lounges at many of the hotels, including the Westin, offer live music. If you've got something a little rowdier in mind, many of the restaurants in the village feature live music, ranging from acoustic folk to electric rock 'n' roll. For starters, check out **Pepi's,** tel. (970) 476-5626, and the **Red Lion,** tel. (970) 476-7676, two definitive Vail après-ski hangouts. Also, watch the *Vail Daily* to see who's playing what kind of music where and when.

CALENDAR

Since the early 1980s, when Vail began seriously to court year-round visitors, its schedule of events has been booked. Indeed, there's a festival, concert, gallery opening, bike or ski race, or tennis or golf tournament almost every weekend. Highlights include **Winterfaire,** an annual winter carnival with dog-sled races, ice sculpture, and music; **VailAmerica Days,** a huge Fourth of July celebration, with fireworks, music, arts and crafts, barbecues; the **Bravo! Colorado Music Festival,** a classical concert series that runs through July and August; and the **Jerry Ford Invitational Golf Tournament,** in late July. In addition, there's the annual **BobFest** in Avon in late May, celebrating "Bob," the "ultimate OK guy." Activities include a Bob-B-Que, and Bobbing for apples. For complete information, phone (970) 476-1000 or 476-9090. You should also watch the *Vail Daily,* available in newspaper racks throughout Eagle County; the paper contains a calendar of weekly events, as well as movie and concert listings.

SHOPPING

Any structure in Vail that's not a restaurant or ski shop is most likely a boutique, gift shop, or gallery. And a fun part of visiting Vail is wandering around the shops. You'll find everything from souvenir and knicknack shops to places selling furs that cost more than your Ford. Also *lots* of jewelry (especially Indian) and T-shirt shops.

In addition to the standard gift shops you'd expect in a resort town, Vail has plenty of specialty stores, with something for every interest— shops selling gifts imported from Alaska, fly-fishing gear, and one devoted entirely to Scotch terriers (and their owners). Even if you're not looking to buy, these stores can be fun to poke your head into, and you should allow at least one afternoon to "do" shopping in Vail Village.

SERVICES

The offices of the **Vail Police Department** are at 75 S. Frontage Rd.; phone (970) 479-2200. Phone the **Eagle County Sheriff** at (970) 949-5620, and the **State Patrol** at (970) 328-6343. The full-sevice **Vail Valley Medical Center,** tel. (970) 476-2451 or 476-8085 (in emergencies), is located in Vail Village at 181 W. Meadow Drive. Vail's main **post office** is at 111 S. Frontage Rd., tel. (970) 476-5217.

Recycling

Recycle aluminum, glass, newspaper, and plastic at **We Recycle,** 111 S. Frontage Rd., Vail, and in Eagle at **Beasely's Food Town,** 212 E. Chambers Road. The **Safeway** in Vail takes aluminum only.

INFORMATION

First-time visitors to Vail should stop at the tourist information center on S. Frontage Rd. in Vail. Signs to it are posted at freeway exits. The center is staffed with friendly people who can answer just about any question you might have, and you'll also find lots of brochures with information on dining, lodging, shopping, and all manner of recreational activities.

You can also get information from the following centers: **Vail Associates,** Box 7, Vail, CO 81658; **Vail Valley Tourism and Convention Bureau,** 100 E. Meadow Dr., Vail, CO 81657, tel. (970) 476-1000, 476-5677, 525-3875, or (800) 775-8245; **Lionshead Visitor Center,** tel. (970) 479-1391; and **Vail Village Visitor Cen-**

ter, tel. (970) 479-1394. The **Activities Desk of Vail and Beaver Creek** can provide information on the area's myriad activities, from hot-air ballooning to chairlift rides to golf. For **road and weather information**, phone (970) 328-6345. For **ski conditions,** phone (970) 476-4888.

TRANSPORTATION

Getting There

Vail is one of Colorado's most accessible resorts, as well as one of the easiest to get around in once you're here. The valley is 100 miles west of Denver, which is serviced by most major airlines. If you fly into Denver International Airport, you can either rent a car there and drive out (less than two hours when the roads are clear) or take a shuttle bus. See the Denver chapter for names and phone numbers of Denver auto-rental agencies, most of which specialize in "winterized" cars (front-wheel- and four-wheel-drive, ski racks).

Vans to Vail, tel. (970) 476-4467 or (800) 222-2212, makes eight trips a day between Vail/Beaver Creek and Denver International Airport. First Vail departure is 7 a.m., the last at 4:30 p.m.; first Denver departure is 9:30 a.m., the last at 7:30 p.m. One-way fare is about $40.

Private charters are available. Other Vail-area shuttle services include **Airport Transportation Service,** tel. (970) 476-7576, and **Colorado Mountain Express,** tel. (970) 949-4227.

You can also fly directly to Eagle County Airport (in Eagle, about 30 miles west of Vail). Phone **American Airlines** at (800) 235-9292; **Delta,** (800) 221-1212; **Northwest,** (800) 225-2525; or **United** at (800) 241-6522. **Skier's Connection,** tel. (800) 824-1104, offers a van-shuttle between Eagle County Airport and Vail.

Getting around the Valley

Getting around once you're in Vail is so easy a car could actually get in the way. Besides, parking, especially in the winter, can be a pain in the neck. **Free shuttles** run daily through the valley, the first bus firing up at 7 a.m. and the last one shutting down at 1:30 a.m. (a bit earlier in the summer and fall); buses run every 10 minutes. For taxi service, phone **Vail Valley Taxi,** at (970) 476-TAXI.

In the Vail area, you can rent cars from **Rent-a-Wreck,** tel. (970) 949-1003; **Budget,** tel. (970) 949-6012; **Hertz,** tel. (970) 476-7707; **National,** tel. (970) 476-6634; and **Thrifty,** tel. (970) 476-8718.

Free parking is provided except during the ski season, with lots conveniently located and well marked.

HIGHWAY 40, UTAH BORDER TO STEAMBOAT SPRINGS

From the Colorado-Utah border to Steamboat Springs is about a 125-mile drive, flat and open with not much traffic. Not a whole lot to look at the first two-thirds of the way, the barren landscape is characterized by miles and miles of flatland, mottled dirty green by the endless sagebrush. Beyond these horizons, though, the Yampa and Green rivers, as well as the Little Snake, carve deep canyons into the plateau.

This is where the land's true colors are seen. Here the canyon walls form tiered mosaics of countless shades of red, ever changing with the angles of the flirting sun. And on the canyon floors, rivers—churning white, brown, then sleeping in still green pools—continue to carve into the stone. Beneath it all are the still darker pools of fossil fuels—oil and coal, as well as natural gas. In Craig, toward the eastern edge of the plateau, smoke and steam rise from the 15-story-high chimneys of the state's largest coal-fired electrical plant, which processes coal from several nearby mines.

In Craig, the plateau tilts, and the highway slowly begins its apparent assault on the Rockies' Western Slope. This 45-mile stretch follows the course of the Yampa River, winding through the valley, the country growing prettier by the meter. By the time you're face to face with Steamboat Ski Area's Mt. Werner and beginning to climb up Rabbit Ears Pass, you're into the Colorado you'll recognize from postcards and calendars—clear mountain streams and green meadows, with a backdrop of snowy, saw-toothed mountain peaks.

DINOSAUR

Three miles east of the Utah border, the town of Dinosaur is little more than a minimart, a cafe, a couple of dinky old motels, and a Colorado Welcome Center. The main drag through town (US 40) is Brontosaurus Blvd., and most other streets are named after dinosaurs as well—Plateosaurus Place, Brachtosaurus Bypass,

Stegosaurus Freeway, even Triceratops Terrace. The little community was known as Artesia until 1965, when it changed its name to reflect its proximity to Dinosaur National Monument.

A **Colorado Welcome Center,** open 8 a.m.-6 p.m. May 1-Nov. 30, has lots of information on things to do and see in the area and throughout Colorado. It is in the center of town on US 40, with friendly and helpful staff, free coffee, and restrooms.

Practicalities

If you're heading east, there's not a whole lot along the 90 miles of US 40 between here and Craig, and if it's getting late you might want to take advantage of Dinosaur's limited lodging options. You can get cheap, no-frills digs at the **Hi-Vu Motel,** tel. (970) 374-2267, or the **Terrace Motel,** tel. (970) 374-2241. RV camping is available at **Blue Mountain RV Park,** tel. (970) 374-2747; plan to roll out your awning, 'cause there's not a shade tree in sight.

Information

For more information on Dinosaur and the area, write Town of Dinosaur, Box 238, Dinosaur, CO 81610.

DINOSAUR NATIONAL MONUMENT

One of the most remote national monuments in the country, Dinosaur National Monument sprawls over 325 square miles of barren and rugged badlands. It straddles the Colorado-Utah border, its distinctly triangular, three-toed shape vaguely resembling a giant dinosaur footprint. A fascinating testimony to the huge reptiles that sloshed through this part of Colorado some 140 million years ago, Dinosaur National Monument is also evidence of the great powers of nature: The Yampa and Green rivers have sliced far into the plateau, leaving narrow 3,000-foot-deep canyons, whose sheer cliffs ensure darkness even at midday.

Though paleontologists had known for years that northwestern Colorado once teemed with dinosaurs of every size and shape, it wasn't until 1909 that Earl Douglass discovered eight brontosaurus tailbones, apparently undisturbed even after millions of years. The find led to several others nearby, including complete skeletons. In 1915, the site was designated a national monument, and in 1938 the monument was expanded to include the Green and Yampa river canyons.

Dinosaur National Monument is not only unique for the sheer numbers of bones and fossils discovered here (some 350 tons of bones have been sent to museums), but also for the number that remain. At the Dinosaur Quarry building, you can view huge femurs, toes, and vertebrae in states of partial excavation, and watch scientists chipping away at the surrounding rock to better display them.

Dinosaur Quarry

This is the only place in the monument to view dinosaur fossils and bones. Located on the Utah side of the monument, the quarry has a visitors center (open daily 8 a.m.-4:30 p.m.; till 7 p.m. in summer) where you'll get a feel for the variety of life that once thrived here, from prehistoric turtles to brontosauruses. In the summer, a shuttle runs daily from the main parking area to the quarry; take your own rig the rest of the year.

The quarry is located seven miles north of Jenson, Utah, on US 149. Phone the quarry visitors center at (801) 789-2115.

Monument Headquarters and Visitors Center

The visitors center on the Colorado side is located a mile east of the town of Dinosaur. From here, a 31-mile road leads into the monument, past several scenic overlooks, dead-ending at Harpers Corner, where you can view the canyons formed by the Yampa and Green rivers.

The center has lots of books, guides, brochures, and other information, as well as rangers to answer your questions. You can also watch a short video about the monument.

Camping

There are two developed campgrounds within the monument, **Split Mountain** and **Green River** (both accessible from the Utah entrance only). Both can accommodate RVs, although neither hookups nor dump stations are available. You can also camp at any of the five free primitive grounds, three of which are in Colorado. **Echo Park Campground,** in the heart of the park 40 miles from Monument Headquarters, offers excellent views of the river and canyons, as well as river access. A ranger station is open summers only. Take Harpers Corner Rd. north from the visitors center, and turn east

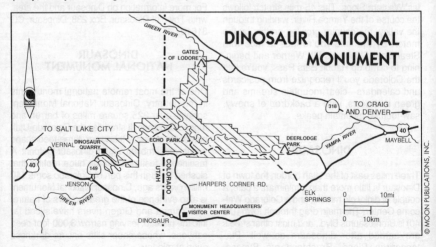

DINOSAUR NATIONAL MONUMENT

GREEN RIVER

GATES OF LODORE

TO CRAIG AND DENVER

318

40

MAYBELL

YAMPA RIVER

TO SALT LAKE CITY

VERNAL

DINOSAUR QUARRY

ECHO PARK

DEERLODGE PARK

40

149

JENSON

GREEN RIVER

COLORADO
UTAH

HARPERS CORNER RD.

ELK SPRINGS

DINOSAUR

MONUMENT HEADQUARTERS/ VISITOR CENTER

0   10mi

0   10km

© MOON PUBLICATIONS, INC.

Hannah visits
the Land Before Time.

on Echo Park Road. **Deerlodge Park Campground** is at the monument's east end and can be reached by turning north on Road 14 at Elk Springs, about 35 miles east of Monument Headquarters. There are no designated sites or drinking water; a ranger station is open summers only as is the campground.

Gates of Lodore Campground is at the far north end of the park and has a ranger station open year round and drinking water available summers only. From the headquarters, take US 40 east for 60 miles to Maybell; then take US 318 another 50 miles west to the campground.

Hiking
You'll find several nature trails in the park, most of which are accessible only from the Utah side. On the Colorado side, you'll find trailheads at Harpers Corner and Gates of Lodor Campground, both leading to stunning gorge views. A half-mile marked trail loops out from Plug Hat Butte picnic area, four miles north of the visitors center (not yet technically in the park).

Information
For more information on Dinosaur National Monument, write Park Headquarters, Box 210, Dinosaur, CO 81610, or phone (970) 374-3000. Be sure to ask for a copy of *Echoes, A Guide to Dinosaur National Monument,* which provides detailed information on hiking, backpacking, camping, rafting, and fishing in the park, as well

as maps and lists of books for further reading. Phone the Dinosaur Quarry Visitors Center (Utah) at (801) 789-2115. You can also get information by writing **Dinosaurland Travel Board,** 235 E. Main St., Vernal, UT 84078, tel. (801) 789-6932 or (800) 477-5558.

Bill Weir's *Utah Handbook* provides detailed descriptions of the monument's geology, history, and recreational opportunities, and also discusses practicalities (accommodations, etc.) in nearby Utah towns. The book is available from Moon Publications, P.O. Box 3040, Chico, CA 95927, tel. (916) 345-5473.

BROWNS PARK NATIONAL WILDLIFE REFUGE

Situated on the Green River north of Dinosaur National Monument, this 6,000-acre marshland is an excellent (if remote) place to see a variety of wildlife in its natural habitat. A nesting area for thousands of migratory waterfowl, including mallards, teal, canvasbacks, and Canada geese, the region is also home to huge numbers of partridge, grouse, wading birds, and hawks, as well as deer and antelope.

The refuge is located off CO 318 about 10 miles east of the Utah border and is open year-round, with two primitive (no water) campgrounds. For further information, write Browns Park National Wildlife Refuge, Greystone Route, Maybell, CO 81640, or phone (970) 365-3695.

RANGELY

A small plateau town that owes its existence almost entirely to the oil and ranching industries, Rangely (pop. 3,000; elev. 5,280 feet), is home to the sixth-largest oil field in the country. Its surrounding landscape, flat and sagey and bleak, dominated by pumpjacks chain-link fenced and nodding round the clock, Rangely is 20 miles southeast of Dinosaur via CO 64.

The town dates from 1880, when it was established as a Ute trading post. In the mid-1880s, ranchers began driving huge herds of cattle to the area, and in 1912 the first shipments of sheep arrived. The first signs of oil were probably seen in 1900, when a local rancher noticed a vague slick on the White River, and the first crude, shallow wells were dug in 1903.

In 1933, the California Company, a subsidiary of Standard Oil, drilled 6,000 feet into the ground and discovered a huge oil deposit, although the well was plugged right away. World War II increased the demand for oil, though, and in 1943, the well was unplugged. By late 1945, 56 wells were in operation.

Today, Rangely is surrounded by Chevron's Weber Sand Unit Oil Field, the largest production field in Colorado, and though some might be offended by the industry's impact on the landscape, Rangely has recently benefitted in other ways from the oilers' presence: The oil companies have made financial retributions, and oil money has gone to build Elk Park, which given the size of the town is one of the nicest in the state, as well as a beautiful hillside rec center.

Rangely Museum

Located in Rangely's first schoolhouse, this small museum has good displays of local rocks, minerals, and Indian artifacts, as well as pioneer clothing and other domestic items. Chevron has an exhibit explaining drilling techniques and technology. Summer hours are Mon.-Sat. 10 a.m.-5 p.m., Sunday 1-5 p.m. Admission is free (donations encouraged). The museum is located just east of town on E. Main (look for the sign just past the college). For more information, phone (970) 675-2612.

Elk Park

This huge town park with rolling lawns (big enough to warrant "no golfing" signs) has picnic tables and barbecue grills, basketball and volleyball courts, and a softball field. Take Stanoland three blocks south of Main.

Rangely's **Recreation Center,** on the hill above the park, features a large indoor swimming pool, weight room, racquetball courts, pool and Ping-Pong table, in addition to jogging and biking trails and an ice-skating rink. Take Stanoland south past Elks Park to the top of the hill. For hours, phone the center at (970) 675-8211.

A pumpjack nods just outside downtown Rangely.

A LOCAL LOOKS AT RANGELY

If you first happen on the Rangely Basin at night, you might believe you were approaching a small metropolis. From the top of Mellen Hill on the western edge of the basin, you can see the lights from over 700 oil wells sprinkle the fifty-square-mile area with a warm, welcoming glow. Only in the harsh reality of daylight do you realize you have been misled. Rangely, situated on the southeast corner of the largest oil field in the Rocky Mountains, is a community of less than 3,000 souls isolated from the rest of civilization by huge tracts of unbroken sagebrush and juniper.

The few travelers who visit Rangely are impressed with the bleak emptiness and lack of flora in the basin. They see the oil wells and gas compression plant and assume the desolation is a result of environmental transgressions by "big oil," but the place hasn't really changed for thousands of years. Sitting on 2,000 feet of Mancos shale, the basin has little topsoil. The winds of spring relentlessly challenge anything green to survive for more than a few weeks. The basin is inhospitable to plant life and supports only sparse vegetation. A quick scan of the photographs in the book *The Raven at Rangely* by G.E. Bud Keeney (Datacolor, 1992) clearly shows little change in the landscape since the earliest photos taken at the beginning of the century.

Oil has always been a part of the landscape of the Rangely Basin. Long before petroleum geologists salivated over the prospect of nearly a billion barrels of crude trapped more than a mile below the surface, shallower deposits of oil were seeping to the surface along the banks of an intermittent arroyo. The oil was a foul-smelling, ugly mess—but it was a natural result of a topography that had eroded down to a shallow petroleum reservoir. The Native Americans dubbed the arroyo "Stinkin' Water Creek," which is the name it carries even today.

To the hurried traveler, Rangely has little to offer. You won't find the blatant, pretentious beauty of the San Juans or Aspens here. Rangely does not share

her beauty capriciously or wantonly with strangers. You have to get to know her—her moods, her whims, the nuances of her soul—before the beauty is manifest. With time, the patient observer will find splendor and elegance in majestic thunderheads towering over Blue Mountain on a brutally hot summer afternoon . . . golden cottonwoods rustling in a gentle autumn breeze carrying the promise of winter . . . the quiet blue light of a frigid January morning . . . or the warm, green glow of the fescue carpeting the basin in the spring.

If you want a sense of the place and can spare a midsummer's evening, I recommend a side trip into the hills south of Rangely. A couple of hours before sunset, turn south at the stoplight at the corner of Main Street and White Avenue (it's not difficult to find—it's the only traffic light in the county). Drive 18 miles on a well-maintained gravel road and watch to the right for the small Bureau of Land Management sign for Rabbit Mountain. Drive up the Rabbit Mountain Road as far as your vehicle and sense of direction will take you. Turn off the car, hug the dog, muzzle the kids, and listen to the absolute silence . . . feel the cool sage-laden air wash over your face . . . close your eyes and let the beauty of the place creep into the edge of your consciousness. If you're not careful, you'll be overwhelmed by the scope of time and space as it surrounds you. The petty concerns you left behind in Camden or Cleveland will snap into perspective and you'll get an inkling—just a hint—of the uncommon beauty found here.

—Jack Matthews

Jack Matthews, an on-again, off-again resident of Rangely since 1988, is an environmental engineer for a major oil company operating in the Rangely Basin. He has written numerous articles for internal company publications and has a voluminous portfolio of letters to editors, public officials, and customer service managers.

Kenny Reservoir

Five miles east of Rangely on CO 64, this small lake offers a cool break from the dry plateau surrounding it—fishing, boating, waterskiing, and swimming, and public restrooms. For information, contact Water Users Association Number One, 2252 E. Main St., Rangely, CO 81648, tel. (970) 675-5055

Petroglyph Tours

The **Rangely Museum Society**, in conjunction with the town of Rangely and Colorado Northwestern Community College, has designated three short self-guided driving tours from which you can view a variety of prehistoric rock art. Petroglyphs include drawings of buffalo, sheep, and deer, as well as many abstract forms and some vaguely resembling humans. The work is from both the Fremont Culture (A.D. 650-1150) and the Ute tribe (A.D. 1200-1880). Recently a series of prehistoric astronomical sites has been discovered; special directions are needed to get to these sites. Tour maps are available from the Rangely Museum.

Practicalities

The **Escalante Trail Motel,** tel. (970) 675-8461, is a favorite of oil-rig crews, who sometimes book half a dozen or more rooms for weeks at a time. Doubles run about $38. The motel is one block off the main drag on S. Grand on the west end of town. The newest and largest motel in town is the 32-room **4 Queens,** tel. (970) 675-5035, where a room for two will run about $45. The **Rangely Motor Hotel,** tel. (970) 675-2257, is located on the east end of town and has seven rooms. You can camp down in the shade of the cottonwoods at **Rangely Camper Park** for $10 a night; there's also a nice lawn and small kids' play area. Turn north on Nichols at the east end of Rangely.

Pretty slim pickin's in terms of food. A couple of small markets and five small restaurants. Try **Magalino's Family Restaurant,** tel. (970) 675-2321, 124 W. Main, or the **Cowboy Corral,** tel. (970) 675-8986, 202 W. Main.

Recycling

Recycle at **Town of Rangely Recycling Program,** 214 E. Main, or 825 E. Main. Phone (970) 675-2413.

Information

For more information, write **Town of Rangely,** 209 E. Main St., Rangely, CO 81648, or phone (970) 675-8469, or the **Rangely Area Chamber of Commerce,** 209 E. Main, Rangely, CO 81648, tel. (970) 675-5290.

CRAIG

Seat of Moffat County, the northwesternmost county in the state, Craig (pop. 8,000; elev. 6,190 feet) lies on the Yampa River 42 miles west of Steamboat Springs and 200 miles west of Denver. Rich in natural resources, particularly coal, oil, natural gas, and uranium, Craig is also rich in prehistory and history, with dinosaur fossils, Native American petroglyphs, and remnants of the Old West all within short drives of town. Craig is also a hub of ranching and agricultural activity, particularly sheep, cattle, and wheat.

We approached Craig from the west on a late January afternoon after spending the previous night in Salt Lake City. The high plains were dotted with snow, ice formed along the edges of streams, and the sagebrush looked brittle in the cold. The sun dropping behind us hung shadows across the land. Suddenly out of nowhere a deer darted into the road in front of us. A big mulie buck. Wild-eyed and frightened. *I've really messed up this time,* he must have been thinking. Fortunately I slammed on the brakes, the car swerved dramatically, and he had time to bound to the shoulder, then into the brush, where he quickly, magically, dissolved into sage and shadows.

No fool, I took this as advice to slow down (not to mention to plan to get my brakes adjusted). And once I did that, and our goal was no longer simply to make Craig before dark, we began to see what was really out there: deer. Dozens of them. Alone, in pairs, threes, and in herds of six, eight, and more. At every turn, over every rise. I'd never seen so many deer in one stretch. Between Elk Springs and Lay, a distance of some 40 miles, we must have seen more than 200 deer, all within 50 yards of the highway. Who knows how many thousands grazed in the brush beyond our small theater?

As you approach Craig, though, the prevalence of Moffat County wildlife might take a backseat to the airborne residue (a towering, thunderheadlike stack of steam) of Colorado's largest coal-fired electrical generating plant, which processes coal from nearby Trapper Mine, as well as from the Colowyo Mine, 27 miles southwest. Providing the power for the lights, stoves, refrigerators, televisions, VCRs, and microwaves of much of northwestern Colorado, the plant also provides work and a solid economic base for Craig and the surrounding area.

© MOON PUBLICATIONS, INC.

In fact, the plant provides weekly paychecks for some 1,200 people.

History

Craig was founded in 1888, seven years after the first homesteader, William Rose, arrived and built a small cabin along Fortification Creek. Though originally called Rose, the community took its current name from the Reverend Bayard Craig, who, along with W.H. Tucker, arrived in 1887 from Glenwood Springs and helped finance and lay out the town. Within a few years, a hotel and saloon had been built, and in 1891 Clarence Bronaugh founded the town's first newspaper, the *Pentagraph*.

On Valentine's eve, 1897, downtown Craig was mostly destroyed by fire. Originating in the town hall, where there was to be a dance and party the next night, the blaze burned out of control up Yampa Avenue. Though devastated by their loss, the citizens of Craig quickly went about rebuilding their town, and within a year most of the buildings had been reconstructed (many with brick this time).

ATTRACTIONS

Museum of Northwest Colorado

Located in the former Armory, at 590 Yampa, this museum documents the history of Craig, Moffat County, and in fact much of the northern plateau. Displays cover early native populations,

cowboys and gunfighters, mining, ranching, and farming, and local flora and fauna. The museum is open Mon.-Fri. 10 a.m.-5 p.m. and Saturday 10 a.m.-4 p.m. (closed Saturday Jan.-April). For more information, phone (970) 824-6360.

Marcia Railway Car

Built for $25,568 in 1906 for David Moffat (the Denver railroad tycoon), this elegant coach once accommodated 12 passengers and two servants. Hauled by winch along specially built tracks to its present site, the Marcia (named for Moffat's daughter) is 68 feet long, 12 feet wide, and features an ornate interior, with African mahogany with oak inlay, two heating systems, and three ice boxes, as well as a kitchen, observation room, and combination dining/sitting/sleeping room. The car is on Victory Way near Craig City Park. Free tours are offered during the office hours of the Craig Chamber of Commerce, 9 a.m.-5 p.m. Mon-Fri, tel. (970) 824-5689.

Sandrocks Nature Trail and Petroglyphs

Sheer sandstone cliffs overlooking the town of Craig, a marked nature trail, and carvings ranging from ancient Anasazi to more recent Shoshone—this nice little side trip will help you better appreciate Moffat County's heritage and natural history. A joint project of Craig-area 4-H'ers, city council members, nearby homeowners, and faculty and staff from Colorado State University, the trail was dedicated in August, 1988. In addition to carvings of hands, paws, lightning bolts, horses and other animals—perhaps symbolic, perhaps simply the recording of daily events—you can also view areas where Native Americans sharpened axes and made arrows and arrowheads. Various plants and bushes—prickly pear, Indian rice grass, and rabbit brush—are identified to help you better appreciate other high-desert exploring you may do. Take 9th St. to Alta Vista Dr., and go west.

Colorado-Ute Power Station
The largest coal-fired plant in the state, this power station generates 1,264 megawatts of power and pays enormous amounts of taxes to Moffat County. Three and a half miles southwest of Craig, in the softly rolling hills of the high plateau, the 25-story main building spews columns of smoke and steam far into the Colorado sky. Meeting or surpassing all environmental guidelines and restrictions, the plant is primarily emitting steam (after electrostatic precipitators have removed 99.6% of particulate matter from the burning coal).

Free tours of the plant are offered by appointment. For information, contact the Craig Chamber of Commerce, tel. (970) 824-5689, or phone the plant at (970) 824-4411. You can also get information by contacting the Communications Group, Colorado-Ute Electric Association, Inc., Box 1149, Montrose, CO 81402, tel. (970) 249-4501.

PARKS AND RECREATION

Town Parks
Located at the corner of 6th and Rose streets, Craig's city park has two swimming pools, tennis and volleyball courts, a playground and picnic facilities. **Loudy Simpson Park,** where S. Ranney crosses the Yampa River, offers fishing, picnicking, a nature trail, jogging paths, a launch area for canoes and rafts, and ice skating.

Elkhead Reservoir
This narrow lake on Elkhead Creek nine miles northeast of Craig is a favorite among sports enthusiasts and folks looking to escape the oftentimes harsh high plains summers. Fishing, boating, waterskiing, and picnicking are all available.

Take US 40 east to County Rd. 29 and go north to the reservoir.

For New Wavers Only
To paraphrase Brian Wilson, "Catch a wave and you're sitting on top of the plains." The public swimming facilities at Craig's city park have recently expanded, adding an adjacent "wave pool," with 180,000 gallons of churning whitewater. Now in addition to swimming laps in the six-lane, 25-meter Olympic pool, you can frolic in Craig's answer to a surfin' safari. Located at 605 Washington. For hours and prices, phone the **Craig Parks and Recreation Department** at (970) 824-3015. The number for the poolside phone is (970) 824-9993.

Golf
The **Yampa Valley Golf Course,** tel. (970) 824-3673, is an 18-hole public course along the Yampa River two miles south of town. Phone for tee times and information. Take Ranney St. south to County Rd. 394.

Hiking
The BLM administers some 1.5 million acres of public land in Moffat County. Six miles north of Craig, Cedar Mountain rises 1,000 feet above "plain-level" and offers good hiking and sightseeing opportunities. Take County Rd. 7 from Craig.

You'll also find hiking trails along the Yampa River at Loudy Simpson Park, off S. Ranney St., and at Sandstone Cliffs (see above). For more information, contact the Craig office of the BLM at 455 Emerson, tel. (970) 824-8261, or the Forest Service district office at 356 Ranney, tel. (970) 824-9438.

Hunting and Fishing
Moffat County is prime hunting and fishing country, home of deer, elk, trout, and other game. The Yampa and Green rivers are well known for good trout fishing, and good-sized northern pike are pulled from Elkhead Reservoir. For tips on hot local hunting and fishing spots, as well as for licenses and supplies, stop in at **Craig Sports,** 124 W. Victory Way, tel. (970) 824-4044. **Nielson's Sports,** 538 Pershing, tel. (970) 824-7021, also carries equipment and licenses. The BLM (455 Emerson, tel. 970-824-8261)

and Forest Service (356 Ranney, tel. 970-824-9458) offices in Craig (see "Hiking" above) can provide maps and further information.

Rafting

The Yampa is a popular rafting and canoeing river. You can put in at Loudy Simpson Park or at the Yampa Valley Golf Course. Both private and public lands flank the 50-mile stretch of raftable water; don't trespass on private property (camping is allowed on public lands).

Tours

The Craig Chamber of Commerce has designed several short self-guiding tours of downtown and the surrounding area. The attractions (and excitement levels) vary widely, from the scintillating pass by Craig High School (on Tour no. 1) to a stop at **Lay Valley Bison Ranch,** where you can pick up a buffalo steak to take home and throw on the barbie. For more information, contact the chamber (360 E. Victory Way, tel. 970-824-5689).

Helicopter tours over the western Rockies are offered through Yampa Valley Regional Airport; phone (970) 276-3723.

PRACTICALITIES

Accommodations

Of the dozen or so motels in Craig, most are on the main drag (US 40) through town and very easy to locate. At the west end of town at the junction of US 40 and CO 13 is a **Holiday Inn,** tel. (970) 824-9455, where doubles for two start at about $55. There's a good-sized indoor pool, jacuzzi, and a children's play area, with toys to ride and climb on. At the same junction, the **A Bar Z Motel,** tel. (970) 824-7066, has rooms for two starting at about $40, and the **Super 8,** tel. (970) 824-3471, has doubles for about $55. Rooms for two at the **Best Western Inn of Craig,** 755 E. Victory (US 40), tel. (970) 824-8101, start at about $35.

Freeman Campground, about 20 miles north of Craig, has 17 sites, pit toilets, nature trails, and fishing on Freeman Reservoir. Go 13 miles north on CO 13, then nine miles northeast on Forest Service Rd. 113 (dirt). The **Craig KOA Kampground,** tel. 824-5105, about two miles

east of Craig on US 40, has 108 RV sites, 13 tent sites, laundry facilities, a small store, and a dump station.

Food

Two restaurants at the Holiday Inn, **Annie Bassett's** and **Cassidy's Bar and Grill,** tel. (970) 824-9455, serve breakfast, lunch, and dinner daily. Dinner entrees include salads, chicken, steaks, seafood. The **Truck Stop Café,** tel. (970) 824-7303, is located downtown at 425 W. Victory and also serves breakfast, lunch, and dinner (American food, reasonable prices). A Safeway and City Market are located on Victory Way.

Shopping

"The shopping hub of Northwestern Colorado," according to the chamber of commerce, Craig has two malls (Centennial and Country) and a downtown shopping center. Included among the de rigueur mall stores are a Kmart (2355 W. Victory Way) and a JCPenney and Anthony's (1111 W. Victory).

Calendar

Craig's **Fall-Color Festival** (mid-September) features a parade, fiddle competition, square dancing, and a pancake breakfast. Firework displays on the Fourth of July. Contact the chamber of commerce for exact dates, times, places, and further information.

Services

The offices of the Craig **Police Department** are at 300 W. 4th St., tel. (970) 824-8111. Phone the **Moffat County Sheriff** at (970) 824-4495. **State Patrol** offices are at 280 S. Ranney, tel. (970) 824-6501. Craig's **Memorial Hospital,** tel. (970) 824-9411, has 24-hour emergency service, as does **Routt Memorial Hospital**, tel. (970) 879-1322, 40 miles east in Steamboat Springs. Craig's main **post office** is at 556 Pershing, tel. (970) 824-5795.

Recycling

Recycle aluminum and glass at **Axis Inc.,** 802 E. 2nd St., and at the **City Market,** 505 W. Victory.

Information

For more information on Craig and Moffat County, write the **Greater Craig Area Chamber of**

Commerce, 360 E. Victory Way, Craig, CO 81625, or phone (970) 824-5689. The **Moffat County Visitors Center** is on the south side of E. Victory Way near the corner of Rose Street. The **Moffat County Library** is located at 570 Green St.; for hours, phone (970) 824-5116. Craig's newspaper, the *Colorado Daily Press,* is published five days a week and runs stories of local and statewide interest. For subscription information, write Box 5, Craig, CO 81626, or phone (970) 824-2600.

For more information on outdoor recreation in the area, contact the **Bureau of Land Management,** 455 Emerson, Craig, CO 81625, tel.

(970) 824-8261, or the Rabbit Ears District Office of **Routt National Forest,** 356 Ranney, Craig, CO 81625, tel. (970) 824-9438.

For **road and weather information,** phone (970) 824-4765.

Transportation

Continental Express, tel. (970) 879-2468, offers passenger service to Yampa Valley Regional Airport (in Hayden, about 20 miles east of Craig) and to Steamboat Springs (40 miles east). The **Greyhound-Trailways** terminal is located at 470 Russell; phone (970) 824-5161.

MEEKER AND VICINITY

Colorado 13 drops south out of Craig, follows the course of the Yampa River for 10 miles or so before the river doglegs to the west, then flirts for a few miles with the western border of White River National Forest. Pagoda Peak (elev. 11,120 feet) and Mount Marvin (elev. 12,045 feet) tower to the east. Be sure to gas up in Craig, as no services are available along the 50-mile stretch to Meeker.

Meeker itself (pop. 2,300; elev. 6,249 feet) is located about midway between US 40 and I-70 at the western base of the White River Plateau. A quiet and picturesque little town with a strong sense of community and civic pride,

Meeker is a favorite among fishers and hunters, especially the latter, who during the fall fill up the town's scattering of lodges and motels, which remain fully booked throughout hunting season.

History

Meeker takes its name from Nathan C. Meeker, an Indian Agent prominent in Colorado affairs. In September, 1879, three years after Colorado achieved statehood, Meeker and 10 of his employees were killed by Utes in what has come to be known as the Meeker Massacre.

Meeker had been appointed to his post at the White River Agency in the spring of the pre-

The White River Museum is located in a 19th-century Army cabin.

vious year. Apparently not much of a diplomat, Meeker presently set about trying to domesticate the Utes, to convert them from a nomadic, hunting people, which they had been for centuries, into a sedentary aggregation of agriculturists.

The Utes resisted. Accustomed to ritual and grace, they couldn't understand Meeker's lack of civility and decorum. In addition, they were already angry at the government, not only for its attempts to yoke them onto the reservation but for not living up to earlier promises of money and supplies. When Meeker plowed an irrigation channel through an Indian horse-race track and then plowed under some of their best pastureland, they'd had enough.

Hearing war drums echoing down the canyons, Meeker sent for troops. Seeing the troops approach, the Utes got even angrier. They attacked the soldiers, and then the agency. Meeker and most of his men were killed, his wife, daughter, and other women taken hostage. A month later, the hostages were released when the Utes and the government negotiated a peace pact, a condition of which was the northern Utes' banishment to a Utah reservation.

After the massacre, the U.S. government established a fort where downtown Meeker now stands. In 1883, it sold the buildings to settlers arriving in the area. Three log cabins, once used as barracks, today house the White River Museum. The massacre site can be viewed from CO 64 about four miles west of town. Look for the marker.

White River Museum
Located in an old log cabin built by soldiers who had come following Meeker's massacre, this museum features five rooms of exhibits, including lots of pioneer artifacts (eyeglasses, sewing machine, tack, guns), Native American artifacts, and a wagon Teddy Roosevelt took from town to the hunting grounds. There are also lots of historical photos, including several of an 1896 bank robbery. Evidently, a group that had been holed up with Butch Cassidy and his gang swept into Meeker, not expecting much violent resistance from the townspeople. Photos show the dead would-be robbers. Nice.

The White River Museum is open Mon.-Sat. 9 a.m.-5 p.m., May 1-Nov. 15. Limited hours the rest of the year; call for hours. You can also

arrange special tours. Phone (970) 878-9982. No admission fee; donations accepted. Located at 565 Park, behind the courthouse.

White River National Forest
The northern unit (Blanco District) of the White River National Forest, once a prime hunting ground of Utes, sprawls to the mountains east of Meeker. Gorgeous country, with several peaks topping 12,000 feet, the forest offers virtually unlimited recreational opportunities. Especially popular are hunting, fishing, and camping; the area's also famous for excellent backpacking, cross-country skiing, snowmobiling, and other activities. Take County Rd. 8 east from Meeker.

Fishing
Excellent stream and lake fishing, and trophy-sized brown, rainbow, brook, and cutthroat trout, lure fishermen to the White River area east of Meeker. (In fact, large trout have been caught on the White River within Meeker's city limits.)

Twenty miles east of town is **Lake Avery,** where fishing is good in summer and winter (ice fishermen do *very* well). Another 30 miles into the park is **Trappers Lake,** which, although remote, still gets lots of traffic. The best way to catch fish here is by boat (no motors allowed), which you can rent at **Trappers Lake Lodge,** tel. (970) 878-3336.

Be sure to check local regulations, as some restrictions apply.

Camping
You'll find several excellent Forest Service campgrounds in White River National Forest

BOB RACE

trainer and sheepdog

east of Meeker, including **North Fork Campground,** right on County Rd. 8 (one mile into the forest, 45 units). Also easily accessible and nearby are **South Fork Campground, Marvine Campground,** and **Himes Peak Campground.** There are four separate campgrounds at Trappers Lake, with a total of nearly 60 sites.

Walking Tour

The Meeker Chamber of Commerce has designed a short self-guided walking tour of the historic downtown area. Included are the Meeker Hotel, the White River Museum, St. James Episcopal Church (built in 1889), and several pre-1900 residences. The tour is described in detail in the chamber's *Visitor Information Guide* (see "Information" following).

Accommodations

Because Meeker draws such crowds during the hunting season, plan to make reservations for an autumn stay well in advance. The **Meeker Hotel,** 560 Main, tel. (970) 878-5062 or 878-5596, is on

the National Register of Historic Places and has nicely appointed rooms at very reasonable rates. Even if you don't plan to stay here, poke your head in. The place hasn't changed all that much since Teddy Roosevelt stayed here on a bear-hunting trip. Located right downtown across from the county courthouse. You can also get rooms (and cabins) at Meeker traditions, the **Rustic Lodge,** 173 Market, tel. (970) 878-3136, and the **Valley Motel,** 723 Market, tel. (970) 878-3656, as well as at the brand new **White River Inn,** tel. (970) 878-5031.

Trappers Lake Lodge, tel. (970) 878-3336, offers definitively rustic cabins—stoves for heating, no plumbing. Common shower and bathroom area. The lodge also offers pack trips, guided fishing, and canoe, rowboat, and horse rentals. Write 7700 Trappers Lake Rd., Meeker, CO 81641.

There are two campgrounds two miles west of Meeker at the junction of Highways 64 and 13. **Rimrock Campground,** tel. (970) 878-4486, is strictly a "passing-through" facility, with basic sites right next to the road. **Stagecoach Park,** tel. (970) 878-4434, offers a bit more privacy, with sites nestled down off the road among the cottonwoods.

Food

The **Sleepy Cat Restaurant,** tel. (970) 878-4413, 20 miles east of town on County Rd. 8, is a 50-year-old Meeker tradition. A classic hunting lodge, its walls lined with trophies, the restaurant is a Meeker favorite, also popular among visiting hunters and anglers and local ranchers. The Sleepy Cat specializes in various beef entrees, but also offers chicken, seafood, and a salad bar.

The **Meeker Cafe,** located next door to the Meeker Hotel on Main, tel. (970) 878-4535, serves burgers and sandwiches for lunch ($3-6) and beef, chicken, and seafood for dinner ($7-10).

Calendar

Meeker's **Range Call Parade, Rodeo, and Pageant,** on the Fourth of July weekend, was begun in 1885 and is the oldest rodeo in the nation. In addition to providing lots of food, music, and rodeo competition, the pageant offers a re-enactment of the Meeker Massacre, with locals acting out the attack, kidnapping, and murders.

The **Meeker Classic Sheep Dog Trials** are held the second weekend in September. The trials attract upwards of 75 competitors and 2,000 spectators, who not only enjoy watching some of the finest dogs and best trainers in the West, but also get to listen to traditional Irish music and take part in other festivities.

Services

The offices of the **Meeker Police Department** are located at 236 7th St., tel. (970) 878-5555. Phone the **State Patrol** at (970) 675-8311. **Pioneers Hospital** is at 785 Cleveland (turn north on 3rd), tel. (970) 878-5047 (in emergencies, 878-5700). The Meeker **post office** is at 656 6th St., tel. (970) 878-5830.

Recycling

Recycle at **Gofer Foods,** 812 Market St., tel. (970) 878-4492.

Information

An excellent source for local information is the chamber of commerce-published *Meeker and White River Country Visitor Information Guide.* Copies are available at the chamber offices on the corner of CO 13 (W. Market) and 7th. Write Box 869, Meeker, CO 81641, or phone (970) 878-5510. The Meeker **public library** is located at 200 Main St., tel. (970) 878-5911.

For information on **White River National Forest,** stop in at the ranger station at 361 7th St., tel. (970) 878-4039.

STEAMBOAT SPRINGS AND VICINITY

Best known for the ski resort that was built here in 1963, Steamboat Springs, seat of Routt County, is a small town (pop. 7,400; elev. 6,695 feet) surrounded by towering mountains and verdant river valleys. With an economy based largely on ranching (sheep and cattle), farming (hay, wheat, oats, barley), and tourism, Steamboat Springs offers a true taste of the old West, where real cowboys still ride the real range, and at the same time lures upscale travelers looking to escape the trappings of some of the state's glitzier resorts.

HISTORY

Though Steamboat Springs' high-rise hotels and sprawling condominiums attest to the town's membership in the club of modern resorts, the area has actually been a playground of sorts for some 600 years. As early as the 1300s, Utes spent their summers here, hunting buffalo and other large game, and, most likely, taking advantage of the 100-plus-degree hot springs in the Yampa River Valley. The name "Steamboat

Steamboat Village, at the base of the ski lifts

STEAMBOAT SPRINGS

TO STEAMBOAT LAKE, HAHN'S PEAK, AND AIRPORT

HOT SPRINGS

ELK RIVER RD.

SEEDHOUSE RD.

TO CRAIG

FOREST SERVICE STEAMBOAT SPRINGS OFFICE

DOWNTOWN STEAMBOAT SPRINGS

STRAWBERRY PARK RD.

40

8th ST.

LOGAN

MISSOURI

7th ST.

6th ST.

AMETHYST RD.

BUD WERNER MEMORIAL LIBRARY

POST OFFICE

FISH CREEK FALLS RD.

HOWELSEN HILL

CHAMBER RESORT ASSOCIATION VISITOR CENTER

LINCOLN AVE.

YAMPA RIVER

SHERATON GOLF COURSE AND CROSS-COUNTRY SKI AREA

CLUBHOUSE DR.

STEAMBOAT BLVD.

PARKING LOT AND SHUTTLE

SKI AREA BASE

MT. WERNER RD.

SHUTTLE STOP

VILLAGE DR.

WHISTLER DR.

NOT TO SCALE

TO RABBIT EARS PASS AND KREMMLING

WALTON CK. RD.

40

© MOON PUBLICATIONS, INC.

Springs," in fact, comes from one of the hot springs: A party of 19th-century trappers heard the waters rumbling and bubbling and thought a steamboat was approaching from downriver.

In 1868, the United States government took claim to the Utes' summer home, yet the Indians resisted relinquishing their land. Between 1868 and 1880, when the Utes were finally forced onto a reservation in Utah, several skirmishes took place between various tribes and white settlers, including the Meeker Massacre of 1879.

The Yampa River Valley's first white settler of record was James Crawford, a Missourian, who homesteaded here in 1875, although Crawford's first home was an abandoned log building, suggesting someone had passed through earlier and had stayed long enough to need solid shelter. Evidently respectful of the Utes and their hunting grounds, Crawford became friends with them, and they left him alone while they attacked other settlements in the area, as well as other settlers passing through. Meanwhile, the Yampa

Valley was becoming increasingly well known for its high-quality native hay, and in the early 1880s, once the Utes had been vanquished from the valley for good, the region began to see a large influx of farmers and ranchers.

In 1885, Crawford, having obtained financial backing from Boulder businessmen J.P. Maxwell and Andrew Mackay, formed the Steamboat Springs Townsite Company, laid out the streets of the small town, and sold lots. By 1888, the number of buildings in Steamboat Springs had grown from half a dozen to nearly 50. Also germane to the town's early development was the introduction of Steamboat's first newspaper, the *Steamboat Pilot*, which was first printed (on a second-hand foot-powered press hauled over from Boulder) on July 31, 1885.

Also at this time, as farmers and ranchers were establishing themselves in the fertile Yampa Valley, a mine at the base of Hahn's Peak, 30 miles to the north, was drawing miners from throughout the area. This further added to Routt County's population, and though some of these miners were transient and would eventually move on (particularly when the Hahn's Peak mine played out in the early 1890s), some would stay in the area permanently.

Still another crucial stage in Steamboat's development was the arrival of the railroad. The talk of the town since the turn of the century, the railroad to Steamboat was completed on December 13, 1908, and the first passenger train chugged into town a month later on the evening of January 19. The *Steamboat Pilot* reported the event the next day: "Steamboat's long-looked-for day has come. . . . Over 75 Steamboat people, including the band, met the train [about eight miles south of town] and rode down, while hundreds more were at the Steamboat Station to cheer it when it arrived."

In 1913, Norwegian cross-country and ski-jumping champion Carl Howelsen arrived in Steamboat and, in 1914, organized the town's first Winter Carnival. Howelsen so impressed locals with his jumping hill and 110-foot leap that many were inspired to try ski jumping themselves. Local lore has it some of the jumpers at the first carnival landed in a herd of startled elk grazing nearby.

By 1940, downhill skiing had become popular among Steamboaters, and in 1943 it was added to the curriculum of the local school. In 1963, Steamboat Ski Area was officially opened for business on Storm Peak three miles south of town. A year later, when one of the town's early Winter Olympians, Buddy Werner, was killed in an avalanche in Switzerland, the peak's name was changed to Mt. Werner. Over the last 30 years, the Steamboat Ski Area has grown dramatically: Lifts and a gondola now spoke out over four different mountains, and the base facilities include everything from a golf course (for summer visitors) to bars, restaurants, condominiums, and a fleet of shuttle buses.

ATTRACTIONS

This is a town that bills itself "Ski Town, USA," and of course the main attraction here is the world-class alpine ski resort three miles from downtown. Which means this is largely a wintersports town, where most everything revolves around the fact the area's meadows, mountains, and moraines are blanketed with snow from November to May. Still, there's lots to do, even if you're not one to strap boards to your boots and go sliding down mountainsides in search of deep thrills—even in the summer, when all the skis in Ski Town, USA are leaning languidly in closets or hanging from garage rafters.

SKIING AND OTHER WINTER SPORTS

Steamboat Ski Area

With 3,600 vertical feet of skiing, 102 runs, 2,500 skiable acres, an uphill capacity of nearly 30,000 skiers an hour, World Cup races, over 300 inches of snowfall per year, and internationally acclaimed tree and powder skiing, this is without doubt one of the best ski areas in the West (many say in the world).

In a sport growing more pretentious and exclusive by the season—a sport of doctors, lawyers, and accountants, turbo Saabs, Volvos, and BMWs—Steamboat is a breath of fresh air. Drawing largely on its Old-West heritage, as well as on the real-life Old-West town down the road, Steamboat has managed to maintain its in-

tegrity and charm—even in the path of an advancing epidemic of condos, high-rises, and boutiques. Oh, there are still boutiques, and ferny bars, and more real estate and property-management companies than you can shake a ski pole at. But still, it all feels more real here than in some of the Rockies' other big resorts.

And it's probably because most everything else here really does take a back seat to skiing. It's a big mountain, and some people come an awfully long way to explore—and, perhaps, master—it. So by day's end, they don't have much energy for shopping. They want to relax, maybe take a hot tub or sauna, and get some food in their bellies for strength for the next day; hardcores with energy left at the end of the day can boogie to live music at several clubs—both on the mountain and in town (see "Entertainment" following).

So, what about that mountain? Well, for starters, it's got a wide variety of terrain for all ability levels, although it's best suited to the intermediate-to-advanced skier, with 54% of its runs designated intermediate (31% are advanced and 15% are beginner). Spread out over four different mountains and rising to 10,385 feet, Steamboat's 2,500 acres of runs and off-piste skiing is serviced by 21 lifts, including an eight-passenger gondola and 17 chairlifts—a quad, seven triples, and nine doubles (which Steamboat returnees claim keep lift lines minimal).

Don't be deceived by what you can see of Steamboat from the base of the mountain. Though it looks big enough, there's lots more. In fact, the majority of the runs and lifts are beyond that first 1,000-foot vertical rise. Experts and advanced skiers will want to check out the runs off of Storm Peak, Sundown, and Priest Creek chair, while Burgess Creek, Sunshine, and Thunderhead offer intermediates a chance to explore and work on their form.

If you can remember back to the 1974 Winter Olympics, or if you read the skiing magazines at all during the late '60s and early '70s, the name Billy Kidd should ring a bell. Perhaps you even have an image of him in your head: the archetypal all-American cowboy-skier, boyish tanned face grinning beneath the brim of his ten-gallon Stetson. Well, Kidd's still around. He's the Director of Skiing at Steamboat, and he's out on the slopes almost every day. And Kidd's not the only Olympian to have cut his ski teeth in the gates of Steamboat. As of 1990, Steamboat had produced 34 winter Olympic athletes, more than any other town in the United States.

Information

The marketing department of Steamboat Springs Ski Resort will gladly send you more information—from maps of the mountain to complete listings of nearby lodges. Write 2305 Mt. Werner Circle, Steamboat Springs, CO 80487, or phone (970) 879-6111. For **Steamboat Central Reservations,** phone (800) 922-2722.

Howelsen Hill

Named for Carl Howelsen, who at Steamboat's 1914 Winter Carnival jumped 110 feet on skis, this is one of the oldest ski areas in the country. Open seven days a week (night skiing Tues.-Fri. 6-9 p.m.), Howelsen Hill, owned and operated by the city of Steamboat Springs, has a 440-foot vertical rise and 30 acres of skiable terrain serviced by two surface lifts.

Best known for its five jumping ramps (20, 30, 50, 70, and 90 meters), Howelsen is the training grounds for the U.S. Ski Jumping Team, and has been the "home field" of many world-class jumpers. Remember "Eddie the Eagle," England's entry in the 1988 Olympic Ski Jumping Competition? Even the Eagle jumped here, having stopped here that year en route to Banff.

The Winter Sports Club, based at Howelsen, offers instruction in downhill, cross-country, and freestyle skiing. There's also an ice-skating rink at the complex, which is located downtown at the south end of the 5th Street Bridge. For more information on Howelsen Hill, phone the Steamboat Springs Parks and Recreation Department at (970) 879-4300, or contact the chamber of commerce at (970) 897-0880.

Backcountry Powder Skiing

For hard-core backcountry skiers and powder-hounds whose idea of graffiti is a series of figure eights in a remote bowl, **Steamboat Powder Cats** will take you by snowcat up into virgin powder—for both day-trips and overnight excursions. Phone (970) 879-5188 or (800) 288-0543.

Cross-Country Skiing

Though better known for its downhill skiing, the Steamboat area also offers excellent opportunities for cross-country skiers—on groomed trails as well as in the backcountry. The **Steamboat Ski Touring Center,** based at the Sheraton Golf Course, has 28 miles of trails winding out over the links and along nearby Fish Creek. The center, which caters to the broadest range of Nordic skiers—from the most cavalier recreational skier to the serious Nordic athlete—is managed by Sven Wiik, who, after immigrating from Sweden in 1949, taught cross-country skiing at Western State College in Gunnison for the next 19 years and coached the United States Olympic team in 1960. Wiik's Scandinavian Lodge offers rentals, lessons, and backcountry tours. For more information, write Steamboat Ski Touring Center, Box 772297, Steamboat Springs, CO 80477, or phone (970) 879-8180.

You'll also find cross-country trails at **Rabbit Ears Pass,** about 10 miles southeast of Steamboat Springs on US 40, as well as at **Clark Store,** tel. (970) 879-3849, 20 miles north of Steamboat on Elk River Rd. (County Rd. 129). Just off Elk River Rd., **Seedhouse Rd.** offers ungroomed trails along the Elk River; and **Howelsen Hill** (see above) offers rentals, equipment, and trails.

In addition, a number of guest ranches in and around Steamboat offer cross-country skiing. Among them: **Hahn's Peak Guest Ranch,** tel. (970) 879-8638; **Vista Verde Guest and Ski Touring Ranch,** tel. (970) 879-3858; **Elk River Guest Ranch,** tel. (970) 879-3843; and **Dutch Creek Guest Ranch,** tel. (970) 879-8519.

For maps and information on ski touring in Routt National Forest, contact the Hahn's Peak District Office, tel. (970) 879-1870, or the Supervisor's Office at 29587 W. US 40 in Steamboat, tel. (970) 879-1722.

Other Winter Sports

Those averse to strapping skis afoot have several other options when it comes to winter recreation in Steamboat. Howelsen Hill Ski Complex also offers bobsledding and ice skating, while snowmobiling, snowshoeing, and ice fishing—**Buggywhips Fish and Float Service,** tel. (970) 879-8033—are also available to the winter sports hound. The various activity and reservations centers, as well as the chamber of commerce, have complete listings and schedules. See "Recreation Information" and "Tours" following.

WHEN THE SNOW MELTS

Don't worry—Ski Town, USA doesn't board up its windows once the chairlifts shut down and wildflowers begin pushing up through the meadows' snowcovers. Quite the contrary. In fact, folks looking for outdoor diversions in the warmer months actually have more to choose from than their winter counterparts do. Golf, for example. Tennis. Cycling (both touring and mountain biking). Rafting. Hiking, backpacking, camping, and fishing. And don't forget hot-air ballooning and horseback riding. You'd have to have the imagination of a hitchin' post not to be able to find something to do in Steamboat once you've put your skis and snowshoes in storage.

Steamboat Lake State Park
Twenty-five miles north of Steamboat Springs on County Rd. 129, this state park on Steamboat and Pearl lakes offers camping, boating, fishing, waterskiing, hiking, and, in winter, snowmobiling. Pit toilets and running water. Phone (970) 879-3922 for more information.

Stagecoach State Recreation Area
South of Steamboat Springs off US 40, this newly opened recreation area at Stagecoach Reservoir has hiking trails, tent and RV camping facilities, fishing for rainbow and cutthroat trout, and a boat ramp. During the winter, Stagecoach is a popular snowmobiling and cross-country skiing site. For more information, write the Colorado Division of Parks and Outdoor Recreation, 1313 Sherman St., Room 618, Denver CO 80203, tel. (970) 866-3437.

Golf
Steamboat has two golf courses, the 18-hole **Sheraton Steamboat Golf Club,** located at the base of Mt. Werner, and the nine-hole public **Steamboat Golf Club,** at the west end of town off US 40. The Sheraton Steamboat is a high-class course, affiliated with the Sheraton Hotel

(Sheraton guests get discounts on the expensive-anyway greens fees) and designed by Robert Trent Jones. Carts are required, Cadillacs or better recommended. Phone (970) 879-1391 for a tee time, prices, and more information. The Steamboat Golf Club is the town's pleb course, with the attendant retrenched prices and lack of ostentation. Phone (970) 879-4295.

Hiking and Backpacking
Routt National Forest, which sprawls from Steamboat Springs north across the Wyoming border and south nearly to Kremmling (another unit lies east of Kremmling in eastern Rio Blanco and Garfield counties), is an Eden of hiking and backpacking trails and backcountry. Part of this million-plus-acre national forest, the Mt. Zirkel Wilderness Area, about 25 miles north of Steamboat Springs in the gorgeous Park Range, offers lots of backcountry to explore. Take Elk River Rd./County Rd. 129 north to Seedhouse Rd., where you'll find one of several trailheads leading into the wilderness area.

The Forest Service supervisor's office in Steamboat Springs, 29587 US 40, tel. (970) 879-1722, and the Hahn's Peak District Office, 57 10th St., tel. (970) 879-1870, can provide maps and information.

One of the more popular short hikes for Steamboat visitors is to **Fish Creek Falls,** a 283-foot waterfall just minutes from town. The quarter-mile trail (restrooms, picnic, and handicap facilities provided) leads to a viewing area, then on to a second waterfall (not nearly as swamped with visitors), and eventually to Dumont Lake, about 11 miles from the trailhead. Take Fish Creek Falls Rd. south from downtown. **Note:** The four-mile road is paved halfway; the second half is a fairly deeply rutted dirt road.

Fishing
The lakes and streams in the Steamboat area offer a wide range of fishing possibilities—from easy-to-fool, recently stocked hatchery fish the size of a large pencil to wily four-pound natives that can tell an artificial fly from the real McCoy at 50 feet. Dumont Lake, on Rabbit Ears Pass 25 miles south of Steamboat via US 40, is stocked regularly with catchable-sized rainbow trout, as is Steamboat Lake, about 30 miles north of Steamboat off County Rd. 129. The Elk

and Yampa rivers also offer good fishing. For guided fishing tours, contact **Buggywhips Fish and Float Service,** tel. (970) 879-8033.

For more information on fishing in Routt County, contact the Steamboat Springs Chamber Resort Association, tel. (970) 879-0880 or (800) 332-3204 (for non-local Colorado calls). Equipment, licenses, and local tips are available at **Steamboat Springs Sporting Goods,** 908 Lincoln Ave., tel. (970) 879-7774; **Straightline,** 744 Lincoln Ave., tel. (970) 879-7568; and **The Grand Tradition,** 906 Lincoln Ave., tel. (970) 879-0916.

Rafting and Kayaking

As you'd expect in a town on two decent-sized rivers, as well as near so many smaller streams, Steamboat is a river rat's paradise, especially those who can settle for water a tad less violent than, say, the Andes' Apurimac. You can put in at a variety of spots along the river, although you need to be careful not to trespass on the private property that flanks much of both rivers.

Buggywhips Fish and Float Service, downtown at 435 Lincoln Ave., tel. (970) 879-8033 or (800) 759-0343, offers a wide range of float trips, from mild to wild. **Mountain Sports Kayak School,** 1835 Central Park Ave., tel. (970) 879-8794, or 879-6910 in winter, provides canoe and kayak rental and instruction. **Mike's Marina** at Steamboat also offers float trips and equipment rentals; phone (970) 879-7019.

Ballooning

Though not cheap, hot-air balloon rides are getting more and more popular each year, with several companies in Steamboat offering quarter-, half-, and full-hour rides daily. **Aero Sports,** tel. (970) 879-7433; **Balloons Over Steamboat,** tel. (970) 879-3298; and **Pegasus,** tel. (970) 879-9191, offer various promotional come-ons (free champagne and transportation, senior and group discounts, personalized flights, etc.) to offset the cost of a bird's-eye view of Steamboat in the quietude of the wind-borne schooner.

Horseback Riding

It should come as no suprise in a town such as Steamboat Springs—whose western heritage oozes from every barn wall, saloon door, and

Stetson hat—that riding is big here. You may find yourself downtown trying on some après-ski boots while across the store some cowpoke with a wad of chew in his lip is eyeing saddles and tack. And though there are some dude ranches in the area, most of the cowboys in Routt County are for real. This is an area that grew up with horses. And horses still work here.

They're also for hire. A stirrup-ful of outfits in and around Steamboat have horses for rent, as well as guides that will lead tours, instructors who will give lessons, and, if you'd rather ride behind than on a horse, sleighs, coaches, and carts are available to make you feel equestrian without risking a bruised posterior. Some of the services provide meals with the trips.

Del's Triangle 3 Ranch, tel. (970) 879-3495 or 879-4109, offers rentals and pack trips, as do **Glen Eden Stables,** tel. (970) 879-3864, and **Steamboat Lake Guides and Outfitters,** tel. (970) 879-3906. **Sunset Ranch,** tel. (970) 879-0954, has horses available for pack trips into the Mt. Zirkel Wilderness Area.

Recreation Information

For more information on what to do in the Steamboat-Routt County area, contact the **Steamboat Activity Center** at (970) 879-2062 or the **Steamboat Springs Chamber Resort Association** at (970) 879-0880 or (800) 332-3204 (for non-local Colorado calls).

Tread of Pioneers Museum

Located in a gorgeous Victorian home built in 1908, this museum displays the history of Steamboat Springs and Routt County beginning with the Utes and finishing up with the story of the ski resort. Exhibits include Native American pottery, ranching and farming implements, medical gear, musical instruments (including a square grand piano shipped from New York in the mid-19th century), firearms, and children's dolls and toys, and the evolution of ski equipment. Videos include footage of early skiing in the area, including jumping off Howelsen Hill and tag-team jorring races (skiers were pulled, water-ski-style behind horses) down US 40 in the early part of the century. The museum is located at 800 Oak (corner of 8th St.). Hours are Tues.-Sat. 11 a.m.-5 p.m. For information, phone (970) 879-2214.

TOURS

In addition to the various outfits offering sleigh rides around Steamboat and balloon rides over it (see above), you'll find everything from snowmobile and jeep tours to pack trips and jaunts to hot springs. The **Steamboat Activity Center,** tel. (970) 879-2062, located downtown at 720 Lincoln and in Gondola Square at the base of the lifts, can arrange just about any kind of tour you have in mind, as can **Let Me Entertain You,** tel. (970) 879-8010. For snowmobile tours, try **Elk River Guest Ranch,** tel. (970) 879-3843, **Emerald Mountain Snowmobile Tours,** tel. (970) 879-8065, **Steamboat Snowmobile Tours,** tel. (970) 879-1551, **Hahn's Peak Guest Ranch,** tel. (970) 879-8638, or **Steamboat Lake Outfitters,** tel. (970) 879-3906 or 879-4404.

Sweet Pea Tours, tel. (970) 879-5820, offers hot-springs tours, which include transportation and admission (bring your own suit and towel).

ACCOMMODATIONS

You won't have an easy time if you go looking for cheap digs in Steamboat Springs—particularly in winter, when some of the best snow in the country has blanketed the runs of Mt. Werner and Sunshine Peak. As in many resort towns, especially those as isolated as Steamboat is, travelers here are more or less at the mercy of the innkeepers and whatever prices they want to charge.

You can save some money, though, by staying in nearby towns. Skiers who don't mind driving 45-60 minutes can get rooms for substantially less in Craig, for example, where rooms at the Holiday Inn start at about $45 (in Steamboat the same room runs $65-145). In addition, advance reservations aren't nearly as crucial if you go outside Steamboat. In town, many rooms are reserved up to a year ahead of time, and in a season of decent snowfall, Steamboat will have fewer rooms available than there were in Bethlehem. Ultimately, you just have to ask (and answer) yourself if the trade-off's worth it. Is what you save by staying 45 miles away worth what you'd gain by staying slope-side, or at least

within walking distance to a shuttle stop? Is saving $50 a day on lodging worth missing out on the experience of hanging out after skiing in one of the West's great winter sports towns?

Hotels, Motels, and Condominiums
The newcomer to Steamboat, especially one who's bought into the resort's claim to being a down-to-earth ski town, will most likely be surprised at the number of high-rise hotels and condominiums sprouting from Steamboat Village and the base of the lifts. The ultimate in convenience for the skier who likes to ski right to her doormat, these rooms provide that fine feeling of knowing when you step out of your skis you're home. No need to worry about finding your car in the parking lot, checking shuttle departure times; no need to fear getting caught in après-ski traffic. In fact, before other skiers have even secured their skis atop their cars, you can be soaking away the day's aches in a hot, swirling jacuzzi as you pull on a cold one. Not a bad way to close the curtain on the day.

Here are just a few of the slope-side lodges at Steamboat (in addition to the nightly rates given here, most Steamboat inns offer ski-and-lodging package deals, which include lift tickets, and sometimes shuttle transportation, meals, equipment, and other enticements): Doubles at the **Best Western Ptarmigan Inn,** tel. (970) 879-1730 or (800) 538-7519, start at about $65 (summer) and $200 (winter). The **Holiday Inn,** tel. (970) 879-2250 or (800) HOLIDAY, has doubles for $65-150. The **Sheraton Resort and Conference Center,** tel. (970) 879-2220, also located at the lifts, has rooms for two starting at $90 and topping out at $290. Right next door, the **Thunderhead Lodge,** tel. (970) 879-9000 or (800) 525-5502, has a range of room—efficiencies to suites, sleeping up to 14—ranging from $90-$500 a night.

In addition to the ski-in/ski-out lodging facilities at the base of the lifts, you'll find a handful of hotels, motels, and condos three miles away in downtown Steamboat Springs. At the **Rabbit Ears Motel,** tel. (970) 879-1150, you can get a double for around $60 summer, $110 winter. The **Western Lodge,** tel. (970) 879-1050, has rooms for two running $60-120.

The **Sky Valley Lodge,** tel. (970) 879-7749, is a resort lodge about eight miles east of town on US 40 offering convention facilities, tennis courts, and deluxe lodging—shuttles to the ski area in winter. Doubles go for $70-140 (two-night minimum).

Bed and Breakfast

The **Clermont Inn,** 917 Lincoln, tel. (970) 879-3083, has several small rooms with adjoining baths starting at about $90 a night. The **Inn at Steamboat Bed and Breakfast,** 3070 Columbine, tel. (970) 879-2600 or 800/872-2601, has rooms for two for about $70 in the summer and $180 in the height of the ski season.

Lodging Information

For more information on the over 50 hotels, motels, and condominiums in Steamboat, as well as complete lists of lodging packages, phone Steamboat Springs Chamber Resort Association's **Steamboat Central Reservations** at (800) 922-2722. Remember, too, during the height of the ski season you're going to need reservations well in advance—though if you find yourself strapped and desperately needing a Steamboat fix within the month, you might call around to see if there've been any cancellations. You can also get lodging information (and make reservations) from the Resort Association's Internet address at **http://www.steamboat-ski.com/ski**.

Camping and RVing

A number of campgrounds are available in and around Steamboat Springs, including three open year-round with RV facilities. **Ski Town KOA campground,** tel. (970) 879-0273, on the Yampa River about two miles west of town on US 40, has 100 RV sites (tent camping on about a quarter of them) and cabins with nightly, weekly, and monthly rates; shuttle service available. **Fish Creek Campground,** tel. (970) 879-5476, a mile and a half east of Steamboat on Fish Creek, has 15 tent and 30 RV sites, laundry facilities, and a rec room. **Steamboat Lake State Park** (see above), 25 miles north of Steamboat, has 200 tent and RV sites on Pearl Lake. For information and reservations, phone (970) 879-3922.

In addition, several Forest Service campgrounds are scattered throughout the area. **Meadows Campground,** 15 miles southeast of Steamboat; **Dumont Lake,** 10 miles east of Meadows (watch for the sign); and **Summit Lake Campground** (no drinking water), about 15 miles northeast of town (take Strawberry Park Rd. to Forest Service Rd. 60), all have tent and RV sites and pit toilets. Phone the Hahn's Peak District Office of the Forest Service at (970) 879-1870 for more information.

FOOD

Start Me Up

A handful of excellent Steamboat breakfast places guarantee a jumpstarted morning. For a light breakfast—muffins, grain cereals, and excellent espresso drinks—try **Off the Beaten Path Bookstore and Coffeehouse,** downtown at 56 7th Street, tel. (970) 879-6830. If you're up for a little hardier breakfast, try **Winona's,** 617 Lincoln, tel. (970) 879-2483, where you'll find homemade granola, pancakes with fruit, and egg dishes. The **Shack Cafe,** 740 Lincoln, tel. (970) 897-9975, is a local favorite, featuring waffles, huevos rancheros, and omelettes.

For something a bit different, check out **Sharon's,** two miles west of town at 30058 W. US 40 (next to Napa Auto Parts). Nothing fancy here, but locals call it "the best dive in town" and rave about the cinnamon rolls. Up at the ski area, try **The Tugboat,** right at the base of the lifts at 1860 Ski Time Square Dr., tel. (970) 879-7070.

Steamboat Traditions

Steamboat abounds in good places to eat, and just about everyone has a favorite restaurant. For Mexican food, try **Dos Amigos,** 1910 Mt. Werner Rd. in Ski Time Square, tel. (970) 879-4270, for excellent fajitas, burritos, chimichangas, and assorted *especiales,* or **La Montaña,** 2500 Village Way, tel. (970) 879-5800, for Mexican and Tex-Mex entrees including chili, fajitas, and enchiladas; entrees at both run $7-17. Also good for Mexican is **Cantina,** 818 Lincoln, tel. (970) 879-0826, serving enchiladas, burritos, and tacos ($6-9), with your choice of red, green, or cheese sauces. Lots of domestic and Mexican beers available to wash down those nachos (no bangers to complement the Watneys and Guinness on tap, though). For dessert, try the flan, cheesecake, or sopaipillas.

Mattie Silk's, in Ski Time Square, tel. (970) 879-2441, serves seafood, beef, veal, duck, lamb, and pasta dishes for $8-22; check out the huge selection of imported beers. **Mazzola's,** 440 S. Lincoln (between the lifts and downtown), tel. (970) 879-2405, is open for lunch and dinner seven days a week. Specialities include pizzas, calzone, lasagna, pastas, and a salad bar; prices range from about $5 for an Italian meatball sandwich to $15 for the "Seafood Medley," various shellfish served in a white sauce over linguine. Another classic is the **Old Town Pub,** downtown at 600 Lincoln, tel. (970) 879-2101. Dinners include burgers, chicken, steak, and seafood ($6-15); also open for breakfast and lunch.

For excellent Italian food, **Riggio's,** 1106 Lincoln, tel. (970) 879-9010, is tough to beat. Choose from a wide range of authentic pasta dishes or one of the entrees, including saltimbocca and vitello. With a reputation for excellent "new American cuisine," **Antares Restaurant,** 57 ½ 8th St., tel. (970) 879-9939, serves a range of salads, grilled foods, and pastas, including a game hen on tomato-and-basil pasta. Entress run $12-18. The **Steamboat Brewery and Tavern,** downtown at 5th and Lincoln, tel. (970) 879-2233, is a lively pub serving burgers, pizzas, salads, and seafood, all of which you should wash down with a homemade beer (maybe the Skull Creek Stout?).

Harwig's, 911 Lincoln, tel. (970) 879-1980, serves a wide array of multi-cultural dishes, including jambalaya, Thai chicken curry, and southwestern chicken, plus steaks, pastas, and seafood, for $8-12. The **Steamboat Yacht Club,** 811 Yampa, tel. (970) 879-4774, serves high-end dinners, including elk, lamb, and seafood at tables overlooking the Yampa River and Howelsen Ski Hill (when it's nice you can sit on the deck outside).

Gurus from the East, Gurus from the West

While Steamboat's older, laid-back baby-boom crowd packs the Steamboat Brewery, the younger, snowboarding, dance-on-the-tables crowd hang at **Heavenly Daze Brewery and Grill,** in Ski Time Square, tel. (970) 879-8080. Pub specials include veggie stir fry and shep-

herds pie, and dinners run $7-12. Excellent homemade beers and ales.

For "true enlightenment," try **Buddha's Burrito's,** 24 5th St. (corner of Yampa), tel. (970) 870-1661. Perhaps the definitive "hole in the wall," Buddha's has four small tables and also serves takeout (open till 1 a.m., will deliver till midnight—perfect for late-night munchies). Hot and cheap ($2-3) burritos and veggie dishes.

Sleigh-Ride Dinners

Departing from the top of the gondola Thursday, Friday, and Saturday nights mid-Dec.-April 1, Ragnar's offers elegant European-style cuisine, live music, and the thrill of an after-dark sleigh ride at mid-mountain at Steamboat Ski Resort. (Sleigh-ride lunches are offered daily.) Child care is available. Call for reservations and prices, tel. (970) 879-6111.

ENTERTAINMENT

Many of Steamboat's clubs, restaurants, and hotels offer a variety of après-ski entertainment. For current listings, pick up a copy of *Steamboat Today,* published daily and available free throughout the area. In addition, the **Steamboat Whistle,** published weekly and also free, lists current happenings, theater showings, gallery openings, etc.

If you've still got energy after a day of skiing, check out **The Inferno,** featuring live music and dancing, as well as stand-up comedy by big-name acts. Located at the base of the gondola; phone (970) 879-5111 for more information. The **Old Town Pub,** 600 Lincoln, tel. (970) 879-2101, has live music Sunday and Monday nights, and a big-screen television showing skiing and other sporting events most of the rest of the time. The **Tugboat,** tel. (970) 879-7070, and **Heavenly Daze,** tel. (970) 879-8080, both in Ski Time Square regularly feature live music.

CALENDAR

There's something going on in Steamboat almost every weekend—from on-skis torchlight parades and ski races to local theater productions and rodeos. One of the highlights is the 80-year-old weeklong **Winter Carnival,** which takes place in early February each year. Among the events are ice-sculpture competitions, ski jumping, hockey games, and a parade on skis. A local tradition, the festival is marked by a general sense of revelry and nuttiness. For more information, phone (970) 879-0695 or 879-0880. In early June, you can join the runners (and walkers) in the Steamboat Marathon (actually a 10-K course), and a month later, the Fourth of July weekend is **Cowboy Roundup Days,** a potpourri of fireworks, community barbecues, a Rocky Mountain Oyster Fry, and a Cowboy Poetry and Storytelling Jamboree. **Strings in the Mountains** is a six-week music festival at the base of the ski lifts offering a range of chamber and other classical music, with musicians from around the world, most days of the week, plus lectures and other activities. Friday is "Different Tempo" night, when you can hear anything from gospel to bluegrass to jazz. **Rainbow Weekend,** at the end of July, is an annual hot-air balloon festival, including arts-and-crafts booths, live music, and food.

For exact dates and more information on these events and many more, phone the **Steamboat Springs Chamber Resort Association** tel. (970) 879-0880. When staying in Steamboat, check out the community calendars in the daily paper *Steamboat Today* and in the weekly *Steamboat Whistle.*

SHOPPING

Though Steamboat's a mecca for lovers of the outdoors, the town and village do offer a variety of gift shops and boutiques as well. While the rest of your party skis, golfs, fishes, balloons, or otherwise explores the area's copious mountains, parks, forests, and lakes, you can venture into the town's world of boutiques, gift shops, galleries, and, alas, tourist traps.

If you drive to Steamboat, you can't miss the zillions of billboards advertising **F. M. Light and Sons,** and most likely you'll be a bit curious. Go ahead and check it out; it's definitely a one-of-a-kind store. Originally a western wear and supply shop dating to the early part of the century, Light's now carries a huge array of apparel—

from lizard-skin cowboy boots to Marlboro-man ponchos, from after-ski boots to I-Heart-Steamboat sweatshirts. You'll also find postcards and other knicknacks.

The **Elephant's Trunk Boutique** in the Torian Plum Building, tel. (970) 879-3468, sells handsome boots for men, women, and children—from fancy dress to after-ski. **Barton's,** also in the village at the base of the lifts, tel. (970) 879-6777, carries a variety of impressive collectibles—dolls, ceramics, Christmas ornaments, shawls, and wall hangings.

You'll also find a dozen or so galleries in the Steamboat area, both in town and at the village. The **Amer-Indian Gallery,** 747 Lincoln, tel. (970) 879-7116, sells paintings, rugs, baskets, sculpture, and jewelry from over 50 Native American tribes. During the ski season, the gallery offers a series of special shows and lectures; call for more information. The **Artisans' Market of Steamboat,** 624 Lincoln, tel. (970) 879-7512, is a local artists' cooperative, selling the work of a variety of Steamboat and Routt County artists. Open daily 9:30 a.m.-8:30 p.m..

SERVICES

The **Steamboat Springs Police Department** is located at 840 Yampa St.; call (970) 849-1144. Phone the **Routt County Sheriff** at (970) 849-1090. **State Patrol** offices are at 29587 W. US 40, tel. (970) 879-4306. Steamboat's **Routt Memorial Hospital** is at 80 Park Ave., tel. (970) 879-1322. The central **post office** is on the east end of town at 200 Lincoln Ave., tel. (970) 879-0363.

Recycling
Recycle aluminum and glass in Steamboat Springs at the **City Market,** 1825 Central Park Avenue. Phone the City of Steamboat **recycling information line** at (970) 879-2060.

INFORMATION

The **Steamboat Springs Chamber Resort Association** is a professional and aggressive group, and a card or phone call will get you on their mailing list, which in turn will get you generous amounts of information (brochures, maps, advertising leaflets, relocation info, etc.). Write Box 774408, Steamboat Springs, CO 80477, or phone (970) 879-0880 or (800) 922-2722. Their Internet address, which can provide you with lodging, dining, and activities information, is **http://www.steamboat-ski.com/ski**.

The **Bud Werner Memorial Library** (Steamboat's public library) is located at 1289 Lincoln Ave., tel. (970) 879-0240; special events are sponsored year-round, including children's storytelling.

For maps and information on hiking, snowmobiling, cross-country skiing, and otherwise exploring Steamboat's backcountry, write the district office of the **Routt National Forest,** 57 10th St., Steamboat Springs, CO 80477, or phone (970) 879-1870.

For **road and weather information,** phone (970) 879-1260. For **Steamboat ski conditions,** phone (970) 879-7300.

TRANSPORTATION

Getting around Steamboat, particularly in the wintertime when the shuttles are running full tilt, is relatively easy, as is getting there. Several major airlines, including **American, United,** and **Northwest,** fly nonstop to Steamboat from cities on both coasts (Los Angeles, San Diego, New York) and in between (Phoenix, Chicago, Dallas, Denver). Check with your travel agent for fares. You might want to fly into Denver instead, as it's considerably cheaper than flying directly into Steamboat, and then either rent your own rig or take a shuttle to the ski area. If you fly into Denver, you can get to Steamboat via **Panorama's Steamboat Express,** tel. (970) 879-3400 or (800) 825-8383.

Once you arrive in Steamboat, whether you're staying downtown or in the village, you don't really need a car to get around. **Steamboat Springs Transit,** tel. (970) 879-3717, has several regular routes around the village, as well as one that runs into town. The "Red Line" and the "Green Line" circle through the condo complexes and will drop you off at the ski area in the morning and virtually at your doorstep at the end of the day. For you night owls, the last bus leaves the village for downtown at 2:03 a.m.

(an hour earlier on Sunday). Phone for more information and for non-ski-season schedules.

Alpine Taxi-Limo, Inc., tel. (970) 879-2800 or (800) 232-RIDE (in Colorado) or (800) 343-RIDE (nationwide), offers standard taxi service as well as charters between Steamboat and Denver International Airport, mountain tours, and shuttles between Steamboat lodges and Yampa Valley Airport.

Rent cars in Steamboat from **Budget,** tel. (970) 879-3103, **Dollar,** tel. (970) 879-5969, **Hertz,** tel. (970) 870-0800, **National,** tel. 879-0800, **Rent-a-Dent,** tel. (970) 879-8737, or from **Sam Taylor Auto Rentals,** tel. (970) 879-0928 or (800) 338-5631, specializing in snow-ready front-wheel- and four-wheel-drive rigs. You can also rent cars at Denver International Airport from all major companies, most of which offer special ski vehicles—4WD, ski racks, etc.

SOUTH TO I-70

US Highway 40 south to the junction with I-70 near Georgetown is absolutely stunning for its variety of breathtaking scenery. Just south of Steamboat, you arc to the east and begin the climb up and over the Continental Divide at Rabbit Ears Pass (elev. 9,426 feet). Just a few miles later, though, the highway dips south again and back onto the western side of the divide at Muddy Pass (8,722 feet). Then the road drops down into the Blue River Valley and into Kremmling, where you can either continue due south to Dillon via CO 9 and Green Mountain Reservoir or bank east to Granby. At the southwestern corner of Rocky Mountain National Park, Granby offers access to US 34 through the park to Estes Park (the road is closed in the winter). Continuing on US 40 south from Granby takes you through the high windswept Fraser River Valley, surrounded by the towering mountains of the deep heart of the Rockies, and into Winter Park. Just past Winter Park, US 40 begins a nasty series of switchbacks, winding and snaking its way up and over Berthoud Pass (11,307 feet). Views along this stretch are unsurpassed (though you need to make sure your brakes are in good working order . . .). From the junction of US 40 and I-70 it's less than an hour's drive to Denver.

Stanley Hotel, Estes Park

NORTH CENTRAL COLORADO

Stretching from the Great Plains west to the Continental Divide and from Winter Park north to the Wyoming border, North Central Colorado displays the state's fascinating geological diversity in all its grandness and at its most breathtaking. Here you'll find scores of peaks topping 12,000 feet and several over 14,000, as well as great expanses of prairie grasslands; narrow one-way mountain passes and long, straight stretches of uninteresting interstate; cold, crisp glacier-carved alpine lakes and the muddy South Platte River, which James Michener's *Centennial* narrator described as "the most miserable river in the west."

In addition, North Central Colorado is home to some of the state's best recreation opportunities, from backpacking in Rocky Mountain National Park to windsurfing on Horsetooth Reservoir, from skiing at Winter Park to fishing in Grand Lake or the Cache La Poudre River. In fact, the area offers an amazing amount of public land

ideal for exploring by foot, mountain bike, horseback, or cross-country skis—Roosevelt, Routt, and Arapaho national forests, along with Colorado State Forest, combine to occupy about half of North Central Colorado's total area.

The showpiece of North Central Colorado is Rocky Mountain National Park. Accessible from US 34 either from the east or west (although the road through the park is closed in winter), this 265,200-acre year-round wonderland attracts nearly three million visitors a year. The park features over 350 miles of hiking trails, excellent opportunities to view Colorado wildlife, including bighorn sheep, elk, and deer, and some of the absolutely most spectacular scenery on the planet—alpine meadows blanketed with wildflowers, massive granite peaks white with year-round snow, and lush valleys vibrantly green from summer rains.

The two largest communities in North Central Colorado are Greeley and Fort Collins, both about an hour's drive north of Denver. Fort Collins is home to the 20,000-student Colorado State University, best known for its agriculture programs. Kept vital by its youthful population, Fort Collins is committed to preserving its past, with several historical museums and the recently renovated Old Town shopping area.

Greeley is a ranching and farming area and the central subject of *Centennial*. In the book, Michener describes it as "nothing less than the soul of America . . . as seen in microcosm."

Which could also be said about the whole of North Central Colorado. From its geology and history to its economy and industry, the area is like a living textbook in American studies.

NORTH CENTRAL COLORADO HIGHLIGHTS

Rocky Mountain National Park: sightseeing, camping, hiking, cross-country skiing

Estes Park: hiking and mountain biking in Roosevelt National Park, cross-country skiing, fishing the Colorado, Arkansas, and Cache La Poudre rivers, museums, shopping, Stanley Hotel (majestic, turn-of-the-century hotel), Long's Peak Scottish Festival

Winter Park: skiing and hiking in Arapaho National Forest, 660 miles of mountain-bike trails, American Music Festival, Rocky Mountain Wine and Food Festival, Famous Flame Thrower High Altitude Chili Cook-off

Grand Lake: entry to Rocky Mountain National Park, fishing, camping, hiking, and skiing in Arapaho National Recreation Area, Indian Parks Wilderness Area

Poudre Canyon: sightseeing, fishing, camping

Fort Collins: Anheuser-Busch, Inc. Brewery, Horsetooth Reservoir, hut-to-hut Nordic skiing along the Never Summer Nordic Yurt System, renovated old-town area, shopping, dining, college-town nightlife, Colorado Brewfest, Balloon Festival

Greeley: Fort Vasquez, University of Northern Colorado, Denver Broncos' summer training camp, summer festivals and fairs, museums, shopping, dining (best Rocky Mountain oysters in the state)

WINTER PARK

Berthoud Pass

The drive up over Berthoud Pass from I-70 to Winter Park is one of the most spectacular in the state. Cutting through sheer canyons and switching back up from the valley floor, finally rising above the timberline and across the Continental Divide, the road affords stunning panoramas of purple mountains and saw-toothed peaks that appear to stretch forever.

At the summit is a plaque marking the Continental Divide. A handful of tables perched precariously on the cliffside let you picnic with a view to the north of Winter Park and on to Rocky Mountain National Park. And if the elevation makes you queasy and you're not sure you can trust your stomach, you can also wait till you get to the bottom, where Midland Picnic Area (in the Arapaho National Forest) will welcome your safe descent.

Located at the foot of Berthoud Pass at the south end of the gorgeous Fraser Valley, Winter Park (pop. 600; elev. 9,000 feet) is a small community devoted almost entirely to tourism and recreation. From Thanksgiving to mid-April, the town is swollen with winter sports enthusiasts of every stripe, while summer sees a proliferation of warm-weather-sports fans, from mountain bikers to trout anglers.

Virtually inseparable from the 54-year-old Winter Park Ski Area, whose runs drop almost to the little town's main drag, Winter Park offers an ideal blend of old-ski-town charm and the latest in high-tech equipment and deluxe lodging facilities. You can stay in a cozy inn or a luxury hotel, take a backwoods sleigh ride or zoom to the top of the mountain via five high-speed detachable quad chairlifts.

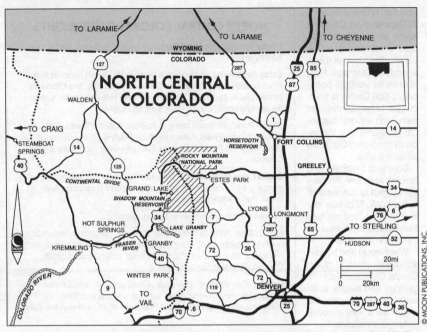

Surrounded by towering mountains and Arapaho National Forest, Winter Park sits at the southern end of the beautiful Middle Park region of the Rockies. Winter Park also provides access to the Fraser River Valley, the resort town of Grand Lake, and the western entrance to Rocky Mountain National Park. In fact, the Denver-to-Denver circle—through Winter Park, Rocky Mountain National Park, Estes Park, Lyons, and Boulder—is one of most breathtaking scenic drives in the country. (Note: The road through Rocky Mountain National Park is closed in the winter.) US 40 through Winter Park is also the best way to get to Steamboat Springs from Denver.

History

The Fraser River Valley was first settled in the mid-1800s, although the area had been explored earlier in the century, and hunters and fur trappers frequented the valley in the 1820s and '30s. The valley's first post office was established in Fraser in 1850, and by the 1870s there

were enough settlers in the area that local Native Americans were beginning to feel intruded upon. By 1883, the Utes had been relocated to a reservation in Utah following the Meeker Massacre.

Winter Park began to come into its own in 1927 with the completion of the $18-million, seven-mile Moffat Tunnel, which bore through the Continental Divide and linked Denver and the Fraser Valley. The tunnel was named for David H. Moffat, a Denver banker who had worked for nearly a quarter century to run the Denver and Pacific Northwestern Railroad through the mountains to provide safer and more reliable passage between Denver and Salt Lake City. The tunnel's western terminus is adjacent to the community of Winter Park, which was originally known as West Portal.

In 1937, the Forest Service built an 800-foot rope tow at Berthoud Pass, and by the end of the decade, some 50,000 skiers a year were descending on the little ski resort. Because the area and skiing were growing so popular with Denverites, the city sought a way to open a municipal "winter park" of its own. West Portal was the perfect locale, and Winter Park Ski Area, under management of the City of Denver, first opened on Jan. 28, 1940. Lift tickets that day were $1.

The city ran into difficulties, however, trying to maintain a park on the other side of the Continental Divide, and during the late 1940s, Winter Park fell into disrepair. Sensing the first wave of Colorado's mid-century ski boom, Denver realized it had the opportunity to take part—if it could make Winter Park a viable resort. In 1950, city officials created the Winter Park Recreational Association (WPRA), a 15-member board of trustees that would work independently of the city and run operations at Winter Park. The nonprofit corporation quickly got to work improving the ski area, beginning with a surface lift. The $167,000 City-of-Denver-financed project increased uphill capacity to 1,600 skiers per hour. Since then, the WPRA has remained nonprofit and self-supporting, successfully managing one of Colorado's best ski areas. The 1991 ski season saw $5.3 million in improvements—including construction of a high-speed quad chair, increased snowmaking capabilities, and the remodeling of on-mountain eating facilities.

Sights
Cozens' Ranch House Museum on US 40 just north of town on the Fraser-Winter Park line was the site of a stage stop and post office dating from 1876. Check out the room commemorating "Doc Suzie," Grand County's first woman doctor, who moved to the area from Cripple Creek in 1907, practiced until 1941, and died in 1960 at age 90. The museum is open Mon.-Sat. 10 a.m.-5 p.m. and 12-5 Sunday, with limited hours during the winter. Admission is $3 for adults, with discounts for seniors and kids. For more information, phone (970) 726-5488.

WINTER SPORTS

Winter Park's accessibility to Denver, just 70 miles away via I-70 and US 40 (broad and well maintained, if a bit steep and harrowing in places), makes it a natural for day-trippers look-

ing for the heart of the snow country. Denver alpine skiers, cross-country skiers, snowboarders, and Telemarkers flock to Winter Park when the snow flies, knowing they can get a good day's skiing in and still be home in time for dinner. In addition, families, honeymooners, and college students from all over the country come to Winter Park for their vacations—by train, plane, and automobile—with the knowledge they'll find some of the state's best skiing here, as well as one of the West's friendliest mountain towns. And non-skiers know there's a lot to do here besides ski. Though the community's too small to offer a whole lot in the way of nightlife and other entertainment, the area affords a wide range of other winter recreational opportunities, from ice skating to moonlight sleigh rides.

Downhill Skiing

Recently ranked 13th among *Snow Country* magazine's top 45 North American ski resorts (Sept. 1991), **Winter Park Ski Area** has earned a solid reputation as one of the state's best family ski areas, with terrain suitable for every ability level, from snowplower to backcountry bowler. In addition, the resort is held in high esteem worldwide for its commitment to skiers with disabilities—amputees, paraplegics, and the blind.

Winter Park Ski Area sprawls across three separate mountain ridges connected by a sophisticated network of lifts and runs. Combined, **Winter Park, Mary Jane,** and **Vasquez Ridge** offer 20 lifts on 1,301 acres of terrain with an uphill capacity of 29,400 skiers an hour (the second largest in Colorado). The longest run is over five miles.

Winter Park and Vasquez Ridge offer the most skiing for intermediate-range skiers, while Mary Jane has the more demanding runs. In

fact, 53% of Mary Jane's runs are designated advanced or expert, and the steep bump runs here are among the nastiest in the state. Only six percent of Mary Jane is designated for beginning skiers.

The true pride of Winter Park, though, is the **National Sports Center for the Disabled.** Founded by Hal O'Leary in the winter of 1969-70, the program started out small. Its goal was to teach children with cancer and leg amputations to ski. Since then, the program has grown to embrace people with over 40 disabilities and provides instruction and adaptive equipment to over 17,000 skiers a year. From single-track skiers (single amputees skiing with outriggers, crutches with short skis on the end) and blind skiers (who follow instructors or partners with bells) to sit skiers (double amputees or paraplegics, who ski in "sleds"), Winter Park's slopes are covered with folks who manage to all but leave their disabilities behind. Don't be surprised to see a single-track skier zip by you demonstrating more élan and control than you can muster on your very best day.

The National Sports Center for the Disabled also offers a number of competitions for disabled skiers, and has recently expanded to offer an array of summer programs, including mountain biking, hiking, and whitewater rafting.

Winter Park Ski Area has a full range of instructional programs for skiers of all abilities

looking east at the Continental Divide from Winter Park

and offers complete rental and equipment-repair services. For more information on ticket prices, hours of operation, or instruction, phone (970) 726-5514. For **snow conditions,** phone (900) 950-5550.

Cross-Country Skiing

The Winter Park-Fraser Valley areas offer nearly unlimited opportunities for the cross-country skier, thanks to the surrounding Arapaho National Forest. Whether you like to follow old logging roads or break your own trails, you won't be disappointed. For maps and information on exploring Arapaho National Forest on Nordic skis, contact the district office in Granby at 62429 US 40, tel. (970) 887-3331 (or 887-3165 for a recorded message).

In addition, the area has a number of groomed public trail systems. **Devil's Thumb Guest Ranch and Cross-Country Center,** offers 90-plus km of trails in the quiet backcountry in the woods along the Fraser River. The center is located east of Fraser at 3530 County Rd. 83. For information, phone (970) 726-5632.

You'll also find excellent groomed cross-country trails at **Snow Mountain Ranch's Nordic Center** about 15 miles north of Winter Park off US 40. The facility has 100 km of trails on some 4,600 acres of woodsy backcountry, with three km lighted for night skiing. Phone (970) 726-4628 for information.

Snowmobiling

The broad Fraser Valley and sprawling expanses of Arapaho National Forest make the area a natural for exploring by snowmobile; several outfits offer rentals and tours. **Trailblazer Snowmobile Tours,** tel. (970) 726-8452, is based in Fraser and provides a range of tours, as does **Sporting Country Guide Service,** tel. (970) 726-9247 (or 887-3255 in Granby). To rent snowmobiles, contact **Mountain Madness** in Fraser Meadow, tel. (970) 726-4529.

Snowcat Tours

You can tour the Winter Park Ski Area by snowcat, with machines leaving the base of the lifts three times daily. For reservations and information, phone the resort at (970) 726-5514.

amputee ski racer at Winter Park

ERIK BAKKE

Totally Tubular

Snow tubing is a Winter Park tradition. One of the best tubing hills in the Rockies is located just north of town on US 40 (you'll see it off to your left). Link 'em together to make tube trains, or go solo. Go head, feet, or butt first. Just dress warm—the wind can *really* whip across that meadow. For rates and information, phone the **Fraser Tubing Hill** at (970) 726-5954.

O'er the Fields We Go

In contrast to the gift shops and high-tech lifts, a horse-drawn sleigh will take you out into the quiet moonlit woods for a short scenic tour or a romantic dinner. **Jim's Sleigh Rides,** tel. (970) 726-5527, offers both afternoon and evening rides, with a stop midway for refreshments and warm-up by the fire. **Dinner at the Barn,** tel. (970) 726-4923, provides dinner and evening entertainment rides to a renovated ranch house. You can also take evening dinner rides from **Devil's Thumb Ranch,** tel. (970) 726-5632. It's not the cheapest way to spend an evening (about $35 adult, $28 child), but ideal for a special celebration.

Ice Skating

You'll find ice-skating rinks at **Fraser Valley Elementary School** in Fraser, **Beaver Village Resort** in Winter Park, tel. (970) 726-5741 or (800) 666-0281, and **Snow Mountain Ranch–YMCA of the Rockies** north of town, tel. (970) 726-4628 or, from Denver, tel. (303) 443-4743. For more information on ice skating in the Winter Park-Fraser Valley area, contact the Winter Park Recreational Association at (970) 726-5514.

WHEN THE SNOW MELTS

Don't let the name deceive you. Though best known as one of the state's winter-sports paradises, Winter Park is fast becoming a year-round resort. When skis get hung in racks, out come the mountain bikes, fishing poles, rafts, backpacks, and saddles and tack. Cross-country ski trails become havens for mountain bikers, and ski lifts are open to sightseers. If the little town were to rename itself, it just might choose Year-round Park.

Mountain Biking

This is without doubt the Fraser Valley area's latest rage, and indications are the sport is here to stay. The old logging trails of Arapaho National Forest offer enough miles of spleen-shaking backcountry riding to keep you rock-hopping all summer, maybe without ever going down the same path twice.

Winter Park's **Fat Tire Society** (FATS) has developed a 660-mile trail system named "best mountain biking system in Colorado" by *Rocky Mountain Sports Fitness* magazine, and the Winter Chamber of Commerce publishes a mountain-biking map available at the chamber and at sports shops around the valley. In addition, several companies offer rentals and guided tours. **Mad Adventures,** tel. (970) 726-5290 or (800) 451-4884, accommodates beginning to advanced riders, with instruction, "Jeep Up/Bike Down" trips, and single-track tours. You can rent bikes at **Alpine Sun,** tel. (970) 726-5107,

and many other shops in town.

Golf

The Fraser Valley's public 18-hole **Pole Creek Golf Course** is 10 miles west of Winter Park. Named "Best New Public Course in America" in 1985 by *Golf Digest,* the 6,230-yard Pole Creek remains on the magazine's list of top 50 American courses. The course hosts several tournaments annually, including the infamous **Bert and Ernie Classic** in September. For information and tee times, phone (970) 726-8847.

Grand Lake Golf Course is located 40 minutes north of Winter Park on the east side of Rocky Mountain National Park. Views from this 18-hole course are some of the best anywhere. Phone (970) 627-8008.

Hiking

You'll find lots of excellent hiking opportunities in the Winter Park area. Hiking's best in the morning, as the sky often clouds up in the afternoon, and hard rains are quite common. **Byer's Peak** (elev. 12,804 feet) towers west of the Fraser Valley and offers a short (just under three miles) but rugged trail to the top. Panoramas are excellent. Go west from US 40 in Fraser.

For information on hiking in Arapaho National Forest, stop in at the information center at the Sulphur District Office in Granby, or phone (970) 887-3331.

Fishing

The Fraser Valley-Grand County area offers a wide range of mountain fishing for trout and kokanee salmon. Free fishing is provided for kids in the small roadside ponds between Winter Park and Fraser; the lakes are stocked regularly by the local chapter of the Lion's Club. More serious (and older) lake anglers should head up to the Three Lakes Area near Granby and the town of Grand Lake. **Grand Lake, Shadow Mountain Reservoir,** and **Lake Granby** are home to some good-size rainbow, cutthroat, lake (Mackinaw), and brown trout, as well as landlocked kokanee. Fishing is best from a boat, but shore anglers have done well too.

Stream fishermen will want to try the **Colorado** and **Fraser rivers.** The Fraser flows through Winter Park, and offers decent fishing

CATHY CARLSON

peregrine falcon

(planters) near the ski area, while a stretch just north of town is designated a Wild Trout Area (be sure to check local fishing restrictions). For information, tackle, and licenses, stop by **Nelson's Fly and Tackle Shop,** north of Winter Park in Tabernash along US 40, tel. (970) 726-8558.

Rafting
With the North Platte, Colorado, and Arkansas rivers all tumbling through the mountains in Grand County, you can bet there's plenty of rafting action. In Winter Park, several companies offer a variety of trips, from mellow floats to serious whitewater. **Mad Adventures,** tel. (970) 726-5290 or (800) 451-4844, **Rapid Transit Rafting,** (970) tel. 627-3062 or (800) 367-8523, and **Timber Rafting,** tel. (970) 887-2141 or (800) 332-3381, book trips (from half-day to three-day) for all levels of ability and interest. Rates usually begin at around $30 for half-day trips.

Horseback Riding
Beaver Stables, tel. (970) 726-8035 or, after 6 p.m., tel. 726-4311, offers a variety of riding packages—from one- and two-hour jaunts throughout the day to evening rides that include chuckwagon dinners. At **Sombrero Ranch Stables** in Grand Lake, tel. (970) 627-3514, you can also book tours and pack trips or rent horses by the hour.

Chairlift Rides
For spectacular views of the surrounding scenery, it's tough to beat an off-season chairlift ride. **Winter Park Ski Area,** tel. (970) 726-5514, runs lifts during the summer for sightseeing.

Alpine Slide
Winter Park's Alpine slide gives summer visitors a chance to crank turns on the slopes in a completely different fashion, though the ride to the top is the same (via chairlift). Located at the base of the ski hill, the half-mile, 30-turn slide is open June-mid-August and costs $4 a ride (multi-ride discounts are available). Children must be at least 45 inches tall. Phone Winter Park Resort at (970) 726-5514 for more information.

ACCOMMODATIONS

Much less developed than some of Colorado's major destination ski resorts, Winter Park nonetheless offers the visitor a wide range of lodging options—from an American Youth Hostel to conventional motels to upscale condos with all the bells and whistles. **Note:** It's necessary to make reservations in winter and highly suggested the rest of the year. Also, prices here should be used for comparison; rates often vary significantly from summer to winter.

Budget
The **Winter Park Hostel,** tel. (970) 726-5356, offers the least expensive beds in town. Bunks start at about $10 (discounts with American Youth Hostel cards), and guests are asked to help out with a chore or two. Located behind Le Ski Lab in downtown Winter Park; write: Box 3323, Winter Park, CO 80482.

A favorite among families is the **Snow Mountain Ranch—YMCA of the Rockies,** tel. (970) 726-4628, which offers a variety of lodging options, from individual cabins (sleeping up to 12) to rooms in the central lodge ranging from $25-250 a night. Kids and their parents love it here, as there's always something to do: go hiking or cross-country skiing (with a lodge guide), play in the indoor pool, or even lose yourself in the lodge library. Located just south of Granby at 1344 County Rd. 53 off US 40, Snow Mountain is a nonprofit operation that's been in business for over 20 years. (YMCA of the Rockies also operates **Estes Park Center**—see Estes Park.) For a brochure with complete information, write Box 169, Winter Park, CO 80482.

Hotels, Lodges, and a Condominium

The **Alpenglo Motor Lodge,** tel. (970) 726-5294, or for reservations only, (800) 541-6130, has rooms in the center of town starting at about $50. The **Olympia Motor Lodge,** tel. (970) 726-8843, also downtown, has doubles for about $40. Rooms for two at **Sundowner Motel,** tel. (970) 726-9451 or (800) 521-8279, start at about $45.

One of the best deals in town is the **Arapahoe Lodge,** tel. (970) 726-8222 or (800) 338-2698, a classic '40s-era ski lodge just north of downtown (on the shuttle line), where the 14 rooms go for $60-70 per person, which includes breakfast and dinner.

One of Winter Park's more upscale condo complexes is the **Iron Horse Resort Retreat,** tel. (970) 726-8851 or (800) 621-8190, located at the base of the lifts between Winter Park and Mary Jane. Rates start at about $80 for two; ski and golf packages are available.

Gasthaus Eichler, tel. (970) 726-5133 or (800) 543-3899, is located downtown and is better known as a restaurant than as a lodge, though there are rooms upstairs, available with or without meals; doubles run $40-140.

Beaver Village Resort, tel. (970) 726-5741 or (800) 666-0281, offers ski packages in the winter, and in the summer, the lodge bills itself as a "Mountain Bike Dude Ranch." Rates start at about $40 and go to $300.

The **Vintage Resort Hotel,** tel. (970) 726-8801 or (800) 472-7017, has a wide range of facilities, from individual rooms to a conference center; golf and ski packages available. Rooms run $65-300.

Another off-the-beaten-track lodge (yet just a few minutes from Winter Park) is **Devil's Thumb Ranch,** tel. (970) 726-5632 or (800) 826-2280 (in Colorado) or (800) 525-3304 (outside Colorado). Located in a huge meadow three miles north of Fraser, Devil's Thumb is first a cross-country ski lodge, but also a perfect base for a riding, mountain biking, hiking, fishing, or just an I-need-to-get-away-from-the-rush vacation. The rustic restaurant overlooking the meadow is open to nonguests as well. Rooms start at $60 d, shared bath mid-November to December 24 and go up to $90 d for a private bath, December 25 to January 2. To get to Devil's Thumb, take County Rd. 83 east from Fraser; then go right at the fork in the road.

For total luxury in backwoods lodging, check out the **C Lazy U Guest Ranch,** tel. (970) 887-3344, "the country's only five-star dude ranch." A year-round resort offering cross-country skiing, snowmobiling, tennis, fishing, horseback rides, cross-country skiing, and many other activities, the C Lazy U is one of the best places around to be pampered. Room prices start around $150, and rise dramatically from there, but include three gourmet meals a day. For complete information, write Box 378B, Granby, CO 80446.

Bed and Breakfasts

Winter Park has a number of bed and breakfasts, all of which do well in winter but slack off once the snow's gone and the lifts have shut down. **Nordic Bed and Breakfast,** tel. (970) 726-8459, **Angel West,** tel. (970) 726-5354, **Alpen Rose,** tel. (970) 726-5039, **Mulligan's Mountain Inn,** tel. (970) 887-2877, **Engelman Pines,** tel. (970) 726-5416, **The Hearthstone,** tel. (970) 726-9710, Beauwest, tel. (970) 726-5145, and **The Pines Inn,** tel. (970) 726-5416, all are within short drives of Winter Park and offer easy access to summer activities. The Winter Park/Fraser Valley Chamber of Commerce will send you a complete list, with descriptions and rates; phone (800) 903-7275.

Camping and RVing

There are several campgrounds—those operated by the Forest Service, as well as privately run camps—in and around Winter Park. **Robbers Roost** is a small Forest Service campground at the north base of Berthoud Pass, just before the turnoff to Mary Jane Ski Area. A few miles farther north, almost right downtown, **Idlewild Campground** also offers Forest Service-run sites. For information, contact the Winter Park Chamber of Commerce, tel. (970) 726-4118, or the Forest Service district office in Granby, tel. (970) 887-3331.

Elk Valley RV Campground, tel. (970) 887-2380, just south of Granby has RV sites with full hookups, as well as cabins (and horses) for rent.

Information and Reservations
Condominium Management Company handles reservations for half a dozen or so properties, including **Hi Country Haus, Braidwood, Hideaway Village, Timber Run, Crestview Place, The Summit at Silver Creek,** and **Trademark;** phone (970) 726-9421 or (800) 228-1025, or (303) 825-0705 from Denver.

Winter Park Central Reservations, tel. (970) 726-5587 or (800) 453-2525, can assist you with booking lodging, as well as air, rail, and shuttle transportation.

FOOD

Start Me Up
One of Winter Park's favorite breakfast spots is **The Kitchen,** tel. (970) 726-9940, at 78542 US 40 on the north end of town, where locals and visitors alike go for the homemade food ranging from muffins to pancakes to traditional egg dishes. **Carlson's Cafe,** on US 40 on the south end of town, is a classic small-town diner, with as much counter space as table space—American breakfasts (delicious pancakes!) run $2-5. Check out the original decor: scores of old ice skates and ice tongs hanging from the ceiling. Note: Hours and days of operation here are rather capricious; be sure to have a plan B if you plan to eat here.

Lunch and Dinner
Deno's Mountain Bistro, tel. (970) 726-5332, downtown on US 40 is part sports bar and part restaurant and has a wide range of food, from chicken-wing appetizers to burgers, fish and chips, steaks, and Cajun dishes. Prices run $5-20 for dinner. Deno's has several television monitors, as well as an excellent beer selection, making it one of the best places in town to catch a game. **The Last Waltz,** tel. (970) 726-4877, on US 40 on the north end of town, serves breakfast, lunch, dinner, and Sunday brunch, specializing in Mexican and home-style American dishes. Prices are very reasonable.

A veritable Winter Park institution, **Gasthaus Eichler,** 78786 US 40, tel. (970) 726-5133, serves lunch and dinner. For lunch try the bratwurst, the quiche of the day, or a salad ($4-7). Dinners include German specialties as well

as beef, veal, and seafood and run to $30 (lobster tail). Another local favorite is **The Divide Grill,** tel. (970) 726-4900, specializing in Italian food, fish, and chicken. Prices range from $7.50 (salad bar) to around $17 (New York steak). At **Hernando's Pizza and Pasta Pub,** tel. (970) 726-5409, pizzas range $7-14, and pasta dinners (spaghetti, ravioli, lasagna, etc.) are around $7. **Lani's Place,** tel. (970) 726-9674, is a long-standing favorite of folks looking for good south-of-the-border food, especially those who've spent a day on the slopes (either on skis or bikes) and are as interested in the margaritas and mingling with the lively crowd as they are in the food. The **Crooked Creek Saloon,** tel. (970) 726-9250, in Fraser has great burgers, salads, and sandwiches.

Finally, if you're looking for a place to take the kids, try **A'Maze,** tel. (970) 726-9555, next to the Safeway in Fraser. In addition to the human maze, in which kids (and adults) can race against the clock, there's also a video arcade and indoor miniature golf. Oh, and food, too: pizzas, burgers, salads, and ice cream.

ENTERTAINMENT

You're much more likely to find night-owl action in Winter Park in the winter, when skiers are looking for places to boogie after a day on the slopes, than in summer, when the clubs are generally only open weekends. If you like things a bit slower and quieter, though, Winter Park's bars can be downright nice in the summer—you won't have to elbow your way through a crowd to order a beer or a plate of nachos. **The Slope,** tel. (970) 726-5727, just north of the base of the lifts, and the **Crooked Creek Saloon** in Fraser, tel. (970) 726-9250, both book live music, and Crooked Creek also has pool tables and darts.

CALENDAR

From first snow till the lifts shut down, and again from early June through August, Winter Park sponsors a wide range of events, from ski races and mountain-bike hill climbs to art shows and concerts.

Among Winter Park's annual highlights: the **First Interstate Bank Cup** features professional ski races in late January, with excellent opportunities to see top competitors. The **High Country Stampede,** Saturdays in July and August, is Fraser Valley's popular rodeo, attracting top professional and amateur riders from around the country.

A Winter Park classic is the **American Music Festival,** mid-July. The stage is set up at the base of the Winter Park Ski Area, and the audience lines the gentle lower slopes; there ain't a bad seat in the house. Lineups feature mostly American music, with a contemporary country bent. Past acts have included Bonnie Raitt, John Prine, Hootie and the Blowfish, the Mother Hips, and Leon Russell (shoulda heard him do "Somewhere Over the Rainbow" just as the rain let up).

Winter Park's late-July **Alpine Art Affair,** first held in 1975, features over 100 juried artists from throughout the western United States, as well as food booths and music. In mid-August, the **Rocky Mountain Wine and Food Festival** offers winetasting and seminars, with over 200 wines and champagnes, as well as gourmet meals prepared by the **Colorado Chefs de Cuisine**—a benefit for the National Sports Center for the Disabled. Also in the food category, the **Famous Flamethrower High Altitude Chili Cook-off** in early September is a high-spirited competition between local chefs vying to represent the Rocky Mountain region in the world chili cook-off.

On Christmas Eve, watch the beautiful **Torchlight Parade** wind its way down the runs of Winter Park Ski Area.

For more information or exact dates, contact the **Winter Park Recreational Association,** tel. (970) 726-5514, or the **Winter Park/Fraser Valley Chamber of Commerce,** tel. (800) 903-7275.

SHOPPING

Though you won't find the busy shopping village of a Vail or Aspen, a number of stores carry gifts, souvenirs, and other items. The main drag through town is rife with ski and sports shops, which often unload the previous season's gear and clothing during the summer at "sidewalk" sales. This can be a good time to pick up a pair of ski boots or a parka for a very good price.

SERVICES

Most Winter Park services, including the police and sheriff departments, are based in Hot Sulphur Springs, about 10 miles west of Granby on US 40. **Police department** offices are at 670 Spring Rd., tel. (970) 726-5666. The offices of the **Grand County Sher-**

Winter Park's Children's Center is one of the best ski-area facilities in the country.

*the Winter Park
Ski Train*

WINTER PARK SKI AREA

iff are at 308 Byers; tel. (970) 726-5666. **Winter Park Medical Center,** tel. (970) 726-9616, is in downtown Winter Park, and **7-Mile Clinic,** tel. (970) 726-8066, is at the base of the lifts of Winter Park Ski Area. The Winter Park **post office** is at 78876 US 40, tel. (970) 726-5495.

Child Care

Winter Park is one of the country's best family ski areas, so it should come as no surprise that children's facilities on the mountain are very highly regarded. A recent article in *Skiing* magazine lauded the resort's **Children's Center,** the oldest in Colorado, giving high praise to the facility's expert and kid-sensitive staff, and to its efficient organization.

The center divides kids into four groups (age three to kindergarten, first to third grade, fourth grade to age 12, and ages 13-16). While the little ones are playing games that acquaint them with the snow, the older ones can ski at their own pace with instructors. The center, operating out of a multistory 32,000-square-foot building, also provides day care for children ages two months to five years. For more information or to make reservations, phone (970) 726-5514, ext. 337.

Recycling

Drop off most recyclables at **Grand Recycles** at the firehouse on US 40 in Fraser. The Safeway in Fraser (on US 40) takes aluminum.

INFORMATION

The **Winter Park/Fraser Valley Chamber of Commerce,** open seven days a week, is an excellent source of information on everything from what to do to where to stay in the area. The office is located in town on US 40 (east side of the road); write Box 3236, Winter Park, CO 80482, or call (800) 903-7275. From among the many brochures, maps, and activity guides, be sure to pick up the Grand County *Exploration Guide,* a listing of over 100 historical and geographical places of interest in the county, as well as a copy of *Trails* (*Tracks* in winter), which lists local events. For Winter Park **Central Reservations,** phone (970) 726-5587 or (800) 453-2525. For electronic information, Winter Park Ski Area's Internet address is **http://www.skiwinterpark.com**.

For **weather information,** tune your radio to AM 930. If you're padding around in the morning waiting for your coffee to brew, tune your television to channel 5 for news about what's going on in the area.

You can also get **road and weather information** by calling (970) 725-3334.

TRANSPORTATION

Winter Park is only 67 miles from Denver and very easy to get to, despite the taxing drive over Berthoud Pass. **Home James,** tel. (970) 726-

5060, offers door-to-door roundtrip (and one-way) shuttle service between Denver and Winter Park (and on to lodges farther north and to Grand Lake). For information on car rentals at Denver International Airport, see "Colorado by Air" in the Introduction. You can rent a car in Winter Park by calling Winter Park Central Reservations at (800) 453-2525.

Without doubt, though, the best way to get to Winter Park is by train. **Amtrak** deposits 26,000 skiers a year at the Winter Park Ski Area station in nearby Fraser. For information, phone (970) 726-8816 or (800) USA-RAIL. From downtown Denver, you can ride the **Winter Park Ski Train,** which has been taking skiers to the slopes for over 50 years. The two-hour ride takes you through 29 tunnels and drops you off 100 yards from the lifts. In the winter of 1990-91, the train carried 25,000 passengers. Tickets are $25 for coach, $40 for first-class. For information and reservations, phone (303) 296-ISKI (4754).

cougar

NORTH OF WINTER PARK

US Highway 40 continues north into the heart of Middle Park, following the Fraser River to Granby then doglegging west toward Hot Sulphur Springs and Kremmling. Just past Granby is the junction with US 34, which continues north past Lake Granby, Shadow Mountain Reservoir, and the town of Grand Lake, before lifting east into Rocky Mountain National Park and over the Continental Divide (closed in winter).

The scenery throughout this area is stupendous, characterized by long broad mountain valleys surrounded by rugged, saw-toothed peaks, many of which are over 12,000 feet high. Towering just east of the town of Grand Lake is Longs Peak, at 14,256 feet one of the highest mountains in the state. To the north is Mt. Richthofen (elev. 12,940 feet), and to the west is Park View Mountain (elev. 12,296 feet).

GRANBY

Granby (pop. 1,200; elev. 7,600 feet) is a small ranching and farming center in the Fraser River Valley about 20 miles north of Winter Park. Once known especially for its mountain lettuce, Granby served as a railroad shipping point for vegetables and cattle, as well as timber. Many of the valley's older ranches have been converted to guest ranches (see "Accommodations" under "Winter Park"), and the town now relies heavily on the tourism industry—skiing in the winter, hunting, fishing, mountain biking, and sightseeing in the summer and fall. Granby's Fourth of July fireworks show is the biggest in the state, usually drawing around 75,000 visitors.

Silver Creek Ski Resort

One of Colorado's youngest and smallest ski areas, Silver Creek opened in 1982 as a primarily beginner and intermediate area catering to families and other folks wanting to get away from the crowds. Four lifts service just over 200 acres of skiable terrain with a 970-foot vertical drop. The terrain is rated 20% beginner, 50% in-

termediate, and 20% advanced, though most sources indicate a certain degree of "slope inflation." (Even the advanced skiing isn't all that challenging at Silver Creek.)

Though barely a decade old, Silver Creek has already established a reputation as a good cross-country area. Nordic skiers can both explore the groomed trails and ride the lifts on the mountain. The **Inn at Silver Creek,** tel. (970) 887-2131 or (800) 526-0590, is a deluxe hotel offering full amenities, including a conference center. Summer rates for two run about $70-95, and $90-120 in the winter.

During the summer, the resort complex offers many other recreational activities. For more information on Silver Creek Resort, phone (970) 887-3384 or (800) 448-9458. The direct line from Denver is (970) 629-1020.

Practicalities

You'll find a handful of small motels in town where you can get clean quiet rooms in the $30-50 range. They include the **Littletree Inn Motel,** tel. (970) 887-2551; the **Blue Spruce Motel,** tel. (970) 887-3300; **Trail Riders Motel,** tel. (970) 887-3738; the **Frontier Motel,** tel. (970) 887-2544; and the **El Monte Motor Inn,** tel. (970) 887-3348 or (800) 282-3348.

Services

The offices of the local **police department** are located west of town in Hot Sulphur Springs, tel. (970) 887-3866. Phone the **State Patrol** at (970) 725-3393. **St. Anthony Hospital Systems Emergency Medical Center** is at 62801 US 40 in Granby, tel. (970) 887-2503. The **post office** is at 54 Zero St., tel. (970) 887-3612.

Information

The **Granby Chamber of Commerce** operates a tourist information booth on the north end of town next to the Blue Spruce Motel. Stop in for maps, activity guides, and dining and lodging brochures, and more information on area guest ranches. You can also write Box 35, Granby, CO 80046, or phone (970) 887-2311 or (800) 325-1661.

WEST TO KREMMLING

US Highway 40 arcs west just outside Granby following the course of the Fraser River to its confluence with the Colorado at Kremmling. The road is flanked by Routt (north) and Arapaho (south) national forests, and passes through the little historical town of Hot Sulphur Springs. In Kremmling, you can either continue north to Steamboat Springs, or turn south onto CO 9, which follows the Blue River into Summit County, past Green Mountain Reservoir, continuing on to Dillon, Frisco, and Breckenridge.

HOT SULPHUR SPRINGS

Seat of Grand County, Hot Sulphur Springs (pop. 400; elev. 7,655 feet) was named for the nearby springs thought by Native Americans to have medicinal powers. According to legend, a Ute chief, whose tribe had left him to die, appealed to his gods for power. The chief built fires below the bubbling waters, bathed and drank in them, was healed, and rejoined the tribe.

Today, Hot Sulphur Springs is the site of the district offices of the Arapaho National Forest, as well as of several local agencies, including police, sheriff, and state patrol. For more information on Hot Sulphur Springs, write **Grand Lake Chamber of Commerce,** Box 57, Grand Lake, CO 80447, or phone (970) 627-3402.

Grand County Museum

Housed in the Hot Sulphur Schoolhouse (1924), this museum exhibits a wide array of historical items, including 8,500-year-old Native American artifacts, pioneer firearms, clothing, utensils, and snow gear (snowshoes, etc.), as well as historical photos. There's also a blacksmith shop, jail, the original county courthouse, and a display commemorating pioneer women and their role in the settling of the area, as well as a recently added 1905 BLM ranger station and a one-room school.

The museum is open daily 10 a.m.-5 p.m. and Sunday noon-5, Memorial Day through Labor Day, as well as Wed.-Sat. 10 a.m.-5 p.m. the rest of the year. Admission is $3 for adults,

with discounts for kids and seniors. For more information, phone (970) 725-3939.

Accommodations

You'll find doubles in the $45 range at the **Canyon Motel,** tel. (970) 725-3395, and at the **Ute Motel,** tel. (970) 725-3326. Both are located on US 40 in town.

KREMMLING

Located on the western side of the Middle Park area at the junction of CO 9 and US 40, Kremmling offers access to a wide range of recreational pursuits. Borders of Arapaho, Routt, and White River national forests are all within 20 miles of Kremmling, and the nearby waters—the Blue, Fraser, and Colorado rivers all pass through Kremmling—are favorites among kayakers and canoers; there's a put-in one mile south of town on CO 9.

You'll find a **visitor information center** on US 40 on the west end of town (corner of Park and Center), as well as a park with picnic tables and playground equipment. **Kremmling RV Park,** tel. (970) 724-9593, is located east of town on US 40 (2200 Central).

NORTH OF KREMMLING

US Highway 40 continues north from Kremmling over Muddy and Rabbit Ears passes to Steamboat Springs, then beelines west across the high plateau toward Dinosaur and the Utah border. Just a couple of miles beyond Muddy Pass you can catch CO 14 north to Walden, the isolated seat of isolated Jackson County. From Walden it's only another 20 miles to the Wyoming border, then 50 miles to Laramie.

WALDEN AND NORTH PARK

The North Park/Jackson County area is a high, intermontane glacial basin and is the location of the headwaters of the North Platte River. The basin is rimmed by stunning mountain peaks, some rising to nearly 13,000 feet. Long a favorite hunting ground of the Utes, North

Park hosts abundant wildlife, although its harsh winters force many of the critters to lower elevations.

Jackson County's economy relies largely on ranching and farming, although the area is being discovered by outdoor enthusiasts who appreciate its backpacking, hiking, fishing, camping, and cross-country skiing opportunities. Walden's **North Park Pioneer Museum** displays the basin's history, from the days of early settlement through Walden's founding in 1890 and into the 20th century.

In Walden you'll find a number of motels and bed-and-breakfast inns, as well as campgrounds and restaurants. The **North Park Motel,** tel. (970) 723-4271, 625 Main (Walden), is open year-round and has 20 units, some with kitchenettes; doubles are $32.

For more information on this remote but gorgeous area, contact the **North Park Tourism Information Center,** Box 489TB, Walden, CO 80480, tel. (970) 723-4344, or the **North Park Chamber of Commerce,** Box 227, Walden, CO 80480, tel. (970) 723-4600.

GRAND LAKE AND VICINITY

Grand Lake (pop. 380; elev. 8,369 feet) is a small summer resort village on the north shore of Grand Lake, the largest natural lake in Colorado. Situated on the western border of Rocky Mountain National Park, the town is a popular stop for tourists heading both into and out of the park. The town itself also attracts its own share of summer visitors, most of whom come to fish and explore the waters and shores of the three nearby lakes, camp in the area's many campgrounds, or hole up in the lodges, guest ranches, and summer homes in town, lakeside, and hidden among the valley's woods and rolling hills. In the summer, the town's population swells to over 3,000. In the winter, things die down considerably, though hardcore outdoorsfolks still prowl the Grand Lake area. Snowmobiling, cross-country skiing, and ice fishing are popular wintertime activities.

Downtown Grand Lake is defined pretty much by the main drag, Grand Ave., which parallels the lake's north shore, and a couple of cross streets that provide access to the water. The downtown section of Grand Ave. comprises three blocks of gift shops, cafes, saloons, Western-art galleries, and Indian pottery and jewelry stores. There's also the proverbial miniature golf, as well as the obligatory proliferation of T-shirt and souvenir shops. As a resort town, though, Grand Lake doesn't feel *quite* as touristy and gimmicky as other western resort towns do. This is perhaps due to its isolation, as well as its link to Rocky Mountain National Park—one of the most rugged backcountry parks in the nation.

History

Although many of Colorado's resort areas were Native American playgrounds or hunting grounds long before white settlers showed up, the Utes avoided this lake, which they called "Spirit Lake," and the surrounding area. According to legend, a Ute village once stood on the shores of Grand Lake, but it was wiped out by invading Cheyenne and Arapahoes who had come to the area to hunt. Ute men were killed, women and children set adrift on a raft as a storm approached. When the raft reached the lake's deep waters, it capsized. Utes believed the mists rising from Grand Lake's surface were the spirits of the drowned villagers.

Grand Lake began to develop as a resort area in the late 19th century. Gold had been discovered nearby, and the community started out as a supply stop for prospectors heading into the high country. In the early 1900s, well-to-do Western families began building summer homes around the lake (which explains the large expanses of private property in the area), and in 1905, the Grand Lake Yacht Club was founded. Rocky Mountain National Park was dedicated in 1915, and Grand Lake, on the park's western border, once again became a supply point—this time for motorists heading up to camp in the park or to cross over into Estes Park via Trail Ridge Road.

In the early 1950s, Colorado completed its Big Thompson Water Project, an irrigation system providing water to the farms and ranches on the state's eastern plains. In addition to a 13-mile tunnel through the mountains, the project in-

*view of the west side
of Rocky Mountain
National Park*

volved a series of reservoirs, including Lake Granby and Shadow Mountain Reservoir. By mid-century, the area was attracting anglers, boaters, and other summer recreation enthusiasts to its three lakes and to the many resort lodges scattered about its woodsy shores.

Kauffman House Museum

Built in 1892, the Kauffman House was one of Grand Lake's first resort hotels, hosting visitors from around the country for nearly 30 years. In 1921, Ezra Kauffman, the log hotel's builder and owner, died, though his wife and family continued to operate it every summer until the end of WW II. The Kauffman house has been restored and is open to the public for tours (summer only), exhibiting artifacts from Grand County's pioneer days.

The Kauffman House is located at 407 Pitkin. For hours, contact the Grand Lake Area Chamber of Chamber of Commerce at tel. (970) 627-3402 or (970) 627-3372.

PARKS AND RECREATION

Rocky Mountain National Park

This is one of the most spectacular national parks in the country, with breathtaking vistas from virtually every point on the main road, as well as hundreds of miles of backcountry climb-ing, hiking, and camping. Encompassing over 265,000 acres, Rocky Mountain National Park is one of the country's true wonders and a must for any traveler who wants to see Colorado at its grandest, and nature at its most spellbinding and wondrous.

Trail Ridge Rd., which winds up into the park out of Grand Lake, across the Continental Divide, and down the park's eastern slope to Estes Park, is one of the most scenic drives in the state, offering above-timberline vistas of the Rockies' grandest peaks, over 70 of which are higher than 12,000 feet. The drive also affords chances to view and photograph a wide array of high-mountain wildlife, including mountain goats, bighorn sheep, elk, moose, black bears, and smaller animals.

Visitors who get away from the roads, though, are the ones who see the park at its best. The park offers nearly unlimited hiking, ranging from short, marked nature trails to extended excursions into the park's most remote areas. Visitor centers at both the park's east and west entrances provide complete information on the park, including history, wildlife, and ecology, as well as hiking, camping, sightseeing, and photography opportunities. The **Kawuneeche Visitors Center** is located on the west side of the park just outside the town of Grand Lake. There you'll find books, tape tours, maps, wildlife displays, and rangers to answer any questions you might have.

For general information on Rocky Mountain National Park, phone (970) 586-2371. For **road and weather information** in the park, phone (970) 586-2385.

Arapaho National Recreation Area

Adjacent to Rocky Mountain National Park's southwestern boundary, Arapaho National Recreation Area covers 36,000 acres surrounding Lake Granby and a number of smaller lakes. Popular particularly among anglers, the area offers several campgrounds and picnic areas with boat ramps and shoreline access.

One of the nicer campgrounds is **Willow Creek Campground,** at Willow Creek Reservoir. Located three miles down a well-maintained dirt road, the campground has both RV and walk-in tent sites, as well as a picnic area and launching ramp. To get there, turn west off US 34 between Granby and Lake Granby (it's well marked). You'll also find picnic areas on the north and south shores of Lake Granby (watch for the signs).

For more information on Arapaho National Recreation Area, phone the Sulphur District Office of Arapaho National Forest in Granby at (970) 887-3331.

Indian Peaks Wilderness Area

Bordered on the west by Arapaho National Recreation Area, on the north by Rocky Mountain National Park, and on the east by the Continental Divide, this triangle-shaped wilderness is very popular with backcountry hikers, backpackers, fishermen, and hunters. Overnight permits are required, and usually need to be reserved well in advance. For information, contact the **Sulphur District Office** of Arapaho National Forest in Granby at (970) 887-3331.

Fishing

Fishing is one of Grand Lake's main draws. The three lakes, Grand, Lake Granby, and Shadow Mountain Reservoir, hold monster trout and kokanee

salmon. Mackinaw (lake) trout running 20-25 pounds are not uncommon (though experienced trout fishermen will tell you that lake trout don't put up nearly the fight that smaller rainbow and cutthroat will, and the latter fish are much more fun to catch).

Because of the amount of private property surrounding the lakes, you're better off in a boat. In addition to the several public launching ramps, you can rent boats from a number of marinas, including **Boater's Choice,** 1246 Lake Ave., tel. (970) 627-9273, or **Trail Ridge Marina,** tel. (970) 627-3586. **Monarch Guides,** tel. (970) 653-4210 or (800) 882-3445, offers a range of guided trips on nearby waters—from a "Twilight Bite" trip to four-day floats, as well as custom excursions.

For tips, tackle, and licenses, stop by **Grand Lake Pharmacy** in downtown Grand Lake, tel. (970) 627-3465, **Lakeview General Store** on Hwy. 34 in Grand Lake, tel. (970) 627-3479, or, along the way, at **Budget Tackle** in Granby or **Nelson's Fly and Tackle Shop** in Tabernash.

Boating

Sailing, windsurfing, and waterskiing are popular on all three lakes, particularly Grand, and public ramps are scattered about the shorelines. At **Boater's Choice,** 11246 Lake Ave., tel. (970) 627-9273, you can rent a range of different boats, including paddleboats, by the hour, or for half-day or full-day outings. You can also rent boats, or take a tour of the lake, at **Spirit Lake Marina,** 1030 Lake Ave., tel. (970) 627-8158, and **Grand Lake Marina,** 1246 Lake Ave., tel. (970) 627-3401.

Rafting

Whitewater rafting is very popular in the Grand Lake area, with many companies offering half-, full-, and multi-day trips on nearby rivers, particularly the Colorado. **Monarch Guides River Adventures,** tel. (970) 653-4210 or (800) 882-3445, is a friendly and professional outfit with offices downtown Grand Lake and Kremmling. Monarch also offers fishing trips (see above).

Golf

Grand Lake Golf Course is an 18-hole course whose greens are carved among tall pines at 8,420

BOB RACE

feet. Turn west from US 40 onto County Rd. 48 just north of the turnoff to Grand Lake. For information and tee times, phone (970) 627-8008.

Camping

Surrounded by national forest, park, recreation, and wilderness areas, Grand Lake offers an abundance of camping opportunities, from RV camping (see "Camping and RVing" following) to remote and rugged hike-in-only sites. Keep in mind that even though the area is indeed remote, it gets a lot of traffic, and reservations are a good idea. For information or to make reservations to camp in Arapaho National Forest, contact the Sulphur District Office in Granby at (970) 887-3331. Contact Rocky Mountain National Park at 16018 US 34, Grand Lake, CO 80447, tel. (970) 627-3471.

In Arapaho National Recreation Area (see above), there are campgrounds at Willow Creek Reservoir, Meadow Creek Reservoir, and the north and east shores of Lake Granby.

Hiking

Grand Lake itself is literally a trailhead for some of the best hiking in the state. Indian Peaks Wilderness Area, east of Lake Granby and south of Rocky Mountain National Forest, offers dozens of miles of marked trails. You can walk along lake shoreline, or hike up into the steep backcountry. Topo maps are available from the Forest Service, tel. (970) 887-3331, and Grand County has published an excellent recreation guide with maps and contact telephone numbers. Pick up a map at any of the Grand County chambers of commerce or visitor centers, or phone the Forest Service.

Cycling

The Grand Lake Metropolitan Recreation District, in conjunction with Arapaho National Forest and local businesses, has recently published a mountain-biking map of the Grand Lake area. The excellent guide, which implores riders to "tread lightly," lists over two dozen different trails (from two to 15 miles long) around the lakes and into the heart of the national forest. Included are degrees of difficulty, lengths, vertical rises, and other useful information. To get a copy of the guide, or for more information, phone the Grand Lake Metropolitan Recreation Dis-

trict at (970) 627-8328 or Arapaho National Forest at (970) 887-3331.

Horseback Rides

This is a very popular way to explore Arapaho National Forest, Indian Peaks Wilderness Area, and Rocky Mountain National Park. Many of the guest ranches have their own stables and provide both rentals and tours. **Sombrero Ranch,** tel. (970) 627-3514, near the turnoff to Grand Lake, offers a range of services, from hourly rentals and evening steak-fry rides to weeklong pack trips. **Winding River Resort,** tel. (970) 627-3215, also offers horseback riding.

Cross-Country Skiing

The Three Lakes area is a natural for cross-country skiing, with miles and miles of trails for all ability levels wandering through mountain meadows and deep into steep woods. The **Grand Lake Touring Center** operates at Grand Lake Golf Course with 25 km of track and skating trails. The center's ski shop offers equipment rentals and lessons; phone (970) 627-8008. You can also get information on cross-country skiing by writing the **Grand Lake Metropolitan Recreation District,** Box 590, Grand Lake, CO 80447.

You'll also find excellent Nordic skiing northwest of Grand Lake in Rocky Mountain National Park. Pick up the free booklet, *Ski Touring in Rocky Mountain National Park,* at the Kawuneeche Visitors Center just north of Grand Lake.

Snowmobiling

Increasing each year in popularity, snowmobiling is a favorite activity of locals and visitors alike. Within minutes/miles of town, snowmobilers can be cruising above the timberline—engines shattering the blissful silence and stillness of the backcountry—where views of the valley below and the sprawling mountains are said to be extraordinary.

The Grand Lake Metropolitan Recreation District publishes the *Grand Lake Snowmobile Trail Map,* which describes nearly 20 different routes. This excellent guide provides directions to trailheads, lengths, specific precautions, and other indispensable information. Write Box 690, Grand Lake, CO 80447, or phone (970) 627-8008.

Rent snowmobiles from **Grand Lake Motor Sports,** 10438 US 34, tel. (970) 627-3806; **Spirit Lake Rentals,** tel. (970) 627-9288; **Snowride,** 724 Grand Ave., tel. (970) 627-8866; or **Grand Lake Snowmobile Rental, Inc.,** 801 Grand Ave., tel. (970) 627-8304.

Other Winter Activities
In addition to offering cross-country skiing and snowmobiling, the Grand Lake area is a favorite of ice fishing enthusiasts and snowshoers. Lake Granby, Grand Lake, and Shadow Mountain Reservoir are all open to ice fishing, and competitions are held annually. For information and equipment stop in at **Lakeview General Store, Grand Lake Pharmacy, Budget Tackle** (in Granby), or **Nelson Fly and Tackle** (in Tabernash). Many of the area's summer hiking trails are ideal for snowshoeing. Pick up maps from the Forest Service or the Grand Lake Chamber of Commerce.

ACCOMMODATIONS

Lodges and Cabins
The **Grand Lake Lodge,** located on the hillside above Grand Lake, tel. (970) 627-3967 or 759-5848, and affording a gorgeous view of the lake and mountains, was established in 1921, and retains an early-20th-century feel about it without compromising modern comforts. Rooms for two start at about $60. The **Spirit Lake Lodge,** 829 Grand Ave., tel. (970) 627-3344, has one- and two-bedroom units (some with kitchenettes) starting at about $55.

Just a couple of miles south of Grand Lake, **Pine Ridge Cabins,** tel. (970) 627-3108 or 693-4217, offers small but nice cabins in the trees near Lake Granby. A single cabin for two people is about $45. **Gala Marina Motel,** tel. (970) 627-3220, is located right on Lake Granby and has kitchenettes, great views, and decks/patios. Rooms start at about $55. To get to both of these, take County Rd. 64 from US 34.

Motels
The **Bighorn Lodge,** 613 Grand Ave., tel. (970) 627-8101 or (800) 621-5923, is a modern and very comfortable motel just a couple of blocks

from the center of town with rooms for two running about $65. Also right downtown is **The Inn at Grand Lake,** 1103 Grand Ave., tel. (970) 627-9234 or (800) 722-2585, where rooms for two start at $45.

Camping and RVing
Shadow Mountain Marina RV Park, 12394 US 40, tel. (970) 627-9971, which offers full-service RV camping as well as tent camping, is located right on the lake. You can also camp at **Winding River Resort Village,** tel. (970) 627-3215, where you'll find 150 sites with horseback rides, volleyball, and other activities.

FOOD

For breakfast, try the **Chuckhole Cafe,** 1119 Grand Ave., tel. (970) 627-5309, serving omelettes, deep-dish pies, and other fare. **Uncle Elmo's Bakery and Cafe,** also on Grand, serves deli sandwiches and a variety of lunch items. The **Red Fox Restaurant,** 411 W. Portal Rd., tel. (970) 627-3418, is a local favorite for upscale lake-view dining. For Mexican food, and the best margaritas around, try **Casa Del Sol,** 827 Grand Ave., tel. (970) 627-8382, a tiny little hole in the wall so family oriented the owners' kids' jackets hang on the coatrack by the door. For cantina-style Mexican dining, try **Aunt Chilada's,** 1101 Grand Ave., tel. (970) 627-8773. Another local favorite for family dining and Mexican food is the **Mountain Inn,** 612 Grand Ave., tel. (970) 627-3385.

In addition, you'll find several boardwalk delis and hamburger stands on Grand Ave., and there are **picnic tables** throughout the Grand Lake area, many near the water, for picnics. The city park on the boardwalk also has picnic tables and a kids' playground.

Entertainment
An evening stroll along the Grand Ave. boardwalk will lead you naturally to the live music, as you hear rock 'n' roll and country wafting through open doors. **EG's Garden Grill,** 1000 Grand Ave., tel. (970) 627-8404, regularly features live music, as does **Grumpy's,** 913 Grand Ave., tel. (970) 627-3149.

CALENDAR

Every January, Grand Lake hosts its **Winter Carnival,** and in mid-February there's a popular Nordic ski race (10k and 20k). Warm-weather events include Fourth of July fireworks, a parade and buffalo barbecue (late July), the **Lipton Cup Sailing Regatta** (early August), and a couple of golf tournaments (mid-August and early September). For more information, contact the Grand Lake Chamber of Commerce (see "Information" following).

SHOPPING

Gift shops, souvenir stores, and art galleries line the two or three blocks that make up downtown Grand Lake Village. Though it's not exactly a shopper's mecca, you can pick up T-shirts and other knicknacks, as well as some quality jewelry and pottery.

SERVICES

Offices of the Grand Lake **Police Department** are located at 308 Byers in Hot Sulphur Springs; the local phone number is (970) 627-3322. The nearest medical facility is **Timberline Medical Center** at 6281 US 40, about a mile from Silver Creek, tel. (970) 887-2503. The **post office** in Grand Lake is at 520 Center, tel. (970) 627-3340.

Recycling
You can drop off most recyclables at **Grand Recycles** in downtown Grand Lake. For information, phone (970) 726-8435.

INFORMATION

An excellent source of information is the **chamber of commerce/tourist information center** on US 34 at the turnoff to downtown Grand Lake. Staff will answer questions about Grand Lake, Grand County, and Rocky Mountain National Park, and you can also pick up helpful brochures and activity guides. Be sure to pick up Grand County's *Sports and Recreation Map,* which has maps of all the nearby communities, as well as various recreation trails (hiking, cross-country skiing, four-wheeling, etc.). You can write the chamber at Box 57, Grand Lake, CO 80447-0057, or call (970) 627-3402 or 627-3372. For a vacation planner, phone (800) 531-1019.

Get information on Rocky Mountain National Park from the administrative offices at 16018 US 34, or phone (970) 627-3471 or (970) 586-2371.

A Word about Money
Keep in mind there's no automatic-teller machine in Grand Lake, odd for a town its size; in fact, the closest one is in Granby 15 miles south. If you're like me, and have gotten in the habit of using ATMs as much as traveler's checks, think again if you plan on having cash at your disposal. I left town with $2.32, and more charged to my credit card than I like.

ESTES PARK AND VICINITY

Estes Park (pop. 3,200; elev. 7,522 feet) is a resort town at the eastern gate to Rocky Mountain National Park. Surrounded by some of the most gorgeous country in the Rockies, Estes Park is a popular base camp for folks heading up into the high country, by tour bus, auto, or hiking boot.

Because Rocky Mountain National Park sees fewer than five percent of its visitors in the winter, Estes Park is naturally a summer-oriented town, and many of its lodges, galleries, shops, and other attractions are only open in the warmer months, usually May through September. During those months, though, the town swells with tourists. Sidewalks swarm with souvenir hunters; traffic through town is often bumper to bumper and directed by traffic police; restaurants and cafes are packed; the town's motels and the valley's many lodges and guest ranches are fully booked; even the backcountry trails and campgrounds can get crowded.

Come winter, though, and the closing of Trail Ridge Rd. (US 34) through the park, most tourists head for more temperate climes, and Estes Park becomes a quiet, laid-back little mountain town. Some lodge owners and gallery operators themselves leave. Other locals, however, know this is the best time to be in the area. Rocky Mountain National Park offers excellent cross-country skiing and snowshoeing, and there's no denying that the Rockies shrouded in snow are at their most visually arresting and spiritually wondrous.

HISTORY

The lush, sprawling mountain valley that is Estes Park was named for cattle rancher Joel Estes, who arrived here with his family in 1859. Though the area, fertile and bountiful, had probably been a hunting ground for nomadic bands of Ute and Arapahoe tribes, the Estes family found few signs of villages or other settlements.

The winter of 1866 was an unusually harsh one, and Estes herded up his clan and cattle and hit the road, heading for warmer climates. The following year, Griffith J. Evans acquired the property and built a handful of cabins that he rented out to travelers, many of whom used the valley as a base camp for ascents of nearby Longs Peak and explorations into what would become Rocky Mountain National Park. One of the area's first visitors was Albert Bierstadt, and travelers familiar with the painter's work will no doubt recognize the inspirations for some of his huge oils.

Another one of Evans's early guests was English nobleman Lord Dunraven. So impressed with the area was Dunraven that he sought to acquire the valley for himself and turn it into a hunting refuge for his fellow aristocrats. However, settlement and land ownership in the valley was controlled by the Homestead Law, which allowed only 160 acres of land per person. Quite used to having his own way, Dunraven found a way around the law, engineering a classic land-grab scheme. He had the deeds to all the 160-acre parcels in the valley transferred to "loafers and drifters," and, apparently, to some folks residing in local cemeteries. Dunraven then "bought" the land from its new owners, offering the live ones piddling amounts of cash or, in the cases of the dead ones, simply taking possession of the property. It was then just a matter of paying the government a small transfer fee and registering what he called the "English Company," a corporation established in England as the Estes Park Company, Ltd.

In 1907, Dunraven sold out to F.O. Stanley and B.D. Sanborn, who split the valley between them. Stanley immediately went to work building the Stanley Hotel and Stanley Manor House. The hotel opened in 1909 and the Manor House the following year.

Stanley, who had invented the Stanley Steamer, ran a line from the closest railroad terminal, 25 miles away in Lyons, to the hotel, and soon began attracting visitors from around the country. With the success of the hotel, a number of other lodges and cabins were built, and Estes Park began to establish a reputation as a premier resort area. In 1915, Rocky Mountain National Park was born, securing Estes Park as a major tourist destination.

ESTES PARK

TO TRAIL RIDGE RD.
AND PARK ENTRANCE

34

ROCKY

MOUNTAIN

NATIONAL

PARK

TO
TRAIL RIDGE RD.

PARK ENTRANCE
RD.

66

TO YMCA OF
THE ROCKIES/
ESTES PARK
CENTER

TO ALLENSPARK
AND NEDERLAND

7

MARY'S LAKE

MACGREGOR
RANCH MUSEUM

MACGREGOR AVE.

ELKHORN AVE.

FALL RIVER RD.

WONDERVIEW AVE.

STANLEY HOTEL
STANLEY VILLAGE

CHAMBER OF COMMERCE/
VISITOR INFORMATION

GOLF
COURSE

ST. VRAIN AVE.

PROSPECT AVE.

HOSPITAL

MOCASSIN
CIRCLE DR.

RIVERSIDE DR.

HIGH DR.

BIG
THOMPSON

MORAINE AVE.

THOMPSON
RIVER

MARY'S
LAKE RD.

PROSPECT MOUNTAIN

H-BAR-G HOSTEL

H-BAR-G RD.

DEVILS GULCH RD.

DRY GULCH RD.

BIG THOMPSON
AVE.

TO
LOVELAND AND
FT. COLLINS

LAKE ESTES

34

BIG
THOMPSON
RIVER

ESTES PARK
AREA
HISTORICAL
MUSEUM

N. ST. VRAIN AVE.

HIGH SCHOOL

STANLEY
AVE.

JUNIOR HIGH
SCHOOL

36

TO
LYONS
AND
BOULDER

GOLF
COURSE

S. ST. VRAIN AVE.

FISH CREEK RD.

PEAKVIEW DR.

NOTE: ONLY MAIN
ROADS SHOWN

NOT TO SCALE

© MOON PUBLICATIONS, INC.

SIGHTS

Estes Park Area Historical Museum

This museum displays Estes Valley's history from its first settlers, Joel Estes and family, through the founding of Rocky Mountain National Park and the incorporation of the village of Estes Park. Exhibits and buildings include the original headquarters of Rocky Mountain National Park, a Stanley Steamer, and lots of pioneer artifacts and historical photos. May-Sept., the museum is open Mon.-Sat. 10 a.m.-5 p.m. and Sunday 1-5 p.m.; limited hours the rest of the year. Admission is $2 ($5 for a family).

The Estes Park Area Historical Museum is located at 200 4th Street. For more information or to arrange tours, phone (970) 586-6256.

MacGregor Ranch
Museum and Education Center

The MacGregor is a working ranch commemorating the Alexander Q. MacGregor family, one of the valley's largest and most influential ranching families, and displaying life in Estes Park from the 1870s through the mid-20th century. Exhibits include historical photos and documentation of MacGregor's staunch opposition to Lord Dunraven's land company, as well as family domestic items, including furniture and silver. Cowhands use century-old equipment to display early ranching techniques.

The museum is located at the foot of Twin Owls on Devil's Gulch Rd. about a mile north of Estes Park. Admission is free, donations encouraged. Hours are Tues.-Fri. 10 a.m.-4 p.m., Memorial Day through Labor Day. For more information, phone (970) 586-3749.

Enos Mills Cabin

The "Father of Rocky Mountain National Park," Enos Mills was a naturalist, writer, and photographer who homesteaded in Estes Park in the late 19th century. Mills's small cabin, which he built in 1885 at the base of Twin Sisters Mountain, today operates as a nature center and museum. His daughter, Edna Mills Kiley, and other docents offer tours of the house, where his books, photos, and other memorabilia are displayed, and nature trails lead out into the 200-acre property. Copies of his books and photographs are sold in the museum's gift shop.

The Enos Mills Cabin is just south of Estes Park on CO 7. Admission is free. Open Tues.-Sun. 11 a.m.-4 p.m., Memorial Day through Labor Day; by appointment the rest of the year. For more information, phone (970) 586-4706 or 586-1016.

Lulu Dorsey Museum

Located at the YMCA of the Rockies, Estes Park Center is a hands-on museum displaying antique children's toys and musical instruments, as well as domestic items of historical interest and historical photos, particularly in relation to the founding of the YMCA of the Rockies (see "Lodges and Cabins," under "Accommodations" following).

The Dorsey Museum is located on the grounds of the YMCA at 2515 Tunnel Rd.; open Mon.-Sat. 9 a.m.-4 p.m. and Sunday 12-4 p.m., Memorial Day through Labor Day. Hours the rest of the year are Mon-Sat. 9 a.m.-4 p.m. Admission is free, though a donation of $1 is encouraged. For more information, phone (970) 586-3341.

Stanley Hotel

Tours of the Stanley Hotel are offered daily at 11 a.m. and 12:30, 2, and 3 p.m. Cost is $5. Sign up in the lobby of the hotel. See also accommodations, below.

PARKS AND RECREATION

Rocky Mountain National Park

This is Estes Park's main draw. Every year thousands of tourists use the little village—and its numerous ranches and motels—as a headquarters for exploring the park. See "Rocky Mountain National Park" below for complete description.

Bicycling

Though mountain biking's not a full-bore craze here yet, like it is in Summit County, Crested Butte, Durango, and some other Colorado resort areas, the region's ideal for the sport. Roosevelt National Forest's 800,000 acres of public land sprawl east of town, providing lots of excellent trails and logging roads (no off-road riding is permitted in Rocky Mountain National Park).

Some of the area's better rides include Crossier Mountain, near Glen Haven, seven miles north of town; Pole Hill, three miles east of town on US 36; and Pearson and Johnny parks, south of town on CO 7.

For maps and more information on cycling in the Estes Park area, stop by the Estes Park Ranger Station at 161 2nd St., tel. (970) 586-3440, or write Roosevelt National Forest, 240 W. Prospect, Fort Collins, CO 80526, tel. (970) 498-1100. You can also get information and rentals from **Colorado Bicycling**, 184 E. Elkhorn Ave., tel. (970) 586-4241.

Golf

The Estes Valley Recreation and Park District maintains two golf courses. The 18-hole **Estes Park Golf Course,** which dates from 1912, is one of the oldest courses in the state. Located at 1080 S. Saint Vrain, the course sprawls through woods at nearly 8,000 feet above sea level. For tee times and information, phone (970) 586-8146. **Lake Estes Executive Golf Course** is a nine-hole course along the banks of the Thompson River, 690 Big Thompson Ave., tel. (970) 586-8176.

Hiking

The Estes Park area is a heaven on earth for hikers, abounding in nature trails to walk, woods to explore, and peaks to climb. The best hiking is in Rocky Mountain National Park, which offers scores of trails with a full range of lengths and difficulty levels. (See complete section on Rocky Mountain National Park, below.) In addition, **Roosevelt National Forest** offers excellent backcountry hiking. Topo maps and information on hiking in the national forest are available from the main office at 240 W. Prospect, Fort Collins, CO 80526, tel. (970) 498-1100, or locally at 161 2nd St., tel. (970) 586-3440. You can also get information, as well as quality equipment, from **Outdoor World,** located in downtown Estes Park Village, tel. (970) 586-2114, and at **The Hiking Hut,** 10 E. Elkhorn, tel. (970) 586-2995.

The **Colorado Mountain Club** has been sponsoring hikes in the Estes Park area since before WW I, and currently runs some 2,000 outings a year. Free literature about the club, including information on hikes, meeting places, degrees of difficulty, etc., is available by phoning (970) 586-6623. You can also get information from their Denver office, 2530 W. Alameda Ave., Denver, CO 80219, tel. (970) 922-8315. The Colorado Mountain Club publishes a monthly newsletter, *Trail And Timberline,* which lists upcoming outings, reviews books on mountains and mountaineering, and tackles sensitive environmental issues.

Reflections of the Rockies Nature Hikes offers naturalist-led hiking tours into Rocky Mountain National Park. For information, write Box 73, Estes Park, CO 80517, or phone (970) 586-8924.

Fishing

Fishing in the Estes Park area ranges from pay-by-the-inch trout farms where no license is required to remote backcountry lakes and streams where wily native trout elude all but the most skilled and patient angler. And of course the scenic rewards of hiking into an isolated lake in Rocky Mountain National Park, even if you get skunked, are far greater for most people than hauling hatchery lunkers from highway-side lagoons.

If you're looking for guarantees, though, you have at least a couple of options. **Trout Haven,** about a mile west of Estes Park on US 36, tel. (970) 586-2955, and **Rock 'n' River Trout Farm,** about 15 miles southeast of town on US 36, stock their ponds with rainbows up to 26 inches. Open daily till dusk April 1 through mid-October.

For anglers looking for more of a challenge, the Big Thompson River east of Estes Park offers good trout fishing and decent-size fish. Some stretches are designated artificial lures and flies only. (Always double-check local restrictions.) There's also fishing (and picnicking) just below the dam at the east end of Lake Estes.

For information on fishing in Roosevelt National Forest, stop by the district office at 161 2nd St., tel. (970) 586-3440.

Rafting

As in most mountain resort towns, whitewater rafting is big here, and several companies offer a range of trips down local rivers. **Estes Park Adventures, Ltd.** books half-, full-, and two-day trips on the Arkansas, Cache La Poudre, and Colorado rivers. Write Box 2924, Estes Park, CO 80517, or phone (970) 586-2303 or (800) 762-5968, ext. 2303. You can also arrange trips with **Rapid Transit Rafting,** Box 4095, Estes Park, CO 80517, tel. (970) 586-8852 or (800) 367-8523; **Mad Adventures,** tel. (800) 451-4844; and **Colorado Wilderness Sports,** 358 E. Elkhorn, tel. (970) 586-6548.

Horseback Riding

This is a popular way to explore both Rocky Mountain National Park and Roosevelt National Forest, and several outfitters in the area offer tours and rentals. **Hi Country Stables,** with two centers within the boundaries of Rocky Mountain National Park, runs a range of tours into some of the park's most scenic spots, including Bierstadt and Bear lakes. Phone (970) 586-5890 or 586-6269. **Sombrero Ranch** offers several types of rides, from one-hour to several-day pack trips, as well as pancake breakfast and evening chuckwagon rides. For information and reservations, phone (970) 586-4577. **Elkhorn Stables** also offers rides, ranging from one to eight hours, some with meals. Phone (970) 586-3291.

Tram Rides

For a bird's-eye view of the Estes Park Valley, as well as of towering Longs Peak and other Rocky Mountain National Park peaks, take the 12-passenger aerial tram to the summit of Prospect Mountain (elev. 8,800 feet). Check out the gift shop and snack bar at the top; open daily mid-May through mid-Sept., 9 a.m.-6:30 p.m. The base of the tram and ticket office are located at 420 E. Riverside Drive. For rates and more information, phone (970) 586-3675.

Cross-Country Skiing
Most visitors to Estes Park come to hike the nearby trails and explore Rocky Mountain National Park backcountry under a warm summer sun. Yet some of those very same trails and woods also offer excellent opportunities for Nordic skiers. The best cross-country skiing is in the park (see "Rocky Mountain National Park" following), although Roosevelt National Forest also has hundreds of square miles of picture-book Nordic terrain. Get maps and information from the Forest Service district office at 161 2nd St., tel. (970) 586-3440; rent equipment and get expert advice from **Colorado Wilderness Sports,** 358 E. Elkhorn, tel. (970) 586-6548. Another excellent source of information on cross-country skiing in the area is the **Colorado Mountain Club,** tel. (970) 586-6623, which sponsors some 2,000 hiking and cross-country skiing trips a year and publishes literature on trails and specific areas.

ACCOMMODATIONS

If you're new to Estes Park, you'll be amazed at the number of inns, lodges, motels, cabins, hotels, and combinations thereof. With its ideal location adjacent to Rocky Mountain National Park, Estes Park has zillions of rooms and campsites available for passers-through, as well as for travelers who want to use the town as a base to do some exploring in the area. For complete listings of available lodging, contact the Estes Park Chamber of Commerce, which publishes several accommodations guides to the area. Their toll-free telephone number is (800) 44-ESTES.

Hotels
Of the first-class lodges in the Rockies, the **Stanley Hotel,** tel. (970) 586-3371 or (800) ROCKIES, is without doubt one of the most elegant and glorious. Standing high on the hillside, castlelike, and looking out over the town, the

valley, and west toward the towering Rockies, the Stanley seems to cast a cynical eye over the rest of Estes Park and some of its more touristy trappings and Johnny-come-lately attendants. First opened in 1909, after three years' construction, the Stanley was the brainchild of F.O. Stanley, whose guests arrived at the lodge via Stanley Steamer, which he invented. At the time, the Stanley was known as one of the most luxurious hotels in the West, and in addition to its fancy furnishings offered guests a golf course, stables, bowling, billiards, and theater.

Though some people claim the hotel was used in the Stanley Kubrick film *The Shining,* anyone who's seen both the movie and the hotel can tell you this isn't true. It is true, however, that the hotel inspired one of its guests, Stephen King, to write the novel upon which the film was based. The filming crew, faced with a lack of snow at the Stanley, shot the movie at the Timberline Lodge on Oregon's Mt. Hood.

During the late 1980s and early 1990s, the Stanley ran into tough times, with the owner finally filing Chapter 11. In May of 1995, the hotel was purchased by the Grand Heritage Hotel chain, whose luxury hotels are scattered about the globe—San Francisco, Paris, London. The Grand Heritage has mounted an aggressive campaign to restore both the hotel and its reputation, beginning with $3 million in renovation.

Double rooms at the Stanley Hotel range from about $90-150 a night, and it's a good idea to make reservations ahead of time.

Though paling in comparison to the Stanley, several other Estes Park hotels offer upscale lodging; among them the **Holiday Inn,** tel. (970) 586-2332 or (303) 534-4775 (from Denver), located in town at the junction of US 36 and CO 7, offers meeting and convention facilities.

Lodges and Cabins
One of the most unusual lodges in the area is **Estes Park Center, YMCA of the Rockies,** tel. (970) 586-3341 or (800) 228-3947 (in Colorado). Like its sister, Snow Mountain Resort (see "Winter Park" above), this is a sprawling, self-contained resort complex offering a huge range of lodging options, facilities, and amenities. Situated on 1,400 acres adjacent to Rocky Mountain National Park, the Estes Park Center has furnished two- and four-bedroom cabins

as well as a variety of lodge-style rooms. Activities include hiking, horseback riding, tennis, cross-country skiing, and snow tubing. Perfect for families, the lodge has lots of kid-oriented programs, as well as its own library, museum, grocery store, and gift shop. For rates and reservations, write YMCA of the Rockies, Estes Park, CO 80511-2550.

The **Deer Crest,** a mile west of town on US 34, tel. (970) 586-2358, has rooms and cottages on the Fall River starting at about $80 for two. Located on the North St. Vrain River 14 miles east of Estes Park, **Shelly's Cottages,** tel. (970) 823-6326, offers convenience and quiet privacy. Cabins for two run about $40-70. You can also get reasonably priced cabins at the family-owned **Edgewater Heights Cottages,** tel. (970) 586-8493, two miles east of Estes Park at 2550 Big Thompson along the Big Thompson River. Another popular Estes Park lodge is the **Longs Peak Inn and Guest Ranch,** tel. (970) 586-2110, about 10 miles south of town at the base of Longs Peak. Longs Peak Inn offers a full range of dude ranch-style amenities, including meals and campfire programs, as well as guided hiking and riding tours, fishing ponds, and day care. The **Aspen Lodge,** about eight miles south of town on CO 7, tel. (970) 586-8133, is a ranch-style inn, with both lodge rooms and cabins available, offering horseback riding, fishing, snowmobiling, and other activities.

Motels

You'll find bizillions of motels in Estes Park, though that shouldn't keep you from making reservations in advance, especially in the height of the summer. Most of the nicer, newer motels are just outside town on US 34 East/Big Thompson Ave., including **Best Western Estes Village Motor Inn,** 1040 Big Thompson Ave., tel. (970) 586-5338; **Silver Saddle Motor Lodge,** 1260 Big Thompson, tel. (970) 586-4476; the **Tyrol Motor Inn,** 1240 Big Thompson, tel. (970) 586-3382; the **Comfort Inn,** 1450 Big Thompson, tel. (970) 586-2358. The **Timberline Motel and Cottages,** 455 S. St. Vrain, tel. (970) 586-4697, is a funky fifties-style motel with among the least expensive rooms in town; doubles start at about $50. **Trappers Motor Inn,** 553 W. Elkhorn, tel. (970) 586-2833, also has doubles in the $50 range. Rooms for two at

the **Alpine Trail Ridge Inn,** 927 Moraine Ave., tel. (970) 586-4585 or (800) 233-5023 (some with kitchens), run $35-90.

Hostel

The **H-Bar-G Hostel,** tel. (970) 586-3688, is a member of the American Youth Hostel system and provides the least expensive lodging in the area ($8 for members, slightly more for nonmembers). Open summers only, the H-Bar-G is just north of Estes Park with a variety of hiking trails leading from the property into Roosevelt National Forest. In addition, the hostel has tennis and volleyball courts and a game room. Write: Box 1260, Estes Park, CO 80517 (May-Sept.) or 700 Flagstaff Star Route, Boulder, CO 80302 (Oct.-late April).

Camping and RVing

Estes Park is surrounded by public campgrounds, administered either by the National Park Service or the Forest Service. **Olive Ridge Campground** is in Roosevelt National Forest about eight miles south of Estes Park on CO 7 (see "Rocky Mountain National Park," following, for camping information).

Privately administered RV campgrounds, generally open May-Sept., include a **KOA,** two miles east of town on US 34, tel. (970) 586-2888; **Park Place Camping Resort,** six miles southeast of Estes Park on US 36 (also cabins), tel. (970) 586-4230; **National Park Campground and Resort,** right at the park's Fall River entrance, tel. (970) 586-4563; and **Estes Park Campground,** about five miles southwest of Estes Park on US 66, tel. (970) 586-4188.

Campers will want to keep in mind that **public showers** are available at Dad's Maytag Laundry, tel. (970) 586-9847, in the Upper Stanley Village Center.

FOOD

A resort town catering to free-spending passersthrough, Estes Park is packed with cafes and restaurants. For breakfast, try **The Other Side,** 900 Moraine Ave., tel. (970) 586-2171, open daily at 7:30 a.m. with a health-conscious menu. Another breakfast spot worth checking out is the **Mountaineer Restaurant,** 540 S. St. Vrain, tel. (970) 586-9001. The Mountaineer opens at 6 a.m. and specializes in biscuits and gravy and homemade cinnamon rolls. The **Topnotch Cafe and Bakery,** in the Stanley Village Shopping Center, tel. (970) 586-0272, specializes in health-oriented breakfasts, including fat-free muffins, veggie omelettes, and "tofu scramble." It's also got excellent espresso drinks and a cozy atmosphere.

A new addition and welcome addition to Estes Park is the **Estes Park Brewery,** 470 Prospect (turn left onto Moraine as you're heading west on US 34), tel. (970) 586-5421. Free samples of the beer, plus beer to go, as well as sandwiches, burgers, and salads served upstairs above the brewery.

For Mexican food, try **La Casa,** 222 E. Elkhorn, tel. (970) 586-2807, a favorite among locals and tourists alike. In addition to Mexican standards, La Casa also serves Cajun and American dishes—outdoor patio seating, too. A nice Italian restaurant, with outdoor seating when weather permits, is **Mama Rose's,** 338 E. Elkhorn, tel. (970) 586-3330. Here classic Italian entrees run $9-14, while pasta dishes run about $7-9. Another favorite for Italian food is the **Dunraven Inn,** 2470 US 66, tel. (970) 586-6409, which calls itself the "Rome of the Rockies." For steak, try **Orlando's Steak House,** 132 E. Elkhorn, tel. (970) 586-9381. About seven miles south of town on US 7, the **Baldpate Inn,** tel. (970) 586-6151, has a reputation for excellent food, particularly the soup-and-salad buffet and homemade breads and pies. The Baldpate also offers bed-and-breakfast accommodations.

If you're looking for picnic fixin's before heading up into Rocky Mountain National Park, stop at the **Safeway** on the hill above downtown, where you'll find a deli and salad bar.

ENTERTAINMENT

The **Gaslight,** 246 Moraine Ave., tel. (970) 586-5978, features live Irish music daily, 4-8 p.m., and dancing to live country music Mon.-Sat. nights 8:30 p.m. till closing. British beers on tap. The **Stanley Hotel,** tel. (970) 586-3371, offers a wide range of music, including a summer music festival and Friday-night big-band dancing. For a classic Colorado chuckwagon supper served with western music and cowboy comedy, try the **Lazy B,** 1915 Dry Gulch Rd., tel. (970) 586-5371. Call for schedule and reservations. You can also enjoy dinner theater with the **Barleen Family,** who offer up rousing family-focused music Mon.-Sat. nights in the summer. Phone (970) 586-5741.

CALENDAR

Estes Park has a rather idiosyncratic lineup of annual events, ranging from the proverbial fireworks-over-the-lake on the Fourth of July to a wild Celtic celebration. Though there are a handful of wintertime affairs, including the **Estes Park Snow Festival** in late March, things don't really kick off until early June, when Trail Ridge Rd. through Rocky Mountain National Park traditionally opens. The Stanley Hotel hosts a variety of music throughout the summer, most notably the classical **Summer Concert Series**; phone (970) 586-3371 for information. The YMCA of the Rockies sponsors its **Summerfest Concert Series,** with music ranging from classical to jazz to bluegrass; phone (970) 586-3341.

Fall's highlight is the two-day Celtic fair in September. Officially known as the Longs Peak Scottish Fair, it usually draws some 20,000 people and features a parade (with over two dozen bagpipe bands), athletic competitions (including the hammer and tree-trunk tosses), and a general craziness that usually lasts into the wee hours. For complete information, phone (970) 586-6308. For more information on Estes Park's wide range of annual events, phone the chamber of commerce at (800) 44-ESTES.

SHOPPING

Estes Park has one of the state's largest concentrations of gift shops and galleries, selling gifts and souvenirs ranging from hopelessly tacky to museum quality. You'll find lots of Native American art, photos and renderings in various other media of Rocky Mountain National Park, as well as Christmas stores, boutiques, and jewelers. Part of the fun is simply wandering around the village, poking your head into the various shops.

A handful of the galleries are particularly worth checking out. The **Art Center,** in the lower level of Stanley Village, features a wide range of quality art, with exhibits changing monthly. The center also offers classes and demonstrations. **Artisans of Colorado,** 157 W. Elkhorn, has work by over 75 of the state's best artists and artisans. The **Ricker-Bartlett Casting Studios and Gallery,** two miles east of town on US 34, is the world's largest pewter-casting studio. Pieces from the studio have been presented to several U.S. presidents, and some are in the Smithsonian Institution. Among the displays is a 300-square-foot re-creation of an American small town at the turn of the century. Phone (970) 586-2030 for complete information.

The **Charles Eagle Plume Gallery and Museum of Native American Arts,** 10 miles south of Estes Park on CO 7, has been around since 1917 and has a huge collection of baskets, jewelry, rugs, and other art and artifacts on display and for sale. Charles Eagle Plume, the shop's owner and curator, graduated from the University of Colorado in 1932 and has been active in Native American rights for the better part of this century. Eagle Plume has been awarded an honorary Doctorate of Humanities from the University of Colorado. The museum and gallery is open summers only. Phone (970) 586-4710 for more information.

The **Fine Arts Guild of the Rockies** publishes the *Estes Park Gallery Guide,* which lists some 20 galleries and shops in town. Write the guild at Box 1165, Estes Park, CO 80517, or phone the chamber of commerce at (970) 586-4431 or (800) 44-ESTES.

SERVICES

The offices of the Estes Park **Police Department** are located at 170 MacGregor; phone (970) 586-5331. Phone the Larimer County **Sheriff** at (970) 586-9511 and the **State Patrol** at (970) 484-4020 (Fort Collins). **Estes Park Medical Center** is located at 555 Prospect, tel. (970) 586-2317. The **post office** is at 215 W. Riverside, tel. (970) 586-8177.

Recycling
The transfer station for **Estes Park Recycling Center** is located on Elm Rd. and will take aluminum, glass, and newspaper. For information, phone (970) 586-3772.

INFORMATION

An excellent place to begin your visit to Estes Park is at the chamber of commerce's **visitor information center,** located at 500 Big Thompson Avenue. You'll find tons of info on Estes, the surrounding area, and Rocky Mountain National Park. You can also write the chamber at Box 3050, Estes Park, CO 80517, or call (970) 586-4431 or (800) 443-7837. The **public library** is at 225 E. Elkhorn, tel. (970) 586-8116. **MacDonald Book Shop,** 152 E. Elkhorn, tel. (970) 586-3450, has a good selection of books on Rocky Mountain National Park, the Estes Park area, and Colorado.

For information on Rocky Mountain National Park, phone the headquarters at (970) 586-2371 or the backcountry office at (970) 586-3440. You can get a 24-hour recorded message by dialing (970) 586-2385.

For **road and weather information** phone (970) 586-4000.

TRANSPORTATION

Estes Park is situated at the junctions of US 34 and 36 and CO 7, making it approachable from the south, east, and west (except during the winter, when US 34 to the west, through Rocky Mountain National Park, is closed). **Charles Limousine Service** runs at least four shuttle buses daily between Estes Park and Denver International Airport; roundtrip fares start at $35. Phone (970) 586-5151 or (800) 950-3274. Charles also provides taxi service in town (tel. 970-586-8440), as well as tours of Rocky Mountain National Park, backcountry 4WD trips, and hiking and fishing tours.

SOUTH OF ESTES PARK

Colorado 7 drops south out of Estes Park, paralleling the eastern border of Rocky Mountain National Park for about 18 miles. Affording excellent views, both of the park (particularly Longs

Peak) and of the valley to the east, the route has several places worth stopping at along the way. The stretch from Estes Park south to Central City, which includes Colorado Highways 7, 72 through Nederland, and 119, has been designated the **Peak to Peak Highway,** and offers breathtaking vistas and panoramas around virtually every turn.

About five miles out of Estes Park is **Lilly Lake Picnic Area,** a day-use-only area administered by Roosevelt National Forest. In addition to picnicking, you can explore the shores of this lovely little alpine lake via a number of hiking trails that begin near the parking lot.

A couple of miles south of Lilly Lake is **Twin Sisters Trailhead,** which leads to Twin Sisters Peak (elev. 11,248 feet) in a small isolated unit of Rocky Mountain National Park east of the highway.

Longs Peak Campground (in Rocky Mountain National Park) is about nine miles south of Estes Park. The campground is designated for tents only. Between Longs Peak Campground and Allenspark (about seven miles), you'll find several Rocky Mountain National Park trailheads, including access to Wild Basin. A mile north of Allenspark is Roosevelt National Forest's **Olive Ridge Campground** (56 sites, pit toilets, no showers).

Allenspark and Ferncliff are two quaint little towns just off the highway at the southeastern edge of Rocky Mountain National Park. You can get rooms at the **Ferncliff Motel and Cabins,** tel. (303) 747-2531, for about $40 and cabins for two for $50. The **Allenspark Lodge,** tel. (303) 747-2552, is a rustic old inn that would be perfect for one of those occasionally mandatory getaways when you just want to shut out the world and not let *anyone* know where you are. Doubles start at about $50.

Four miles south of Allenspark the road arcs east, and you can either continue on to Lyons or catch CO 72 south for Nederland, where you can shoot into Boulder the back way.

ROCKY MOUNTAIN NATIONAL PARK

Without doubt one of the most gorgeous and breathtaking of Colorado's natural wonders, Rocky Mountain National Park includes over 265,000 acres of towering peaks, rolling alpine meadows, pristine lakes, and dense forests of aspen, fir, spruce, and pine. A paradise for hikers, backpackers, mountain climbers, and sightseers, the park attracts nearly three million visitors a year, the greatest percentage of whom come between May and October as the main road through the park—see "Driving through the Park" following—is closed in winter.

A microcosm of the greater Rocky Mountains' geology, Rocky Mountain National Park is like a giant wedge of cheese, gently sloping up from the west, then dropping dramatically at the Front Range to the flatlands below. Within the boundaries of the park are more than 75 peaks towering 12,000 feet or more above sea level, including several over 13,000. The highest point in the park is Longs Peak, at 14,255 feet. Trail Ridge Rd., the main road through the park, passes through 12,000-foot-high meadows, with wildflowers and grasses waving softly in moun-

tain breezes. Five small alpine glaciers, vestiges of the great ice floes that carved valleys and lakes from the heaving mountains, remain within the park's boundaries.

Not surprisingly, the park is full of wildlife: bighorn sheep, mountain goats, elk, deer, bear, and many smaller animals, from marmots and beavers to coyotes and mountain lions. Thankfully, no hunting is allowed.

History
Rocky Mountain National Park's history dates from just after the turn of the century, when naturalist, writer, and photographer Enos Mills, who had been living in a small cabin just outside Estes, began a campaign to protect the land. Although Mills soon had enough support to convince the Federal government to set aside some land, the first designation was as a national forest. But conservationists were not yet satisfied. A small but vocal group, spearheaded by the newly founded Colorado Mountain Club, sought national park status, against the wishes of the Forest Service and landowners.

The group, led by Mills, and the club, got its way. In January 1915 the land was officially designated Rocky Mountain National Park.

One of the park's most influential administrators was its third superintendent, Roger Toll, who took office in 1920. Toll, an avid mountain climber and preservationist, made first ascents of many of the park's peaks and wrote the park's first climbing guide, *Mountaineering in Rocky Mountain National Park* (Department of the Interior), as well as the classic *The Mountain Peaks of Colorado* (Colorado Mountain Club). Toll also oversaw construction of Bear Lake Rd. (1920), Trail Ridge Rd. (1932), and many of the park's first trails, which opened up much of the backcountry to visitors. Toll served until 1936, when he was killed in a car crash en route to Mexico to consult with U.S. and Mexican authorities about establishing game preserves along the border. In 1940, the name of Ute Horn was changed to Mt. Toll, and in 1941, the Toll Memorial was erected on Sundance Mountain near Trail Ridge Road.

VISITOR CENTERS

There are excellent visitor centers at both the east and west entrances to Rocky Mountain National Park, as well as at the summit of Trail Ridge Road. You'll find a wide range of books, maps, and brochures, as well as staff members to answer all questions. The **Park Headquarters Visitors Center** is located on US 36 just west of Estes Park, tel. (970) 586-1206. Also on the Estes Park side is the **Moraine Park Museum,** tel. (970) 586-3777, where you can study the park's geology, history, and wildlife, and take a hike on a half-mile, self-guided nature trail. The museum is open mid-May-September.

The **Kawuneeche Visitors Center,** tel. (970) 627-3471, is located on the park's west side just north of Grand Lake. The **Alpine Visitors Center,** tel. (970) 586-4927, is near the top of Trail Ridge Rd. at Fall River Pass (elev. 11,796 feet) in the heart of the park. You'll find exhibits about the surrounding alpine tundra, plus other park information. Closed in winter.

For more information, write Rocky Mountain National Park, Estes Park, CO 80517. You can also phone (970) 586-1206 (headquarters), (970) 586-1333 (recorded information), or (970) 586-1242 (backcountry office).

In your car, tune your radio to AM 1610 for recorded visitor information.

DRIVING THROUGH THE PARK

The main road through Rocky Mountain National Park is **Trail Ridge Rd.,** a 48-mile stretch highway that offers some of the most spectacular scenery on the planet. Its summit at 12,183

Rocky Mountain National Park's Trail Ridge Road rises well above the treeline on its 12,183-foot summit.

ROCKY MOUNTAIN NATIONAL PARK

NOTE: THIS MAP IS INTENDED FOR ORIENTATION ONLY. UPON YOUR ENTRANCE TO THE PARK, YOU WILL BE GIVEN A DETAILED MAP SHOWING ALL CAMPGROUNDS, PICNIC AREAS, HIKING TRAILS, ETC.

feet, Trail Ridge Rd. lifts up past the treeline and meanders along the ridgetop through meadows of alpine tundra. Allow three to four hours, as along the way you'll want to get out of your car to take pictures or simply appreciate the scenery. There are also several short hikes to scenic overlooks.

Old Fall River Rd. is the original road through the park. Completed in 1920, the one-way (east-to-west) 11-mile gravel road parallels Trail Ridge

Rd. from Endovalley to the Alpine Visitors Center. Don't expect the sweeping panoramas you get on Trail Ridge. Motor homes over 25 feet and trailers are not allowed.

Bear Lake Rd. leads from the Moraine Park Museum to Bear Lake, where a number of trails lead to waterfalls and other lakes. The road is paved and gets a lot of traffic, and the parking lot at the lake is usually full in the summer in mid-day. To avoid parking hassles, you can take a

Park Service shuttle from Glacier Basin Campground, about three miles past the museum (watch for the signs).

At the visitor centers you can pick up cassette tapes with recorded information on the drive through the park. The narrator points out areas of geological and historical interest, and also discusses regional wildlife and Native American legends. Tapes cost about $12 and include maps. They're available at the park visitor centers, as well as at gift shops in Estes Park. You can order tapes from **CCInc. Auto Tape Tours,** Box 631, Goldens Bridge, NY 10526, tel. (914) 232-0322.

Tours

If you'd rather leave the driving to someone else, you can tour the park with **Charles Tour and Travel Services,** which offers several different types of trips, including 4WD tours. For information and reservations, phone (970) 586-5151.

HIKING AND BACKPACKING

You could spend a lifetime exploring the trails and backcountry of Rocky Mountain National Park (and some folks have). Over 350 miles of marked trails weave in and out of forests and meadows, up mountainsides, and along meandering streams. They range from short paths between parking lots and scenic overlooks, to trails that cross the park from one side to the other, *over* the Continental Divide. Your best bet is to stop in at one of the visitor centers to check out the several available hiking guides. They range from the brief Park Service-published brochure to full-blown books with maps, charts, descriptions, difficulty levels, and any information you could possibly need. A popular (very!) short hike is the half-miler around **Bear Lake.** Take Bear Lake Rd. to the trailhead. In addition to the short Bear Lake Trail, several other hikes of varying lengths and degrees of difficulty begin here.

The **Sprague Lake Five Senses Trail** is specifically designed with disabled visitors in mind; the half-mile trail is level, wide enough to accommodate wheelchairs, and encourages appreciation of the park, and nature, through all five senses. Take Bear Lake Rd. about three miles past the Moraine Park Museum.

Just west of the Fall River Entrance Station (on US 34), you'll find a turnoff to Aspenglen Campground. Several trails wander through this lush valley and along the Fall River (this is before the road begins to climb up to Trail Ridge). There are also hiking and nature trails at all the visitor centers.

At the other end of the spectrum are the **Longs Peak trails.** The highest peak in the park (elev. 14,255 feet), Longs can be reached by at least two routes. The most popular is the main trail from the Longs Peak trailhead, located south of Estes Park just off CO 7. The 16-mile roundtrip is for experienced hikers only, although no climbing equipment is generally needed in July and August; allow about 12 hours. **Note:** The Park Service recommends getting an early start and being on your way down by early afternoon to avoid the almost-every-afternoon summer storms.

Remember, too, that hiking in Rocky Mountain National Park is serious business, and even though you don't need a permit for a day hike, you should always let someone else know where you're going and when you expect to return. Backcountry hiking is limited to seven nights June-Sept. (15 nights the rest of the year). Camp in designated areas only, unless authorized by permit, available at the visitor centers, tel. (970) 586-1242.

Camping

Rocky Mountain National Park has five campgrounds. **Longs Peak, Moraine Park, Glacier Basin,** and **Aspenglen** are out of Estes Park on the east side of Fall River Pass; **Timber Creek Campground** is on the west side, out of Grand Lake. Not one of the campgrounds has electrical outlets or water or sewer connections, and all are full by noon (earlier in June, July, and August). Longs Peak Campground is designated tents only, and stays are limited to three days. You can camp up to seven days at the others.

Permits to camp in the backcountry are available at the visitor centers. Be sure to read regulations carefully and to follow them closely. They're designed for your safety and the health of the park. For more information, phone park headquarters at (970) 586-1206.

CROSS-COUNTRY SKIING

The lower valleys of Rocky Mountain National Park are perfect for exploring on cross-country skis, and roads to several of the lower trailheads are plowed throughout the winter. Moraine Park, Longs Peak, and Timber Creek campgrounds are open year-round, providing access to a wide range of excellent trails and woodsy backcountry. There are also trails at Glacier Basin Campground and at Bear Lake.

For more information on cross-country skiing in Rocky Mountain National Park, stop by **Colorado Wilderness Sports,** 358 E. Elkhorn in Estes Park, tel. (970) 586-6548. You can also get information from the **Colorado Mountain Club,** tel. (970) 586-6623. The club, founded in 1912 as an offshoot of the Colorado Mountain Climbing Club (itself founded in 1896), sponsors a wide range of trips into the park each season.

GREELEY AND VICINITY

Located near the confluence of the Cache La Poudre and South Platte rivers about 60 miles north of Denver, Greeley (pop. 68,000; elev. 4,663 feet) is a proud and civic-minded community whose roots are in cattle ranching and agriculture. Weld County, of which Greeley is the seat, comprises two million acres and ranks fourth in the nation and first in the state in the value of its agricultural products, primarily corn, wheat, and alfalfa.

Greeley is home to the University of Northern Colorado as well as the summer training camp of the Denver Broncos. Several Fortune 500 companies, including Hewlett Packard and Eastman Kodak, have facilities nearby. Greeley's size and western plains location ensures a laid-back, small-town lifestyle and a relatively mild climate. At the same time, it's just an hour from the Denver nightlife or the rugged backcountry of Rocky Mountain National Park.

In 1989, Greeley scored a major coup. In May of that year it was selected as one of the 10 All-American Cities by the National Civic League of Chicago. Focusing primarily on the candidates' senses of community, the 40-year-old program seeks "to encourage and recognize civic excellence." Among the 10 judging criteria are citizen participation, community leadership, government performance, volunteerism, and civic education.

Walking the streets of Greeley, you can see it. There's a genuine wholesomeness and classic Western friendliness here. And there's an almost palpable sense that folks who live here are proud of themselves and their community, and wouldn't live anywhere else.

History
Greeley was named for *New York Tribune* editor Horace Greeley, who visited Colorado Territory in 1859 and returned with his exhortation, "Go West, young man, and grow with the country." Impressed by the land's immense potential for farming, Greeley, along with his agriculture editor, Nathan Meeker, campaigned to establish a utopian community in Colorado based on religion, temperance, and cooperative farming. According to the WPA's 1930 Colorado guidebook, Meeker circulated flyers and advertised in eastern papers, emphasizing that "the idle, immoral, intemperate, or inefficient need not apply." In 1869, Meeker bought 12,000 acres of land on the banks of the Cache La Poudre River in the South Platte Valley, with provisional title to another 60,000. The following year he led a group of 50 New England families to the site, traveling from Cheyenne on the newly completed Denver Pacific Railroad. There the group established the Union Colony, each member paying $5 to belong and $150 for no more than 160 acres of land. A 100-by-150-foot townsite was also laid out.

Work began immediately on housing and irrigation ditches, though one of the first construction projects on the agenda was a church, in which services were held within two weeks of the colonists' arrival. One of the new community's commandments was, "Thou shalt not sell liquid damnation within the lines of Union Colony."

By the mid-1870s, homes, stores, and office buildings had been built, and water was being run into the fields to irrigate tomatoes, potatoes, melons, cucumbers, and fruit trees. In October of that year, Horace Greeley visited for the first time the town that had taken his name.

In 1877, Greeley was designated seat of old Weld County, which included almost all of what is now northeastern Colorado, including Logan, Washington, Morgan, Sedgwick, Phillips, and Yuma counties. Weld County, named for Lewis Leyard Weld, whom Abraham Lincoln appointed Colorado Territory's first Secretary in 1861, was reduced to its present size in 1899.

During the last quarter of the 19th century and into the 20th, Greeley began to grow proportionately more potatoes, and "Greeley Spuds" earned a national reputation. In addition, the surrounding area began to develop as a ranching center, with huge herds of beef cattle blanketing the plains. In 1890, Greeley citizens matched $10,000 in state funding to establish the University of Northern Colorado, which opened its doors in 1899.

Shortly after the turn of the century, farmers in Weld and other Platte River Valley counties began to contract with sugar companies to grow sugar beets. Sugar factories were built in Greeley and other nearby towns. From the early 1900s

through the 1930s, the area attracted large numbers of immigrants, who came to work in the newly built factories and in the productive fields, as well as to take advantage of homesteading opportunities. According to a recent edition of *Greeley Style Magazine,* many current residents' German, Russian, Japanese, and Hispanic roots date to early 20th-century recruiting.

Greeley remained true to the vision of its founding fathers for its first 100 years, and it wasn't until 1969 that the sale of liquor was allowed within the city limits. In the 1980s, James Michener lived in Greeley while he researched and wrote *Centennial,* his fictionalized account of the history of the town and area. Anyone looking to learn more about Greeley and Weld County would do well by Michener's novel.

SIGHTS

Meeker House Museum
Listed on the National Register of Historic Places, this was the home of Greeley founder Nathan Meeker, who built the two-story brick

house in 1870. The museum offers docent-led tours of the adobe building and offers an opportunity to view some of Meeker's personal belongings and furniture, as well as other artifacts collected from the area.

The Meeker Museum is located at 1324 9th Avenue. Memorial Day through Labor Day, the museum is open Tues.-Sat. 10 a.m.-5 p.m., and the rest of the year it's open Tues.-Sat. 10 a.m.-3 p.m. Admission is $3 (discounts for kids six to 12 and seniors 60 and older). Costs also include admission to Centennial Village (see below). For more information, phone (970) 350-9221.

Historic Centennial Village

This multi-structure museum complex occupies five acres and offers an interpretive history of Greeley and Weld County from 1860 to 1920. Exhibits and buildings include an 1863 log courthouse, an 1872 cottage, and a turn-of-the-century church and one-room schoolhouse, as well as displays emphasizing the importance of agriculture, such as a granary and an early-20th-century sugar beet shanty. Guided tours take about an hour. There's also a small gift shop, where you can buy souvenirs, books on local history, and homemade candy.

The Centennial Village Museum, at 1475 A St., is open Memorial Day through Labor Day, Tues.-Sat. 10 a.m.-5 p.m. and Sunday 1-5 p.m. The rest of the year it's open Tues.-Sat. 10 a.m.-3 p.m. Admission is $3—discounts for kids and seniors—which includes entrance to the Meeker House Museum (see above). For more information, phone (970) 350-9224.

Greeley Municipal Museum

A gallery and research center, this museum exhibits traveling displays and stores archives on the history of Greeley and Weld County. In addition, the museum houses the Colorado Collection: rare, out-of-print, and contemporary books and journals on all aspects of the state. The museum is located at 919 7th St. and is open Tues.-Sat. 9 a.m.-5 p.m. Admission is free, tours available. For more information, phone (970) 350-9220.

Fort Vasquez

Located on US 85 in Platteville, about 18 miles south of Greeley, this National Historical Society site is a WPA-constructed model of the original Fort Vasquez, which was built in 1835. Originally established as a trading post where mountain men and Plains tribes swapped furs, weapons, and tools, the Fort Vasquez enterprise was a relatively short-lived one. Today the visitor center next to the fort offers an overview of early-19th-century South Platte Valley fur trade. In addition to viewing the displays in the visitor center, you can also tour the fort itself.

Fort Vasquez is open to visitors Memorial Day through Labor Day, Mon.-Sat. 10 a.m.-5 p.m. and Sunday 1-5 p.m.; in September Thurs.-Sat. 10 a.m.-5 p.m. and Sunday 1-5 p.m.; and Oct.-May, Thurs.-Sat. 10 a.m.-5 p.m. For more information, phone (970) 785-2832.

PARKS AND RECREATION

City Parks

Greeley's got over two dozen city parks scattered within its boundaries. **Lincoln Park,** across the street from the downtown mall, has lush lawns and shade trees and is perfect for picnicking. Another nice city park is **Bittersweet Park,** at 16th St. and 35th Ave., which has lawns, shade, and playground equipment. For more information on Greeley's city parks, contact the **Parks and Recreation Department,** 651 10th Ave., tel. (970) 350-9400.

Golf

Greeley's **Highland Hills Municipal Golf Course** is located on the west side of town off 20th St. (2200 Clubhouse Dr.). For information and tee times, phone (970) 330-7327. The **Eaton Country Club,** in Eaton about 10 miles north of Greeley on US 85, is an 18-hole "championship course" with a restaurant and banquet room. Phone (970) 454-2106.

ACCOMMODATIONS

You'll find accommodations in Greeley ranging from mom-and-pop motels to convention-center complexes and a bed and breakfast. The **Sterling House,** tel. (970) 351-8805, is a very tastefully done bed and breakfast in a gorgeous 1886

Victorian home at 818 12th St. (only two rooms available). Full breakfast included, and evening meals can be arranged with advance notice. A **Motel 6,** tel. (970) 351-6481, is located on the south side of town at 3015 8th Avenue. The **Best Western Ramkota Inn and Conference Center,** tel. (970) 353-8444, is right downtown kitty-corner from the Greeley Mall; doubles run about $60. At the Greeley **Holiday Inn,** 609 8th Ave., tel. (970) 356-3000, you can also get doubles for around $60.

Greeley Campground and RV Park, tel. (970) 353-6476, a mile east of town on US 34, has 95 sites on 10 acres.

FOOD

Bruce's

Call them what you will, bull fries, prairie oysters, swinging steaks, or the more popular Rocky Mountain oysters, but the best, well, bull testicles around are (reportedly!) served up at Bruce's, located west of Greeley in Severance. Sliced thin, breaded, and deep fried, Bruce's fries are very popular—folks go nuts for 'em. In fact, Bruce's owners Ruth and Betty Schott sell between 20 and 25 tons of the things a year and have been known to let patrons think they were eating "headless and tailless shrimp." A recent *Rocky Mountain News* article quoted Schott as saying, "I always tell people to come to Severance and have a ball." Travelers watching their weight or red-meat intake might want to try the turkey variety.

Like something out of *Thelma and Louise,* Bruce's doubles as a Western bar and has been open since 1958. Regular customers include members of the Denver Broncos, whose summer training camp is in Greeley. Outside the restaurant are murals of bulls holding picket signs reading "Unfair" and "Very Unfair." Inside is a painting of a rather startled and angry-looking bull experiencing "the procedure." Saturday nights, locals come to dance and drink beer. You can also get a freshly shot goose cleaned for $6.

To get there, take US 85 north about 10 miles to Eaton, and go west another nine miles. Phone (970) 686-2320.

Other Greeley Food

If you don't have the stomach for Rocky Mountain oysters, or don't feel like driving up to Severance, you'll find plenty of more conventional cuisine in Greeley—lots of fast-food places, franchises (Red Lobster, Golden Corral), and other restaurants. The best coffee shop in town is **Margie's Java Joint,** 931 16th St., tel. (970) 356-6364, where you can pick up espresso coffees, muffins, pastries, and beans in bulk. A favorite dinner restaurant is **Potato Brumbaugh's,** 2400 17th St., tel. (970) 356-6340, named for the fictional owner of Brumbaugh Feed Lots in *Centennial.* Specialties include steaks, chicken, and seafood. For Mexican food, try **Mirasol,** 627 8th Ave., tel. (970) 351-7357.

ENTERTAINMENT

With the 10,000-student University of Northern Colorado (UNC) in town, Greeley offers more in the way of entertainment than the many other plains communities that roll up the sidewalk when the sun goes down. In addition to clubs that book live dance music—from bluegrass to rock 'n' roll—Greeley also has a philharmonic orchestra, chamber orchestra, and a number of community theater groups, including **Greeley Civic Theater** and **Encore Theater,** as well as the **Children's Theater of Gridley.** A good bet for finding out what and who's playing when is *Greeley Style Magazine,* published by the chamber of commerce and available at their offices and around town. You can also get a copy by writing Box 5195, Greeley, CO 80631-0195.

There's also always a lot going on over at UNC, from dance to jazz to opera. UNC's **Little Theater of the Rockies** has been producing plays since 1934. For information and schedules regarding UNC performances, write Little Theater of the Rockies, College of Performing and Visual Arts, University of Northern Colorado, Greeley, CO 80639, or phone (970) 351-2200.

CALENDAR

Semana Latina ("Latin Week") in early May is a weeklong celebration of the area's Hispanic heritage. Festivities include music, dance, and

CATHY CARLSON

No urban cowboys, Greeley's bull riders are the real McCoy.

poetry readings, and exhibits demonstrate contributions to politics, education, and other aspects of Greeley and Weld County life. The event is designed to highlight Cinco de Mayo. For more information, contact the Greeley Cultural Affairs Office, 919 7th St., Greeley, CO 80631, tel. (970) 353-6123.

One of Greeley's most popular annual events is the **Greeley Independence Stampede,** running from late June through the Fourth of July. The eight-day celebration features rodeos, barbecues, lots of live music, and a Fourth of July parade, culminating with an evening of fireworks displays. For information, phone (970) 356-BULL. The **Weld County Fair** in August pro-

vides a forum for local farmers and ranchers to display their prize crops and critters, as well as for local bakers, canners, and sewing hobbyists to compete for best pies, peaches, and quilts. Contact the Weld County Extension Office, tel. (970) 356-4000.

For more information or for a complete calendar of events, contact the convention and visitors bureau, tel. (970) 352-3566 or (800) 449-3866.

SHOPPING

Greeley's downtown mall is a very pleasant retail shopping area, with a full range of shops and boutiques, as well as cafes, benches, and shade trees. Ideally located across the street from Lincoln Park, the mall offers an excellent opportunity to stroll about to get a feel for Greeley and its people.

The newly built Greeley Mall is a generic mall located at the Hwy. 34 bypass and 23rd Avenue. You'll find what you expect: Sears, JCPenney, Joslin's, etc.

SERVICES

Phone the **Greeley Police** at (970) 350-9605, the **Weld County Sheriff** at (970) 356-4000. **North Colorado Medical Center** is located at 1801 16th St., tel. (970) 352-4121. The Greeley **post office** is at 925 11th Ave., tel. (970) 353-0398.

Recycling
You can drop off most recyclables in Greeley at the **King Soopers** store at 2712 11th Ave., or at **Greeley-Weld Recycle** with locations at 310 8th St. and 2699 47th Avenue. For more information, phone (970) 352-8312.

INFORMATION

The **Greeley Convention and Visitors Bureau** publishes several guides and directories you'll probably find very useful. Stop by their offices at 1407 8th Ave., or phone (970) 352-3566 or (800) 449-3866. Be sure to ask for a copy of *Greeley Style Magazine,* which runs stories on Greeley and Weld County history, reviews restaurants, and profiles local businesspeople. For subscription information, write Box 5195, Greeley, CO 80631.

The **Greeley Municipal Museum** contains the Colorado Collection: new, rare, and out-of-print books on the area and state. The museum is located at 919 7th St. and is open Tues.-Sat. 9 a.m.-5 p.m., tel. (970) 350-9220. The **UNC Book Store** is located on campus in the University Center at 2045 10th Ave., tel. (970) 351-2136. You can also get information on Greeley, Weld County, and Colorado at the Greeley **public library,** 917 7th Street.

TRANSPORTATION

The **Greeley/Weld County Airport** is located at 600 Crosier Ave., tel. (970) 356-9141. Rent cars from most national agencies, plus **Econo Rent-A-Car,** 1030 7th Ave., tel. (970) 351-6969, and

Garnesy and Wheeler Rent-A-Car, 1108 8th Ave., tel. (970) 353-1111. For taxi service, phone **Shamrock Taxi** at (970) 352-3000.

Public transportation is available on Greeley's "The Bus," which has routes throughout town. For schedule information, phone (970) 350-9BUS.

NORTH OF GREELEY

US Highway 85 continues north from Greeley, paralleling I-25 all the way to Cheyenne. Between Nunn and Rockport, a distance of about 20 miles, the highway skirts the western edge of **Pawnee National Grassland.** The area is open to the public and offers the amateur geologist a fascinating case study. For a description of the region, see "The Interstate 76-South Platte Corridor" in the following chapter. You can get information and maps from the Grasslands headquarters, located in Greeley at 660 O St., tel. (970) 353-5004.

beaver

ANNE LONG

FORT COLLINS AND VICINITY

Fort Collins (pop. 94,000; elev. 5,004 feet) is located 60 miles north of Denver on the Cache La Poudre River just east of sprawling Roosevelt National Forest. A college town, Fort Collins offers plenty of outdoor as well as indoor activities: What better way to wind up a day on the lake than by quaffing a locally made ale and digging a local blues band's rendition of "Good Mornin', Little School Girl"?

Though the Fort Collins-area economy has traditionally relied on ranching and farming for its stability, the last decade has seen an influx of modern industry, with several large companies, including Hewlett-Packard and NCR, building plants nearby. In addition, Colorado State University has a growing reputation as a center for high-caliber research and has been instrumental in linking academia and agriculture. The result has been an increase in the efficiency and productivity of local farmers and a state-of-the-art agricultural technology that Fort Collins proudly exports. About 20,000 students attend the university, which is the city's largest employer (nearly 8,000).

Fort Collins's plains location guarantees a fairly moderate climate (local boosters claim the sun shines some 300 days a year), yet the city is close enough to the Front Range of the Rockies to allow for day-trips to some of the state's best hiking, backpacking, mountain biking, skiing, and other sports. One of the highlights of the downtown area is the newly renovated Old Town, a couple of square blocks where you can visit boutiques and bookstores, gift shops and galleries, and pubs and restaurants with fountain-side outdoor seating perfect for people-watching. Cart vendors also sell a variety of items, from tie-dyed T-shirts and novelty sunglasses to frozen yogurt.

HISTORY

As one of the last stops for fur trappers heading west into the rugged Rocky Mountains, the prairie lands surrounding what is now Fort Collins, as well as the various local waterways and routes leading into the high country, were well known by early-19th-century mountain men and the Native Americans with whom they traded and sometimes fought. In fact, the Cache La Poudre River, which runs north of town, takes its name from the French trappers who, to lighten their loads before heading up into the snow, often stashed their powder barrels in the lower river basin.

The Colorado gold rushes of the mid-1800s brought the first real settlers to the Fort Collins area—many of them frustrated miners who hadn't hit pay dirt in the mountains. In 1862, Camp Collins (named for U.S. Cavalry Lt. Col. William O. Collins) was established to protect traders traveling the Overland Trail, which passed about five miles north of present-day Fort Collins. On June 9, 1864, the camp was wiped out by flood, and three months later a new post (Fort Collins) was established downstream. During the 1870s and '80s, a series of irrigation canals was built in the area, allowing for much more efficient farming—primarily wheat, oats, and barley—and establishing the economic base that still exists. By 1872, Fort Collins could claim a hotel, general store, and post office.

In 1876, the town was hit by a horde of grasshoppers, which, along with the failure of Fort Collins's first bank, almost destroyed it. In fact it might have, were it not for the Colorado Central Railroad, which arrived the following year. In 1879, the first building of what would become Colorado State University was constructed—on land donated by the townspeople—and the Agricultural College of Colorado opened its doors for the first time in September of that year.

By the end of the 19th century, local farmers had begun to harvest sugar beets and alfalfa, and in the early 1900s the area was also prime cattle- and sheep-raising country. In 1910 the population of the town was over 8,000; by that time, however, Fort Collins's population had divided itself into two disparate camps, the "wets" and the "drys," the infamous Blue Laws having been enacted in 1896 (Fort Collins remained "dry" until 1969).

FORT COLLINS, DOWNTOWN

W. VINE DR.
TO CHEYENNE AND
HWY. 14 WEST
E. VINE DR.
LAPORTE AVE.
CHERRY ST.
MOUNTAIN AVE.
CITY PARK
CHAMBER OF COMMERCE
OLD TOWN SQUARE
OAK ST.
OLIVE ST.
MAGNOLIA ST.
CONVENTION AND VISITORS BUREAU
FORT COLLINS MUSEUM
MULBERRY ST.
MYRTLE ST.
LAUREL ST.
NORTH DR.
COLORADO STATE UNIVERSITY
LOCUST ST.
W. ELIZABETH ST.
SOUTH DR.
MERIDIAN
E. ELIZABETH ST.
HELMSHIRE INN
PITKIN ST.
ROOSEVELT NAT'L FOREST HQ
PROSPECT RD.
TO I-25
DRAKE RD.
HORSETOOTH RESERVOIR
OVERLAND TRAIL
CTY. RD. 42 C
TAFT HILL RD.
SHIELDS ST.
COLLEGE AVE.
LEMAY AVE.
HORSETOOTH DR.
NOTE: ONLY MAIN ROADS SHOWN
0   0.5mi
0   0.5km
CTY. RD. 38E
TO LOVELAND AND US 34

© MOON PUBLICATIONS, INC.

The addition of a college to Fort Collins proved fortuitous, as students and professors worked together on projects that greatly improved farming conditions and the quality of the crops. Eventually, the school began to earn a reputation as a frontrunner among the nation's agricultural colleges and began to attract students from beyond the nearby fields. Colorado State University, as it came to be known, was largely responsible for the town's increase in population, which doubled in the 1950s and '60s.

During the 1970s, the people of Fort Collins began to realize the importance of their own past (the Fort Collins Historical Society was

founded in 1974), and by the 1980s the town was at work restoring itself: Old Town Square was an early '80s project that sought at once to recognize the town's history and to attract shoppers and tourists by restoring the downtown area.

SIGHTS

Fort Collins Museum

Specializing in historical artifacts pertinent to the settling of the Fort Collins area, the Fort Collins Museum also curates a handful of the area's original buildings, which have been moved to the Library Park site just off College Avenue. A log cabin built by fur trapper Antoine Janis and purportedly one of the oldest buildings in the state, a stone cabin from the 1860s, and a schoolhouse built in 1884 have all been dismantled and moved to the park. The museum also houses an excellent selection of Folsom points found north of town in the 1920s and '30s.

The museum sits on a city block surrounded by lawn and shade trees, with picnic tables and a playground—the perfect post-museum-tour picnic site.

The Fort Collins Museum, located at 200 Matthews St. (two blocks east of College), is open Tues.-Sat. 10 a.m.-5 p.m. and Sunday 12-5 p.m. Admission is free. For more information, phone (970) 221-6738.

Avery House

Listed on the National Register of Historic Places, the sandstone Avery House was built in 1879 by Franklin C. Avery, a Fort Collins architect and banker. Descendants of Mr. Avery lived in the house until 1962, when it was obtained by the city, restored, and turned into a museum. The house contains original Avery-family furniture and decorations, in addition to other authentic period pieces.

The Avery House is located at 328 W. Mountain and is open the second and fourth Wednes-

days of each month. For more information, contact the convention and visitors bureau.

Historical Walking Tours

The Fort Collins Convention and Visitors Bureau has designed a 22-site walking tour of some landmarks of historical Fort Collins. Included are the Avery House, several of the first Colorado State University buildings, and an early church, drugstore, and hotel. For a list of the sites and addresses, contact the convention and visitors bureau.

Anheuser-Busch, Inc. Brewery

Free tours of the state's fastest brewery (not to be confused with its largest, the Coors plant in Golden, or its best, the Wynkoop in Denver) are offered at this facility year-round. (Smaller-quantity and home brewers scorn both speed and size; how much beer and how fast you can make it are generally in opposite proportion to its quality.) In addition to viewing the brewing and packaging processes, visitors also get to see the Budweiser Clydesdales and taste some beer before browsing in the gift shop (natch!).

A relative newcomer to Colorado brewing, having opened for production in 1988, the Bud brewery is open to visitors daily 10 a.m.-5 p.m., May-Oct., and Wed.-Sun. 9 a.m.-4 p.m., Nov.-April. To get there, take I-25 north from town to Mountain Vista Dr. (Exit 271), and turn right onto Busch Drive. For more information, phone (970) 490-4691.

Fort Collins Museum is just two blocks from Old Town.

PARKS AND RECREATION

Fort Collins's location at the foot of the Rockies and virtually in the shadow of Rocky Mountain National Park guarantees plenty of year-round outdoor activity for residents and passers-through. Not to be overlooked, though, are the great numbers of recreational possibilities outside the park and mountains—from fishing in nearby lakes and streams to cycling, hiking, and golf in the warmer months to cross-country skiing in the winter.

City Parks

Fort Collins has several large city parks and many smaller neighborhood parks. **City Park,** 1500 W. Mulberry, has lots of lawns for tossing Frisbees or napping, picnic facilities, a fitness course, and fishing (at the small lake). For tennis or horseshoes, try **Edora Park,** 1420 E. Stuart, where you'll also find a public swimming pool and ice-skating rink. **Lee Martinez Park** features picnic facilities, tennis courts, and softball fields. You can also visit Martinez Park's 12-acre farm and experience first-hand the responsibilities of raising animals and harvesting crops (kids can pet the animals). For information, phone (970) 221-6665. **Roland Moore Park,** 2201 S. Shields, has indoor handball and racquetball courts, in addition to hiking and biking trails and a picnic area.

For more information on Fort Collins city parks, phone the **Parks and Recreation Department** (north of town) at (707) 221-6640.

Horsetooth Reservoir

Horsetooth Reservoir is a popular recreational area just southwest of Fort Collins. The 4,000 acres of water and its rocky shoreline attract lots of outdoor enthusiasts, particularly in the warmer months when folks flock to the water to escape the heat. **Horsetooth Mountain Park** borders the lake and offers fishing (for bass, trout, and landlocked salmon), waterskiing, windsurfing, picnicking, horse-back riding, mountain biking, and backcountry camping. For information, contact the **Larimer County Parks Department** at (970) 226-4517.

Lory State Park is located on the northwest shore of Horsetooth Reservoir. In addition to hiking and mountain biking on the park's two-dozen-plus miles of trails, you can explore the area on horseback. At **Double Diamond Stables** you can rent horses by the hour, join a group on a breakfast, lunch, or dinner ride, or rent a carriage. For information, write 710 Lodgepole, Bellvue, CO, or phone (970) 224-4200. Lory State Park also offers fishing and birdwatching and is a favorite place to check out the wildflowers in spring and early summer. For more on Lory State Park, contact the **Colorado Division of Parks and Outdoor Recreation,** 3842 S. Mason, Fort Collins, CO 80525, tel. (970) 226-6641.

To get to Horsetooth, head west from downtown to Overland Trail; then take County Rd. 42C (which runs into Overland between Prospect and Drake). You can also get there by heading west on US 287 through Laporte and turning west at the Bellvue exit.

Colorado State Forest

Located about 70 miles west of Fort Collins via US 287 and CO 14 (and 10,276-foot Cameron Pass), Colorado State Forest offers excellent hiking and backpacking, as well as camping, fishing, and sightseeing. Write Colorado State Forest, Star Route Box 91, Walden, CO 80480, or phone (970) 723-8366.

Cycling

Any self-respecting college town's got to have its share of bike paths and mountain-bike trails, where students can go to alleviate post-exam stress (or avoid thinking about an exam on the horizon). No exception, Fort Collins has nearly 60 miles of city bikeways, and the city is dedicated to making cycling safe and convenient. The *Tour de*

BOB RACE

Fort Bike Guide is a city map that designates a variety of interconnecting routes, including some set aside for pedestrians and cyclists only. The guides are available at local bike shops, as well as from the chamber of commerce and the convention and visitors bureau.

Local mountain bikers like to head into Roosevelt National Forest or Colorado State Forest, west of town via CO 14. For maps and information on biking in the national forest, stop by its headquarters at 240 W. Prospect, or phone (970) 498-1100. State forest information is available from the main office in Walden; phone (970) 723-8366.

The **Never Summer Nordic Yurt System** is a hut-to-hut cross-country skiing system open in the summer to mountain bikers. There are three yurts (small cabins that sleep six) and an interconnecting series of trails. The area is located in Colorado State Forest about 70 miles west of Fort Collins (east of Walden). For reservations and more information, write Box 1254, Fort Collins, CO 80522, or phone (970) 484-3903.

Closer to town, **Horsetooth Reservoir** offers a decent amount and range of off-road cycling on 2,100 acres of public land (county maintained). Small entrance fee.

Golf

The city of Fort Collins maintains three municipal golf courses, and there are a handful of private courses in the area. **City Park Nine** is a nine-hole course at City Park (411 S. Bryan). For information and tee times, phone (970) 221-6650. The other two city courses are **Collindale Golf Course,** 1441 E. Horsetooth, tel. (970) 221-6651, and **Southridge Greens,** 5750 S. Lemay, tel. (970) 226-2828, both 18-hole courses.

Link-N-Greens, 777 E. Lincoln, tel. (970) 221-4818, is a public course offering nine holes and a lighted driving range. Private courses include the **Fort Collins Country Club,** north of town on Country Club Dr. (off College), tel. (970) 482-1336.

Hiking

Fort Collins is located close to some of the state's best hiking areas. Rocky Mountain National Park and Roosevelt National Forest offer hundreds of miles of trails to wander, woods to explore, and peaks to bag.

The **Colorado Mountain Club,** based in Estes Park, hosts day and overnight trips into the backcountry. Phone their main office at (970) 586-6623; for the name and number of the current Fort Collins Outing Chairman, phone the Denver office at (303) 922-8315.

The **Mountain Shop,** 632 S. Mason, tel. (970) 493-5720, is an excellent source for expert advice and quality equipment; they also carry maps and rent gear.

Fishing

Several of the lakes in the Fort Collins area offer good fishing for bass, crappie, walleye, and other warm-water species. At Horsetooth Reservoir, you can cast for warm-water fish as well as trout and kokanee salmon; the reservoir is especially well regarded for its large lake trout. There are public boat launches and marinas at Horsetooth, though fishing can be productive from the shore as well. Kids might enjoy fishing for panfish at the small lake at City Park.

If you'd rather not take chances of getting skunked (or if you don't want to buy a license), **Frank's Trout Pond,** 2912 W. Mulberry, tel. (970) 482-5102, is stocked with hungry fish you pay for by the inch. (See also "West of Fort Collins," following.)

Rafting

Several companies in Fort Collins and the surrounding area offer whitewater rafting trips on the Cache La Poudre, Arkansas, and Green rivers. Phone **Adrift Adventures** at (970) 493-4005 or (800) 824-0150 (from Denver). Trips are also offered by **Wildwater, Inc.,** tel. (970) 224-3379, and **Wanderlust Adventures,** tel. (970) 484-1219.

Cross-Country Skiing

Excellent cross-country skiing opportunities await the Fort Collins-area three-pinner—from the woods of Roosevelt National Forest to the valleys of Rocky Mountain National Park, and a lot closer to town as well, including the trails around Horsetooth Reservoir.

The **Never Summer Nordic Yurt System** offers hut-to-hut Nordic skiing in Colorado State Forest. Sleeping six people each, the three yurts are connected by an intricate series of backcountry trails. For reservations and more information, write Box 1254, Fort Collins, CO 80522, or phone (970) 484-3903.

The best source for information on Nordic skiing around Fort Collins is **The Mountain Shop,** 632 S. Mason, tel. (970) 493-5270. In addition to providing advice, rental gear, and maps, the store also stocks quality equipment and clothing.

You can also get information and maps from Roosevelt National Forest Headquarters, 240 W. Prospect, Fort Collins, CO 80526, tel. (970) 498-1100.

ACCOMMODATIONS

You'll find a range of lodging options available in Fort Collins, from a handful of low-budget motels to high-end chain hotels. A cluster of motels and hotels is located on E. Mulberry, at the I-25 junction (Exit 269). Among them: **Motel 6,** tel. (970) 382-6466; **Ramada Inn,** tel. (970) 493-7800; **Days Inn,** tel. (970) 221-5490; **Sleep Inn,** tel. (970) 484-5515; **National 9,** tel. (970) 482-1114; and the **I-25 Holiday Inn,** tel. (970) 484-4660.

Doubles at the **Inn at Fort Collins,** just south of the college at 2612 S. College Ave., tel. (970) 226-2600, start at about $45. The **Helmshire Inn,** tel. (970) 493-4683, on College Ave. right across from the school, offers rooms for two in a converted hotel for about $80, which includes a continental breakfast and access to health club facilities. A second **Holiday Inn** is located at 425 W. Prospect, tel. (970) 482-2626, and the Fort Collins **Marriott** is at 350 E. Horsetooth, tel. (970) 226-5200 or (800) 548-2635.

The Fort Collins **Mile High KOA** campground, tel. (970) 493-9758, is located about 10 miles northwest of town on US 287.

FOOD

Start Me Up

For breakfast, it's tough to find a place with a better reputation than the **Silver Grill Café,** 218 Walnut, tel. (970) 484-4656. Serving the residents of Fort Collins since the 1930s, the Silver Grill specializes in gargantuan cinnamon rolls, and it dishes up other standard American fare as well.

The **Patio Café** in Old Town Square is also a very nice place to relax over breakfast. With seating on the mall (and inside as well), this little restaurant specializes in dishes with a Southwestern bent (breakfast burritos), as well as elegant egg dishes (various versions of eggs Benedict); prices range $4-6.50.

For your espresso-and-pastry-while-you-read-the-paper-and-listen-to-jazz fix, check out **Pour La France,** at the corner of Mountain and College. Meanwhile, the younger, body-pierced-in-weird-places crowd might prefer **Paris on the Poudre Coffee House** across College at 15 Old Town Square, where the proverbial little short-haired brown dogs lie waiting patiently for their rasta mastas.

Lunch and Dinner

If you're looking for a lunch spot with lots of local flavor, stop in at **Coopersmith's Brew Pub,** tel. (970) 498-0483, in Old Town Square. Quaff a beer (Scottish Ale, India Pale, or Oatmeal Stout) while you munch on bangers and mash, fish and chips, bratwurst, or a burger with artichoke hearts, scallions, and sour cream. Coopersmith's also serves stir fry, steaks, salads, and homemade desserts; lunches and dinners run $6-10. Open Mon.-Sat. 11 a.m.-2 a.m. and Sunday 11 a.m.-midnight.

Across the square, **Old Town Ale House,** tel. (970) 493-2213, also serves pub fare—soups, salads, and sandwiches run $5-10—with one of the best beer selections in town, including several British Isle beers on tap. **Chesterfield, Bottomsley, and Potts,** 1415 W. Elizabeth, tel. (970) 221-1139, is a sports bar (eight big-screen TVs) very popular with the college crowd. Over 50 imported beers, and the local paper's pick as "best burger in town" for three years in a row.

One of Fort Collins's hot spots for south-of-the-border fare, and famous for the best margaritas in town, is the **Rio Grande Mexican Restaurant,** 150 N. College, tel. (970) 224-5428, which serves traditional Mexican food, as well as Tex-Mex, with dinners running $5-8; lunch specials are $4-6, and you can get a mini-margarita for 99 cents. (The Rio Grande has a sister restaurant in Boulder just below the Pearl Street Mall.)

Another standby is **Old Chicago,** 147 S. College, tel. (970) 482-8599, serving pizza, pastas, salads, over 125 types of beer, and offering patio dining. Open for lunch and dinner. Prices range $5-12.

Also popular for Italian food is **Canino's,** 613 S. College, tel. (970) 493-7205. A longtime family-owned favorite, Canino's offers takeout and delivery as well.

If you start feeling guilty after gorging yourself on pub fare, pasta, *burritos de pollo,* and local brew, and you're looking for something healthful to pack for the road, stop in at **Fort Collins Food Co-op,** 250 E. Mountain (just around the corner from Old Town Square), tel. (970) 484-7448. The little shop carries organically grown fruits and vegetables, in addition to juices, nuts, breads, and other goods.

For the best Rocky Mountain oysters in the area, check out **Bruce's** in Severance, just southeast of Fort Collins (see "Food" under "Greeley and Vicinity" above).

ENTERTAINMENT

Any college town has got to have places where folks can let loose on weekends, and Fort Collins doesn't disappoint. **Mishawaka Inn,** tel. (970) 482-4420, located about 14 miles up Poudre Canyon north of town, regularly features surprisingly big-name acts; summer of 1995 saw Leon Russell, Jerry Jeff Walker, 10,000 Maniacs, and Los Lobos.

In Old Town Square, the **Old Town Ale House,** tel. (970) 493-2213, features live music most nights, while just across the mall, the **Comedy Works,** tel. (970) 221-5481, books local and club-circuit comics. The **Crown Pub,** 134 S. College, tel. (970) 484-5929, has live music—acoustic rock, jazz, blues—Thurs.-Sunday.

A favorite of the college crowd is **Fort Ram,** 450 N. Linden, tel. (970) 482-5026—live music from time to time, but other nights, DJs play dance music. **Linden's,** 214 Linden, tel. (970) 482-9291, specializes in blues—Chicago and Delta—and also books pure rock 'n' roll bands. Open jam sessions Monday nights.

For up-to-date information on clubs and other entertainment, check out *The Scene,* a free monthly distributed around town in racks, hotel lobbies, and cafes. Also, take a look at the entertainment section of the *Fort Collins Coloradoan,* the local daily (35 cents in racks).

CALENDAR

There's an event or festival of one kind or another almost every weekend in Fort Collins, either at the university or downtown. Highlights include the **Colorado Brewers' Festival** in late June, where you can sample the pilsners and porters of Colorado's many microbreweries, munch from a wide range of food booths, and listen to a variety of ethnic music. On the **Fourth of July** there's a fair with food, music, and fireworks at City Park, and in mid-September balloons from the Fort Collins **Balloon Festival** fill the sky. The **Octoberfest,** during the first week of October, features street dancing, traditional food and drink, and a general sense of revelry and carrying on.

For a complete calendar of Fort Collins's annual events, contact the chamber of commerce or convention and visitors bureau. See "Information" following.

SHOPPING

Old Town Square, located in one of Fort Collins's original financial centers, is one of the town's true delights. Built in the early 1980s, with a fountain to keep it cool and several cafes with patio seating, the little shopping mall offers several different retail shops, galleries, as well as cart vendors selling T-shirts, jewelry, and souvenirs. **Children's Mercantile** has tons of kids' games, toys, and an exceptional selection of books. **Colorado Classics** carries menswear and specializes in Western duds, particularly Pendleton shirts. **Trimble Court Artisans** and **Walnut Street Gallery** are worth poking your head into if you're interested in prints, posters, and art by local craftspeople.

Farmers Market

Every Wednesday 3-6 p.m., local farmers (and remember, this is one of the agricultural capitals of the state) sell their freshly picked wares in the parking lot at the corner of College Ave. and History Cabin.

SERVICES

The offices of the Fort Collins **Police Department** are at 300 Laporte, tel. (970) 221-6540. Phone the Larimer County **Sheriff** at (970) 221-7000; offices are at 200 W. Oak. **State Patrol** offices are at 2412 E. Mulberry, tel. (970) 484-4020. **Poudre Valley Hospital,** tel. (970) 482-4111 or (800) 284-5241, is located at 1024 S. Lemay Avenue.

Fort Collins's main **post office** is in the Federal Building, tel. 482-2837.

Recycling

The **King Soopers** stores at 1015 Taft Hill Rd. and 2325 S. College take aluminum, glass, newspaper, and plastics.

INFORMATION

The offices of the **Fort Collins Convention and Visitors Bureau,** tel. (970) 482-5821 or (800) 274-FORT, are at 420 S. Howes St., Suite 101, where you'll also find the Fort Collins Information Center; the folks here are always good for information on things to do and see (and where to spend your money) in the area. The **Fort Collins Chamber of Commerce,** tel. (970) 482-3746, is located at 225 S. Meldrun, across College Ave. from Old Town Square. Be sure to pick up a copy of *The Guide to Fort Collins,* which contains listings of parks, restaurants, nightclubs, shopping centers, and other attractions. The Fort Collins **public library** is at 201 Peterson, tel. (970) 221-6740. **Stone Lion Books,** tel. (970) 493-0030, in Old Town Square, has a wide selection of books on local and state history, as well as on recreation.

The local daily is the *Fort Collins Coloradan,* a Gannett paper. For subscription information, phone (970) 224-7730.

TRANSPORTATION

America West, Continental, and **Delta** airlines fly into **Fort Collins-Loveland Municipal Airport,** tel. (970) 221-1300, about five miles south of town

off I-25. Private-plane pilots can fly directly into **Fort Collins Airpark,** located near the downtown area, tel. (970) 484-4186 or 482-6588.

Airport Express, tel. (970) 482-0505, has shuttle service between Denver's airport and Fort Collins (as well as between Fort Collins and Cheyenne and Fort Collins and Laramie). Fort Collins's public transportation is **Transfort,** with regular routes throughout town; phone (970) 221-6620 for rates and route information. For taxi service, phone **Yellow Cab** at (970) 493-8200 or **Shamrock Taxi** at (970) 224-2222.

Rent cars in Fort Collins from **Altra Auto Rental,** 115 E. Harmony Rd., tel. (970) 226-3171; **Budget,** 516 S. College Ave., tel. (970) 484-5574; **Choice Rent-a-Car,** tel. (970) 226-6772; **Econo-Rate Rent-a-Car,** 3836 S. College Ave., tel. (970) 221-2722; **Hertz,** 1235 N. College Ave., tel. (970) 484-0077; **National,** 3404 E. Harmony, tel. (970) 229-0704; **Rent-a-Wreck,** 134 W. Wilcox, tel. (970) 224-3478; or **Ugly Duckling,** 602 S. College Ave., tel. (970) 484-7443.

WEST OF FORT COLLINS

US Highway 287 continues north through Fort Collins for a couple of miles, hooks to the west, then meanders north again, crossing the border into Wyoming and rolling into Laramie.

Fourteen miles northwest of Fort Collins, you can catch CO 14 west through the Poudre River Canyon, Roosevelt National Forest, and Colorado State Forest, eventually arriving in the small town of Walden. This is a wonderfully scenic route, taking you along the shores of the Cache La Poudre, past some excellent fishing spots, camping and picnic areas, through the Medicine Bow Mountains, and over Cameron Pass (elev. 10,276 feet) near the northwest corner of Rocky Mountain National Park. Along the 80-mile stretch from Laporte to Gould are numerous Forest Service access roads leading to more campgrounds. Be sure to check local fishing regulations with the Colorado Division of Wildlife, tel. (303) 297-1192, or local sporting goods stores as some stretches of the Cache La Poudre have special restrictions.

Forest Service campgrounds along CO 14 include **Ansel Watrous,** 18 miles west of Laporte (open all year, pit toilets, no showers); **Kelly Flats,** 30 miles west (open mid-May to mid-Nov., pit toilets, no showers); and **Chambers Lake** (60 miles west, open June-Oct., pit toilets, no showers). In addition, camping is available in the **Red Feather Lakes** area northwest of Fort Collins, where a series of lakes offers good trout fishing just north of the Poudre River Canyon. Be sure to check local regulations; some of the waters have special restric-

tions. To get there, turn north onto Feather Lakes Rd. at Rustic.

For information on lodging and camping in the Feather Lakes Area, write **Poudre River— Red Feather Lakes Tourist Council,** Box 505, Red Feather Lakes, CO 80545, or phone (800) 462-5870. For information on the other Forest Service campgrounds accessible from CO 14, contact the offices of **Roosevelt National Forest,** 240 W. Prospect Rd., Fort Collins.

black bear

Sterling

NORTHEASTERN COLORADO

This is not the Colorado most imagine when they think of the state. It's not John Denver's "Rocky Mountain High" or Boulder's progressive politics and New Ageism; nor is it Cripple Creek's Victorian shops or Colorado Springs' mountain vistas. Yet this Colorado offers the

NORTHEASTERN COLORADO HIGHLIGHTS

Fort Morgan: museum, Pawnee National Grassland, Pawnee Buttes

Sterling: Overland Trail Museum, parks, boating, fishing, Sugar Beet Days

Tamarack Ranch State Wildlife Area (Crook): 7,000-acre refuge

Limon: Twilight Train rides

Burlington: museum and Kit Carson County Carousel (national historic register)

traveler something just as much a part of the state's soul and heartland: the plains, where people have been farming, ranching, and drawing their livelihoods from the soil and the sky for generations. It's a place where bumper stickers advise you to Eat Beef, where acres of sugar beets and alfalfa stretch as far as you can see, where folks haul ass on long, straight unpaved back roads in pickups and Cadillacs, like characters out of Larry McMurtry novels. It's a place where you can get not only a sense of rural Colorado and hard-working Coloradans but a very real taste of something that is truly and uniquely American as well.

Just listen to the names of some of the towns out here: Yuma, Burlington, Holyoke, Sedgwick, Heartstrong, Haxtun, Crook—most of them blink-and-you'll-miss-it burgs where things are so slow and the citizenry so insulated that if you do slow down you're likely to be given the once-over by just about everyone you pass on the street, from the kid in the high-school letter jacket and his young adoring girlfriend to the retired rancher in his pickup. That's not to say the people out here aren't friendly. On the contrary, they welcome passers-through, and they'll usually go out of their way to help you find a restaurant or coffee shop, campground, park or picnic area. In fact, get a local talking about his town—or, more accurately, his county—and you'll have a tough time getting him to stop. These are proud people, and they love their county fairs, livestock shows, and harvest festivals.

Long before the white man arrived here, these grasslands had been home to roaming bands of Cheyenne and Arapahoe, who hunted the prairie's great herds of buffalo. As early as the 1820s, though, traders and trappers began infringing on Native American lands, working the

South Platte area for beaver pelts (which parallels present-day I-76 from Julesburg to Fort Morgan, then veers northwest to Greeley) and building a series of forts and trading posts. Like the buffalo, though, which within a few years would be all but extinct on the American plains, the beaver, which had once been abundant in the South Platte, were quickly too few to be very profitable. By the 1850s, interest in trapping along the South Platte was dying out.

Toward the end of the 1850s, however, gold was discovered at Pikes Peak and Cherry Creek (near what is now Englewood, a suburb of Denver), and prospectors began streaming across Colorado, many of them following the South Platte corridor. In 1860, Julesburg became a stop on the short-lived Pony Express

Trail, and though that enterprise only lasted a year, when the Union Pacific Railroad arrived in Julesburg in 1867, the sleepy little hamlet was transformed almost overnight: Its dance halls and saloons, prostitutes and gamblers earned it the nickname, "the wickedest little town in the West." (Actually, the present town of Julesburg is not in the same location as the Julesburg of the 1860s; there were, in fact, four separate Julesburgs, the current one having been founded in 1881.)

During the early 20th century, the South Platte Valley became prized for its sugar beets, and although other crops—including alfalfa, wheat, and other grains—are grown out on these plains, it's the beets that have been sweetening the local economy for most of the century. Several northeastern Colorado towns, including Haxtun, Sterling, Merino, and Atwood, have relied heavily over the years on the annual beet harvest (beginning in October) for their economic survival. And even the towns whose economies are primarily livestock related also rely on the beets; ranchers in Fort Morgan, for example, fatten sheep on beet pulp.

Traveling through Northeastern Colorado today, whether by interstate or back road (the latter is advised), is in a way like stepping back in time. The pace in these little towns is a lot slower than it is in Denver, Colorado Springs, or Boulder. The stockyards are much the same as they were a hundred years ago, though ranching has changed considerably. Today, ranchers buy and sell by computer and telephone (don't be surprised to see them sitting in coffee shops or behind the wheels of their pickups, talking into cellular phones), though the weather, with its ability to capriciously determine fates, still dominates conversation.

But don't write Northeastern Colorado off as strictly a bunch of lazy cowtowns. Even if you're just passing through on your way to Vail, take the time to get off the main highways. Check out the Fort Morgan Museum, with its Glenn

Miller display (Miller grew up in Fort Morgan), the Overland Trail Museum in Sterling, or the Kit Carson County Carousel (a hand-carved merry-go-round) built in 1905 and designated a National Historic Landmark). Or just take the time to drive through the grasslands, imagining a time when the country wasn't in such a hurry.

Northeastern Colorado Information

You'll find a **Northeast Colorado Gateway Information Center** at the Julesburg exit off of I-76. Pick up brochures and publications promoting areas of historical and recreational interest, as well as information on lodging, dining, and sightseeing throughout the northeastern part of the state.

The **Northeast Colorado Visitor Information Center** is located just east of downtown Sterling between I-76 and the Platte River (take the Sterling exit). Farther south in Burlington, check out the **State of Colorado Welcome Center,** where you can get information on northeastern Colorado as well as on the rest of the state. Be sure to pick up a copy of the *Northeast Colorado Travel Guide,* which discusses the area's history, highlights specific areas of interest, and suggests several different tours. The publication is available at visitor centers, as well as at the Logan County and Sterling chambers of commerce. You can also get a copy, and more information, by writing **Northeast Colorado Travel Region,** 451 14th St., Burlington, CO 80807, or by phoning (800) 777-9075.

Further Reading

James Michener's typically sprawling historical novel *Centennial* explores in great depth and detail the history of this part of Colorado, as well as the area just to the west. As in most Michener novels, in which the setting becomes a central character, the plains play a pivotal part. Locals claim the town in which most of the book takes place was based on Greeley, Colorado (see "North Central Colorado").

THE INTERSTATE 76-SOUTH PLATTE CORRIDOR

Interstate 76 angles from Denver up to a point about as close to the precise northeastern corner of Colorado as you can get. The drive northeast from Denver to Julesburg, just two miles from the Nebraska border, is a little over 200 miles and it's flat, fast, and arrow straight. Without stopping, it will take less than four hours. Along the way, though, are a handful of museums and other diversions that are well worth exploring if you've got the time. The Overland Trail Museum in Sterling, for example, with its displays from the 19th century, will give you a better sense of the area's history and of its land and people. Another good way to appreciate the region is to stay off the interstate entirely: A series of two-lane highways parallels both the South Platte and I-76, from Fort Morgan to Julesburg, passing through several tiny farming and ranching towns and communities along the way. The little general stores and watering holes provide great opportunities to experience local color.

FORT MORGAN AND VICINITY

Fort Morgan (pop. 8,628; elev. 4,330 feet) is the seat of Morgan County, one of the small-est (1,296 square miles) but most agriculturally rich counties in the state. Producing a wide variety of crops, including sugar beets, wheat, beans, alfalfa, onions, barley, and potatoes, Morgan County relies on Fort Morgan as a shipping and distribution hub. The area is also known for its beef, sheep, and dairy ranches.

Founded in 1864 as a military post to protect gold rushers and other travelers on the Overland Trail, Fort Morgan was originally called Camp Tyler, then Camp Wardell. The town assumed its present name in 1866 in honor of Colonel C.A. Morgan, the post's first commanding officer. The town today is one of quiet tree-lined streets, many with beautiful, well-maintained homes and large lush yards. Fort Morgan is also the home town of Glen Miller (see below) and Philip K. Dick, the well-known science-fiction writer and author of the short story on which the film *Total Recall* was based. Dick is buried in the Fort Morgan cemetery.

Fort Morgan Museum
Depicting Morgan County from the first nomadic bands of hunters up to bandleader Glenn Miller, who grew up here, this small museum displays artifacts and photos that testify to the area's

The Northeastern Colorado Visitor Center in Sterling is a good source for advice and literature on the area.

LA JUNTA

TO ROCKY FORD
AND PUEBLO
ARKANSAS RIVER
50
10
TO WALSENBURG
ANDERSON
SAN JUAN AVE.
SANTA FE AVE.
COLORADO AVE.
RATON AVE.
2nd ST.
TO
BENT'S
OLD FORT
AND LAS
ANIMAS
50
10th St.
CITY PARK
350
TO TRINIDAD
14th ST.
OTERO JUNIOR COLLEGE
KOSHARE INDIAN MUSEUM
NOTE: ONLY MAIN
ROADS SHOWN
NOT TO SCALE
109
109

© MOON PUBLICATIONS, INC.

varied history. Particularly worth checking out is the Koehler Site display, which explains the 1980 discovery at a nearby landfill of a prehistoric campsite. Also on display are Plains tribe moccasins, belts, and pipes, as well as an exhibit devoted to Miller, with many intriguing photos of him as a teenager and young man (Miller graduated from Fort Morgan High School in 1921), as well as a re-created soda fountain from the old Hillrose Drugstore, and a room reserved for traveling exhibits (usually with Western themes, from Navajo blankets to Charles Russell's paintings).

Museum hours are Mon.-Fri. 10 a.m.-5 p.m., Tues.-Thurs. evenings 6-8 p.m., and Saturday 11 a.m.-5 p.m. Admission is free, with donations encouraged. The Fort Morgan Museum is at 414 Main St., also the site of the city library. For more information, phone (970) 867-6331.

Riverside Park and Canfield Recreation Area

This large and beautiful city park just off the freeway (Exit 80) tempts the weary road warrior with shaded lawns, picnic tables, restrooms, volleyball, basketball, and tennis courts, horseshoe pits, and (for winter travelers) an ice-skating rink, as well as tons of playground equipment. The park is a perfect stop for a quick leg-stretch or maybe even a long afternoon nap under a shade tree. In addition, the park offers free overnight camping and has a swimming pool that's free and open to the public.

Pawnee National Grassland And Pawnee Buttes

The two separate units of Pawnee National Grassland sprawl on the plains of northern Weld County, north of Greeley and Fort Morgan. Desolate, dry, and sparsely populated, the grasslands don't offer the traveler much in the way of views, especially when compared to the eastern slope of the Rockies looming just to the west. There are two startling exceptions, though, to all this flatness: Pawnee Buttes.

Rising over 250 feet above the plain, the two buttes, composed of sedimentary rock protected by a layer of hard sandstone, have resisted the forces that have eroded the surrounding area. Of great interest to paleontologists and anthropologists, the buttes have yielded several prehistoric animals, including *Alticamelus,* a giraffe-like camel, and *Amphycyon,* a large animal that would appear today part dog and part bear, as well as an abundance of Native American artifacts (the area was once the hunting grounds of the Pawnee).

The Pawnee National Grassland and Buttes are open to the public, though getting to the Buttes does require some back-roading. The dirt road leading to them is fine for passenger cars, but gets thick with mud when rainstorms hit. For more information and specific directions, see Lee Gregory's excellent book, *Colorado Scenic Guide, Northern Region.* You can also get more information, including maps, from the Pawnee National Grassland Office of the Forest Service, located in Greeley at 660 O St., tel. (970) 353-5004.

Golf

The **Fort Morgan Municipal Golf Course,** tel. (970) 867-5990, is adjacent to the Fort Morgan Country Club, 17856 County Rd. T, and is open to the public.

Accommodations

You can get good clean rooms right downtown at the **Park Terrace Best Western,** 725 Main St., tel. (970) 867-8256, as well as the **Econo Lodge**, 1409 Barlow (Exit 82), tel. (970) 867-

9481 or (800) 446-6900; the **Super 8 Motel,** 1220 Main St., tel. (970) 867-9443; the **Central Motel,** 201 W. Platte Ave., tel. (970) 867-2401; and the **Madisson Hotel,** 14378 US 34, tel. (970) 867-8208.

If you've got the time and the inclination to get off the beaten path and see this part of the country close up, the **Elk Echo Ranch Bed and Breakfast,** offers home cooking and tours of the backcountry ("elk tours") on the southern edge of Pawnee National Grasslands. For information on rates and tours, write Elk Echo Ranch, Stoneham, CO 80754, or phone (970) 735-2426.

Food

You'll find the requisite fast-food and franchise restaurants in Fort Morgan, including Pizza Hut, Kentucky Fried Chicken, and Hardee's. In addition, the Best Western Park Terrace motel has a dining room. For Mexican food, check out **Delgado's II,** 300 E. Platte, tel. (970) 867-0404.

Services

Fort Morgan Police can be reached at (970) 867-5678. The offices of the **Morgan County Sheriff** are at 400 Warner, tel. (970) 867-2461. Reach the **State Patrol** at (970) 867-6657. **Colorado Plains Medical Center** is at 1000 Lincoln, tel. (970) 867-3391. The central **post office** in Fort Morgan is at 300 State, tel. (970) 867-7111.

Recycling

The **Safeway,** 620 W. Platte, takes aluminum. For more information on recycling in the Fort Morgan area, phone **All Trash Recycling** at (970) 867-6196.

Information

The Fort Morgan **public library,** tel. (970) 867-9456, is located next door to the Fort Morgan Museum at 414 Main Street. For more information on Fort Morgan and Morgan County, phone the **Fort Morgan Chamber of Commerce,** tel. (970) 867-6702, or write 300 Main St., Box 971, Fort Morgan, CO 80701. For **road and weather information,** call (970) 522-4848.

STERLING

The largest town in the ranching and farming country of the northeastern corner of Colorado, Sterling (pop. 1,200; elev. 3,945 feet), seat of Logan County, is a quiet little community with towering shade trees and old homes with long front porches. Only the southwestern end of town has been invaded by the proverbial Wal-Mart, Kmart, Taco John's and other fast-food franchises. Its economy supported by cattle, sugar beets, corn, and alfalfa, Sterling hosts several agricultural and livestock festivals each year; the whole town'll turn out for a 4-H show or the annual alfalfa festival.

You might have trouble finding tofu burgers in parts of Colorado.

one of Brad Rhea's
"living" sculptures

Calling itself the "City of Living Trees," Sterling is particularly proud of the dozen or so sculptures scattered around town, carved "on location" by Brad Rhea out of, well, living trees. These include "Skygrazers," a herd of giraffes stretching skyward; "The Dreamer," a clown; "Minute Man," and "The Golfer," the latter located, of course, at the Sterling Country Club.

In 1871, railroad surveyor David Leavitt passed through the area and was impressed enough with the valley to return the following year to begin ranching. The town of Sterling was founded a decade later in 1881, and originally settled by pioneers from Mississippi and Tennessee. The little town's riverside location led to rapid growth, and throughout the early- and mid-20th century, it served as a hub for area beet farmers. Today, many of Sterling's buildings, including the Logan County Courthouse, are on the National Register of Historic Places. Sterling's Northeastern Junior College, founded in 1941, offers a wide variety of fully accredited two-year programs in several different fields, including agriculture, humanities, business, sciences, and social sciences. For information on admissions or visiting the college, phone (970) 522-6600, ext. 651.

Overland Trail Museum
One of the best small-town museums in the state, the Overland Trail Museum features excellent displays of Native American clothing, tools, and weapons, pioneer clothing and domestic uten-

sils, a grand piano shipped from Mississippi to Sterling in 1889, and, out back, a reconstructed blacksmith's shop with tools and items typically made by a smithy (horseshoes, spades, plow hardware, etc.). Also out back is an old schoolhouse used these days as a summer school by Sterling teachers and students, who dress as pioneers. Be sure to spend a few minutes looking over the native grasses display between the parking lot and front door. There's also a nice shaded picnic area next to the museum.

The Overland Trail Museum is open April 1-Oct. 1, Mon.-Sat. 9 a.m.-5 p.m. and Sundays and holidays 10 a.m.-5 p.m. Call (970) 522-3895. Admission is free.

Parks and Recreation
Columbine Park, on US 6 between S. 3rd Ave. and Division Ave., is huge, shady, and lawny, with picnic tables, swings, and other playground equipment, as well as two of the "Living Tree" sculptures. **Pioneer Park,** two miles west of downtown on Main St., offers horseshoe pits, tennis courts, a merry-go-round, a series of nature trails among 14 acres, and campsites. For more information, contact the **Sterling Recreation Department,** 421 N. 1st St., tel. (970) 522-9700. You can phone the offices of Pioneer Park at (970) 522-0441.

Other Recreation
North Sterling Reservoir, as well as nearby Jumbo and Prewitt reservoirs, offers fishing for

catfish, bass, walleye, and other warm-water fish. Even if you're not into waterskiing, boating or fishing, take a drive out to the lake in the evening. It's quiet out here, except for the sound of an occasional fish rising, and the prairie seems to stretch endlessly, to the horizon and into the past—it's easy to forget the 20th century, and imagine yourself a westbound pioneer, one of the first settlers crossing the Great Plains.

Sterling also has four golf courses, including the public **Riverview,** tel. (970) 522-3035, and the private **Sterling Country Club,** tel. (970) 522-5523. For swimming, racquetball, and other indoor sports (the pool is indoor, with a $5 fee for nonresidents), check out the **Sterling Recreation Center,** 808 Elm, tel. (970) 522-7882.

Accommodations

Several motels cluster near the I-76/US 6 junction just east of downtown Sterling. The most upscale of them is the **Best Western Sundowner,** tel. (970) 522-6265 or (800) 528-1234. Doubles start at about $70. The **Ramada Inn,** tel. (970) 522-2625, also just off the freeway, has rooms for two in the $50-60 range.

Buffalo Hills Camper Park, tel. (970) 522-2233, has tent and RV sites, laundromat, recreation room, and heated pool.

Food

A favorite hangout for local ranchers and merchants, the **J and L Café,** 423 N. 3rd, tel. (970) 522-3625, has been serving meals for nearly 40 years. A classic small-town cafe—its atmosphere defined by cigarette smoke and formica—the J and L serves breakfast, the meal it's best known for, all day. Steak and eggs are $4.50, German sausages $3.75, and hot cakes, rolls, and other standard fare run $2-4. For lunch, try **Fergie's,** 324 W. Main, tel. (970) 522-4220, a small bar and restaurant specializing in sandwiches (Italian subs and barbecue beef), soups, and nachos. Hours are Mon.-Fri. 11:30 a.m.-2 a.m. While you're waiting, amuse yourself with the *Far Side* cartoons on the back of the menu.

Cocina Alvarado, 713 W. Main, tel. (970) 522-8884, is an authentic Mexican restaurant, with daily specials running $4-6. There are also full-service restaurants at the **Ramada Inn,** tel. (970) 522-2625, and the **Best Western Sundowner Inn,** tel. (970) 522-6265.

Calendar

Among Sterling's annual events are the **Northeastern Junior College Rodeo** in May, **Hay Days** in June, the **Heritage Festival** July 4, the **Logan County Fair** in August, and **Sugar Beet**

Days the third weekend in September. For specific dates, contact the **Logan County Chamber of Commerce,** tel. (970) 522-5070 or (800) 544-8609, or the Northeastern Colorado Visitor Information Center at (800) 544-8609.

Services
Phone the **Sterling Police** at (970) 522-3512, the **Logan County Sheriff** at (970) 522-1373, and the **State Patrol** at (970) 522-4693 (Fort Morgan). **Sterling Regional MedCenter** is located at 615 Fairhurst, tel. (970) 522-0122. A larger facility, **Fort Morgan Community Hospital,** is in Fort Morgan at 1000 Lincoln, tel. (970) 867-3391. The main **post office** is at 306 Poplar, tel. (970) 522-1105.

Recycling
Recycle aluminum at **Pioneer Distributing,** 915 State St., tel. (970) 522-0706. **Disposal Services, Inc.,** 18211 Iris Dr., recycles aluminum and newspapers.

Information
The independently published *Journal-Advocate,* tel. (970) 522-1990, is Sterling's daily newspaper, a good source to get a feel of the town, as well as to find out about what's going on in the area, from movies to alfalfa fairs. Published weekday afternoons and Saturday mornings, the paper is available in racks around town.

You'll find a Northeastern Colorado **Visitor Information Center** just east of town between I-76 and the South Platte (across the street from the Overland Trail Museum). Pick up brochures and other information on Sterling, Logan County, and much of the northeastern corner of the state. Phone them at (970) 522-7649 or write Box 1683, Sterling, CO 80751.

The **Logan County Chamber of Commerce** is in Sterling at 109 N. Front St.; phone (970) 522-5070 or (800) 544-8609, or write Box 1683, Sterling, CO 80751.

The Sterling **public library,** tel. (970) 522-2023, is located at the corner of 5th and Walnut. For **road and weather information,** phone (970) 522-4848.

JULESBURG

If you're heading east on I-76, Julesburg will be the last you'll see of Colorado before lifting up over the border into Nebraska (two miles from town). At various times over the history of the region, the name Julesburg was given to three different communities in the same vicinity. It was finally affixed to the present townsite in 1881, when the town was founded as a division point on the main line of the Union Pacific Cutoff to Denver. Today, Julesburg is one of the area's major agricultural shipping stations.

The **Fort Sedgwick Depot Museum,** 202 W. 1st St., tel. (970) 474-2264, is open from the week before Memorial Day through the week after Labor Day and exhibits prehistoric and Native American artifacts, pioneer gear (from bullets and casings found at battle sites to hat pins and carriages), and historical photos. Hours are Mon.-Sat. 9:30 a.m.-4:30 p.m. and Sunday 11:30 a.m.-4:30 p.m. Tours are also offered by appointment; phone (970) 474-3682. Admission is $1 for adults, 50 cents for kids under 12. There's a nice picnic area right next door.

If you're looking to spend the night, you can get lodging at the **Platte Valley Inn Motel,** tel. (970) 474-3336. A popular local chow house is **Dan's Seafood and Steak House,** tel. (970) 474-3757, at the junction of I-76 and US 385.

HIGHWAY 34 TO NEBRASKA

BRUSH

Ten miles from Fort Morgan, where US 34 forks off of I-76 and shoots due east into the heart of the plains, Brush is a small plains town that has historically been dependent on agriculture and the local beef industry. Huge ranches and muddy stockyards packed with lowing cattle punctuate the surrounding prairie, and billboards claim Nothing Satisfies Like Beef. Ranchers in dusty Ford pickups, often with Queensland blue heelers or border collies in the back, zoom down highways and bump over rutted dirt back roads.

Named for Jared L. Brush, one of northeastern Colorado's pioneer cattlemen, Brush also relies heavily on agriculture, particularly sugar beets. The town itself is one of quiet streets shaded by huge numbers of fir, pine, and cedar trees, obviously not indigenous to the area and looking a bit incongruous against the prairie backdrop. You'll find free camping, with electrical hookups for RVs, at **Brush City Campground** (take Clayton St. four blocks south of US 34), as well as shaded lawns, picnic tables, playground equipment, a pool, showers, and restrooms. Brush's **Best Western Inn** is located at 1208 N. Colorado, tel. (970) 842-5146.

For more information on Brush, write the **Brush Area Chamber of Commerce,** 301 Edison St., Brush, CO 80723, or phone (970) 842-2666.

AKRON

About midway between Brush and Yuma, Akron has been a division point on the Burlington Railroad since 1882, when it was the only townsite on the line. Akron is the seat of Washington County. You'll find a picnic area with barbecue grills and restrooms at the corner of US 34 and Custer. Lodging is available at the **Crestwood Manor Motel,** tel. (970) 345-2231, and at the **4 B's Motel,** tel. (970) 345-2028.

YUMA

Incorporated in 1887, Yuma is located on the western edge of Yuma County, where the local economies are chiefly dependent on agriculture and ranching; Yuma County grows more corn than any other county in the state. Other crops include oats, winter rye, wheat, pinto beans, soybeans, sunflowers, and alfalfa. At one time, Yuma was known for the Federal Agricultural Experiment Station here, which developed new methods of soil conservation. Tourist information is available at the **Yuma Chamber of Commerce,** 413 S. Main St., tel. (970) 848-2704. The **Yuma Historical Society Museum,** at the corner of CO 59 and E. 3rd Ave., is open weekends only.

WRAY

Seat of Yuma County, Wray is a sort of oasis on the prairie flatlands: It's got actual hills, shaded with indigenous trees, and the North Fork of the Republican River tumbles through town. The **Wray Museum,** 205 3rd St., tel. (970) 332-5063, displays Native American arrowheads, barbed wire, local brands, a 1907 switchboard, dolls, and military uniforms and weapons. Hours are Tues.-Sat. 10 a.m.-5 p.m. Admission is $1.

Free tent camping is available at West City Park on US 34 on the west end of town, where you'll also find a picnic area with barbecue grills, a playground, and restrooms. You can get lodging in Wray at the **Butte Motel,** tel. (970) 332-4828, and the **Traveler's Inn,** tel. (970) 332-4848, both located on US 34 in town. The **Sandhiller Restaurant,** tel. (970) 332-4134, has an all-you-can-eat lunch buffet daily 11 a.m.-2 p.m. for $4.25. Dinners (chicken, steak, seafood) run $8-22. **Augustino's,** tel. (970) 332-3177, serves sandwiches, lasagna, stews, and chili for $2-4, and pizzas run $4-13; the salad bar is $4. There's a **Safeway** on the east end of town.

For more information on Wray, phone the chamber of commerce at (970) 332-4609. Tourist information is also available at the Butte Motel.

OTHER PLATTE RIVER CORRIDOR TOWNS

If you take US 6 from Fort Morgan up to Sterling and then continue on US 138 to Julesburg, you'll pass through a handful of intriguing little towns, including Merino, Atwood, Iliff, Proctor, Sedgwick, and Crook. If you want to get even more off the beaten path, you can explore CO 113 north (where you'll find the little town of Peetz, just a few miles from the Nebraska border), or US 6 east (where you'll pass through Fleming and Haxtun before arriving in Holyoke, the seat of Phillips County).

For specific information on any of these towns, call or write the **Centennial Country** branch of the Colorado Tourism Board, Box 1683, Sterling, CO 80751, tel. (800) 544-8609.

MERINO

Originally known as "Buffalo," and the site of the area's first school (1874), Merino was given its present name in 1881 by railroad workers who saw sheep grazing on the nearby plains. Though Merino is in the heart of traditional farming and ranching country, one ranch has animals you won't see on others. Ostriches, llamas, and draft and miniature horses are raised by the Vogt family, who will be happy to show you around if you call ahead; phone (970) 522-0936. Merino is also home to Brad Rhea, who does the "Living Trees" sculptures in Sterling.

ATWOOD

Just southeast of Atwood is the **Summit Springs Battlefield**, site of the last major battle between the United States Cavalry and the indigenous Plains people. On July 11, 1869, Cheyenne Chief Tall Bull and his warriors were attacked by eight companies of the Fifth Cavalry and 150 Pawnee scouts—the Cheyennes, in a last desperate attempt to fend off the encroaching whites, had kidnapped two white women on a "rampage" through Kansas. Fifty-two Cheyennes, including Tall Bull, were killed in the battle, and the soldiers took 12 Indian pris-

oners. According to reports, one of the kidnapped women was rescued, though the other died, having been tomahawked before the battle began.

PEETZ

Just south of the Nebraska border on CO 113, Peetz is a tiny community made up largely of ranchers and farmers who are descendants of the area's original white settlers. Though this part of Colorado is mostly flat prairie, grasslands seeming to roll oceanlike forever toward all horizons, the plain is broken up, and quite dramatically, about 15 miles west of Peetz. There, the plain breaks, and the Chimney Canyons rise, their mesa-tops towering 250 feet above the prairie, in stark contrast to their flat surroundings. To get there from Peetz, take County Rd. 74 west to 37, then 37 south to I-70 and go west again.

First settled in 1885, by homesteaders Peter Peetz and Nick Treinan, the town has a reputation for mischief that's belied by today's quiet community. Local legend has it early 20th-century residents, particularly those living in the area during Prohibition, were a fiercely independent folk and did not take kindly to the restrictions the feds attempted to levy on their lifestyles. Some say there was a "still over every hill." There's even a story of one woman who supposedly took out the backseat of her Model T, which she then filled with her homemade potables, making housecalls along the area's dusty country back roads. In keeping with the town's bibulous tradition, the **Hot Spot**, tel. (970) 334-2265, is a watering hole popular among locals throughout the county.

CROOK

Best known in the area for the **Tamarack Ranch State Wildlife Area,** a hunting and bird- and wildlife-watching refuge (wild turkeys, geese, pheasant, deer, antelope, etc.) on 7,000 acres of river-bottom land, Crook is another small ranching and farming community in the fertile Platte River valley. Two Overland Trail stage stops, Spring Hill and Lillian Springs stations, both designated with historical markers, are just outside Crook on the Tamarack Ranch. For more information on the Tamarack Ranch State Wildlife Area, phone (970) 671-4500 or (800) 365-2267.

In town, named for General George F. Crook, to whom Geronimo surrendered in New Mexico in 1866, you'll find the **Crook Museum**, tel. (970) 886-2782 or 886-2992. The museum dis-

plays pioneer artifacts, local brands and tack, and a gorgeous 19th-century rosewood piano originally purchased for 50 cents. The museum is open Sunday 2-4 p.m., Memorial Day to Labor Day, and by appointment. There's also a small community park and picnic area in Crook, as well as **Bobbi's Tavern**, tel. (970) 886-3241, which serves wild game (goose, wild turkey, antelope, etc.) in season. Another restaurant popular among locals is **Nelson's Cafe**, tel. (970) 886-2402.

HIGHWAY 6 TO NEBRASKA

FLEMING

Sitting 20 miles east of Sterling on US 6, Fleming was first settled in the 1880s and incorporated in 1917. Another agriculture-dependent small town, Fleming relies heavily on wheat, alfalfa, and corn. The town has two small museums of interest to passers-through. The **Fleming Heritage Museum and Park**, tel. (970) 265-2591, at the old Burlington Northern Train Depot, displays items of local historical interest (the park has restrooms, playground equipment, and picnic shelters). **Al's Country and Western Museum** has antique wagons, surreys, carriages, and automobiles. Ask locals for information on and directions to some of the area's first homesites: a rock house, "soddies" (early sod houses), and two homes ordered pre-cut from an early-20th-century Sears-Roebuck catalog.

HOLYOKE

Holyoke, at the junction of Highways 6 and 385, is a small town of beautiful brick homes with nicely maintained yards. Very young mothers push strollers along the sidewalks of sleepy, shady streets. *It's a Wonderful Life* could have been filmed here.

Just 15 miles from the Nebraska border, Holyoke, seat of Phillips County, is a hub for area ranchers and farmers; the main crops are alfafa, wheat, and corn. Passers-through will find two nice parks, one on the north end of town (on US 385), with a picnic area and kids' playground; the other, on the town's south end (also on US 385), is a bit bigger and also has tennis and basketball courts, and a swimming pool. You can get lodging at the **Cedar Motel**, tel. (970) 854-2525. For more information on Holyoke, write the Information Center at 100 Emerson, Holyoke, CO 80734, or phone (970) 854-3517.

EAST ON INTERSTATE 70

LIMON

Limon (rhymes with "rhymin'") is located in the heart of Colorado's "outback" about midway between the Rockies' Front Range and the Kansas border. If you're westbound on I-70, you can either continue on the interstate at Limon (pop. 1,800; elev. 5,360 feet) where it veers north toward Denver (about 75 miles), or you can catch US 24 and drop southwest to Colorado Springs (also about 75 miles).

Ordinarily a typically quiet little plains community, Limon roared and crashed and turned topsy-turvy for about 10 minutes one evening in the summer of 1990. On June 6, the skies over Colorado's plains began to darken and churn—not particularly unusual for that time of the year—and a series of tornadoes was reported touching down in remote plains locations. What was unusual that night, though, was the winds didn't settle down; they got angrier, and one of the tornadoes happened to choose to twist, moving slowly and forcefully, right through the middle of downtown Limon, demonically, like some hell-born evil bent on destruction, spitting hail and turning almost everything that had been Limon to rubble.

When the tornado was gone, so was most of the town: Homes had been slashed apart (70 mobile homes were destroyed). Town Hall totaled. Retail stores and banks leveled, or pummeled beyond recognition (23 businesses were destroyed). Cars upended, lifted clear off the ground, and dumped like toys in heaps. Crops and fields ruined (agricultural damage was estimated to be well over $1 million). Total damage: over $20 million.

As you'd expect in a small farming community such as Limon, the townspeople banded together, offering moral, emotional, and financial help to each other. The Salvation Army and the American Red Cross also helped out, as did Colorado grocery stores (including Albertson's, King Soopers, and Safeway) and other businesses, and Limon has mostly recovered. In fact, within weeks, most businesses (especially those on the edges of town, where the damage wasn't so severe) were back to normal operations. By late spring, 1991, even most of downtown had been rebuilt, and in June the governor came to dedicate "New" Limon.

Limon Heritage Museum and Railroad Park
Located in the original Limon depot of the Union Pacific Railroad, this small museum displays a wide range of artifacts relating to local history, including three box cars, an 18-foot-tall replica of a Cheyenne teepee, over 30 cowboy saddles, a reconstructed one-room schoolhouse. The museum, located at the corner of East Ave. and First St., is open daily in June, July, and August 1-8 p.m. Admission is free. Phone (719) 775-2373 for hours.

Practicalities
Passers-through looking for lodging in Limon have several options. The **Budget Host Silver Spur Motel,** tel. (719) 775-2807, and the **Preferred Motor Inn,** tel. (719) 775-2385 (both at Exit 361 off I-70), have rooms starting at $35. Downtown, the **Midwest Motel and Country Inn,** tel. (719) 775-2373, also has rooms for around $35.

For more information on points of interest, events, and services in the Limon area, write the **Limon Chamber of Commerce** at Box 101, Limon, CO 80828. Chamber Representative Harold Lowe can be reached at the Midwest Motel and Country Inn.

BURLINGTON

Thirteen miles from the Kansas border, Burlington (pop. 3,000; elev. 4,160 feet) is home to a historic carousel still offering rides to the public, and Old Town, a reconstructed frontier town featuring a museum and twenty historic buildings (some are restorations, some are new). Seat of Kit Carson County, Burlington was once the largest grain-shipping point between Omaha and Denver. If you're arriving from the east, be sure to stop at the **State Welcome Center** just off the interstate, where you can get brochures and information on the Burlington/Kit Carson County area, as well as on the rest of Colorado.

Kit Carson County Carousel

Built in 1905 by the Philadelphia Toboggan Company for Denver's Elitch Gardens (where it operated until sold to Kit Carson County in 1928), the carousel is a National Historic Landmark. Among the 46 hand-carved animals on whose backs you can ride are horses, giraffes, zebras, camels, goats, and a "hippocampus" (seahorse), all of which parade in lines of three to the robust and throaty music of a Wurlitzer Monster Military Band Organ, built in 1909. The details on the animals, including tigers' snarling mouths, lions' saddles adorned with cherubs, and a snake crawling up a giraffe's neck, are exquisite.

The Kit Carson County Carousel is open from Memorial Day to Labor Day 1-8 p.m. and is located at the Burlington Fairgrounds. A ride will set you back all of a quarter.

Old Town Museum

With melodrama, cancan girls, gunfights, and hayrides, as well as a saloon, drugstore, blacksmith shop, and bank, Burlington's Old Town Museum offers an attractive break from the tedium of long-haul cross-plains travel. (You can also take a wagon ride from Old Town to the Kit Carson County Carousel.)

In winter, Old Town Museum is open Mon.-Sat. 9 a.m.-6 p.m., and Sunday noon-6 p.m.; summer hours are extended. Admission is $4 adults, $3.50 for seniors, $2 ages 12-18, and $1 ages three to 11. For information, phone (800) 288-1344. Signs throughout town will direct you there.

Bonny State Recreation Area

About 22 miles north of Burlington off US 385, this 7,000-acre park offers picnicking, camping, fishing, birdwatching, and boating. Four different campgrounds (with 200 sites) range from rather primitive (pit toilets) to more developed (flush toilets, showers, and laundry facilities). Camping is free on weekdays; a small fee is charged on weekends. At the Bonny Marina, tel. (970) 354-7306, you can rent boats and buy fishing tackle, licenses, and groceries.

For more information on Bonny State Recreation Area, write Box 78-A, Idalia, CO 80735, or phone the Bonny Marina. You can also get information from the Colorado Division of Parks and Recreation, 1313 Sherman St. no. 618, Denver, CO 80203.

Accommodations

You'll find a handful of motels just off the interstate in Burlington. Try the **Burlington Super 8,** 2100 Fay, tel. (719) 346-5627 or (800) 843-1991; the **Burlington Inn,** 450 S. Lincoln, tel. (719) 346-5555; the **Kit Karson Motel,** 118 8th

Old Town Museum in Burlington

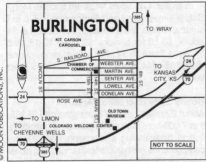

St., tel. (719) 346-8613; or the **Western Motor Inn,** 222 Rose Ave., tel. (719) 346-5371. You'll also find several campgrounds, suitable for either tents or RVs: **Campland,** 4th and Rose, tel. (719) 346-8763; and **Sloan's Trailer Park,** 1901 Rose, tel. (719) 346-5333.

Food

Like most out-in-the-middle-of-nowhere American towns, especially those that lie along interstates, Burlington has its share of fast-food restaurants—a Pizza Hut, Dairy Queen, Sonic Drive In, Arby's, and Burger King. You can also get decent grub at the **Hoof and Horn Restaurant,** tel. (719) 346-7107 (about a mile west of town on US 24); the **Interstate House,** tel. (719) 346-8010 (at the junction of I-70 and US 385—open 24 hours); and at the restaurant at the **Western Motor Inn,** tel. (719) 346-9974 (junction of US 24 and US 385). The **Main Street Donut and Deli** offers its wares at 415 14th Street.

Services

The **Burlington Police Department** is at 1394 Webster, tel. (719) 346-8353. The offices of the **State Police** are located at 179 Webster, tel. (719) 346-5430. **Kit Carson County Memorial Hospital** is at 286 16th St., tel. (719) 346-5311. The main **post office** is at 259 14th St., tel. (719) 346-8964.

Information

For more information on Burlington and Kit Carson County, contact the **Burlington Chamber of Commerce** at 415 15th St., Burlington, CO 80807, tel. (719) 346-8070. The **public library** is at 321 14th St., tel. (719) 346-8109.

pronghorn

BOB RACE

SOUTHEASTERN COLORADO

At first glance, Southeastern Colorado may appear much like the northeastern corner of the state. Both comprise vast prairie land stretching from the Rockies' Front Range to the state's eastern border, and both are primarily agricultural regions, divided by important waterways, which, with headwaters in the Rockies, eventually reach the Missouri-Mississippi River system and the Gulf of Mexico. A closer inspection, however, will reveal significant differences in the two eastern corners of Colorado—in their histories, people, and even in the geology and the composition of the prairie itself.

If you come into southeastern Colorado from the north, you'll note gradual changes in the flora of the plains. Its makeup shifts from waving wheat fields and rolling grasslands to desert stretches of yucca and sage, and the hills are dotted with juniper and piñon. This is the southwestern United States, and it looks a whole lot more like New Mexico than it does Kansas.

In addition, as you get farther south into Colorado, you'll find the proportion of people of Spanish descent increases dramatically. This is reflected in the region's place names (the towns of La Junta, Las Animas, Granada, and Campo, as well as Baca and Otero counties) and its cooking (you tend to see more authentic Mexican restaurants out this way than you do burger shacks). Why the change in demographics? Is it simply because you're that much closer to Mexico? In part, yes. But the reason's also historical: From the early 1820s until the late 1870s, the Santa Fe Trail cut across this part of Colorado, linking Santa Fe, New Mexico—then *old* Mexico's major northern trade center—with Independence, Missouri. Goods, and people, were transported along the rutted dirt highway, creating a natural amalgamation of cultures.

Settlement of Southeastern Colorado began in the late 1820s, when traders Ceran St. Vrain and Charles and William Bent built a trading post along the Santa Fe Trail between what are now

TO LIMON
AND DENVER

TO BURLINGTON

SOUTHEASTERN
COLORADO

71

40

287

385

40

94

PUNKIN
CENTER

CHEYENNE WELLS

TO OAKLEY

TO
COLORADO
SPRINGS

KIT CARSON

EADS

96

385

287

TO PUEBLO

96

ORDWAY

BENT'S
OLD
FORT

SANTA FE TRAIL

TO
GARDEN CITY

71

50

266

198

JOHN
MARTIN
DAM

LAMAR

GRANADA

ARKANSAS RIVER

50

ROCKY FORD

LAS
ANIMAS

JOHN MARTIN
RESERVOIR

KANSAS
COLORADO

LA JUNTA

10

287

TO WALSENBURG

385

COMANCHE
NATIONAL
GRASSLAND

109

350

TO TRINIDAD

TO DODGE CITY

0   15mi

0   15km

SPRINGFIELD

160

COMANCHE NATIONAL GRASSLAND

160

389

287

BRANSON

385

TO CLAYTON
AND AMARILLO

COLORADO
NEW MEXICO

COLORADO
OKLAHOMA

© MOON PUBLICATIONS, INC.

Crested Butte is one of the country's great ski towns.
(Crested Butte Mountain Resort Association, Grafton Marshall Smith)

(top) totally tubular, Fraser tubing hill north of Winter Park; (bottom) over the river and through the woods, near Redstone (both photos: Stephen Metzger) the cities of La Junta and Las Animas. A major hub of trading activity—for mountain men, Cheyennes, and Mexican and American troops—the outpost at one time employed over 100 men. The fort was abandoned in 1852, although it has since been reconstructed and is an excellent stop for modern travelers interested in the history of the West (see "Bent's Old Fort National Historic Site" under "Las Animas" following).

The railroad arrived in Southeastern Colorado in the 1870s, and during the 1880s the area was prime cattle-grazing country, with huge herds of longhorns roaming freely. It was largely this cattle-ization and railroad-ization of eastern Colorado that marked the end of the area as a wilderness populated by the great indigenous animals: Bison and bears fell victim to sharpshooters, government, and bounty hunters. "It was the livestock industry that finished off the grizzly [bear] in the more arid states," writes Doug Peacock in his excellent book *Grizzly Years*. "The principal reason given for killing grizzlies was protection of livestock. But few bears actually preyed on domestic animals, though the reprisals were always unrelenting and unforgiving. Bears were shot on sight out of ignorance, irrational hatred, and because of illusions about what constituted duty or sport."

By the early 20th century, the great cattle roundups had gone the way of the bison, wolf, grizzly, and Indian. Ranchers and farmers had turned to poultry, lamb, dairy cattle, and irrigated crops, particularly melons and sugar beets. Holly, after the sugar company of the same name, and Sugar City are both located in this part of the state.

In many ways, Southeastern Colorado has not changed much since its conversion from cattle-grazing country to agriculture. Melons and sugar beets are still primary crops, and the little towns and farming communities, miles and miles from the state's sprawling metropolitan centers and chic resort areas, remain slow paced, close knit, and timelessly and essentially yoked to the earth and their own landscape.

Travelers in Southeastern Colorado, though not afforded the mountain vistas and cultural centers of other parts of the state, can take advantage of several museums, including the restored Bent's Fort and a fascinating Native American museum in La Junta. In addition, motorists can follow the route of the Old Santa Fe Trail, from Holly, near the Kansas border, to Trinidad, where the route drops down into New Mexico. Campers and fisherpersons can explore the Arkansas River, as well as John Martin Reservoir, where the river is dammed, about midway between Las Animas and Lamar.

Before You Go

If you're coming into the area from the south, stop in Trinidad at the state welcome and tourist center, where you'll find information not only on Southeastern Colorado but on the rest of the state as well. Pick up brochures on everything from historical sites to recreation. There's also a welcome center in Burlington that provides lots of information on eastern Colorado. For information on specific towns and areas in Southeastern Colorado, contact the local chambers of commerce, whose phone numbers and addresses follow.

ARKANSAS RIVER CORRIDOR AND HIGHWAY 50

Dropping down out of the Rocky Mountains west of Pueblo and slicing across the Southeastern Colorado plains to the Kansas border, the 2,000-mile Arkansas River, which drains nearly 190,000 square miles, is the greatest tributary of the Missouri-Mississippi river system. US Highway 50 follows this main artery of Southeastern Colorado, passing through a number of small towns and communities, including Holly, about four and a half miles from the border, Lamar, Las Animas, and La Junta: US 50 and the Arkansas continue to run parallel west through Pueblo, Cañon City, and Salida, where the river drops down from its headwaters near Leadville.

LAMAR

Named for L.Q.C. Lamar, President Cleveland's Secretary of the Interior, Lamar (pop. 9,500; elev. 3,500 feet) still feels like the rowdy cowboy town it was during the late 19th and early 20th centuries. As late as 1928, four bank robbers rode into Lamar, held up the First National Bank (shooting the president and his son and kidnapping an employee, who was also eventually shot), and escaped with nearly a quarter of a million dollars.

Today Lamar is the seat of Prowers County, as well as home to Lamar Community College. In the fall, the town, which calls itself the "Goose Hunting Capital of the World," fills up with bird hunters, who pour into town by the barrel, fill

---

SOUTHEASTERN COLORADO HIGHLIGHTS

Bent's Old Fort: "living" museum in Santa Fe Trail fort dating from 1830s

La Junta: Native American and historical museums

John Martin Reservoir: fishing and camping

---

up most of the motels, and spend their days working the sprawling fields and wetlands.

Big Timbers Museum

Admission is free to this pioneer museum, named for a stretch of the Animas River where William Bent and company had camps during the height of their trading empire (see "Bent's Old Fort National Historic Site" following). In addition to historical photos, you'll find an array of domestic tools and equipment, as well as clothing from the mid-19th century. The museum is open daily 1:30-4:30 p.m. It's located at 7515 US 50 just north of Lamar. Phone (719) 336-2472 for more information.

Practicalities

The nicest lodging in town is the **Cow Palace Inn Best Western,** 1301 N. Main, tel. (719) 336-7753. Doubles start at about $60. You'll find less expensive rooms (doubles about $35) at the **El Mar Motel,** 1210 S. Main, tel. (719) 336-4331. The dining room at the **Cow Palace Inn** has good food at reasonable prices. **Ranchers 24-Hour Family Restaurant,** tel. (719) 336-3445, at the Lamar Truck Plaza, three miles west of town at the junction of US 50 and 287, serves BIG truckers' breakfasts for $2-5, sandwiches and burgers for $3-6, and there's a soup and salad bar. Sunday hours are limited 11 a.m.-2 p.m., while Friday evenings you can find Mexican specialties on the menu.

The Lamar **KOA** campground, tel. (719) 336-7625, is located about five miles west of town on US 50. **Hud's Campground,** tel. (719) 829-4344, about 15 miles west of Lamar, has nice RV sites in the shade of cottonwoods as well as a small grocery store. Sites with full hookups are $14.

Services

The offices of the **Lamar Police Department** are located at 505 Main St., tel. (719) 336-4341. Reach the **Prowers County Sheriff** at (719) 336-5234 and the **State Patrol** at (719) 336-7403. **Prowers Medical Center** may be found

LAMAR

LAMAR TRUCK PLAZA

TO LAS ANIMAS
AND LIMON

COW PALACE INN

50
287

MAPLE ST.

8th ST.
7th ST.
6th ST.
5th ST.
4th ST.
3rd ST.
2nd ST.

BEECH ST.

CHAMBER OF
COMMERCE/VISITOR
INFORMATION CENTER

50

TO
GARDEN CITY

← TO THE AIRPORT

OAK ST.

PARMENTER ST.

MAIN ST.

14th ST.

EL MAR MOTEL

FORT BENT ST.

TO SPRINGFIELD
AND AMARILLO

MEMORIAL DR.

287

NOT TO SCALE
NOTE: ONLY MAIN
ROADS SHOWN

© MOON PUBLICATIONS, INC.

at 2101 S. Memorial Drive, tel. (719) 336-4343. The central **post office** is at 300 S. 5th St., tel. (719) 336-4421.

Recycling

Recycle aluminum at the **Safeway,** 405 E. Olive St., and aluminum and glass at the **Lamar Area Hospice,** 1001 S. Main.

Information

The **Lamar Chamber of Commerce** is downtown at 109-A E. Beech St, tel. (719) 336-4379.

The **public library** is at 104 E. Parmenter, tel. (719) 336-4632. Tourist information is also available from the KOA campground west of town.

LAS ANIMAS

US Highway 50 beelines due west for 30 miles from Lamar to Las Animas, following the courses of the Arkansas River, the Santa Fe Trail, and the Atchison, Topeka, and Santa Fe Railroad. Not a whole lot to look at along here—mostly dry, brown, and flat—though you can pull off at John Martin Reservoir to camp or do some warm-water fishing. Also watch along the highway for communities of prairie dogs.

Las Animas (pop. 2,800; elev. 3,900 feet) was founded in 1869 at the confluence of the Arkansas and Purgatoire rivers and near the site of Fort Lyon, a U.S. Army post built in 1860 to house cavalry troops and to protect Santa Fe Trail travelers. Between the mid-1870s and about 1915, the Las Animas area was the scene of huge cattle roundups, though the region has long been rich in agriculture as well. As early as 1866, Thomas O. Boggs and John Prowers were experimenting with irrigated crops on a farm two miles south of present-day Las Animas. Boggsville, as the community came to be known, eventually became a regional center for cattle, sheep, and a variety of crops, and it was the first seat of Bent County. Kit Carson died in 1868 in a cabin in Las Animas and was buried near Bent's Fort with his third wife, Maria Josefa Jaramarillo, though their remains were later moved to Taos, New Mexico. The abandoned Boggsville was acquired in 1985 by the Pioneer Historical Society of Bent County, which is in the process of restoring the community.

Kit Carson Museum

If you think this place is odd to look at, with the word "MUSEUM" spelled out on letters atop tall poles, like an advertisement for some tacky motel, get a load of the building's history: Built of adobe in 1940, it originally housed German prisoners of war captured in North Africa. After the war, it was home to Jamaican field workers, and later became a home for widows and the poor. Don't expect upscale displays here with high-tech dioramas and fancy collections. This is a pioneer museum pure and simple. Wander through the historical displays of the main building—Native American artifacts, early farming equipment, domestic gear. Then wander out back to the several historical buildings that have been moved onto the site: the first Las Animas jail, built in 1882; the original Bent County Jail; an 1860s log stage station, originally located between Bent's Fort and Pueblo; a one-room school; a blacksmith shop; and a carriage house. Be sure to check out the replica of the gallows in the field across the street from the museum.

Kit Carson Museum is open Memorial Day through Labor Day and is located on 9th St. near the junction of US 50 and Colorado 101. Watch for the sign (you can't miss it). For more information, phone the Las Animas/Bent County Chamber of Commerce at (719) 456-0453.

John Martin Reservoir and Lake Hasty

Located about 15 miles east of Las Animas, this large reservoir and smaller, nearby lake offer a variety of water sports, as well as sightseeing, picnicking, and camping, with lots of very nice campsites right on the water. Originally part of a federal flood-control and irrigation project, the dam was completed in 1946. It's over two miles long and rises over 100 feet above the river; the spillway is over 1,000 feet

The familiar Canada goose; look for them near water.

long. Seventy-five-acre Lake Hasty is immediately downstream and was formed when earth was moved to build the dam.

Stop in at the visitor center in the Project Office, where you can pick up maps and other information about the facilities. Tours can also be arranged by calling in advance. For information, or to book tours, phone (719) 336-3476, or write John Martin Reservoir Resident Office, U.S. Army Engineers, Star Route, Hasty, CO 81044.

Bent's Old Fort National Historical Site

Anyone with even a moderate interest in history will find this fort absolutely fascinating, definitely one of the highlights of a visit to this part of the state. Completed in 1833, the adobe fort was for nearly 20 years a critical trading hub—the most important stop between Independence, Missouri, and Santa Fe, New Mexico—where Native Americans, mountain men, U.S. Army troops, and Mexican soldiers gathered to swap furs, manufactured goods, and tales of life in the rugged West, as they swigged the notorious Taos Lightning.

The trading company was the brainchild of two brothers, Charles and William Bent, along with Ceran St. Vrain, the three of whom had left St. Louis to make their fortunes in fur trading. William Bent, historians tell us, was unusually sensitive to the Native Americans, whose lands their trading empire encompassed (Southern Cheyenne, Arapahoe, Ute, Northern Apache, Kiowa, and Comanche). The business-savvy William went to great lengths to ensure the post saw large numbers of traders; he encouraged rival tribes to make peace with each other, and in 1837 he even married a Cheyenne woman, apparently to look better in the eyes of potential native traders.

By the late 1840s, Santa Fe Trail trade was already on the wane—due to the Mexican-American War, increasing native uprisings, Charles's death in Taos, St. Vrain's departure, and finally, in 1849, cholera, which decimated the tribes upon which William relied for trade.

Bent's Old Fort has been restored to approximate its 1830s prime, and it's one of the best examples in the West of a "living museum." A costumed guide takes visitors through the fort's many rooms—blacksmith's shop, military and trappers' quarters, billiard room, and warehouse—while employees, also in costume, quietly go about their work, as though it were a

Don't miss Bent's Old Fort between Las Animas and La Junta.

century and a half earlier. Be sure to check out the orientation film before going through the fort (if only to hear the attempt at a French accent by whoever's doing the voice of Ceran St. Vrain).

The fort is open daily 8 a.m.-5 p.m., Memorial Day through Labor Day, and 9 a.m.-4 p.m. the rest of the year. Closed New Year's Day, Thanksgiving, and Christmas. Admission is $2. To get there take CO 194 or US 50 west from Las Animas, or US 50 east from La Junta, and watch for the signs. A 200-yard paved walkway leads from the parking lot to the fort; rides are provided for disabled visitors. For more information, phone (719) 384-2596, or write 35110 US 194 East, La Junta, CO 81050-9523.

Practicalities

In addition to a handful of independently run motels in Las Animas, you can get rooms at the **Best Western Bent's Fort Inn,** 10950 US 50, tel. (719) 456-0011; doubles run about $40. The **Troll Haus Restaurant,** 616 Locust, tel. (719) 456-0062, is a local favorite.

Services

The **Las Animas Police Department** is located at 326 Prowers Court, tel. (719) 456-1313. Contact the **Bent County Sheriff** at (719) 456-1363 and the **State Patrol** at (719) 384-2562 (La Junta). The nearest hospital is the **Arkansas Valley Regional Medical Clinic** in La Junta at 1100 Carson Dr.; phone (719) 456-2088 from Las Animas, (719) 384-5412 from La Junta. The Las Animas **post office** is at 513 W. 6th St., tel. (719) 456-0310.

Recycling

Recycle aluminum and glass in La Junta at **Greenstreet Distributing Company,** 706 E. 1st St. (call ahead: 719-384-8761), or at **Safeway,** 315 W. 2nd Street.

Information

For more information on the Las Animas area, write **Las Animas/Bent County Chamber of Commerce,** 332 Ambassador Thompson Blvd., Las Animas, CO 81054, or phone (719) 454-0453. In town, stop by the Las Animas **public library** at 308 W. 5th St., tel. (719) 456-0111.

LA JUNTA

Seat of Otero County, La Junta (Spanish for "The Junction," though mispronounced La-HUNT-a) is located about 20 miles west of Las Animas, at the junction of the old Navajo and Santa Fe trails. At La Junta (pop. 7,600; elev. 4,050), US 350, following the Santa Fe Trail, splits off US 50 and drops down through the Comanche National Grassland to Trinidad. La Junta is also at the junction of the Santa Fe Railroad's main line and its Denver branch, and so has long been an important shipping town. It was founded in 1875 and originally called Otero, after Spanish settler Miguel Otero.

One of the prettier towns on the southeastern plains, La Junta is characterized by huge hillside homes and nicely kept lawns and gardens. Its city park is perfect for a picnic and/or an afternoon snooze.

FORT MORGAN

SOUTH PLATTE RIVER

CANFIELD RECREATION AREA
RIVERSIDE PARK
76
TO STERLING
TO DENVER

W. RIVERVIEW AVE.   E. RIVERVIEW AVE.

W. 7th AVE.   MAIN ST.   STATE ST.   E. 7th AVE.

W. PLATTE AVE.   E. PLATTE ST. AVE
                                        WARNER

CITY LIBRARY
AND MUSEUM

NOT TO SCALE

NOTE: ONLY MAIN
ROADS SHOWN

© MOON PUBLICATIONS, INC.

Koshare Indian Museum

It might be tempting to zip through La Junta without stopping, but it'd be a shame to miss this wonderful museum. Among the highlights are Crow, Cree, Shoshone, and Flathead buckskin clothing, moccasins, and hide paintings, in addition to Zuni pottery, Hopi, Zuni, and Navajo silver, Hopi Katchina, and Hupa baskets. There's also a full-size model of a kiva, where a local Boy Scout troop performs authentic Native American dances Saturday evenings in the summer and during holidays (the group started in the 1930s and has earned a national reputation for itself, performing around the country). A gift shop sells quality Native American artwork, as well as souvenirs and knicknacks.

The museum is open Tues.-Sat. 10 a.m.-5 p.m. and Sunday 12:30-5 p.m. June-Aug., and Tues.-Sat. 12:30-4:30 p.m. the rest of the year. Admission is $2 for adults, with discounts for seniors and kids. It's located on the Otero Junior College campus. Take Santa Fe Ave. south to 18th St. (Santa Fe is interrupted by the city park; circle around it). Small entrance fee. For more information, phone (719) 384-4411, or write 115 W. 18th St., Box 580, La Junta, CO 81050.

Otero Museum

This pioneer museum, located in a turn-of-the-century building listed on the National Register of Historic Places, displays artifacts from the area's history, emphasizing the arrival of the railroad and the development of agriculture. Exhibits include grocery items (the building was originally a grocery store), farming and ranching tools and equipment, and even a mid-19th-century stagecoach.

The museum, located at 2nd and Anderson, is open daily 1-5 p.m. June through September. Phone (719) 384-7500 for more information.

City Park

Just north of the Koshare Museum and Otero Junior College is a large city park with hilly lawns, shade, picnic tables, and a large pond.

Practicalities

You'll find a handful of motels and inns in La Junta. For about $50 you can get a double at the **Days Inn**, US 50 W, tel. (719) 384-4408, and at the **Quality Inn**, 1325 E. 3rd St., tel. (719) 384-2571.

Predictably, there are *muchos restaurantes Mexicanos* in La Junta. Try **El Azteca**, 710 W. 3rd. St., tel. (719) 384-4215; **El Cid**, 1617 Ratón Ave., tel. (719) 384-9818; or **Felicia's**, 27948 Frontage Rd., tel. (719) 384-4814. There's also a McDonald's, Kentucky Fried Chicken, and K-Bob's Steak House.

Services

You can reach the **La Junta Police** at (719) 384-2525, the **Otero County Sheriff** at (719) 384-5941, and the **Colorado State Patrol** at (719) 384-8981. La Junta's **Arkansas Valley Regional Medical Center** is located at 1100 Carson Ave., tel. (719) 384-5412. The main **post office** is at 4th and Colorado, tel. (719) 384-5944.

Recycling

Recycle aluminum and glass at **Colorado Beverage,** 706 E. 1st St., tel. (719) 384-8761 (call ahead), and aluminum at **Safeway,** 315 W. 2nd Street.

Information

La Junta's **Woodruff Memorial Library** is located at 522 Colorado Ave., tel. (719) 384-4612. The **La Junta Chamber of Commerce** may be found at 110 Santa Fe Ave., tel. (719) 384-7411. Check the **Book Stop,** 318 Santa Fe, tel. (719) 384-8839, for books of local interest.

WEST OF LA JUNTA

If you've been out poking around on the eastern plains you're probably growing a bit weary of all the flatness and barrenness and seeming nothingness. Driving west out of La Junta, then, offers cheap thrills. To wit: an actual, bona fide view of mountains. Yes, whether you take US 50 to Pueblo, CO 10 to Walsenburg, or US 350 to Trinidad, somewhere about a half hour out of La Junta (sooner on clear days) you see them: the Rockies, looming snowcapped in the distance. Truly a sight for sore eyes.

The 65-mile stretch of US 50 from La Junta to Pueblo takes you through a handful of small farming towns and communities, including Swink, Rocky Ford, Manzanola, Fowler, and Avondale. Pueblo sits at the foot of the Front Range, and from there it's just a half-hour or so before you're winding up into some serious mountains.

Rocky Ford

This little agricultural community, about 15 miles west of La Junta, is known nationwide for its melons. The Rocky Ford cantaloupe, particularly, but locally grown watermelons as well, attract buyers from throughout the country. Each summer, in mid-August, Rocky Ford hosts the Arkansas Valley Fair, which celebrates the region's multicultural heritage and agricultural harvests.

Information

For more information on Rocky Ford or the Arkansas Valley Fair, write the **Rocky Ford Chamber of Commerce,** 105 N. Main St., Rocky Ford, CO 81067, or phone (719) 254-7483.

La Junta to Walsenburg and Trinidad

From La Junta to Walsenburg it's about 75 miles, the drive straight and unbroken, with little to amuse, save for two exciting crosses over county lines. Best, then, simply to get on with it.

La Junta to Trinidad is about an 80-mile drive, US 350 following the Santa Fe Trail southwest then dropping nearly due south at Trinidad and the junction with I-25. From there it's just 90 miles to Ratón Pass and the New Mexico border. In fact, along this stretch of US 350 the landscape begins to look even more Southwestern, the brown bluffs and mesas dotted with yucca and cane cholla. Then, just about 15 miles out of Trinidad, the flora turns dramatically green, the valleys lush and fertile. Readers heading on to New Mexico and heartbroken about having to glovebox the witty traveling companion that has guided them thus far, or those simply intrigued with the mystery and seductiveness of that wonderful state, would do well to invest 15 bucks in the critically acclaimed *New Mexico Handbook,* by yours truly (and humbly); it's available at your local bookstore, or from Moon Publications, P.O. Box 3040, Chico, CA 95927, tel. (916) 345-5473.

Anasazi pottery

BOB RACE

SOUTH CENTRAL COLORADO

The diversity of South Central Colorado makes it in a very real sense a microcosm of the rest of the state. This one region, stretching north from the New Mexico border to Colorado Springs and Fairplay and west from the Great Plains to the towering Rocky Mountains, offers fascinating lessons in the state's geology, history, and demographics, as well as myriad sightseeing and recreation opportunities.

South Central Colorado is split lengthwise by I-25, which crosses over from New Mexico at Ratón Pass, then follows the plains' western edge north through Trinidad, Pueblo, and Colorado Springs, and continues on through Denver and up into northern Wyoming. US Highway 50 bisects I-25 at Pueblo, cutting east to west across South Central Colorado from the plains up into the foothills of the Cañon City area and then on to Salida, Gunnison, Grand Junction, and west to California. Just north of the New Mexico border, between Del Norte and the Sangre de Cristo Mountains, is the San Luis

Valley, a 50- by 125-mile pocket of austere beauty surrounded by mountains—the San Juans, Sangre de Cristos, La Garitas, and Conejos-Brazos.

This was the first part of Colorado to be explored by nonnative peoples. Perhaps as early as the mid-16th century, Spanish expeditions were pushing up from the south. San Luis, a small community a half-hour from the New Mexico border at the junction of CO 159 and CO 142, is the oldest town in the state. Because the Spanish were the first to explore and settle this area, it still maintains its Hispanic heritage—evident in its architecture, cooking, folk art, and the surnames of a large proportion of the people.

In the mid-19th century, South Central Colorado was the scene of important mining activity. The mines of Cripple Creek, in the high mountains west of Colorado Springs, produced millions of dollars in gold and silver and made fortunes for their owners, who built palatial homes,

SOUTH CENTRAL COLORADO

TO DENVER

285

CONTINENTAL DIVIDE

FAIRPLAY

25

67

24

87

85

FLORISSANT

WOODLAND PARK

MANITOU SPRINGS

TO LIMON

TO LEADVILLE

24

FLORISSANT FOSSIL BEDS NAT'L MONUMENT

PIKES PEAK (14,110 ft.)

TO HWYS. 40 AND 287 →

94

COLORADO SPRINGS

CRIPPLE CREEK

VICTOR

PHANTOM CANYON RD.

115

285

50

SALIDA

ROYAL GORGE

CAÑON CITY

FLORENCE

67

LAKE PUEBLO STATE RECREATION AREA

PUEBLO

TO LA JUNTA

SANGRE DE CRISTO RANGE

69

96

25

50

TO GUNNISON

114

96

SAGUACHE

17

WESTCLIFFE

SILVER CLIFF

COLORADO CITY

165

10

GREAT SAND DUNES NAT'L MONUMENT

69

GARDNER

TO LA JUNTA

MONTE VISTA

285

160

150

WALSENBURG

160

350

TO PAGOSA SPRINGS

ALAMOSA

LA VETA

25

160

239

FORT GARLAND

87

SAN LUIS

12

TO SANTA FE

142

ANTONITO

285

TO TAOS

159

TO SANTA FE

160

TRINIDAD

COLORADO
NEW MEXICO

0   20mi

0   20km

© MOON PUBLICATIONS, INC.

opera houses, and resorts in Denver and Colorado Springs.

Today South Central Colorado offers the traveler lots to see and do. Drive up to the top of Pikes Peak. Visit the United States Air Force Academy or ProRodeo Hall of Fame in Colorado Springs. Explore the old mining towns of Victor and Cripple Creek, or a stretch of the Old Santa Fe Trail. Camp in the gorgeous San Isabel and Pike national forests. Take a narrow-gauge train over into New Mexico. Wander into the tallest sand dunes in the country. Or just enjoy some of the prettiest scenery in the state.

Before You Go

If you're coming in from the south, stop at the **Colorado Welcome Center** in Trinidad, 309 N. Nevada Ave., tel. (719) 846-9512. You'll find a friendly staff and lots of information and brochures on things to do and see in the area, as well as the rest of the state. The center, open daily 8 a.m.-6 p.m., also provides information about lodging and camping. Be sure to pick up a copy of *Spirit: The Magazine of Southern Colorado.*

TRINIDAD

Situated just east of the Sangre de Cristo ("Blood of Christ") Mountains and 20 miles from the New Mexico border, Trinidad (pop. 9,500; elev. 6,025 feet), seat of Las Animas County, maintains a strong sense of its Spanish heritage. Its narrow, hilly brick streets, stone churches, and mellow, Old-World pace, as well as the nearby place names (Segundo, Aguilar, Isabel, Cuchara, La Veta) indicate the town's ties to the Spanish Colonial era and, later, to the period when the surrounding area was part of the Territory of New Mexico.

The hub of several highways, Trinidad is a funny town to drive in, as I-25, US 160 and 350, and CO 12 and 239, not to mention the railroad, all convene near the river, winding linguine-like before heading out again in their different direc-

tions. The downtown area, Corazón de Trinidad ("Heart of Trinidad"), is an excellent spot to spend a few hours poking around and getting a feel for a part of the state that's very different from the resort towns and sprawling urban centers to the north. Also, take a few minutes to drive up into the hills on Trinidad's east side above the Pioneer Museum; the brick streets are truly unique and add a distinct flavor to the little town.

HISTORY

The Trinidad area, including the Sangre de Cristos and the Purgatoire River Valley, was long a hunting and ceremonial ground for various Indian tribes, and though the town was never actually attacked, early European settlers were accustomed to threats by Ute war parties. Long before the Comanches, Utes, and other groups arrived, prehistoric people lived in caves and crude shelters in the nearby hills.

Shortly after 1598, when Juan de Oñate arrived in the Santa Fe area from Spain, he led a group north into the Purgatoire River Valley. Over the next two centuries, Spanish priests, explorers, and soldiers continued to probe the area north of Santa Fe, and between 1822 and the late 1870s, Trinidad was the last stop on the Santa Fe Trail before Ratón Pass and the drop down into Santa Fe.

On May 13, 1847, the United States declared war on Mexico, and a month later, Stephen Watts Kearny, after passing through what is now Trinidad, arrived in Santa Fe and took control of that town without resistance. In 1859, New Mexican Gabriel Gutierrez came north to Trinidad to herd sheep, and his cabin was the first building of record.

Gradually, Trinidad saw more and more settlers, at first mostly from the south. Soon, though, people began to arrive from the north as well, and for a time the rambunctious town seemed to symbolize the larger frictions between the United States and Mexico; fights between the two groups were commonplace. On Christmas Day, 1867, nearly a thousand people took part in a rumble of sorts, which resulted in several deaths and could only be brought under control by the U.S. cavalry, who declared martial law. That year also saw the opening of Trinidad's first coal mine.

The arrival of the railroad in the late 1870s helped encourage cattle ranchers to come to the area, boosting the local economy; the town was incorporated in 1877. On April 20, 1914, striking coal workers, with support from the United Mine Workers, battled U.S. militiamen, who had been called in to keep the peace. During the ensuing gunfight, which took place about 12 miles north of Trinidad, six coal miners were shot, and 11 children and two women killed when the tent in which they were hiding burned. (If you find this period of history interesting or are *horses grazing in the Purgatoire River Valley near Weston on CO 12*

intrigued by the early American labor movement, see Peter Weir's excellent film *Matewan,* which, based on a true story, examines the deplorable working conditions in the mines and the resistance labor organizers met when they tried to improve them.)

The United Mine Workers of America erected a monument near the Ludlow Exit north of Trinidad in recognition of those killed. In June 1990, the 100th anniversary of the founding of the UMWA, labor leaders from around the country gathered at the site of the monument to commemorate the massacre.

MUSEUMS

Trinidad History Museum

This three-museum complex occupies the 300 block of E. Main Street. A small entrance fee gets you a guided tour of all three buildings.

The **Baca House,** made of adobe and dating from 1869, is the oldest still-standing building in Trinidad. Built by Pennsylvanian John S. Hough and sold a year later to Felipe Baca, a Spanish sheep rancher, shipping tycoon, and politician, the house has been redecorated with period furnishings.

The 13-room **Bloom House** is reportedly the state's best example of Second Empire French architecture; it was built in 1882 for cattle rancher and banker Frank L. Bloom. All of the furnishings in the mansion are either originals or exact duplicates. Bloom House highlights include elaborate draperies and wallpapers and a Victorian garden, complete with waterfall.

Occupying what were once the stables and servants' quarters for the Baca House, Trinidad's **Pioneer Museum** displays an array of artifacts from the Santa Fe Trail and from Trinidad's past, including Indian arrowheads, carriages, guns, and historical photos.

The museum complex is open May 1-Sept. 30, Mon.-Sat. 10 a.m.-4 p.m. and Sunday 1-4 p.m.; Oct. 1-April 30 by appointment only. For information on all three museums, write 300 E. Main St., Trinidad, CO 81082, or phone (719) 846-7217.

Louden-Henritze Archaeology Museum

Housed in the library of Trinidad State Junior College, this small museum features dioramas of nearby Trinchera Cave, which was occupied thousands of years ago by nomadic hunters. The museum also displays arrowheads, fossils, and samples of local gems and minerals. Some of the artifacts come from a 1962 excavation of hundreds of sites now deep beneath the waters of Trinidad Reservoir.

The museum is open daily June-Aug., 12-4 p.m. Admission is free. For more information, phone (719) 846-5508.

Trinidad Children's Museum

Located in an old firehouse, which was also the town's first city hall and jail, this is a museum full of hands-on displays, including a firecart, fire engine, and primitive alarm system.

The museum, at 314 N. Commercial Street, is open June-Aug., Mon.-Fri. 10 a.m.-2 p.m. Admission is free. For more information, or to book tours, phone (719) 846-7721 or 846-8418.

A.R. Mitchell Memorial Museum and Gallery

Famous for his Western paintings, as well as the scores of covers he did for Western dime novels, Arthur Roy Mitchell died in 1977. The Trinidad gallery displays some 200 of his original oils, in addition to work by other Western-style painters, including Harvey Dunn and Grant Reynard. The museum also exhibits a collection of Spanish folk art, and a gift shop sells jewelry, paintings, cards, and souvenirs. Admission to the museum, at 150 E. Main, is free. Hours are Mon.-Sat. 10 a.m.-4 p.m., mid-April through September. For more information, phone (719) 846-4224.

PARKS AND RECREATION

City Parks

Kit Carson Park, northwest of the downtown area at San Pedro St. and Kansas Ave., has picnic facilities, lawns, shade trees, and a playground, as well as a turn-of-the-century bandstand and a statue of Carson. **Central Park,** west of I-25 at Stonewall and San Juan, has softball fields, a small lake, picnic tables, a playground, and a jogging trail. **Southside Park,** on Benshoar Dr., has a jogging trail, horseshoe pits, softball fields, picnic tables, and a playground. For more information, phone the Trinidad Community Center at (719) 846-4454.

Trinidad Lake State Recreation Area

This 2,300-acre park, with a 900-acre lake, about four miles west of Trinidad on CO 12, offers a wide range of recreational activities, including hiking, fishing, boating, picnicking, swimming, and camping (tenting and RVing). You'll find 62 campsites, running water, flush toilets, and hot showers, as well as laundry and RV-dumps. Fish for rainbow and brown trout, largemouth bass, channel catfish, bluegill, walleye, and crappie. Two short nature trails (Carpios Ridge Trail, one mile, and Levsa Canyon Trail, 1.5 miles) have been laid out for hikers.

For more information on Trinidad Lake State Recreation Area, write 32610 US 12, Trinidad, CO 81082, or phone (719) 846-6951. Call to reserve campsites or group picnic areas. You can also get information from the **Colorado Division of Parks and Outdoor Recreation,** Department of Natural Resources, 1313 Sherman no. 618, Denver, CO 80203, tel. (303) 866-3437.

State Highway 12
and San Isabel National Forest

State Highway 12, which winds west out of Trinidad, up into the gorgeous Sangre de Cristo Mountains of San Isabel National Forest, over 9,941-foot Cucharas Pass, then back down through La Veta and into Walsenburg, offers excellent camping (three Forest Service campgrounds lie just east of Cucharas Pass) and fishing opportunities, as well as spectacular sightseeing. The 82-mile drive is discussed in detail under "North to Walsenburg Via Highway 12" following. Monument Lake Resort, about 35 miles west of Trinidad, is owned by the city. For further information on San Isabel National Forest, write 1920 Valley Dr., Pueblo, CO 81008, or phone (719) 545-8737.

Golf

The **Trinidad Municipal Golf Course,** tel. (719) 846-4015, just south of town, is a nine-hole course open year-round and sponsors various local tournaments.

PRACTICALITIES

Accommodations

A **Days Inn,** tel. (719) 846-2271, is just off I-25 (Exit 13B) and has doubles starting around $60. Doubles at the **Best Western Country Club Inn,** tel. (719) 846-2215, Exit 13A, will run $45-65 depending on the season. There's also a **Holiday Inn,** tel. (719) 846-4491 or (800) HOLIDAY; take Exit 11. Downtown at the corner of Main and University, the **Inn on the Santa Fe Bed and Breakfast,** tel. (719) 846-4636, offers seven rooms in a converted 19th-century brick building that served as medical offices throughout much of the early 20th century. All rooms have private baths; rates are $45 for one, $65 for two.

Food

For Mexican food, try **El Capitan**, 321 State St., tel. (719) 846-9903, and **Maria's**, 219 W. Main St., tel. (719) 846-4962. **Aspen Court**, 220 W. Pine, tel. (719) 846-2000, Trinidad's most upscale restaurant, serves rack of lamb, seafood, pastas, and steaks, as well as Sunday brunch ($10.95); the restaurant claims to have the "most extensive wine list in a 150-mile radius." You can get Italian food at **Nana and Nano's Pasta House,** 415 University St., tel. (719) 846-2697, over on the west side of town en route to Trinidad Lake. Right next door, **Monteleone's Deli** sells homemade Italian sandwiches (meatball, Italian sausage, etc.).

Calendar

Each June (usually around the second weekend), Trinidad sponsors the **Santa Fe Trail Festival,** featuring arts-and-crafts shows, costume competitions, and lots of food and live entertainment. There's also a staged melodrama. For information and exact dates, contact the chamber of commerce (309 Nevada St., tel. 846-9285).

Services

The offices of the **Trinidad Police Department,** tel. (719) 846-4441, and the **Las Animas County Sheriff,** tel. (719) 846-2211, are downtown next to city hall on N. Animas. Reach the **Colorado State Patrol** in Trinidad at (719) 846-2227. **Mt. San Rafael Hospital** is at 410 Benedicta, tel.

(719) 846-9213. The main **post office** is at 301 E. Main, tel. (719) 846-6871.

Recycling

Recycle aluminum at the **Las Animas County Rehabilitation Center,** 1205 Congress Dr., and at **Safeway,** 457 W. Main.

Information

In addition to the Colorado Welcome Center in Trinidad, you'll find a Trinidad **visitor center,** in the train caboose in the parking lot between Safeway and city hall. Pick up information on recreation, dining, lodging, as well as maps of the area and of a self-guided historical walking tour. Write the **Trinidad Chamber of Commerce** at 309 Nevada St., Trinidad, CO 81082, or phone (719) 846-9285.

Trinidad's historical **Carnegie Public Library** is at 202 N. Animas, tel. (719) 846-6841. Pick up Trinidad's daily newspaper, the *Chronicle-News,* tel. (719) 846-3311, for listings of current events and other happenings.

For **road conditions,** phone (719) 846-9262.

Transportation

Although Trinidad's a weird town to drive in, with all the different highways converging, the downtown area is pretty square and easy to walk. To make it even easier to get around, the city offers the **Trinidad Trolley,** with stops at parks and historical sites. Departures are hourly from the parking lot next to the city hall (summer only).

pika

NORTH TO WALSENBURG VIA HIGHWAY 12

Though this route will take you at least an hour and a half out of your way (I-25 to Walsenburg takes 40 minutes, max), this scenic byway, one of the prettiest in the state, is definitely worth the extra time. The highway first drops southwest out of Trinidad, passes Trinidad Lake State Recreation Area and the historical mining town of Cokedale, winds through the lush Purgatoire River Valley, then begins to climb up into the high mountains, offering breathtaking vistas along the way. You'll pass through a number of tiny resort communities, San Isabel National Forest, up over 9,941-foot Cucharas Pass, and past several pristine alpine lakes near, or above, timberline. Linguists take note: Occasionally in the Purgatoire River Valley, you'll see the word "Picketwire" in place names. This is an Anglo bastardization of "Purgatoire," French for Purgatory.

Cokedale

Now a National Historic District, Cokedale was founded in 1906 by the American Refining and Smelting Company. Though the community bustled with work and workers during the early part of the century, when coke from the town's ovens was shipped to Leadville, today the town's all but abandoned. Dirt streets wind past dilapidated houses—some still occupied—which cling to the hillside in last-gasp efforts to remain standing.

Segundo

About 10 miles past Cokedale, the tiny town of Segundo is little more than a gas station, small market, and deli (Ringo's). Earlier in the century, citizens of Spanish descent painted the doors and window frames of Segundo homes and businesses bright blue to keep the devil away.

Stonewall

Named for the gigantic granite stone wall you can see through the trees on the west side of the highway, this town was established by Juan Gutierrez (nephew of Gabriel Gutierrez, one of Trinidad's founding fathers) in the late 1860s. Long a resort community for fishermen, as well as for people simply wanting to escape the heat of the lowlands, Stonewall still offers a couple of inns tucked away in a beautiful valley setting, highlighted by the rushing river, green meadows, and tall pines and cottonwoods. The **Picketwire Lodge,** tel. (719) 868-2265, has rooms with kitchens and is open year-round for hunting, fishing, and cross-country skiing. The **Stonewall Guest Ranch,** tel. (719) 868-2270, has cabins, RV sites, a playground, and a trout pond. The **Mountain Inn Motel,** tel. (719) 868-2294, has cabins, RV sites, and a small store with groceries and basic camping and fishing supplies.

You can also get fishing licenses and equipment, as well as tips on how to catch the big ones, from **The Shopping Bag,** a small grocery store and cafe in Stonewall.

Monument Lake

With a large granite stone sticking straight up out of its deep blue waters, Monument Lake is a perfect place to stop and picnic and set up camp for a couple of days. **Monument Lake Resort and Campground,** tel. (719) 868-2226 or (800) 845-8006, owned and operated by the city of Trinidad, offers a full range of accommodations, from tent and RV sites to cabins and luxury rooms in the adobe lodge; there's also a full-service restaurant, lounge, and gift shop. Tent sites run about $10, cabins and rooms start at about $50 for two. Write Star Route no. 1, Box 81A, CO 81091, for more information.

Cucharas Pass

The views from this pass are stunning. In the early summer, columbines sheet the steep meadows, and the mountainsides are mottled green with aspen, fir, spruce, and pine. Several of the lakes along the road offer excellent fishing, although you should check the restrictions—some allow flies or artifical lures only. Just north of the pass is a turnoff to a rocky dirt road leading to three Forest Service campgrounds (pit toilets only, no showers). The first, **Cucharas Pass** (22 sites), is a half mile from the highway, **Blue Lake** (15 sites) is four miles, and **Bear Lake** (14 sites) is five.

Spanish Peaks is a private campground also on the north side of the pass, with nicely sheltered tent and RV sites ($8 and $13, including showers).

Cuchara

Cuchara is a 90-year-old resort between the gorgeous Cucharas Pass and the lush Cuchara Valley. With a boardwalk, saloon, gift shops, and a "trading post," as well as a disproportionate number of real-estate offices, the little village is making a brave attempt to make it in the fickle world of year-round resorts.

Though primarily a summer resort, the area began to attract winter visitors in 1981, when the small Panadero Ski Resort opened up the road. The name was soon changed to Cuchara Valley Resort, and in 1985 the area was expanded to cover 135 acres with 24 runs and a vertical drop of 1,562 feet. In 1986, the resort's loan was foreclosed upon. Its new owners? Summit Savings in Dallas, which operated the area until November 1989, when it announced quite unexpectedly that it was shutting down the lifts.

Then in 1991, the ski area was purchased by Dick Davis, a Texas businessman whose goal was to turn Cuchara Valley Resort into a family-oriented area that emphasized affordability and fun. Unfortunately, Davis' venture didn't last either, and the resort didn't open for the 1994-1995 ski season, one of the best in recent memory. In the summer of 1995, the ski area's re-opening seemed uncertain, and locals I talked to seemed skeptical at best.

You'll find a variety of lodging options in Cuchara, including **Yellow Pines Guest Ranch,** 15846 CO 12, Cuchara, CO 81055, tel. (719) 742-3528; **Misty Haven Cabins,** 178 Hill Rd., Cuchara, CO 81055, tel. (719) 742-3433; the **Cuchara Inn,** tel. (719) 742-3685; and the rustic **Cuchara Lodge,** tel. (719) 742-3254. For information on lodging at the Cuchara Valley Resort (ski area), phone (719) 742-3163 or (800) 227-4436. You can also get information on the area at **Cuchara Valley Sports Guides,** tel. (719) 742-5544, where you can also book 4WD tours, hire fly-fishing guides, and rent mountain bikes.

The Cuchara Valley

Just past Cuchara, CO 12 drops down out of the high mountains and begins its gentle roll through the Cuchara Valley back toward I-25 and the western edge of the plains. During the summer, the valley meadows are ablaze with wildflowers—especially impressive are June's wild irises and July's columbines. This verdant valley offers spectacular views of the Spanish Peaks, or Las Cumbres Españolas, which have been landmarks for travelers for hundreds of years. To the Native Americans, the mountains were known as Huajotolla (which I've seen translated both as "the Twins" and as "the Breasts of the World"), and as early as 1654 New Mexico governor Diego de Vargas reported having spotted them on a trip north from Santa Fe. The mountains, rising 13,610 and 12,669 feet, have also been called Dos Hermanos ("Two Brothers"), the Mexican Mountains, and Twin Peaks.

LA VETA

This kick-back little resort town and artists' community sits in the shadow of the Spanish Peaks and on the banks of the slowly tumbling Cucharas River. Founded in the mid-19th century, La Veta ("The Vein") served as a trading center for about a hundred years. Today, La Veta caters to folks looking to escape lowland heat and urban craziness, whether they come to rejuvenate for a weekend or to relocate for a lifetime. Passersthrough can stop in at the town's impressive historical museum, play a round of golf at the club, or camp at one of the many nearby campgrounds.

Fort Francisco Museum

Built in 1862 by Colonel John M. Francisco and Judge Henry Daigre, both to serve as a trade center and to protect local settlers from Indian attacks, this was the first structure in the Cuchara Valley. In 1871, the area's first post office opened at the fort. When the railroad arrived in the valley in the late 1870s, and the depot was built a few blocks north, the community's merchants and traders all but abandoned this once-thriving hub.

In 1957, the Huerfano County Historical Society obtained the fort and shortly thereafter opened it as a museum. Many of the buildings and furnishings are original, and descendants of local settlers have donated artifacts of historical interest. Exhibits include the old saloon (which over the years also served as a pool hall, restaurant, post office, roller rink, and general store), barbershop, one-room school, blacksmith shop, and mining museum. The museum, open daily Memorial Day to October 3, 9 a.m.-5 p.m., has an excellent collection of historical letters and documents, including Kit Carson's will. Admission is $2. A gift shop sells souvenirs, cards, and locally made crafts.

The Gallery

Established in 1975, La Veta's Friends of the Arts Guild displays and sells work by local artists. The Gallery, on W. Ryus, was built in 1983. In addition to exhibiting artwork, the building also serves as a classroom and meeting place for guild members who are spread throughout the area. Ordinarily, the Gallery displays the work of over two dozen artists, with media ranging from charcoal and pencil drawings to weaving, woodwork, and stained glass. For information and business hours, contact the La Veta/Cuchara Valley Chamber of Commerce (Box 32, La Veta, CO 81055, tel. 719-742-3676).

Golf

La Veta's **Grandote** (gran-DOH-tay) **Golf and Country Club** is an 18-hole course designed by famous golfer Tom Wieskopf. One of the state's newest golf courses (it opened in 1986), Grandote hosts a number of tournaments throughout the summer and fall. For information on greens fees and tee times, phone (719) 742-3123.

Outdoor Adventures

The recently opened **Wahatoya Base Camp,** at 22 Main St. in downtown La Veta, offers a wide range of outdoor classes, trips, and adventures, some of which are taught in conjunction with Trinidada State Junior College. Included are classes in edible and medicinal plants of Colorado, geology of the Spanish Peaks region, five-day mountain-bike tours, and birdwatching. Wahatoya also rents and sells outdoor gear and equipment. For information on classes, call (719) 742-5578, or stop by the shop on W. Ryus.

Practicalities

For such a small community, La Veta offers a relatively large number of accommodations options, from RV campgrounds to bed and breakfasts. The **1899 Inn,** tel. (719) 742-3576, is an extremely nice and unassuming little getaway on Main St.; rooms with private baths start at about $50 (about $35 for shared bath). A *huge* breakfast is included. The **Hunter House Bed and Breakfast,** 115 W. Grand Ave., tel. (719) 742-5577, also offers comfortable bed-and-breakfast accommodations. **Circle the Wagons** RV Park, tel. (719) 742-3233, offers RV sites for $9, plus, for square dancers, a variety of "dance packages." You can also get rooms at the **Log Haven RV Park and Motel,** tel. (719) 742-3252, and the **La Veta Motel,** tel. (719) 742-5598.

The **Positively Main Street Cafe,** in downtown La Veta right next door to the Wahatoya Base Camp, is a local favorite as well as for passers-through—the outdoor patio is especially nice. The **Covered Wagon Steakhouse,** 205 S. Main, tel. (719) 742-3679, serves a variety of beefy entrees, fowl, salads, etc. If you're looking for a place to grab a hot dog, some fries, and a cold one, try the new **Sports Pub and Grub** at 923 Oak, tel. (719) 742-3093, open Sun.-Thurs. 11 a.m.-midnight and Friday and Saturday 11 a.m.-2 a.m.

Recycling

Recycle aluminum, glass, and newspapers at 121 E. Ryus.

Information

The **La Veta/Cuchara Valley Chamber of Commerce,** Box 32, La Veta, CO 81055, tel. (719) 742-3676, has assembled a thorough package of tourist information, including a *La Veta/Cuchara Tour Map and Guide,* which features hot springs, hiking trails, geological highlights, and other points of interest in the area. The chamber can also provide a complete list of restaurants, retailers, accommodations, and other information services.

You can also get information on the area from the **Cuchara Tourist Association.** Write Box 2111, Cuchara, CO 81055, or phone (719) 742-3685 or 742-3450.

WEST ON US 160

US Highway 160 runs west out of Walsenburg, up over North La Veta Pass (elev. 9,413 feet), then cuts across northern Costilla County, through Fort Garland, Blanca, and into Alamosa. The 75-mile stretch follows pretty closely the Denver and Rio Grande Western Railroad route.

This southern prairie pocket of Colorado, roughly 125 miles north to south and 50 miles across, is the San Luis Valley, long a hunting area for Utes and Comanches. One of the first parts of Colorado to be explored by the Spanish, as early as 1761, the San Luis Valley still claims a great many Hispanic citizens, many of whom are descendants of original mid-18th-century Mexican land-grant settlers.

As you approach Fort Garland, watch the mountains to the north. Four "14ers" are clustered within a few miles of each other: Mt. Lindsey (14,042 feet), Little Bear Peak (14,037 feet), Blanca Peak (14,345 feet), and Ellingwood Point (14,042 feet).

FORT GARLAND

The first U.S. outpost in the San Luis Valley was Fort Massachusetts, built in 1852 about five miles northeast of Fort Garland. The fort only saw active duty for six years, as it was built on swampland, and the army had trouble providing fresh drinking water for the troops. Fort Garland, named for Brigadier General John Garland, was built in 1858, when Fort Massachusetts was abandoned. For some 25 years, Fort Garland served both to protect settlers from Utes, who were attempting to save their land and herds, and also to provide a social and trading center in an otherwise lonely and barren region. Kit Carson was assigned to the fort from 1866-67; it was his last military post.

Sixteen miles south of Fort Garland on CO 159 is the little town of San Luis, the oldest community in the state.

Fort Garland Museum
Reconstructed to provide visitors with a genuine sense of life on the lonesome frontier in

the mid-19th century, the old fort displays a wide range of Native American, Mexican, and Anglo historical artifacts, including original military uniforms and weaponry. There's also a sampling of Hispanic folk art from the area.

The museum is at the junction of US 160 and CO 159. For hours and more information, write Box 368, Fort Garland, CO 81133, or phone (719) 379-3512.

ALAMOSA

Alamosa (pop. 9,500; elev. 7,544 feet) is the largest town in the San Luis Valley. It's also the closest town to Great Sand Dunes National Monument. Long a hub town and shipping center, particularly for potatoes, the San Luis Valley's principal crop, Alamosa ("Cottonwood Grove") today is the seat of Alamosa County, as well as home to Adams State College, a four-year state university.

History
In 1878, Alamosa's founding father, A.C. Hunt, president of the Denver and Rio Grande Construction Company, loaded up flatcars with stores, churches, and houses and moved them from Garland City—which until then had been the railroad's terminus—and plunked them down at the site of the new one. *Voilà*. Alamosa.

A rambunctious town from the get-go, early Alamosa saw more than its share of ramblers, gamblers, and frontier crazies, particularly the notoriously rowdy railroad construction workers. Lynchings are said to have been commonplace, with one particular riverside cottonwood designated the "hangin' tree."

Later, things mellowed out some, and Alamosa became a central shipping point for San Luis potatoes, as well as wheat, oats, alfalfa, lettuce, cauliflower, and peas, which were commonly fed to hogs, another Alamosa-area export.

Great Sand Dunes National Monument
Created by winds blowing Rio Grande-eroded particles of valley floor east across the San Luis

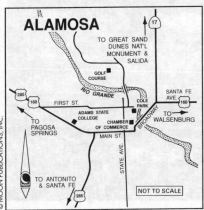

Valley and up against the Sangre de Cristo range, these sand dunes, which reach heights of 800 feet, are the tallest in the country. A true geological oddity, the 52 square miles of dunes stand in stark contrast to both the snowcapped mountains behind them and the desert valley at their base.

Great Sand Dunes National Monument offers year-round camping (both in developed and in primitive backcountry areas), picnicking, and hiking, as well as a chance simply to goof around in this huge and most unlikely of sandboxes. Though much of the dune area is off limits, a short hike from the parking lot, one mile past the visitors center, will take you into sand completely undisturbed by anything save the wind and the handful of small critters that make their homes there.

The visitors center, open daily 8 a.m.-5 p.m. (with extended summer hours) has brochures, maps, books, wildlife and geology displays, explanatory videos, a touch screen, and a self-guided nature trail, as well as rangers to answer your questions.

To get to Great Sand Dunes National Monument, take US 160 16 miles east from Alamosa and then CO 150 20 miles north. You can also go north 14 miles from Alamosa on CO 17 and turn east on County Lane 6 one mile north of Mosca. For more information, phone (719) 378-2313.

City Park

Alamosa's **Cole Park** is at the east end of town on the banks of the upper Rio Grande. You'll find huge lawns, cottonwoods for shade, and picnic tables—all just yards from the Alamosa Chamber of Commerce tourist information center, located in the depot building.

Golf

Four public golf courses lie within driving distance of Alamosa. **Alamosa Golf Course** is an 18-hole course at 6678 River Rd., tel. (719) 589-5330. The **Monte Vista Golf Club** (nine holes) is in Monte Vista west of Alamosa via US 160; phone (719) 852-9995. North of town, off CO 17 in Crestone, is **Los Cumbres Golf Course,** another nine-hole course, tel. (719) 256-4856. **Great Sand Dunes Country Club and Resort** is about seven miles south of Great Sand Dunes National Monument, tel. (719) 378-2357.

Where Are We, the Everglades?

No, but you're near Colorado's next best thing, the **Two Mile Creek Wildlife Habitat and Colorado Alligator Farm.** That's right, in geothermal ponds (87° F) 80 alligators nap, yawn, and grin for visitors. In addition, the habitat area offers fishing, hiking, and picnicking, plus a gift shop where you can pick up smoked fish and, ahem, alligator meat. It's open daily 7 a.m.-7 p.m. June-Aug. and 10 a.m.-3 p.m. Sept.-May. Admission is $2 for adults, $1.50 for kids six to 12. For more information, phone (719) 589-3082.

Accommodations

Not a whole lot to choose from here, although since it's most likely not your honeymoon you shouldn't be too disappointed. The least expensive rooms are probably at the **Sky-Vue Motel,** tel. (719) 589-4945, on the east end of town at 250 Broadway. For about $50 a night you can get a room at any of a handful of places, including the **Alamosa Inn Best Western,** 1919 Main, tel. (719) 589-2567; the **Lamplighter,** 425 Main, tel. (719) 589-6636; and the **Days Inn,** 224 O'Keefe Parkway (US 160 on the east side of town), tel. (719) 589-9037. The Alamosa **Holiday Inn,** tel. (719) 589-5833, offers doubles for about $55. The **Alamosa Super 8,**

*cooling off in the
creek at the base of
the sand dunes*

2505 Main, tel. (719) 589-6447, has doubles
running $40-60.

Camping and RVing

There are RV campgrounds both on Alamosa's
east and west side. A **KOA,** tel. (719) 589-9757,
is on US 160 as you pull into town from the
east, and **Navajo Trails Campground**, tel.
(719) 589-9460, on the west side of US 160
offers mini golf. There's also camping at Great
Sand Dunes National Monument, about 35
miles northeast of Alamosa (see above). **Great
Sand Dunes Oasis and RV Park,** tel. (719)
378-2222, is three miles south of the visitors
center on CO 150. There's also a small grocery and souvenir store, and you can book
scenic 4WD tours. **Blanca RV Park,** tel. (719)
379-3201, is about 30 miles south of the park in
Blanca.

Food

Passers-through can fill up ice chests at the
City Market and Safeway in Alamosa (west side
of town, US 160). If you'd rather sit down and eat
than buy picnic fixin's, **Oscar's,** right downtown
at 710 Main, tel. (719) 589-9320, serves Mexican lunches and dinners daily 11 a.m.-9 p.m. For
Asian food, try **Hunan Chinese Restaurant** at
419 Main, tel. (719) 589-9002—serving Hunan,
Szechuan, and Cantonese dishes. You'll find a
handful of other restaurants and cafes in downtown Alamosa.

Shopping

The **Rio Grande Art Market,** downtown at the
corner of State and Main streets, carries a wide
range of traditional and contemporary work from
artists throughout the San Luis Valley—from
traditional weavings to jewelry, pottery, furniture, basketry, and bronze. Hours are Mon.-
Sat. 10 a.m.-8 p.m.; phone (719) 589-5557.

Services

The offices of the **Alamosa Police Department**
are at 425 4th St., tel. (719) 589-2548 (589-5807
in emergencies). Phone the **Alamosa County
Sheriff** at (719) 589-6608 (589-5807 in emergencies). The **State Patrol** offices are at 1205
West, tel. (719) 589-2503. The **San Luis Valley
Regional Medical Center** is in Alamosa at 106
Blanca Ave., tel. (719) 589-2511. There are also
branch clinics in La Jara, tel. (719) 589-3000,
and in Monte Vista, tel. (719) 589-3658.

Alamosa's **post office** is behind the chamber
of commerce at 505 3rd St., tel. (719) 589-4908.

Information

At Cole Park, along the Rio Grande just off US
160 on the east side of town, the **Alamosa
County Chamber of Commerce** has lots of
brochures, maps, and other information on
Alamosa and the San Luis Valley. Write Alamosa Chamber of Commerce, Cole Park, Alamosa, CO 81101, or phone (719) 589-3681 or
(800) BLU-SKYS. For maps and information on
the San Luis Valley, write the **Bureau of Land**

Management, 1921 State Ave., Alamosa, CO 81101; or phone (719) 589-4975.

A book's throw across the parking lot is the Alamosa **Southern Peaks Public Library,** 424 4th St., tel. (719) 589-6592. **Narrow Gauge Newsstand,** 604 Main St., tel. (719) 589-6712, carries books on the area, its history, and recreational guidebooks.

Alamosa's daily newspaper is the *Valley Courier,* which serves the San Luis Valley. For information or subscriptions, write Box 1099, Alamosa, CO 81101, or phone (719) 589-2553 or 359-0742.

For **road and weather information,** phone (719) 589-9024.

Transportation

Alamosa lies at the junctions of US 160 running east to west, US 285 running north to south, and CO 17, which runs north from Conejos (northbound termination point of the Cumbres-Toltec Railroad), through Alamosa, and north toward Salida.

Air transportation is provided by **United Express,** tel. (719) 589-3804, to San Luis Valley Airport (tel. 719-589-2593)—connecting flights from Denver International. You can rent cars in Alamosa from **L and M Auto,** tel. (719) 589-9027; **Hertz,** tel. (800) 654-3131; and **Spradley Ford,** tel. (719) 589-9063.

Tours

You can arrange 4WD tours of the Great Sand Dunes area through **Great Sand Dunes Oasis and RV Park,** tel. (719) 378-2222. May through September, tours are offered at 10 a.m and 2 p.m. Cost is $14 adults, less for kids.

MONTE VISTA

Monte Vista is a small shipping and agricultural center on the western side of the San Luis Valley. The town is a gateway to Rio Grande and San Juan national forests, which sprawl to the north and west, as well as to Wolf Creek Pass, about 60 miles west on US 50. Monte Vista's annual Ski-Hi Stampede (late July) is Colorado's oldest rodeo. A small visitor center on US 50 on the east side of town has information on Monte Vista and the surrounding San Luis Valley.

Practicalities

The Monte Villa Historic Inn, 925 1st Ave., tel. (719) 852-5166, is a unique, 40-room stone lodge built in 1929. Doubles run about $40-50. The inn also has a dining room, coffee shop, and lounge. You can also get rooms at the **Movie Manor Inn Best Western,** 2830 W. Hwy. 60 (two miles west of town), where a room for two will run about $45-60.

SOUTH TO ANTONITO AND NEW MEXICO

From Alamosa, it's only a half-hour drive south on US 285 to Antonito and the northern terminus of the Cumbres and Toltec Scenic Railroad, and from there it's just five miles to the New Mexico border. A fairly straight shot this, beelining down along the western side of the San Luis Valley.

A mile north of La Jara, or about 14 miles out of Alamosa, you'll find the **Conejos Peak Ranger Station** for the Rio Grande National Forest, where you can get maps and information on camping in the forest (which stretches to the west from Del Norte nearly to Silverton). At the junction of CO 142, about seven miles past La Jara, you can turn east to Manassa, birthplace of

Jack Dempsey, the "Manassa Mauler," and visit the **Jack Dempsey Museum.** Though Dempsey left the tiny town as a young teenager to fight in the mining camps to the north, and by 1950 was famous worldwide as one of the greatest heavyweight boxers of all time, he kept in close contact with his friends and family in Manassa, until he died in 1983. The museum, located downtown, displays boxing artifacts and photos of young Jack and his family. For hours and more information, write Box 130, Manassa, CO 81141.

From Manassa, continue east to San Luis, one of the oldest towns in Colorado. Founded in 1851 by Spanish settlers, the town has remained largely isolated, and its citizenry is still almost entirely Hispanic. The **San Luis Museum, Cultural, and Commercial Center** there displays Hispanic folk art, as well as graphic explanations of the culture of the San Luis Valley. The museum, at 402 Church Place, is open weekdays year-round 10 a.m.-5 p.m. and in the summer on weekends 11 a.m.-5 p.m. For information, phone (719) 672-3611.

For more information on San Luis, write the **San Luis Visitor Center,** Box 307, San Luis, CO 81152, or phone (719) 672-4441.

Antonito

The northern terminus of the **Cumbres and Toltec Scenic Railroad,** Antonito is little more than a train depot and a couple of motels and small cafes. Beginning in Chama, New Mexico, the 1880-vintage railroad winds 64 miles through some of the most beautiful country in the Rockies—through tunnels and pristine vales,

and across high trestles over deep mountain gorges—crisscrossing the border several times. The summit is 10,022-foot Cumbres Pass, where the Spanish first entered Colorado.

From Antonito to Chama is a full-day ride, and you can return by van. Another option is to stop at Osier, the halfway point, for lunch, and to return to Antonito. Either way it's one full day. Fare from Antonito to Chama, including return by van, is about $50. Reservations are highly recommended. For more information, contact Cumbres and Toltec Scenic Railroad, Box 668, Antonito, CO 81120, tel. (719) 376-5483, or Box 789, Chama, NM 87520, tel. (505) 756-2151.

The **Antonito Tourist Information Center and Chamber of Commerce** is at the south end of town across from the railroad tracks. Write to Box 427, Antonito, CO 81120, or phone (719) 376-5441. You can get lodging in Antonito at the **Narrow Gauge Railroad Inn,** tel. (719) 376-5441.

black-footed ferret

BOB RACE

WALSENBURG AND VICINITY

About 17 miles separates La Veta and Walsenburg (pop. 6,200; elev. 6,186 feet), and CO 12 joins US 160 about 12 miles west of town. Predictably, it gets flatter and drier as you drop back down onto the prairie. About five miles west of Walsenburg, you'll pass Martin and Horseshoe lakes and Lathrop State Park, where you'll find facilities for camping, boating, fishing, swimming, and other activities (see below).

Founded by Spanish farmers in the mid-19th century as Plaza de los Leones, Walsenburg was renamed in the 1870s for Fred Walsen, one of the town's early merchants. Today it's a

true hub town, at the junction of I-25, US 160 and 85, and CO 10.

Lathrop State Park

With a commanding view of Spanish Peaks in the distance, this recreation area offers a watery and scenic respite from the heat of the plains. Whether it's waterskiing, sailing, windsurfing, fishing (for trout, bass, catfish, walleye, bluegill, and crappie), swimming, camping, picnicking, golfing, or just plain sightseeing, the two lakes and surrounding area offer a bit of relaxation for just about everyone. The two campgrounds, **Piñon** and **Yucca,** offer a total of nearly 100 campsites, and much of the park is handicapped accessible.

Even if you're just passing through, you might want to stop at the visitor center, where nature trails help you identify local flora and you can pick up maps, books, area guides, and postcards. For more information, write Lathrop State Park, 70 County Rd., Walsenburg, CO 81089, or call (719) 738-2376. For information on the golf course, phone (719) 738-2730.

City Park
You'll find a nice, lawny, shady park as you come into town from the west. The park has a public pool, picnic facilities, and playground equipment.

Accommodations
The **Rio Cucharas Inn,** tel. (719) 738-1282, is the first lodge you'll see if you're coming in from the west. From I-25, take Exit 52 to the **Best Western Rambler,** tel. (719) 738-1121; doubles run \$55-80 (low in winter, high in summer). You can get nice rooms in town at the **Anchor Motel,** 1001 S. Main, tel. (719) 738-2800, for about \$35 for two. Campers can either pull in at **Lathrop State Park** (see above), **Dakota Campground,** tel. (719) 738-9912, or **Budget Host,** tel. (719) 738-3800 (the latter two are north of town on Pueblo Rd./US 85-87). There's a **Day's Inn,** five miles north of Walsenburg just off I-25, tel. (719) 738-2167. A handful of other motels are situated on the north end of Walsen Ave. on the way to I-25.

Malachite Farmstay
The Malachite Farm and School is a nonprofit education organization focusing on nature and humanity's "responsibility to build anew and to cultivate healthy relationships between people and the planet through an awareness that all we create comes from within." Located west of Gardner and surrounded by gorgeous peaks, the school offers bed-and-breakfast, dorm-style accommodations (\$20 per person) and camping (\$12 per person). Dinner and lunch menus feature locally grown organic produce and farm-raised rabbit, chicken, pork, and beef.

To get there, take CO 69 west 25 miles to Gardner, and then turn south on the west side of town at the sign for Redwing. Continue south for five miles, and then turn left when you see the row of mailboxes. Follow the dirt road for a mile, and watch for the sign for Malachite.

For more information, write Malachite School and Farm, 8055 County Rd. 570, Gardner, CO 81040, or phone (719) 746-2412.

Food
The **Alpine Rose Café,** downtown on Main St., tel. (719) 738-1157, is a classic small-town eatery, offering breakfast, lunch, and dinner at reasonable prices. For Mexican food, try **Corine's,** on Main between 8th and 9th, tel. (719) 738-1231.

Services
You'll find the **Walsenburg Police Department** at 202 W. 6th St., tel. (719) 738-1044. The **Huerfano County Sheriff** is at 112 W. 5th St., tel. (719) 738-1600. The **State Patrol** offices are at 500 S. Albert, tel. (719) 738-1600. The **Huerfano Medical Center**, tel. (719) 738-5100, is five miles west of Walsenburg on US 160. The main **post office** is at 204 E. 6th, tel. (719) 738-2100.

Recycling
Recycle aluminum at the **Walsenburg City Hall** at 525 Albert.

Information
The **Huerfano County Chamber of Commerce** provides extensive information on Walsenburg, Huerfano County, and the surrounding area, including local histories and dining, lodging, and recreation guides, as well as helpful information if you're thinking of relocating. Write to the chamber at 400 Main St., Walsenburg, CO 81089, or phone (719) 738-1065. If you're in town, stop by the offices (closed weekends) in the train depot on Main St. between 4th and 5th. The Walsenburg **public library** is at 323 Main St., tel. (719) 738-2774. The local paper is the *Huerfano World,* tel. (719) 738-1720, with offices at 111 W. 7th.

NORTH FROM WALSENBURG

The 50-mile, less-than-an-hour stretch of I-25 from Walsenburg to Pueblo is largely nondescript, save for the impressive views of the Wet Mountains, a Rockies' sub-range, standing massive and snowcapped to the west. Two miles north of Walsenburg, CO 69 shoots northwest off the interstate, follows the Huerfano River to Gardner, snakes between the two largest units of San Isabel National Forest, passes through the beautiful Wet Mountain Valley and Westcliffe, then intersects with US 50 west of Cañon City and Royal Gorge. To the west, just south of Westcliffe, you'll be able to see five mountain peaks topping 14,000 feet. Known collectively as the Crestone Needle Peaks, they include Kit Carson Mountain (14,165 feet), Crestone Peak (14,294 feet), Crestone Needle (14,191 feet), Challenger Peak (14,080 feet), and Humboldt Peak (14,064 feet). At both Westcliffe and Hillside you can turn west off US 69 to campgrounds in San Isabel National Forest.

WESTCLIFFE

At the junction of US 69 and 96 and nestled between the Wet and Sangre de Cristo mountains, Westcliffe is the seat of Custer County, long one of Colorado's important ranching regions. Westcliffe was founded in 1885 by transplanted Englishman Dr. J.W. Bell, who named it after Westcliffe-on-the-Sea, where he was born. Today Westcliffe, along with its sister city, Silver Cliff, once a booming silver town a mile east, is a base for hikers, backpackers, anglers, cross-country skiers, climbers, and hunters heading either west or east up into the mountains. It's also one of the prettiest spots on the planet, nestled in a lush and verdant valley between the towering Sangre de Cristos to the west and Wet Mountains to the east.

Bishop Castle

A legitimate candidate for Ripley's "Believe It Or Not," this is one of the state's most unlikely attractions—a three-story (and growing!) medieval stone castle, complete with buttresses and ornamental iron. The obsession of one man, Jim Bishop, who has been building it at a rate of 1,000 stones a year since 1969, the as-yet-uncompleted castle stands nearly 60 feet tall, less than half as high as it's projected to be upon completion. (It will also have a moat and drawbridge.)

Bishop Castle, which stands partially hidden among the mountain pines and firs, is about 28 miles southeast of Westcliffe and open to the public free of charge. Take CO 96 east, turn south on 165, and watch for the signs. For more information, write Bishop Castle, HCR 75, Box 179, Rye, CO 81069.

Practicalities

Lodging is available in Westcliffe at the **Westcliff Inn,** tel. (719) 783-9275, the **Antler Motel,** tel. (719) 783-2426, and the **Alpine Lodge,** tel. (719) 783-2660. **Purnells' Rainbow Inn Bed and Breakfast,** tel. (719) 783-2313, has four rooms that rent for $50-65 and an adjacent coffeehouse and small store, where you can get espressos and muffins as well as fishing licenses and USGS maps. For more information on lodging, dining, camping, etc. in the Custer County area write the **Custer County Chamber of Commerce** at Box 81, Westcliffe, CO 81252, or phone (719) 783-9163.

PUEBLO AND VICINITY

Pueblo (pop. 102,000; elev, 4,690 feet) is situated on the very edge of America's Great Plains. Just a couple of miles west of town, the Rockies begin their gradual yet unrelenting ascent from foothills to deep forested mountains. Short drives west from Pueblo take you into some of Colorado's most scenic, as well as most historically significant, areas. In fact, one of the best ways to get to Cripple Creek is to head west from Pueblo and then just east of Cañon City to take Phantom Canyon Road (well-maintained gravel) up into Victor and the historic high mining country; in fact, with the advent of gambling in Cripple Creek, shuttle service now runs between the two towns, with regular departures from the Pueblo Visitor Center (see below).

HISTORY

Long a popular hunting ground for bands of plains and mountain native tribes, particularly Comanche, Kiowa, Arapahoe, Cheyenne, and Ute, the Pueblo area was first explored by Europeans in the mid-17th century, when Spaniards from Santa Fe came looking for gold and convertible pagans, as well as to investigate rumors that the French were beginning to colonize the area. The first recorded accounts of actual encampments at the site of present-day Pueblo are from 1706, when a group of Santa Feans rested here briefly on their quest for escaped Native American slaves. Over the next century, the area was explored by trappers, soldiers, prospectors, and Spanish priests.

In 1806, Lieutenant Zebulon Pike erected Pueblo's first structure—a five-foot-high log shelter in which his party camped for a week—and in 1822, Major Jacob Fowler and a small party of trappers and traders built a three-room log house on the banks of the Arkansas River. Twenty years later, James Beckwourth and his party built a small trading post, attracting to the site a couple of dozen settlers, whom Beckwourth put to work building a small adobe fortress, which he dubbed Fort Pueblo.

Between 1842 and 1854, Pueblo attracted a wide range of settlers, from a splinter group of a westbound Mormon party to Indian agents, trappers, traders, and rambunctious pioneers. One of the most famous traders to pass through Pueblo was Richens Lacy "Uncle Dick" Wooten, who would later make a fortune building a 27-mile road over Ratón Pass into New Mexico, erecting a tollgate, and charging every trader, trapper, soldier, and outlaw that passed through.

the Rosemount
House Museum

In 1854, a year after he had driven 9,000 head of sheep from New Mexico to California, Wooten settled briefly in Pueblo. At Christmas that year, the inhabitants of the fort, against Wooten's advice, invited local Utes to join in their celebrations. The Utes, taking advantage of the Puebloans' drunkenness, massacred all of them save for three children and one man. By 1855, Pueblo was all but abandoned, former traders avoiding it, believing it haunted by the ghosts of the Christmas massacre.

Pueblo City was actually established in 1860. By 1863, the town had its own post office and by 1868 its first newspaper. The town was incorporated in 1870. Two years later the narrow-gauge Denver and Rio Grande Railroad arrived, and four years after that the rails of the Atchison, Topeka, and Santa Fe railroad were laid to Pueblo. The late 19th century saw the development of Pueblo as an industrial area, with the construction of several smelters, and in the early 20th century a number of steel mills were built.

One of the city's most painful memories can still be recalled by Pueblo old-timers: On July 3, 1921, the Arkansas River overflowed its banks, submerging the downtown area in over 10 feet of water. Hundreds of homes and businesses were washed away, destroyed, or damaged, and scores of people were killed. Two years later the capricious river was rerouted, domesticated with concrete channels and levees.

Today, Pueblo is on the heels of much of the rest of Colorado in its move to clean up its neighborhoods and downtown historical district. Many of the old buildings have been converted to gift shops and cafes, and homes are getting facelifts and paint jobs. And though parts of town still appear run down, in many ways Pueblo is a very pleasant little city, with quiet tree-lined streets, stunning Victorian homes, and a population that's quite happy here, thank you, and wouldn't live anywhere else.

MUSEUMS

Rosemount House Museum

This gorgeous 37-room Victorian was built in 1893 for banker and merchant John A. Thatcher, who amassed his fortunes in mining, ranching, and farming. The 24,000-square-foot house is constructed of pink rhyolite stone and features extensive marble and silverplate tile, elaborate gold, silver, and brass lighting fixtures, and an oak dining table that seats 36. The house cost $60,000 to build.

Tours of the home, located at 419 W. 14th St., are offered during the summer every half hour, Tues.-Sat. 10 a.m.-3:30 p.m. and Sunday 2-3:30; the rest of the year tours are Tues.-Sat. 1-3:30 p.m. and Sunday 2-3:30. It's closed in January. Admission is $3 for adults, $1 for ages six to 16. For information, phone (719) 545-5290.

El Pueblo Museum

Operated by the Colorado Historical Society, this museum displays the history and culture of Pueblo and Pueblo County. Included are both permanent exhibits (Native Americana, the contributions of iron and steel to the area, and a section of the town's "hanging tree," a 388-year-old cottonwood cut down in 1883 to make way for Union St.) and traveling displays. The museum occupies the actual site of a trading post built in 1842. During the school year, the museum works with local educational groups, offering a variety of historical programs.

El Pueblo Museum, at 324 W. 1st St., is open Mon.-Sat. 10 a.m.-4:30 p.m. and Sunday 12-3 p.m. Admission is $2.50 for adults and $2 for kids and seniors. You can also arrange group tours. For more information, or to book tours, phone (719) 583-0453.

Fred E. Weisbrod Aircraft Museum

At the airport east of town, this outdoor museum lets you wander among a wide array of once-important aircraft, including a Lockheed F-80 fighter plane, a B-29 (with original crew members listed on display stand), an F-101 Voodoo, a Douglas C-47 Skytrain, and the B-47E "Might in Flight." Statistics, including passenger or load capacity, crew, special uses, etc., about each craft displayed on plaques. Open daily 9 a.m. to sunset, tel. (719) 948-9219; admission is free.

International B-24 Memorial Museum

Across the street from the Aircraft Museum, the B-24 Museum is dedicated to the crews of WW

II B-24 Liberators. Exhibited here are historical photos, uniforms, documents, and other artifacts. Open Mon.-Fri. 10 a.m.-4 p.m. and Saturday 10 a.m.-3 p.m.; admission is free. For information, phone (719) 948-9219.

Pueblo Fire Museum

Located at 102 Broadway, this museum displays historical fire-fighting gear, including an 1881 hand-drawn fire-hose cart, a fire truck from 1917, a collection of helmets from around the world, as well as ladders, nozzles, rescue equipment, and historical photos. Open by reservation only; admission is free. For more information, phone (719) 544-4548, or write Box 4127, Pueblo, CO 81004.

Historical Walking Tours

Local historical groups have developed self-guided walking tours of two Pueblo districts. The **Union Avenue District** tour includes homes and businesses in the Union and Grand Avenue areas, many dating from the 1880s. Some 40 buildings are listed on the National Register of Historic Places. The **Mesa Junction** tour, on the other side of the Arkansas River, explores the 1880s shopping area where two trolley lines met.

Maps and more information on the tours, as well as detailed discussions of the buildings, are available from the Pueblo Chamber of Commerce (see "Information" following).

Sangre de Cristo Arts and Conference Center

This two-building complex at 210 N. Santa Fe, with four art galleries, a 500-seat theater, and a hands-on children's museum, attracts upwards of 200,000 visitors a year. The galleries feature both permanent and traveling displays, and the center offers dance and music workshops, as well as a summer concert series. There's also a gift shop.

The center's art galleries are open Mon.-Sat. 11 a.m.-4 p.m. The children's museum is open Mon.-Sat. 11 a.m.-5 p.m. For information, or to arrange free tours, phone (719) 543-0130.

PARKS AND RECREATION

Lake Pueblo State Recreation Area

An excellent place to beat the heat of a Pueblo summer afternoon, Pueblo Reservoir offers a variety of water sports, including sailing, windsurfing, fishing, and swimming (permitted only in the Rock Canyon Swim Area), in addition to camping, horseback riding, hiking, wildlife viewing, and sightseeing. Though its 60-mile shoreline is mostly barren, surrounded by treeless bluffs and rocky cliffs, the lake still affords a stark, highplains sort of beauty, especially against the massive Rockies in whose shadow it lies.

PUEBLO

NOTE: ONLY MAIN ROADS SHOWN

© MOON PUBLICATIONS, INC.

First open in the early 1970s, the recreation area has several different campgrounds, with hot water, flush toilets, and RV hookups—nearly 300 campsites all told. Fish for trout, black bass, crappie, and bluegill, from the shore or boat, or hoist a sail and run on the wind. You can also tour the fish hatchery. To get there, take US 50 west and watch for the signs. For information, write 640 Pueblo Reservoir Rd., Pueblo, CO 81004, or phone (719) 561-9320.

Greenway and Nature Center
Situated on the Arkansas River below the Pueblo Reservoir Dam, the center offers picnicking, fishing (from a large deck out over the river), volleyball courts, and raft, kayak, and canoe put-ins. Cyclists will enjoy the 20 miles of bike trails, while hikers can follow the short nature trail (wheelchair accessible). Canoes and bikes are available to rent.

Above the greenway is a small nature center displaying much of the flora and fauna found in the area, and the nearby Raptor Rehabilitation Center cares for injured hawks, owls, falcons, and eagles, with the hope of returning them to the wild. The Nature Center, tel. (719) 545-9114, is open daily 9 a.m.-5 p.m., and the Raptor Rehabilitation Center, tel. (719) 545-7117, is open daily 11 a.m.-4 p.m. To get there, take US 50 west to Pueblo Blvd./CO 45, turn south, and follow the signs.

City Park and Zoo
This is a very popular weekend destination for locals as well as passers-through. Highlights include a carousel built at the turn of the century (moved to its present site in 1940), a small lake (open for fishing to kids 15 and under and disabled people only), and a train that loops you out around the lake. The park also has other amusement-park rides, playground equipment, tennis courts, a softball field, golf course, and picnic facilities.

The **Pueblo Zoo,** adjacent to the park, houses over 70 different kinds of animals, including Bengal tigers, camels, American bison, and an Andean condor, as well as the state's largest herpatology display. The zoo is open in the summer 10 a.m.-5 p.m. and the rest of the year 9 a.m.-4 p.m. A nominal admission fee is charged. To get there from US 50, take Pueblo Blvd.

south to Goodnight (do not go gentle. . .). From downtown, take 4th St. west to Pueblo Blvd.; then go north to Goodnight.

Mineral Palace Park
This huge city park, with gorgeous gardens, lawns, and tall shade trees, is frequently the site of weddings. A perfect place to picnic after wandering around Pueblo, the park also has a public swimming pool and exercise course. From downtown, take Santa Fe or Main north; from Elizabeth or Greenwood, turn east on 17th.

Golf
Pueblo's 18-hole municipal golf course is at City Park at Pueblo Blvd. and Thatcher. For information and tee times, phone (719) 561-4946. Other area courses include the **Pueblo West Golf Club,** eight miles west of town off US 50 in the Pueblo West development, tel. (719) 547-2280; **Walking Stick,** 4301 Walking Stick Blvd., tel. (719) 584-3400; and the **Hollydot Course,** 25 miles south of Pueblo on I-25 (Exit 74), tel. (719) 676-3341.

Cycling
The Pueblo area has miles and miles of biking trails. For maps, contact the chamber of commerce or the **Pueblo Parks and Recreation Department,** 800 Goodnight Ave., Pueblo, CO 81005, tel. (719) 566-1745. For maps of cycling trails in Pueblo, Colorado Springs, Cañon City, and Trinidad, write **Colorado Division of Parks and Outdoor Recreation,** 1313 Sherman St., Denver, CO 80203, or phone (303) 866-3437.

ACCOMMODATIONS

Motels and Hotels
Pueblo has several franchise-type lodges easily accessible from I-25, many of which are at the junction of I-25 and US 50 west. They include a **Motel 6,** 4103 N. Elizabeth, tel. (719) 543-6221; a second **Motel 6,** around the corner at 960 US 50, tel. (719) 543-8900; **Super 8,** 1100 Hwy. 50 W, tel. (719) 545-4104; **Holiday Inn,** 4001 N. Elizabeth, tel. (719) 543-8050; and **Hotel Pueblo,** US 50 E and Hudson Ave. (I-25 Exit 100A), tel. (719) 542-3750; and the **Pueblo Motor Lodge** 800 US 50 W, tel. (719) 543-

6820. The **Inn At Pueblo West Best Western** is eight miles west of town on US 50, tel. (719) 547-2111.

Bed and Breakfast

The **Abriendo Inn,** at 300 W. Abriendo, tel. (719) 544-2703, in the elegant and beautifully restored 1906 home of brewing magnate Martin Walter, is one of the classiest and most comfortable bed and breakfasts around. Hostess Kerrelyn Trent serves up huge and delicious homemade breakfasts, the menu changing daily. If your timing's right, there just might be some bearclaws or poppyseed cake waiting for you in the sunny dining room. Doubles at the Abriendo range $50-85.

Camping and RVing

In addition to the campgrounds at **Lake Pueblo State Recreation Area** (see above), the Pueblo **KOA** campground, tel. (719) 542-2273, is five miles north of town off I-25 (take Exit 108).

FOOD

Start Me Up

A popular morning hangout among the Abriendo-area business crowd, the **Pantry Restaurant,** 107$\frac{1}{2}$ E. Abriendo, tel. (719) 543-8072, is a down-home and home-style restaurant. For a taste of local blue-collar color, try **Don's Café,** tel. (719) 543-5814, on Elizabeth just a couple of blocks south of the US 50 W exit from I-25 (and near both the Holiday Inn and Motel 6s). A classic diner, Don's serves American breakfasts (including pork chops and eggs) for $2-4, and lunch and dinner (sandwiches, liver and onions, chicken, soup and salad) for $5-12. An excellent place to hang with locals and get a taste of the remodeled Union Street Historical District is at **Lane's B-Street Cafe,** 121 W. B St., tel. (719) 583-9239, where you can get good-size breakfasts (omelettes, pancakes, lox and bagels) for $4-7, or just sip a latte and munch on a piece of nine-grain toast. Lane's also serves lunch (sandwiches, salads, fish, and lamb) for about $5-8.

Mexican Food

As you'd expect, Pueblo has lots of excellent Mexican restaurants, ranging from neighborhood

holes in the wall to upscale dining rooms. A sure bet is **El Valle Mexican Restaurant,** 208 W. Northern, tel. (719) 564-9983, a family-run joint in business since 1937. Open every day but Thursday, El Valle offers huge lunch specials for about $5, while combination dinners run $7-9. You can also get shrimp, pork, chicken, avocado, and beef burritos for about $6; a bowl of *menudo* is $3.25. For dessert, try the *conchas—sopaipillas* stuffed with apple, pineapple, or cherry for $1.75. El Valle is on Central Ave. near the junction with I-25. From the freeway, take the Central Ave. exit and go north one block. Another Mexican favorite is **Jorge's,** 1319 E. Evans, tel. (719) 564-6486. Famous for burritos, Jorge's also serves enchiladas Tejanas (with eggs and chicken) and tamales and stuffed *sopaipillas* for $3-5. Jorge's is also open for breakfast, serving Mexican and American food for $3-5. **Nacho's,** 215 N. Main, tel. (719) 544-0733, is yet another favorite, serving lunch and dinner burritos, tostadas, and taco plates for $2.50-4.50. A bowl of *menudo* is $2.95. A bit more upscale, in fact, described by a local as a "California-style Mexican restaurant—you know, great atmosphere, lots of lettuce, fruit, stuff like that . . . ," the **Cactus Flower,** 2149 Jerry Murphy Rd., tel. (719) 545-8218, serves blue-corn enchiladas, *pollo* dishes, as well as *carne asada,* crab chimichangas, and *pescado Veracruz* for $7-11.

Other Mexican standbys include **Los Hombres,** 3015 W. Northern, tel. (719) 561-8800, and **Stifino's,** 625 W. Abriendo, tel. (719) 544-4019.

"But I'm Tired of Mexican Food"

Understandable. But fear not. Though this town is no San Francisco, there *are* alternatives. (In fact, Pueblo bills itself as, ahem, "a cultural cornucopia.") And though you might not find much in the way of, say, Senegalese food in town, you will find restaurants serving food besides tacos. To wit: The **Irish Pub and Grille,** 108 W. 3rd, tel. (719) 542-9974, serves, according to Pueblo gourmands, excellent (I'm not making this up) Chinese food. Locals swear by the fried rice, chicken chow mein, huge beer selection, and friendly after-work atmosphere. The fried chicken is also said to be good.

Hardcore meat lovers might forego the Mexican food, no matter how highly recommended, for the equally highly touted steaks at **Park East,** 720 Goodnight Ave., tel. (719) 561-8707—also serving seafood, chicken, and prime rib. Prices run $7-16.

For Italian food, try **Ianne's Pizzeria,** 515 W. Northern, tel. (719) 542-5942. In addition to pizza, you can get a variety of pasta, including homemade lasagna, as well as chicken and barbecued ribs (about $8), and good salads. There's also an **Ianne's** at 2912 N. Elizabeth, tel. (719) 543-3230. Another down-home friendly place, highly respected for its "home-style cooking" is **LaTronica's,** at the corner of E. Mesa and Abriendo, tel. (719) 542-1113. The **Gold Dust Saloon,** 130 S. Union (Historical District), tel. (719) 545-0741, is a cozy neighborhood sports bar and saloon serving up dynamite burgers and fries with which to chase your beer.

La Renaissance, 217 E. Routt Ave., tel. (719) 543-6367, is one of Pueblo's more upscale restaurants, serving prime rib, baby-back ribs, and seafood (about $11-30) in a church dating from 1888.

If you happen to be near (or in) the Rosemount House Museum around lunchtime, try **Lindy's Restaurant,** right next door, tel. (719) 544-9593. Specials include gourmet salads (asparagus mousse, for example) and sandwiches. Open Mon.-Fri. 11 a.m.-2 p.m.

ENTERTAINMENT

The Bars

Downtown Pueblo is a strange blend of modern-looking office buildings and neighborhood taverns, ranging from biker bars to sports pubs. Some of the downtown joints feature live music on weekends. **The Gold Dust Saloon,** 130 S. Union, tel. (719) 545-0741, is a friendly little place where you can munch popcorn or peanuts while tossing darts or catching a game on one of the several television screens.

Pueblo Pooch Races

A popular Pueblo pastime is dog racing. At **Pueblo Greyhound Park,** at Lake Ave. and Pueblo Blvd. South, tel. (719) 564-5274, you can participate in parimutuel greyhound racing. Call for starting times and information.

CALENDAR

Pueblo's big annual event is the **Colorado State Fair.** In addition to offering the standard rides, livestock shows, and booths where you can win a mirror etched with a likeness of Elvis or of a large-breasted woman on a Harley, this huge and highly anticipated fair also features big-name entertainment. Headliners at recent fairs include Bob Dylan and Wayne Newton, and other acts included Waylon Jennings, Kenny Rogers, and Los Lobos. Held in late August, the Colorado State Fair attracts thousands of people from all over the Southwest. For information, phone (719) 561-8484 or (800) 444-FAIR.

Pueblo also hosts a number of other events over the course of the year, from arts-and-crafts and home-and-garden shows to rodeos and concerts. For information on what's going on in Pueblo, check the *Pueblo Chieftain,* or phone the city Events Line (weekly listing) at (719) 542-1776, or the Community Calendar (coming events) at (719) 542-1704.

SHOPPING

Downtown Areas

Combine your shopping with historical tours at three downtown shopping areas, **Mesa Junction, Downtown,** and **Union Avenue Historic District.** You'll find gift shops, bookstores, boutiques, and other specialty shops in restored 19th-century buildings. There are also restaurants and neighborhood pubs for refreshment.

Pueblo Mall

The Pueblo Mall, at I-25 and US 47 East, has (surprise!) a JCPenney, Mervyn's, Ward's, Joslin's, 10 shoe stores, seven jewelers, and a whole lot of other stores. A slew of strip malls is near the corner of Pueblo and Northern—Kmart, Wal-Mart, SuperCuts, fast-food franchises, etc.

SERVICES

The offices of the **Pueblo Police Department** are at 130 Central, tel. (719) 549-1200. The **Pueblo County Sheriff** is at 909 Court, tel.

(top) rock climber in Garden of the Gods, near Colorado Springs;
(bottom) Glenwood Hot Springs Pool (both photos: Stephen Metzger)

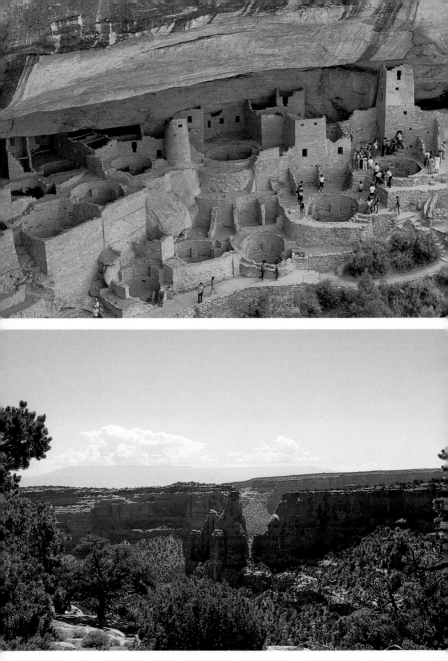

(top) Visitors explore cliff dwellings at Mesa Verde National Park. (Durango Chamber Resort Association and Mesa Verde National Park); (bottom) stark cliffs and spires in Colorado National Monument (Stephen Metzger)

(719) 546-1123. Phone the **Colorado State Patrol** in emergencies at (719) 544-2424 (546-5465 in nonemergencies). **Parkview Episcopal Medical Center** is at 400 W. 16th (Exit 99B off I-25), tel. (719) 584-4000. **St. Mary-Corwin Regional Medical Center** is at 1008 Minnequa (Exit 96 off I-25), tel. (719) 560-4000. The main **post office** is at 421 Main St., and there's also one at 6th and Central.

Recycling

Recycle aluminum, glass, newspapers, and plastic at the **King Soopers** stores: 3050 W. Northern and 102 W. 29th. Recycle aluminum at the **Safeway:** 1322 E. 8th St., 617 W. 29th St., and 1231 S. Prairie.

INFORMATION

Chamber of Commerce and Tourist Information

Contact the Pueblo **Chamber of Commerce** at 302 N. Santa Fe, Pueblo, CO 81003, tel. (719) 542-1704. The **Visitor Information Center** in the Kmart parking lot at US 50 W and Elizabeth St. (from I-25, take Exit 101), tel. (719) 543-1742, is an excellent place to begin your visit. You'll find a friendly staff, plus lots of brochures and other information on what to and where to stay in the area. A shuttle to Cripple Creek departs from the visitor center six times a day. Rate is $15, with $7 in gambling tokens returned on your delivery to Cripple Creek. For information, phone (719) 545-8687. The offices of the **Parks and Recreation Department** are at 800 Goodnight Ave., tel. (719) 566-1745. Offices for **Pike** and **San Isabel** national forests are at 1920 Valley Dr., tel. (719) 545-8737.

For **road and weather information,** phone (719) 545-8520.

Bookstores and Libraries

The **Bookery,** 129 E. Abriendo, tel. (719) 544-1135, has a good selection of books on Colorado—history, travel, etc. For used books and rare books, check out **Tumbleweed Books,** 687 S. Union, tel. (719) 544-3420, which specializes in, among other subjects, Western Americana. There's a **Waldenbooks** in the Pueblo Mall.

The main branch of the **Pueblo Library District** is at 100 E. Abriendo, tel. (719) 543-9600. There are also branches at 1515 Bonforte, tel. (719) 544-5040, and 2525 S. Pueblo, tel. (719) 564-8382.

The independently published *Pueblo Chieftain,* first printed in 1868, comes out Mon.-Sat. and is available in racks around town. Its offices are at 825 W. 6th Street. Write Box 4040, Pueblo, CO 81003, or phone (719) 544-3520.

TRANSPORTATION

Pueblo is an easy town to get around in, though it does get a bit messy downtown, where streets change names and loop around each other. It helps to remember when driving that the main north-south arteries are Elizabeth, Greenwood, Abriendo, Santa Fe, and, on the west side, Prairie and Pueblo. East-west thoroughfares are Northern, 4th St. (which, heading west, turns into Lincoln, which turns into Thatcher), Midtown, 29th St., and US 50. Remember, too, that the numbered *streets* run east to west and the numbered *avenues* run north to south.

Pueblo Airport is served by **United Express,** tel. (719) 948-4423. **Greyhound-Trailways** has passenger service to Pueblo, tel. (719) 544-6295. Rent cars in Pueblo from **Avis,** tel. (800) 331-1212; **Budget,** tel. (719) 948-3363; **Hertz,** tel. (719) 948-3345; **National,** tel. (719) 948-3343; and **U-Save,** tel. (719) 544-6222.

WEST TO CAÑON CITY

On the north side of Pueblo, US 50 rises up out of the plains and into the scrubby Rocky foothills, loosely following the courses of the Arkansas River and the Atchison, Topeka, and Santa Fe Railroad. Eight miles out of Pueblo, you'll pass the planned community of Pueblo West, a sprawling development of newer homes, many owned by retirees. You can turn south here, wind your way through Pueblo West and down to Lake Pueblo State Recreation Area (see above), where you'll find boating, camping, and fishing opportunities. Forty miles out of Pueblo, CO 115 tees into the highway, dropping back to the northeast to Colorado Springs, and following the western boundary of Fort Carson en route. Turn south at this junction onto Colorado 115 to **Florence,** site of the oldest continually producing oil well in the world. Long an important oil and coal town (Petroleum Ave. is one of the main north-south streets), Florence (pop. 3,000) today is the seat of Fremont County. The **Price Pioneer Museum** on the corner of Pikes Peak and Front St. displays mining and domestic artifacts. Open June through mid-September. You'll find a city park and public swimming pool on Pikes Peak between 3rd and 4th. For information about Flo-

rence, write **Florence Chamber of Commerce,** Rialto Theatre Building, Box 145, Florence, CO 81226, or phone (719) 784-3544.

Four miles past the junction with 115, you can turn north onto **Phantom Canyon Road**, which follows the old Denver and Rio Grande Railroad line up into the historic mining towns of Victor and Cripple Creek. A seldom-used route, this well-maintained dirt road takes you gradually up into the high mountains, offering some excellent scenery along the way. From this turnoff it's about eight miles to Cañon City.

CAÑON CITY

As a gateway town, Cañon City (pop. 25,000; elev. 5,332 feet) offers access to some excellent recreational and sightseeing opportunities: thousands of square miles of national forest land (for camping, hiking, cross-country skiing), as well as some of Colorado's favorite stretches of white water, and the 1,000-foot-deep, eight-mile-long Royal Gorge. Not really sure how to define itself, Cañon City is at once both proud of its fascinating history and scenic wonders and at the same time somehow determined to exploit them in silly and embarrassing ways.

HISTORY

With its mild climate and proximity to so much natural bounty, the Cañon City area was a favorite hunting ground and base camp of Utes long before the first white settlers showed up. The first nonnatives to explore the area were most likely Zebulon Pike and his party, who camped here in December, 1806 (although he mistook the Arkansas River for Texas's Red River). The next half century or so, though, the area remained solely Ute land, and it wasn't until 1859 that the first miners started to arrive.

The early town's economy was a hybrid, derived from both mining (gold and silver) and agriculture (fruits and vegetables). Writer Joaquin Miller was one of Cañon City's first administrators, serving as mayor, judge, and minister.

In 1868, Colorado Territory gave Cañon City a choice. It could be the site of either the state university or the state penitentiary. Cañon City

chose the latter, figuring attendance would be better at prison than at school. The university, of course, went to Boulder. And, as the University of Colorado has largely given definition to the city of Boulder since then, so has Colorado State Penitentiary defined Cañon City. Today, the Department of Corrections is Fremont County's largest employer, and the townspeople thank the prison system for the stability it provides.

In the late 1870s, as the West's railroads

competed for rights to key routes, Cañon City, because of its choice location—near the mouth of Royal Gorge, a crucial passage west—became an unwitting participant in the fray. The Denver and Rio Grande and the Santa Fe railroads went to court over the rights to the canyon, with the rights ultimately awarded to the Denver and Rio Grande. The Santa Fe had to run its line south from Pueblo and then west from Ratón.

In 1908, Cañon City acquired Royal Gorge Park, and in 1929, a suspension bridge, still the highest in the world (1,053 feet), was built across it. Since then, Cañon City has appealed to tourism, attracting upwards of a half million visitors a year, who, in addition to being awed by the bridge, also appreciate the canyon's sheer beauty, the aerial tramway across, and the railroad rising 1,500 feet from the river to the canyon's rim.

SIGHTS

Colorado Territorial Prison Museum and Park

A genuinely unique and perversely intriguing experience, a tour of this museum offers a realistic view of the 120-year history of Colorado State Penitentiary. Originally a single, two-story stone structure, the prison saw 77 executions (45 by hanging, 32 by gas) and a number of escapes and riots; the bloody aftermath of one of which has been re-created with broken cell doors and blood on floors. There's also a fascinating collection of historical photos, including shots of Alferd Packer (who served 15 years for cannibalism), John Dockerty (Colorado's first convicted abortionist), and Anton Wood (at 11, the state's youngest prisoner of record—sentenced to 25 years for murdering a neighbor in a dispute over a watch). The grisliest photos are of the hanging of one George Witherall.

The Colorado Territorial Prison Museum and Park, at 1st and Macon, is open daily 8:30 a.m.-6 p.m. Admission for adults is $3.50, $3 for seniors, and $2 for kids six to 12. For more information, phone (719) 269-3015.

Cañon City Municipal Museum

Housed in a complex that includes the second floor of the Cañon City municipal building, as

Cañon City still has a number of fine bars.

COLORADO HISTORICAL SOCIETY

well as two historic buildings behind the city hall, this museum displays a wide range of items from the Fremont County area's history. Included are rocks and minerals from the region, the mounted heads of the last of the area's buffalos (shot by poachers in 1897), Ute artifacts, replicas of a saloon and blacksmith shop, as well as antique furniture and clothing and other personal belongings and domestic items.

The museum, at Royal Gorge Blvd. and 6th St., is open May 6-Sept. 3, Tues.-Sun. 10 a.m.-4 p.m.; Sept. 4-May 5, the museum is open Tues.-Sat. 10 a.m.-4 p.m. Admission is $1 for adults, 50 cents for kids six to 12. For information, phone (719) 269-9018.

PARKS AND RECREATION

Surrounded by lush national forests, steep mountains, and countless lakes, streams, and rivers, Cañon City is an outdoor-lover's paradise. Particularly popular is river rafting, with several guide services offering half- and full-day trips on the Arkansas and other area rivers.

Of course, the scenery, too, is wonderful, and the area offers excellent sightseeing opportunities.

City Parks

Twelve miles north of Cañon City is 500-acre city-owned **Red Canyon Park,** characterized by its bizarre redrock formations. It offers sightseeing, hiking trails, and picnic facilities. Take Field Ave. north from town.

Temple Canyon Park, also owned by Cañon City, offers picnicking, hiking, and sightseeing as well. A natural amphitheater along one of the hiking trails is reportedly an ancient Ute ceremonial site. Take 1st St. south from town.

Hiking and Biking

The Cañon City area abounds in hiking and biking trails, and the city, in conjunction with the Forest Service, publishes a map with dozen different routes. Pick up maps at the visitor information center in Centennial Park off US 50 on the west side of town, as well as at bike shops in town, including **Bike Tech,** 922 Phay, or **Otero Cyclery,** 722 Main Street.

Whitewater Rafting

The section of the Arkansas River between Cañon City and Salida is a favorite among river rats, and even those new to the sport can get in on the fun. Half- and full-day trips can be arranged. No problem finding an outfitter/guide, as the countryside, particularly right at Royal Gorge, is studded with billboards advertising the services. Rafting companies include **Brown's Royal Gorge Rafting and Helicopter Tours,** tel. (719) 275-5161 or 275-7238; and **Lazy J Resort and Rafting Company,** tel. (719) 942-4274. Prices usually start at about $35 per person (half day).

An excellent place from which to view rafters is an over-the-water observation deck at **Five Points Arkansas Headwaters Recreation Area,** about eight miles west of Royal Gorge; public restrooms and picnic tables are available.

Scenic Drives

Eight miles east of Cañon City is the junction with **Phantom Canyon Road,** where you can turn north and drive into Victor and Cripple Creek

the back way. The twisting, turning, well-maintained 35-mile dirt-and-gravel road, which follows the old Denver and Rio Grande Railroad line, is not recommended for large (over 35 feet) RVs. Three-mile **Skyline Drive,** built in 1906 with convict labor and stones from every state in the union, takes you 800 feet above the town. The one-way road begins just west of Cañon City on US 50; follow the signs.

Camping

With San Isabel National Forest to the south and southwest, and Pike National Forest to the west and north, Cañon City offers almost unlimited camping possibilities (in addition to the RV camping at Royal Gorge—see that section, following). For maps and information, stop by the Forest Service office in town at 300 Dozier, tel. (719) 275-4119, or the BLM office at 3170 E. Main, tel. (719) 275-0631.

Golf

The private **Shadow Hills Golf Club** is open to nonmembers with some restrictions. Built shortly after WW II, the course has long been a local favorite. Take 4th St. south from town; phone (719) 275-0603 for tee times and information.

Horseback Riding

This is another activity popular in the Cañon City-Royal Gorge area, with several companies offering rentals and rides. Among them: **Buckskin Joe,** tel. (719) 275-5149, and **Lazy-J Resort and Rafting Company,** tel. (719) 942-4274, headquartered in Coaldale, about 35 miles west of Cañon City on US 50.

PRACTICALITIES

Accommodations

Among the many motels in Cañon City is the **Best Western Royal Gorge Motel,** 1925 Fremont, tel. (719) 275-3377, where doubles range $45-$80, depending on the season. Doubles at the **Cañon Inn,** at US 50 and Dozier, tel. (719) 275-8676, run $50-85, while rooms for two at the **Super 8,** 209 North 19th, tel. (719) 275-8687, cost between $40 and $60.

In addition to the RV campgrounds at Royal Gorge (see that section, following), you can also camp at **RV Station and Campground,** in town at 3120 E. Main, tel. (719) 275-4576. Much more isolated, in fact pretty much out in the proverbial middle of nowhere, **Indian Springs Ranch Campground,** tel. (719) 372-3907, is at the end of a four-mile dirt road that forks off Phantom Canyon Rd. east of Cañon City (no vehicles over 25 feet).

Food

A longstanding local favorite restaurant is **Merlino's Belvedere,** 1330 Elm/CO 115, tel. (719) 275-5558, which specializes in Italian food and steak and seafood, as well as homemade soups. Entrees run $8 (pastas) to $25 (steak and lobster). **Ortega's,** 2301 E. Main, tel. (719) 275-9437, is an authentic Mexican *restaurante,* where burrito, enchilada, and tamale dinners run $5-8. For sandwiches, nachos, green-chile burritos, and a taste of the local scene (albeit a bit of a smoky one), stop in at **My Brother's Place,** tel. (719) 275-9954, 625 Main—also great for a cold beer and a game of pool. For what locals claim are the best burgers around, try the **Burger Baron,** 1006 Royal Gorge, tel. (719) 275-8513; it also serves milk shakes and ice cream. The **Dragon Gate,** 507 Main, tel. (719) 275-0684, has a daily all-you-can-eat Chinese buffet lunch.

For picnic packin', there's a **City Market** on US 50 on the east end of town.

Shopping

One of the joys of researching travel books is discovering bizarre little businesses with bizarre little names. This one in Cañon City tops 'em all, though: **Fluff 'em, Buff 'em, and Stuff 'em.** Representing a true milestone in the history of marketing, advertising, promotion, and taste, this little place offers one-stop hairstyling, car restoration, and taxidermy.

If you'd rather stick to more conventional shopping, you might want to wander the Main Street area, where you'll find a handful of boutiques and galleries, including **RSVP,** at 515 Main, which carries some nice Native American art and jewelry.

SERVICES

The offices of the **Cañon City Police Department** are at 816 Royal Gorge Blvd., tel. (719) 275-8638. Phone the **Fremont County Sheriff** at (719) 275-2000 or 275-1553. The **Colorado State Patrol** can be reached at (719) 275-0015 or 275-1558. Cañon City's **St. Thomas More Hospital** is at 1019 Sheridan, tel. (719) 275-3381. The main **post office** is at 505 Macon, tel. (719) 275-6877.

Recycling

Recycle aluminum and glass at the **City Market** on the east end of town off US 50. Recycle aluminum, cardboard, glass, newspapers, tin, and more at **Recycling Opportunities,** in the Alco Parking lot, Saturday 10 a.m.-4 p.m., and at **Florence Super Foods,** (in Florence) Tuesday 12-4 p.m.

INFORMATION

You'll find a tourist information booth just off US 50 on each end of town. Pick up information on lodging, recreation, and other attractions. You can also get information from the **Cañon City Chamber of Commerce,** 403 Royal Gorge. Write Box 749, Cañon City, CO 81215, or phone (719) 275-2331.

To learn more about the history of the town and surrounding area, visit the **Local History Center,** tel. (719) 269-9020, which collects newspapers (from 1860); historical periodicals, journals, and photographs; oral histories and transcripts; and maps and extensive prison records and publications. It's downstairs in the **Cañon City Public Library,** 516 Macon, open Mon.-Fri. 12-5 p.m. and Saturday 10:30 a.m.-2 p.m.

The Book Corral, 621 Main, tel. (719) 275-8923, carries an excellent selection of books about Colorado, from histories to recreational and backcountry guides. The local newspaper, the *Daily Record,* comes out weekday afternoons and Saturday mornings. Watch for the weekly insert "This Week in the Royal Gorge Region," which lists current events and highlights particular points of interest. For information, phone (719) 275-7565.

For information on the Pike or San Isabel national forests, contact the district offices at 300 Dozier, Cañon City, CO 81212, tel. (719) 274-4119. Or write the central offices at 1920 Valley Dr., Pueblo, CO 81008, tel. (719) 545-8737.

The local office of the BLM is at 3170 E. Main, tel. (719) 275-0631.

For **road and weather conditions**, phone (719) 545-8520.

ROYAL GORGE

A bizarre blend of absolutely stunning scenery and god-awful promotion and exploitation, Royal Gorge can be enjoyed on a number of levels, and for a range of prices. If you've got the time and money ($10 admission), you can take in the entire experience: Take the aerial tram, the "Scenic Railway," the train to the bottom, and/or a helicopter tour; view a "25-minute sight and sound extravaganza" in the Royal Gorge "Plaza Theatre"; buy some deer food "for a buck" from the human-type beings dressed as a chipmunk and a miner; stay at "Yogi Bear's Jellystone Park RV Camp and Resort" (I'm not kidding).

Or . . .

Drive up to the tollgate, turn around, park, and walk over through the piñons to the cliffside (protected with chain-link fence), and take a look. For free. There's also a free picnic area just east of the tollgate. The problem is, you may have already been turned off by the tackiness of it all, the way the natural beauty has been subjugated, hidden away behind the waterslide and the billboards advertising "buffalo burgers" and "Pepsi, the Official Soft Drink of

Royal Gorge." What's truly stunning is that nature still manages, somehow, to awe and inspire despite it all. But just think what it must have been like in the days B.C. (Before Commercialism).

Buckskin Joe's

This theme park next to Royal Gorge offers gold panning, gunfights (11 a day!), horseback riding, and country music. For information, phone (719) 275-5149.

Steam Train and Antique Car Museum

This museum features a collection of hand-built steam trains, as well as a gondola, a caboose, tank cars, box cars, and cattle cars. The collection also includes many beautifully restored vintage American automobiles. Open daily through the summer. For information, contact the Cañon City Chamber of Commerce, tel. (719) 275-2331.

Accommodations

Although a number of private RV campgrounds at Royal Gorge vie for your patronage, you can

suspension bridge over 1,053-foot-deep Royal Gorge

camp free at what's probably the nicest area anyway. **Cañon City Campground** is a sprawling area with isolated sites (no water), located between the turnoff from US 50 and the tollgate about a mile down a well-maintained dirt road. Among the private campgrounds: **Camp Eight Eighty,** tel. (719) 269-3211; **KOA,** tel. (719) 275-6116; **Royal View RV Campground,** tel. (719) 275-1900; and **Yogi Bear Jellystone Park RV Camp and Resort,** tel. (719) 275-2128.

Food

The **Grandview Steakhouse,** at the US 50 turnoff to Royal Gorge, tel. (719) 269-3594,

serves steaks, seafood, and pastas. There's also a restaurant at Buckskin Joe's and a cafeteria and a beer and pizza garden inside the tollgate at Royal Gorge Bridge.

Information

For more information on Royal Gorge, write Box 549, Cañon City, CO 81212-0549, or phone (719) 275-7507. To make reservations for whitewater rafting or helicopter tours, phone (719) 275-5161 or 275-7238. You can also get information from the **Cañon City Chamber of Commerce,** Box Bin 749, Cañon City, CO 81215-0749, tel. (719) 275-2331.

male elk

COLORADO SPRINGS

Snug up against the Rocky Mountains' forested eastern slope, with Pikes Peak rising towerfully just a few miles to the west, Colorado Springs (pop. 291,000; elev. 6,035 feet) is one of the state's more popular tourist destinations. With a huge variety of historical, recreational, and geological attractions, Colorado Springs could keep a traveler charmed for weeks.

A planned community dating from the late 1880s, Colorado Springs still reflects its original design—the downtown streets are wide, the sidewalks broad, and lush parks dot the city. You'll find a scattering of outdoor cafes, buildings that have been remodeled but not overly gentrified, and small shops. The centerpiece of the downtown area is Acacia Park, a lovely central park and plaza that looks like something out of *The Music Man* or a Norman Rockwell painting. Until recently the park had gone to seed (locals dubbed it "Needle Park"), but it has been "reclaimed," and on summer evenings these days is full of families, young couples, and old-timers. Some sit on benches enjoying ice cream cones from Michelle's across the street; others pack the shuffleboard courts or just idly watch the wonderfully summer-paced competition.

HISTORY

Between modern downtown Colorado Springs and Manitou Springs is Colorado City, or "Old Town." Founded in 1858 as "El Paso" (the site was chosen for its location at the base of popular Ute Pass Trail) by a group of Kansas miners, the town changed its name to El Dorado City just a year later, when a second group of Kansans laid out streets and housing sites. By the late 1850s the community was known as Colorado City, and by the early '60s it had some 300 homes and cabins; for a few short years Colorado City was the territorial capital.

In 1871, William J. Palmer, a Denver and Rio Grande Western Railroad baron and former Civil War general, bought 10,000 acres of land east of Colorado City and went about designing what he foresaw as a thoroughly modern and "up-

right" community, complete with schools, parks, and churches. Calling his new town Fountain Colony, Palmer discouraged industry of all kinds, as well as saloons and gambling houses, which he believed were better left to the still-wild-and-woolly Colorado City. In fact, the new town was so bent on maintaining a "temperate" community that all city deeds had specific contracts disallowing the manufacture and sale of alcoholic beverages. Colorado Springs remained "dry" until the repeal of the 18th Amendment in 1933.

Little London

Although one of Colorado Springs' original aims was to set itself apart from the rowdy Manitou Springs, a road between the two communities was built within a year of the construction of Palmer's first buildings. Soon visitors, drawn to Colorado Springs by the railroad companies' boasts of pure, medicinal mineral waters and a dry and healthful year-round climate, were regularly making the short trek to Manitou. Meanwhile, Colorado Springs grew from its original buildings—a post office, hotel, and railroad office—to a bustling resort community with elegant mansions, polo and cricket fields, and golf courses. So popular was Palmer's Colorado Springs with easterners and Europeans, who gave it a decidedly cosmopolitan flair, that Palmer's resort city earned itself the nickname, "Little London." During these same years, several sanatoriums were built to accommodate the increasing numbers of tuberculosis patients moving to the area. Evidence of Colorado Springs' TB days can be seen today in the huge porches on hillside houses, as well as in the immense number of towering trees, originally planted to increase the city's air quality.

Like many Colorado cities and towns, early Colorado Springs was shaped to a large degree by the railroad (or, more precisely, the railroads). In the mid-1880s, the Colorado Midland Railroad ran a line west from Colorado Springs to facilitate ore transportation from the thriving mountain camps, and four years later, the city was designated as the far-western stop on the Chicago, Rock Island, and Pacific Railway. In

COLORADO SPRINGS

U.S. AIR FORCE ACADEMY

SOUTH GATE BLVD.

TO DENVER

WOODMAN RD.

CENTENNIAL BLVD.

GARDEN OF THE GODS RD.

GARDEN OF THE GODS

TO PIKES PEAK AND LEADVILLE

AUSTIN BLUFFS PKWY.

30TH ST.

FILLMORE ST.

MANITOU AVE.

MANITOU SPRINGS

OLD COLORADO CITY

31st ST.

COLORADO AVE.

21st ST.

CASCADE AVE.

NEVADA AVE.

TEJON ST.

WAHSATCH AVE.

UNION BLVD.

CIRCLE DR.

UINTAH ST.

ACADEMY BLVD.

TO LIMON

OLYMPIC SPORTS COMPLEX

McALLISTER HOUSE MUSEUM

PLATTE AVE.

BEAR CREEK PARK AND NATURE CENTER

LOWER GOLD CAMP RD.

CONVENTION AND VISITORS BUREAU

PIONEER'S MUSEUM

VERMIJO ST.

CIMARRON ST.

PIKES PEAK AVE.

MEMORIAL PARK

AIRPORT RD.

FOUNTAIN BLVD.

NORTH CHEYENNE CANYON PARK

CHEYENNE BLVD.

LAKE AVE.

BROADMOOR HOTEL

MUNICIPAL AIRPORT

N. CHEYENNE CANYON RD.

S. CHEYENNE CANYON RD.

CHEYENNE MTN. BLVD.

WILL ROGERS SHRINE

CHEYENNE MTN. ZOO RD.

CHEYENNE MOUNTAIN ZOO

TO CAÑON CITY

TO PUEBLO

0   1.5 mi

0   1.5 km

NOTE: ONLY MAIN ROADS SHOWN

© MOON PUBLICATIONS, INC.

1890, a cog railway was built to the top of Pikes Peak (see "Pikes Peak Area" following).

The Town Hits Pay Dirt

The development of Colorado Springs ground to a near standstill in the early 1890s when the silver market went bust; at the same time, the once-thriving Colorado City all but shut down. A few years later, however, things picked up again when the mines of Cripple Creek began producing vast quantities of gold. By the end of the century, Colorado Springs, as well as Colorado City, was back on its feet.

Colorado Springs continued to grow as a resort town, attracting large numbers of wealthy investors and vacationers. In addition, many of the miners who had struck it rich in the Rocky Mountain mines moved to the young town, built huge homes, and established an upscale social order, the remains of which can still be seen today in their palaces around the Broadmoor Hotel (see "Accommodations" below) and in the almost Old-World-like separation of the people who live in them from the working class. From 1900 to 1910, Colorado Springs' per-capita wealth was the highest in the country.

Meanwhile, Colorado City, whose economy relied largely on wages and on those who did the grunt work for the mine owners, ran into hard times when the mines played out. By the 1920s, most of the community's mills had been shut down and its saloon doors boarded up.

During the early 1940s, Colorado Springs began to take on the shape it has today, as military presence grew more and more part of the city's personality. In 1942, Fort Carson (originally called Camp Carson) was built to the south, and a few years later Peterson Air Force Base and the North American Aerospace Defense Command were part of the city's landscape. Work on the United States Air Force Academy, today the state's third most popular tourist attraction (see "Vicinity of Colorado Springs" following), began in 1954.

Modern Colorado Springs

The 1970s and '80s saw a huge boost in Colorado Springs' appeal to tourism. Many of Colorado City's and Manitou Springs' old buildings were converted to specialty shops, and the area's many geological wonders—from Royal Gorge and Pikes Peak to Garden of the Gods and Cave of the Winds—began to solicit visitors with more aggressive pitches, from elaborately slick brochures to monstrously hideous billboards that often screened off and scarred the mountains' otherwise scenic landscapes.

By the late '80s and the beginning of the century's last decade, Colorado Springs had taken on the feel of so many of the country's larger urban centers. Though the mountains keep the town from sprawling very much to the west, and the downtown area is nicely preserved, the east side has fallen victim to suburban blight, with miles and miles of housing developments, all looking very much alike, seeming to roll forever toward the plains. In addition, the mid- to late 1990s saw the city creeping southward as well. New housing now flanks much of CO 115 south of town, many of the homes scrunched onto the tiniest of lots, to make room for more.

SIGHTS

Pioneers Museum

Don't let the name mislead you: The Pioneers Museum, though basically historical in concept, displays a wide range of artifacts from the Pikes Peak area. The museum's highlights are temporary exhibits (often on loan from places such as the Smithsonian), as well as several permanent displays: Pikes Peak Natives, for example, which includes Paleo-Indian and more modern Native American cultures; and a look at the area's medical history, with an emphasis on tuberculosis—patients and cures. There's also a gift shop, which stocks an excellent selection of books. Also unique to this museum is its location: in the old El Paso County Courthouse, which opened in 1903, was restored in 1972, and dedicated as Pioneers Museum in 1979. Today the exhibits are in the original courtrooms; mock trials, open to the public, are held from time to time.

The Pioneers Museum, at 215 S. Tejon St., is open Tues.-Sat. 10 a.m.-5 p.m. and Sunday 1-5 p.m. Admission is free.

McAllister House Museum

Built in 1873 by Henry McAllister, one of General Palmer's protégés and an early civic leader, this was one of early Colorado Springs' first landmarks and showplaces. Listed on the National Register of Historic Places, the house had three white marble mantlepieces, shipped from Philadelphia, as well as running water. The home has been restored to its original elegance and appointed with authentic Victorian furnishings and decorations.

Today the McAllister House, at 423 N. Cascade (on the east side of the street; park in the alley), is open for tours and viewing. Hours are Wed.-Sat. 10 a.m.-4 p.m. and Sunday 12-4 p.m. (May-Aug.); Thurs.-Sat. 10 a.m.-4 p.m. (Sept.-April). Admission is $2 for adults, $1 for seniors and students.

Colorado Springs Fine Arts Center

With both rotating and permanent exhibits, this museum displays a wide array of 19th-century, modern, and postmodern art. The Charles Russell Room contains sketches and letters by the artist, as well as original manuscript pages from his autobiography. The museum also houses pieces by Georgia O'Keeffe, Peter Hurd, and Edward Hopper.

The museum, at 30 W. Dale (one block off N. Cascade), is open Tues.-Fri. 9 a.m.-5 p.m., Saturday 10 a.m.-5 p.m., and Sunday 1-5 p.m. Small admission charge. For more information, phone (719) 634-5581.

U.S. Olympic Sports Complex

Colorado Springs is one of the most outdoors- and sports-oriented areas in the country, so it's no surprise that the city is home to this 36-acre training complex, which also serves as headquarters for the U.S. Olympic Committee. Stop by to watch athletes working out (the thin air at 6,000 feet is ideal for training)—at everything from fencing to gymnastics to volleyball. Guided 90-minute tours take you through the facilities, beginning with a 90-minute film on the Olympics. There's also a gift and souvenir shop.

The complex, at 1750 E. Boulder, offers tours during the summer Mon.-Sat. 9 a.m.-5 p.m. and Sunday 10 a.m.-4 p.m.; the rest of the year Mon.-Sat. 9 a.m.-4 p.m. and Sunday 12-4 p.m. Admission is free. Phone the visitors center at (719) 578-4618 or the **Events Hotline** at (719) 578-4644.

World Figure Skating Hall of Fame and Museum

A true special-interest museum, this complex commemorates the history of ice-skating and honors famous skaters such as Sonja Henie and Peggy Fleming (who hails from Colorado Springs and the rink at the Broadmoor Hotel). Besides costumes, medals, and trophies, the museum also houses a library of ice-skating books and what it claims is the world's largest collection of ice-skating art.

Summer hours are Mon.-Sat. 10 a.m.-4 p.m., and Mon.-Fri. 10 a.m.-4 p.m. the rest of the year. No charge for admission. It's near the Broadmoor Hotel at 20 1st Street. For information, phone (719) 635-5200.

Carriage House Museum

This is a real sleeper—not many people even know about it. But right across Lake Circle from the main building of the Broadmoor Hotel, this little museum displays the carriage (and other vehicle) collection of Spencer Penrose, who built the Broadmoor Hotel in 1918. In perfect condition, all 33 of them, they include a one-horse *carromat* and *caliza* (from the Philippines), an 1890 opera bus (for two or four horses), an Abbott Downing and Company Concord Coach, built in 1850 and shipped around the Horn to be used for mail service in Mendocino County, California. There's also a beautiful 1928 Cadillac and an antique gun collection, including several examples of dueling pistols. A bonus is the two friendly and knowledgeable gentlemen who tend the museum. As classy as the carriages themselves.

The museum is open daily 9 a.m.-noon and 1-5 p.m. Admission is free, though donations are accepted.

Cheyenne Mountain Zoo

Perched on the hillside above the Broadmoor complex and southern Colorado Springs, this small zoo features some 800 animals in a natural setting lush with flora. Wind your way from cage to cage along narrow pathways overgrown with tall bushes. Highlights: gorgeous snow leopards, giraffes that eat out of your hand, and a monkey house.

Of course, a zoo is a zoo, and particularly on hot days one tends to wonder at the absurdity of locking wild animals in cages hundreds of times

*Not known for their
sense of humour,
giraffes just can't keep
tongue in cheek.*

smaller than what they'd ordinarily need to sustain themselves. But given that, this zoo tends to be environmentally responsible, with attention drawn to the plights of endangered species (many of which are represented here), as well as scheduled workshops for local school groups.

Zoo hours are 9 a.m.-6 p.m. Memorial Day through Labor Day and 9 a.m.-5 p.m. the rest of the year. The admission ($6 adult, $3 child) also gets you into the Will Rogers Shrine (see following). To get to the zoo, take Lake Ave. from S. Nevada (CO 115), and follow the signs. The route is well marked. For information, phone (719) 475-9555.

Will Rogers Shrine of the Sun

Even if you're not necessarily interested in Will Rogers, a drive up to this shrine is well worth your time. Clinging to the steep mountainside above southern Colorado Springs, the stone tower, made of indigenous gray-pink granite, offers excellent views of the city, particularly of the Broadmoor area (from here, you can really see the property's sprawling majesty).

Begun in 1934 and dedicated to the entertainer in September, 1937, the shrine was commissioned by Spencer Penrose, who owned the Broadmoor Hotel. When Penrose's friend Will Rogers died in 1935, Penrose decided to name the tower in his honor. (One story, perhaps apocryphal, is that Penrose—not known for his modesty—originally intended to honor himself with the shrine.)

Today, a tape of a Will Rogers monologue plays continually, and the interior of the tower is decorated with lots of photos of Rogers, including the plane crash that took his life, as well as with painted murals depicting Colorado's history. The shrine is open to the public Memorial Day through Labor Day 9 a.m.-5:30 p.m.; 9 a.m.-4:30 p.m. the rest of the year. Follow Mirada Rd. through Cheyenne Mountain Zoo (see above), admission to which includes entrance to the shrine.

Seven Falls

This is a beautiful series of seven waterfalls cascading into a tiny pool. If you've been faithful to your stairmaster, or are in moderately good shape, you can climb the *steep* steps to the tops of the two viewing platforms. The first clings to the canyon's side across from the falls (there's a snack bar and gift shop at the top); the second climbs the granite alongside the falls themselves and takes you to a trail that follows the meandering upper creek back into the woods. Native American dances are performed at the falls' base several times daily.

Admission is $6.25 for adults, $3 for kids six to 12. Take Cheyenne Blvd. and watch for the signs. For information, phone (719) 632-0741.

PARKS AND RECREATION

Near some of the finest outdoor recreation areas in the country, Colorado Springs is a natural for just about any sport or activity you can name (well, maybe not *surfing . . .*). And the folks who live here take advantage of it. They're an outdoorsy bunch—runners, skiers, hikers, climbers, cyclers, golfers, all enjoying that crisp mountain air and fabulous scenery.

Several city-maintained parks are scattered around town, offering grass, shade, and picnicking. **Memorial Park** is near downtown Colorado Springs (at Pikes Peak and Union) and has a public swimming pool, tennis courts, picnic facilities, huge lawns, shade trees, and a small lake. **Quail Lake Park,** just east of Nevada Ave./US 115 on Cheyenne Mountain Rd., is a very nice little community park with lush lawns, picnic tables, grills, hiking and biking trails, boating and fishing, and a wonderful kids' playground. **North Cheyenne Canyon Park,** on the west side of town at the end of Cheyenne Canyon Rd., offers hiking trails, guided nature walks, and interpretive programs, as well as rock-climbing and picnicking. For information, phone (719) 634-9320 or 578-6640. At **Bear Creek Regional Park,** 245 Bear Creek Rd., you can hike the five miles of nature trails, join in a guided walk, or explore the **Bear Creek Nature Center.** For more information, phone (719) 520-6387.

Golf

Colorado Springs has several excellent golf courses, public and private. The courses at the Broadmoor Hotel complex, tel. (719) 634-7711, attract some of the best (and wealthiest) golfers in the country. Open to members and hotel guests only. The 18-hole Robert Trent Jones course at the **U.S. Air Force Academy** is open to military personnel only (including retirees). Phone (719) 472-3456 for information and tee times. **Colorado Springs Country Club** is at 3333 Templeton Gap Rd., tel. (719) 473-1782.

If you've got neither the bucks nor the connections to play a private course, don't be putt off: the city has places for plebes too. **Pine Creek Golf Club,** 9850 Divot Dr., tel. (719) 594-9999, is an 18-hole public course open year-round, as are the **Patty Jewett Golf Course,** 900 E. Espanola, tel. (719) 578-6825, and **Valley-Hi Golf Course,** 610 S. Chelton Rd., tel. (719) 578-6926.

Hiking

Hiking and backpacking opportunities in the Colorado Springs area range from nature walks at the city parks (see above) to full-bore excursions into serious backcountry and treks to the top of Pikes Peak. The most popular route up Pikes Peak is **Barr Trail,** which begins above the hydroelectric plant in Manitou Springs off Ruxton Avenue. You'll find overnight shelters along the 13-mile (one way) trail at the 6.8-mile (Barr Camp Cabins) and 8.5-mile (Timberline A-frame) points. For information on camping, phone the Pike National Forest office at (719)

The Will Rogers Shrine of the Sun offers excellent views of Colorado Springs.

636-1602. **North Cheyenne Canyon Trail** will take you on an easy 10-mile (roundtrip) day hike with good views of Colorado Springs and the mountains. Look for the trailhead just past the entrance to North Cheyenne Canyon at the end of Cheyenne Canyon Road.

For more information on hiking and backpacking in the Colorado Springs area, write the **El Paso County Parks and Recreation Department** at 1045 W. Rio Grande, Colorado Springs, CO, or phone (719) 520-6375.

Swimming

Public swimming pools in Colorado Springs include the **Manitou Springs Pools,** 202 W. Manitou in Manitou Springs, tel. (719) 685-9735, and more than a half dozen Colorado Springs municipal pools, including **Memorial Park Pool,** tel. (719) 578-6634, and **Valley-Hi Pool,** tel. (719) 471-9085. For a complete list of municipal pools, phone the County Parks and Rec. Dept. at (719) 520-6375.

Cycling

As in the rest of the country, bicycling is enjoying a renaissance in Colorado Springs. This is due in large part to the overnight explosion in the popularity of mountain biking, though the interest in touring has also been rekindled. The city has published a wonderful map, *Pikes Peak Area Trails Map and Recreation Guide,* available at bike shops, outdoor shops, and the Colorado Springs Convention and Visitors center. For information on mountain biking and touring in the area, stop by **Mountain Chalet Sports,** 226 N. Tejon; **Criterium Bicycles,** 829 N. Tejon or 5660 N. Academy; **Mountain Tour Cycles,** 1813 N. Circle (where you can also rent mountain bikes; phone 719-389-0780).

Climbing

The steep sandstone spires and cliffs of the **Garden of the Gods** attract highly skilled rock climbers, as well as photographers and others awed by these athletes' arachnid ability to cling to vertical surfaces. Climbers must register at the visitors center before heading up.

Mountain Chalet Sports, 226 N. Tejon in Colorado Springs, tel. (719) 633-0732, carries climbing equipment, maps, and local guidebooks, and also rents gear.

Skiing

Colorado Springs is close enough to the state's major resorts that (weather permitting) serious shredders can head up for the day and be stepping into skis at, say, Monarch or A-Basin when the lifts open.

Cross-country skiers need not go all the way to Summit County to find some good fluff, as some excellent trails await in nearby **Pike National Forest.** For cross-country rentals, as well as advice on where to head, stop by **Mountain Chalet Sports,** 226 N. Tejon.

TOURS

Gray Line, tel. (719) 633-1181, offers tours to Pikes Peak, Royal Gorge, and other area attractions, including Seven Falls and Cave of the Winds. Gray Line also offers whitewater-rafting trips.

Pikes Peak By Bike, tel. (719) 633-6399 or (800) 798-5954, will haul you to the top of Pikes Peak for a ride down (19 miles). The company also offers other bike tours of the area.

ACCOMMODATIONS

Hotels

Without doubt one of the grandest of all hotels west of the Mississippi, **The Broadmoor,** tel. (719) 634-7711, will take your breath away even if you've prepared yourself to be impressed. Built in 1918, and added onto and renovated several times over the years, the 30-building complex—looking more like an Italian villa than an American hotel—sprawls beautifully at the foot of the Rocky Mountains.

Of course, none of the 700 rooms here is cheap, but for those rare occasions when you really want to toss caution to the wind, the Broadmoor offers you first class all the way. Doubles start at about $120 low season (Oct.-May); suites range $220-1540. Lodging plans range from no-frills digs to packages that include meals, champagne, golf, skiing, and tours of the area.

To get there, take Nevada Ave. south from downtown, and turn right on Lake Ave. (you'll see the signs).

the Broadmoor Hotel, one of the classiest lodges in the West

Another Colorado Springs institution is **The Antlers Double Tree Hotel,** 4 S. Cascade Ave., tel. (719) 473-5600, originally built in 1883 by William Palmer and for many years a rival to the Broadmoor. Recently bought and completely remodeled by the Doubletree chain, the hotel offers luxurious rooms starting at about $90 for two.

You'll also find many of the chain hotels in Colorado Springs. Doubles at these usually run about $50-90, with lower rates on weekends, when business people, whose companies are picking up their tabs, are less likely to be traveling. The following hotels all offer easy access for travelers: **Embassy Suites,** tel. (719) 599-9100 (Exit 149 from I-25); **Hampton Inn,** tel. (719) 593-9700 (Exit 149); **Hilton Inn,** tel. (719) 598-7656; **Marriott,** tel. (719) 260-1800 (Exit 147 from I-25); and two **Ramada Inns,** tel. (719) 596-7660 (at the airport), and tel. (719) 594-0700 (Exit 146 from I-25).

Motels

Colorado Springs has a wide range of motels, from historical places with lots of character to sterile freeway-side numbers that are nonetheless fine for a night's shut-eye for passers-through. Most of the city's chain motels are at or near the major freeway exits from I-25. You'll find two **Holiday Inns,** tel. (800) HOLIDAY, one at Exit 141, and one north, at Exit 145; rooms for two start around $45. At the Colorado Springs **Comfort Inn,** tel. (719) 598-6700 (Exit 150A),

and **Quality Inn,** tel. (719) 593-9119 (Exit 146), doubles run $45-65.

In addition, you'll find at least two "motel rows" in Colorado Springs. You can get cheap rooms at any of several motels along S. Nevada near the railroad tracks, as well as along US 24 west of town between Colorado City and Manitou Springs.

Bed and Breakfasts

The Colorado Springs area has several wonderful bed-and-breakfast inns. In fact, right downtown you'll find one of the nicest and best-known in the state, **The Hearthstone,** 506 N. Cascade, tel. (719) 473-4413. Remodeled from two side-by-side Victorians, now joined by what was originally a carriage house, the Hearthstone has 25 different rooms, each beautifully decorated in a specific theme and most with private baths. Rates range from about $60 for "The Dormer," the smallest room (no bath), to $140 for "The Fireside," which has a fireplace and its own private porch.

The **Holden House,** 1102 W. Pikes Peak Ave., tel. (719) 471-3980, is another elegantly restored Victorian (built in 1902). Named for historically important Colorado towns (Cripple Creek, Silverton), the Holden House's rooms are decorated with authentic furnishings from Colorado's past. Rates run about $60-90.

Youth Hostel

Colorado Springs' **American Youth Hostel,** tel. (719) 475-9450, is at Garden of the Gods Campground in Manitou Springs. Over 100 tent sites, as well as a dozen cabins with bunks. AYH members only; beds run about $10 for adults.

Camping and RVing

You'll find virtually limitless camping opportunities in **Pike National Forest** west of Colorado Springs, from improved areas with running water to backcountry sites where no one else may have ever camped. For maps and information on Pike National Forest, stop by the district ranger office at 601 S. Weber, or phone (719) 636-1602. Another great source is **Mountain Chalet Sports,** 226 N. Tejon, tel. (719) 633-0732, where you can pick up books and maps and talk to experts on camping and exploring the Colorado backcountry.

There's also lots of RV camping in the Colorado Springs area. Situated on 1,000 isolated acres four miles south of town on CO 115, **Golden Eagle Ranch RV Park,** tel. (719) 576-0450, has 500 RV campsites. It's also right next to the May Museum of Natural History (see "Vicinity of Colorado Springs" following). **Garden of the Gods Campground,** tel. (719) 475-9450, is adjacent to Garden of the Gods in Manitou and has 300 RV sites, as well as tent sites and cabins. Bus and trolley service to Manitou Springs and lots of social events (barbecues, watermelon feeds, Sunday pancake brunches). You'll also find several RV campgrounds west of Colorado Springs on US 24 (between Green Mountain Falls and Woodland Park).

FOOD

Start Me Up

Thankfully, Colorado Springs has jumped on the espresso bandwagon, and while looking for gourmet coffee in the Springs was once like looking for burgers in a Zen monastery, these days it's a lot easier. In fact, downtown is home to more than a handful of excellent espresso-and-baked-goods shops, where you can linger over the morning's paper (I recommend the *Denver Post* over the Colorado Springs paper) or your itinerary of the day's events. There's a **Starbuck's** at the corner of Tejon and Bijou and **Boulder Street Coffee Roasters** a block

north at Tejon and Boulder. Both, as well as the several other coffee shops downtown, have tables outside, and if Pikes Peak weren't looming just to the west you might think you were in North Beach. If you're out in old Colorado City, try **La Baguette,** 2417 Colorado Blvd., tel. (719) 577-4818, for gourmet coffees and a variety of pastries and breads. (La Baguette faithfully donates unsold bread to homeless shelters.) You can also get coffee and pastries at **La Creperie,** 204 N. Tejon, tel. (719) 632-0984, as well as crepe specials (stuffed with chicken, turkey, asparagus, etc.) for dinner ($6-8).

Downtown's **Country Kettle,** 23 S. Tejon, tel. (719) 520-0449, serves breakfast daily from 6 a.m. **The Olive Branch,** 333 N. Tejon, tel. (719) 475-1199, specializes in healthful breakfasts, including vegetarian dishes (there's a second Olive Branch at 2140 Vickers).

Inexpensive to Moderate

A favorite among both locals and passersthrough, particularly families, is **Giuseppe's,** tel. (719) 635-3111, serving good solid Italian food at reasonable prices—in the Old Depot (just a couple of blocks from downtown), where trains roar by regularly just outside the back door (ask for a window table to get the best view of the tracks). Specializing in pasta dishes (the lasagna is superb), sandwiches, and pizzas, as well as prime rib, steaks, and seafood, Giuseppe's also has a soup and salad bar and desserts (if you're not yet dragging your caboose).

Giuseppe's is at 10 S. Sierra Madre. From downtown, go about three blocks west—it's between the train tracks and old Engine 168, the power that pulled the first passenger train from Denver to Ogden, Utah, on May 21, 1883.

Another favorite for Italian food is **Old Chicago,** downtown at 118 N. Tejon, tel. (719) 634-8812, serving excellent pasta dishes, deep-dish pizzas, and Italian sandwiches ($5-10). The place does tend to get a bit crowded, especially on Friday evenings (when the downtown business crowd flocks in to wind down), but waiting for a table here is half the fun. The bar features over a hundred different kinds of beer from around the world, as well as a couple of television sets usually tuned to the seasonally appropriate sport. Old Chicago also offers takeout.

Speaking of beer and fun, if these two concepts interest you, don't miss the **Phantom Canyon Brewing Company,** 2 E. Pikes Peak Ave. (corner of Cascade), tel. (719) 635-2800, where you can wash down excellent sandwiches, pastas, salads, and traditional pub fare such as shepherds pie and fish and chips with some of Colorado's best microbrewery ales, beers, and stouts, as well as novelties, such as raspberry ale. A very popular local hangout.

At 222 N. Tejon is another hoppin' place, **Jose Muldoon's,** tel. (719) 636-2312, serving steaks, seafood, chicken, and Mexican and New Mexican food for $6-12. The **Ritz Grill,** 15 S. Tejon, tel. (719) 635-8484, serves pastas, fish, and stir-fry for $5-14, as well as soups, sandwiches, and salads for $2-6. **Luigi's,** 947 S. Tejon, tel. (719) 632-7339, is a family-owned Colorado Springs tradition, where you can get chicken, veal, pastas, and pizzas for $6-13. Specials include homemade lasagna Wednesday and manicotti Friday.

Another Colorado Springs tradition and favorite for Mexican food is **Henri's,** 2427 W. Colorado in Colorado City, tel. (719) 634-9031, serving stuffed *sopaipillas,* shrimp chiles rellenos, and other dinners ($7-9), as well as a la carte tacos, tostadas, etc. for $2-4. Also highly regarded by locals for Mexican food is **El Tesoro,** 10 N. Sierra Madre (right next door to Giuseppe's), tel. (719) 471-0106, where you can get blue-corn enchiladas, chile verde, and some of the best margaritas in town; dinners run $4-6. Also try **La Casita,** 1321 S. Nevada, tel. (719) 633-9616, a gas-station-turned-restaurant famous for its salsa bar, fresh tortillas, and *menudo.* For Thai, try **Little Bangkok,** 109 E. Pikes Peak Ave., tel. (719) 442-6546, where the food is hot and the coffee cold (iced).

For classic American food, you have several excellent choices. Rated by in-the-know Colorado Springs gourmets as one of the best downhome restaurants in the area, **Juniper Valley Ranch,** tel. (719) 576-0741, 15 miles south of town on CO 115, has served fried chicken, baked ham, and other American standards at reasonable prices for over 40 years. For closer-to-town American food (burgers, chicken-fried steak, fried catfish), try **Gunther Toody's Diner,** 3952 N. Academy, tel. (719) 597-1950. Dinners are $3-8. If you'd rather eat on the lighter (and

more healthful) side, check out the **Dale Street Cafe,** 115 E. Dale St., tel. (719) 578-9898. Salads (Caesar, Niçoise, spinach, tabbouleh, etc.), pastas, and Mediterranean pizzas run $5-8.

More Expensive

As a resort town founded primarily by big money, Colorado Springs claims its share of upscale restaurants, most notably those located in the Broadmoor Hotel. In fact, the Broadmoor complex includes eight separate restaurants, ranging from casual (relatively speaking) dining rooms off the golf course to those in the main buildings, with dress codes and don't-ask-the-prices menus.

The Broadmoor's classiest, fanciest, and most expensive restaurant is **Charles Court,** tel. (719) 577-5774, in the west lobby. The **Penrose Room,** tel. (719) 577-5773, in Broadmoor South, specializes in continental cuisine. Both require coats and ties for men and dresses or skirts for women. The **Tavern,** tel. (719) 634-7711, in the Broadmoor Main, serves excellent food—steaks, prime rib, and seafood, as well as daily specials—at more affordable prices (dinners run about $12-24). Live music nightly.

For more information on dining at the Broadmoor Hotel, phone (719) 577-5252.

The **Steaksmith,** 3802 Maizeland Rd., tel. (719) 596-9300, is said to have the best steaks in town, as well as excellent seafood and desserts. Dinners run $12-22.

ENTERTAINMENT

Colorado Springs is a big enough city that you're likely to find live music and other entertainment just about every night of the week, ranging from lounge music to comedy to hardcore rock 'n' roll. Check the *Gazette-Telegraph,* Colorado Springs' daily newspaper, for listings of who's playing where and when. Friday's edition carries the "Scene" supplement, geared specifically to entertainment. Also check the weekly *Independent.*

Clubs

A great place to go with family and friends is the **Golden Bee,** in the International Center at the Broadmoor. Gather round a table, order up a yard-long schooner of beer, pass around the house songbooks, and join the crowd accompanying the tavern's pianist.

To quaff a few with the downtown locals, stop by **Old Chicago,** 118 N. Tejon, tel. (719) 634-8812, especially on a Friday around happy hour.

The local favorite for comedy is **Laff's Comedy Corner,** 1305 N. Academy Blvd., tel. (719) 591-0707, where acts range from Springs' stand-ups to big-name stars on tour.

Take Me Out to the Ball Game

As anyone who's been to a minor league baseball game knows, these games have a charm and attraction all their own. You don't have to fight crowds, all the seats are good (and cheap!), the young players, while working hard to make it to the Bigs, are having great fun, and the fans are absolutely *rabid.* The Colorado Skysox are the AAA team of the Colorado Rockies and play 72 games in the springs. Take in an afternoon or evening game and watch these young players on their way up (and some on their way down . . .). Box seats are $6, general admission $4. For information and tickets, phone (719) 597-1449.

CALENDAR

From chili cook-offs to rodeos, auto races, and arts-and-crafts festivals, there's something going on nearly every weekend in Colorado Springs. The town's biggies are the **Air Force Academy Graduation,** in late May; the **Fourth of July Celebration and Fireworks;** the **Pikes Peak Auto Hill Climb,** in July (past winners include Bobby and Al Unser and Mario Andretti); **Pikes Peak or Bust Rodeo,** in mid-August; and the **International Balloon Classic,** Labor Day Weekend. Watch the *Gazette-Telegraph* for listings of events. You can also get up-to-date information by phoning the convention and visitors bureau's **FunFone Events Line,** (719) 635-1723.

SHOPPING

Colorado Springs-area shopping is essentially clustered in three areas: downtown Colorado

Springs, Colorado City, and Manitou Springs. Downtown in the Springs, you'll find everything from upscale gift shops and boutiques to western traditions—hardware stores, shoe stores, and uniform stores. Be sure to allow some time to explore Old Colorado City, a National Historic District between the 2400 and 2700 blocks of Colorado Ave. (west of downtown). Lots of boutiques, art galleries, and cafes are housed in 1860s-era buildings that once served as supply stores and saloons for Cripple Creek miners. Check out **Michael Garman Galleries,** tel. (719) 471-1600, for miniature figurines and dioramas of street scenes. Equally impressive is **Simpich Character Dolls,** tel. (719) 636-3272, where you can get (or just look at) exquisitely detailed, handmade ceramic and fabric miniature dolls, with an emphasis on Christmas figures. The dolls come to life in the **Simpich Marionette Theatre,** where past productions include *A Christmas Carol, Heidi,* and *Beauty and the Beast.* Phone the theater at (719) 636-3539 for more information.

You'll also want to spend some time exploring the boutiques, galleries, and arcades in Manitou Springs. Shops range from some rather tacky rubber-tomahawk "trading posts" to legitimate and classy galleries and boutiques selling quality jewelry, pottery, and other crafts and artwork. When you're done shopping, or just need a break, there are lots of sidewalk cafes, as well as vendors selling soft drinks and saltwater taffy.

Colorado Springs' main mall is at US 24 and Platte and includes a Mervyn's, JCPenney, and scores of the other traditional mall shops—Victoria's Secret, Eddie Bauer, B. Dalton, and Foot Locker.

SERVICES

In emergencies in Colorado Springs, always dial **9-1-1.** For nonemergencies, phone the **Colorado Springs Police** at (719) 635-6611; the **El Paso County Sheriff** at (719) 390-5555; and the **Colorado State Patrol** at (719) 635-3581.

Colorado Springs' **Memorial Hospital** is at 1400 E. Boulder, tel. (719) 475-5000. The **Penrose-St. Francis Healthcare System** maintains three separate facilities: **Penrose Community**

Hospital, 3205 N. Academy, tel. (719) 591-3000; **Penrose Hospital,** 2215 N. Cascade, tel. (719) 630-5000; and **St. Francis Hospital,** 825 E. Pikes Peak, tel. (719) 636-8800. For information, phone their **Healthline** at (719) 630-5555.

The downtown branch of the **post office** is at 210 E. Pikes Peak; phone (719) 570-5343. For information, or for locations of other branches, phone (719) 570-5339.

Recycling

Colorado Springs is a relatively big city, and there are scores of places to recycle just about anything you've managed to collect on your trip. Recycle aluminum, glass, newspapers, and plastic containers at all Colorado Springs **King Soopers,** including those at the following sites: 1750 W. Uintah, 2720 Palmer Park, 6930 N. Academy, and the corner of Hancock and Academy. You can also recycle aluminum, glass, and newspaper, at two **Recycle America** locations (419 E. Vermijo and 1965 Commercial), as well as at **Springs Recycling,** 3436 W. Colorado Avenue. Colorado Springs **Safeways** will recycle aluminum and grocery bags.

For more information on where to recycle in the Colorado Springs area, contact **Waste Management of Colorado Springs,** tel. (719) 632-8877.

INFORMATION

For more information about Colorado Springs and the Pikes Peak-Manitou Springs area, contact the **Colorado Springs Convention and Visitors Bureau,** tel. (719) 635-7506 or (800) 88-VISIT. The bureau's offices are downtown at 104 S. Cascade (free parking at entrance on Colorado Ave. and camper parking one block west). Stop in to pick up brochures on area attractions, as well as dining, lodging, and events guides; particularly useful is the free Colorado Springs *Official Visitors Guide.* Write the **Colorado Springs Chamber of Commerce** at Drawer B, Colorado Springs, CO 80901, or phone (719) 635-1551.

The information center for the **Pikes Peak Library District** is at 5550 N. Union Blvd., tel.

(719) 531-6333. The district's downtown branch is the **Penrose Public Library,** tel. (719) 473-2080, at Kiowa and Cascade.

One of the area's best bookstores is **The Chinook Bookshop,** downtown at 210 N. Tejon, tel. (719) 635-1195. It stocks an excellent selection of books (travel, recreation, histories, etc.) on the Colorado Springs area, as well as on the rest of Colorado and the West, including a large section of Native American works. For used books, check out **Poor Richard's,** 324 N. Tejon, tel. (719) 578-0012, where you'll also find a cafe and espresso bar. Another excellent used bookstore is **Four Corners Bookshop,** 425 Bijou, directly across from the downtown plaza.

Colorado Springs' daily newspaper is the *Gazette-Telegraph.* For subscription information, phone (719) 632-5511 or write Box 1779, Colorado Springs, CO 80901. The city's weekly alternative, *The Colorado Springs Independent* is a refreshing change from the *Gazette-Telegraph,* with profiles of locals, restaurant reviews, and stories with environmental-libertarian perspectives.

For information on **road and weather conditions,** phone (719) 635-7623.

Internet Information

The Colorado Springs Convention and Visitors Bureau can also provide information to subscribers for various electronic information servers. The web address is: **http://www.coloradosprings-travel.com/cscvb.**

Further Reading

One of the best histories of the area is Marshall Sprague's *Newport of the Rockies.* Available in most Colorado Springs-area bookstores, this book documents the city from its beginnings under General William Palmer, through its popularity with health- and cure-seekers, particularly tuberculosis patients, and into the later 20th century. Sprague's *Money Mountain, the Story of Cripple Creek Gold* will also interest travelers who want to learn about the area's past. Sprague writes as though he were telling you yarns as you sat around a campfire at the base of Pikes Peak.

TRANSPORTATION

Getting There

Colorado Springs Airport is a small, user-friendly facility that has seen huge increases in customers since Denver International Airport (DIA) opened in early 1995. With United's virtual monopoly at DIA, as well as DIA's distance from downtown, many Denver-area travelers are finding it's both cheaper and easier to drive to Colorado Springs, which is served by several major carriers, including **American Airlines, America West, Continental, Delta, Reno Airlines, TWA, Western Pacific,** and **United Express.** For a free flight guide, phone (800) GO-CSPG. **Colorado Springs Airport Shuttle Services, Inc.,** tel. (719) 578-5232, offers regular shuttles from the airport to Colorado Springs hotels and private residences. **Colorado Springs Ski Lift,** tel. (719) 593-5921 or (800) 972-2690, specializes in service to the nearby ski areas, including Breckenridge, Copper Mountain, and Keystone. Colorado Springs' bus terminal is at 327 S. Weber; phone **Greyhound-Trailways** at (719) 636-1505 or (800) 527-1566.

Automobile rentals are available both downtown and at the airport. Rent from **Avis,** tel. (719) 596-2751; **Budget,** tel. (719) 473-6535; **Dollar,** tel. (719) 591-6464; **Hertz,** tel. (719) 596-1863; **Payless,** tel. (719) 597-4444 (airport) or 471-4444 (downtown); and **Thrifty Car Rental,** tel. (719) 574-2472. Phone **Yellow Cab** at (719) 634-5000.

Getting Around

Getting around in Colorado Springs is not difficult. **Colorado Springs Transit** buses serve most of the metropolitan area. For route information, phone (719) 475-9733.

When driving, remember the major north-south arteries are I-25, CO 115, Academy/CO 83, Wahsatch, Nevada, Tejon, and Cascade; major east-west arteries include Fountain, US 24/Platte, Colorado (which connects Colorado Springs and Manitou Springs and becomes Pikes Peak Blvd. east of US 24), Constitution, Fillmore, and Austin Bluffs Parkway. It's helpful, too, to keep a bit of history in mind: Queen Palmer, wife of founding father General William Palmer, named Colorado Springs' original north-south streets, or those parallel with the Rockies, after other mountain ranges (Cascade, Sierra Madre, Wahsatch) and east-west streets after rivers (Cimarron, Cuchara, Rio Grande, Las Animas, Colorado, Platte, Willamette). Finally, remember that Pikes Peak and the Rocky Mountains are always to the *west*—you couldn't ask for a better landmark.

VICINITY OF COLORADO SPRINGS

In addition to the many things to do and see in town, the surrounding area has a wide range of other attractions, from museums, railways, and shopping areas to mountains, forests, and redrock canyons—enough to keep the budding naturalist exploring happily for weeks on end. Whether your bent is to watch white-capped cadets marching in formation at the U.S. Air Force Academy or to hike to the top of Pikes Peak and take in the incredible vistas, you're sure to find plenty to do.

SIGHTS

United States Air Force Academy

One of Colorado Springs' main tourist attractions, this 18,000-acre officer-training campus is impressive (even if you're not a military buff) for its military importance, its intriguing architecture and layout, and the gorgeous grounds, rife with wild game, in the forests at the foot of the Rocky Mountains.

Though much of the campus is off-limits to visitors, you can take a self-guided driving tour through the grounds, with a number of stops along the way. The huge visitor center, open daily 9 a.m.-5 p.m. (till 6 in summer), has displays on the academy's beginnings (founded in 1954), a map with pins showing hometowns of current cadets, textual and photo exhibits of the school's educational programs, the requisite display showing how being a cadet "builds character," and a gift shop, where you can get Air Force sweatshirts and other souvenirs. Regularly scheduled guided tours are offered free of charge. Admission to the visitor center is also free.

To get there, take Exit 156B from I-25 to the academy's north entrance, and follow the signs. At the gate, you'll be given a map to help guide you through the grounds and to the visitor center and other parts of the campus open to tourists, including the chapel, planetarium, parade ground, and nature trail.

For more information, write **Visitor Services Division,** Directorate of Public Affairs, HQ USAFA/PAV, USAF Academy, CO 80840-5151; or phone (719) 472-2025.

ProRodeo Hall of Fame and Museum

Even if you didn't grow up ropin' and ridin', and even if the closest you've come to a rodeo is the pages of a Larry McMurtry novel, you'll still get a boot out of this museum.

Displays include works by Gary Morton, of New Mexico's Bell Ranch (paintings), who's

B-52 Bomber displayed on the campus of the U.S. Air Force Academy

statue outside Colorado Springs' ProRodeo Hall of Fame and Museum

also a cowboy ("I'll keep on ridin' for my pleasure and paintin' the cowboy's domain"); a memorial to Casey Tibbs, with memorial by Charlie Daniels (his gold record for "Simple Man" and a poem, "Casey's Last Ride" dedicated to Tibbs); and lots of great photos, including shots of clowns *working* (saving bronc riders in BIG trouble), trophies, silver spurs, gold buckles, and beautifully tooled saddles.

The museum, north of town at Exit 147 off I-25, is open daily 9 a.m.-5 p.m. Admission is $5 for adults; group rates available. For information, phone (719) 593-8847.

Western Museum of Mining and Industry

A nonprofit and low-key outfit, this is one of Colorado Springs' true gems, one that avoids the touristy trappings of some of the other attractions. Tours begin with a short slide show (sponsored in part by the National Endowment for the Humanities) on the history of western mining, and then you're taken through displays of various steam engines (which your tour guide will fire up), and even to a sluice box (where you'll learn how to pan for gold). In all, there are over 15,000 square feet of exhibits in several different

buildings. An 8,000-volume library is open to museum members and students (by appointment only).

Admission, including the tour, is $5 for adults, $4 for seniors and students, and $2 for kids five to 12. Group rates (the museum is a natural for field trips!) are available. Hours are Mon.-Sat. 9 a.m.-4 p.m. and Sunday 12-4 p.m.

Take Exit 156A (Gleneagle Dr.) from I-25 and follow the signs (east side of highway). For more information, phone (719) 488-0880.

May Museum of Natural History And Space Museum

A couple of the area's quirkiest museums, these two display the lifetime collections of artifacts owned by John May. The Museum of Natural History actually specializes in entomology, as you would have guessed from seeing the giant beetle at the turnoff. But even for non-bug fans, this is some interesting stuff—butterflies, moths, spiders, and beetles of every imaginable size, shape, color, and attitude, all well displayed and safely dead, thank you. Check out the 20-inch-long Karabidionaustrala monster from New Guinea (something like a giant praying mantis), the megasoma beetle from South America (just smaller than a Volkswagen), a Peruvian tarantula scarfing a hummingbird, and foot-long Venezuelan centipedes.

There's also a small gift store, where you can pick up an odd assortment of souvenirs—how 'bout a shiny gold black widow lapel pin?

The Space Museum, off in the woods a hundred feet or so from the bug museum, is even more peculiar—but for entirely different reasons. First of all, it's in an old musky-smelling house trailer, with warped paneling, and then there are the displays—model airplanes and photos and maps, most of which look like they were picked up in dime stores and in gift shops at other museums. There's also an early-flight exhibit, and a display, with news clippings and photos, of the American space program.

Again, a quirky little place, where a sense of humor will get you a long way. Entrance fee to both museums is $4.50. Open 8 a.m.-5 p.m. in May; 8 a.m.-9 p.m. June through September; closed the rest of the year. To get there, take CO 115 south of town, past Fort Carson, and watch for the giant beetle on the west side of the road.

The Golden Eagle Ranch RV Park is adjacent to the museum and administered by the same people—see "Accommodations" under "Colorado Springs" above. For more information, phone (719) 576-0450.

PIKES PEAK AREA

Of course, the main attraction here is Pikes Peak itself, the flagship of the Front Range. First spotted in 1806 by Zebulon Pike, the mountain had been known to the Utes for years as "The Long One." In the 1850s, the mountain was a welcome sight to westbound gold seekers, whose covered wagons often bore their motto, "Pikes Peak or bust." Pikes Peak was also the "purple mountain . . . above the fruited plains" to which Katherine Lee Bates was referring when she wrote *America the Beautiful.* Each summer in July, top race-car drivers from around the world compete in the Pikes Peak Hill Climb, or the "Race to the Sky." There's also an annual footrace to the top.

Pikes Peak Highway

In 1916, a road was cut to the top of Pikes Peak, and for the next 20 years was maintained with funds collected at the tollgate ($2 per car), providing a popular, if somewhat nerve-rattling, manner in which to test the guts, and brakes, of early motorcars. Between 1936 and 1948, the Forest Service took over the highway's operations and allowed passage free of charge, although without the funds to maintain the road, it quickly fell into a state of decline. The City of Colorado Springs took over the highway in 1948 and has been managing it since.

Pikes Peak Highway is open daily April-Oct. (weather permitting). The nearly 20-mile (one way) route, which rises about 7,000 feet, is paved the first third of the way, and is gravel-dirt the rest. Allow at least two hours roundtrip. At the 13-mile point is the **Glen Cove Inn,** where you'll find a snack bar, souvenirs, and restrooms. The road quickly gets steep, zigzagging dramatically up the mountainside, past the treeline, then rolling out onto some positively lunar landscape. Watch for bighorn sheep, deer, and marmot, as well as figure eights made by skiers. The views along the way, of Denver, the San Juans, the plains, are stunning.

At the top is the **Summit House,** a second gift shop, and a doughnut shop and snack bar. If you plan to get out, bring a sweater: It may be warm down in Colorado Springs, but it'll be *cold* up top, most likely with a biting wind.

Unfortunately, the toll is per person, not per car, so it can get a bit steep, although all proceeds go to road maintenance. Toll: Age 12 and up, $5; age six to 11, $2; five and younger, free. The tollgate is open 9 a.m.-3 p.m. in April and May and 7 a.m.-6:30 p.m. through the summer. Be sure to get a map and information

looking down on Pikes Peak Highway from near the summit

brochure, and pay attention to its driving tips. To get there, take US 24 west from Manitou Springs to Cascade Rd. and watch for the signs. For more information and road conditions, phone (719) 684-9383.

Hiking Trails

The in-shape and adventurous can hike to the summit of Pikes Peak, something Zebulon Pike wrote would never be possible. Many hikers take Barr Trail (named for Fred Barr, the trail's designer) and allow two days to make the 26-mile roundtrip. You can spend the night at either of two camps about halfway up from the trailhead (see "Hiking" under Colorado Springs above). For maps and more information, stop by the office of Pike National Forest, 601 S. Weber St., or phone (719) 636-1602.

Pikes Peak Cog Railway

If you don't trust your rig, or your nerves, you can instead get to the top of Pikes Peak by rail. The seven-mile ride offers equally stunning views and takes just over three hours roundtrip (the old Swiss-made trains chug s-l-o-w-l-y up the 26% grade). The train runs about every hour and a half 8 a.m.-5:20 p.m., departing from Manitou Springs. At the top is a snack bar and gift shop. Cost is $21 for adults and $9.50 for kids five to 11; no charge for kids five and younger if they're held on laps.

Pikes Peak Cog Railway

To get to the depot, take Manitou Ave. to Ruxton, go left, and watch for the signs. For information, write Manitou and Pikes Peak Railway, Box 351, Manitou Springs, CO 80829, or phone (719) 685-5401.

North Pole/Santa's Workshop

Located in a beautiful mountain setting at the foot of Pikes Peak, this amusement park offers a variety of rides, shows, and other diversions for kids from one to ninety-two. You can pet Santa's reindeer and other animals, see toys being made for Christmas delivery, ride the antique carousel, take a train ride, and then stop for a milk shake or hot chocolate in the ice-cream parlor.

The North Pole is open mid-May until Christmas Eve. In May, hours are Fri.-Wed. 9:30 a.m.-6 p.m.; June 1-Aug. 31, daily 9 a.m.-6:00 p.m.; and Sept. 1-Dec. 24, Fri.-Tues. 10 a.m.-5 p.m. Admission is $7.95, with discounts for kids and seniors. Phone (719) 684-9432.

MANITOU SPRINGS

Located about 10 miles west of Colorado Springs on US 24, Manitou Springs was named for the two dozen mineral springs that have been attracting health seekers for centuries.

Long before white settlers arrived in the mid-19th century, Native American hunting parties visited the springs when passing through the area. In the 1860s and '70s, miners heading into or out of the Cripple Creek area would stop here. Many of them eventually settled, turning Manitou into a sort of frontier resort.

Manitou Springs today is part artists' community, part resort, and part tourist trap—a blend of galleries, gift shops, quiet city parks, tastefully remodeled Queen Anne homes, and Coney Island-type arcades. A National Historic District, Manitou Springs offers a wide range of history-oriented attractions, from turn-of-the-century stone castles and old stagecoach stops to "trading posts," wax museums, and reproductions of Anasazi cliff dwellings.

Garden of the Gods

One of the most popular attractions in the Colorado Springs area, Garden of the Gods is a geologic oddity of bizarre red Morrison sandstone rock formations, some angry, jagged, and jutting, others softly and sensuously eroded. American novelist and campaigner for social justice Helen Hunt Jackson described the gardens in the 1880s as "colossal monstrosities looking like elephants, like gargoyles, like giants . . . all motionless and silent, with a strange look of having been stopped and held back in the very climax of some supernatural catastrophe." Dedicated in 1909, this city park is not only a geologist's dream come true, but it's also a hiker's, horseback-rider's, and climber's paradise. And—here's the best part—this 1,350-acre registered National Natural Landmark is absolutely *free.* An oddity in itself in a region where it's routine to shell out 20 bucks so the family can view paraffin approximations of American historical figures waxing nostalgic under museum lights.

The lunarlike landscape of the Garden of the Gods began to take shape some 300 million years ago, long before the Rockies pushed up to their modern (in geological terms) elevation and eminence. Some of the spires you see standing above the garden floor—the tallest of which is 300 feet—have withstood the eroding powers of wind and rain that long.

A series of loop roads will take you out into the gardens (past several picnic areas), and even if you don't get out and do much exploring, you ought to stop in at the new **visitor center** (opened in May 1995). You'll find a variety of geology, history, and wildlife displays there, as well as a small theater where an excellent multimedia show ($1.50) explains the geology of the region. You can also sign up for guided nature walks. Rock climbers must register with rangers here. The Garden of the Gods Trading Post is the largest gift shop in the Pikes Peak area and sells a range of artwork, jewelry, and souvenirs, including work by highly regarded Native American artists such as R.C. Gorman.

Garden of the Gods is open year-round. Summer hours are 5 a.m.-11 p.m.; reduced hours the rest of the year. To get there, take US 24 from Colorado to Manitou Springs, turn north on Ridge Rd., and follow the signs. You can also get there by taking Garden of the Gods Rd. off I-25 to 31st St. and following the signs. For more information on Garden of the Gods, write 1401 Recreation Way, Colorado Springs, CO 80905, or phone (719) 578-6640. Call the Trading Post at (719) 685-9045.

Glen Eyrie

This sprawling estate and castle, listed on the National Register of Historic Places, was built in 1904 by Colorado Springs' founding father William Palmer for his wife, Queen. The property includes stables, lagoons, a schoolhouse, and a dairy, as well as the castle itself, decorated with furnishings from Europe and heated by 24 fireplaces, many of which were also brought from abroad—one was carved by Benedictine monks in the late Middle Ages.

Tours of Glen Eyrie, which begin at 1:00 p.m., take approximately 75 minutes and cost $5, less for kids and seniors (no charge for ages 12 and younger). Reservations are highly recommended. Sunday afternoons, High Teas are offered for $8.95 ($11.95 with tour), and Mon.-Fri English Teas are offered for $5.95 ($8.95 with tour).

For information and reservations, phone (719) 594-2268. To get there, take Garden of the Gods Rd. west from I-25, and turn left on 30th St., or take 30th or 31st north from Colorado Ave. in Manitou. Glen Eyrie is just north of Garden of the Gods.

Miramont Castle Museum

If Garden of the Gods is Manitou Springs' geologic oddity, then Miramont Castle is its architectural one. Dating from just before the turn of the century, this four-story, 14,000-square-foot structure, with its two-foot-thick stone walls, looks like it's part medieval castle, part Swiss chalet, and part San Francisco Victorian. In fact, the castle's original design drew on nine distinct architectural styles.

Commissioned in 1895 by Father Jean Baptiste Francolon, an ailing but wealthy French priest who came to Manitou with his mother for the mineral springs, the castle has 46 rooms ranging from open and airy sitting rooms to small and dark bedrooms barely bigger than closets. After the priest died, the castle served as a sanatorium and later as an apartment building. It was put on the National Register of Historic Places in 1977.

Today, the castle is open to the public. Some of the rooms have been restored to approximate their original flavor, while others house various displays—a doll museum, railroad museum, and a miniature reproduction of turn-of-the-century Colorado Springs, complete with an in-progress baseball game. The castle also has a restaurant and hosts weddings and other groups and parties.

Summer hours are daily 10 a.m.-5 p.m., the restaurant serving 11 a.m.-3 p.m. by reservation only, while Sept.-May the castle is open 1-3 p.m. daily. Small admission fee to the castle. For more information, or to book tours, phone (719) 685-1011. You can also write Miramont Castle, 9 Capitol Hill Ave., Manitou Springs, CO 80829. To get there, take Manitou Ave. west to Ruxton, turn left, and then go right on Capitol Hill Road.

Cave of the Winds

A strange blend of nature at its most impressive and commercialism at its most shameless, Cave of the Winds is a mile-deep cavern, tours of which are so orchestrated and slick that you feel more like you're at Universal Studios than deep underground. Look beyond the fancy lights and talking rocks, though, as well as the corny group photo and the push to buy a print at tour's end ($4), and you'll find the cave quite fascinating. Discovered in 1880 by children who were playing nearby, the cave is named for the sound the wind makes as it whistles through the subterranean tunnels.

Of particular interest is the nature display, where area birds and minerals are identified, and kids can use blocks to make wolf, deer, raccoon, coyote, and other animal tracks in the sand. The gift and souvenir shop sells the standard key chains, mugs, T-shirts, and Native American jewelry; there's also a snack bar. A brand new Wild Winds Tour is available to visitors who want to go beyond where most visitors get and to do some genuine spelunking (reservations, old clothes, flashlight, and $30 required).

Cost for the regular tour is $8 for adults, $4 for kids six to 15 (tours last 45 minutes). Take US

24 west and watch for the signs. For more information, phone (719) 685-5444.

Manitou Cliff Dwellings

Not to be mistaken for the real McCoys—in New Mexico, Arizona, and southwestern Colorado—these cliff dwellings were built here in 1906, some 600 years after the last Anasazi packed his spare loincloth into his Samsonite, checked out of his room, and climbed down off Mesa Verde. Actually a decent facsimile, the dwellings were made of rocks hauled from the Four Corners area with the best of intentions—to preserve the remains of a culture that was disappearing as fast as its people once did. Regular dances by Plains (?) Native Americans suggest a possible nomination for an Unclear-on-Concept Award.

In addition to the dwellings, there's a small museum, where you can get a sense of 13th-century pueblo life, as well as of the dwellings' construction, by viewing dioramas and Anasazi and Mogollon pottery and other artifacts.

Summer hours are daily 8 a.m.-9 p.m.; in May, September, and October, the museum's open 10 a.m.-5 p.m. Admission is $4, less for kids and seniors. For information, phone (719) 685-5242.

Ghost Town

Though a bit on the gimmicky side, Ghost Town offers a wide array of authentic historical artifacts and knicknacks, arranged to simulate an American frontier town. There's a general store, with candy jars, hog tonic, hats, corsets, and washbowls, a barbershop, jail, post office, bank, and a stagecoach that ran between Denver and Cheyenne in 1868. You can also view Roosevelt's 1942 bullet-proof Lincoln limousine (and wonder what the hell it's doing here), as well as the proverbial two-headed calf. Exit, of course, through the "Trading Post" (read, gift shop).

Summer hours are weekdays 9 a.m.-7 p.m. and Sunday 1-6 p.m. Also open weekdays 9 a.m.-5 p.m. and Sunday 1:30-5 p.m. May 1 through Memorial Day and Labor Day through mid-October. Admission for adults is $3.75, less for kids and seniors. To get there, turn south on 21st St. from US 24 West. For more information, phone (719) 634-0696.

Buffalo Bill Wax Museum

Offering a general overview of the West, this museum features wax likenesses of many of the characters from western American history and mythology, many of them acting out the scenes for which they're most famous. See Black Bart in mid-holdup, the shoot-out at the OK Corral, Black Jack Ketchum's hanging in Clayton, New Mexico—also Buffalo Bill and Annie Oakley (good taste precludes a re-creation of what *they* were best known for . . .), the James Gang, mountain men Jim Bridger and Jim Bowie, and western writers Mark Twain, Bret Harte, and Ned Buntline. A highlight is the authentic western music, a la Sons of the Pioneers.

Buffalo Bill Wax Museum is in Manitou Springs at 404 W. Manitou. In summer, it's open daily 8 a.m.-5:30 p.m.; in April, May, and September daily 8 a.m.-5 p.m. Admission is $3.50 for adults and $1.50 for kids six to 16—no charge for children five and younger. For information, phone (719) 685-5900.

Hall of the Presidents Living Wax Studio

Featuring wax figures from Madame Tussaud's London studio, Hall of the Presidents depicts U.S. presidents (and other political figures) through Reagan at historical moments: Thomas Jefferson signing the Declaration of Independence, John Adams and Benjamin Franklin at the Court of Versailles in 1782, the assassination of Garfield in 1881, and Reagan nodding off during a summit conference. The museum also has a wax Pinocchio, Alice in Wonderland, and Snow White and the Seven Dwarfs.

Hall of the Presidents, at 1050 S. 21st Street, is open daily in the summer 9 a.m.-9 p.m. and Oct.-April Thurs.-Mon. 1-5 p.m., Saturday 10 a.m.-5 p.m. Admission is $4 for adults, less for kids and seniors. For more information, phone (719) 635-3553.

Pikes Peak Auto Hill Climb Museum

This small museum displays race cars and motorcycles that have raced in the annual 4th of July Pikes Peak Hill Climb since the 1920s. The brief tour, which takes you from the first cars (a 1920 Lexington, a 1936 Coniff Special) to very recent high-tech jobs (including several that were built and raced by Bobby Unser), winds up at a small sitting room where you can see video

a wax Richard Nixon at the Hall of Presidents Living Wax Museum, but no mention of his checkered past

footage (ESPN) of recent races. There's also a small gift shop with hats, jackets, banners, and other race mementos. The museum is at 135 Manitou Ave. in Manitou Springs. Admission is $4 for adults, with discounts for kids and seniors. For more information, phone (719) 685-5996.

Van Briggles Art Pottery

Billed as an art studio offering free instructive tours, Van Briggles has been in business since 1899, and the uniquely gorgeous pottery is one of the prides of Manitou. Paris-taught founder Artus Van Briggle was world famous and won numerous awards for his work, many of which are on display in the studio.

Maybe I'm naive to the ways of the business world, but I was expecting more from my visit than a sales pitch. Most of the five-minute "free tour" is spent watching a potter at work on a wheel while your tour guide explains the process of "throwing"—the whole thing really just a gimmick to get you into the "showroom" and the clutches of too many eager salespeople. Too bad, because the work is beautiful, and it'd be nice to be able to enjoy it without feeling pressured.

The studio, at the corner of Colorado Ave. and 21st St., is open Mon.-Fri. 8 a.m.-5 p.m. and Saturday 8:30 a.m.-5 p.m. For more information, phone (719) 633-7729.

Flying W Ranch

The Flying W is a working cattle ranch where you can get an authentic chuckwagon dinner before settlin' in for a western stage show featuring The Flying W Wranglers, a western band that plays swing, gospel, and country favorites and dishes a healthy portion of corn-pone humor. The dinner, which includes baked beans, beef, homemade biscuits, and apple sauce (delicious!), and show are offered rain or shine (indoors if it's wet, outdoors otherwise) at long picnic-style tables, where you can get a chance to meet and talk with some of the 1,400 guests the Flying W serves nightly. While you wait for the dinner and show, you can wander around the grounds, which include a reconstruction of 19th-century old-west town, with a blacksmith shop (watch the smith at work between 6 p.m. and 7 p.m. daily), jail, and other outbuildings/gift shops, selling everything from old-west cookbooks to western wear to Native American jewelry (our favorite was the book of John Wayne paper dolls at the bookstore). Reservations are required for dinner, seatings for which are at 7:15 p.m. daily mid-May through September. October through May, shows are offered Friday and Saturday nights only, with seatings at 5 p.m. and 8 p.m. (the Flying W is closed in January and February). Cost for dinner and show is $21 for adults, $11 for kids. Phone (719) 598-4000 or (800) 748-3999. To get there from I-25, take Garden of the Gods Rd. west to 30th St., turn right, and then go left on Flying W Ranch Road. From Manitou, take 30th St. north past Garden of the Gods to Flying W Ranch Road.

Manitou Springs-Area Lodging

The adobe **El Colorado Lodge,** tel. (719) 685-5485 or (800) 442-4884, is a rustically handsome motel on the east end of Manitou Springs.

Doubles range $35-70. Also in Manitou are **Garden of the Gods Motel,** 2922 W. Colorado Ave., tel. (719) 636-5271, where doubles run about $30-50, and the **Apache Motel,** 3401 W. Pikes Ave., tel. (719) 471-9440, where you can get a room for two for starting at about $30. At the **Manitou Super 8,** 229 Manitou Ave., tel. (719) 685-5898, doubles run $50-90. The **Two Sisters Inn,** 10 Otoe Pl., tel. (719) 685-9684, was built in 1919 and is a half block from the center of town. Stay in one of the five bedrooms in the main house ($60 with shared bath, $70 with private) or the separate cottage ($90).

Manitou Springs-Area Dining

Manitou Springs is home to several excellent restaurants, and a good number of small cafes, many with sidewalk seating. **The Stagecoach Inn,** 702 Manitou Ave., tel. (719) 685-9335, is located in an 1880s-era stagecoach stop that was also a summer home for novelist Helen Hunt Jackson. The perfect place for a light, casual lunch, the Stagecoach specializes in salads, soups, and quiches, and also serves dinner. The **Briarhurst,** 404 Manitou, tel. (719) 685-1864, is a high-end restaurant ($12-18 for entrees) housed in a stone mansion built in 1878 and serving continental cuisine cooked with organically home-grown herbs, fruits, and vegetables, and home-smoked meats and fish. **Antonio's,** 301 Garden of the Gods Rd., tel. (719) 531-7177, serves chicken, veal, and pasta dinners, in addition to several vegetarian specialties. Prices run $7-16. For good, homestyle cooking try **Above and Beyond,** 733 Manitou, tel. (719) 685-4234, where you walk through the kitchen to the second-floor dining room with views of the mountains and downtown.

If you're out wandering around in Manitou Springs and feel like snacking but aren't in the mood for the cotton candy, fudge, and caramel corn the arcades are pushing, check out **Market La Rue Too** just off the main drag at 102 Canyon. This unpretentious little grocery store sells organically grown produce, natural sodas, and other healthful treats.

Manitou Springs Information

The **Manitou Springs Chamber of Commerce** is at 354 Manitou Ave., Manitou Springs, CO 80829, tel. (719) 685-5089. Write or stop by for maps and brochures.

WEST OF COLORADO SPRINGS

US Highway 24 West from Colorado Springs rises quickly into beautiful mountain country, skirts the northeast flank of Pikes Peak, and passes through the southern section of Pike National Forest. About midway between Colorado Springs and Woodland Park, you'll pass turnoffs to Cascade, Chipeta Park, and Green Mountain Falls—small resort communities nestled at the base of Pikes Peak.

Cascade was founded in 1886 by transplanted Kansans, who built a number of small cottages along Fountain Creek. Among those who spent summers here was Indiana lawyer John Milton Hay, assistant secretary to President Lincoln. Hay wrote much of his ten-volume *Abraham Lincoln: A Life History* in Cascade, as well as his *Pike County Ballads.* Chipeta Park was named after Ute Chief Ouray's wife, Chipeta.

In Green Mountain Falls, you'll find a nice shady picnic area just off the highway, as well as a public swimming pool and a small lake with a tiny island and gazebo. The **Outlook Lodge,** tel. (719) 684-2303, in Green Mountain Falls is a quiet bed and breakfast on a forested hillside. Rooms with private baths start at about $45 (call ahead—the eight rooms book up way in advance). The **Falls Motel**, tel. (719) 684-9745, is situated right on the lake and has rooms (many with kitchens) starting at about $35.

In Woodland Park, you can either turn north onto CO 67, which will take you up through the national forest to the little fishing/resort village of Deckers, or you can stay on US 24, which continues west over Ute and Wilkerson passes, to Buena Vista and Leadville. Seven miles past Woodland Park is the turnoff to Cripple Creek, an important western historical site and one of Colorado's most popular tourist attractions.

Colorado 67 South to Cripple Creek is one of the highlights of exploring this part of the state. Winding up through Pike National Forest, along aspen- and spruce-sided mountains, and through a rickety, log-lined one-way tunnel, the 20-mile stretch offers more great views per mile than many of even the most famously scenic of Colorado highways. It's also one of the state's least nerve-wracking high-mountain passes, the road unfolding gently across above-timberline alpine meadows—you half expect to hear distant singing, and then to see the Von Trapp family appearing blonde and knickered over a windswept knoll.

WOODLAND PARK

Woodland Park (pop. 4,300; elev. 8,500 feet) is an attractive and vital mountain community just 20 miles west of Colorado Springs. With its crisp mountain air and omnipresent view of Pikes Peak, Woodland Park attracts many Colorado Springs workers, who find the under-half-an-hour commute a fair price to pay for the slower and more healthful mountain lifestyle. The town was founded in the early 1880s, and until the early 20th century was an important lumber supply center, serving both Cripple Creek and Colorado Springs.

Woodland Park Practicalities

You can get good inexpensive rooms at **The Lofthouse,** tel. (719) 687-9187, located at 222 E. Henrietta on the hillside above the downtown area. The rooms, some of which have kitchenettes, are smoky, well stocked with murder mysteries, and feel like the kind of places where Officers Gannon and Friday might stay while investigating some insidious crime. A reader sent me a brochure for the **Woodland Inn Bed and Breakfast,** 159 Trull Rd. tel. (719) 687-8209 or (800) 226-9565, which she highly recommends. Sitting on 12 woodsy acres, the inn offers four rooms running $45-75.

If you're passing through Woodland Park in the early hours, stop in at the locally popular **Donut Mill** at 310 W. US 24. In addition to doughnuts and fritters, you can get biscuits and gravy, as well as eggs with burritos—all for under $3. **Grandmother's Kitchen** at 212 US 24 serves early-bird specials 6-8 a.m. (all breakfasts except steak and eggs are $2). For dinner, try **Pazano's Italian Restaurant,** 730 E. US 24, tel. (719) 687-9898, where you can get complete dinners (excellent lasagna) for $5-10. **Tres**

Hombres Tex-Mex Cantina, 116½ Midland (US 24), tel. (719) 687-0625, serves good burritos, chimichangas, etc. for $4-7; live music most nights.

For more information on Woodland Park and the surrounding area, stop by the **chamber of commerce** at the junction of US 24 and CO 67 North. You can also write Box W, Woodland Park, CO 80866, or phone (719) 687-9885.

CRIPPLE CREEK

To get a proper perspective on Cripple Creek's importance to the state, as well as to the history of the west, consider: Between 1891 and 1916, Cripple Creek produced $340 million worth of gold. By 1952, 625 tons, or 20 million ounces, of the stuff had been taken from Cripple Creek mines for a total value of over $413 million (figured at the long-running mid-century rate of $20.67 an ounce). Cripple Creek produced twice as much gold as California's famed Mother Lode, and nearly $100 million more than Nevada's Comstock produced in gold and silver combined. Alaska's and the Yukon's gold camps—Klondike, Fairbanks, Nome—pale in comparison to Cripple Creek's. In fact, no single geological deposit on earth has produced as much gold as Cripple Creek.

According to Colorado Springs historian Marshall Sprague, Cripple Creek's population increased from 15 to 50,000 between 1891 and 1900, its monthly payroll from $50 to $1,000,000. During the same period, the town's annual production went from "$2,000 worth of calves to $20 million worth of gold bricks." Among those who cashed in on Cripple Creek's boom was Winfield Scott Stratton, who left his $3-a-day carpentry job in Colorado Springs, staked a claim in Cripple, and later sold his mine for $10 million. According to the WPA guide to Colorado, just after the turn of the century, Cripple Creek had 41 assay offices, 91 lawyers, 88 doctors, 70 saloons, and 14 newspapers.

Today, Cripple Creek is a major tourist destination, many of the old buildings having been converted to boutiques, restaurants, and gift and specialty shops. Walking Cripple Creek's main drag, and touring mines where huge fortunes were made, you can easily imagine how it must have been a century ago, when the camp was roaring with gambling saloons, bars, and brothels, and the very existence of every citizen and visitor—from wealthy mine owner to exploited mine worker, from postal clerk to pickpocket—was inextricably linked to the goldfields. In fact, seeing Cripple Creek—a small town so germane to the development of the state—crystalizes one's understanding and appreciation of Colorado.

In part because here you can also see close up the ugly side of it all.

In addition to bringing wealth and prosperity to Colorado, mining—and its myopic policymakers—also caused great environmental harm. One need not look awfully hard to see the scars and ugly mine dumps that remain on the bare mountainsides surrounding the little town. Look a little more closely, or talk to people who live in the area, and you'll come to know mining's more subtle and perhaps longer-ranging consequences: the contamination of soils and waters from gold mining processes. In short, there's a much bigger lesson in a visit to Cripple Creek. As Sprague wrote in 1952, "Cripple's story . . . is a capsule history of the United States from country bumpkin to world power." He might add today that its subsequent fall—marked by depression, environmental destruction, desperate appeal to tourism through commercial exploitation, and, finally, in a last-ditch effort to prop itself back up, legalized gambling—resembles the recent sad stumble this country's taken.

Today during the summer, Cripple Creek's sidewalks are packed with visitors clinging to shopping bags, and its sidestreets are lined with motor homes with out-of-state plates and Volvo station wagons piled high with ice chests, tents, lawn chairs, and tricycles—while the casinos bulge with folks pulling slot-machine handles, marking keno cards, and watching the dealer draw to a 21.

History
During the 1860s and early '70s, the valley in which Cripple Creek lies was known as Poverty Gulch, through which meandered a small stream. Actually the crater of a long-extinct volcano, the valley was blessed with sides steep enough to contain cattle, and the first settlers in the area were ranchers, one of whom was Levi

Cripple Creek's first newspaper office, 1892

Welty, who, according to a perhaps apocryphal story, gave the town its name.

One day Welty and his three sons were building a cabin in the valley when they lost their grip on a heavy log, which rolled into one of the boys. In the commotion, Levi Welty's shotgun discharged, injuring his hand and frightening a pet calf grazing nearby. The calf tried to jump the stream, but stumbled and broke its leg. His son, his hand, and his calf all injured, Levi later supposedly lamented, "Well boys, this sure is some cripple creek!"

One of the valley's more colorful characters was Bob ("Crazy Bob") Womack, a cowboy who had come to Colorado from Kentucky and taken over the Welty ranch. Apparently rarely sober—which is probably why his claims of gold in the area were not taken seriously—Womack in 1886 did finally manage to haul some gold out of a Poverty Gulch mine, the El Paso. Womack sent specimens to an assayer's office in old Colorado City, where it was found to be of high quality. On a Christmas morning years later, after watching tiny Poverty Gulch transform into the bustling Cripple Creek Mining District, Bobby Womack would stand on a street corner in Cripple Creek, drunk and holding the $500 for which he had sold his share of the mine the night before. There, in the cold of that wintry morning, Womack handed out a one-dollar bill to each child that passed by, until a long line formed and Womack realized he was giving money to adults. At that point, an embittered Womack

slugged the next person in line, who slugged back, knocking Womack to the ground. Womack was taken home by the deputy sheriff and the next day left Cripple Creek, never to return. The El Paso would go on to produce gold worth over $5 million.

By 1896, 10,000 people were living in Cripple Creek, and the little town's reputation for wild times and wilder women, particularly those employed at the "pleasure palaces," was well known throughout the country. On a Saturday afternoon in late April of that year, a couple fighting in their apartment above the Central Dance Hall knocked over a lighted gasoline stove, igniting a fire in the building that quickly spread up and across the street. The fire, which lasted only three hours but abetted by stiff breezes, destroyed some 40 homes, the Cripple Creek Mining Exchange, the First National Bank, the post office, and several "one-girl cribs," including "The Library" and "Old Faithful." By the time it was over, 1,500 people were homeless.

A determined and uneasily daunted lot, Cripple Creek residents quickly set about rebuilding their town. The Cripple Creek *Times* moved into a new office and put out a paper the very next day; carpenters began construction on new buildings; and many of the dance halls, some partly burned, were once again raucous and rolling.

For three days.

Then on Wednesday another fire broke out. This one, buffeted by even stronger winds, destroyed 10 saloons and numerous other homes, stores, and businesses. Many people were seriously injured, including six firemen hurt when a boiler exploded, and 5,000 people were left without homes. Still, the cloud of fires had its silver lining: The phoenix that rose from the ashes was largely brick and built to last. Cripple Creek was less a mining camp now, bastion of rascals and con artists, and much more a legitimate town, an alliance of businesspeople and civic leaders.

Which isn't to say Cripple Creek became an instant model of righteousness. Indeed, though the town did take more pride in itself, the lowlife faction was decidedly still extant. Just before the turn of the century, the murder rate rose from one to eight a month.

In the early 1900s, labor-management relations in Cripple Creek began to grow strained. Workers' attempts to unionize were violently resisted. According to some reports, as many as 500 laborers simply "disappeared" from Cripple Creek's streets.

By 1915, the price of gold had fallen, and Cripple Creek's mines were mostly played out. In 1920, fewer than 10% of the district's mines were in operation. Still, ore continued to be taken from the hillsides, though by mid-century most of the remaining mines were owned by large conglomerates. The days of individual ownership—the days of Womack, Stratton, and the rest—were long gone. In the 1970s and 1980s, Cripple Creek began to appeal to tourism. Mine tours were offered, artisans opened up shop in some of the old buildings, and boutiques and gift shops appeared in others. Town boosters hoped the tourist dollar would facilitate a second boom for the little mountain town.

Then, in the late summer of 1990, holding what it hoped was one last wild card up its sleeve, Cripple Creek looked its tourists in the eye and upped the ante. Cripple Creek, along with Central City and Black Hawk, legalized gambling. Though limited in scope, especially compared to the virtually-anything-goes wagering you'll find in Nevada, gambling is now a major part of Cripple Creek's personality, with many of the old buildings having been converted to casinos. In addition, the community has built a new mini-mall, and larger grocery stores have sprung up to accommodate the increase in visitors.

Meanwhile, Coloradans—from legislators to investors to nickle-slot players—are keeping a close eye on what happens. For if gambling does for Cripple Creek what proponents claim it will, if it increases the town's draw and helps breathe new life into the economy, then it's likely that other Colorado historical districts—Leadville, Georgetown, and others—will follow suit.

Cripple Creek District Museum

With a large collection of mining artifacts, including equipment and tools, ore samples, mine models, and a reconstructed assay office, this small museum offers an opportunity to see what made Cripple Creek tick between 1890 and the early 20th century. Also on display are domestic items and Victorian-era clothing. Open daily 10 a.m. to 5 p.m., May 30 to mid-October, weekends noon to 4 p.m. the rest of the year. It's on Bennett Ave. (east end); a small admission fee is charged. For more information, phone (719) 689-2634.

Historical Tours

The Cripple Creek Chamber of Commerce designed a self-guided historical tour of the Cripple Creek Mining District, including the town of Victor (see that section, following). The 18-mile (roundtrip) auto tour takes about 45 minutes. For a map and guide, stop by the office at 107 E. Eaton. **Ghost Town Tours** offers guided trips through the area. Legitimate historians (not college kids doing summer work), the guides provide in-depth explanations of the mining district and the various mines. The hour-and-a-half tours, beginning at 451 E. Bennett, are offered daily 8:30 a.m.-5 p.m.; $6 for adults. When you're finished, stick around for the 30-minute "Story of Cripple Creek" video. For more information, phone (719) 689-3000.

Mollie Kathleen Mine Tour

In continuous operation between 1892 and 1961, "the Mollie" now offers miner-led tours 1,000 feet into its recesses. View the equipment miners used to extract the gold and convey it to the surface; listen to stories and explanations of how the shafts were dynamited. Take a look at what real gold looks like before it finds it way to earrings and necklaces. Learn what to look for should you find yourself getting "the fever."

Tours of the Mollie Kathleen are offered daily 9 a.m.-5 p.m., May-October. Admission is $8 for adults, with reduced rates for kids. Take Bennett Dr. east, turn north on CO 67, and follow the signs. For more information, phone (719) 689-2465.

Cripple Creek and Victor Narrow Gauge Railroad

This four-mile run from Cripple Creek to Anaconda provides an authentic way to get a sense of the mining district's past (at one time 56 ore-laden trains left Cripple Creek daily). The coal-burning steam engine hauls you out past several abandoned mines (and the attendant dumps and junk piles), and offers views of many historical sites, including Bobby Womack's "Poverty Gulch." Trains run daily 10 a.m.-5 p.m. Memorial Day through Labor Day, departing from the Cripple District Museum; the trip takes 45 minutes. Cost is $6.50 for adults, $6 for seniors, and $3.25 for kids. For more information, phone (719) 689-2640.

Imperial Hotel Melodrama

Established in 1948, this old-time theater group is one of the most famous in the country, having been written up in *Time, The New York Times,* and many other publications. Season is mid-June through Labor Day; show times are Tues.-Sat. 2 p.m. and 7:45 p.m., and Sunday 1 p.m. and 4 p.m. Tickets run $8-12, with discounts for kids and at matinees. It's in the Imperial Hotel and Casino, 123 N. 3rd St.; for reservations or more information, phone (719) 689-7777.

Shopping

Downtown Cripple Creek consists of several blocks of turn-of-the-century (and earlier) buildings, and though many have been recently converted to casinos and restaurants, others house boutiques, gift shops, and souvenir shacks. Which means, of course, there's no shortage of places to pick up T-shirts, mugs, hats, and key chains. Yet a handful of the shops carry quality gifts and artwork. **Phenix Rising Gallery** [*sic*] sells contemporary painting, sculpture, and pottery with a Southwestern and Native American feel. The **Scott Stearman Gallery** has contemporary Native American bronze sculptures. **John's Jewelry** carries an excellent selection of Hopi work, including rings, bolos, pendants, bracelets.

Scenic Drives

If you're in Cripple Creek, you've taken at least one scenic drive: there's no way to get here without passing through some of the state's most beautiful country. If you've come in from the north and are looking for an alternative route out, you have several (well-maintained gravel)

*shops and hotels
in downtown
Cripple Creek*

options. **Phantom Canyon Road** runs south out of Cripple Creek through Victor and down toward Cañon City. **Gold Camp Road** follows the old rail line between Cripple Creek and Colorado Springs. Both of these offer gorgeous views and exceedingly light traffic.

Accommodations

For a real taste of historic Cripple Creek, the **Imperial Hotel**, 123 N. 3rd St., tel. (719) 689-7777, has doubles running $60-80. Built in 1896, it's the only one of Cripple Creek's original hotels still standing. The Imperial also hosts melodrama theater during the summer (see above). A brand new **Holiday Inn Express**, tel. (719) 689-2600, has been built on the hill above town; rooms about $70-100. You can also get lodging at the **Cripple Creek Motel,** 201 Bison, tel. (719) 689-2491; the **Best Western Gold Rush Hotel and Casino,** 209 E. Bennett, tel. (719) 689-2646; the **Midnight Rose Hotel and Casino,** 256 E. Bennett, tel. (719) 689-2865 (also has a kids' arcade); the **Palace Hotel and Casino,** 2nd and Bennett, tel. (719) 689-2992, and the **Longbranch Saloon and Casino,** tel. (719) 689-3242 (featuring stand-up comedy).

For bed-and-breakfast accommodations, try the three-bedroom **The Victorian Lady,** 127 W. Carr, tel. (719) 689-2143.

Two miles northeast of town on CO 67, **Cripple Creek Gold Campground,** tel. (719) 689-2342, offers very nice secluded campsites, for both tents and RVs. A couple of hundred yards down the road at the junction of CO 67 and Co. Rd. 81 is a **KOA** campground, tel. (719) 689-3376, with 60 RV sites and 20 tent sites.

Food

You'll find on-site restaurants at most of the hotel/casinos, including the **Gold Rush,** tel. (719) 689-2646; **Bronco Billie's,** tel. (719) 689-2142 (which also has a sports bar); and the **Midnight Rose,** tel. (719) 689-2865. The **Imperial Hotel and Casino,** tel. (719) 689-7777, has a long-standing tradition of excellent dinners, with specialties including beef, seafood, and chicken. Another favorite is the **Red Lantern,** 353 Myers, tel. (719) 689-2519, where you can get steaks, burgers, and barbecued chicken dinners for $8-12. **Goldie's,** upstairs in Johnny Nolon's Saloon, serves sandwiches,

steak, and salads (prime-rib special, $4.99), and they also have a selection of locally brewed beers and ales on tap.

Note: Many of the casinos have excellent food and even better prices. Remember, however, a casino's prime directive: to get folks in the door. Your $1.99 burger can quickly turn into ten or twenty bucks if you stop at the slot machines or the blackjack tables. I stopped in at Johnny Nolon's recently for a salad and a beer that ended up costing me about $25 (shouldn't have doubled down on that pair of fives. . .).

Services

The offices of the Cripple Creek **Police Department** are in the city hall building on E. Bennett, tel. (719) 689-2655. Phone the **Teller County Sheriff** at (719) 689-2644. The **post office** is at the corner of 2nd St. and Masonic, tel. (719) 689-2423.

Information

The **Cripple Creek Chamber of Commerce** provides extensive visitors packages, with complete information on attractions, lodging, dining, etc. Write Box 650, Cripple Creek, CO 80813, or phone (719) 689-2169 or (800) 526-8777. Cripple Creek's **Franklin-Ferguson Memorial Library** is on the northwest side of town at the corner of B St. and Galena, tel. (719) 689-2800.

VICTOR

The second-largest city in the Cripple Creek Mining District, Victor was once home to 18,000 people. Lowell Thomas spent a good portion of his youth here, jump-starting his journalism career by delivering newspapers in the town's red-light district. Jack Dempsey once trained and fought in the city hall building. Today fewer than 300 people live in Victor.

History

Though over the years Victor and Cripple Creek have been rival cities, Victor was largely to thank not only for helping put out Cripple's 1896 fires but also for sending men and supplies and for helping shelter the 6,000-plus residents the fires left homeless. Victor's streets are said to be

The Lowell Thomas Museum offers illuminating glimpses into frontier Colorado.

literally "paved with gold": In the district's early days only the highest-grade ore was trucked out, the low grade used for road surfacing.

In 1893, after mine owners attempted to reduce the district's $3-a-day wage, some 800 Cripple Creek and Victor members of the Western Federation of Miners went on strike. Arbitration, and the National Guard, kept things from getting out of hand, and the workers' wages remained unchanged. In 1903, some of the mines began shipping ore to a nonunion mine in Colorodo City, and Cripple Creek and Victor members of the WFM struck in sympathy. Tension escalated, with many miners refusing to work while others broke strike and kept working. In September, the militia was called in, and by December the entire Cripple Creek Mining District was under martial law.

In early 1904, there were both a "mysterious" mine explosion and a mine "accident" involving a broken cable hoist. Many men were killed, management claiming the mines had been sabotaged and workers claiming management was attempting to discredit the union. Two more men were killed when rioting broke out in the streets of Victor. Eventually, troops were again called in, and union members unconvinced it would be in their best interest to leave of their own accord were escorted down off the mountain. The Cripple Creek Mining District's chapter of the WFM was effectively dismantled.

Victor today is a crumbling remnant of its once-booming self. Though a couple hundred of the old red-brick buildings still stand, they lean tiredly and wistfully into the hillside. Still, Victor has its own special draw, in part its refreshing lack of tacky souvenir shops. Walking the steep streets of Victor one can, perhaps more easily than in Cripple Creek, imagine ghosts of Victorian-era miners lurking in doorways and dissolving before the future's great wash.

Lowell Thomas Museum

This is at once both a monument to Victor's history and to the early life of Lowell Thomas, who moved here with his family just after the turn of the century. Thomas delivered the *Denver Post* and the *Victor Daily Record* in the area, worked in the mines in 1911, and for a short time was editor of the *Victor Daily News*. He left Victor in 1912.

In addition to old miners' gear, a fire truck, slot machine, mail-order catalogs, quilts, dolls, clocks, typewriters, and historical photos, the museum displays Lowell Thomas memorabilia, including various editions of the many books he wrote. Some of the rooms have been reconstructed to approximate the Thomas family's home.

Admission is $1. For hours and more information, phone the Cripple Creek Chamber of Commerce at (719) 689-2169.

Lodging in Victor

The four-story red-brick **Victor Hotel,** tel. (719) 689-3553, is a converted late-19th-century bank building with 30 rooms with private baths. Rates run $70-100. For more information on lodging in Victor, contact the Cripple Creek Chamber of Commerce, Box 650, Cripple Creek, CO 80813, tel. (719) 689-2169.

UTE PASS WEST TO FAIRPLAY

Ute Pass (elev. 9,165 feet) has long been an important gateway between the central Rockies and the eastern foothills. Until 1859, when whites came looking for gold, the pass was a stronghold of the Utes, who took advantage of its narrowness and steep granite walls to keep the Plains tribes at bay. Even into the early 20th century, Utes maintained small fortresses in the area. Today, US 24 climbs up out of Divide, over the pass, winds through a broad alpine valley, through the tiny towns of Florissant and Lake George, and then climbs up again, over Wilkerson Pass (elev. 9,507 feet), before dropping down into the South Park basin. There, the highway crosses CO 9, which shoots north through the basin to Fairplay (18 miles) or south to meet US 50 between Cañon City and Royal Gorge (50 miles).

Florissant Fossil Beds National Monument

Just three miles south of Florissant lies this natural paradise for the budding paleontologist. Between 26 and 38 million years ago, the area was lush waterland, with palm trees, towering redwoods, and tall birches and willows lining the shores of Lake Florissant. There were also thousands of species of insects. Toward the end of that period, volcanoes began spewing ash and lava into the air, which settled onto the thriving ecosystem, preserving it and providing for visitors today one of the world's most extensive fossil records.

Visiting Florissant Fossil Beds is a good way to get an overview of what life in Colorado was like during the Oligocene Period. The visitors center has excellent fossil displays and books, and also offers guided walks out into the fossils. In addition, you can take a self-guided tour on a series of hiking trails, ranging from one-half to four miles long, where you can view petrified redwood trees (some estimated to have been 350 feet tall) and other 35-million-year-old specimens. It's open daily; small admission

fee. For more information, write Box 185, Florissant, CO 80816, or phone (719) 748-3253.

Lake George

This small town is little more than a roadside market and a couple of RV campgrounds, **Stage Stop Campground**, tel. (719) 748-3393, and **Homestead Motel and Campground**, tel. (719) 748-3822. Just past Lake George is the turnoff to Pike National Forest's **Round Mountain Campground**, where you'll find a couple of dozen sites nicely set back in the aspens and ponderosas (pump water and pit toilets only).

Forest Service Information

You'll find a district office for Pike National Forest at Wilkerson Pass. Stop in for information on camping and other activities in the area, as well as for maps.

FAIRPLAY

Though not as well known as Cripple Creek or Leadville, Fairplay, too, was once a thriving mining town. Named by prospectors who'd been run out of Tarryall, another gold camp, about 20 miles east, Fairplay (pop. 500; elev. 10,000 feet) is the seat of Park County and the largest community in South Park. From Fairplay, you can continue north on CO 9 to Summit County (about 35 miles to Frisco), turn south on US 285 to Buena Vista (35 miles), or head back to Denver on US 285 (85 miles). All routes guarantee breathtaking scenery—high mountain passes and lush forests.

South Park City Museum

Comprising 30 different buildings, this museum is a model of a Victorian-era town, with artifacts from throughout the state. Included are a general store, assay office, drugstore, saloon, and brewery, all furnished with authentic period artifacts. Open daily mid-May through mid-October; small admission fee. For more information, phone (719) 836-2387.

Practicalities

Two historic hotels in the Fairplay area offer accommodations and dining in genuine Victorian-era settings. The **Fairplay Hotel**, at 500 Main St., tel. (719) 836-2565, offers reasonably priced rooms with and without private baths; the hotel also has a dining room and saloon. The **Hand Hotel,** 531 Front St., tel. (719) 836-3595, has 10 bed-and-breakfast rooms and a dining room. The town is also home to two motels, three secluded guest cottages, and a handful of restaurants.

Cross-Country Skiing

The **Fairplay Nordic Center,** tel. (719) 836-2658, offers 20 km of groomed trails with views of the South Park area. Instruction and rentals available.

Fishing

Ten miles south of Fairplay is the **Middle Fork of the South Platte River,** a designated Gold Medal trout stream known for its 20-inch (and larger) fish.

Information

For more information on activities in the Fairplay area, as well as on lodging and dining, contact the **Park County Tourism Office,** Box 220, Fairplay, CO 80440, tel. (719) 836-4279.

BOB RACE

rattlesnake

SOUTHWESTERN COLORADO

Most folks who know Colorado have soft spots in their hearts for the southwestern corner of the state. They know this area offers as much scenic beauty, history, culture, and recreation as any similar-sized area in the country—perhaps more. From the towering peaks of the San Juan Mountains to the deep gorges of Black Canyon of the Gunnison, from the sharp Continental Divide to the gently falling Western Slope, from the high lakes of Grand Mesa to the western reaches of the San Luis Valley, and from the cliff dwellings at Mesa Verde National Park to the trendy boutiques in Aspen, Southwestern Colorado offers enough to see and do to keep you here for weeks on end, or for a lifetime, to which many transplanted locals will testify.

The first thing that'll most likely strike you is the pure scenic wonder of the area. Drive in from the south, over Wolf Creek Pass, or down out of Carbondale, through the Crystal River Valley. Head north from Durango over the "Million Dollar Highway" to Silverton and Ouray, or

explore the Maroon Lakes area just outside Aspen. Out here, even cynics shake their heads and mutter things about "God's Country."

The history, rich with railroads and mining, is fascinating as well. Drive up to Leadville and take a tour of the famous Matchless Mine. Ride an 1880s coal-powered narrow-gauge train from Durango to Silverton. Stay in an historic hotel in Telluride or Aspen, or toss back a shot and a beer at a 19th-century bar in Crested Butte.

And then check out the culture: 1,000-year-old Anasazi ruins, as well as museums and heritage centers in the Four Corners area; film, jazz, rock, and bluegrass festivals in Telluride; film, classical music, and wine and food festivals in Aspen. Plus scores of local historical society museums scattered about the area, many with excellent displays of Native American, mining, and railroad artifacts.

And *then* there's recreation: world-class snow skiing at Telluride, Aspen, and Crested Butte, as well as excellent skiing at out-of-the-way areas such as Wolf Creek Pass and Purgatory; jeep touring over high mountain passes and through ghosts of 19th-century mining towns; fly-fishing for wily native rainbow trout or trolling for landlocked salmon; whitewater rafting in Class V rapids; and if that's not enough, there's hiking, snowshoeing, hot-air ballooning, camping, golfing, horseback riding.

And the nice thing is that much of Southwestern Colorado is remote enough that you won't be fighting the crowds to see it. Oh, sure, Aspen gets packed with tourists, summer and winter alike, and when the train's running in Durango, it's tough sometimes just to find a place to park in the little town. But for the most part, Southwestern Colorado—and its sprawling San Juan, Rio Grande, Gunnison, Uncompahgre, and Grand Mesa national forests—offers the traveler an excellent opportunity to lose herself. To get away from the trappings of this fast-paced and overcrowded world. To simply enjoy being outside in one of the country's prettiest spots.

SOUTHWESTERN COLORADO

GRAND JUNCTION

Grand Junction (pop. 30,000; elev. 4,590 feet) is the largest town between Salt Lake City and Denver. Situated in the irrigated Grand Valley at the junction of the Colorado and Gunnison rivers, Grand Junction is mainly a small industrial and agricultural community; its major crops are corn, alfalfa, and fruit, particularly apples and peaches. Other important crops include beans, small grains, pears, cherries, and apricots. The Grand Valley also supports large herds of cattle, and many sheep ranchers summer their animals in the area.

Grand Junction and the Grand Valley are surrounded by remarkable landscapes. To the northeast are the Little Bookcliffs, a miles-long row of mesa-side cliffs that drop dramatically to the valley floor. East of town, the Colorado River carves deep canyons into the rugged Colorado Plateau, and to the southeast, Grand Mesa, the world's largest flat-topped mountain, rises powerfully into the clouds. Just a half hour from Grand Junction, Grand Mesa National Forest is a treasure of alpine lakes, pine, fir, and aspen trees, and that invigorating high-country air. To the west you'll find the soft redrock canyons, stark sandstone spires, and juniper- and piñon-dotted mesa-tops of Colorado National Monument.

Which adds up to lots of wonderful country to explore. Whether by foot, Nordic skis, mountain bike, horse, or car, the Grand Junction area offers plenty of open space to wander in. As well as wonderfully friendly folks to point you in the right directions.

HISTORY

Although white settlement didn't begin in the Grand Valley and surrounding area until 1881, several Spanish and United States exploration parties had passed through in the late 18th and mid-19th centuries. The first Spanish explorers in the area, friars Francisco Antanasio Dominguez and Silvestre Velez de Escalante, traveled through in search of a route connecting the missions of New Mexico with those in California. In 1821, after Mexico won its independence from Spain, the region was claimed for the United States, and in 1853, the area was partially mapped by two U.S. expeditions—those of John C. Frémont and John Gunnison—attempting to establish a cross-country railroad route. The United States Geological Survey studied the area in detail

---

SOUTHWESTERN COLORADO HIGHLIGHTS

Grand Junction: Colorado National Monument, museums, mountain biking along Kokopelli's Trail (125 miles), camping, fishing, and other recreation

Aspen: downhill skiing on Buttermilk Mountain, Snowmass, Aspen Mountain and Aspen Highlands, hut-to-hut Nordic skiing on the 10th Mountain Trail Association Hut System, dogsledding, fishing along the Roaring Fork River, hiking in the White River National Forest, festivals such as Winteröl, and the Aspen-Snowmass Food and Wine Classic

Leadville: mining tours on the Leadville, Colorado, and Southern Railroad, hiking up Mt. Elbert (state's highest peak), museums, camping, fishing, skiing, Oro City Festival

Salida/Buena Vista: rafting on the Arkansas River, museums, camping, hot springs, Aspen-Salida Music Festival, Yard-of-the-Month Awards

Crested Butte/Gunnison: alpine skiing at Mt. Crested Butte, fishing in the Taylor, East, and Gunnison rivers, 4WD tours, biking, hiking, camping, American Indian Cultural Festival, Fat Tire Week, Festival of the Arts

Ouray/Silverton/Durango: Durango-Silverton Narrow Gauge Railroad, hiking, mountain biking in the San Juan National Forest, fishing and rafting on the Animas River, Purgatory Ski Area, Trimble Hot Springs, Durango Cowboy Gathering, Mesa Verde National Park

Telluride: skiing, mountain biking, 4WD tours, film and music festivals in the early 1870s, and the resulting book of maps, the Hayden Survey, was published and sold across the country in 1876.

Settlers began to arrive in September 1881, once the Utes had been moved to the reservation, and within four months irrigation projects were underway, a store had been built and the town of Grand Junction was incorporated. Its first winter, the new town could claim just 150 residents. But 1882 saw the the arrival of the Denver and Rio Grande Railroad, as well as the town's first hotel, and soon nearly a thousand citizens were supporting a bustling business district, including a drugstore, two blacksmith

shops, and five hotels and restaurants. By the end of the year, 11 more saloons went up, providing rest and recreation for cowboys who worked ranches in the area (from 15 to 75 miles away) and would come to town to hit the saloons and red-light districts.

As Grand Junction's downtown area continued to grow, increased irrigation in the surrounding Grand Valley led to successful peach, pear, and apple orchards. Farming continued to provide stability to Grand Junction's economy into the 20th century, as improved irrigation turned the valley into one of the lushest and most productive in the state—the area was now exporting cherries, apricots, grapes, and other crops as well. The Grand Valley area drew to the nation's attention again in 1911, when Colorado National Monument was established.

During the early and mid-1900s, oil and uranium wells were drilled throughout the northern Western Slope area, from Rangely south to the Grand Junction area. Grand Junction, as the largest town between Salt Lake City and Denver, again became an important shipping center, for both product and workers, and the area saw a cycle of booms and busts. The biggest boom, fueled by the post-war demand for uranium, brought worldwide publicity to Grand Junction, though the bust of the early 1960s caused major social and economic problems.

Most recently, Grand Junction has begun to capitalize on its nearby recreation, and to appeal to tourism. Still defined largely by farming, the Grand Junction area nonetheless is becoming better known for its excellent hiking, mountain biking, and other sports, as well as for the gorgeous forests and startlingly beautiful mesa lands and canyons nearby. At the same time, downtown Grand Junction has begun to honor its history and celebrate its diversity, with museums, galleries, art shows, and various festivals throughout the year.

MUSEUMS

Museum of Western Colorado

This museum complex includes the main museum downtown, the Dinosaur Valley paleontology center, and the Cross Orchards Historic Site.

The small but interesting **Main Museum** displays the geology, prehistory, history, and culture of western Colorado. Exhibits include a Colorado timeline (1880-1950), with tools, clothing, and artifacts from each era; Ute baskets, beadwork, and bows and arrows; Fremont culture petroglyphs, awls, fetishes; and Mimbres pottery. The museum also has a gift-and-book store, specializing in Colorado history. The museum, at 248 S. 4th Street (corner of Ute), is open Mon.-Sat. 10 a.m.-4:45 p.m., Memorial Day through Labor Day; Tues.-Sat. 10 a.m.-4:45 p.m. the rest of year. Admission is $2 for adults, $1 for kids two to 17. For more information, phone (970) 242-0971.

Dinosaur Valley, on the Main Street Mall at 362 Main, presents a veritable course in dinosaurs and paleontology. Follow the huge green footprints past several *large* animated dinosaurs, including a *Stegosaurus, Allosaurus,* and *Tyrannosaurus rex,* all of which move in startlingly lifelike fashion and growl ferociously. Other features include reconstructed dinosaur skeletons, fossilized eggs and footprints, timelines explaining when the different dinosaur periods were, a video room, and an explanation of continental drift. Don't miss the life-size reconstructed head of a *Tyrannosaurus rex;* it's downright scary (in fact, though the museum is wonderful for kids, some of the younger ones might be a bit put off by all the growling and moving). The museum is open daily 9 a.m.-5 p.m. Memorial Day through Labor Day; Tues.-Sat. 10 a.m.-4:30 p.m the rest of the year. Admission is $4.50, $2.50 for kids two to 12.

The adjoining gift shop sells a variety of dinosaur-oriented items, including dinosaur kites, coffee mugs, T-shirts, backpacks, books, posters, and even inflatable dinosaurs. For more information, phone (970) 241-9210.

Cross Orchards Historic Site offers thorough tours of a working apple orchard, operating since the late 1890s. Founded by Isabelle K. Cross of Massachusetts (heiress to the Red Cross Shoe Company fortune), the Cross once reigned as one of the largest and most productive orchards in the country; it covered nearly 250 acres when the average orchard was fewer than 10.

An ideal school field trip, a Cross Orchards tour demonstrates planting and harvesting techniques and also takes you into the workers' bunkhouses, a dining room, and kitchen. Tour participants get to taste apples (in season) and munch on fresh-baked sugar cookies. After the tour, visitors are free to wander through several other exhibits: a barn packed with tools and equipment from an early-20th-century family farm, including wagons, plows, pitchforks, and domestic items, as well as photos and original farm records and receipts; a collection of early-20th-century road-maintenance equipment; and several cars, a partial track, and a reconstructed trestle from the Uinta narrow-guage railroad, used from 1904-39 to carry Gilsonite out of the moutains to the switch yard west of

Grand Junction. A gift shop sells cards, crafts, candy, and other items. A number of annual events take place here, including a quilt show, pumpkin hunt, and "country Christmas." Cross Orchards also plans to plant another six and a half acres of adjacent land with 5,500 experimental apple species, including Fujis, to help raise revenue for the site.

Cross Orchards is open to the public daily 10 a.m. to 4 p.m., mid-May through November 1, as well as during special events. Admission is $1.50 for kids two to 12, $3 for ages 13-59, and $2.50 for seniors. For more information, write Cross Orchards Historic Site, 3073 Patterson/F Rd., Grand Junction, CO 81504, or phone (970) 434-9158.

The museum also administers **Dinosaur Hill** and **Riggs Hill,** sites of historic dinosaur excavations. One-mile loop trails provide access to both of these historic quarries. **Rabbit Valley Research Area and Trail Through Time** is administered by the museum and the BLM. Dinosaur bones, plant fossils, and geology can be seen along this 1.5-mile self-guided trail.

For more information on the Museum of Western Colorado complex, write 248 S. 4th St., Box 20000-5020, Grand Junction, CO 81502, or phone (970) 242-0971.

Devil's Canyon
Science and Learning Center
Full-scale animated replicas of dinosaurs from throughout the Mesozoic period roar and growl, snort and feed in a range of incredibly lifelike displays at this museum in Fruita just west of Grand Junction. With an emphasis on education for kids and teens, Devil's Canyon features dozens of hands-on activities: buttons to push, footprints to make, clay for creating your own dinosaur. That's if you can concentrate with the huge creatures growling beside you and swaying their long necks through the air. Check out the Thalassomedon (a 45-foot-long marine reptile), or the (apparently) hungry Apatusaurus. In addition, there are replicas of more recent creatures, including a wooly mammoth and a 25-foot great white shark, plus, you can stand on an earthquake simulator and watch the plate tectonics demonstrate how the earth's crust changed over the years. In a separate room, videos explain how and where the dinosaurs lived, how excavation is done, and how the models were made.

There's also a gift shop with T-shirts, stuffed dinosaurs, and kids' books.

And, if that's not enough, you can also sign up to go on an actual dinosaur-quarry dig. **Dinosaur Discovery Expeditions** offers you the chance to go out and assist paleontologists on-site. Learn about excavation techniques and lab research; accommodations, transportation, and meals included.

Dinosaur Valley is open seven days a week Memorial Day through Labor Day, 8:30 a.m.-7 p.m.; the rest of the year 9 a.m.-5 p.m. Admission is $5 for adults, $3.50 for kids and seniors. To get there, take the Fruita exit from I-70 and follow the signs. For more information, phone (970) 858-7282. For information on the expeditions, phone (800) DIG-DINO.

Western Colorado Center for the Arts
Located at 1803 N. 7th St., this museum features a wide variety of rotating displays. Though the emphasis is on Western and Native American art, the museum also exhibits other works in various forms from around the country. On permanent display is an excellent collection of Navajo rugs. This is also a center for performing arts, with concerts held throughout the year. Hours are Tues.-Sat. 10 a.m.-5 p.m. For more information, phone (970) 243-7337.

PARKS AND RECREATION

Colorado National Monument
Sheer redrock cliffs, sandstone spires rising dramatically up from valley floors, desolate mesas, and shadowed canyons dotted with juniper and piñon—Colorado National Monument sprawls just west of Grand Junction over 32 square miles of some of the Southwest's most austerely beautiful landscapes. **Rimrock Drive,** the main road through the park, rises from the lowlands of the Colorado River Valley through the canyons to the top of a broad plateau. The 23-mile road provides access to the park's visitor center, a campground, several picnic areas, over a dozen hiking trails, and many scenic overlooks.

Be sure to stop in at the visitor center, where you'll find displays of the park's geology, flora, and fauna. You can also get information on *hiking trails in Colorado National Monument*

guided nature walks and campfire programs, and pick up books, maps, and other useful literature. **Saddlehorn Campground** has 81 sites available on a first-come, first-served basis; flush toilets, no showers, $7 per night. Backcountry camping is also allowed throughout the park; some restrictions apply.

Hiking trails in Colorado National Monument range from short nature walks and quarter-mile paths leading to scenic overlooks, to seven- and eight-mile backcountry routes through remote canyons. Some of the trails offer excellent cross-country skiing in the winter.

You can reach the monument from the east and west. To get to the east entrance, take Monument Road west from downtown. To get to the west entrance, take Broadway west from downtown or I-70 west to Fruita and follow the signs. Admission is $4 per vehicle for a seven-day pass.

For further information, write Colorado National Monument, Fruita, CO 81521, or phone (970) 858-3617.

City Parks
Lincoln Park, on N. 12th between North and Gunnison, is the community's largest and best town park. Volleyball courts, swimming pools, picnic areas, a great kids' playground, huge lawns, and shade trees add to its appeal. Smaller, but also nice, is **Hawthorne Park,** at 5th and Gunnison; you'll find a picnic area, playground, lawns, and shade trees. For more in-

formation on Grand Junction parks, phone the **Parks and Recreation Department** at (970) 244-3866.

Child's Play
Grand Junction is a wonderfully "kid oriented" town. In addition to the excellent city parks, the community offers two unique diversions for kids. **Moon Farm** is a day and summer camp catering to kids ages five to 12. Originally founded over 30 years ago when the Moon family hosted son Dave's end-of-the-year kindergarten party, the farm, situated on a huge spread west of town, has grown to include a huge and bizarre array of things for kids to do, with an emphasis on multicultural understanding. They can try on wooden shoes at the Dutch House; play in the "saloon"; explore the Egypt House (and learn about papyrus painting and the Egyptian alphabet); learn about Arabic cultures in the Middle East House; dig in a real fossil pit; feed the many animals, from Vietnamese pigs to goats and peacocks. Kids can also play soccer, volleyball, basketball, go horseback riding, practice archery, make videos, explore the Witch's Castle—with 180-200 other children (with one employee per 15 kids).

Moon Farm offers both daily and weekly programs, with bus service provided from downtown Grand Junction; you can either stay with your kids or turn them over to trained staff. Day-camp rate is $10 per child per day. For more information on rates, hours, and special programs, write Moon Farm, Inc., 1360 18¹/₂ Rd., Fruita, CO 81521, or phone (970) 858-7176. To visit Moon Farms, go south on US 50 to 18¹/₂ Road.

On a smaller scale, but equally attractive, the **Doo Zoo Children's Museum** offers a wide range of diversions for kids from about age three to eight. From play cars to a "sea" of blue plastic balls for "swimming," from a post office to a grocery store, the Doo Zoo offers enough to keep kids occupied for hours. Hands-on learning toys abound, including typewriters and computers. A small admission fee is charged, and parents should stay with their kids.

The Doo Zoo is right downtown at 635 Main. Hours are Mon.-Sat. 10 a.m.-5:30 p.m. For more information, phone (970) 241-5225.

Cycling

The Grand Junction area offers excellent touring and mountain biking. Rimrock Drive through Colorado National Monument is a wonderful if admittedly arduous road tour. The route rises 2,000 feet from the valley floor to the top of the plateau and back down in 23 miles; the loop from Grand Junction through the park and back to town is about 36 miles.

Kokopelli's Trail, a recently developed mountain-bike trail, winds 128 miles from Grand Junction to Moab, Utah. Kokopelli's Trail (named for the humpbacked, flute-playing Anasazi god of fertility) begins 15 miles west of Grand Junction at Loma (Exit 15 from I-70), parallels the interstate for about 40 miles then drops south at Cisco, Utah, winding down just south of Arches National Park. The trail is just one leg of the Colorado Plateau Mountain-Bike Trail System, which also includes the **Tabeguache Trail** to Montrose and when completed will ultimately comprise a half dozen other routes interconnecting Crested Butte, Aspen, Telluride, Grand Junction, Montrose, Moab, and Green River. The designers of the system are dedicated to political awareness and environmental preservation (Kokopelli's Trail is largely old jeep trails, so little actual construction had to be done). For a map of Kokopelli's Trail or more information on the Colorado Plateau Mountain-Bike Trail Association, write Box 4602, Grand Junction, CO 81502, or phone (970) 241-9561. Information is also available from the BLM, 764 Horizon Dr.,

Grand Junction, CO 81506, tel. (970) 244-3000, as well as from Grand Junction-area bike shops, including **The Bike Peddler,** 710 N. 1st, tel. (970) 243-5602; and **Tompkins Cycle Sports,** 301 N. Main, tel. (970) 241-0141.

Golf

Grand Junction's public golf courses include the small, nine-hole **Lincoln Park Golf Course** in town at 12th and Gunnison, tel. (970) 242-6394, and the 18-hole **Tiara Rado Golf Course** between Grand Junction and Colorado National Monument (go west on Broadway), tel. (970) 245-8085.

Hiking

The Grand Junction area's two best hiking areas are **Colorado National Monument** and **Grand Mesa** (see "Grand Mesa," following, for information on hiking in Grand Mesa National Forest). Colorado National Monument offers excellent hiking for all levels of ability and dedication. A half dozen or so short marked trails (from one-quarter- to one-mile long) will get you out of the car for a breather, while backcountry trails ranging four to eight and a half miles take up to 16 hours roundtrip. The park has published a map and guide with descriptions of the different trails, including lengths in miles and approximate time allowances. You'll receive the guide when you enter the park. You can also get information on hiking in the park from the visitor center or by writing Colorado National Monument, Fruita, CO 81521; or call (970) 858-3617.

Just west of the national monument lies little-known **Rattlesnake Canyon,** a desolate and rugged area accessible only by foot or 4WD vehicle. Hardy backcountry hikers will be rewarded with some of the most austere beauty on the Western Slope—sandstone cliffs, piñon-dotted mesas, and several natural arches. For information on Rattlesnake Canyon, contact the regional BLM office at 764 Horizon Dr., Grand Junction, CO 81506, tel. (970) 243-3000.

Fishing

The Colorado and Gunnison rivers probably once brimmed with healthy lunker trout, though as victims of irrigation and mining, the rivers don't offer much to modern anglers. The Grand Mesa area (see that section, following) has over 200 lakes and offers decent fishing. For information and licenses in Grand Junction, stop in at **Surplus City,** 1st and Grand, tel. (970) 243-3604.

Rafting
Grand Junction's Western Slope location makes it ideal as a base for river running, from kayaking in boiling whitewater to floating down broad, lazy stretches of calm riverwater. **Adventure Bound, Inc.** is a Grand Junction-based company offering trips on the Colorado, Yampa, and Green rivers in Colorado and Utah. Trips range in length from one to five days. Explore the canyons of Dinosaur National Monument and Utah's Green Wilderness. For a brochure with more details, including prices and reservation information, write Adventure Bound River Expeditions, 2392 H Rd., Grand Junction, CO 81505, or phone (970) 241-5633 or (800) 423-4668.

You can also book raft trips on the Colorado River through **Rimrock Deer Park and Outdoor Center.** Rates range from $13 (1.5-hour trip) to $135 (two days). You can also rent canoes. Write Box 604, Fruita, CO 81521, or phone (970) 858-9555.

Horseback Riding
Grand Junction's roots are in ranching and farming, and it remains a very Western town—lots of Stetsons, string ties, and horse trailers. Several outfitters in the area rent horses and offer tours, one of the best ways to see Colorado National Monument. **Rimrock Deer Park,** whose stables are near the west entrance to the monument, offers one- and two-hour rides, as well as half-day, full-day, and overnight pack trips. In addition, rodeos are held every Tuesday evening in the summer, and Rimrock rents canoes and rafts and can provide transportation to and from put-in spots. Rates for horseback rides start at about $15 an hour. For further information, phone (970) 858-9555.

Downhill Skiing
One of Colorado's lesser-known ski resorts, **Powderhorn,** is just 35 miles from Grand Junction via I-70 and US 65. Powderhorn and the surrounding Grand Mesa National Forest also offer good Nordic skiing. For information on skiing Powderhorn, see "Grand Mesa," below.

TOURS
If you've got time, you'll want to explore the Grand Junction area a bit, from the peach orchards on the east side of town of the barren backcountry to the south. Poking around by car is a great way to do it, as you'll constantly come across landscapes, farmhouses, vineyards, or tiny little towns you hadn't realized existed. Or you can hook up with one of several outfits in the area that will guide you where you want to go.

Winery Tours
Though not all that new to the valley—the first arrived in the late 1970s—the wineries of the Grand River Valley have only fairly been discovered by tourists in the past couple of years. What's more, these wines are good: Several of the local wines won major awards at national competitions in recent years.

You'll find six wineries in the Palisade region (seven miles east of Grand Junction) alone, including a "meadery." A wonderful way to spend an afternoon is tasting the local product and touring the operations. Because these wineries are small, you're apt to get talking to the person pouring your sample only to discover she is the winemaker/owner herself. Tours and tastings are free, and in addition to selling wine, the shops stock novelties, such as T-shirts, gift baskets, wine racks, and wine glasses. If you happen to be around in late September, check out the **Winefest,** an annual celebration of grapes, the harvest, and good wine, with special tastings tours, entertainment, and other events in both Grand Junction and Palisade.

The Grand Junction Visitor and Convention Bureau provides a complete list of the area wineries, maps and other information, as well as exact dates of the Winefest.

Commercial Tours
Among the companies offering tours of the Grand Junction area is **Coopertours,** tel. (970) 434-0224. Owner David Cooper will take you on history tours, archaeology, or photography tours—either one he's designed, or one you customize to your own interests. **Eagletree Tours,** tel. (970) 241-4792 or (800) 818-3928, features river- and mountain-bike shuttles, sag

wagons, and fully catered tours, as well as individual hiking or biking tours of Colorado National Monument.

ACCOMMODATIONS

Hotels and Motels
Most of Grand Junction's hotels and motels are concentrated on Horizon Drive just off I-70 (airport exit, Exit 31). You'll find a **Days Inn,** tel. (970) 245-7200; **Ramada Inn,** tel. (970) 241-8411; **Holiday Inn,** tel. (970) 243-6790; **Super 8,** tel. (970) 248-8080; **Sandman Best Western,** tel. (970) 243-4150; **Horizon Inn Best Western,** tel. (970) 245-1410; **Budget Host Inn,** tel. (970) 243-6050; **Hilton,** tel. (970) 241-8888; **Motel 6,** tel. (970) 243-2628; and several others.

The closest motel to Colorado National Monument is the **West Gate Inn,** at I-70 Exit 26, tel. (970) 241-3020. Doubles run about $40-50.

Bed and Breakfasts
The **Junction Country Inn,** 861 Grand Ave., tel. (970) 241-2817, is a centrally located bed and breakfast in a remodeled 1907 home. Within walking distance of many of the city's parks and other attractions, the inn is also on a relatively busy (for Grand Junction) street. Also on Grand Avenue is the **Cider House,** 1126 Grand, tel. (970) 242-9087. If you'd rather be out and away from the hustle and bustle of town, try the **Orchard House,** 3573 E-1/2 Rd. (Palisade), tel. (970) 464-0529. About 10 miles east of Grand Junction on a hillside above the little town of Palisade, the Orchard House looks out over the farms and orchards of the Grand Valley.

Hostel
The least expensive lodging in town can be found at the Melrose Hotel's **International Hostel,** 337 Colorado Ave., tel. (970) 342-9636, where a bed in a dorm will run you $10, and a double with private bath is $30—all rates include breakfast. In addition, you can arrange packages that include various tours of the Grand Junction, eastern-Utah/western-Colorado area.

Camping and RVing
In addition to Saddlehorn Campground at Colorado National Monument (see above) and the Forest Service campgrounds on Grand Mesa (see that section, following), the Grand Junction area also offers several privately owned camping areas. The Grand Junction/Clifton **KOA** campground, tel. (970) 434-6644, is just east of town at 3238 E. Business-70 (take Exit 37 from I-70). On the other side of town are the **Junction West RV Park,** 799 Rd. 22 (Exit 26 off I-70), tel. (970) 245-8531, and **Fruita Junction RV Park and Campground,** tel. (970) 858-3155, off I-70 in Fruita adjacent to the Colorado Welcome Center and near the west entrance to Colorado National Monument.

FOOD

Start Me Up
If you're just passing through, you'll find plenty of fast-food restaurants at the major exits off I-70, particularly at the airport exit (Exit 31). **Good Pastures,** tel. (970) 243-3058, at the Friendship Inn at 733 Horizon Dr. (Exit 31 from I-70), is Grand Junction's version of a health food restaurant. Beginning with fresh juices (celery, carrot, apple, etc.), Good Pastures offers several low-fat, healthful dishes, including some vegetarian specials; at breakfast, you have your choice of sausage, Canadian bacon, or "soysage." Downtown, try the European-style **Jitters Espresso,** 504 Main, tel. (970) 245-5194, where you can find excellent pastries, as well as full breakfasts, in addition to gourmet coffees. Just up the street at 6th and Main is **Main Street Bagels,** serving a variety of bagels and coffees.

Other Restaurants
Fortunately, the microbrewery bandwagon didn't pass Grand Junction by. The brand new (1995) **Rockslide Restaurant and Brewery,** 401 Main, tel. (970) 245-2111, serves excellent beer, as well as typical pub fare (burgers, fish and chips), plus dinner specials—seafood, prime rib, and pastas. Another very good restaurant is **The River City Cafe and Bar,** 748 North, tel. (970) 245-8040. Offering an eccentric menu with an emphasis on healthful foods, River City serves pizzas (with eggplant and feta cheese), soups, salads, and a variety of Mexican and Southwestern dishes. River City specializes in black-bean and other vegetarian dishes, including de-

licious black-bean burgers. Dinners run $5-12.

One of the Western Slope's more intriguing restaurants is **Grits,** 2704 US 50, tel. (970) 243-8871, recently converted from a '50s-type diner to an upscale place serving a range of nouveau cuisine. The kick here is that the formica and overall feel of the old place remains, contrasting wonderfully with the progressive menu, which features pastas, meat dishes, soups, and salads, all excellent. Dinners run $8-12.

The **7th Street Cafe,** 832 S. 7th, tel. (970) 242-7225, is Grand Junction's retro '50s diner. Decorated with posters of James Dean, Marilyn, and Elvis, as well as old 45s (a 45 is thin, round, black vinyl disk a bit larger than a CD, on each side of which is a single groove from which a tiny needle would produce music. . .).

For authentic Mexican food, try **La Mexicana,** 1310 Ute, tel. (970) 245-2737. Dinners run $4-7, and Friday and Saturday nights, the stage comes alive with authentic Mexican folk dancing, focusing on a different state in Mexico each evening. Also good for Mexican food is **Dos Hombres,** 421 Brach, tel. (970) 242-8861, and at 569 Rd. 32, tel. 434-5078, both of which are more cantina style than the smaller La Mexicana.

Just Desserts
Pappy's Ice Cream Parlor, on the Main Street Mall at 560 Main, tel. (970) 241-5600, features excellent homemade ice cream (using Ben and Jerry's recipes), fresh-squeezed lime-lemonade, fresh-ground coffees, and gourmet candies.

ENTERTAINMENT

Those expecting Boulder-like nightlife in Grand Junction will be disappointed. Though there are a handful of places to listen to live music, your choices are limited, and you're probably better off taking advantage of the area's daytime recreational opportunities. If nighttime does find you antsy to get out, try the **The Rose,** 2993 North Ave., tel. (970) 245-0606, where you can dance to live country-and-western music; **Bailey's,** at the Ramada Inn, 2790 Crossroads, tel. (970) 241-8411, a nightclub/disco with DJ dancing; **Cinnamon's,** in the Holiday Inn, 755 Horizon, tel. (970) 243-6790. **Charade's,** in the Hilton, 743

Horizon, tel. (970) 241-8888, features live comedy on Tuesday nights. The **River City Cafe and Bar,** 748 North, tel. (970) 245-8040, also books live music from time to time, as does the **Blue Moon,** 120 N. 7th St., tel. (970) 242-4506.

CALENDAR

From music festivals to baseball tournaments to bike races, Grand Junction's got something going on just about every weekend. The best sources for what's happening when and where are the *Daily Sentinel* and the Grand Junction Area Chamber of Commerce.

Among the highlights: The **JUCO** (Junior College) **Baseball World Series** in late May; the **Hot-Air Balloon Rally** early June; the **Colorado Stampede** (rodeo, music, cowboy poetry), mid-June; **Country Jam USA Music Festival** late June or July (a week of music featuring big-name acts such as Willie Nelson); **Dinosaur Days,** late July; the **Mesa County Fair,** early August; **Palisade Peach Festival,** late August; **Renaissance Faire,** mid-September; and the **Colorado Mountain Winefest,** late September.

Throughout the summer, downtown Grand Junction features **Art on the Corner,** with a diverse group of the state's sculptors displaying their work outside on streetcorners. The **Grand Junction Symphony Orchestra** hosts a concert series each year, with special shows attracting big-name guest conductors and musicians. For information, phone the symphony at (970) 243-6787.

SHOPPING

Try to allow yourself some time to explore downtown's Main Street Mall. Though the street has been remodeled, it's refreshingly free of Yupscale boutiques and trendy (and pricey) shops. Instead, you'll find classic small-town clothing, band-instrument, shoe, stationery, and gift stores. There's even a nurses' uniform store, a formalwear rental shop, and a Woolworth's. Be sure to check out **A Haggle of Vendors Emporium**, 510 Main, where every imaginable nook and cranny is packed with imports, antiques, and junk—everything from toys and fabrics to picture frames, plates, mugs, and glassware.

SERVICES

The offices of the Grand Junction **Police Department** are located at 625 Ute, tel. (970) 244-3538. The Mesa County **Sheriff** is at 215 Rice, tel. (970) 244-3500. Both of Grand Junction's hospitals offer emergency and nonemergency medical care. **St. Mary's Hospital and Regional Medical Center** is at the corner of 7th and Patterson, tel. (970) 244-2273. **Grand Junction Community Hospital** is at 12th and Walnut, tel. (970) 242-0920. Grand Junction's main **post office** is at 241 N. 4th; for information on other branches or Grand Junction-area zip codes, phone (970) 244-3400.

Recycling

Recycle at **United Waste and Recycle,** 2948 I-70 Business, and **Western Colorado Recycling,** 2379 G Road. You can also drop off most recyclables at Grand Junction's **City Markets,** 2770 US 50, 1909 N. 1st St., 569 32nd Ave., and 200 Rood Avenue.

INFORMATION

Just west of town in Fruita is a Colorado State **Welcome Center,** where you can pick up brochures on what to do and see in the Grand Junction area, as well as in the rest of the state.

The **Grand Junction Visitor and Convention Bureau** has a beautiful new information center located just off I-70 at Horizon Drive. The center is staffed with helpful volunteers and has scads of literature and other information on what to do, where to stay, and where to eat in Grand Junction. Phone the offices (970) 244-1480 or (800) 962-2547.

One of the best places in town for Colorado books, maps, and magazines is **Readmore Book and Magazine Stand,** 344 Main St., downown on the Main Street Mall. The shop carries an excellent selection of everything from coffee-table-size photo books to small-press

histories, with a special section of books by local authors. The main branch of the **Mesa County Public Library** is in Grand Junction at 530 Grand Ave., tel. (970) 243-4442.

Grand Junction's *Daily Sentinel,* which comes out weekday afternoons and Saturday and Sunday mornings, has information on current events, local movie and television listings, and weather. For subscription information, phone (970) 242-5050.

Electronic Information

Information on lodging and exploring the Grand Junction area is available through the convention and visitors bureau's Internet address: **http://grand-junction.net**.

TRANSPORTATION

Just south of Interstate 70 about 250 miles west of Denver, Grand Junction is easily approachable by either car or bus. The **Greyhound-Trailways** bus depot is downtown at 230 S. 5th; for information on rates and schedules, phone (970) 242-6012. You can also get to Grand Junction via **Amtrak,** whose passenger station is at 2nd and South Ave.; for information, phone (970) 241-2733 or (800) 872-7245.

Grand Junction's **Walker Field Airport** is the largest airport in the state west of Denver and is serviced by several major airlines, with flights from cities around the country as well as connecting flights from Denver. Phone the airport at (970) 244-9100. For airport transportation services, phone **A Touch With Class,** tel. (970) 245-5466.

Most of the major car-rental agencies have booths at Walker Field, including **Avis,** tel. (970) 244-9170; **Budget,** tel. (970) 244-9155; **Hertz,** tel. (970) 243-0747; and **National,** tel. (970) 243-6626. Offices of **Thrifty Rental,** tel. (970) 243-7556, are at 752 Horizon.

For taxi service in Grand Junction, phone **Sunshine Taxi** at (970) 245-TAXI.

SOUTH AND EAST OF GRAND JUNCTION

COLORADO 141 SOUTH

Colorado 141 winds south from Grand Junction to Dove Creek, coursing through western Colorado's remote canyon country and passing through a handful of ramshackle old mining towns. Along the way, the 150-mile stretch of highway flirts with the Utah border, twice approaching within 10 miles of the state line. Known as the **Unaweep/Tabeguache Byway**, the road slices below Grand Mesa, across the Uncompahgre Plateau, and follows the course of the Dolores River for some 30 miles. Ribboning through ancient Native American hunting grounds, the route takes its name from the Utes: "Unaweep" means "Canyon With Two Mouths," and "Tabeguache" ("TAB-a-wash") means "Place Where The Snow Melts First."

Unaweep Canyon is a harshly scenic draw that slices through the plateau nearly from Whitewater to Gateway. Its floor lush, green, and sometimes seemingly endless, its walls towering sharp and sheer, the canyon possesses that unmistakably familiar ability to help travelers find perspective. Out here, where the lines between nature's beauty and her cold indifference become blurred, you, and your problems, can seem awfully small.

In the late 1880s, a seven-mile wooden flume was built along the Dolores River just north of Uravan. Used to carry water from the San Miguel River to the Lone Tree Placer Site, **Hanging Flume** clings precariously to the sheer sandstone cliffs 150 feet above the water's surface. A turnout and interpretive sign provide an excellent view, as well as historical background.

Uravan was a company town founded in 1936 and named for the two elements found in the area's carnotite ore: uranium and vanadium. During the 1940s, the U.S. Army sent uranium from the tailings from the vanadium mill to Los Alamos, New Mexico, where Oppenheimer and crew used it in the Manhattan Project, the world's first atomic bomb. The mill shut down in 1984.

For a complete guide to the Unaweep-Tabeguache Byway, contact the Grand Junction Visitors and Convention Bureau. The thorough and well-written guide describes 35 points of interest along the route from Whitewater to Placerville and also provides information on the geology, history, and wildlife of the area. Write 360 Grand Ave., Grand Junction, CO 81501, or phone (970) 244-1480 or (800) 962-2547.

Nucla, Naturita, and Norwood

Naturita is a small town west of the junction of CO 141 and CO 145 with several businesses flanking the highway for a couple of blocks. The town, founded in 1882, now serves as a supply center for nearby ranchers and farmers. In addition, a handful of small motels provide base camps for the hunters who find their way out here in the summer and fall. **Children's Memorial Park** is just off the highway (at 2nd St.), next to the **Rimrock Historical Museum** (for hours and more information phone the Naturita Town Hall at 970-865-2286).

Five miles northeast of Naturita is the town of Nucla. Shortly before the turn of the century, the Colorado Cooperative Community established the town as an experiment in communal living. Designed as a community where "equality and service rather than greed and competition [would be] the basis of conduct," Nucla was made up of cooperatively owned businesses. In addition, labor was evenly divided, and any product of community labor—the town's irrigation ditch, for example—became community property. Nucla was chosen for the town's name as its founders saw it as the nucleus of a socialist society that would eventually spread throughout the country. But it was not to be—the experiment was short-lived.

About 20 miles southeast of the junction of CO 145 and CO 141 is the little mesa-top ranching town of Norwood. Popular with outdoor enthusiasts, particularly hunters and anglers, the Norwood area is one of Colorado's little pockets of relatively undisturbed natural beauty. You can enjoy fishing and boating at nearby Miramonte Reservoir. For information on the area, phone the **Norwood Chamber of Commerce** at (970) 327-4238.

GRAND MESA

Less than an hour east of Grand Junction via I-70 and CO 65, Grand Mesa appears startling in its contrast to the Grand Valley sprawling at the base of its steep sides. Here a mountain highway winds, climbs, and switches back from the scrubby canyon country up into the firs, spruces, and aspens of Grand Mesa National Forest. The mesa is 10,000 feet above sea level (and over 5,000 feet above Grand Junction) and covers over 50 square miles.

With over 200 lakes, 15 campgrounds, and miles of riding, hiking, snowmobiling, and cross-country ski trails, as well as Powderhorn downhill ski area, Grand Mesa offers some of the best recreational opportunities in the region. In addition, the mesa affords absolutely spectacular scenery. On the drive down the back side of the mesa, several spots afford views of the San Juan Mountains shouldering massively into the sky over a hundred miles to the south. Oftentimes in the summer, as late-afternoon storms roll in, cold rains angle across the sky, washing the needles and leaves of the trees, and the sunlight plays strange tricks with the mist and the distant clouds. Rainbows arc across the sky, and the greens shine electric.

A word of caution: Even when it's warm in the valley, it can get downright cold on the mesa. I drove up one day in mid-June when it was pushing 90° F in Grand Junction, and by the time I got onto the mesa it was *snowing*. Even if it seems crazy, bring a coat or sweater.

Grand Mesa Lodging

The **Grand Mesa Lodge,** tel. (970) 856-3250, offers cabins that sleep up to six ($60 a night; $75 for one with a fireplace; two-night minimum or pay extra $15). **Mesa Lakes Resort,** tel. (970) 268-5467, has small rustic cabins (no running water), larger, more modern cabins, and a central motel. Rates start at $40 a night (smaller cabins) and range to $110 for the larger cabins; doubles in the motel are $49.50. The lodge has a small restaurant and grocery and tackle shop. Lodging is also available at **Powderhorn Ski Resort,** where summer promotional rates are attractively low, $40 and up a night. Phone (970) 242-5637 or (800) 241-6997 for information or reservations.

Camping

Grand Mesa's campground's are generally open only from Memorial Day through Labor Day, thanks to the large amount of snowfall. Sometimes, there's even too much snow to open the areas until mid-June or later. **Jumbo** and **Spruce Grove** campgrounds have tent and RV sites, pit toilets, and access to hiking trails.

Hiking

Grand Mesa National Forest offers hundreds of miles of trails and backcountry to explore. One of the more popular trails is **Crag Crest Trail** on the highest point of Grand Mesa. The 10-mile trail provides access to broad clearings, where you'll want to stop and take in the view, as well as to dense forests and beautiful mountain lakes. The Forest Service can provide topo maps and more information on specific parts of the mesa that are best for hiking.

Fishing

Open year-round, the lakes on Grand Mesa even draw die-hard trouters for the ice fishing. Most of the lakes are quite small and get a lot of traffic; the shores of the more accessible lakes lined with hopeful anglers, their RVs parked nearby. Even the more remote lakes are rather heavily fished.

For licenses, tackle, and information on current hot spots, stop in at the **Mesa General Store** in Mesa on CO 65 on the north slope.

Skiing

Though primarily an intermediate area, Powderhorn offers good skiing away from the pomp and snobbery of some of the state's better-known resorts. Powderhorn skiers are also afforded some of skiing's more interesting and expansive views; because the mesa rises so dramatically from the valley below, the view becomes a mosaic of snowy mountain meadows, deep forests, and far-off canyonlands and arid desert.

Powderhorn's four lifts service 240 acres of trails and a 1,650-foot vertical drop. Terrain is 20% beginner, 60% intermediate, and 20% advanced. Lessons and rental equipment are available, as is limited on-site lodging, though plans for expansion exist. For information, phone (970) 268-5700. For lodging reservations, phone (800)

241-6997. For a recorded **snow report,** phone (970) 242-SNOW.

Information

For maps and complete information on Grand Mesa and Grand Mesa National Forest, stop by the Grand Junction district office of the Forest Service at 764 Horizon Dr., Grand Junction, or phone (970) 242-8211. Information is also available from the Grand Mesa National Forest Headquarters, 2250 US 50, Delta, CO 81416, tel. (970) 874-7691.

Cedaredge

Cedaredge (pop. 1,200; elev. 6,100 feet) is a robust and colorful small town between the lower slopes of Grand Mesa's south side and the flatlands of the Uncompahgre and Gunnison river valleys. Backed up against the mesa, Cedaredge offers excellent views of the sprawling valleys and orchards and, on clear days, the San Juan Mountains far to the south. **Pioneer Town** is a reconstructed 19th-century western village run by the local historical society. The village features a mining and Native American museum, plus a blacksmith shop, jail, chapel, and one-room schoolhouse. Pioneer Town is open Memorial Day through Labor Day, Mon.-Sat. 10 a.m.-4 p.m. and Sunday 1-4 p.m.

You'll find a nice city park right downtown on Main St./CO 65, with picnic facilities, shade trees, and tennis courts.

COLORADO 133

Colorado US 133 winds northeast from Hotchkiss along the North Fork of the Gunnison River, past Paonia Reservoir, over McClure Pass (elev. 8,755 feet), and then through the Crystal River Valley past Redstone and on to Carbondale. Weather permitting, this is the best and shortest route between much of Southwestern Colorado and Denver, bypassing the Grand Junction-to-Glenwood Springs stretch of I-70 and cutting an hour or more off the trip. Colorado Highway 133 is also the best route connecting Telluride and the ski areas of Central Colorado, and during the winter you'll see a lot of ski-racked Subarus and Jeeps buzzing back and forth along the highway.

The first third of the way is mostly orchard and ranching country. Fertile orchards dominate the open, rolling landscapes, and grazing cattle dot the fields. Elk, commonly seen from the roadway, also graze throughout this area. At Paonia Reservoir, the road doglegs due north and lifts up over McClure Pass, where you'll find trailheads of some excellent cross-country skiing trails. The highway then drops down over the back side of the pass and through the beautiful White River National Forest and the Crystal River Valley, the Crystal River ribboning through the firs and gleaming argentine at roadside.

Paonia

Paonia (pop. 1,670; elev. 5,675 feet), founded in 1882, was named for the abundance of flowers in the area. The name is a bastardization of "peonie," probably resulting from misread handwriting. Agriculture, its major industry, yields excellent peaches, apples, cherries, and other fruits. Several mines can also be found nearby.

Paonia is also the rather unlikely site of the offices of one of the West's boldest, angriest, and most progressive and intelligent environmental newspapers, *High Country News.* Published out of an old one-story storefront building on Main St., the *News,* whose motto is, "A Paper for People Who Care about the West," is supported almost solely by subscriptions and grants, including one from the Grateful Dead's Rex Foundation. This allows the paper the freedom to confront sensitive issues head-on without fear of advertisers pulling their ads. The result is a scrupulous press that does thorough investigative pieces on subjects ranging from overgrazing on New Mexico public lands to the official federal stand on grizzly bears in Yellowstone Park, and on all aspects of the West's often-destructive industries—mining, drilling, logging, and the military-industrial complex. For subscription and other information, write Box 1090, Paonia, CO 91428, or phone (970) 527-4898.

If you're looking for a good place to eat in Paonia, try **La Casa** on Main St., where you can get Mexican and Italian food, as well as sandwiches, burgers, and salads for $5-8. Lodging is available at the **Redwood Arms Motel,** just west of town on CO 133, tel. (970) 527-4148. Doubles start at about $40.

For more information on Paonia, write the **Paonia Chamber of Commerce,** Box 366, Paonia CO 81428, or phone (970) 527-3885. There's also a tourist information booth on CO 65 at the turnoff to town.

Yule Marble Quarries

Some of the world's purest marble was mined at this National Historic Site. First discovered in 1870, the marble from this area has been used in government buildings around the country, including the Denver capitol. In addition, deposits here provided the largest single piece of marble ever quarried in the world: the 100-ton brick used for the Tomb of the Unknown Soldier in Arlington National Cemetery in Washington, D.C. Marble from the Yule quarries was also used in the construction of the Lincoln Memorial.

Though inactive for years, the quarries are open to the public. Wander around the old mill, view huge slabs of flawless marble once used in mill buildings, or hike along Yule Creek, where crystal-clear water polishes the marble's swirling veins and faded pastels. But be careful: Some of the old pits are deep, so use caution when exploring and keep an eye on kids.

The Yule marble mill and quarries are accessible only by foot or 4WD vehicle. Turn south from CO 133 onto County Rd. 3 (the turnoff is marked), and continue two miles to the town of Marble. From there it's about four miles to the quarries. You can arrange 4WD tours to the Yule quarries through **Crystal River 4x4 Tours,** 116 Main St., Redstone, tel. (970) 963-1991.

Redstone

Redstone, a tiny resort community on the banks of the Crystal River, dates from the turn of the century, when coal baron John Cleveland Osgood (cousin of Grover Cleveland) built a village here made up of several small cottages and one magnificent "castle." Osgood, founder and director of the Colorado Fuel and Iron Company, was at one time one of the country's most successful industrialists, his peers (and houseguests) including John D. Rockefeller and Theodore Roosevelt. Osgood was reportedly worth some $40 million.

The town of Redstone was built as a model industrial community. Cottages were construct-

John Cleveland Osgood

DENVER PUBLIC LIBRARY, WESTERN HISTORY DEPARTMENT

ed to house the families of his employees who worked in the nearby coal mines, while the large Redstone Inn was for "bachelors and guests." He built the 42-room, 16-bedroom Cleveholm Manor for himself, decorating it with the finest furnishings from around the world—Tiffany chandeliers, Persian rugs, and Italian oil paintings, as well as lots of goldleaf and marble. Osgood and Roosevelt are said to have sat on the front porch shooting deer that the gamekeeper released on the lawn.

Today, Redstone consists of a single narrow road paralleling the highway across the Crystal River. A handful of vacation homes and several gift shops, mostly specializing in antiques, dolls, woodcarvings, and glass, can be found there; also some vacation lodges, a general store, and a small park and playground.

Cleveholm Manor is open for tours and lodging. Suites run $155-180, rooms with private baths $125, and rooms with shared baths $95-105. For information, stop in at the Redstone Country Store, or phone (970) 963-3463 or (800) 643-4837.

The **Redstone Inn** is the lodge built to accommodate Osgood's bachelor workers and is on the National Register of Historic Places. Though not as opulent or huge as the Castle, the inn is still impressive in its grandeur and elegance. If you're looking for a great place to hole up away from daily life's hustle and bustle, you'd be hard-pressed to find a better spot (doubles start at about $70; slightly less for shared bath). The Inn also serves excellent dinners, and is famous for its Sunday brunch. Even if you're just passing through, take a few minutes to look around and maybe have a Bloody Mary in the bar, which is decorated with original Victorian furnishings. Passers through can get a taste of the inn's elegance by stopping for a bite at the main dining room, where you can get steaks, seafood, and lamb, or at the less formal **Patio Grill,** serving salads, sandwiches, and burgers. For more information and reservations, phone (970) 963-2526 or (800) 748-2524.

ASPEN

If there is an Avalon of Colorado, it is Aspen, a place where myth and reality circle round each other like freewheeling falcons under a cobalt sky. And this is the town's real charm—the way it exists as though dismembered from the rest of the world, and how in a strange way it doesn't much matter what's real and what isn't. Though you might feel more grounded after having visited, it's due not as much to the town itself but to the perspective it provides. Like Hemingway said of journalism: Aspen is good for you, if you get out in time.

Of course some people stay longer than others. Though if you plan to stay, you need nearly to be independently wealthy. In the first quarter of 1990, the average price of a home was $1.16 million. In the middle of the same year, the cheapest house on the market was priced at $365,000; the house was under 1,000 square feet.

Which, of course, is why Aspen is almost synonymous with celebrity: Don Henley, Glenn Frey, Goldie Hawn, Jack Nicholson, Hunter Thompson, Oprah Winfrey, and John Denver are but a few who either live in the area or spend time here.

And it's not just housing. Walk around the downtown mall—you can almost smell the money. The boutiques and specialty shops aren't here for working people, who are, however, free to window shop and imagine a lifestyle they'll probably never experience.

What is there, then, for the untitled, the *unentitled?* Just this: Some of the most magnificent

*downtown Aspen and
Aspen Mountain*

scenery and greatest recreational opportunities on the planet. Though best known as a ski resort—in fact, Aspen (pop. 7,000; elev. 7,908) is probably the country's quintessential ski town—the area offers untold riches for hikers, mountain bikers, anglers, and anyone else willing to explore a bit. White River National Forest literally surrounds Aspen, its woods, streams, lakes, towering peaks, and old logging roads inviting endless hours of exploration, whether you go with a group or prefer the meditative nature of solitude.

Situated in a winter-locked box canyon on the Roaring Fork River, Aspen traces its history, as do many Colorado mountain towns, to late-19th-century mining, and the town's homes and other buildings reflect that. Cozy Victorian homes—most of them tastefully remodeled and, in the summer lobelia, pansies, and other colorful flowers spilling out of planters and window boxes line the town's side streets. The Hotel Jerome, at one time one of the most elegant lodges in the west and still defined by glorious opulence, stands sentrylike on Main St., its solid, red-brick sides providing constancy to the pulsing, dynamic community that surrounds it.

Over the last half century, Aspen earned a reputation as a center of sophistication and progressive cultural education. The permanent population is among the best educated in the Rockies, with 55% holding bachelor's degrees or better (as opposed to 20% nationwide), and *Snow Country Magazine* rated its school system number one among 47 ski towns. Also, a number of institutes, arts centers, and annual festivals—music, film, food and wine—bring famous writers and directors, professors and lecturers, chefs and winemakers to town every summer. In addition, the large number of well-known artists, musicians, and actors who live permanently or part-time in or near Aspen guarantee the area will remain a cultural mecca, if an overpriced one, well into the future.

HISTORY

The first mines were staked in the Roaring Fork Valley in the summer of 1879, when prospectors seeking silver arrived from Leadville by way of

Independence Pass. By fall of that year, word spread that these mines, at the bases of Smuggler and Aspen mountains, were producing respectable amounts of ore. The valley's first community, originally called Ute City, was established by Midwesterner Henry Gillespie, who stopped in Leadville en route to the valley just long enough to purchase rights to the mines from the original prospectors. Gillespie didn't stay long, deciding to go to Washington, D.C. to try to raise money and establish postal service for his camp. In February 1880, B. Clark Wheeler arrived in Ute City, having skied into the valley on "Norwegian snowshoes," and, in Gillespie's absence, changed the name of the camp to Aspen.

That summer, great numbers of miners descended on the Roaring Fork Valley camps, and with them came merchants and others opening shops and services. It was reportedly a rowdy time, the lawless camp attracting men with little regard for social convention or propriety. When winter rolled around, though, and temperatures and snow fell, all but a handful hit the road for more hospitable climes. The few who stayed established the town's first newspaper, organized a Sabbath School, and sponsored regular dances and shows.

For the next three years, Aspen's ore production was kept to a minimum. The camp's remote location made hauling in equipment and domestic items difficult at best—with the nearest railroad 40 miles east, just about anything shipped into or out of the valley came via burro.

In 1883, Jerome B. Wheeler, a New York businessman vacationing in Manitou Springs, arrived in Aspen and immediately saw its investment potential. Wheeler (not related to B. Clark Wheeler) bought controlling interest in several local mines, built the town's first bank, and resurrected an abandoned smelter, which allowed for greatly increased ore production. Shortly after Wheeler's arrival, the little town's annual silver production was $1.25 million.

When the Denver and Rio Grande Railroad arrived in 1887, Aspen's population was approximately 15,000, making it the third-largest town in the state. Local mines, particularly the Molly Gibson, Durant, Midnight, Montezuma, and Smuggler I and II, were producing nearly 100% pure silver, and the value of the area's annual output had increased to $6 million. In addition, the town had earned an international reputation for free-spending wild times and wilder women. Jerome Wheeler opened the Jerome Hotel and the Wheeler Opera House in 1889 at the pinnacle of Aspen's prosperity.

Aspen's boom was destined to be silenced, however. The silver market crashed in 1893, the mines closed down, and folks packed up lock, stock, and barrel, and headed out—some hiked over Independence Pass to Leadville. For the next half decade, Aspen was little more than a handful of crumbling shacks and hardy holdouts hoping good times would return. In the early 1930s, Aspen's population dwindled to approximately 250.

Within a few years, however, the first seeds of the valley's second growth spurt were beginning to be sown. In the summer of 1936, American bobsled racer Billy Fiske and his partner Ted Ryan created the Highland-Bavarian Corporation, with plans to develop the area into the kind of ski area the two had seen in Europe. They built the valley's first inn, the Highland Bavarian Lodge, and hired Andre Roche, a Swiss mountaineer, to survey the mountains for possible ski runs. By 1939, Fiske, Ryan, and Roche had organized the town's first ski club, cut the first trail on Aspen Mountain, and hosted the Rocky Mountain Ski Racing Championships. In 1941, Aspen served as the site of the U.S. Nationals.

Throughout the 1940s, Aspen Mountain continued to host races, and its reputation as an excellent training mountain spread throughout the country. The summer of 1949 saw the founding of the Aspen Institute for Humanistic Studies, the town's first of many forays into the cultural arena. The following winter, Aspen Mountain became the first American site to hold the World Alpine Ski Championships. The little community was now on the international map.

In 1958, the Aspen Skiing Corporation expanded, opening Buttermilk Mountain just south of Aspen. Buttermilk, with gentler slopes than Aspen Mountain, developed primarily as a teaching and beginner-to-intermediate area. Aspen Highlands opened the same winter, and Snowmass Ski Area opened 10 seasons later, in the winter of 1967-68.

MUSEUMS AND "CULCHA"

Since 1949, when Aspen developer Walter Paepcke organized an international celebration in honor of Johann Wolfgang von Goethe's 200th birthday, Aspen has been a center for a wide range of cultural and educational events and permanent institutes, from music and film festivals to various seminars, workshops, and conferences. June through September, the tenor of the town is decidedly intellectual, approaching highbrow, as well-known professors, critics, writers, and artists convene in Aspen to share ideas and to explore the parameters of their disciplines and media. In addition, there are enough museums and galleries, many with a Native American and Southwestern flavor, to keep you occupied for days on end.

Wheeler-Stallard House Museum

Located in the restored private residence of Aspen pioneer Jerome B. Wheeler, this museum displays furniture, clothing, toys, and other period pieces collected by the Aspen Historical Society. Docent-led tours provide insights into Wheeler's life, public as well as private, and offer a keen sense of life in the Roaring Fork Valley before it became a winter playground for the rich and famous. You can also arrange guided walking tours of historic Aspen or pick up a map and take a self-guided tour. The Aspen Historical Society can also recommend and direct you to tours of nearby ghost towns, including Ashcroft and Independence.

The Wheeler-Stallard House Museum, at 620 W. Bleeker St., is open daily 1-4 p.m. mid-June-Sept., and during the ski season (mid-Dec. through mid-April). Small admission fee. For more information, phone (970) 925-3721.

Aspen Art Museum

Located along the Roaring Fork River and the Rio Grande hiking and biking trail, the Aspen Art Museum displays rotating exhibits by well-known artists from around the country, as well as the work of local artists, many of whom are highly respected and widely acclaimed. A variety of media is represented, from architecture and design art to sculpture and paintings.

With its creekside location and adjacent Rio Grande Park, the museum provides an ideal picnic spot and also offers a complimentary wine-and-cheese reception and gallery tour each Thursday evening at 5:30. The museum, at 590 N. Mill, is open for a small entrance fee Tues.-Sat. 10 a.m.-6 p.m. and Sunday noon-6 p.m. For more information, phone (970) 925-8050.

Institutes and Galleries

In addition to these museums, the Aspen area is home to several academic and environmental institutes, arts centers open to the public, and a score or more of commercial galleries. The **Rocky Mountain Institute** is an experiment in environmentally responsible architecture and lifestyles. The 4,000-square-foot center, entirely solar heated, displays techniques in conserving energy and water. The center is in Snowmass at 1739 Snowmass Road. For information on tours, phone (970) 927-3851. The **Aspen Center for Environmental Studies,** on the Roaring Fork River behind the post office, includes a 25-acre wildlife sanctuary and a bird-rehabilitation center, both open to the public. Phone (970) 925-5756 for information and hours. The **Anderson Ranch Arts Center,** at 5263 Owl Creek Rd. in Snowmass Village, displays works of visiting photographers, painters, woodworkers, and other artists and also offers workshops in various media. An example of the caliber of talent here was a recent "Winter Landscapes" workshop taught by Galen Rowell and Robert Glenn Ketchum. For information on touring the center, or on upcoming workshops, phone (970) 923-3181.

Commercial galleries in Aspen and Snowmass range from shops specializing in prehistoric Native American art to places displaying campy art deco and art nouveau, with everything imaginable in between—large-format photography, Southwestern sculpture, 19th-century watercolors, and prints and originals by such names as Picasso, Renoir, Matisse, and Miró.

DOWNHILL SKIING

First, a clarification: there is no *one* Aspen. "Aspen" is actually four separate mountains, all of which—Aspen Mountain, Buttermilk, Aspen Highlands, and Snowmass—are owned by the Aspen Skiing Company. To further complicate things, three of the ski areas—Aspen Mountain, Aspen Highlands, and Buttermilk—lie within two miles of the *town* of Aspen. The fourth, Snowmass, is about 12 miles northwest of Aspen at Snowmass Village, not to be confused with the tiny *town* of Snowmass, about halfway back to Carbondale. Got that? Now, the ski areas, one at a time.

Aspen Mountain

First off, Aspen's terrain is designated 30% expert, 35% advanced, 35% intermediate, and 0% (!) beginner. That's not to say it should be avoided by all but the most advanced skiers, but this *is* where you'll see the polish, the finesse, the graceful speed—skiers who look like they were born on the mountain (indeed, many virtually were). Rated the third best American ski resort by a 1991 *Ski* magazine readers' poll, Aspen Mountain is truly one resort that every skier should hit at least once.

As with many European ski resorts, Aspen Mountain's base—the gondola, the lift ticket window, the ski school—is right in town. This is why you see skiers walking down sidewalks with skis ashoulder, and why half of those not carrying skis *are* wearing ski clothing (whether they've been skiing or not). It also creates a problem, though: parking. The relatively few on-street spaces in town are limited to 90 minutes and are closely monitored. Your best bet is to park in the newly built parking garage next to the Aspen Resort Chamber (two blocks north of Main St. off Mill) and then take a free bus to the lifts.

Assuming your first ascent of Aspen Mountain is via gondola (recommended), you'll probably be surprised at how far back, and up, the lift takes you. It seems never to end. In fact, Aspen Mountain's 625 skiable acres are disproportionately lanky compared to other resorts' layouts, and most of the 75 trails are long, narrow, and steep—covering a 3,267-foot vertical drop. In addition to the gondola, Aspen Mountain offers seven other lifts designed to connect the different runs on the top half and lower north side of the mountain.

Buttermilk Mountain

Designed as Aspen's teaching mountain, Buttermilk is divided into three distinct, lift-connected sections. Offering sharp contrast to Aspen Mountain's advanced- and expert-oriented terrain, Buttermilk is geared almost entirely toward beginning and intermediate skiers. Six lifts service 410 acres with 45 trails rated 35% beginner, 39% intermediate, and 26% advanced.

Buttermilk is also much better suited to families than is Aspen Mountain, with lots of wide-open, treeless runs ideal for group cruising, or, after a decent dump, practicing those figure eights. Three-pinners not up to Aspen Mountain can tune their chops on Buttermilk's gentler slopes and take Telemark lessons through the area's ski school.

Snowmass

The Roaring Fork Valley's newest ski area, Snowmass is located 12 miles "down valley" from the town of Aspen. Like Buttermilk, Snowmass best suits to intermediate skiers and families—the mountain's skiable acres rate 10% beginner, 51% intermediate, and 39% advanced and expert. In fact, *Snow Country* magazine's Resort Editor Abby Rand described Snowmass as "the intermediate's paradise" in the January/February 1991 issue. Sixteen lifts service 2,500 acres of skiable terrain with a 3,612-foot vertical drop.

In addition, things are a little more laid-back here than they are in town, and Snowmass attracts folks not interested in the pretensions and celebrity of Aspen. And that's a lot of the area's skiers: in the winter of 1988-89, 50% of the Aspen area's skier-days were spent at Snowmass.

Rated 19th among U.S. ski areas by a *Snow Country* reader survey, Snowmass is popular for its long runs, one of which stretches over four miles, as well as for its child care facilities and large number of ski-in/ski-out lodges and condominiums.

Aspen Highlands

Of all the Aspen-area ski resorts, Aspen Highlands offers the longest vertical drop (3,800 feet), and the most even distribution of terrain: 50% intermediate, 20% beginner, 30% advanced and expert.

Aspen Highlands is on Maroon Creek Rd. just north of the town of Aspen and the Castle Creek bridge. Situated "upvalley," Aspen Highlands generally gets plenty of snow (an average of 300 inches), and though its snowmaking capabilities are minimal, during seasons of limited snowfall its slopes often stay in better shape than those at Snowmass or Buttermilk. Aspen Highlands has nine lifts and 55 trails on 619 acres of skiable terrain.

Alpine Skiing Information

For complete information on Aspen Mountain, Buttermilk, Aspen Highlands, or Snowmass, write the **Aspen Skiing Company,** Box 1248, Aspen, CO 81612, or phone (970) 925-4444 or (800) 825-6200. For **ski-school information,** phone (970) 925-1220. For the company's **snow report,** phone (970) 925-1221.

CROSS-COUNTRY SKIING

Though Aspen is better known as a mecca of downhill skiing and skiers, the area also offers excellent opportunities for the Nordic skier, with miles and miles of groomed trails and vast unbroken forests and meadows where you can cut your own path. The **Aspen/Snowmass Nordic Trail System** maintains 80 km of trails between the town of Aspen and Snowmass Village. Trailheads dot the southern Roaring Fork Valley, including those at the Aspen Club, Aspen High School, the Aspen Cross-Country Center (22475 West CO 82), and the Snowmass Club Touring Center. Transportation to the trailheads is available on the Roaring Fork Transit Agency's buses. You can get detailed maps of the trail system from the visitor center in the Wheeler Opera House, 328 E. Hyman, or by writing Box 10815, Aspen, CO 81612, or calling (970) 925-2145. Contact the Snowmass Touring Club at 02329 Club Circle, Snowmass Village, CO 81615, tel. 923-3148.

Twelve miles west of Aspen on Maroon Creek Rd., the **Ashcroft Ski Touring Center** offers 30 km of groomed trails in the gorgeous Castle Creek Valley. After a day on the trails, return to the center's **Pine Creek Cookhouse,** where you can get a fixed-price gourmet dinner or take a sleigh ride before skiing back to your car. For complete information on ski trails, dinner, and sleigh rides, phone (970) 925-1044.

Skiers looking for the ultimate cross-country experience can choose from two of the county's best backcountry trail systems. With difficult trails at high elevations, these systems are not for beginners. Skiers must be accomplished, physically fit athletes, and able to carry heavy packs.

The **10th Mountain Trail Association Hut System** offers European-style hut-to-hut skiing on 300 miles of trails stretching from Aspen to Vail and throughout much of the White River National Forest. On-trail accommodations are provided at 12 huts and lodges three to eight miles apart. The association owns eight rustic huts and maintains four privately owned lodges. Reservations are generally required months in advance. (For a complete description, see "Winter Sports" under "Vail and Beaver Creek" in the Northwestern Colorado chapter.) For information, write 1280 Ute Ave., Aspen, CO 81611, tel. (970) 925-5775.

The United States Ski Association operates the **Alfred A. Braun Hut System,** the trailhead of which you'll find on Maroon Creek Rd. near Ashcroft. Each of the six huts accommodates up to 18 skiers (or hikers—the center is open year-round), with a minimum of four per hut. For information or reservations, write Box 7937, Aspen, CO 81612, tel. (970) 925-7345.

For information on cross-country skiing in the surrounding White River National Forest, stop in at the district office at 806 W. Hallam St., Aspen, or phone (970) 925-3445. You can also get information at any of the town's retail shops, including **Ute Mountaineer,** 308 S. Mill, tel. (970) 925-2848, and **The Hub of Aspen,** 315 E. Hyman, tel. (970) 925-7970. For guide service, contact **Elk Mountain Guides,** tel. (970) 923-6131, which offers tours of the 10th Mountain Trail Association and the Alfred A. Braun huts and trails, as well as other half-, full-, and multiday trips into the backcountry.

OTHER WINTER SPORTS

Snowmobiling

The **T-Lazy-7 Ranch** has become almost an institution in Aspen, with visitors returning year after year. The ranch offers snowmobile tours up into the Maroon Bells backcountry, as well as rides to ghost towns and historic mining camps. You can also take a ride up the back side of Aspen Mountain to meet skiing friends for lunch at the top of the gondola. The T-Lazy-7 also offers sleigh rides and, in the summer, stagecoach rides. For more information, phone (970) 925-4614 or 925-7040.

You can also rent snowmobiles or join tours (three-hour or half-day) at **Western Adventures** north of Aspen at Woody Creek. For information, phone (970) 923-3337.

Skating, Dogsledding, and Sleigh Rides

Aspen Ice Gardens is a 16,000-square-foot indoor rink at 233 W. Hyman, tel. (970) 925-7485. Open year-round, except for April and May, the rink offers instruction, rentals, repair, and sales. The **Silver Circle** outdoor ice rink is located at 433 E. Durant, tel. (970) 925-6360.

Dogsledding in Aspen goes back to just after WW II, and **Krabloonik Kennels** carries on the tradition. Krabloonik is owned and operated by Iditarod racer Don MacEachen, who named the kennels after the first lead dog he ever raised— Krabloonik means "Big Eyebrows" and is the Eskimo term for "White Man."

Sleds pulled by 13-dog teams take visitors on full- and half-day tours through the Maroon Bells area, beginning at the ranch at 1201 Divide Rd., Snowmass Village, where MacEachen keeps over 300 dogs. Full-day trips include lunch on the trail, and half-day trips include lunch at the center. Prices start at $185 for a two-hour ride, including lunch. For information and reservations, phone (970) 923-4342 or 923-3953.

If you're feeling more nostalgic than Yukony, you can also tour the Aspen area by horse-drawn sleigh, with several companies offering tours (over the river and) through the woods, as well as through town. **Aspen Carriage Company**, tel. (970) 927-3334, has sleighs as well as carriages, with scenic and historic tours available. You'll see the rigs parked in town at the corner of Cooper and Galena. **Snowmass Stables**, tel. (970) 923-3075, offers nightly rides to a backwoods cabin, where guests are served dinner and treated to live entertainment. Sleighs depart at 5:30 and 8 p.m. Phone for reservations, as the rides are very popular.

Another longtime favorite for sleigh rides is the **T-Lazy-7 Ranch**, tel. (970) 925-7040 or 925-4614. Offering Maroon Creek Valley rides ranging from daytime scenic tours to evening dinner rides where you grill your own meat and enjoy live music, the T-Lazy-7 has sleighs that accommodate up to 24 people.

You can also take sleigh rides at **Ashcroft Ski Touring Center**, tel. (970) 925-1044 (lunch and dinner rides), and at **Moon Run Ranch**, tel. (970) 923-3244. The latter offers afternoon and evening rides with food and live entertainment; the rides are designed specifically for large groups and are available by reservation only.

WHEN THE SNOW MELTS

Aspen's countenance changes considerably when the lifts shut down, when running shoes and golf spikes replace ski boots as the footwear of choice and aloha shirts replace sweaters and parkas. Still, there's a common thread: a youthful vigor and an obsession with the outdoors. Running, rafting, biking, ballooning, hiking, tennis, golf, and all sorts of water sports, from fishing to windsurfing, abound. And for those who get their thrills shopping instead of rock hopping, Aspen's pricy boutiques and specialty shops offer plenty of breathtaking thrills (like coats that cost as much as Jeep Cherokees).

Hiking

Aspen locals like to say, "You come here for the winter, but you stay for the summer," and indeed, many of Aspen's year-round citizens originally came with plans to spend a season ski bumming and then return to more serious pursuits when the resorts closed down. And the hiking in the area is without doubt one of the reasons folks stick around.

Aspen is literally surrounded by National Forest land. The Aspen Ranger District of the White River National alone comprises 260,00 acres and containes three wilderness areas—the Maroon Bells-Snowmass, Collegiate Peaks, and Hunter-Frying Pan regions near the Roaring Fork Valley. This means there's no shortage of excellent hiking in the area—from short nature walks to serious backcountry expeditions.

One of the area's easiest and more popular hikes, the **Rio Grande Trail,** begins where Mill St. crosses the Roaring Fork River. The two-mile trail continues northwest along Cemetery Lane and the river, offering a peaceful stroll and good views of the valley. It's also a popular mountain-bike trail.

The **Braille Trail** is a quarter-mile nature walk along the Roaring Fork River east of Aspen. Blind walkers follow a nylon rope to some two dozen stations with braille as well as printed-text explanations. The trailhead and parking lot are on the south side of CO 82 about 10 miles east of Aspen. For the rough and tumble crowd, try the five-mile **Sunnyside Trail,** which begins near the Slaughterhouse Bridge off the Rio Grande Trail. The 2,000-foot vertical rise (to almost 10,000 feet) is guaranteed to give the old ticker a workout, while affording views of spectacular scenery. And speaking of which: the 1.5-mile-long **Maroon Lake Scenic Trail** follows Maroon Creek to Maroon Lake to a view of Maroon Bells (whew!) and some scenery that will take your breath away. Take Maroon Creek Rd. about eight miles west of CO 82 (summertime day-trippers will have to take the shuttle, as the road is closed except to travelers heading into the campgrounds or lodges).

Other nearby trails include the Ute Trail, American Lake Trail, and Hunter Valley Trail. For complete information on these and other trails, see *Aspen-Snowmass Trails: A Hiking Trail Guide,* by Warren Ohlrich, available in local bookstores and outdoors shops. For information and maps of White River National Forest, stop by the district office at 806 W. Hallam, or phone (970) 925-3445. You can also get maps, as well as gear and equipment, at **Ute Mountaineer,** 308 S. Mill, tel. (970) 925-2849; **Ute Alpinist,** 605 E. Durant, tel. (970) 925-2489; and **Aspen Sports,** 408 E. Cooper, tel. (970) 925-6331; and in the Snowmass Center, tel. (970) 923-3566.

Elk Mountain Guides, tel. (970) 923-6131, and **Aspen Alpine Guides,** tel. (970) 925-6680, are both licensed outfitters offering guided day hikes and backpacking trips into the Aspen-area backcountry. **Naturalist Walks** offers half- and full-day naturalist-led walks and hikes—wildflower walks, high-mountain-lakes hikes, wildlife viewing, kids-only walks. Phone (970) 923-3649 for information and reservations.

Cycling

Not surprisingly, cycling is extremely popular in the Aspen area, and mountain biking especially has caught on big in recent years. Road bikers can take any number of local passes and valley drives, although you need to exercise extreme caution: Not only are many of these roads very narrow, some with steep drop-offs, but you've also got to watch out for tourists more interested in sightseeing than bike-rider seeing.

Roadsters looking for a real workout, with an equally rewarding view, can head up Independence Pass east of Aspen. The 20-mile ride from town to the summit gains 4,000 feet in altitude, and there are excellent photo ops along the way, not only of the valley east of the pass (from the top), but of the tumbling Roaring Fork River (from just a few miles east of Aspen). Castle Creek Rd. to Ashcroft and Maroon Creek Rd. to the Maroon Lake trailhead are shorter and less demanding—each is about 10 miles and gains only 1,500 feet. The Maroon Creek Rd. ride can be especially nice, as it's closed during the summer except to shuttle buses and travelers heading to the campgrounds and lodges, and the lack of traffic is a refreshing respite from the hustle and bustle of town.

Mountain bikers, who have gradually begun to eclipse road bikers in the area, have far more opportunities than their skinny-tire predecessors. First of all, White River National Forest, which surrounds Aspen, is full of old logging and mining roads, fire trails, and other areas to explore. In addition, the ski areas themselves now solicit mountain bikers, with access roads and ski runs open for fat-tire exploration, expedition, and exhibition.

One of the more popular is the **Richmond Ridge Trail,** which is accessible either from the gondola at Aspen Mountain or via Aspen Mountain access roads (including Summer Road). Other good rides include the **Rio Grande Trail,** beginning near the post office on Puppy Smith St., **Owl Creek Trail,** which connects Aspen and Snowmass Village on the west side of CO 82, and the **Fisherman's Trail** tour north along the Roaring Fork from Aspen to Woody Creek.

For more information on cycling in the Aspen area, stop in at any of the excellent shops, including **Aspen Velo Bike Shop,** 465 N. Mill, tel. (970) 925-1495; **Aspen Sports,** 408 E.

Cooper, tel. (970) 925-6331, and in Snowmass Center, tel. (970) 923-3566; **The Hub of Aspen,** 315 E. Hyman, tel. (970) 925-7970; or the **Sport Stalker,** 204 S. Galena, tel. (970) 925-9237. These shops, and dozens more in the area, also rent bicycles.

To arrange guided tours, all equipment and transportation provided, contact **Timberline Bicycle Tours,** tel. (970) 925-9237; **Aspen Velo,** tel. (970) 925-1495; **Blazing Pedals,** tel. (970) 923-4544; or **Elk Mountain Guides,** tel. (970) 923-6131.

Golf

What better way to spend a warm summer afternoon in the Roaring Fork Valley than strolling about the links, taking in the great views and the crisp mountain air, and feeling the warmth of the high-altitude sun? Of course, the summer afternoon won't be all you'll be spending. Golf is a high-end sport, Aspen's a high-end resort town, and when you put the two together the results are predictable: high-end greens fees.

Then again, you probably didn't come to Aspen to cut corners. You came to enjoy yourself. So swing away.

The **Aspen Golf Course** is a 7,000-yard-plus, 18-hole course across CO 82 from the turnoff to Maroon Bells. The municipal course, known for its water hazards, offers a number of discounts (twilight play, multi-day passes, etc.). For tee times and information, phone (970) 925-2145.

The **Snowmass Golf Club Course** is geared toward guests of the Snowmass Lodge but is open to the public on a space-available basis. Designed by Arnold Palmer and Ed Seay, the 18-hole course is part of the large recreation facility that also includes

tennis, racquetball, and squash courts, as well as a gym and athletic club with all the luxuries you'd expect in Aspen. Greens fees range from $50 (May 1-June 14 and Sept. 16-closing) to $95, with discounts on twilight play (after 4 p.m.) and for guests staying at affiliated properties. Phone the pro shop at (970) 923-3148 for tee times and information.

Tennis

Several private tennis court complexes serve the Aspen-Snowmass area, including the **Aspen Club,** tel. (970) 914-8900, and the **Snowmass Club,** tel. (970) 923-5600. In addition, the area offers a handful of public courts, though you'll still have to pay $4-5 per hour to use them. You'll find public courts on Maroon Creek Rd. at Iselin Park and at Aspen Highlands Ski Area, as well as at Aspen Meadows, 25 Meadows Road.

Fishing

Aspen's Roaring Fork Valley is both home to and surrounded by better trout fishing than many people realize. In addition to the two stretches of specially restricted Gold Medal streams, several other rivers and lakes in the Aspen area also offer good fishing—for rainbow, brown, cutthroat, and brook trout, as well as hybrids.

The **Roaring Fork River** flows through the town of Aspen and down the valley to its confluence with the Colorado at Glenwood Springs. The river has a fair amount of public access (respect private property) and, though it gets quite a bit of traffic, can pay off for the patient and savvy angler. The **Frying Pan River,** located northeast of Aspen, runs through Ruedi Reservoir to Basalt and is famous for its BIG fish and accessible water. The stretch west of the reservoir is particularly good, with fish topping eight pounds caught regularly. Other streams worth checking out are **Maroon Creek** and **Castle Creek. Important:** Stretches of both the Roaring Fork and the Frying Pan are governed by special regulations, with specific size limits, bait restrictions, and catch-and-release rules. Pick up a copy of the regulations at local sporting-goods stores or from the **Colorado Division of Wildlife,** 6060 N. Broadway, Denver, CO 80216, tel. (970) 297-1192.

BOB RACE

rainbow trout

Several lakes in the area can also provide excellent fishing. In addition to **Ruedi Reservoir** east of Basalt, several smaller, tougher-to-get-to high-country lakes can be rewarding. The best sources for information on where to go when are the local shops, many of which offer guide services as well as top-quality instruction and equipment. Among the outfits with good reputations are **Taylor Creek,** 555 E. Durant, tel. (970) 920-1128 (or 970-927-4374 for the store in Basalt); **Aspen Rod and Gun Company,** 519 E. Cooper, tel. (970) 920-2140; **Aspen Trout Guides, Inc.,** 614 E. Durant, tel. (970) 928-1050; **Frying Pan Anglers,** 302 Midland (Basalt), tel. (970) 927-3441; **Oxbow Outfitting Company,** 675 E. Durant, tel. (970) 925-1505 or (800) 421-1505.

Camping

Aspen is in the heart of the White River National Forest and literally surrounded by excellent Forest Service campgrounds. And considering how packed the town and valley can get, the campgrounds tend to stay relatively uncrowded. Maybe picnic tables, sooty barbecue grills, and pit toilets are beneath the dignity of the monied noblesse, but I've driven through town on Friday afternoons when the streets were jammed with tourists and plenty of sites were available at nearby campgrounds, particularly those east of town along the upper Roaring Fork.

The following Forest Service campgrounds can be found on CO 82 and the Roaring Fork River between Aspen and Independence Pass; all are quite nice: **Difficult,** 47 sites, five miles from Aspen; **Weller,** 11 sites, nine miles from Aspen; **Lincoln Gulch,** seven sites, 11 miles from Aspen; and **Lostman,** nine sites, 15 miles from Aspen. In addition, there are four campgrounds on Maroon Creek Rd.: **Silver Bar,** four sites, no trailers; **Silver Bell,** four sites, no trailers; **Silver Queen,** six sites; and **Maroon Lake,** 44 sites.

For complete information on the Forest Service campgrounds in the Aspen area, stop by the Aspen Ranger District Office at 806 W. Hallam, or phone (970) 925-3445. For 24-hour recorded information, phone (970) 920-1664.

River Running and Windsurfing

With so many rivers and streams in the area, it will come as no surprise that kayaking and rafting are very popular and that several outfitters capitalize on the quality water by offering a full range of trips. Among the popular nearby rivers are the **Roaring Fork, Colorado, Arkansas** (over Independence Pass from Aspen), and **Crystal** (west of Aspen via CO 133). **Caution:** In the spring and early summer, these rivers swell with snowmelt, and their capriciousness is the stuff of legends. Scores of people, including experienced river rats, have been killed. Check with local authorities, and don't get in the water if you don't know what you're doing.

For guided raft tours, contact **Aspen Whitewater,** tel. (800) 873-8008; **Blazing Paddles/Snowmass Whitewater,** tel. (970) 925-5651 or 923-4544 (the Snowmass number); **Colorado Rift-Raft,** tel. (970) 925-5405 or 923-2220 (Snowmass); or **River Rats,** tel. (970) 925-7648.

Windsurfing and skiing seem to go hand in hand somehow—get a group of skiers together, and it's very likely at least a couple of them will talk about spending the "off season" sailboarding. And though Aspen doesn't offer the thrills of the Columbia River or the Hawaiian Islands, Aspenites do find places to catch the wind. **Ruedi Reservoir** (east of Basalt) and **Twin Lakes** (east of Aspen via Independence Pass) are among the popular spots.

Horseback Riding

A dozen or so outfitters offer rides into the Aspen mountains and Roaring Fork-area backcountry. You can either rent an animal and explore the areas on your own, or take guided tours, which range from short, two-hour trips and dinner rides with chow on the trail to multiday pack trips into wilderness areas. The best-known is probably the **T-Lazy-7 Ranch,** whose Maroon Creek Road location provides excellent access to the Maroon Bells valley; for information and reservations, phone (970) 925-7040. You can also rent horses and book tours through **Brush Creek Stables,** tel. (970) 923-4252; **Moon Run Ranch,** tel. (970) 923-3244; **Snowmass Stables,** tel. (970) 923-3075; **Pioneer Springs Ranch,** tel. (970) 923-4252; and **Diamond J Ranch,** tel. (970) 927-3222 (located on the Upper Frying Pan River above Ruedi Reservoir).

Ballooning

The Roaring Fork Valley sprawls lush and rolling at the base of the towering Elk Mountains and, I imagine, is rather breathtaking from the air. A balloon ride offers the opportunity to see the landscape from an eagle's perspective without the in-your-face roar of an airplane engine (though the flatulent hot-air balloons themselves get awfully loud). **Adventures Aloft,** tel. (970) 925-9497, **Aspen Balloon Adventures,** tel. (970) 923-5749, and **Unicorn Balloon Company,** tel. (970) 925-5752, all offer tours of the area's skies, with a variety of incentives to offset the price ($150-200 per person), including transportation, food, champagne, and video filming.

Recreation Information

The Aspen Visitors Center in the Wheeler Opera House at 328 E. Hyman has walls of brochures, fliers, pamphlets, and other information on the area's vast recreational opportunities. Another good source is the **Aspen Resort Chamber,** at 425 Rio Grande Place near the downtown parking garage, tel. (970) 925-1940. Warren Ohlrich's *Aspen-Snowmass Guide to Outdoor Activities* is an excellent book of tips on everything from golf to ice climbing, running trails to snowshoeing, as well as maps and phone numbers for further information. The book is available at Aspen-area bookstores.

ACCOMMODATIONS

As you've probably heard, it's not cheap to stay in Aspen. And as in most of Colorado's resort towns, rates for accommodations fluctuate with the season. High season runs from mid-December until just after the first of the year. Rates also go up around holidays and three-day weekends. In April, May, October, and November, when there's not a whole lot going on in town—it's too warm for snow and most people consider it too cold to hike, mountain bike, and otherwise explore the outdoors—you can get excellent rates on rooms. In fact, sometimes the lodges and inns offer promotional rates of $30 a night.

One of the easiest ways to book a room is through **Aspen Central Reservations,** which handles the full range of accommodations in town. Phone them at (970) 925-9000 or (800) 262-7736. You can also stop in at their offices at 425 Rio Grande Place.

If you're looking for cheap, basic, bargain-basement digs, you might check out lodging in Glenwood Springs, 40 miles back down the canyon (north on CO 82), where you can usually find a room for $30-40.

Ski Lodges

Staying in a ski lodge can be a relatively inexpensive way to go, and most of them make up in cozy charm what they lack in luxury. The **Heatherbed Lodge,** tel. (970) 925-7077 for information, or (800) 356-6782 for reservations, is a funky old '50s-style ski lodge directly across the road from the parking to Aspen Highlands and nestled down in the pines along Maroon Creek. Heatherbed rooms start at $90, which includes breakfast and after-ski chili. The recently renovated **Mountain House Lodge,** 905 E. Hopkins, tel. (970) 920-2550, features a hot tub and large lounge area; rooms run about $50-250, which includes full breakfast in the ski season and a buffet-style continental breakfast in the summer. The Mountain House is an easy three- or four-block walk to downtown shopping and the base of the lifts at Aspen Mountain.

Also located in downtown Aspen are the **Skier's Chalet,** 203 Gilbert, tel. (970) 920-2037, and the **Aspen Manor Lodge,** 411 S. Monarch, tel. (970) 925-3001, where rates range $60-150. The **Alpine Lodge,** 1240 East CO 82, tel. (970) 925-7351, has small but comfortable rooms within walking distance of the lifts. With rates running $40-100, the Alpine offers among the least expensive digs in town—so it's often booked *way* in advance.

Hotels

The hotel for the ultimate Aspen experience is without doubt the **Hotel Jerome,** 330 E. Main, tel. (970) 920-1000 or (800) 925-2784. Built in 1889, this gorgeous building has been completely restored and is worth a look around even if you don't plan to stay. The lobby is furnished with plush Victorian-era chairs and sofas, and the bar is a classic place where hip Aspenites rub elbows. Rates at the Hotel Jerome, which has over 90 rooms (about two-thirds of which have been added to the original building), range (top) downtown Crested Butte in summer; (bottom) Mountain bikers explore the Crested Butte area. (both photos: Crested Butte Mountain Resort Association, Grafton Marshall Smith)

Victorian home in Georgetown (Stephen Metzger)

Aspen's Hotel Jerome

from about $160 to $1650 for suites and the Grand Parlor.

Aspen's most upscale hotel is probably the Aspen Skiing Company-owned **Little Nell,** 675 E. Durant, tel. (970) 920-4600. Located at the base of Aspen Mountain's gondola and offering unabashed opulence and every possible amenity, the hotel has rooms, suites, and "executive apartments." Cheap rooms in the off-season start at about $175. The new **Ritz-Carlton,** 315 E. Dean, tel. (970) 920-3300, is another upscale downtown lodge, where doubles start at $145.

Other classic Aspen hotels include the **Hotel Lenado,** 200 S. Aspen, tel. (970) 925-6246; **Independence Square Hotel,** 404 S. Galena, tel. (970) 920-2313; and **Hotel Aspen,** 110 W. Main, tel. (970) 925-3441.

Bed and Breakfasts

The Roaring Fork Valley has a number of bed and breakfast inns that have earned reputations for offering a combination of quiet charm and Aspen luxury. One of the larger and better known is the **Molly Gibson Lodge,** 101 W. Main, tel. (970) 925-2580. The 50 units vary from hotel-type rooms to suites with kitchens; almost half have fireplaces; there are two jacuzzis and one heated outdoor pool. Doubles start at about $150 and go to $350. The **Sardy House,** 128 E. Main, tel. (970) 920-2525, is a longtime Aspen favorite famous for its gourmet breakfasts, high-class decor, and overall elegance. Rooms start at about $250.

Camping and RVing

In addition to the many Forest Service campgrounds near Aspen (see "Camping" above), the Roaring Fork area offers a handful of privately run, RV-oriented campgrounds, though none in the immediate Aspen vicinity. The closest is 18 miles northwest, the **Aspen Basalt Campground** just west of Basalt; for reservations or information, phone (970) 927-3532.

FOOD

There's no shortage of excellent restaurants in Aspen, and many have become little institutions of their own—places to see and be seen, and to catch up on all the important local skinny. Thankfully, many of Aspen's restaurants post their menus on the door or an outside window, providing not only a sense of the type of food and specials but of prices as well. An enjoyable way to spend part of an evening in Aspen, no matter what the season, is strolling about the downtown area "researching" the different dinner houses. In addition, *Aspen Magazine* publishes an Aspen-area *Menu Guide,* which reproduces the menus of scores of the valley's restaurants. The guides are free and available at most hotels and lodges, as well as at many gift shops.

Start Me Up

One of the best ways to get your morning off to an optimistic start is over a cappuccino and croissant at **Pour La France,** 411 E. Main, tel. (970) 920-1150. A favorite of locals looking for a quick caffeine fix, or just wanting to linger leisurely over the morning paper, this little European-style cafe serves a variety of pastries and coffees—croissants and bran muffins, teas, espressos, and decaf. Smaller and with a more neighborhoody feel, **Zélé,** 121 S. Galena, (970) 925-5745, also has excellent gourmet coffees and teas, scones, muffins, and other pastries, plus three or four outside tables. If you're looking for something more stick-to-your-ribsable, a couple of local favorites are **Poppycock's,** 609 E. Cooper, tel. (970) 925-1245, and **Hickory House,** 730 W. Main, tel. (970) 925-2313.

Dinner Restaurants

Anyone who's spent much time in ski towns knows that Mexican restaurants are always very popular, not only for their food, but for their casually festive ambience—rehash the day over a plate of nachos with margaritas or Dos Equis.

As perhaps America's definitive ski town, Aspen claims at least three first-rate Mexican restaurants, all with excellent reputations and popular with locals and tourists alike. The **Cantina,** 411 E. Main, tel. (970) 925-3663, offers a comfortable, laid-back atmosphere and huge windows looking out on Main Street. The relatively new **Flying Dog Brew Pub,** 424 E. Cooper, tel. (970) 925-7464, serves burgers, seafood, and Mexican dishes. **La Cocina,** 308 E. Hopkins, tel. (970) 925-9714, specializes in New Mexican food, including blue-corn tortilla dishes.

Other distinctive and highly recommended Aspen-area restaurants include **Little Annie's,** 517 E. Hyman, tel. (970) 925-1098, for reasonably priced burgers, salads, ribs, etc.; **Asia,** 132 W. Main, tel. (970) 925-5433, which serves excellent Chinese food in a classic Aspen Victorian (also delivers); the **Stewpot,** in Snowmass Village, tel. (970) 923-2263, where you can fill up on homemade bread and excellent beef stew for under $10.

Uniquely Aspen

Krabloonik, in Snowmass, tel. (970) 923-3953, a restaurant-cum-Yukon-style dog kennel (the owner keeps 300 dogs and regularly competes in the Iditarod) specializes in wild game (moose, boar, and elk). The **Pine Creek Cookhouse** at the Ashcroft Touring Center, tel. (970) 925-1044, serves gourmet meals to diners who (in winter) arrive after a cross-country ski trek or sleigh ride. In downtown Aspen, the **Ajax Tavern,** at the base of the gondola, tel. (970) 920-9333, features locally raised lamb and beef, seafood and pasta dishes, and one of the best wine lists in the area. The slope-side location offers diners the opportunity to watch skiers winding up their days on the mountain, and in the summer, to catch end-of-the-days rays on the outdoor deck.

If you're out exploring the Roaring Fork Valley, you couldn't do much better for lunch than the **Woody Creek Tavern** (watch for the signs along CO 82 north of the turnoff to Snowmass), tel. (970) 923-4585, a little roadhouse where the food (burgers, Mexican, salads) is excellent and the atmosphere festive and friendly.

Un-Uniquely Aspen

Aspen has recently been **Planet Hollywood**ed, with a restaurant at 312 S. Galena, tel. (970) 920-3900, and the **Hard Rock Cafe** is just down the street at 210 S. Galena, tel. (970) 920-1666. There's also a McDonald's in the mall at 416 S. Mill Street.

Groceries and Picnic Fixin's

The small **City Market** on E. Cooper Ave. is Aspen's grocery store and a sort of social hub as well. The store has neither a salad bar nor deli (unlike most City Markets), but you can pick up sandwich makings and other picnic supplies. **Clark's Market Deli,** 300 N. Mill St., tel. (970) 925-8046, and **Charcuturie and Cheese Market,** 520 E. Durant Ave., tel. (970) 925-8010, are good places to stop in for to-go, deli sandwiches, pasta salads, and soups.

Snowberry's Natural Food Store, next door to City Market at 719 E. Cooper Ave. (downstairs), carries juices, bulk grains, fresh produce, and healthful snacks and other groceries, as well as natural cosmetics, soaps, and toiletries. There's also a juice-and-salad bar inside the store.

ENTERTAINMENT

Aspen is at once both a rowdy and a sophisticated town, and the entertainment options here run the gamut from smoky pool saloons to opera. If you're looking to tear things up a bit, try the **Cooper Street Pier,** 508 E. Cooper Ave., tel. (970) 925-7758, an often-raucous local watering hole. The **Wheeler Opera House** books a wide range of live music, often big-name acts passing through town on otherwise big-venue tours; past acts have included Bonnie Raitt and Lyle Lovett. Phone the ticket office at (970) 920-5770.

The bar at the **Hotel Jerome,** 330 E. Main, tel. (970) 920-1000, is worth stopping by, not only for its elegant Victorian decor but also to check the pulse of high-end Aspen society. The **Woody Creek Tavern,** about 10 miles north of Aspen in Woody Creek, is a great place to go for a burger and a beer. Neighbors Hunter Thompson and Don Henley stop in from time to time when in town.

CALENDAR

Detailing Aspen's myriad of cultural and recreational annual events goes far beyond the scope of this book—the town's world-famous affairs virtually merit a book of their own. To find out what's going on, phone or write the **Aspen Chamber Resort Association,** 425 Rio Grande Place, Aspen, CO 81611, tel. (970) 925-1940, or (800) 262-7736. You can also phone the **Aspen Visitors Center** at (970) 925-5656. Once you're here, read the *Aspen Times,* one of the best small-town papers in the country, for complete listings of what's happening and numbers of whom to contact for more information.

Annual Highlights

Among the highlights of Aspen's annual events: **Winterskol,** a crazy winter festival featuring everything from a canine fashion show to ski competition to a pancake breakfast; **The Food and Wine Magazine Classic at Aspen,** with chefs, winemakers, and food writers from around the world (early June); **Aspen Music Festival,** with outside concerts ranging from chamber music to jazz (late June through August); **Snow-**

mass **Hot-Air Balloon Festival** (late June); and the **Aspen Film Festival** (late September).

SHOPPING

Confirmed shoppers will be in hog heaven in Aspen. Though nothing's cheap here—you'll find "sales" but not many bargains—there are oodles of shops to wander around in. Lots of jewelry stores, with emphases on the Southwest and Native Americana; gift shops, specializing in bath oils, kitchenry, and woodcarvings; boutiques, ranging from lingerie to fur; and a T-shirt or sports-apparel shop around every corner.

Part of the fun of Aspen, of course, is simply exploring aimlessly, wandering from one shop to the next. A handful, though, are specifically worth checking out. One of my favorites, **Stars,** 525 E. Cooper Ave., tel. (970) 920-2920, specializes in "historical documents, Hollywood collectibles, and rock 'n' roll memorabilia" (*very* high-end stuff—I just look). Guaranteed to make any history buff, sports fan, or pop-culture nut drool, Stars sells jerseys, cleats, helmets, bats, hockey sticks, footballs, baseballs, basketballs—all worn and signed by famous athletes, from Mickey Mantle to O.J. Simpson. The shop also displays guitars played and signed by the likes of B.B. King, Bob Dylan, and Stevie Ray Vaughan, as well as platinum records awarded to musicians. In addition, Stars sells historical documents—letters to and from U.S. presidents, for example.

Another intriguing little shop, **Curious George,** 410 E. Hyman Ave., specializes in collectible Western Americana. Lots of ceremonial Native American clothing—beaded moccasins and leggings—as well as frontier firearms including 1880s Colts and Winchesters; when I stopped by, there was even a matching pair of 18th-century dueling pistols, the same model used by Alexander Hamilton and Aaron Burr.

SERVICES

The main offices of the Aspen **Police Department** and the **Pitkin County Sheriff** are at 506 E. Main Street. Phone the police at (970) 920-5400 and the sheriff at (970) 920-5300. Phone

Aspen's Wheeler Opera House and Visitor Information Center

the Colorado **State Patrol** at (970) 945-6198 (Glenwood Springs). The full-service **Aspen Valley Hospital** is located at 200 Castle Creek Rd., Aspen, tel. (970) 925-1120.

The Aspen area's two **post offices** are in town at 235 Puppy Smith St., tel. (970) 925-7523, and in Snowmass Village at 1106 Kearns Rd., tel. (970) 923-4266.

Just Kiddin'
Aspen-area kids' programs range from day care to weeklong race camps. Snowmass offers **Snow Cubs** for children 18 months to four years, and **Big Burn Bears** (ski instruction) for kids four through kindergarten, as well as evening child care; phone (970) 923-1220. At Buttermilk, kids three to six can play inside or take ski lessons through **Powder Pandas**, tel. (970) 925-6336 or 923-3959. Aspen Highlands' **Snowbunnies** offers both day care and lessons; phone (800) 525-6200.

Babysitting services not affiliated with the ski resorts include **Super Sitters, Inc.,** tel. (970) 923-6080, and **Georget's Babysitting,** tel. (970) 923-2988.

Recycling
The following **Pitkin County Drop-Off Sites** take aluminum, glass, newspaper, plastic, and tin and steel cans: the county landfill, Aspen High School, Woody Creek Tavern, Basalt Library. You can also recycle aluminum at the City Market at 711 E. Cooper Ave., tel. (970) 920-5215.

INFORMATION

A branch of the **Aspen Chamber Resort Association** is right downtown in the Wheeler Opera House, 328 E. Hyman (corner of Mill). You'll find staff to answer questions, as well as scores of brochures and other publications promoting just about everything there is to do in the area—snowmobiling to trout fishing. Parking in the area can be tough, but directly in front of the building are several 15-minute spaces reserved for center visitors. Phone the visitor center at (970) 925-5656. The chamber's main offices are at 425 Rio Grande Place; phone (970) 925-1940. For **Aspen Central Reservations,** phone (800)-26-ASPEN.

The **Pitkin County Public Library** is at 120 N. Mill St., tel. (970) 925-7124; hours are Mon.-Thurs. 10 a.m.-9 p.m., Friday and Saturday 10 a.m-6 p.m., and Sunday 12-6 p.m. The **Basalt Regional Library** located in Basalt, is at 99 Midland Ave., tel. 927-4311.

For **road and weather information** phone (970) 945-2221 (Glenwood Springs).

Electronic Information
You can also get Aspen information—from ski conditions to lodging—through the Internet. The address is **http://www.aspenonline.com**.

Bookstores
Aspen, which claims one of the most educated citizenries in the country, isn't real big on book-

stores. One would expect, as in Boulder, several nooked and crannied holes-in-the-wall with easy chairs for customers, shelves spilling over into disarray, and shopkeepers more interested in reading George Eliot or Joseph Conrad than in designing window displays. But Boulder this is not.

Nonetheless, Aspen does have a couple of bookstores worth checking out. The best is **Explore, Bookseller and Bistro** at 221 E. Main St., tel. (970) 925-5336. Housed in an old Aspen Victorian, the shop devotes each room to a category. What must have been a parlor or sitting room at one time is now the literature room; another room is for kids' books (very possibly at one time a child's room). Upstairs, you'll find the bistro . . . and more book rooms. In fact, the tables are scattered throughout the upstairs rooms, and you can sit over a meal in, for example, the "Travel Room."

Up the hill on the mall is **Unicorn Books.** Very big on travel, outdoor recreation, and Colorado, especially with a local angle, Unicorn also carries kids' books, self-help, and reference, as well as magazines. The store is at 400 E. Cooper Ave., tel. (970) 925-7500. **Aspen Bookstore,** located at the Little Nell Hotel at the base of Aspen Mountain, tel. (970) 925-7427, also carries travel, Colorado, self-help, and magazines, as well as a decent selection of oversized art books. **Timberline Books** is at 425 E. Hyman Ave., tel. (970) 925-2719.

Forest Service Information

For information on White River National Forest, stop by the **Aspen District Office** at 806 W. Hallam, tel. (970) 925-3445. You can also write or visit the main offices at 9th and Grand, Box 948, Glenwood Springs, CO 81602, or phone (970) 945-2421.

TRANSPORTATION

Getting There

United Express offers daily flights connecting at Denver International Aiport; phone (970) 925-3400 or (800) 241-6522.

Aspen is also easily accessible by car. The most scenic route from Denver is via I-70 to Copper Mountain, south on CO 91 to Leadville, south on US 24 from Leadville to the CO 82 junction, then west on CO 82 over Independence Pass. This route offers absolutely spectacular views and relatively little traffic. However, Independence Pass is closed in the winter, and if you're coming to ski, the only way to get to Aspen is via I-70 to Glenwood Springs then CO 82 south to Aspen (40 miles).

Amtrak offers passenger service to Glenwood Springs, where you can either rent a car or hop a Roaring Fork Transit Authority bus. Phone the Glenwood Springs depot at (970) 945-9563 or the central reservations office at (800) 872-7245.

Getting Around

Roaring Fork Transit Authority offers free buses around town and during the ski season, also runs buses from the town of Aspen to Aspen Highlands, Buttermilk, and Snowmass, as well as to the cross-country centers. Pick up shuttles at the Rubey Park Bus Station (on Durant between Galena and Mill) and at the shuttle stops throughout town. RFTA buses also service most of the Roaring Fork Valley, with routes extending north to Glenwood Springs—fee charged for non-City Route rides. Buses depart from the Rubey Park bus station to the different ski areas. For information on schedules and fares, phone (970) 925-8484.

Aspen Limousine and Bus Service, tel. (970) 925-9400 or (800) 222-2112, runs daily trips to Glenwood Springs, Vail, and Denver, and **High Mountain Taxi and Limousine,** tel. (970) 925-TAXI, offers taxi and van shuttle service throughout the area. **Rocky Mountain Rent-A-Car,** tel. (970) 925-2880 or (800) 525-2880, and **Eagle Rent-A-Car,** tel. (970) 925-2128 or (800) 282-2128, specialize in 4WD skier vehicles.

LEADVILLE

The highest incorporated town in the United States, Leadville (pop. 3,000; elev. 10,430 feet) lies in a broad mountain valley at the base of Colorado's two tallest peaks, Mts. Elbert (elev. 14,433 feet) and Massive (elev. 14,421 feet). Once the state's second-largest community, Leadville claims a history firmly rooted in mining. Its stories were written by some of the West's most colorful characters, and its mines yielded some of the world's greatest fortunes—some wisely invested, some squandered.

Though modern Leadville is tame in comparison to the wild days of the late 19th century, when its muddy streets bustled with prospectors and prostitutes, the town still offers excellent views into the past. Tourists can visit a wide range of museums, from the spanking new National Mining Hall of Fame and Museum to the Healy House and Dexter Cabin State Museum to the Matchless Mine (where Tabor made part of his $12 million). In fact, the town is virtually a museum in itself. Stroll the sidewalks of Leadville's main street (Harrison Ave.), wander into the old Tabor Opera House, and hike up

COLORADO HISTORICAL SOCIETY

Horace A. Tabor

the little side streets, all the while taking in that thin 10,000-foot air and the indescribably beautiful scenery—there's not much better place to get a feel for what it must have been like to live in a wild western mining town during the burlesque of Colorado's most important decade.

HISTORY

The story of Leadville is one of the most fascinating in the state, if not the country, as well as one of the most important in the tapestry of world mining history. It's a story of gold and silver, of rowdy miners determined to strike it rich, of lusty saloons and busy brothels, gambling halls and opera houses, and huge fortunes won and lost, and sometimes won and lost again.

Gold was first discovered in the Leadville area in the spring of 1860, and by that summer, Oro City, as the camp was called, had a population of 5,000. The gold proved particularly difficult to extract, however, and within a couple of years most of the miners had lit out for more promising lodes and the camp was all but abandoned. In 1875, "Uncle Billy" Stevens and his partner, metallurgist A.B. Wood, explored some of the deserted mines and, finding traces of silver, staked new claims. Word soon got out, and Oro City experienced a second rush, though this one on a much smaller scale. When Leadville was incorporated in 1878, postmaster H.A.W. Tabor estimated the population at about 200 people.

Tabor had been part of the Pikes Peak gold rush in 1859, having arrived in Colorado from Vermont with his wife, Augusta, and their son. A stonecutter by trade, Tabor had had little luck in the Colorado gold and silver fields and by the late 1870s had pretty much given up on ever finding the big one. In addition to acting as postmaster, Tabor worked as a storekeeper as well.

"Hey, Look Vat Ve Found!"
One day, two German shoemakers, George Hook and Auguste Rische, whom Tabor had grubstaked for partial interest in any ore they discovered, helped themselves to a jug of the

black cigars," fights, vigilantes, rowdy gambling halls where the mine owners played for huge stakes, and a general sense of silver-induced frenzy. Mines, and anything remotely resembling one, including simple holes in the ground, were sold and resold at huge profits, often over the course of a single day. One winter a gravedigger hit a silver vein while preparing to bury a body, and the cemetery was immediately staked out—the dead man was left in a snowbank, frozen stiff, until spring.

Meanwhile Tabor had become very much a public figure. He was elected lieutenant-governor, built opera houses in both Leadville and Denver, and served for a brief period as a U.S. senator, filling in between Senator Henry M. Teller's appointment as Secretary of the Interior and the election of a new senator 30 days later. Tabor also divorced his wife, Augusta, and in 1883 married Elizabeth McCourt Doe, a Leadville woman with whom he had apparently been trysting for some time.

Leadville and Tabor went into the skids at the same time, and for the same reason: the devaluation of silver. In 1893, panicking investors sold interest in their mines, banks went under, and Tabor's empire crumbled. He died in 1899,

Augusta L. Tabor

storekeeper's booze, climbed up a hill, and started digging. What they drunkenly happened upon, almost immediately, was what would later be known as the Little Pittsburg. Almost overnight, Tabor's fortunes from the silver mine totaled $500,000; within a year he had sold his interest in it for $1 million and invested his profits in other lodes. One of them turned out to have been "salted," although digging at the site led to the discovery of the huge Chrysolite lode. More important was Tabor's investment in the famous Matchless silver mine, which would result in his becoming the district's first multimillionaire; his empire would eventually be worth $12 million. The great productivity of the Matchless also led to Leadville's being overrun, again, by prospectors, and by 1880, the town's population had surged to 25,000-60,000, the figure officially reported by the Leadville *Chronicle*.

During the early 1880s, Leadville was a rambunctious town with three breweries, brass bands playing every night along State St., drunken women driving carriages and "smoking long

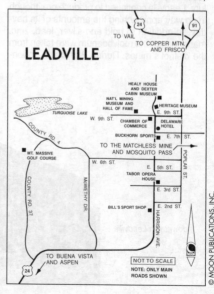

the course of his life having run full circle—he was nearly broke his last years, and working as a civil servant, as the postmaster in Denver. His last words to "Baby Doe," as his second wife came to be known, are reputed to be "Hang on to the Matchless."

"Baby Doe" Tabor went on to become one of Leadville's most well-known citizens, albeit a reclusive and, some say, insane one. Though there were occasional reported sightings of her, she spent over three decades alone in a tiny cabin beside the mine. She was found in 1935, lying on the floor, her body frozen.

One of the strangest chapters in Leadville history was written in the early winter of 1895, when local merchants organized a "Crystal Carnival." According to the WPA guide to Colorado, they built a "castellated structure of Norman design [that] covered five acres." Its ice walls were eight feet thick and 50 feet high and enclosed a "ballroom, a skating rink, a restaurant, peep shows, and curio shops. Frozen into the walls were specimens of ore, produce, and meat; ice and snow statues graced the interior. The palace, visited by thousands, remained open until March 28, 1896, before it melted away."

Throughout the first quarter of the 20th century, Leadville continued to produce ore, though in no way approaching the amounts of its heyday. In addition to gold and silver, lead, zinc, manganese, and molybdenum were taken from the district's mines. During Prohibition, moon-shiners set up shop in the old shafts, and "Leadville Moon" earned a reputation as one of the best whiskeys in the West.

MUSEUMS

Leadville probably has more museums per square foot, and certainly per capita, than any other town in Colorado. And, with the exception of the Matchless Mine, they are all within an easy walk to the center of town.

Historic Slide Show

Presented by the Leadville Chamber of Commerce, "The Earth Runs Silver—Early Leadville," is a six-projector slide show offering a dramatized glimpse of the area's history, from the gold and silver rushes of the late 19th century to modern restoration and tourism.

Showings daily 10 a.m.-5 p.m. Screenings are in the old church next to the chamber of commerce, 809 Harrison. Admission is $3 for adults—discounts for seniors and kids. For more information, phone (719) 486-3900.

National Mining
Hall of Fame and Museum

Examining every aspect of U.S. mining, as well as bits and pieces from around the world, this fascinating museum displays a wide range of exhibits. Highlights include a state-by-state ex-

downtown Leadville

*interior of the
Tabor Home*

planation of Western states' ores, production rates, and mining methods, as well as important tools and equipment. There are also dioramas showing different extraction techniques and surveying methods, a reproduction of a cableway system near Bordeaux, France, and a display of Egyptian mining techniques. The Hall of Fame, in the same building, features plaques dedicated to various pioneers of the industry.

The museum is at 120 W. 9th St., open daily 9 a.m.-5 p.m. (with limited winter hours). Admission is $3.50 for adults. For more information, phone (719) 486-1229.

Matchless Mine and Baby Doe's Cabin

Up on the hill away from the T-shirt and souvenir shops of Harrison St., this is an excellent place to get a sense not only of the famous mine but of how Baby Doe spent the second half of her life. Guided tours take you into the mine's entrance, where original heavy equipment still sits. In addition, there's a good display of miners' tools, forged in the blacksmith shop on-site, as it was too expensive to ship them from Denver. The rickety one-room cabin, where the frozen body of Baby Doe was found in 1935, still contains her meager furnishings, and the walls display the last known photos of her.

The mine and cabin are open daily 9 a.m.-5 p.m., Memorial Day through Labor Day. Admission is $2 for adults. To get there, take 7th St. two miles east from downtown. For more information, phone (719) 486-0371.

Tabor Opera House

Built in 1879 when Leadville was home to at least 25,000 people, the Tabor Opera House was at one time one of the most elegant buildings in the West. Hosting a wide range of well-known performers, from Harry Houdini and Oscar Wilde to the New York Metropolitan Opera, the Tabor Opera House originally included boutiques, a saloon, and a suite for visiting artists. Private booths were reserved for Tabor and his guests, who entered from the adjacent hotel via a second-floor walkway.

The Tabor Opera House is downtown at 308 Harrison, open for self-guided tours Memorial Day through Labor Day 9 a.m.-5:30 p.m.; closed Saturday. For more information, phone the chamber of commerce at (719) 486-3900.

Healy House and Dexter Cabin

Offering self-guided tours of an early Leadville boardinghouse and a private residence, this museum shows a side of Leadville history apart from that of the ubiquitous H.A.W. Tabor. The Healy House was built in 1878 by successful St. Louis mining engineer August Meyer and his wife Emma. Between 1897 and 1902, the structure served as a boardinghouse, primarily for area schoolteachers.

James V. Dexter built the cabin in 1879 as a social club and poker hall. Don't be deceived by the cabin's Daniel Booney-like facade; inside it's lavishly furnished, reflecting Dexter's fortune and his passion for quality art and furniture.

The Healy House and Dexter Cabin, at 912 Harrison, St. are open Memorial Day through Labor Day 10 a.m.-4:30 p.m. daily. Admission is $2.50 for adults. For information, or to book off-season tours, phone (719) 486-0487.

Heritage Museum and Gallery
Offering an in-depth view of Leadville's boom days, the Heritage Museum and Gallery features mining dioramas, historical photos, Victorian furniture, a scale model of the 1896 Leadville Ice Palace, a 10th Mountain Division display, domestic items, and other late-19th-century artifacts. The art gallery diplays rotating exhibits of Colorado artists and craftspeople. The museum is located at 9th and Harrison streets and is open daily 10 a.m.-6 p.m., May through October, with limited hours of operation the rest of the year. Admission is $2.50 for adults. For more information, phone (719) 486-1878.

Leadville, Colorado, and Southern Railroad Company
This narrow-gauge railroad is the highest in the U.S., leaving from the Leadville depot and twisting and curving and switching back to its 11,120-foot summit. Both morning and afternoon trips are available. Daily tours Memorial Day through Labor Day, weekends only through fall.

Non-reserved seating is available on a first-come, first-served basis. For reservations or further information, write Leadville, Colorado, and Southern Railroad Company, 326 E. 7th St., Box 916, Leadville, CO 80461, or phone (719) 486-3936.

Leadville National Fish Hatchery
Established in 1889, the Leadville hatchery raises brook, rainbow, and cutthroat trout for stocking in a wide range of Rocky Mountain waters, including those in national parks and forests and Indian reservations, as well as lakes and streams under state jurisdiction. In addition to viewing hatchery operations, visitors can hike on the one-mile nature trail, where local wildflowers, trees, and other flora are identified. There's also a picnic area on the property.

To get to the hatchery, go south from Leadville on US 24 for about two miles, then west on CO 300 (the turnoff is well marked). For hours and information, phone (719) 486-0189.

Note: Recently the fish hatchery has been threatened by federal budget cuts. Call before visiting.

PARKS AND RECREATION

Surrounded by sprawling acres of national forest and some of the state's highest and most impressive peaks, Leadville is as rich in outdoor recreation opportunities as it once was in ore. Though the historic district offers excellent insight into the town's past, the surrounding area offers chances to hike, mountain bike, ski, golf, fish, and sightsee in one of Colorado's most scenic areas.

Cycling
Tourers looking for a place to train for high-altitude competition need look no further than the roads and passes of the Leadville area. Excellent-though-grueling rides include the 60-mile Leadville-to-Aspen route, which winds up over Independence Pass (elev. 12,095 feet). The route drops south and down out of Leadville, follows the upper Arkansas River, then lifts west past Twin Lakes and up over the pass. You could also head north out of Leadville on CO 91, which will take you over Fremont Pass (elev. 11,320 feet), past the mines, titanic machinery, tailings, and rusting detritus of Climax, and down into Summit County. The stretch along Ten-Mile Creek is beautiful, and provides access to Summit County's other bike trails, including the path over Vail Pass (see "Cycling" under "Vail and Beaver Creek" in Northwestern Colorado). From Leadville to the junction of I-70 is about 25 miles.

There are also excellent trails for mountain biking in the region, thanks particularly to the plethora of old mining roads spider-legging over hillsides and along ridges. One good ride is up E. 7th St. into the Fryer Hill and Matchless Mine area. The route, first cut in the late 1870s, eventually takes you up and over Mosquito Pass (elev. 13,186 feet) and then down into South Park, connecting with CO 9 just north of Fairplay. For maps and information on mountain biking in the Leadville and Lake County area, stop by the chamber of commerce at 809 Harrison Ave., or contact the **Leadville Ranger District Office** of the Forest Service at 2015 N. Poplar St., Leadville, CO 80461, tel. (719) 486-0749.

Golf
Claiming to be North America's highest golf course, **Mount Massive Golf Club** (elev. 9,700 feet), is about four miles west of town at the foot of the appropriately named Mt. Massive (elev. 14,421 feet). Only nine holes, but some of the prettiest sights you'll ever see from manicured lawns—deer, bear, elk, and cougar (but no lynx) have been spotted from from the course. For tee times and information, phone (719) 486-2176.

Hiking
Hiking in the Lake County area ranges from a short nature trail at the Leadville National Fish Hatchery to serious and physically demanding backcountry excursions, including at least three specific marked routes to the top of **Mt. Elbert,** Colorado's highest peak (elev. 14,443 feet). Elevation gains on Mt. Elbert trails are in the 4,000-5,000-foot range, and the trails are four to six miles long. In addition, the **Colorado Trail** passes just west of Leadville.

The most popular route up Mt. Elbert, the **North Trail,** begins from Halfmoon Campground (go west on CO 300 two miles south of Leadville, then south on Forest Service Rd. 110 to the campground).

For maps and more information on hiking in the area, stop by the Ranger District Office at 2015 N. Poplar St., Leadville, or phone (719) 486-0749. Another excellent source of information is **Bill's Sports Shop,** 225 Harrison St., tel. (719) 486-9739 (the store also carries ski equipment and rents, repairs, and sells mountain bikes). In addition, you can get gear and information from **Buckhorn Sporting Goods,** 616 Harrison St., tel. (719) 486-3944.

Horseback Riding
You can rent horses by the hour or day, or book tours that include breakfast and/or lunch, at **Pa and Ma's,** on Tennesee Rd., tel. (719) 486-3900 (Leadville Chamber). Rates are $12 an hour for kids, $14 for adults.

Fishing
Turquoise Lake, three miles west of Leadville via CO 300, and **Crystal Lakes,** four miles south of town on US 24, are both stocked regularly. Though fished fairly heavily, the waters produce

rainbow, brown, and cutthroat trout, as well as kokanee salmon, in decent numbers and occasionally of respectable size. There is also fishing at the Leadville National Fish Hatchery. Stream fishers might want to try **Halfmoon Creek,** west of Leadville off CO 300.

For licenses and tips on local hot spots, stop in at **Buckhorn Sporting Goods,** 616 Harrison St., tel. (719) 486-3944.

Camping
Excellent Forest Service campgrounds surround Leadville, many of which are situated on or near Turquoise Lake. For a complete list, contact the Ranger District Office at 2015 N. Poplar St. in Leadville, or phone (719) 486-0749 or 486-0752.

To get to the following Turquoise Lake campgrounds, go south from Leadville on US 24 two miles, then west on County Rd. 37 and watch for the signs. **Baby Doe Campground** has 50 sites, all RV-suitable, on 13 acres. **Belle of Colorado Campground** is also on the lake, though its 19 sites are designated tents only. Other Turquoise Lake campgrounds include **Dexter** (26 sites), **Father Dyer** (26 sites), **May Queen** (34 sites), and **Silver Dollar** (45 sites).

Halfmoon Campground (24 sites, also maintained by the Forest Service) is on Halfmoon Creek just south of Turquoise Lake.

WINTER SPORTS

Downhill Skiing
One of Colorado's lesser-known downhill resorts, but a favorite of locals, as well as of Denverites wanting to avoid the crowds and pretensions of some of the state's larger resorts, **Ski Cooper** is just ten miles from Leadville. The mountain offers four lifts serving 312 acres, a 1,200-foot vertical drop (11,700-foot top), and excellent views. Terrain is rated 30% beginner, 40% intermediate, and 30% advanced.

Ski Cooper also offers rentals, lessons, and the "Panda Patrol" children's ski school (for ages three to five). In addition, advanced skiers can take the "Chicago Ridge" snowcat tour to some first-rate backcountry skiing, either bowls or trees—half- and full-day tours available.

For more information on Ski Cooper, write Box 896, Leadville, CO 80461, or phone (719)

486-3684. For information on snowcat tours, phone (719) 486-2277.

Cross-Country Skiing

Plenty of Nordic skiing can be found in the Leadville area, from Turquoise to Twin Lakes. **Ski Cooper** features a Nordic center with 35 km of groomed trails, as well as access to the lifts. Nordic and Telemark lessons and rentals are available. For information, phone (719) 486-2277. There are also cross-country trails at the **Leadville National Fish Hatchery,** tel. (719) 486-1089.

At the Leadville/Lake County Chamber of Commerce, 809 Harrison Ave., you can pick up the *Winter Recreation Trails* guide, which lists and describes 27 cross-country trails in the immediate area. You can also get information, as well as gear, from **Leadville Ski Country,** 116 E. 9th St., tel. (719) 486-3836.

Other Winter Activities

Though known to relatively few, the Leadville area is truly a winter wonderland, with plenty to do outside when the mercury falls. Ice fishing is popular, particularly on Turquoise Lake, as is snowmobiling in the high valley's open meadows.

For more information on the area's winter recreation opportunities, stop by the chamber of commerce at 809 Harrison Avenue. For maps and information on skiing or snowmobiling on Forest Service land, contact the Ranger District Office, 2015 N. Poplar St., tel. (719) 486-0749.

ACCOMMODATIONS

Leadville offers a wide range of accommodations options, whether you're looking for an intimate bed-and-breakfast hideaway, a historic hotel, or a no-frills motel room, whether you're just passing through or want digs for the season.

Bed and breakfasts include the **Apple Blossom Inn,** 120 W. 4th St., tel. (719) 486-2141, with rooms for $60-80 d, and one with a kitchenette for $118; **Leadville Country Inn,** 127 E. 8th St., tel. (719) 486-2354, an ornately restored 1880s mansion and carriage house ($49-130 d); **Wood Haven Manor,** 807 Spruce, tel. (719) 486-0109, originally two late-19th century homes, now combined to house two suites and

six rooms for $49-95 d (some with private baths); and **Peri and Ed's Mountain Hideaway,** 201 W. 8th, tel. (719) 486-0716, another restored Victorian right downtown, where you'll find six rooms ($45-85 d) some with private baths and majestic mountain views.

You can also stay at the historic **Delaware Hotel,** 700 Harrison Ave., tel. (719) 486-1418 or (800) 748-2004 ($65-75 d). Built in 1888, the hotel was at one time one of the classiest in town; after Leadville's fall from grace, it served as a dry goods store, and has only recently been restored and reopened for lodging. Rooms are reasonably priced and include breakfast.

Motels in Leadville include the **Silver King Motor Inn,** 2020 N. Poplar St., tel. (719) 486-2610, where doubles run $45-60, and the **Timberline Motel,** 216 Harrison Ave., tel. (719) 486-1876 (about $40 for two).

In addition to the many Forest Service campgrounds in the Leadville and surrounding areas, the **Leadville RV Corral,** 135 W. 2nd St., tel. (719) 486-3111, is just a block off Harrison Ave. and offers 28 full-service RV sites. **Sugar Loafin'** is another privately owned campground with RV hookups and tent sites, also offering gold panning. To get there, take US 24 south to mile marker 177, and go three miles west on Rd. 4. For information and reservations, phone (719) 486-1031.

For more information on accommodations in the area, contact the **Leadville-Twin Lakes Lodging Association,** tel. (800) 748-2057.

FOOD

Start Me Up

For breakfast, try the **Leadville Diner,** 115 W. 4th St., tel. (719) 486-3812, specializing in natural and fresh ingredients and homemade dishes; **Mom's Place,** 612 Harrison Ave., tel. (719) 486-1108, for good standard American breakfasts; or the **Tabor Grand Coffee House,** 711 Harrison Ave., tel. (719) 486-1317, for espresso coffees and muffins and pastries.

Lunch and Dinner

A favorite for Mexican and New Mexican food is **La Cantina,** a mile south of town on US 24, tel.

(719) 486-9927. La Cantina features home-made tamales and tortillas, as well as stuffed *sopaipillas,* and the wonderful green chili of the Southwest. **The Prospector,** three miles north of town on US 91, tel. (719) 486-3955, another local favorite, features homemade soups and bean dishes, as well as rack of lamb and Cajun food; the restaurant's mining theme includes ore samples on the ceiling. **Callaway's,** 700 Harrison Ave., tel. 486-1418, serves salads, pastas, and steak dinners ($6-16). The **Silver Dollar Saloon,** 315 Harrison Ave., tel. (719) 486-9914, decorated with historic photos and western artifacts, is a great place for a cold one, a burger, and a sense that you never left the 19th century. Another place for good ol' American burgers is the **Pastime Saloon,** 120 W. 2nd, tel. (719) 486-9914.

CALENDAR

Leadville's annual calendar isn't exactly packed back-to-back with events, but those that are scheduled tend to be big, rowdy, and well known. On weekends in late June and early July, the city hosts the **Oro City Festival,** which re-creates Leadville/Oro City's boom days. Visitors can pan for gold, sample frontier "grub," listen to plenty of good old-fashioned mountain music, and just generally cut loose in the manner of the town's founding rowdies, miners, painted ladies, and entrepreneurs. The event is sponsored by Colorado Mountain College (Timberline Campus) and takes place just south of downtown. For information, phone the college at (719) 486-2015, or contact the chamber of commerce at (719) 486-3900.

Another Leadville classic is **Boom Days** in early August, which includes a parade, food, music, drilling competitions, and the famous **International Pack Burro Race,** in which participants—teams of burros and humans—haul, er, ass to the top of Mosquito Pass and back to Leadville.

The **Leadville Trail 100** (mid-August) is America's highest hundred-mile footrace (9,200 to 12,600 feet). Following back roads and trails deep into the woods, the course is famous among distance runners around the world as one of the most grueling.

For more information on Leadville's annual events, contact the chamber of commerce, tel. (719) 486-3900.

SHOPPING

You won't come up empty-handed if you go looking for souvenirs in downtown Leadville. Harrison Avenue is packed with T-shirt and poster shops, as well as places to pick up everything from postcards to Native American jewelry. Allow yourself time to stroll both sides of the four- or five-block Harrison Avenue boardwalk.

SERVICES

Offices of the Leadville **Police Department** are downtown across from the chamber of commerce at 800 Harrison Ave., tel. (719) 486-1365. Phone the Lake County **Sheriff** at (719) 486-1249. Leadville's **St. Vincent General Hospital** has 24-hour emergency service and is located at W. 4th and Washington streets, tel. (719) 486-0230. The Leadville **post office** is at 130 W. 5th St., tel. (719) 486-1667.

Recycling

You can recycle aluminum at the **Safeway** on the north end of town and at the Coors warehouse.

INFORMATION

Probably the best place to begin your visit to Leadville is at the **chamber of commerce** at 809 Harrison Avenue. Pick up maps, brochures, and other information on things to do and see in the area. You can also purchase tickets for the multi-media historical presentation shown next door (see preceding). Write the chamber at 809 Harrison Ave., Leadville, CO 80461, or phone (719) 486-3900.

For books, stop in at **The Book Mine,** 502 Harrison Ave., tel. (719) 486-2866, where you'll find a good selection of local, state, and Western history. The Lake County **public library** is at 1115 Harrison Ave., tel. (719) 486-0569.

Tours

For a bird's-eye view of the Leadville mining district, you can take a **Leadville Air Tour** plane ride. Tours include passes over Turquoise Lake, Twin Lakes and Independence Pass, and the Leadville mines, including the Matchless and Climax. Phone (719) 486-2627. **Dee Hive Tours,** tel. (719) 486-2339, offers more down-to-earth tours, both historical and scenic.

SOUTH OF LEADVILLE

US Highway 24 drops almost due south out of Leadville, slicing through the beautiful Arkansas River Valley and following the tracks of the Denver and Rio Grande Western Railroad. Probably the single best place in the state to see Colorado's wealth of towering peaks, this route affords stunning—somehow humbling, even—views of the majestic Collegiate Range, a north-south formation of "14ers" paralleling the highway from the turnoff to Independence Pass to Salida.

In addition to Mounts Harvard (elev. 14,420 feet), Columbia (elev. 14,073 feet), Yale (elev. 14,196 feet), Princeton (elev. 14,197 feet), and Oxford (elev. 14,153 feet), the range includes at least seven other peaks over 14,000 feet. There are several places to pull your car off the road to take pictures or simply to enjoy the commanding views.

Just north of Salida, US 24 forks: You can either veer southeast for Salida, then catch US 50 east for Royal Gorge and Cañon City, or you can continue south on US 285, which passes through Poncha Springs, climbs up over Poncha Pass (elev. 9,010 feet), and then beelines through the San Luis Valley and Alamosa before dropping down into Santa Fe, New Mexico.

TWIN LAKES AREA

About 12 miles south of Leadville is the junction with CO 82, which connects the Arkansas River Valley with Aspen via Independence Pass (12,095 feet; closed in winter). South of the road are the two Twin Lakes, home to some of the largest trout in the state; patient Mackinaw anglers have taken 30-pounders. For those more interested in fight than weight, Twin Lakes are also regularly stocked with rainbow and cutthroat trout. You'll find several boat ramps, as well as lakeside picnic areas.

If you feel like holing up for a while, the lakes also offer a handful of very nice Forest Service campgrounds, and the area's moderately remote location keeps them from filling up as quickly as do many of the more easily accessible campgrounds. **Lakeview Campground** is at the east end of the lower lake, with 59 tent and RV sites (flush toilets). Other Twin Lakes campgrounds include **Parry Peak** (26 sites), **Twin Peaks** (37 sites), and **White Star** (64 sites). None of the Twin Lakes Forest Service campgrounds has showers. For information, phone the **Leadville District Office** of San Isabel National Forest at (719) 486-0752 or 486-0749, or the Pueblo headquarters at (719) 545-8737.

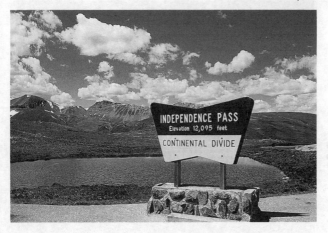

Independence Pass between Leadville and Aspen is closed in the winter.

The **Twin Lakes Nordic Inn** offers lodging in a restored 19th-century stagecoach stop and brothel—rooms are furnished with feather beds and antiques. The inn also has a restaurant serving German and American food, and a cross-country ski center (rentals available). For reservations and information, write Twin Lakes Nordic Inn, Twin Lakes, CO 81251, or phone (719) 486-1830 or (800) 626-7812.

BUENA VISTA

The name of this town is no lie—this area offers some of the prettiest views in the Rockies (those who know Spanish will cringe when they hear the local pronunciation: It's "BYOO-na VIS-ta" here, not "BWAY-na VEES-ta").

Lying in the rich, green Upper Arkansas River Valley, at the confluence of Cottonwood Creek and the Arkansas River, Buena Vista (pop. 2,075; elev. 7,954 feet) is surrounded by massive mountains, affording views that nearly take your breath away. West of town, Mts. Yale and Princeton rise over 6,000 feet up from the valley floor to their 14,000-foot-plus peaks, providing the town with a constant reminder of nature's power and beauty. And when the sun of a late afternoon washes over the mountains' flanks, and the mist of a distant rainstorm softens their far ridge lines, well, it's almost enough to make a Believer out of you.

Silver miners founded Buena Vista in 1879, establishing it as the seat of Chaffee County the following year when they absconded with county records that had been stashed in a brewery in Granite 20 miles upriver. In 1881, an ore-sampling plant and smelter were built in Buena Vista, attracting large numbers of laborers, and through the 1880s the town was notorious throughout the West for its rowdy dance halls, gambling parlors, and brothels.

Today, Buena Vista's fortunes lie in tourism. Billing itself the "Whitewater Capital of Colorado," Buena Vista each summer attracts tens of thousands of visitors who come to sample the wide variety of runnable river water, from long stretches of calm water to nasty narrows and Class III, IV, and V rapids.

Buena Vista Heritage Museum

This four-room historical museum on the east end of Main St. features a variety of displays spanning a range of interests. Railroad buffs will dig the miniature reconstruction of the Upper Arkansas River Valley and the working model of the three railroads that served the area in the late 19th century. One of the rooms is devoted to mining and minerals, while you others display clothing and domestic utensils from the 1880s through the 1920s, as well as historical photos.

The Buena Vista Heritage Museum is open daily 9 a.m.-5 p.m., Memorial Day through Labor

Buena Vista Heritage Museum

Day. Admission is $1 for adults. For more information, phone (719) 395-2515 or 395-8458.

City Parks
A shady lawn area on US 24 behind the chamber of commerce is perfect for picnicking. You'll also find picnic tables, lawns, and shade trees at the small city park at the corner of US 24 and Main St.—kids can fish in the small lake.

River Running
This is modern Buena Vista's raison d'être and pretty much defines the town during the summer. Several rafting companies offer a wide range of trips on the Arkansas River, from no-experience-required sightseeing tours to serious trips requiring not only previous experience but top physical ability and strength as well. The following Buena Vista-based outfits are well established and have good reputations: **American Adventure Expeditions,** (719) 395-2409 or (800) 288-0675; **Buffalo Joe River Trips,** tel. (719) 395-8757 or (800) 356-7984; **Noah's Ark,** tel. (719) 395-2158; **Art/4 Corners Rafting,** tel. (719) 395-4137 or (800) 332-7238; and **Wilderness Aware,** tel. (719) 395-2112 or (800) 462-7238.

If you'd rather watch than ride, one of the best places to view whitewater rafters is an observation deck at **Five Points Arkansas Headwaters Picnic Area,** west of Salida on US 50 about eight miles east of Royal Gorge.

Hiking
You could pretty much head out in any direction from Buena Vista and, being careful to avoid private property, find yourself in primo hiking country. If you feel like gaining some altitude, head west 12 miles on County Rd. 306 from the stoplight in downtown Buena Vista to the Denny Creek trailhead. From there, a four-mile trail leads to the top of Mt. Yale (an elevation gain of 4,300 feet).

Another approach to Mt. Yale is just a few miles north; the trail circles south from the trailhead up to a saddle, where you can either turn around or head on up to the peak. It's a four-mile hike to the saddle (elevation gain: 2,600 feet), six to the peak (gain: 4,900 feet). To get to the trailhead, go north three blocks from the light in downtown Buena Vista, and turn left on Cross-

man (County Rd. 350). Go west two miles, until you reach County Rd. 361, and turn left. After one mile, turn left on County Rd. 365, and look for the trailhead about three miles up the road on the left.

For additional information on hiking in the Buena Vista area, contact the **Salida Ranger District Office** at 325 W. Rainbow Blvd., Salida, or phone (719) 539-3591.

Mountain Biking
Any area with this much excellent hiking will no doubt afford good mountain-biking opportunities as well. For maps and information on logging roads in the area, as well as single-track trails, contact the Salida Ranger District Office (see "Hiking" above). In addition, several of Buena Vista's rafting companies are "crossing over" and offering mountain bike tours, ranging from half- and full-day outings to combination "pedal-and-paddle" trips. Both **American Adventure Expeditions,** tel. (719) 395-2409 or (800) 288-0675 and **Buffalo Joe,** tel. (719) 395-8757 or (800) 356-7984, can arrange guided tours that include meals, bike, and helmet rental.

Other Outdoor Activities
Buena Vista's location in the gorgeous Arkansas River Valley makes it ideal for a wide range of other recreational activities, from cross-country skiing and snowmobiling to fishing and jeep touring. For more information contact the Buena Vista Chamber of Commerce, Box P, S. US 24, Buena Vista, CO 81211.

Accommodations
A small resort town just a few blocks long, with a motel on nearly every one, Buena Vista often fills up in the evenings with visitors and passersthrough—especially in the summer, when tourists need dry beds after spending a day on the river, and cross-country travelers need soft beds before heading back out on the trail in the morning. One of the first to fill up is the **Sumac Lodge,** tel. (719) 395-8111, at 428 US 24 (south end of town). Doubles go for about $32 in the winter, $63 in summer. The **Topaz Lodge,** tel. (719) 395-2427, across the street and a couple of blocks north, offers large inexpensive rooms—nothing fancy, but clean and comfortable. A room for two is about $34 in summer, $55 in winter.

The **Adobe Inn Bed and Breakfast,** 303 N. US 24, tel. (719) 395-6340, is a small southwestern-style inn decorated with Mexican and American southwest furniture and art, featuring large breakfasts of green chile, sausage, eggs, and Mexican hot chocolate. Also in town, the **Meister House Bed and Breakfast,** 414 E. Main, tel. (719) 395-9220, is a two-story brick lodge built in the late 19th century as a hotel; all five rooms are on the second floor and run $50-75. Just southwest of town right on the Arkansas, the **Blue Sky Inn Bed and Breakfast,** tel. (719) 395-8862, is a nice, quiet home in the country; the two rooms run $70 and $80.

RVers can camp at the **Mt. Princeton RV Park,** tel. (719) 395-6206, a mile north of town.

Food

You'll find a handful of good restaurants in Buena Vista, ranging from Italian to Oriental to Mexican, as well as down-home American. You can get authentic solid Mexican food at **El Duran's,** 301 Main St., tel. (719) 395-2120. Dinners (enchilada, burritos) run $5-9, but nightly specials, with drinks, go for under $5. Also recommended is **Casa del Sol,** on N. US 24, tel. (719) 395-8810, where the food is a bit more expensive, but the menu offers more to choose from (Mexican-style scampi and steak).

Delaney's Depot, S. US 24, tel. (719) 395-8854, is a decent place for families, with a railroad theme and serving standard American fare at reasonable prices.

Entertainment

This is also a town full of river rats who need to unwind after spending their days guiding tourists downriver in rafts. And there are a couple of bars where you might stumble on some action. The **Blue Parrot** at 304 E. Main St. is usually packed with locals pounding beers; also on Main, between the highway and the Blue Parrot, the **Lariat** (whose motto is "We sell and service hangovers") seems to cater to more serious drinkers.

For the kids, **Rolling Wheels Skate Center** offers indoor skating and miniature golf.

Services

The offices of the Buena Vista **Police Department** are located at 101 Park Ave.; phone (719) 395-2451 (in emergencies, phone 719-395-8098). The nearest hospital is the **Heart of the Rockies Regional Medical Center,** 448 E. 1st St., Salida, tel. (719) 539-6661. The Buena Vista **post office** is at 100 Park Lane, tel. (719) 395-2445.

You can recycle aluminum at the **Circle Super Food Center,** 428 US 24.

Information

The **Buena Vista Chamber of Commerce** is in the center of town on US 24 and offers lots of information on things do and see in the area, as well as on places to eat and sleep. Stop in for brochures or to ask questions of the staff. Phone the offices at (719) 395-6612.

Another good source for local information is the weekly *Chaffee County Times.* In addition to running local news and listing events, the paper focuses on outdoor sports—watch particularly for discussions of nearby hiking trails. The paper costs 35 cents in racks throughout Chaffee County. For subscription information, phone (719) 395-8621. The Buena Vista **public library** is at 131 Linderman, tel. (719) 395-8700.

SALIDA

Salida (pop. 5,200; elev. 7,036 feet) was founded in 1880 as a division point on the Denver and Rio Grande Railroad, although for years prior the area served as a stopping point for travelers passing through the mountains via the Arkansas River Valley. Throughout the late 19th century, Salida, like Buena Vista, its sister town upriver, had a reputation for rowdy, shoot-'em-up streets, and saloons and brothels famous throughout the Rockies. The railroad based its maintenance and repair operations in Salida into the second half of the 20th century.

Mount Shavano (elev. 14,229 feet), about 14 miles northwest of Salida (pronounced Sa-LIE-da), is the town's dominant landmark, named for the Ute Chief Shavano. In the spring, the mountain's melting snow is said to take the form of the "Angel of Shavano," who appeared to the Ute chief as he prayed for his dying friend, trader Jim Beckwourth, founder of the town of Pueblo.

Today, motels and fast-food joints surround a quiet, narrow-streeted historic downtown area defined in part by antique shops, jewelers, and old taverns. Salida's definition is completed by the focus on the Arkansas River, running along the east side of town, and the many rafting and kayaking companies offering trips to tourists.

Salida Museum

Adjacent to the chamber of commerce on US 50/Rainbow Blvd. (west side of town), this small historical museum displays a variety of Native American and pioneer artifacts from the Salida-Arkansas Valley area, with exhibits highlighting the region's mining and railroad histories. The museum is open daily, 11 a.m.-7 p.m. Memorial Day through Labor Day. For more information, phone the Heart of the Rockies chamber of commerce at (719) 539-2068.

Parks

Salida is a true gateway to some of Colorado's best recreation areas and activities. The Arkansas River, one of the best whitewater-rafting streams in the state, flows right through town, south from Leadville then east toward Royal Gorge. To the northwest of town is the Collegiate Range and Colorado's biggest concentration of "14ers"—excellent hiking, climbing, and cross-country skiing. Also, Salida's surrounded on three sides by national forest—Pike to the north and San Isabel to the south and and west. In addition, Gunnison and Rio Grande national forests sprawl through Saguache County to the southwest of Salida, offering more camping areas and backcountry to explore.

kayaker

City parks include **Riverside Park,** on the Arkansas River downtown at 1st and E streets. The park has nice lawns and shady cottonwoods and offers good fishing and picnicking, as well as a place to watch rafts go by. **Alpine Park,** a neighbornhood park at the corner of 4th and F streets, has picnic tables, a playground, and a large lawn. There's also a small park with a playground and tennis courts adjacent to the chamber of commerce.

River Running

Like Buena Vista, Salida is a paradise for river rats, offering an exceptional base camp for a range of waters. Brown's Canyon in the Arkansas River Valley to the north is famous for its Class III and IV rapids. To the east, the Arkansas cuts through the mountains at Royal Gorge, sheer cliffs rising 1,200 feet up from the riverbed. Stretching along a 148-mile section of this river lies **Arkansas Headwaters State Recreation Area,** which has established a number of campgrounds, kayak and raft put-ins, picnic facilities, and hiking trails for use by the public. You can get a guide and map to the area by writing Box 126, Salida, CO 81201, or by calling (719) 539-7289.

In addition, several private companies offer a range of river trips, with one to suit just about every budget, desire, and ability. **Dvorak's Kayak**

downtown Salida

and Rafting Expeditions, based in Nathrop (about 18 miles north of Salida), books half- to 17-day trips not only on the Arkansas but on rivers throughout Colorado, Idaho, New Mexico, and Utah, as well as Hawaii, New Zealand, Australia, and Mexico. Dvorak's also offers fishing, mountain biking, and pack trips. For their catalog, write 17921-B US 285, Nathrop, CO 81236, or phone (719) 539-6851 or (800) 824-3795. Other Salida-area-based rafting companies include **American Adventure Expeditions,** (719) 539-4680 or (800) 288-0675; **Independent Whitewater,** tel. (719) 395-2642 or (719) 539-4057; **Timberwolf Whitewater Expeditions,** tel. (719) 539-7508 or (800) 843-8448; and **River Runners, Ltd.,** tel. (800) 332-9100 (in CO) or (800) 525-2081 (outside CO).

Hot Springs
Salida Hot Springs, Colorado's largest indoor hot-springs pool, is next to the chamber of commerce building at US 50 and Rainbow Boulevard. The pools were built in 1937 by the WPA. You'll find a lap pool, wading pool, and private tubs. Salida Hot Springs is open year-round, but hours vary. For times and information, phone (719) 539-6738.

Mt. Princeton Hot Springs is between Salida and Buena Vista, five miles west of Nathrop. In off-and-on operation since the late 19th century, the hot springs, lodge, and restaurant are very popular with locals and passers-through alike. In addition to three swimming pools and several private tubs, there are rock-lined pools on Chalk Creek below the lodge. For reservations or information, write 15870 County Rd. 162, Nathrop, CO 81236, or phone (719) 395-2447.

Skiing
Just west of Monarch Pass, about 15 miles west of Salida on US 50, **Monarch Ski Area** offers a low-key, family-oriented alpine resort atmosphere with some of the best skiing in the Rockies (see "Monarch Pass" following).

Golf
Salida Municipal Golf Course is a nine-hole course open year-round. For tee times and information, phone (719) 539-6373.

Accommodations
You'll find a "motel row" on US 50 on the west side of town with plenty of places to choose from, including the **Best Western Colorado Lodge,** 352 W. Rainbow Blvd., tel. (719) 539-2514, where doubles run about $55-80. The **Super 8 Motel,** 525 W. Rainbow Blvd., tel. (719) 539-6689, features an indoor pool and hot tub and very reasonably priced rooms ($35-50). The **Friendship Inn of Salida,** 7545 W. US 50, tel. (719) 539-6655 or (800) 453-4511, has rooms for two running about $35-55.

There are also a number of motels on the east side of town, including the **Circle R Motel,** 304 E. Rainbow Blvd., tel. (719) 539-6296 ($40-45 for doubles), and the **Days Inn,** 407 E. US 50, tel. (719) 539-6651 ($35-50).

The **Poor Farm Country Inn,** 8495 County Rd. 160, tel. (719) 539-3818, is a bed and breakfast located in a three-story brick country home built in 1892. Situated on the west bank of the Arkansas River, the cozy little lodge offers excellent mountain views and a peaceful escape from the demands of late-20th-century life. Doubles with full breakfast start at about $50.

Several other bed and breakfasts recently opened in the Salida area, many of them in gorgeous remodeled turn-of-the-century Victorian homes. Among them are the **Century House,** 401 E. 1st St., tel. (719) 539-7064, in downtown Salida with four guest rooms, and the **Thomas House,** 307 E. 1st St., tel. (719) 539-7104, built in 1888 to house railroad workers today offers five rooms to visitors. The **Tudor Rose,** 6720 Paradise Rd. (Box 89), tel. (719) 539-2002 or (800) 0899, is just south of town and sits on 37 sprawling acres, with horse stabling and rentals available.

Heart of the Rockies RV and Tent Campground, tel. (719) 539-4051 or (800) 496-2245, is located on US 50 (10 miles west of Salida) and has 45 RV sites, 20 tent sites, pool, playground, and excellent access to rafting, horseback riding, and sightseeing tours.

Food
A great place to head for a pre-raft-trip breakfast is the **First Street Cafe,** 137 E. 1st St., tel. (719) 539-4759. Located in the historic downtown section of Salida, the building was con-

structed in the late 19th century and has served as a boardinghouse, barber shop, and Ford auto garage. The cafe today is hipper (less smoky, for example) than most small-town joints and serves several vegetarian specials (stir-fry, etc.) in addition to traditional fare. Very reasonably priced. The First Street Cafe is also open for lunch and dinner. For good and inexpensive Mexican food, try **El Palacio, 1015** E. US 50/Rainbow Blvd., tel. (719) 539-3784, where lunch entrees run $4-6 and dinners $6-10. El Palacio also serves burgers and sandwiches (lunch) and steaks and seafood (dinner).

Entertainment
You'll find live music in several of the downtown bars and restaurants, especially on summer weekends, in addition to the annual festivals also featuring live music (see below). The **Steam Plant,** located in one of the country's first electrical-engineering plants and converted to a theater, offers a regular series of music and drama, ranging from western swing to modern dance and repertory theater. For schedules and prices, write Box 758, Salida, CO 81210.

Services
The offices of the Salida **Police Department** and **Chaffee County Sheriff** are at 217 E. 3rd St., tel. (719) 539-2596. Phone the **State Patrol** at (719) 275-0015 (Cañon City). **Heart of the Rockies Regional Medical Center** is located at 448 E. 1st St., tel. (719) 539-6661. The Salida **post office** is on the corner of 3rd and D streets.

Recycle aluminum at the **Safeway,** 232 G St., and at **Wal-Mart,** 201 E. Rainbow Blvd.

Calendar
The **FIBArk Boat Races** in mid-June kick off Salida's summer whitewater season (FIBArk = First in Boats on the Arkansas). In addition to a 26-mile kayak and raft race, the four-day event features footraces, novelty races (bed races, for example), a pancake breakfast, and a parade. A couple of weeks later, the town sponsors an "old-fashioned Fourth of July" with music, street dancing, a chili cook-off, and fireworks. In late summer (beginning early July), the **Aspen-Salida Music Festival** is a series of concerts featuring classical ensembles from the world-famous Aspen concert series.

For more information on these and other Salida events, contact the Heart of the Rockies Chamber of Commerce.

Information
The **Heart of the Rockies Chamber of Commerce** is a good place to get information not only on Salida but on the wealth of recreational opportunities available in the Arkansas River Valley. Offices are located at 406 W. Rainbow Blvd. (US 50), tel. (719) 539-2068.

For information on camping, hiking, and other national forest activities, contact the **Salida Ranger District Office** of the Forest Service, 230 W. 16th St., tel. (719) 539-3591.

For **road and weather information,** phone (719) 539-6688 or 275-1637 (Cañon City).

HIGHWAY 50 WEST

Highway 50 continues west from Salida, connecting the Arkansas River Valley with Gunnison and Montrose. In Montrose, the highway doglegs north, joining US 550 and ribboning up between the Uncompahgre Plateau and Grand Mesa through Delta to Grand Junction. The Salida-to-Gunnison section of US 50 is particularly scenic, rising up into Gunnison National Forest, lifting over Monarch Pass, then following Tomichi Creek. Along the way you'll find several Forest Service roads—some paved, some gravel—that lead to campgrounds and provide access to backcountry. For information on camping in Gunnison National Forest, contact the main office at 2250 US 50, Delta, CO 81416, tel. (970) 874-7691, or the Ranger District Office, 216 N. Colorado, Gunnison, CO 81230, tel. (970) 641-0471.

Poncha Springs
Five miles west of Salida, the little junction town of Poncha Springs has a couple of motels and cafes, including the **Poncha Truck Stop,** a classic little coffee shop/diner open at 6 a.m. daily. In addition to excellent breakfasts (burritos, steak and eggs, etc.), the place serves lunch and dinner (Mexican food, steak, and fried chicken), as well as their monstrous "Alaska burger." There's also a small gift shop and bookstore, as well as public showers for a small

fee. Rooms are available in Poncha Springs at the **Jackson Hotel,** built in 1878 as a stage stop; claim is that Jesse James, Billy the Kid, and Teddy Roosevelt all stayed here. Rates run about $35-50.

Monarch Pass

Highway 50 crosses over the Continental Divide at Monarch Pass (elev. 11,312 feet). One of the highest and most scenic highway summits in the United States, the pass affords excellent views and photo ops. To the south are the Sangre de Cristo and San Juan mountains, both ranges continuing across the border into northern New Mexico; to the north are the Ruby Mountains and the towering peaks of the Collegiate Range, several over 14,000 feet. In fact, from Monarch Pass you can see at least a dozen of Colorado's "14ers."

If the view from the roadside isn't enough, you can take the **Monarch Aerial Tram** to almost 12,000 feet. At the top is an enclosed observation tower, from which you'll have one of the best views in the Rockies. Maps and telescopes help you orient yourself and identify distant peaks. The tram is open daily 9 a.m.-4 p.m.,

mid-May through mid-October. For more information, phone (719) 539-4789.

Monarch Ski Area, one of Colorado's classic off-the-beaten-path ski areas, is a favorite among locals, who are hip to its low-key atmosphere, relatively low prices, and uncrowded slopes. In addition, the resort's 10,800-foot base guarantees that its 350 average inches of snowfall are as fluffy as the downy flake in a Robert Frost poem—the stuff that makes converts out of pagan powder-hounds.

With four lifts on 600 acres of terrrain, Monarch's 1,000-foot vertical drop offers good skiing for just about every ability level. The trails are designated 22% beginner, 44% intermediate, and 33% advanced (and, no, I don't know where that last one percent disappeared to . . .). Instruction and rentals are available, and though there is no on-site lodging, you can stay down the road at the **Monarch Lodge,** tel. (719) 539-2581 or (800) 332-3668, where you'll find a full-service restaurant, indoor swimming pool, jacuzzi, exercise rooms, and many more amenities.

For more information on Monarch Ski Area, phone (719) 539-3573. For snow conditions, phone (800) 228-7943.

cliff palace at Mesa Verde

GUNNISON AND VICINITY

Gunnison (pop. 5,785; elev. 7,700 feet) is located in the broad Gunnison River Valley about midway between Montrose and Salida. Home of Western State College and center for some of Colorado's finest recreation, Gunnison is a youthful and outdoor-oriented town whose roots are in ranching and mining.

Seat of Gunnison County, Gunnison has long served as a trade center for many of the smaller communities in the surrounding area. Today, the town's economy relies largely on the tourism industry and education for its stability: Tourism brings in roughly $35 million annually and education $26 million; ranching brings in another $8 million.

Though Gunnison claims the sun shines almost every day, it still manages to get damn cold in the winter. This is due largely to its valley location: Average temperatures in town are generally at least several degrees lower than in nearby towns such as Crested Butte, which lies at a higher elevation but is nestled against the mountainside. Gunnison has on occasion recorded the coldest temperature in the nation.

History

The first nonnative people to explore the Gunnison area were probably those in the Escalante-Dominguez party, who in 1776 followed the Gunnison River west in their search for an overland route connecting the missions of Santa Fe, New Mexico, and Monterey, California. During the early and mid-19th century, the region was trapped and hunted by mountain men who would trade their furs at Taos and Bent's Fort.

On September 6, 1853, Captain John W. Gunnison, a government surveyor, and his party camped along the Gunnison River near present-day Gunnison after having crossed the mountains in search of a transcontinental railroad route. The Gunnison party continued west into Utah, following roughly what is today the route of CO 50. On October 25, while looking for a place to hole up for the approaching winter, the group was attacked by Native Americans, and Gunnison and all but four of his men were killed.

In the early 1860s, prospectors began to arrive in the Gunnison area, and in 1869, the region's Utes were removed to the Los Piños Indian Agency, clearing the valley for white settlement. It wasn't until the mid-1870s, though, that farmers and ranchers moved into the region in significant numbers. In 1874, Dr. Sylvester Richardson, a Denver physician, established the town site and organized the first town company. Gunnison became the official seat of Gunnison County on May 22, 1877.

Meanwhile, local creeks, particularly Tomichi and Quartz, were beginning to produce quality gold and silver in large amounts, and thriving mining camps were springing up in the nearby mountains. Gunnison was a natural supply center. In 1880, the railroad arrived, a godsend not only to miners but to Gunnison Valley ranchers and farmers as well.

In 1909, Gunnison's Colorado State Normal School was founded; in 1915 its name was changed to Western State College.

kokanee salmon

BOB RACE

Throughout this century, Gunnison has been a popular gateway to some of Colorado's best recreation areas. As early as the mid-1900s, the area's waterways—Taylor River and Tomichi and Cebolla creeks—were known for some of the best trout fishing in the Rockies. In 1963, with the opening of Crested Butte Ski Area, Gunnison became a destination for some of the best downhill skiers in the country—today, direct flights from Dallas, Chicago, Atlanta, Houston, and Denver offer easy access to the slopes.

Pioneer Museum

Gunnison's historical museum complex includes a restored turn-of-the-century schoolhouse, the town's first post office, and a railroad depot. There are also displays of railroad artifacts, Native American arrowheads, pioneer farming equipment, and lots of old photos.

The Pioneer Museum is located at S. Adams and E. Hwy. 50 and is open Mon.-Sat. 9 a.m.-5 p.m. and Sunday 1-5 p.m., Memorial Day through Labor Day. For more information, phone (970) 641-9963.

Western State College

Undoubtedly one of the first things you'll notice in Gunnison is the huge "W" on the side of Tenderfoot Mountain on the north side of town. Reportedly the world's largest college emblem, the "W" is made of white-washed flat rocks, carried up the mountain by students and faculty in 1923. Each line of the letter is 16 feet wide and 400 feet long; the overall dimensions are 320 by 420 feet.

For more information on the school's wide range of programs, write Western State College, Gunnison, CO 81230, or phone (970) 943-2119.

PARKS AND RECREATION

Gunnison is surrounded by some of nature's most gorgeous landscapes. Tumbling trout streams, mountain lakes, dense fir woodlands, granite peaks shouldering high above the timberline, broad valleys that come springtime are vibrant with wildflowers and shimmering waves of green—there's enough here to keep the outdoor lover grinning blissfully all year round.

Gunnison's very pleasant **city park** is located on the east side of town on CO 50 and has large lawns, lots of playground equipment, and public restrooms.

Fishing

This is one of Gunnison's main draws. In fact, on March 1, 1988, the state record brown trout, weighing 30.5 pounds, was taken from a pond near the East River just north of Gunnison. Though some of the best water in the area flows through private property, there is plenty of excellent easy-to-get-to public-access water in the region. In addition, the area's full of trouty backcountry streams that locals know are well worth the effort to reach.

Some of the best fishing in the area is found at **Blue Mesa Reservoir** about seven miles west of town. The 15-mile-long lake, formed when Blue Mesa Dam was built on the Gunnison River, yields lunker rainbow trout, as well as trophy-size lakes (Mackinaws) and browns. Fishing is best in early spring, shortly after the ice breaks up, and you can troll and jig from boats or work the shoreline, which ranges from rocky cliffs to sandy beach. The reservoir also has a decent population of kokanee salmon—usually caught by trolling. Rent boats at either of the reservoir's two marinas. For more information, see "Curecanti National Recreation Area," following.

Taylor Reservoir, 30 miles northeast of Gunnison at Taylor Park, is another favorite of local lake anglers, who fish for lake, brown, rainbow trout, and kokanee salmon. You can rent boats and pick up fishing supplies and groceries at Taylor Park Boathouse. To get there, take CO 135 north from Gunnison about 10 miles and watch for the turnoff on your right.

The Gunnison area also boasts some of the best stream fishing in the state. The **Taylor River,** above Taylor Reservoir, offers good fly-fishing, while pools below the reservoir are large and deep enough for spinners and other lures. The **East River,** whose headwaters are near Schofield Pass north of Crested Butte, merges with the Taylor at Almont. The East is one of the area's best fly-fishing streams, producing good rainbow, brown, and brook trout (special restrictions apply on some stretches).

The **Gunnison River,** between Blue Mesa Reservoir and Gunnison, and north of town along CO 135, is one of the state's best known and most productive stretches of water. Anglers have been pulling trophy brown and rainbow trout out of holes and riffles here for years, on both flies and lures.

For more information on fishing in the Gunnison area, as well as for licenses and equipment, stop in at **Gene Taylor's Sporting Goods,** 201 W. Tomichi, tel. (970) 641-1845. To arrange guided trips, contact **Three Rivers Resort and Outfitting,** Box 339, Almont, CO 81210, tel. (970) 641-1303.

Cycling

Gunnison's proximity to Crested Butte, one of the mountain-bike capitals of the country, guarantees there will be plenty of great rides nearby. Road bikers don't have as many options, though, as there are really only two roads that go anywhere from town: US 50, with major, high-speed traffic in both directions; and CO 135 to Crested Butte, a *far* better place to take the touring bike for a spin. In fact, a bike path parallels the highway several miles north of town, and though it gets narrow after that, it would still be a rewarding ride.

For more on mountain biking in the area, see "Crested Butte," following.

Golf

The **Dos Rios Golf Course** is an 18-hole course named for the *dos rios* (two rivers) at whose confluence it lies: Tomichi Creek and the Taylor River. To get there, take US 50 two miles west from Gunnison and watch for the sign on your left. For information and tee times, phone (970) 641-1482.

Rafting and Kayaking

With so much river water nearby, the Gunnison area is a natural for whitewater sports. Kayakers, rafters, and canoers enjoy the Gunnison River from Almont to Blue Mesa Reservoir, as well as the Taylor River from Taylor Park Reservoir to Almont. Caution: River water in this area can get awfully fast and brawly during the snowmelt of late spring. The Taylor, particularly, can get mean and should only be attempted by experienced river rats or with guides.

Companies in the Gunnison area offering guided trips include **Three Rivers Resort and Outfitting,** tel. (970) 641-1303, and **Scenic River Tours,** 703 W. Tomichi, tel. (970) 641-3131.

Camping

At least 30 National Forest and National Recreation Area campgrounds can be found within an hour or so of Gunnison. Gunnison National Forest alone includes a couple of dozen, both north of town in the Taylor Park region and south around Lake City. In addition, Curecanti National Recreation Area, west of Gunnison, offers a dozen or so more.

County Rd. 742, which parallels the Taylor River from Almont to Taylor Park, is virtually lined with Forest Service campgrounds, with at least 10 along this stretch alone. Among them: **Almont Campground,** just south of Almont off CO 135 (10 sites); **Taylor Canyon,** about halfway to Taylor Reservoir (five sites, tents only); and **Lottis Creek,** just below the Taylor Reservoir dam (27 sites). Several other Forest Service campgrounds are located at Taylor Park Reservoir. In addition, you'll find Forest Service campgrounds at the towns of Pitkin and Ohio.

Curecanti National Recreation Area campgrounds include **Cimarron,** 22 sites, dump station; **Dry Gulch,** 10 sites, pit toilets, no showers; **Elk Creek,** 179 sites, flush toilets, dump station, boat ramp and marina, visitor center; and **Lake Fork,** 87 sites, dump station, flush toilets, boat ramp and marina, visitor center.

The Forest Service has published a detailed chart and map that lists all the campgrounds in the area and includes information on fees, number of sites, water availability, and fishing and hiking access. Write Gunnison National Forest, Taylor and Cebolla Ranger Districts, 216 N. Colorado, Gunnison, CO 81230, or phone (970) 641-0471. For information on Recreation Area campgrounds, write Curecanti National Recreation Area, 102 Elk Creek, Gunnison, CO 81230, or phone (970) 641-2337.

Sailing and Windsurfing

Though the several dams on the Gunnison River have changed forever this once wild and scenic stream, the trade-off has been an increase in the amount of available area for recreational activities, including sailing and windsurfing. **Curecanti National Recreation Area,** which flanks the Gunnison River west of town, includes three reservoirs. You'll find boat ramps on Blue Mesa Reservoir, while hand-carried boats only are allowed on Crystal Lake and Morrow Point Reservoir. For maps and information, stop in at any of the three visitor information centers: **Elk Creek** (16 miles west of Gunnison), **Lake Fork** (26 miles west of Gunnison), and **Cimarron** (20 miles east of Montrose).

Skiing

Gunnisonites are fortunate to live close to one of Colorado's best ski resorts, Mt. Crested Butte, just over 30 miles north of town. Offering excellent skiing for all abilities, this out-of-the-way and laid-back resort promises an honest good time, relatively uncrowded slopes, and some of the state's most breathtaking scenery. See "Crested Butte," following, for a complete description.

TOURS

Scenic Drives

Gunnison is a wonderful starting point for several of the Rockies' most scenic drives. And if you've got a 4WD rig, you could spend an entire summer exploring little-used high mountain passes. Several unpaved Forest Service roads begin near Taylor Park, affording back-way access to Buena Vista, Salida, and Aspen. One of the most visually arresting drives in the area is up over Kebler Pass and down to CO 133. Though unpaved, this is a well-maintained road, suitable for most vehicles (see "Crested Butte," following).

Another highly recommended drive is the loop over **Cumberland Pass** via Taylor Park. Take CO 135 north to Almont, and turn east on County Rd. 742. At the east end of Taylor Park Reservoir, turn south for Tincup, a mining town dating from 1880 (when it was known as Virginia City). Continue south over Cumberland Pass (elev. 12,000 feet), then down through Pitkin and Ohio, sites of late 1870s silver strikes. Continue to Parlin; then catch CO 50 back to Gunnison.

One of Colorado's most fascinating engineering marvels is located east of Gunnison near Pitkin. **Alpine Tunnel,** a 1,771-foot bore under the Continental Divide, was completed in 1881 by the Denver, South Park, and Pacific Railroad and last used in 1910. Though the tunnel's west entrance has collapsed, you can view the remains of several old buildings, including water tanks and a boardinghouse, as well as the site of Woodstock, where the telegraph station and coal platform were located. The access road is about two miles north of Pitkin (watch for the sign).

For maps and more information, contact the **Taylor River and Cebolla Ranger District of Gunnison National Forest,** 216 N. Colorado, Gunnison, CO 81230, tel. (970) 641-0471. In addition, the Gunnison Country Chamber of Commerce has published a map and guide to 20 scenic tours in the area. Write Box 36, Gunnison, CO 81230.

Historical Walking Tour

The Gunnison Country Chamber of Commerce has published a map and tour guide to historical Gunnison. Included are residences and commercial buildings dating from the 1880s, as well as several from the turn of the century. The guide, which explains each structure's architectural and historical significance, is available from the chamber.

ACCOMMODATIONS

Gunnison's US 50 location, its reputation for abundant nearby recreation, and the fact that it's a college town needing digs for parents and visiting professors guarantee plenty of lodging in the area, most of it reasonably priced. Motels, guest lodges, cabins, bed and breakfasts, in town, in a country meadow, or beside a mountain trout stream—the area should have something to suit your needs.

The Gunnison Country Chamber of Commerce has published an accommodations guide, with descriptions and photos of over 30 places to stay in the area. You can have one sent to you by writing Box 36, Gunnison, CO 81230, or by phoning (800) 274-7580.

Motels and Lodges

The **ABC Motel,** 212 E. Tomichi, tel. (970) 641-2400 or (800) 341-8000, is located near the center of town and has among the least expensive rooms in town, doubles start at about $35. Two blocks east, **Bennett's Western Motel,** 403 E. Tomichi, tel. (970) 641-1722, has rooms for two starting at about $45. At the **Holiday Inn,** 400 E. Tomichi, tel. (970) 641-1288, doubles run $45-70, and you can get rooms with kitchens at the **Mountain View Lodge,** 117 N. Taylor, tel. (970) 641-1799, for around $50.

Two riverside Gunnison-area lodges are the **Lost Canyon Resort,** 8264 CO 135, tel. (970) 641-0181, where cabins start at about $50 a night, and **Three Rivers Resort and Outfitting,** in Almont, tel. (970) 641-1303, where cabins run $50-90. Three Rivers also has RV and tent sites, as well as a guide service, fly shop, and equipment rentals.

Harmel's Ranch Resort, Box 944, Gunnison, CO 81230, tel. (970) 641-1740, is a classic Rocky Mountain dude ranch northwest of town on the Taylor River. Harmel's has an excellent reputation, and your stay can include everything from meals to hayrides and campfire singalongs. Doubles start at about $135.

Hot Springs/Guest Ranch

Dating from the mid-19th century, **Waunita Hot Springs,** 8007 County Rd. 887, tel. (970) 641-1266, offers first-class road-less-traveled digs and a range of activities, from horseback riding to hot-springs relaxing. In the late 1890s, the springs was developed into a commercial health spa, and over the next several decades, cabins, a guesthouse, a swimming pool, and a hospital were built, though the spa went under in the late 1920s. Some of the buildings remain and in

the early 1960s, when the current owners purchased the property, they were restored. Weekly rates are $950 a week (per person), with discounts for kids.

Camping and RVing

In addition to the dozens of National Forest and National Recreation Area campgrounds in the area (see "Camping," above), there are many private campgrounds where you can fetch up for weeks on end. **Sunnyside Campground,** tel. (970) 641-0477, is located 12 miles west of Gunnison on Blue Mesa Reservoir. If you'd rather be streamside, you can get RV and tent sites, as well as cabins, at **Three Rivers Resort and Outfitting,** tel. (970) 641-1303, located 10 miles north of town where the Taylor and East rivers merge to form the headwaters of the Gunnison. A **KOA** campground is located just west of town on the Gunnison River, tel. (970) 641-1358.

FOOD

For a small ranching town, Gunnison has a fairly decent number of good, reasonably priced restaurants. That might be due in part to the presence of Western State College: Students get tired of dorm food and Top Ramen and love to go out to eat—on a budget.

For breakfast, try either the **Sidewalk Cafe,** 113 W. Tomichi, tel. (970) 641-4130, serving eggs, pancakes, and other hearty fare, or **Hi-Kountry Kitchen and Bakery,** 302 N. Main, tel. (970) 641-1489, specializing in pastries, breads, and doughnuts.

Mario's Pizzeria, 213 W. Tomichi, tel. (970) 641-1374, is a local favorite for thick or thin, white- or wheat-crust pizza, as well as pastas and other Italian dinners. Free delivery. For Mexican food, try **Cactus Jack's,** 9th and Rio Grande, tel. (970) 641-2044, and for Chinese, **Hunan Chinese Restaurant,** 405 W. Tomichi, tel. (970) 641-3600, serving several provincial cuisines, including Szechuan, Cantonese, Mandarin. If you're leaning more toward red meat, a big ol' steak, or a slab of prime the size of a Cadillac, it's tough to beat the **Cattlemen Inn,** 301 W. Tomichi, tel. (970) 641-1061.

CALENDAR

The main event on Gunnison's calendar is **Cattlemen's Days** in mid-July, which includes a rodeo, livestock shows, a parade, and street barbecues. There's also a parade, barbecues, and fireworks on the Fourth of July.

For complete information on Gunnison's annual events, write the chamber of commerce at Box 36, Gunnison, CO 81230, or phone (970) 641-1501.

SERVICES

The offices of the Gunnison **Police Department** are located at 201 W. Virginia, tel. (970) 641-8000. Phone the Gunnison County **Sheriff** at (970) 641-1113 and the **State Patrol** at (970) 641-1242. **Gunnison Valley Hospital** is at 214 E. Denver Ave., tel. (970) 641-1456. The **post office** is at 200 N. Wisconsin, tel. (970) 641-1884.

Recycling

You can recycle aluminum at the **City Market,** 401 W. Georgia, and the **Safeway,** 112 S. Spruce. Gunnison's **Citizens for Recycling** is at 702 W. Tomichi, where you can drop off aluminum, glass, and plastic; for more information, phone (970) 641-2137.

INFORMATION

The **Gunnison Country Chamber of Commerce,** 500 E. Tomichi, is a good place to

begin your visit. Pick up lodging and recreation guides, as well as other brochures, maps, and information. Be sure to get a copy of *Gunnison River Territory Magazine,* a free tourist-oriented publication with historical articles, profiles of locals, and pieces on exploring the Gunnison-area outdoors. Write the chamber at Box 36, Gunnison, CO 81230, or phone (970) 641-1501.

For information on recreational activities in Gunnison National Forest, stop by the Tomichi District Office at 216 N. Colorado, tel. (970) 641-0471.

The Book Worm, 211 N. Main, tel. (970) 641-3693, specializes in books on the outdoors, recreation, and wildlife, and also sells maps. you'll find the **Ann Zegelder Library** (public) at 307 N. Wisconsin, tel. (970) 641-3485.

For **road and weather information,** phone (970) 641-2896.

TRANSPORTATION

United Express provides passenger service to Gunnison County Airport, with increased flights during the ski season. You can also get here by bus; the terminal for **TNMO Bus Lines,** tel. (970) 641-0060, is located at The Gunnison County Airport.

Rent cars in Gunnison from **Budget,** 212 W. US 50, tel. (970) 641-4403, or **Hertz,** 708 S. 12th, tel. (970) 641-2881. **Alpine Express,** tel. (970) 641-5074, offers transportation between Gunnison County Airport and Crested Butte Ski Area.

CRESTED BUTTE

A Sunday evening in June, 1991. The sun has just set over Kebler Pass, and the last light of the day is disappearing from the massive flanks of Mt. Crested Butte. I've been eating pasta and drinking red wine at Angello's and watching the Bulls beat the Lakers in the NBA play-offs. I decide to take one more stroll about town. Up Elk Avenue, past Mountain Earth Natural Foods, Coal Creek Sports, and Kochevar's, then north on 2nd and back down Maroon. And as I walk past the Union Congregational Church at the corner of 4th, I see a single image that says more about Crested Butte than any collage or long-playing study: There, in the weedy lot in front of the church, are some two dozen mountain bikes—some parked, some sprawled, all muddy, dusty, and well ridden, their riders, obviously, inside. There are fewer than six cars.

Surrounded by jagged mountain peaks and the million-plus-acre Gunnison National Forest, Crested Butte (pop. 1,200; elev. 8,885 feet) is one of Colorado's true gems. A young town with a hundred-year history, Crested Butte is famous for some of the best downhill skiing in the state and is quickly gaining a reputation as its mountain bike capital. Crested Butte is actually two communities: the town of Crested Butte, which was founded in 1880, and the village of *Mt.* Crested Butte, founded nearly a century later, when Mt. Crested Butte Ski Area opened. Separated by a three-mile road and connected by a free shuttle system, Crested Butte and Mt. Crested Butte offer just about everything you could want in a vacation—history, outdoor activities, scenery, a wide range of restaurants and lodging, and friendly, down-to-earth locals.

Crested Butte's mining-era heritage is obvious from first glance: Elk Ave., the town's main drag, is lined with Victorian homes and buildings that once served as saloons, banks, and supply shops. Today, many of them still *are* saloons, banks, and supply shops, though the supplies have changed from pickaxes and gold pans to ski poles and biking shorts. And though many of the buildings have been restored, the town has resisted gentrification, thanks in large part to the locals' respect for their history, as well as the town's off-the-beaten-path location.

History

Crested Butte dates to the early 1880s, when it was a thriving gold camp and supply headquarters for the mines in the nearby mountains, particularly in Washington Gulch, where the boom was launched when prospectors found $350,000 in gold nuggets. In the late 1880s, coal was discovered in the area, providing an economic base that would carry the community into the mid-20th century (unlike most Colorado mining camps, which were all but abandoned when ore prices fell in the 1890s).

In the early 1960s, Mt. Crested Butte Ski Area opened, changing forever the tenor of the town.

CRESTED BUTTE AND MT. CRESTED BUTTE

© MOON PUBLICATIONS, INC.

Mount Crested Butte and Mount Crested Butte Village

GRAFTON MARSHALL SMITH

At the base of the ski resort, condominiums and hotels sprang up, as did upscale restaurants and after-ski bars and pizza places. Thankfully, the town of Crested Butte was designated a National Historic District in 1974, guaranteeing the preservation of the old buildings, and an architectural review board was established to monitor renovation and new construction.

In the late 1970s and early 1980s, mountain biking came to Crested Butte big-time, and the area's personality shifted again. In fact, by the late 1980s, Crested Butte, along with Durango, was one of the three or four world mountain-bike meccas. In addition to attracting more athletes to the area, both to live and visit, the new sport is contributing greatly to the area's transformation to a year-round resort area. Though winter is still high season out here, summer is not far behind. And it probably won't be too much longer that local lodge owners feel compelled to lower their rates when the lifts shut down.

WINTER SPORTS

During the winter, the town of Crested Butte, the village of Mt. Crested Butte, and Crested Butte Ski Area virtually become one— ndeed, they're connected every 15 minutes by free shuttle. And during the winter, just about everything revolves around winter sports: Restaurants and lodges swell with vacationing skiers,

students from Western State College in Gunnison cut classes and hit the slopes, and the equipment retail and rental shops do brisk business in boots and bindings, poles and parkas, sweaters and sunscreen. And for good reason: The area claims some of the finest skiing in the Rockies—cross-country and downhill—and some of the prettiest winter scenery this side of the Swiss Alps. In addition, there's a certain sense of abandon here, a nearly palpable feeling of communal *carpe diem,* the result of which is an on-the-edge inventiveness that has spawned sports indigenous only to Crested Butte, like dog fishing and "board joring." Dog fishing came about as a pragmatic solution to the town's notorious dog overpopulation. Though Crested Butte's dog fishermen have now mostly retired, they once trolled in the backs of pick-ups with fishing poles and Milk Bones, hoping to land lunker Labradors and trophy terriers (on the off-chance a poodle was hooked, it would be ceremoniously tossed back). "Board jorists" ride snowboards, water-ski-like, clinging to ropes pulled by horses galloping across meadows.

Downhill Skiing

Crested Butte might not be as well known as Aspen, as big as Vail, or as easy to get to as Winter Park, but there's no denying the friggin' great snow, the runs that range from long, gentle trails to steep-ass chutes and gnarly bump runs, and one of the friendliest, most kick-back attitudes you'll ever find at a ski resort.

With an average of 229 inches of snow falling annually on Crested Butte's 1,160 acres of ski-able terrain, this mountain guarantees that if any place in the state has snow, it'll be here. In addition, there's good skiing for all ability levels, with 13 lifts providing access to 86 trails, although at Crested Butte the expert definitely has the home-court advantage: Since the mid-1980s, Crested Butte has targeted extreme skiers, focusing development on black-diamond and double-black-diamond runs, and recently opening up 550 acres of backcountry chutes, bowls and cornices. Since 1992, Crested Butte has hosted the U.S. Extreme Skiing Championships, and in 1995 hosted the first U.S. Extreme Skiing Snowboarding Championships.

Two of Crested Butte's real prides are its ski school, which was chosen by *Rocky Mountain Sports and Fitness Magazine* as the best in the state, and its overall user-friendliness: A recent *Ski* magazine reader poll ranked Crested Butte 10th in the nation in customer service. Additionally, the resort's **Program for the Physically Challenged** caters to disabled skiers, with instructors trained to teach sit and mono-skiing, three- and four-track techniques, as well as to work with blind, deaf, and developmentally disabled skiers. Handicapped skiers can also rent adaptive equipment such as outriggers.

For more information on Mt. Crested Butte Ski Area, phone (970) 349-2222 or (800) 544-8448. For ski-school information, call (970) 349-2252. Phone the Program for the Physically Challenged at (970) 349-2296.

Cross-Country Skiing

From Telemarking in untracked backcountry bowls to speed skating on groomed track, the Crested Butte area offers plenty of high-quality Nordic skiing. Folks who want to explore the woods have the entire Gunnison National Forest at their ski tips; you can explore old logging and mining roads or take off through the trees. Several of the high mountain passes are ideal for short or extended outings—experienced cross-country. For maps and information, contact the Forest Service District Office, 216 N. Colorado, Gunnison, tel. (970) 641-0471.

You can also get information, as well as equipment, at any of the area's ski shops, in-cluding **Paradise Bikes and Skis,** 224 Elk Ave., Crested Butte, tel. (970) 349-6324, and **Gene Taylor's Sporting Goods,** 19 Emmons Loop, at the base of the lifts in Mt. Crested Butte, tel. (970) 349-5386.

The **Crested Butte Nordic Center,** based at the corner of 2nd St. and Whiterock Ave. in downtown Crested Butte, has 30 km of cross-country track and skating lanes. The center offers lessons (private and group) in all types of Nordic skiing, equipment rental, and guided tours. For information or reservations, phone (970) 349-1707. **Mt. Crested Butte Ski Area** is a favorite among local three-pinners, and its ski school offers lessons and equipment rental; phone (970) 349-2252 for more information.

Other Winter Sports

Though you'll probably want to leave Crested Butte's more innovative winter sports, such as dog fishing and "board joring," to the locals, there are several more conventional winter activities available in the area. **Snowmobile** tours and rentals are offered by a couple of companies. Phone **Action Adventures in Snowmobiling** at (970) 349-5909 or **Burt Rentals and Snowmobile Tours** at (970) 349-7423.

Backcountry powder skiing is available via both helicopter and snowcat at **Irwin Lodge,** tel. (970) 349-5308. With 2,000 skiable acres and a 1,200-foot vertical drop, the lodge offers trips for both intermediate and advanced skiers (also see "Accommodations," following). **Paradise Sleigh Ride Dinners** leave from the Grande Butte Hotel for Bubba's on the mountain on Tuesday, Thursday, and Saturday nights, with dinner including rib, lamb, and lobster; phone (970) 349-2211 for rates and reservations. There are also two ice rinks in town.

For a complete description of the area's winter activities, contact the Crested Butte-Mt. Crested Butte Chamber of Commerce (see "Information," following).

WHEN THE SNOW MELTS

Mountain Biking

Colorado mountain biking was born in Crested Butte. Following the lead of riders from Marin County, California, Crested Beauties attached motorcycle brakes and multiple gears to old "clunkers" and hit the trails. The first outings were over Pearl Pass to Aspen, but the huge number of old logging and mining roads in the area soon spawned a boom in the sport. Today, Crested Butte is one of the true mountain-bike capitals of the world.

Fat Tire Week each summer draws some of the country's best riders to a wide array of competitions, from serious dual slalom on the ski slopes to novelty events like a limbo, a "slow race" (be the *last* one to cross the finish line, without putting your foot down), and mountain-bike polo. The week also provides an opportunity for newcomers to the sport to become better and more knowledgeable riders: Clinics, workshops, and tours are offered daily. (See "Calendar," following, for more information.)

The rest of the summer, too, mountain biking is big in these little communities. Tourists and locals alike explore gravel roads and single-track trails that snake through the valleys and over the ridges of the surrounding mountains. A couple of the classic rides are over **Pearl Pass** to Aspen and **Kebler Pass** to CO 133 near Paonia. Both are steep and demanding, though physical fitness is more important than technical riding ability.

As you'd expect, there are a disproportionate number of bike shops in Crested Butte, all of which are happy to talk bikes and trails. In the town of Crested Butte, stop in at **Paradise Bikes and Skis,** 224 Elk Ave., tel. (970) 349-6324; at Mt. Crested Butte, check out **Crested Butte Sports—Ski and Bike Shop,** in the Evergreen Building at the base of Keystone lift, tel. (970) 349-7516.

Golf

Crested Butte's **Skyland Resort and Country Club** includes a 7,200-yard 18-hole course designed by Robert Trent Jones, Jr. Located on 200 acres at the base of Mt. Crested Butte, Skyland is a full-service resort complex, with tennis courts, private lake, and exercise room, as well as course-side condominiums and homes (also homesites, if you really fall in love with the place).

For tee times and information, phone the pro shop at (970) 349-6131. For accommodations information, phone (970) 349-7541.

River Running

Several rivers in the Crested Butte area offer excellent opportunities for river rats. The lower Taylor River, which flows from Taylor Park Reservoir down through Taylor Canyon to its confluence with the East River at Almont (where the Gunnison River is born), is a kayaker's delight, with rapids ranging from Class II to V. The Gunnison River, slower and broader, is better suited to rafts.

A handful of outfits in the area offer guided tours of local waters, ranging from short float trips to extended backcountry excursions for experienced river runners only. **C B Rafting And Adventures,** 309 Gothic Rd., Crested Butte, tel. (970) 349-7423, has a full-course menu of tours. The company can also arrange horseback, mountain-biking, and snowmobile tours, as well as sleigh rides and dogsledding.

Horseback Riding

Though the area's chief recreation has taken a decidedly different tack of late, and the saddle of choice has changed from the type found on horses to the type found on mountain bikes, Crested Butte remains the quintessential Western community—ranches sprawl in the surrounding valleys, and horses stand in lots a quarter mile from downtown. And by horseback is still one of the best ways to see the high country—the Elk Mountains, the Sawatch Range, the lush river valleys.

The following are among the stables and outfitters offering horses for rent, as well as guided tours, from half-day rides to multi-day pack trips: **C B Rafting and Adventures,** tel. (970) 349-7423; **Fantasy Ranch,** tel. (970) 349-5425; **Harmel's Ranch Resort,** tel. (970) 641-1740; **Just Horsin' Around,** tel. (970) 349-9822; and **Teocalli Outfitters,** tel. (970) 349-5675.

Ballooning

Big Horn Balloon Company offers balloon tours of the Crested Butte area year-round. Flights (guaranteed 30 minutes, usually 45-60 minutes) are $110, and extended flights are $180. Write Box 361, Crested Butte, CO 81224, or phone (970) 349-6335.

Jeep Tours

Located in the heart of high-mountain mining country, with some of Colorado's most spec-

(top) downtown Aspen—boots by Tony Lama? (bottom) Denver's Union Station after dark
(both photos: Stephen Metzger)

frozen fountain in Redstone (Stephen Metzger)

tacular scenery beckoning, Crested Butte is an ideal base from which to explore via 4WD vehicle. In fact, some of the best tours, though they'll take you off the pavement, are perfectly suitable for conventional-traction automobiles (see "Tours," following).

If you are equipped with 4WD, however, you've got substantially more options. Though it's nearly 200 miles from Crested Butte to Aspen by paved road, as the crow flies it's barely 30—just north from town, up over the Elk Mountains, and across the county line. With a 4WD rig, you can at least approximate the general direction of Mr. Crow, by crossing over the mountains at Taylor Pass or Pearl Pass. Topo maps, with 4WD routes indicated, are available at the Gunnison Office of the Gunnison National Forest, 216 N. Colorado, tel. (970) 641-0471.

Camping

Literally surrounded by Gunnison National Forest, the Crested Butte area offers limitless camping opportunities, whether you hike in to a secluded backcountry spot or set up at one of the many nearby Forest Service campgrounds. **Lost Lake Campground** (10 sites, pit toilets, no drinking water) is located about 15 miles west of Crested Butte just south of Kebler Pass Rd. among some of the area's finest scenery. **Cement Creek Campground** (13 sites, pit toilets) is southeast of Crested Butte via CO 135 and Forest Service Rd. 740.

You'll also find Forest Service campgrounds along the Taylor River and at Taylor Park Reservoir (25-40 miles from Crested Butte), as well as National Park Service and privately owned campgrounds west of Gunnison. For more information on Crested Butte-area Forest Service Campgrounds, phone (970) 641-0471.

Other Summer Activities

If the area's mountain biking, horseback riding, golf, four-wheel-driving, and hot-air ballooning aren't enough for you, there's still more. You'll find excellent **fishing** in nearby lakes and streams, particularly the Taylor, East, and Gunnison rivers, and Taylor Park and Blue Mesa reservoirs. For licenses and information, stop in at **Gene Taylor's Sporting Goods** at the base of the lifts at Mt. Crested Butte, tel. (970) 349-5386. For information on guided fly-

fishing trips in the area, try **Coal Creek Sports,** 207 Elk Ave., Crested Butte, tel. (970) 349-6166.

The area is also fraught with excellent **hiking** opportunities. Serious backpackers have the whole of Gunnison National Forest, including the beautiful Elk Mountains and the mighty Sawatch Range, while nature trailers and day hikers can wander any of the region's shorter and more accessible trails.

Several trails near Cement Creek Campground are perfect for day outings. Go south on CO 135 for seven miles and turn east on Cement Creek Road. You'll also find excellent hiking possibilities west of Crested Butte in the Kebler Pass area; **Lost Lake Campground** is a good base for hikes through aspeny hillsides to views that'll knock your socks off. A good source for information and equipment is **The Alpineer,** 419 6th St., Crested Butte, tel. (970) 349-5210. You can also get information and maps from the Forest Service District Office in Gunnison.

ACCOMMODATIONS

Accommodations are available in both the town of Crested Butte and the village of Mt. Crested Butte. In the village, slopeside lodges and condos provide the ultimate ski-in/ski-out experience, though regular shuttle service from the smaller and more colorful inns in town makes lodging there nearly as convenient.

Keep in mind that lodging rates in the Crested Butte area, like those at most ski resorts, vary tremendously from summer to winter: rates will be highest during the peak times of the ski season (Christmas vacation, weekends, etc.) and lowest when the lifts shut down. In fact, many of the lodges offer special off-season incentives just to keep their help busy.

For complete information on lodging packages, including air and ground transportation, lift tickets, equipment, and instruction, phone **Mt. Crested Butte Reservations** at (800) 544-8448, or write Box 1288, Crested Butte, CO 81225. You can also get lodging information from the **Crested Butte/Mt. Crested Butte Chamber of Commerce,** Box 1288, Crested Butte, CO 81224, tel. (800) 545-4505.

Many Colorado lodges offer rooms with kitchenettes.

COLORADO HISTORICAL SOCIETY

For condominium information or reservations, phone **Crested Butte Accommodations** at (800) 821-3718. For condominiums and vacation homes, phone **Rocky Mountain Rentals** at (970) 349-5354.

Mt. Crested Butte Lodging

The **Grand Butte Hotel,** tel. (970) 349-4000 or (800) 642-4422, is located 35 yards from the base of the lifts and features 262 rooms, each with whirlpool, wet bar, and other luxuries. Doubles start at around $150 during the ski season. The smaller (27-room) **Nordic Inn,** tel. (970) 349-5542, is 300 yards from the lifts. Doubles during the ski season start at about $60, which includes continental breakfast and après-ski wine and hors d'oeuvres.

The **Crested Butte Lodge,** tel. (800) 544-8448, is also located in the village and has a large indoor pool, as well as a sauna and outdoor hot tub. For a real winter-wonderland ski vacation, try the **Irwin Lodge,** tel. (970) 349-5308 or (800) 2-IRWIN-2, which during the ski season is accessible only by snowmobile, snowcat, or skis. In addition to offering cozy out-of-the-way lodging and an on-site restaurant, the Irwin also features snowcat ski tours on 1,400 acres of terrain (2,100-foot vertical drop). Call for rates and information packages and other activities.

In Town

Located just a couple of blocks from downtown Crested Butte, the **Cristiana Guesthaus Bed and Breakfast,** tel. (970) 349-5326 or (800) 824-7899, is a classic little ski lodge offering very comfortable rooms, a large downstairs lobby with fireplace, and a sauna and outdoor hot tub with a wonderful view of the mountains. Doubles run about $55-90.

Billing itself a "unique" bed and breakfast, the **Claim Jumper,** tel. (970) 349-6471, is guilty of nothing but understatement. This place is packed floor to ceiling with one of the strangest assortments of odds and ends you'll ever see. Not only is the lobby full of antiques and parlor games, but each room has a bizarre theme and the decor to match: "Ethyl's Room" has a Shell gasoline pump and a jukebox; "Soda Creek" is dedicated to Coca Cola memorabilia; and the best room of all, the "Sports Fan Attic," is packed with mementos and souvenirs from baseball, football, hockey, and other sports—signed game jerseys worn by Jose Canseco and John Elway, signed baseball cards, and, in a separate room, a *putting green.* Doubles run $90-125 in winter ($80-120 summer). Phone for reservations or a brochure describing each room in detail.

The least expensive rooms in the area are probably at the two modest motels, the **Old Town Inn,** tel. (970) 349-6184, and **Forest Queen,** tel. (970) 349-5336. Doubles run the $45-55 range.

FOOD

When the Denver *Post* wrote that Crested Butte "has more fine restaurants per capita than any town in America," the marketing people ate it up (sorry); you'll see the quote all over the area's promotional material. It's not hyperbole, though. There truly are an amazing number of excellent places to eat here—from burger-and-beer joints to upscale, stiff-napkin dining establishments. Some have been around forever; some are brand new; some will probably be gone by the time you read this. At any rate, *salut i force canut.*

Start Me Up
The **Bakery Cafe,** at 3rd and Elk in downtown Crested Butte, tel. (970) 349-7280, opens at 7:30 a.m. daily and is a longtime favorite for breakfast, specializing in fresh baked goods (no preservatives) and gourmet coffees. The Bakery is also open for lunch and dinner, serving pastas, stuffed croissants, and homemade soups and chili.

Dinner Joints
For good Italian food at reasonable prices, try **Angello's,** 501 Elk, tel. (970) 349-5351, serving pizzas, pastas, and antipasto salads. For a slightly more upscale Italian restaurant, try the **Gourmet Noodle,** 411 3rd St., tel. (970) 349-7401; pastas run around $10, and specials (veal, chicken, seafood) are about $12-15. **Giovanni's,** tel. (970) 349-4000, in the Grande Butte Hotel also serves Italian food, its prices, though steep, are said to be fair for the quality of food and service.

You'll find two good Mexican restaurants in Crested Butte. **The Powerhouse Bar y Grill,** 130 Elk, tel. (970) 349-5494, is the more authentic of the two, while **Donita's,** 330 Elk, tel. (970) 349-6674, a cantina-style restaurant, specializes in atmosphere and can really get to hopping when the lifts shut down.

A wonderful after-ski (or after-any-other-activity) hangout is the **Idle Spur,** 226 Elk, tel. (970) 349-5026, one of the best microbrewpubs in the state. The huge interior, with rough-hewn beams and blazing fire allow you to join the rowdy crowd or find a cozy corner. The menu, Mexican food, burgers, salads, and pastas, runs $7-12.

The same *Post* article that lauded Crested Butte's many excellent restaurants singled out **Soupçon,** 2nd and Elk, tel. (970) 349-5448, as one of the area's best. Specializing in French country cuisine, this restaurant has a rotating menu featuring appetizers such as oysters aioli, shrimp Dijon, and duckling mousse, and en-

trees of seafood, veal, or beef. Ideal for an anniversary or other celebration. Another special-occasion dining experience is the **Paradise Sleigh Ride,** which begins at the Grande Butte Hotel at Mt. Crested Butte and takes you up to the ski resort's on-mountain restaurant, where fixed-price dinners include veal, beef, lamb, and seafood. Phone (970) 349-2211 for rates and reservations.

Crested Butte's oldest saloon, the **Wooden Nickel,** 222 Elk, tel. (970) 349-6350, attracts a rowdy and hungry post-slope crowd (bar opens at 3 p.m.; happy hour is 4:30-5:30). Dinners include steak, soups and chili, burgers, seafood, and ribs. For good Chinese food, try **Jimmy Wong's,** tel. (970) 349-4399, at the base of the lifts at Mt. Crested Butte.

ENTERTAINMENT

Crested Butte's a young town, with lots of folks doing some short-term ski and mountain bumming before facing real-world responsibilities—and of course they need places to spend the money they're saving for college. In addition, skiers and other tourists count on at least a certain degree of nightlife as part of their vacation packages. Though this is no Aspen (which is *good* news to most), the area does offer its fair share of places to let off steam.

The Rafters, at Mt. Crested Butte, conveniently located between the bus stop and the base of the Silver Queen lift, is the ski area's main bar and has a classic ski-lodge sundeck. Live music Tuesday through Sunday during the ski season, both in the afternoon for the après-skiers, then later, rockin' and rowdy—also pool and video games, as well as sandwiches and fajitas for when the munchies kick in. You'll also find live music at the **Avalanche Bar and Grill,** tel. (970) 349-7195, and the **Artichoke Bar and Dining Room,** tel. (970) 349-6688, both right at the base of the lifts.

In town, **Kochavar's** at 127 Elk, tel. (970) 349-2299, is another local favorite, where music from live bands often spills out onto the streets. The **Wooden Nickel,** 222 Elk, has been in the hangover business (breeding and nursing) since 1929.

CALENDAR

As Crested Butte grows from a winter-only to a year-round resort, more and more events and activities are being scheduled. Throughout the winter, Mt. Crested Butte Ski Area hosts several races and other slope-side fiestas. On opening day of Mt. Crested Butte Ski Area, usually in late November, lift-ticket prices are rolled way back and the hills are alive with the euphoria induced by winter's return. For complete information on winter activities at Crested Butte Mountain Resort Ski Area, write Box A, Mt. Crested Butte, CO 81225, or phone (800) 544-8448.

One of Crested Butte's popular summer events is **Fat Tire Week** in early to mid-July, when the town, already mountain-bike crazy, becomes the hub of the country's mountain-bike activity. Attracting riders from recreational novices to hard-core racers, events include a dual-slalom race on Mt. Crested Butte's ski slopes, a bicycle rodeo, bicycle polo, clinics and workshops, tours of nearby mountain-bike trails, including Pearl Pass, the dirt road to Aspen that gave birth to Colorado mountain biking back in the mid-'70s. For information and registration forms, write Fat Tire Week, Box 782, Crested Butte, CO 81224, or phone (970) 349-6817.

In addition, several other events and programs punctuate the summer in Crested Butte and Mt. Crested Butte, from softball tournaments and "fun runs" to art shows and wildflower festivals. Highlights include Fourth of July festivities, with street music, food booths, parade, and fireworks; **Aerial Weekend,** a hot-air balloon festival in late July; and the **Festival of the Arts,** a juried art show with street music, food booths, etc. in early August. For a complete calendar of special events in the Crested Butte area, write the Crested Butte-Mt. Crested Butte Chamber of Commerce, Box 1288, Crested Butte, CO 81224, or phone (970) 349-6438.

SERVICES

The office of the Crested Butte **Police Department** is at 409 2nd St.tel. (970) 349-5231. Phone the **State Patrol** in Gunnison at (970) 641-6382. The nearest hospital is **Gunnison Valley Hospital,** 214 E. Denver Ave., Gunnison, tel. (970) 641-1456. Limited medical facilities are available at **Crested Butte Medical Clinic,** 611 Gothic Rd., tel. (970) 349-6651. The clinic specializes in (appropriately enough) sports injuries and medicine.

The Crested Butte **post office** is at 217 Elk Ave., tel. (970) 349-5568. There's also postal service in Mt. Crested Butte at the 3 Seasons Building, tel. (970) 349-7310.

Recycling

For recycling information in Crested Butte, phone **Sunshine Garbage,** (970) 349-5957. You can also drop off recyclables in Gunnison, at the **Citizens for Recycling** drop-off, 702 W. Tomichi, the **City Market,** 401 W. Georgia, and the **Safeway,** 112 S. Spruce.

Child Care

Mt. Crested Butte Ski Area's **Buttetopia Children's Program** offers a range of supervised activities for kids six months to 12 years. Programs include day care for kids six months to six years (no skiing), beginning group ski instruction for kids three to six, private lessons for kids two to six, and "Tag-a-Long" lessons for kids two to 12 and their parents—follow the class and learn how to continue instructing your child in technique and chairlift safety. For reservations or more information, phone (970) 349-2259.

TOURS

Though a trip to Crested Butte is a scenic tour unto itself, several roads in the area offer icing on the cake. Of course, you're limited in the winter, when all but the area's main routes are closed, but during the summer, assuming you don't mind getting off the pavement, you can really do some exploring. Allow a couple of hours to tour one of my favorite routes in the state, **Kebler Pass Rd.,** which lifts up from downtown Crested Butte, winds up over Kebler Pass, past Mt. Baldy, and then drops down to CO 133; there you can either turn north for Redstone and Glenwood Springs or continue west toward Paonia, Delta, and Grand Junction. A wide and well-maintained gravel road, Kebler Pass Rd. features enough vertical rise that you can literally watch the aspens change colors. In the spring, those at lower elevations are green and leafy, while nearer the summit they're still wintry and bare; in the fall, watch them change from green to gold to crimson.

Another interesting drive, and one that's less of a commitment, is the short jaunt to the ghost town of **Gothic,** a Victorian-era silver-mining town with superb views of the East River valley. Gothic, which was pretty much abandoned by the late 1880s, is located about seven miles northeast of Crested Butte; take Forest Service Rd. 327 from Mt. Crested Butte.

Other scenic drives in the area include the Alpine Tunnel tour and the Gunnison, Taylor Park Reservoir, Pitkin, and back to Gunnison loop.

Walking Tour

Crested Butte was designated a National Historic District in 1974, and many of the buildings lining Elk Ave. and some of the side streets date from the late 19th century. The Chamber of Commerce publishes a map and guide to historical Crested Butte, with over 40 sites, many open today as restaurants, inns, and other small businesses. Full of anecdotal history, the little pamphlet is useful and intriguing whether you just want to know the history of the bar at which you plan to plant yourself or you intend to take the full tour.

INFORMATION

As you approach Crested Butte by car (assuming you come in via CO 135, the main route, and not in the back way, over one of the several unpaved mountain-pass roads), you'll meet almost head-on with a chamber of commerce **visitor informa-**

tion center. This is a good place to stuff your pockets with brochures on things to do and see while you're in the area, as well as to pick up lodging and dining guides. To stock up before your visit, write **Crested Butte-Mt. Crested Butte Chamber of Commerce,** Box 1288, Crested Butte, CO 81224, or phone (800) 545-4505. For good selections of books on recreation and wildlife in the area, check out **Heg's Place,** tel. (970) 349-5304, in Crested Butte, or stop on your way into town at **The Book Worm,** 211 N. Main (CO 135), Gunnison. The **Crested Butte Library,** tel. (970) 349-6535, is located in the Old Rock Schoolhouse and is open Monday, Wednesday, and Friday 1-5 p.m. and Tuesday 6-8 p.m.

For information on **Gunnison National Forest,** stop by the ranger station at 216 N. Colorado, Gunnison, or phone (970) 641-0471.

For **road and weather information,** phone (970) 641-2896.

TRANSPORTATION

American Airlines, United Express, Delta, Continental, and **Continental Express** offer regular passenger service to Gunnison, with daily nonstop flights during the ski season from Chicago, Atlanta, and Dallas/Ft. Worth, as well as connecting flights from Denver. Most hotels in Crested Butte offer free airport shuttle service for guests. In addition, you can arrange ground transportation between Gunnison and Crested Butte with **Alpine Express,** tel. (970) 641-5074 or (800) 822-4844.

The village of Mt. Crested Butte and the ski area are located three miles from the town of Crested Butte. Free shuttle buses run between the two about every 15 minutes till midnight during ski season.

CURECANTI NATIONAL RECREATION AREA

Paralleling the Gunnison River from Gunnison to Black Canyon of the Gunnison National Monument, Curecanti National Recreation Area includes three reservoirs, 10 separate campgrounds (with over 300 sites), 18 picnic areas, and four visitor centers, as well as marinas, boat ramps, and hiking trails. Extremely popular with anglers—who know the lakes' depths hold lunker rainbow, brown, lake, and brook trout, in addition to kokanee salmon—the area is also excellent for wildlife watching: Ducks and geese and other waterfowl are common in the area, as are bald and golden eagles and great blue herons, and elk, bighorn sheep, and mule deer can be seen in the area in winter.

The three-dam system was designed to provide irrigation water and to generate hydroelectric power. Though the dams' construction met (understandably) with opposition from environmentalists and conservationists, the result has been the development of one of the state's best all-around recreation areas.

Blue Mesa, where you'll find the majority of recreational activities, is the largest of the three lakes and the system's main storage reservoir. Morrow Point and Crystal reservoirs generate power and control water flow through Black Canyon of the Gunnison. Dozens of creeks flow into the three lakes and the stretches of Gunnison between them; the streams flowing into

Blue Mesa Reservoir form long arms gouging into the surrounding mesas and plateaus and creating a fjordlike appearance to the waterway.

Camping

The four largest and most developed campgrounds at Curecanti are **Elk Creek, Lake Fork, Stevens Creek,** and **Cimarron.** Other smaller campgrounds, some nestled in the lakes' narrow arms, are better suited for getting away from crowds, and several of the campgrounds offer access to hiking and self-guided interpretive trails. Group camping is available at **East Elk Creek Campground** (by reservation only). To make camping reservations, or for more information on camping at Curecanti National Recreation Area, phone (970) 641-2337.

Fishing

Though rainbow trout are the most commonly caught fish in the park, the waters also hold brown, lake (Mackinaw), and brook trout, and kokanee salmon. Fishing is best in spring, shortly after ice-out, and again in the fall, when big browns head up into the tributaries to spawn. Kokanee can be legally snagged beginning in October (check regulations at nearby sporting goods stores or with the Division of Wildlife).

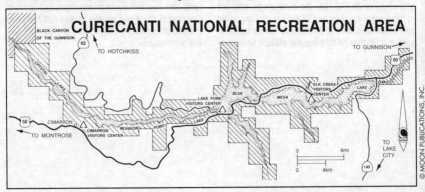

The area can be productive from both shore and boat, though the latter is the better way to go, especially if you're looking to hook into one of the monster lake trout, which prefer the cold, deep water (45-70 feet and deeper). Rental boats are available at Elk Creek and Lake Fork.

Water Sports
Blue Mesa Reservoir offers the broadest range of water sports and boating, with waterskiing and windsurfing popular in the summer when the water (and air) warms up. In addition, the lake is large enough—20 miles long, with three separate basins—and contains enough arms and inlets to offer sailors plenty of water to explore. Boating on Crystal and Morrow Point lakes is restricted to hand-carried craft.

Swimming is permitted at Curecanti, but keep in mind this water's *cold*. Also, remember swimming is not permitted from docks, launch ramps, and unanchored boats.

Boat Tours
If you want to get out on the water but neither have your own boat nor feel like renting, you can take a tour with an interpreter/naturalist, who discusses the area's geology, history, and wildlife, as well as the role of the dams in irrigation and power generation. Tours are offered regularly throughout the summer. For information and reservations, phone the Elk Creek Marina at (970) 641-0402.

Winter Sports
Winter activities in Curecanti National Recreation Area include ice fishing, snowmobiling, and cross-country skiing. Be sure to check with rangers to make sure the ice is thick enough (four inches to support an adult, seven to support a snowmobile). The area's nature trails are perfect for Nordic skiing, or you can break your own trail. You'll find a specifically designated beginning cross-country ski trail at the Elk Creek Visitor Center.

Information and Visitor Centers
The **Elk Creek Visitor Center** is the best place to get oriented. In addition to viewing a slide/tape presentation on the area, you can pick up maps and other publications and ask questions of the rangers. There are also visitor information centers at Cimarron and Lake Fork. At Cimarron, you can view a restored 19th-century Denver and Rio Grande Railroad engine and cars.

For more information on Curecanti National Recreation Area, write Superintendent, Curecanti National Recreation Area, 102 Elk Creek, Gunnison, CO 81230, or phone (970) 641-2337.

BLACK CANYON OF THE GUNNISON NATIONAL MONUMENT

A jagged incision—2,000 feet deep and 53 miles long—in the rocky Gunnison Uplift, Black Canyon of the Gunnison is without doubt one of the Southwest's most startling natural wonders. Named for the gorge's primarily dark gray Precambrian rocks of gneiss and schist, Black Canyon is a haven for hikers, campers, backpackers, and especially rock climbers. Black Canyon of the Gunnison National Monument was established by President Herbert Hoover on March 2, 1933, and encompasses one of the most stunning stretches of the gorge—a 12-mile length of river and sheer canyon wall. It includes two specific scenic drives (one of which, North Rim Rd., is closed in winter). In addition, the monument includes two campgrounds, a handful of nature trails, view points, picnic areas, and a visitor center.

Formed over some two million years by the erosive powers of the Gunnison River, Black Canyon was known 10,000 years ago to nomadic bands of Folsom people, who hunted deer and other game along the gorge's rim. Later, in the 17th, 18th, and 19th centuries, Utes also hunted in the area, chasing deer and buffalo to the canyon's rims, where they'd trap and kill the animals at close range or force them off the cliffs so they'd fall to their deaths.

Members of the Hayden Expedition of 1873-74 were probably the first nonnatives to see the canyon. Then toward the end of the 19th century, a survey crew for the Denver and Rio

Hayden Expedition, 1870—pausing for espressos and croissants

Grande Railroad proposed diverting water from the Gunnison River west to the Uncompahgre Valley for irrigation. In 1900, surveyors entered the canyon by boat, but their efforts were largely unsuccessful. A year later, two explorers lashed gear and belongings onto a rubber mattress and, after floating, swimming, and scrambling for nine days and 33 miles, emerged on the far side with the opinion that a tunnel was indeed possible. In late 1904, work was begun, and over five years later, in September of 1909, the seven-mile Gunnison Diversion Tunnel was completed.

When visiting Black Canyon, don't miss the visitor center, just inside the National Monument boundary. Here you'll find exhibits on the area's geology, history, flora, and fauna, and you can join regularly scheduled nature walks to the very edge of the canyon's rim, where a ranger discusses the gorge's formation and natural history and will answer questions. The visitor center is

open daily May-Sept., with reduced hours of operation in spring and fall; closed in winter.

To get to Black Canyon of the Gunnison National Monument, take US 50 west from Gunnison 60 miles or east from Montrose six miles and turn north on CO 347. During the summer only, you can get to the North Rim by taking CO 92 east from Delta or north from its junction with US 50, about 30 miles west of Gunnison.

For more information, write 223 E. Main, Montrose, CO 81402, or phone (970) 249-7036 (main office) or 249-1915 (visitor center).

Camping
Both campgrounds in Black Canyon National Monument are open May through October. **South Rim Campground** (102 sites), located near the visitor center off CO 347, is the most accessible of the two. During the winter, you can't even get to **North Rim Campground** (13 sites), as the gravel road in from CO 92 is closed.

DELTA

Located at the junction of US 50 and CO 92, and smack dab in the middle of some of Colorado's richest ranch land, Delta (pop. 3,900; elev. 4,980 feet) is a natural hub for travelers and ranchers alike and is also the headquarters for Grand Mesa, Uncompahgre, and Gunnison national forests. Not exactly a tourist destination in itself, Delta does offer several motels, cafes, and markets for travelers looking to rest for a while or to pull off the road for the night. It's also got a couple of nice city parks.

Billing itself "The City of Murals," Delta displays seven different murals on downtown buildings. The paintings, done by local artists, depict the history, economy, and recreational activities in the area. Examples include a pair of elk in a mountain meadow and a collection of fruit labels used by Delta County growers. Watch for the murals on Main St. (US 50) as you arrive either from the north or south.

Delta County Historical Museum

A good place to get a sense of Delta's past, this museum displays an array of ranching and farming tools, including harnesses and saddles, as well as dolls and other domestic items and historical photos. Entomologists take note: The museum's butterfly collection includes specimens that are extinct and are the only known surviving examples.

The museum, located one block east of Main St. at the corner of 3rd and Palmer, is open Tues.-Sat. 10 a.m.-4 p.m., Memorial Day through Labor Day, limited hours the rest of the year. Admission is $1. For information, or to arrange special tours, phone (970) 874-3791.

Fort Uncompahgre

This is a living-history recreation of the original fort built in 1826 by French fur

trader Antoine Roubideau. Costumed docents explain, demonstrate, and allow visitors to experience firsthand the variety of activities that defined frontier life for early 19th-century Colorado pioneers.

The museum is located at Confluence Park just north of Delta. Take US 50 north to Gunnison River Dr., and turn west. Admission is $3.50 for adults, with discounts for kids and seniors.

History as Theater

Thunder Mountain Lives, billed as a "Saga of the Old West," is an outdoor drama production that brings to life the history of Delta and the surrounding area. See and hear the stories of the Southern Utes, Alferd Packard, and Captain John Gunnison, and visit a model of a 19th-century fur-trading post.

Performances run mid-June through Labor Day at Confluence Park, just off US 50. Tickets are $7.50 for adults and $4.50 for kids (slightly less if bought in advance—available at the Delta Visitor Center, see below). For tickets or information, write the Delta Chamber of Commerce, 301 Main St., Delta, CO 81416, or phone (970) 874-8616.

Delta Dinosaurs

Delta County is the site of several important dinosaur-fossil discoveries. In 1971, paleontologists discovered the humerus of a brachiosaurus, and in 1979, a nine-foot scapula and a 48-inch-wide vertebra from an ultrasaurus were discovered.

Delta resident Vivian Jones, who has been collecting dinosaur bones and fossils for 40 years, welcomes visitors to her small private museum. Reservations are required. Phone (970) 874-8909.

Ute Council Tree

Included in the book *Famous and Historic*

Ute Council Tree

BOB RACE

DELTA

Trees of the United States and recognized as a Colorado Landmark, the Ute Council Tree is an over 200-year-old cottonwood in north Delta. Between 1852 and 1887, Ute Chief Ouray and his wife, Chipeta (the only woman allowed to sit at the tree), met with white settlers in attempts to bring peace to western Colorado. The Ute Council Tree is 85 feet tall and seven feet in diameter.

To get there, watch for the small sign on US 50 just north of the bridge across the river.

Ute Trail
This four-mile hiking trail, which follows one of the main routes used by Utes for centuries before settlers arrived, takes you from the south rim of the Gunnison Gorge down to the Gunnison River. This is an excellent area to view the geology of the area, as the trail switches back several times in its 1,200-foot descent, displaying sedimentary rocks, as well as metamorphic and igneous formations. In addition, bighorn sheep and river otters (both recently introduced by the Colorado Division of Wildlife) can be seen in the canyon.

To get to the trailhead, where you'll find picnic tables and a parking lot, take CO 92 five miles east to Austin, and go south for three miles on County Rd. 2200. At County Rd. 2450, go east for five miles and watch for the sign to the access road (two miles of dirt; recommended for high-clearance vehicles only).

PRACTICALITIES

Accommodations
The **Sundance Best Western,** tel. (970) 874-9781, on the south end of town at 903 Main (US 50) has rooms starting at about $40. A new **Comfort Inn,** on the north end of town, 180 Gunnison River Dr., tel. (970) 874-1000, has doubles running about $45. Just across the Gunnison River is the **Riverwood Inn and RV Park,** tel. (970) 874-5787. East of town on US 92, you'll find the Delta **KOA** campground, tel. (970) 874-3918.

Food
A classic western junction town, Delta offers more than its share of cafes and fast-food restaurants. In addition, you'll find a number of specialty restaurants. **Pony Espresso,** 447 Main, tel. (970) 874-1774, serves breakfast and lunch, specializing (of course!) in espresso drinks, but also offering sandwiches, salads, and homemade soups. **Daveto's,** 520 Main, tel. (970) 874-8277 is a favorite for Italian food, with pizzas and pastas running $6-16. **Sun Wah,** 142 Eaton, tel. (970) 874-4884, has Cantonese and Hunan food, with entrees in the $7 range (weekdays there's an all-you-can eat buffet for $4.99). You'll also find the old standby, **City Market,** at the corner of Main and 6th, for deli food and a salad bar.

Information
The **Delta Chamber of Commerce and Visitors Center,** tel. (970) 874-8616, is right downtown at 3rd and Main. An RV parking lot is located directly behind the building; turn west from Main. For information on camping, fishing, hiking, etc. in any of the surrounding National Forest lands, stop in at the headquarters for the Grand Mesa, Uncompahgre, and Gunnison national forests, located about a mile south of town on US 50; phone (970) 874-7691.

HIGHWAY 50/550 SOUTH

US Highway 50 drops south out of Grand Junction, shooting down between the Uncompahgre Plateau on the west and Grand Mesa on the east. The Gunnison River follows the 40-mile stretch of highway from Grand Junction to Delta, while the Uncompahgre parallels the 48-mile Delta-to-Ridgway stretch. In Montrose, US 50 doglegs to the east, while 550 continues south.

Just south of Ridgway, the highway begins to lift up into the mountains, and then, suddenly, at Ouray, you're facing an apparently unpassable wall of mountain granite. Don't worry: The road continues. In fact, at Ouray, US 550 begins a dramatic series of switchbacks up over Red Mountain Pass (elev. 11,008 feet), then drops down again into Silverton before winding back up over Molas Divide (elev. 10,910 feet) and through some of the state's most gorgeous scenery. Fifty miles south of Silverton, US 550 slips into Durango.

This is one of the Western Slope's most well-traveled roadways. Not only do many motorists take advantage of the quick northern section, which provides the best access between Grand Junction and Telluride, but many drive the southern route for its scenery alone. The Ouray-to-Silverton section, known as the Million Dollar Highway, offers unparalleled views of the Colorado Rockies at their most dramatic.

MONTROSE

The seat of Montrose County, Montrose (pop. 8,884; elev. 5,794 feet) is a small crossroads town in the center of the fertile Uncompahgre Valley on the Rocky Mountain's stark Western Slope. Used during the late-19th century as a supply point for miners working the Uncompahgre River, which flows through the valley, as well as those probing the 14,000-foot San Juan Mountains to the south, Montrose today serves as a hub for ranchers, hunters, and others exploring the vast recreational opportunities afforded by the southwestern Rockies, particularly Black Canyon of the Gunnison National Monument, and the Native American ruins of the Four Corners area.

Just over a mile above sea level, Montrose is blessed with a fairly moderate year-round climate, the town's lowest average temperatures scarcely dropping into the high 30s (in January) and its highs maxing out at about 90° (in July). Average maximum temperature is 63°, and local boosters like to brag about Montrose's 250 or so annual days of sunshine.

History

Like most of the country's most desirable areas, the Uncompahgre Valley was once Native American land. Southern Utes had farmed and hunted in the region for centuries before Europeans arrived, Chief Ouray and his wife Chipeta overseeing local Utes in the fertile river valley in the mid- to late-19th century—until the tribe was "removed" in 1881 by the United States government.

Oliver D. "Pappy" Loutsenhizer was one of the first white settlers in the valley, arriving first in the fall of 1873 with a group of gold-seeking

MONTROSE

TO DELTA

50

MOST MONTROSE ACCOMMODATIONS

LOCUST ST.

50

N. 1st ST.

N. TOWNSEND AVE.

MAIN ST.

S. 1st ST.

TO BLACK CANYON OF THE GUNNISON

UNCOMPAHGRE RIVER

MONTROSE CO. HISTORICAL MUSEUM

SELIG AVE.

S. TOWNSEND AVE.

PARK AVE.

MESA AVE.

90

CHIPETA DR.

E. OAK GROVE RD.

BLM INFORMATION CENTER

VISITOR INFORMATION CENTER

ANDERSON RD.

789

TO OURAY AND TELLURIDE

550

UTE INDIAN MUSEUM

NOT TO SCALE

© MOON PUBLICATIONS, INC.

COLORADO HISTORICAL SOCIETY

Colorado State Prison was Alferd Packard's home for several years after his conviction on charges of culinary impropriety.

adventurers led by Alferd Packard. Though Loutsenhizer and part of the group eventually turned back (at the urging of Ouray), Packard continued, even as winter temperatures and snow began to fall. Ultimately, Packard was convicted of cannibalizing five members of his splinter group after they became snowbound near Lake City (see "Lake City," under "North of Pagosa Springs" following).

Loutsenhizer returned to the valley several years later and, in 1881, with his friend Joseph Selig, laid out what was to become the town of Montrose—first dubbed "Pomona," after the Roman goddess of fruit, but later renamed after the Duchess of Montrose, a character in a Walter Scott novel. Shortly after its founding, Montrose saw two big changes that would have great effects on its face and character. The first was the railroad, which pushed through in 1882, providing opportunities for local farmers to ship their crops, especially cotton and sugar beets, to destinations throughout the United States. The second was the Gunnison Diversion Tunnel.

Begun in 1904 and completed in 1909, the seven-mile passage provided irrigation water from the Gunnison River northeast of town to Uncompahgre Valley farmers whose increasing croplands were requiring more and more water. One of the Bureau of Reclamation's first projects, the tunnel had a much-celebrated inauguration, with the dedication conducted by President Taft.

Ute Indian Museum And Ouray Memorial Park

Dedicated in 1956 by the Colorado Historical Society, this small museum sits on land once farmed by the Southern Ute chief Ouray and displays artifacts from the Ute culture as well as dioramas and exhibits describing European exploration of the area, including the Dominguez-Escalante expedition of 1776. In addition to the collections of ceremonial artifacts, some of which once belonged to Ouray himself, the museum and park include a monument to the chief and the grave of his wife, Chipeta, as well as picnic facilities for passers-through.

The museum is located two miles south of the town center on US 550 and is open Mon.-Sat. 10 a.m.-5 p.m. and Sunday 1-5 p.m., May 15-Sept. 30. The rest of the year, the museum is open for school groups and pre-arranged tours. Admission is $2 for adults and $1 for kids and seniors. For more information, phone (970) 249-3098, or write 1736, Montrose, CO 81402.

Montrose County Historical Museum

Providing a general history of the Uncompahgre Valley and the Western Slope—from Ute occupation through 20th-century irrigation and development—this museum highlights the late-19th-century pioneer and settler. Especially impressive are the museum's excellent displays of historical photos, particularly of Chief Ouray and his wife, Chipeta, and of the early days of the railroad—as well as the collections of artifacts, including Ute arrowheads and domestic items, from toys to medical equipment to musical instruments. Also of interest are replicas of nearby petroglyphs and a full-size homesteader's cabin with original furnishings. The museum's library includes Montrose newspapers from 1896-1940, photos, and several historical publications.

The Montrose County Historical Museum is open Memorial Day through September Mon.-Sat. 9 a.m.-5 p.m. The museum is on W. Main St.; admission is $2 for adults, with discounts for kids and seniors. For more information, phone (970) 249-2085.

PARKS AND RECREATION

Golf

Montrose's 18-hole golf course (1350 Birch St., by way of Hillcrest Dr.) is open to the public 7 a.m.-7 p.m. For information and tee times, phone (970) 249-8551.

River Running

Rafting and float trips are also popular on Montrose-area rivers, including the nearby Gunnison and Uncompahgre. Most outfits also book trips to other Colorado waters as well. Go for a half day, or take a three- or four-day excursion. Prices start around $60.

Several Montrose companies offer trips, including **Gunnison River Expeditions,** tel. (970) 249-4441.

ACCOMMODATIONS

Hotels and Motels

Montrose's "Motel Row" is on the east end of town on Main St./US 50 E, where you'll find a dozen or so places to bed down. There are newer hotel-type lodges, as well as mom-and-pop places. The **Best Western Red Arrow Inn,** 1702 E. Main, tel. (970) 249-9641 or (800) 468-9323, is one of the more fully appointed lodges in town (exercise room, fax and copy services, convention facilities, etc.) and has 60 rooms ranging in price from about $70 to $100. Also on US 50 E, the **Black Canyon Motel,** 1605 E. Main, tel. (970) 249-3495 or (800) 453-4911, has good clean rooms for about $35-60. At the **Super 8,** 1705 E. Main, tel. (970) 249-9294, rooms run $40-65; RV and truck parking available.

The **San Juan Inn,** 1480 US 550 S, tel. (970) 249-6644, is one of the first you'll come to as you approach from the south; rooms for two start at $45. The indoor pool and jacuzzi are especially nice after a day on the road.

Camping and RVing

Though it gets a bit cold on the Rockies' Western Slope for winter camping, from late spring to early fall the weather's much more accommodating, and the Montrose area offers a number of campgrounds, both private and government run. The **Hangin' Tree RV Park,** 17250 US 50, tel. (970) 249-9966 has laundry facilities, showers, and a convenience store, and sites with full hookups for $10-15; open year-round. The Montrose **KOA,** 200 N. Cedar, tel. (970) 249-9177, is open Memorial Day through Labor Day and has both tent and RV sites, showers, laundry, pool, and small store; rates run $12-16.

In addition to the campgrounds at Black Canyon of the Gunnison and Curecanti National Recreation Area (see above), you'll find a number of Forest Service campgrounds near Cimarron, in the Uncompahgre National Forest about a half-hour east of Montrose: **Big Cimarron Campground** offers free camping at 16 sites along the Big Cimarron River—no drinking water available; **Beaver Lake Campground** has 16 sites on Beaver Creek; the 60 units at **Silver Jack Campground** on Silver Jack Lake provide access to good boating and fishing on the reservoir, as well as to hiking into the Big Blue Wilderness Area. To get to all three campgrounds, take US 50 about 24 miles east of Montrose and then Owl Creek/Cimarron Rd. (dirt) 20 miles south.

FOOD

Montrose offers a decent number of non-franchise, non-fast-food restaurants. **The Whole Enchilada,** 44 S. Grand, tel. (970) 249-1881, serves a variety of Mexican and Southwestern dishes, including fajitas, chimichangas, and blue-corn enchiladas. Most dinners are under $10. If you're more in the mood for a classic steak-and-seafood joint, try the **Backwoods Inn,** 103 Rose Ln., tel. (970) 249-1961. Entrees include prime rib, steaks, lobster, and chicken. Live entertainment Wednesday through Saturday evenings. For Italian food, try **Sicily's,** 1135 E. Main, tel. (970) 240-9199, specializing in homemade pizza and pastas and, weather permitting, serving on a cozy outdoor patio.

A favorite among truckers and other passers-through is **Starvin' Arvin's,** tel. (970) 249-7787, on US 50 on the south side of town, right next door to the San Juan Inn. This moderately priced family-style restaurant serves breakfasts, lunches, and dinners daily 6 a.m.-10 p.m.. For those on the run, **El Sombrero,** tel. (970) 249-0217, offers Mexican takeout Tues.-Sat. 11 a.m.-9 p.m. and Sunday 11 a.m.-10 p.m. For an early-morning caffeine and sugar fix, stop in at **Daylight Donuts,** 219 N. 1st—fresh-baked doughnuts and coffee to get your motor runnin'.

SERVICES

Phone the **Montrose Police Department** at (970) 249-6609 and the **Montrose County Sheriff** at (970) 249-6606. The offices of the **State Patrol** are at 2420 N. Townsend, tel. (970) 249-4392. **Montrose Memorial Hospital** is at 800 S. 3rd St., tel. (970) 249-2211. Montrose's main **post office** is at 321 S. 1st Street.

Recycling

Drop off most recyclables at **Montrose Recycle Center,** 1215 N. Townsend. The **City Market,** 128 S. Townsend, and **Safeway,** 1329 S. Townsend, will take aluminum.

Calendar

Montrose is busy with events throughout the year. A few highlights are the **Fourth of July** parade and fireworks display, the **Montrose County Fair** (August), and a number of **Christmas shows and pageants** (December). For a complete listing of annual events, write the Montrose Chamber of Commerce (50 N. Townsend, Montrose, CO 81401).

TOURS

The Montrose Chamber of Commerce has delineated several specific scenic day-trips from town and has published maps with mileages, average driving times, and other tips. Visit Ridgway State Recreation Area, Black Canyon Na-tional Monument, Curecanti National Recreation Area, or Grand Mesa National Forest—all of which are also discussed in this book. For maps and information, contact the chamber at 550 N. Townsend, Montrose, CO 81401, or phone (800) 873-0244.

For guided tours, contact **San Juan Mountain Tours,** 2850 Star Ridge Court, Montrose, CO 81401, or phone (970) 249-1535.

INFORMATION

You can obtain further information about the Montrose area by stopping by or writing the visitor information center, 2490 S. Townsend, Montrose, CO 81401, or by phoning (970) 249-1726—the visitor center is open seven days a week, May through October only. You can also write the Montrose County Chamber of Commerce, 550 N. Townsend, Montrose, CO 81401, or call (970) 249-5515 or (800) 873-0244—open Mon.-Fri. 8 a.m.-5 p.m. Be sure to ask for the *Montrose Visitors Guide,* which includes a full listing of lodging and restaurants, as well as information sources for various recreational pursuits (hunting to scuba diving).

Montrose's daily newspaper is the independently owned **Montrose Daily Press** (not published weekends or holidays), available for 25 cents in racks around town. For subscription information, write 535 1st St., Montrose, CO 81401, or phone (970) 249-3444.

For **road conditions and weather information,** phone (970) 249-9363 or (800) 821-4765.

TRANSPORTATION

United Express/Mesa Airways, tel. (970) 249-8455, offers passenger service to **Montrose Airport,** tel. (970) 249-3203, located on the north end of town, where you can also rent cars. Phone **Budget** at (970) 249-6083, **Hertz** at (970) 249-9447, or **Dollar,** (970) 249-3770.

The Montrose **bus depot** is at 132 N. 1st, tel. (970) 249-6673. For taxi service, phone (970) 249-8880.

RIDGWAY

Located at the junction of US 550 and CO 62, Ridgway (pop. 370; elev. 6,900 feet) marks the point where scenery for southbound travelers begins to get absolutely breathtaking. Telluride-bound travelers will turn west at Ridgway, ascending the 8,970-foot Dallas Divide Pass before dropping back down to CO 145 and looping back into the little box canyon from the west. As you rise up out of Ridgway toward the pass, look back over your shoulder to your left at the towering Mt. Sneffels Range, the highest point of which is 14,150-foot Mt. Sneffels.

If you're continuing south from Ridgway, you'll follow the course of the Uncompahgre River for 10 miles before reaching Ouray, a tiny Swiss-like village at the foot of Red Mountain Pass. From Ouray, you'll begin a switchback assault on the pass, climbing almost 3,500 feet in about a half dozen miles.

Ridgway dates from 1891, when it was a link on the Rio Grande Southern Railroad's route to Durango (175 miles to the south). Throughout the 20th century, Ridgway has served as a supply center for miners working claims scattered in the San Juan Mountains. In addition, the little town is a natural hub for cattle ranchers in the surrounding valley.

Rail service to Ridgway was halted in 1951, when shipping rates became prohibitively expensive, though the little town still sees plenty of travelers, due in large part to its "gateway" location. In the early 1970s, the movie *True Grit* was filmed in Ridgway.

Ridgway State Park
This recently opened (1989) recreation area two miles north of Ridgway surrounds a 1,000-acre reservoir on the Uncompahgre River. Though the area is still being developed, current facilities include a campground with almost 200 sites, a boat-launching ramp, picnic facilities, and a visitor center. Plans call for additional campsites, as well as increased fishing and picnic facilities, plus a special area for windsurfing.

For information or to reserve campsites, phone (970) 626-5822.

Food
Passing through Ridgway en route to a day at Telluride? Need a lift? Try **Linda's Bakery,** 520 W. Sherman, tel. (970) 626-5803 (south side of the road). Large coffees, sugary pastries, muffins—to go or eat in the little cafe. Brought to you by San Juan Mommas, Inc.

For Mexican food, try the **Adobe Inn,** 251 Liddell Dr., tel. (970) 626-5939. Other Ridgway options include the **Sunset,** 153 N. US 550, tel. (970) 626-5494, which features classic American fare for breakfast, lunch, and dinner. At the **Ridgway Mountain Market,** tel. (970) 626-5811, on CO 62, you can build your own sandwich (and pay by the pound), or choose from other deli items, including chicken, ribs, and, well, "everything from wieners to caviar." **The True Grit Cafe,** 123 N. Lena, tel. (970) 626-5739, displays a variety of memorabilia from the film.

Accommodations
The **Adobe Inn,** 251 Liddell, tel. (970) 626-5939, is a hostel with three rooms. The **Sunset Motel,** 153 N. US 550, tel. (970) 626-5494, has rooms for two for under $30. There's also a **Super 8 Lodge,** at 373 Palomino Trail, tel. (970) 626-5444, where doubles are about $45.

Information
For more information on Ridgway, write the **Ouray County Chamber of Commerce,** Box 145, Ouray, CO 81427, tel. (970) 325-4747 or (800) 228-1876. Be sure to ask for a copy of the *Ouray County Vacation Guide,* a very thorough guide (60 pages) to communities in the area, including lodging, dining, and recreation opportunities. The **Ridgway Visitor Center** is located at 102 Village Square West, tel. (970) 626-5868.

OURAY

Nestled in a natural amphitheater in a narrow box canyon and surrounded by peaks that tower 5,000 feet above the valley floor, Ouray (pop. 700; elev. 7,800 feet) is known as the "Little Switzerland of America." Approached from either the north or the south, Ouray will certainly arrest the eye. As you enter the valley from the north, the high walls seem to close in on you, and as you pass through the quiet little town—its streets lined with Victorian-era homes and lavish old hotels—you can't help but be struck by the seemingly unpassable pass ahead. All around you the mountains rise: to the west, White House Mountain (elev. 13,493 feet); to the south, Hayden Mountain (elev. 13,100 feet); and to the northwest, Cascade Mountain (elev. 12,100 feet). Ouray (pronounced "you-RAY") seems trivialized by nature.

If you arrive from the south, you'll be switchbacking down Red Mountain Pass and looking at the town from almost straight above. This is when it really seems like a Little Switzerland, the colorful buildings and green meadows at the base of these towering peaks looking like something right off a calendar or the cover of a travel magazine. The view is breathtaking.

Don't let it take so much of your breath that you forget to keep your eyes on the road; this is a steep sucker, with dramatic horseshoe turns. Look away from the road for too long and you could end up taking the shortcut to town. Instead, take advantage of the turnouts provided for sightseeing and picture taking.

The town takes its name from the Southern Ute Chief Ouray, whose people had been coming to the valley for centuries before the white men came to mine and ranch. The hot mineral waters that bubble up from the ground in several different places were said to have healing powers. Today those same waters soothe the aches of road-weary motorists, as well as hikers, cross-country skiers, horseback riders, and others who enjoy relaxing in the hot mineral waters after a day of recreation. You'll find hot springs at several local lodges as well as the municipal pool and park at the north end of town.

History

Ouray dates from 1875, when prospectors entered the valley and discovered a number of rich silver lodes in the nearby mountains. The town was incorporated in the fall of the next year and named for Chief Ouray, universally praised for his intellect and attempts to bring whites and Native Americans together in harmony. Soon, the Uncompahgre area's first newspaper, the *Ouray Times,* was founded after a wagon train hauled type and presses from Cañon City.

Ouray boomed in the early 1880s but then went temporarily belly up when the silver market crashed in 1893. In 1896, however, carpenter Thomas F. Walsh discovered gold in the Camp Bird silver mine, bought rights to the mine for $20,000, and quickly became one of Colorado's

Ouray (the Arrow), the Southern Ute Chief for which the town is named

laborer-turned-millionaires. Until 1902, the mine yielded ore worth between $3 and $4 million a year, sometimes matching Walsh's initial investment in a single week. By 1910, the mine had produced $26 million in gold.

Many of the Ouray-area mines are still worked, although as costs of extraction have increased disproportionately to the price of gold, the industry has become less and less important. Instead, Ouray and Ouray County rely on tourism and ranching to keep local economies vital.

ATTRACTIONS

Bachelor-Syracuse Mine

Named for three bachelors and a group of miners from Syracuse, New York, this mine produced $90 million in gold and $8 million in silver, as well as respectable amounts of lead, zinc, and copper. Tours of the mine, which take you 3,350 feet into the side of Gold Hill, offer an excellent sense of Ouray's early (and dangerous!) mining days. Be sure to bring a sweater, as the temperatures inside stay right about 50° Fahrenheit.

The Bachelor-Syracuse Mine is open to the public late May through mid-September. Tours are on the hour 9 a.m.-6 p.m. late June through August and 10 a.m.-5 p.m. the rest of the season. Rates are $8.95 for adults, kids and seniors discounted. For an added fee, you can pan for gold and keep what you find. For information or reservations, write Bachelor-Syracuse Mine Tour, County Rd. 14, Drawer 380W, Ouray, CO 81427, or phone (970) 325-4500.

Ouray County Historical Museum

With an emphasis on the area's mining and railroading history, this museum, housed in an old hospital dating from 1887, also features exhibits highlighting contributions of the Southern Utes, ranchers, educators, doctors, and other settlers. The museum is located at the corner of 5th St. and 6th Ave. and is open daily. For exact hours or other information, phone (970) 325-4576.

Walking Tour

Ouray is small enough (downtown is about six by four blocks) that you can easily tour the town by foot in an afternoon—it is hilly, though. The

Ouray County Chamber of Commerce has designated a specific walking tour of the National Historic District, with over two dozen buildings of historical significance. Among them: **St. Elmo Hotel,** 426 Main, built in 1898, recently restored, and today operating as a restaurant and inn; the **Western Hotel** (est. 1891), 220 7th Ave., Ouray's original deluxe lodge; and **Wright's Opera House** (est. 1888), fascinating for its Romanesque and Greek Revival architecture. Pick up a map and detailed guide at the visitor center next to Ouray Hot Springs Pool, or write the chamber of commerce, Box 145, Ouray, CO 81427.

Million Dollar Highway

In the early 1880s, Otto Mears built a toll road over Red Mountain Pass to make it easier to get Ouray ore out of the valley; the road greatly increased the efficiency of mining in the Ouray-Silverton-Telluride District. Today, US 550 from Ouray to Silverton follows the old route much of the way and is known as the Million Dollar Highway. Why? No one seems to be able to say for sure, though there are at least three explanations you'll get, depending on which "expert" you talk to: The road was paved with gold-bearing gravel, the value of which was not discovered until the project was completed; the road was so steep and so precarious that an early traveler was heard to claim, "You couldn't pay me a million dollars to go back over that pass"; or, the road cost about $1 million to pave in the mid-20th century.

PARKS AND RECREATION

Ouray Hot Springs Pool and Park

Ideal for soaking away a day's hiking or skiing aches, or cooling off after a long day's driving, this municipal facility features hot springs soaking pools as well as cool-water lap and goof-around pools. And the location couldn't be better: Kick back in the 104° F water and dig the towering peaks that rise 5,000 feet from the valley floor and box Ouray into the canyon.

If you don't feel like getting wet, there's a spacious grassy lawn, perfect for tossing the Frisbee about, as well as picnic facilities and a playground. The hot springs and park are located right on US 550 at the north end of town. The pools are open Mon.-Sat. 9 a.m.-9 p.m. and Sunday 9 a.m.-7 p.m. in the summer, Wed.-Mon. noon-9 p.m. in the winter. For more information, phone (970) 325-4638.

Box Canyon Falls and Park

With the waters of Clear Creek crashing nearly 300 feet into the narrow granite-walled Box Canyon, this city-owned park offers spectacular views and hiking trails. In addition, a steel suspension footbridge across the canyon affords a stunning view of the falls and creek. There are also restrooms and picnic facilities.

The falls and park are located just south of town off US 550 (watch for the signs). Hours are 8 a.m.-dusk mid-May through mid-October. Admission is $1.25 for adults and 75 cents for kids. For more information, phone (970) 325-4464.

Jeep Touring

This is one of the primary reasons folks come to Ouray. Scores of rocky back roads wind into remote canyons, past abandoned mines, through ghosts of old mining camps, and along cliffsides with sheer dropoffs to valley floors thousands of feet below. Trips range from the fairly easy tour to **Yankee Boy Basin** to the more difficult (and dangerous) drive over **Imogene Pass** to Telluride. The Yankee Boy Basin tour begins on Camp Bird Road just south of Ouray, follows Canyon Creek to the Camp Bird Mine (five miles from Ouray), and then veers west toward a series of wildflower-laden valleys at the base of Dallas and Gilpin peaks and Mt. Emma. The Imogene Pass road begins at the Camp Bird Mine and winds up over the 13,509-foot summit, affording views of some of the best scenery in one of most scenic areas of the state.

If you're looking to explore on your own, pick up Forest Service maps at the **Ouray Ranger District Office,** 2505 S. Townsend, Montrose, tel. (970) 249-3711. You'll also find a 4WD map and descriptions of routes in Ouray County's *Vacation Guide.*

San Juan Scenic Jeep Tours, in operation since 1946, offers half- and full-day tours throughout the area. Go on a predesigned tour, or make your own itinerary. Prices start at about $25 for adults for half-day trips. You can also

rent vehicles. For reservations or information, write Box 143, Ouray, CO 81427, or phone (970) 325-4444 or 325-4154.

Several other companies in Ouray also offer Jeep rentals and 4WD tours. Among them are **Switzerland of America,** Box 184, Ouray, CO 81427, tel. (970) 325-4484, and **Colorado West,** 332 5th Ave., tel. (970) 325-4014. You can also rent Jeeps at the **KOA** campground north of town.

Hiking

The woods, peaks, and steep canyons of the Ouray area are ideal for exploring by foot, and hikers will find a wide variety of trails. The following are but a sampling of the hikes in the area. The *Ouray County Vacation Guide* describes a dozen or so more, providing lengths and degrees of difficulty. **Lower Cascade Falls Trail** is a short (half mile) but fairly rugged trail that begins at the top of 8th Avenue and takes you down into the canyon to the bottom of Cascade Falls—expect to do some scrambling over boulders, and be careful of slick spots caused by melting snow. For something a little longer, although not as demanding, try the five-mile **Portland Trail,** which begins on the east side of town at Amphitheater Campground in Portland Basin. **Upper Cascade Trail** also begins at Amphitheater Campground and though half as long gains more than twice the altitude (1,500 as opposed to 700 feet). Great views of the valley, as well as of waterfalls on Cascade Creek.

For more information on hiking in the area, stop by the Ouray Visitors Center next to Ouray Hot Springs Pool, or contact **Uncompahgre National Forest,** either at its headquarters at 2250 US 50, Delta, tel. (970) 874-7691, or at the **Ouray Ranger District Office,** 2505 S. Townsend, Montrose, tel. (970) 249-3711.

Fishing

Ridgway Reservoir at the recently established **Ridgway State Recreation Area,** about 12 miles north of town on US 550, is regularly stocked with rainbow and brown trout. Fish the 1,000-acre lake either from shore or from a boat; launch your own boat from the six-lane ramp near the main entrance, or rent a boat from **San Juan Skyway Marina** on the lake, tel. (970) 626-5480. You can also fish for trout at the tiny but scenic **Molas Lake** on the Silverton side of Molas Pass, where you'll also find camping and picnicking facilities (fee charged, except for in a very small public area). The **Uncompahgre River** between Ouray and the reservoir is also stocked, though much of the river passes through private property.

For more information on fishing in the Ouray-San Juan-Uncompahgre area, or for licenses or guide service, stop by Telluride's **Olympic Sports,** 150 Colorado Ave., tel. (970) 728-4477, or **Duranglers of Telluride,** 666 W. Colorado Ave., tel. (970) 728-3895. You can also get licenses and information at **Outdoor World,** 1234 Greene St., Silverton, tel. (970) 387-5628.

Cross-Country Skiing
The nonprofit Ouray County Nordic Council operates **Red Mountain/Ironton Park Cross-Country Trails,** with several designated routes and loops that wind among eight historic landmarks and sites. There are both beginner and intermediate trails. For information, write Box 468, Ouray, CO 81427.

Other Activities
Though one could devote most of a summer to hiking or Jeep touring in the Ouray area, there are other things to do. One of the best ways to get into the heart of the backcountry is by horseback. **San Juan Mountain Outfitters,** whose stables are along the Uncompahgre River two miles north of town, offers half- and full-day trips, as well as overnight camp-out rides and full-service hunting pack trips. Reservations required. Write 2882 County Rd. 23, Ridgway, CO 81432, or phone (970) 626-5659.

Ouray Livery Barn has one- and two-hour and half-day rides along some of the nearby area's hiking trails, including Oak Creek and Portland Trail. Located on Main St. in Ouray, tel. (970) 325-4606.

San Juan Balloon Adventures offers half- and one-hour balloon tours of the Uncompahgre River Valley, as well as a "Balloon-N-Brunch" flight; soar out to a secluded picnic brunch, sip champagne with your meal, and climb back aboard for the trip home. Reservations required at least 12 hours in advance. Write Box 66, Ridgway, CO 81432, or phone (970) 325-4257 or 626-5495.

ACCOMMODATIONS

Ouray is a wonderful little hideaway town, a perfect place to hole up after a particularly demanding job project or semester of graduate school. Personally, I've always wanted to rent a little room in town, set up my word processor, and write all those scripts I've been telling myself Hollywood is aching to produce. If I ever do set up camp here, however, it's more likely I'll be working on updating this book. Whatever, I couldn't think of a better place.

Ouray offers a variety of accommodation options, with one common denominator: They all tend to fill up. Don't expect to be choosy if you're looking Friday afternoon for digs for Friday night. In fact, you might not be able to find anything at all, at least in the summer, when Southwestern Colorado swells with sightseers and vacationers. Call ahead for a room.

The small **Antlers Motel,** right downtown at 407 Main St., tel. (970) 325-4589, has no-frills doubles starting at $60. The **Best Western Twin Peaks Motel,** 125 3rd Ave., tel. (970) 325-4427, has a natural hot-springs whirlpool and doubles for $60 and up. Both the Antlers and the Twin Peaks are closed in the winter. You'll also find natural outdoor hot tubs at **Box Canyon Lodge and Hot Springs,** 45 3rd Ave., tel. (970) 327-5080; rooms for two run $50-75.

Located in the center of town at 426 Main St., the **St. Elmo Hotel,** tel. (970) 325-4951, was built before the turn of the century and has recently been remodeled into a bed-and-breakfast inn with 11 rooms furnished with Victorian-era antiques. Doubles start at about $70. You can also get bed-and-breakfast accommodations at **Damn Yankees Bed and Breakfast,** 100 6th Ave., tel. (970) 325-4219 or (800) 845-7512.

For more information on lodging in Ouray, write the Ouray Chamber of Commerce, Box 145, Ouray, CO 81427, or phone (970)325-4746 or (800) 228-1876.

Camping and RVing
Ouray Rotary Park on US 550 at the north end of town offers free overnight camping and picnicking. **Amphitheater Campground,** tel. (970) 249-3711, located immediately south of town

(east side), is operated by Uncompahgre National Forest and has 30 sites, pit toilets, and no showers.

A **KOA** campground, tel. (970) 325-4736, is four miles north of Ouray—110 tent and RV sites, plus a few cabins. You can also camp at **Timber Ridge Motel and Campground,** located just north of town on US 550, tel. (970) 325-4523. Motel rooms have fireplaces and steam rooms.

FOOD

Ouray has a respectable number of good restaurants, some of which draw folks from throughout the Uncompahgre Valley area. The **Grounds Keeper Coffee House** at 6th and Main, tel. (970) 325-0550, has wonderful health-oriented breakfasts and lunches, including homemade cobblers, soups, and salads, for $3-6. The recently opened **Ouray Brewing Company,** at 6th and Main, has classic pub fare and its own microbrews. For Mexican food, try the dining room at the **Western Hotel,** 210 7th St., tel. (970) 325-4645. In addition to south-of-the-border favorites, such as enchiladas and chiles rellenos, you can also get buffalo, elk, and venison. Entrees are in the $10-18 range. Another longtime favorite is the **Bon Ton Restaurant,** next door to the St. Elmo Hotel at 426 Main, tel. (970) 325-4951. The Bon Ton specializes in Italian food, as well as steaks, seafood, and chicken, with dinners ranging from $12 to $20. Sunday brunch is served 10 a.m.-1 p.m. for the set price of $6.95. The **Outlaw,** 610 Main, tel. (970) 325-9996, is a classic Western steakhouse that was spotlighted by *National Geographic Traveler* in 1990. You can also get seafood and chicken dinners. Dinners are $10-18.

ENTERTAINMENT AND EVENTS

As the commercial, recreational, and cultural center of Ouray County, Ouray offers lots of goings-on throughout the year, from arts-and-crafts shows to music festivals to the **Jeepers Jam-**

boree. Highlights include the **Music in Ouray** classical concert series (mid-June); the **Imogene Pass Run** footrace up Imogene Pass, which connects Ouray and Telluride (early September); and the **Octoberfest** (early October). Write the Ouray County Chamber of Commerce (see "Information," following) for a complete calendar of annual and special events.

The **San Juan Odyssey** is a 15-projector, five-screen slide show examining the San Juan Mountains in all their rugged glory. Written and narrated by Ouray mayor and country musician C.W. McCall (remember "Convoy"?), the show, which has been running nightly in summer since 1976, features a soundtrack by the London Symphony. Shows are at 8:30 p.m. in the Opera House at 5th and Main. Admission is $5 for adults, $3 for kids 12 and younger. For information, phone (970) 325-4020.

INFORMATION

If you're passing through, be sure to stop at the **tourist information center** on the north end of town next to Ouray Hot Springs and Pool. If you're planning to visit, write **Ouray County Chamber of Commerce,** Box 145, Ouray, CO 81427, or phone (970) 325-4746 or (800) 228-1876. Be sure to request a copy of the *Ouray County Vacation Guide,* which is full of maps, suggestions for hiking and jeep-touring trails, and listings of accommodations, restaurants, and other businesses. For information on Uncompahgre National Forest, phone the main office in Delta at (970) 874-7691, or stop by the **Ouray Ranger District Office,** 2505 S. Townsend, Montrose, tel. (970) 249-3711.

You can also get maps (topo, 4WD, hiking, etc.), as well as books on local and regional history at **Big Horn Mercantile,** 609 Main St., tel. (970) 325-4257.

The *Ouray County PlainDealer* newspaper is published weekly and is available in racks and shops throughout the area. For subscription information, write Box 607, Ouray, CO 81427-0607, tel. (970) 325-4412.

SILVERTON

Silverton (pop. 790; elev. 9,300 feet) is the seat of San Juan County and the center of the Las Animas Mining District. Situated in a tiny pocket between Molas and Red Mountain passes, and literally ringed with towering mountain peaks, Silverton began as an isolated mining camp, became a railroad supply center, and between 1880 and 1910 had a reputation as one rip-roarin' town, where whoring, drinking, and gun-fighting went on around the clock.

Known as the "mining town that never quit," Silverton finally shut down its last mine in August, 1991, after a century and a quarter of silver, gold, lead, zinc, and copper production. Eureka, Howardsville, Red Mountain, and other once-thriving mountain communities are accessible by back roads; get information and maps from the Silverton Visitors Center on the west end of town.

Silverton is also known today as the northern terminus of the Durango and Silverton Narrow Gauge Railroad, and for the dozens of gift shops, as well as restaurants and hotels, that occupy 100-year-old buildings. In the summer, passengers take the winding railroad up from Durango, spend a few hours wandering through the shops of Silverton (or spend the night), and then get back on the train for the trip back to Durango (you can also begin the trip in Silverton; see "Attractions," following). The Silverton Gun-fighters Association entertains tourists every evening at 5 with gunfights in the street.

History

A mining camp dating from 1871, when the first lodes were discovered here, Silverton was originally known as Baker's Park, after Captain Charles Baker, who had explored the area in the early 1860s. According to local legend, the town's name was changed in 1874 when a local mine operator announced, "We may not have gold here, but we have silver by the ton."

The camp prospered in the late 1870s and early '80s. Several large hotels and other buildings were constructed, among them the Grand Imperial Hotel and the gold-domed courthouse. In 1882, the Denver and Rio Grande Railroad arrived in town, greatly improving accessibility to the little community. During this time, Silverton's Blair St., one block east of Greene, was a hotbed of brothels, saloons, and gambling houses. Madams such as Mamie Murphy, Kate Starr, and Jew Fanny operated 24-hour-a-day "pleasure palaces" that drew huge numbers of miners and other callers from throughout western Colorado. Things got so wild, in fact, that Silverton eventually recruited Bat Masterson from Dodge City to "clean up the town."

Silverton fared better during the silver crash of 1893 than did many of Colorado's ore-dependent towns, its mines continuing to produce an average of $2 million a year. In fact, Silverton prospered well into the next century; the population in 1910 was 2,153, more than twice what

downtown Silverton in the late 19th century

it is today. By 1918, over $65 million in silver had been taken from Silverton-area mines.

ATTRACTIONS

Durango and Silverton Narrow Gauge Railroad

Though the vast majority of tourists catch the train at its southern terminus, Durango, you can also begin in Silverton. Options include one-day, roundtrip tours; roundtrip tours with an overnight layover in Durango; one-way trips; and combination bus-train roundtrip tours. Reservations highly recommended. Roundtrip fares are about $40 for adults. Phone the Durango depot at (970) 247-2733, or write Durango and Silverton Narrow Gauge Railroad Company, 479 Main Ave., Durango, CO 81301. Also see "Attractions" under "Durango," following.

San Juan County Museum

Located in the old San Juan County jail, this small museum, operated by the San Juan County Historical Society, is geared mostly toward the area's railroad and mining history. The first floor of the building, constructed in 1902, served as the sheriff's living quarters, while the jail cells, which have not been removed, are on the second floor.

The San Juan County Museum, located on Greene St. between 15th and 16th, is open daily 9 a.m.-5 p.m., Memorial Day through Labor Day, and thereafter daily 10 a.m.-3 p.m. through mid-October. Admission is $1.50 for adults. For information, phone (970) 387-5838.

Historical Walking Tour

Whether you realize it or not, if you're walking around Silverton, you're taking a historical walking tour. You can't help it: Silverton *is* history. The two main north-south streets—Greene and Blair—offer a tour of the town's past, from its most elegant to its most indecorous; while most of the "respectable" businesses were on Greene, Blair was known for its brothels and wild saloons.

The Silverton Chamber of Commerce and the San Juan County Historical Society have printed a map and thorough description of historic Silverton. Included are over 50 structures

within a few short blocks of each other. Among the buildings on the tour are the **Grand Imperial Hotel,** 1221 Greene, which was built in 1883; the **Exchange Livery,** 1244 Greene, built in 1906 (buggies and wagons were stored downstairs, horses upstairs); and **Natalia's,** 1161 Blair, and the **Shady Lady,** 1154 Blair, both of which were popular brothels around the turn of the century.

The map and guide are published in the back pages of the *Silverton-San Juan Vacation Guide,* available at the chamber of commerce visitor center at the town's entrance.

Christ of the Mines Shrine

Dedicated to Silverton's miners, past and present, this statue of a 12-ton Rio-like Jesus stands arms spread in a stone alcove on the hillside above Silverton. Erected in 1959, the statue, made of Italian marble, is thought to have been the source of several local "miracles," including the fact that no workers were present when a local mine exploded one Sunday night. To get there, take 10th St. west from downtown Silverton.

RECREATION

Hiking

Silverton is surrounded by the San Juan National Forest and is just northwest of 405,000-acre Weminuche Wilderness Area, the state's largest and most visited. This is steep and high country, though, with the Continental Divide passing just a few miles east of town, and hikers should know what they're doing. For topo maps of the area, and for suggestions on hiking, contact the **Animas Ranger District Office** of the Forest Service, 701 Camino Del Rio, Durango, CO 81301, tel. (970) 247-4874. The Silverton Visitors Center also has information and maps, as does **Outdoor World,** 1234 Greene, Silverton, tel. (970) 387-5628.

Though you can get into the backcountry by walking from downtown Silverton, you can also take the Durango-Silverton Railroad. Certain runs stop for backpackers (to let you on or off). For information, phone (970) 387-5416 (Silverton) or 247-2733 (Durango).

Jeep Tours

Like Ouray, Silverton is a four-wheel-driver's paradise, and the old cliff-hanging mining roads are litmus tests for driving skills. One popular trail is the **Alpine Loop,** which connects Silverton, Lake City, and Ouray and crosses **Engineer Pass** (elev. 12,800 feet) and **Cinnamon Pass** (elev. 12,620 feet). The 65-mile route is designated a **Backcountry Scenic Byway,** is not one of the more treacherous in the area.

Several companies in the area offer 4WD rentals. Try **Rent-A-Jeep** at the Conoco Station at 864 Greene St., tel. (970) 387-9990, or **Silver Lakes Campground,** just north of town at the junction with CO 110, tel. (970) 387-5721. For guided tours along the Alpine Loop, phone **San Juan Tours** at (970) 387-5565.

Pick up 4WD and topo maps at **Outdoor World,** 1234 Greene, tel. (970) 387-5628.

ACCOMMODATIONS

For such a tourist-oriented town, Silverton has a number of good places to stay at decent rates, from hotels in century-old buildings to modern motels. There's not a whole lot in terms of numbers, though, and you'd be wise to make reservations ahead of time. Remember, too, that things slow down in Silverton considerably during the winter, and some of the lodges are available mid-May through September only.

Hotels and Motels

The **Alma House,** 220 E. 10th., tel. (970) 387-5336, is a small (11-room) inn two blocks from the train depot and one block from Greene. Built in 1902 and empty for years, the old stone hotel has been recently restored. Rooms are $32. Owned and operated by the same couple, the red sandstone **Wyman Hotel,** 1371 Greene, tel. (970) 387-5372, was built in 1902 and is located in the upper-downtown area. Rooms are $58. Smoking is not allowed at either the Alma or the Wyman.

You can also get rooms in the **Alpine House,** 1234 Greene, tel. (970) 387-5628 (about $60 for two). The **Teller House Hotel,** 1250 Greene, tel. (970) 387-5423, was built in 1986 and is located upstairs from the French Bakery; rooms with shared bath are $31, with private bath $47.

Camping and RVing

Molas Lake Park, tel. (970) 387-5410, five miles south of Silverton on US 550, is a privately run campground with 60 sites on a 40-acre trout-stocked lake. The area gets a certifiable A+ for scenery. **Silverton Lakes Campground,** tel. (970) 387-5721, has tent and RV sites right next to town at the junction with CO 110. **South Mineral** Forest Service campground just north of town has 23 sites and flush toilets (no showers). Take US 550 four miles north, then Forest Service Rd. 585 five miles west. Phone the Durango District Office of San Juan National Forest at (970) 247-4874 for reservations or more information.

FOOD

An excellent place to get started in the morning is at the **French Bakery,** 1250 Greene, tel. (970) 387-5423. Get standard American fare, as well as fresh-baked goods. The large windows looking out on Greene St. make it an ideal people-watching place. You can also get breakfasts in the Gold King dining room at the **Grand Imperial Hotel,** 1221 Greene, tel. (970) 387-5527, where you can get traditional eggs-and-bacon dishes, as well as fancy pancakes and waffles (topped with berries and whipped cream). Prices run $4-7. The Gold King is also open for lunch and dinner (seven days a week).

For Mexican food, try **Romero's Restaurant y Cantina,** 1151 Greene, tel. (970) 387-5561. Specializing in margaritas, Romero's also serves *menudo* (a sure sign the place is authentic!). Dinners are in the $5-7 range.

Another recommended Silverton restaurant is **Handlebars,** 117 E. 13th St., where lunch salads (spinach, pasta, and veggie) run about $5 and soups, burgers, and sandwiches are $5-7. Dinners, which include beef and chicken plates, range $7-15.

ENTERTAINMENT AND EVENTS

Although Silverton is absolutely beautiful during the snowy months, its location and elevation make it less a winter than summer destination. Among the highlights of the summer season are the **Jubilee Folk Festival,** late June; **Fourth** of July, with a parade and fireworks; **Kendall Mountain Run,** a 13-mile footrace up Kendall Mountain (4,000-feet altitude gain) in mid-July; and the **Hardrockers Holiday Mining Celebration,** with tugs-o'-war, drilling competitions, wheelbarrow races, etc., in mid-August; and the **Great Rocky Mountain Brass Band Festival,** mid-August. In addition, the **Silverton Theatre Group,** which began producing plays in 1988, has a half dozen or so offerings each season, ranging from standards by Neil Simon and George Bernard Shaw to lesser-known and sometimes locally penned works. Performances are in the Miners Union Theatre, at the corner of 11th and Greene; $7 for adults, $4 for kids. For information and reservations, phone (970) 387-5337 or (800) 752-4494.

For more information on these and other Silverton events, contact the Silverton Chamber of Commerce at (970) 387-5654.

SHOPPING

Though Silverton was at one time defined by miners, saloons, gambling halls, and brothels, today the little town is defined by tourists, restaurants, gift shops, and more gift shops. Like several other Colorado mining-camps-turned-tourist-towns (Cripple Creek, Georgetown), Silverton relies heavily on the out-of-town dollar to keep the head of its struggling economy above water, and its main drag (Greene St.) is virtually lined with gift and souvenir shops. So, if you're looking for something to bring home, look no further. And even if you're not, allow yourself a couple of hours to wander up and down Greene St., and down the side streets. Poke your head into the little specialty shops; you'll find the owners very friendly and laid-back (no high-pressure selling in this low-key little town).

In addition to the shops you'd find in most tourist-oriented towns (Christmas, jewelry, minerals, T-shirts, Native American art), Silverton also has a handful of stores specializing in the area's history.

INFORMATION

You'll want to stop in at the two chamber-of-commerce visitor centers in Silverton. The main one, at the town's entrance, is stocked with literature on Silverton and the surrounding area, and there are staff members to answer questions—open year-round. The second one, the Blair Street Information Booth, on Blair between 12th and 13th, has brochures and information on local businesses, including the menus of many of Silverton's restaurants. There are also picnic tables and public restrooms—open summer only.

You can get information before your visit by writing the **Silverton Chamber of Commerce,** Box 565, Silverton, CO 81433, or by calling (970) 387-5654. Be sure to get copies of the *Silverton-San Juan Vacation Guide* (published by *The Silverton Standard* and *The Miner*), which includes coupons good at local gift shops, as well as stories on Silverton's history and suggestions for things to do in the area.

TELLURIDE AND VICINITY

A mining town that has turned world-class resort village, Telluride (pop. 1,400; elev. 8,745 feet) is full of juxtapositions and ironies: Gingerbread Victorian homes stand in the shadows of ultra-modern condominium complexes; grizzled life-time locals share bar space with Austrian ski racers named Wolfgang, while young WASPy passers-through with wannabe dreadlocks hang out on benches on the sidewalk; chic boutiques, new-age bistros, and Southwestern art galleries line the streets; and, in perhaps the most potentially explosive stand-off of all, developers, no- and slow-growthers debate the town's future according to their own visions.

Situated at the end of a box canyon deep in the San Juan Mountains, Telluride almost overnight has mushroomed from a sleepy little community with summer music and film festivals and some of the best uncrowded skiing in the country to a hot spot attracting the likes of Tom Cruise and Donald Trump. Which, of course, is why there are such strong feelings among the community. Locals have seen real estate prices skyrocket in recent years (a *modest* restored Victorian in town can fetch anywhere from $500,000 to $1,500,000, and nearby ranch homes and ski lodges run a couple of mil . . .), and people fear the little town will become another Aspen.

In addition to their ambivalence about the gentrification and possible overdevelopment of the town of Telluride, locals are split over the development of Telluride Village, the new mega-bucks resort at the base of the ski area. Though the deluxe hotels and other lodging promise to pump big money into the economy, and to provide more jobs for Telluridians trying to eke out a living in the canyon, the new housing is clearly aimed at outside budgets. As Telluride Village began to take shape in the late 1980s, and the cost of living in town zoomed skyward, many local workers were forced to move "down valley," where housing was still affordable.

Apparently things have slowed down a bit, though, and real estate, for example, has reached a sort of plateau. In addition, several nearby housing develpments, including Lawson Hill (two miles from Telluride; three-bedroom duplex: $155,000), have put home ownership within the reach of locals. Plus, some of the housing is "deed restricted," meaning new homes are designated for purchase by locals only, and they must meet several criteria, including living and working within the local school district, to qualify.

Still, the supply of developable land is scarce and demand for it high, so you can expect housing to continue to command top dollar. And though Telluride's future hangs uncertain, it's still one of the prettiest and classiest places in Colorado. And on a dark, cold December night with a light snow falling softly on deserted side

downtown Telluride
shortly after a light
January snowfall

streets and firelight flickering in windows of century-old Victorians, the place becomes truly magical. If you plan to hit the slopes in the morning, it's easy to think you've found paradise.

HISTORY

Telluride's history dates from 1875, when it served as a supply center for several mines—including the Sheridan, Ajax, and Smuggler—that had been staked in the high mountains just east of the little box canyon. Originally known as Columbia, Telluride took its name from tellurium, a sulphurous compound prevalent in the district and often found in the gold itself. (There's little evidence to support the claim of barstool historians that the name comes from "To Hell You Ride," a saying that apparently once quite accurately described the nature of the trip to the rugged and rowdy little town.)

The Rio Grande Southern Railroad arrived in Telluride in 1890, making the camp far more accessible. Almost overnight, the tents and shacks that had lined Colorado Avenue were replaced by homes, shops, brothels, and hotels. By some estimates, over 5,000 people were living in Telluride in the early 1890s.

The New Sheridan Hotel was constructed between 1890 and 1895. Typifying the lavishness of Colorado's mining-industry-financed hotels, the New Sheridan offered luxurious accommodations for passers-through, as well as a dining room said to rival that at Denver's Brown Palace. Sarah Bernhardt and Lillian Gish were among the hotel's early guests.

Telluride's boom was short-lived, however. After the silver market crashed in 1893, many of the town's mines shut down, and homes and businesses were abandoned. By the last years of the 19th century, overall productivity had greatly decreased and the remaining miners were disgruntled; the euphoria of the early part of the decade had vanished. In 1901, mine owners presented workers with new contracts, and guess what? They stipulated more money to owners and management and less to labor. The union struck, though nonunion miners were brought in, resulting in intense standoffs and violence, with the National Guard being called in during the winter of 1904 to impose peace on the town.

Though a handful of mines remained open through the first part of the 20th century, the Bank of Telluride closed, and all but a few people left town. The population in 1930 was 512. Still, Telluride's contribution to Colorado mining history had been impressive. By 1909, the district had produced more than $60 million in gold, silver, copper, lead, and zinc.

Telluride lay remote and mostly idle for most of the mid-century, though its second boom was on the horizon. As early as 1938, the town was realizing its potential as a winter resort area, although poor snowfalls and WW II combined to discourage the idea's first backers. However, in 1945, after the war, Telluride's first rope tow was built. The lift ran for two seasons, lay inoperative for over a decade, and then was rebuilt in 1958 using an old car engine for power. That winter, season passes sold for $5.

It was still another decade before Telluride would make the transition from a tiny ski area used almost exclusively by locals to one ultimately attracting some of the best and most sophisticated skiers from around the world. In 1968, in a move that could eventually be seen as disconcertingly prophetic, businessman Joe Zoline arrived in Telluride from Beverly Hills with plans to develop a "winter recreation area second to none." Work began almost immediately, and Telluride Ski Area was dedicated in April, 1971.

For the next 15 years or so, although the town was again hitting pay dirt, it enjoyed a relatively downscale and unpretentious elegance, guaranteed by its remote location. Though it had a reputation for some of the best skiing—as well as some of the best music and film festivals—in the state, you had to really *want* to go there: While Denver skiers could get to Winter Park in an hour and a half, Telluride was a six- or seven-hour drive, more if the weather was at all threatening.

Then in the late 1980s, Telluride Regional Airport was built, and it became as easy to get to Telluride as to get to Vail or Aspen. Regular flights were offered from Los Angeles, Phoenix, and Albuquerque, and express jets were flying into Telluride daily from Denver. The face and tenor of the town changed dramatically and permanently. By 1990, local waiters and ski-lift operators were no longer renting cheap rooms in town; there weren't any. By now, property values had skyrocketed, and working people for the most part couldn't afford to live in town. Huge resort complexes—hotels and conference centers—were springing up at Telluride Mountain Village. Movie stars and rock musicians were being seen in shops buying sealskin after-ski boots; realtors found themselves dealing with a whole new breed of buyer, folks who flew into town in their own jets.

Still at least as of last inspection, Telluride has managed to survive the onslaught of outside money. As long as local music promoters continue to book (and sell tickets to) acts like James Taylor, Emmy Lou Harris, and John Prine, and as long as the mountain continues to attract skiers to whom nothing matters but deep snow and steep slopes, the town should retain most of its integrity and charm, and should remain one of Colorado's true treasures.

Historical Walking Tours

The Town of Telluride has published a map and guide to historical Telluride. With over a dozen sites, the tour includes the **San Miguel County Courthouse** (in use since 1887), the **town hall** (built in 1883), the **New Sheridan Hotel** (early 1890s), as well as several private residences dating from before the turn of the century. The map and guide are printed in the vacation guide in *Telluride Magazine* and are available at the Telluride Visitor Center and most real estate offices. **Historic Tours of Telluride** offers guided tours of town, including both famous and lesser-known Telluride landmarks. Catch them at 10 a.m. daily from Elk's Park June to September.

Cost is $8 per person. Phone (970) 728-6639 for reservations and information.

PARKS AND RECREATION

This is why folks both live and visit here. Located in one of the prettiest pockets of Colorado's gorgeous San Juan Mountains, Telluride offers a range of activities guaranteed to satisfy even the most demanding outdoor enthusiast. Though best known for its downhill skiing, Telluride is also an excellent base for myriad other recreational pursuits as well, from hiking, horseback riding, and mountain biking to jeep touring, fishing, and whitewater rafting. In addition, it's a great place just to experience *being* outdoors. In the fall, when the aspen leaves turn to gold and crimson, there may not be a lovelier place on earth.

Downhill Skiing

Known until recently as a mountain geared mostly toward advanced (and better!) skiers, Telluride has spent the last several summers cutting more trails and opening things up for intermediate and beginning skiers as well. The mountain straddles a high ridge, which provides two separate base areas. Two lifts are based in town and take skiers up the steep face that looks down on Telluride's streets; the main base area is accessible by driving around the ridge to Telluride Mountain Village, where you'll find the ski school, administrative offices, and other base facilities. A free skier shuttle runs regularly between the two areas.

Olympic gold medalist Phil Mahre crosses the finish line just ahead of his dual-slalom competitor.

Telluride Mountain Village under construction in January 1991

Generally, the advanced and expert skiing is on the town-of-Telluride side. Several of these runs—Spiral Stairs, for example—offer some of the steepest, nastiest lift-serviced skiing in the country. In addition, you'll find excellent bump skiing over here, as well as the best powder—the northern exposure means snow staying in better shape longer. Meanwhile, the Telluride Mountain Village side caters more to intermediate and beginning skiers, with lots of long, sweeping runs, perfect for GS-style cruising, in packs or all by your lonesome.

With 11 lifts servicing 1,055 acres, Telluride has one of the longest vertical drops in the state: 3,522 feet. In addition, recent *Snow Country* magazine reader polls ranked Telluride's lift lines the state's shortest and the bumps the west's best. The terrain is officially designated 21% beginner, 47% intermediate, and 32% advanced and expert. **Free tours** of the mountain are offered daily at 10 a.m. Look for the guides in the turquoise ski parkas. The Telluride Ski School includes instruction in Telemarking and snowboarding.

For more information on Telluride Ski Area (ski school, lift tickets, etc.), phone (970) 728-4424 or (800) 525-3455. For **snow conditions,** phone (970) 728-3614.

Cross-Country Skiing

Nordic skiing in all its forms is very popular in Telluride. Telemarkers, skaters, and tourers can all find plenty of action. If you just want to get some fresh air and check out the valley a little bit, try the **Town Park and River Trail,** which is maintained by the city and runs east from town park along the San Juan River. **Telluride Resort Nordic Center** is a full-service center located at Telluride Mountain Village. Sunshine Express lift at the ski area provides access to over 30 km of excellent trails of varying ability levels. You can also arrange guided backcountry tours. Phone (970) 728-4424.

For the more ambitious, **San Juan Hut Systems** offers a series of backcountry cabins linked by cross-country ski trails. The huts are five to six miles apart, and the scenic trails are skiable even for beginning Nordic skiers. For information or reservations, phone (970) 728-6935.

WHEN THE SNOW MELTS

City Parks

Located on the east side of town on the San Juan River, **Telluride Town Park** is perfectly befitting the little community's character and charm. In addition to some two dozen campsites (no hookups, small fee), the park has picnic facilities, volleyball, basketball, and tennis courts, playground equipment, a skateboard park, and a small lake where kids can catch trout recently arrived from the hatchery. For information phone (970) 728-3071. An alternative picnic area is the very nice little **San Miguel County Park** on the San Miguel River in Placerville, about 15 miles northwest of Telluride (no overnight camping).

Cycling

The old mining roads twisting and slicing throughout the San Juan Mountains make Telluride a natural for mountain biking, and the sport has really taken off in recent years. For the ultimate southern Colorado mountain-bike experience, check out **San Juan Hut Systems'** Telluride-to-Moab trip. This 215-mile weeklong tour features stops at six cabins along the way, and all you have to do is ride (you can go with or without a guide). The huts are 35 miles apart and each has 12 padded bunks (with blankets), a propane stove, kitchen utensils, a wood-burning stove, and firewood. You can also arrange day-trips through San Juan Hut Systems. Guided tours start at about $30 a day. For information or reservations, write Box 1663, Telluride, CO 81435, or phone (970) 728-6935. In town, stop by 224 E. Colorado.

For accessories, tips on biking in the Telluride area, or to rent bikes, stop in at **Paragon Ski and Sports,** 217 W. Colorado, tel. (970) 728-4525; **Telluride Sports** 150 W. Colorado, tel. (970) 728-4477, or **Freewheelin',** 101 E. Colorado, tel. (970) 728-4734.

Guided bicycle tours are available through Paragon Sports and Telluride Sports. Get topo maps of Uncompahgre National Forest from the **Norwood Ranger District Office,** 1760 Grand, Norwood, CO 81423, tel. (970) 327-4261.

Golf

The 18-hole, 7,009-foot **Telluride Golf Course** is located at Telluride Mountain Village, five miles south of town. For information and tee times, phone (970) 728-8000.

Hiking

Hiking is one of the best ways to get out and enjoy Southwestern Colorado, and the Telluride area offers a wide array of trails, from short walks to backcountry excursions. The town's de rigueur outing is to **Bridal Veil Falls.** This relatively easy two-mile roundtrip walk on a dirt road takes about two hours, and leads to the largest waterfall in the state where water cascades off a 425-foot cliff. Begin at Pandora Mill

on the east end of town. Total elevation gain is about 1,000 feet. The two-mile **Judd Weibe Trail** begins at the north end of Aspen St., where it crosses Cornet Creek. Allow up to three hours, but expect excellent views. Along the way, you'll also pass the remnants of Telluride's old "pesthouse," where horse-drawn wagons once carried Telluride's contagious to quarantine. Another hike known for its stunning scenery begins in town at Pine St. and climbs two miles and 1,300 feet in elevation through **Bear Creek Canyon** to a multi-tiered waterfall.

For complete information on hiking in the area, pick up a copy of Susan Kees's *Telluride Hiking Guide* (Pruett Publishing Co., Boulder), available in bookstores and some outdoors shops in the area. Get topo maps from the Forest Service District Office in Norwood, tel. (970) 327-4261.

Fishing

With lots of good fishing in Southwestern Colorado, particularly in the San Juan Mountains, Telluride's as good a place as any to base yourself. Though you won't find the lunker Mackinaw that you might at Blue Mesa or Shadow Mountain Reservoir, there's plenty of good stream fishing, especially for those who'd rather entice a native fish to rise to a hand-tied fly than hook a larger hatchery fish on bait or hardware.

The west fork of the **Dolores River,** which parallels CO 145 south of town, has rainbows, browns, and cutthroats. Fish for rainbows in the faster water and rapids below pools; fish for browns in deeper, slower water. Closer to town, the **San Miguel River** is regularly stocked with pan-size rainbows, as is the little lake at **Town Park,** an excellent spot to give younger kids their first lessons in the sport (fishing here is for kids 12 and younger only).

Popular lakes in the area include **Alta Lake, Priest Lake,** and **Trout Lake,** all accessible via CO 145 south of town; **Woods Lake** is west on CO 145 toward Placerville.

For information, licenses, equipment, and guided fly-fishing trips, stop in at **Telluride Sports,** 150 W. Colorado Ave., tel. (970) 728-4477, or **Telluride Outside,** 666 W. Colorado, (970) 728-3895, the latter also offering a fly-fishing school.

TELLURIDE

TO TELLURIDE MTN.
VILLAGE, RIDGWAY,
AND AIRPORT

VISITOR
INFORMATION
CENTER

145

JUDD WIEBE TRAIL

CORNET CREEK

COONSKIN
SKI LIFT

DAVIS

TOWNSEND

COLUMBIA

GALENA

TOMBOY
RD.

TO
IMOGENE
PASS

MEDICAL
CENTER

COLORADO AVE.

ASPEN

HISTORICAL
MUSEUM

GREGORY AVE.

SAN MIGUEL RIVER

PACIFIC

OAK

SPRUCE

OAK ST.
SKI LIFT

SAN JUAN

FIR

PINE

LIBRARY

WILLOW

TO BRIDAL
VEIL FALLS

NOT TO SCALE

NOTE: ONLY MAIN ROADS SHOWN

FESTIVAL GROUNDS

KIDS' FISHING POND

TOWN PARK

© MOON PUBLICATIONS, INC.

Rafting

Though most Telluride-area streams are too small for rafting, you can book a range of trips on other southwestern Colorado rivers—the Gunnison, Dolores, Animas—through **Telluride Sports,** tel. (970) 728-4477, or **Telluride Outside,** tel. (970) 728-3895.

Four-Wheel-Drive Tours

Four-wheel-drive rigs and Southwestern Colorado go together like motor scooters and Bangkok. Not only are they ideal for simply getting around in the winter, but in the summer they're the only (well, okay, quickest and easiest . . .) way to some of the region's more secluded and scenic spots.

The mountains around Telluride are interlaced with old mining roads perfect for four-wheeling. And since the roads have already been cut, your contribution to environmental damage is limited.

(Do stay on those roads, though. As tempting as it might be to take a short cut across a high-mountain meadow, keep in mind how vulnerable and fragile these ecosystems are.)

Imogene Pass (elev. 13,509 feet) is the cliff-hanging historical route connecting Telluride and Ouray (about 18 miles). You'll pass both the abandoned Tomboy Mine and the remains of Fort Peabody, which was a guard station during the labor-management conflicts at the turn of the century. For neither the timid nor the amateur back-roadster, the pass is as difficult as it is scenic. Experienced drivers: Take Oak St. north, and turn east onto the Forest Service-maintained pass road.

A much easier and less dangerous 4WD route is **Ophir Pass** (elev. 11,740 feet), an 1881 toll road that connected Telluride and Silverton. Today, it's one of the most popular backcountry scenic routes in the area. Note: This is a one-way road, with traffic moving east to west. Start in Silverton, and go north on US 550 about five miles; the road is unmarked, but directly across from it is a sign for Red Mountain Summit (five miles). From Silverton to Ophir is about 15 miles.

For information, tours, and 4WD rentals, contact **Telluride Outside,** tel. (970) 728-3895. **Skip's Taxi,** tel. (970) 728-6667, **Mountain Limo,** tel. (970) 728-9606, and **Dave's Jeep Tours, Inc.,** tel. (970) 728-4316, all offer 4WD backcountry tours.

ACCOMMODATIONS

Because of Telluride's remote location, and the fact that it's grown increasingly popular in recent years, especially in winter, lodge owners can pretty much get whatever they want for a room. Though not yet on a par with Aspen, rooms in Telluride are expensive (winter high season is from mid-December till just after the first of the year; summer rates go up during festivals and special events). If you can, plan to come when things are slower. During January, for example, rooms are the least expensive (of the ski season), and the skiing's at its best.

For a complete listing of accommodations available in Telluride, or to make reservations, contact **Telluride Central Reservations** at (800) 525-3455.

Rooms in Town
For a real taste of Telluride, try the recently remodeled (1995) **New Sheridan Hotel,** tel. (970) 728-4351. Rates for doubles range from about $65 (shared bath, low season) to $195 (private bath, high season, five-day minimum)—quite a jump from the early '70s when a room here ran 80 bucks a month (of course only 500 people lived in Telluride then, and it was sort of an outpost-on-the-frontier resort). The **Victorian Inn,** tel. (970) 728-6601 or (800) 537-2614, though built in 1976, blends in gracefully with the surrounding 19th-century structures and is located within a short walk of Coonskin and Oak Street lifts. Rooms go for about $40-110.

Another distinctly Telluride inn is the **San Sophia,** tel. (970) 728-3001 or (800) 537-4781. This elegant bed and breakfast is located right downtown near the base of the lifts and has doubles running $95-195. You can also get good, comfortable rooms at comparatively reasonable rates ($60-190) at the **Bear Creek Bed and Breakfast,** tel. (970) 728-6681.

Bargains?
You'll probably find the least expensive rooms in town at the **Oak Street Inn,** tel. (970) 728-3383. A member of Youth Hostels of America, this little lodge, located one block off the main drag, offers rooms starting at about $25 (shared bath). Don't expect anything fancy and you won't be disappointed. Discounts offered to AYH members. Showers $3 for nonguests.

Lodging at Telluride Mountain Village
The newly developed Telluride Mountain Village has plenty of lodging in condominium complexes and upscale hotels. Though they don't offer the charm of staying in one of Telluride's historical hotels or refurbished old homes, they do offer convenience and just about every amenity you can imagine, including ski and golf packages. The newest and fanciest hotel is **The Peaks at Telluride Resort and Spa,** tel. (970) 728-6800, a 200-room, $60-million number with a huge athletic club, as well as conference and banquet facilities. Rates for rooms range from $150 to $500 a night.

Pennington's Mountain Village Inn, tel. (970) 728-5337, is a smaller and less imposing lodge (12 units) on a grassy knoll; one of the more attractive inns at the village, Pennington's has been the site of many weddings and other gatherings. Doubles start at about $140.

FOOD

Gone Skiing?
Telluride is first and foremost a ski town, and if there's been a good dump during the night, it's not unusual for a restaurant to shut its doors for the day. Don't be surprised when looking for breakfast to find signs on doors that read, "Powder day. Closed. See you this afternoon."

Start Me Up
The **Excelsior Cafe,** right downtown at 200 W. Colorado, tel. (970) 728-4250, serves espressos, cappuccinos, and other coffees guaranteed to

put a bite in your morning, as well as pastries and other goodies. Another local favorite is **Maggie's Bakery** 217 E. Colorado, tel. (970) 728-3334, where you can get espressos, regular coffees, pastries, and complete breakfasts. A casual cafe attracting everyone from white rastas on the road to longtime Telluridians, Maggie's also serves lunch and dinner, with an emphasis on health and vegetarian dishes.

Other Telluride Restaurants

The **Roma Bar and Cafe,** 133 E. Colorado, tel. (970) 728-3669, serves excellent Italian food in an anything-but-pretentious atmosphere (listen to the pool balls smacking each other in the next room). Entrees are in the $9-13 range, and you can also order off the appetizer-pizza menu (pizzas start at about $10). The Roma Bar also offers a skier's breakfast special—eggs, toast, and potatoes for around $2. **Floradora,** tel. (970) 728-3888, supposedly named after a couple of Telluride pioneers (Flora and Dora, who worked the Red Light District), serves excellent lunches and dinners at reasonable prices. From burgers to steaks, chicken, and Mexican dishes, with specials daily and a soup du jour. Great bar for munching nachos and watching a game.

Another Telluride favorite is **Eddie's,** 300 W. Colorado, tel. (970) 728-5335. In addition to pizza, either whole or by the slice, Eddie's serves great salads, sandwiches, burgers, and pasta dinners ($5-14). The **One World Cafe,** tel. (970)

728-5530, has quickly earned a solid reputation for good grub. For Asian food, try **Honga's Lotus Petal,** tel. (970) 728-5134.

Grocery Stores

The Natural Source, 124 E. Colorado, tel. (970) 728-4833, sells organic produce, bulk foods, vitamins, and other health products. **Rose Food Mart,** 700 W. Colorado, tel. (970) 728-3124, and **Village Market,** 157 S. Fir, tel. (970) 728-4566, both carry meats, produce, and other grocery products, with emphases on natural and health foods.

ENTERTAINMENT

And a Good Saloon in Every Single Town

Sometimes you're in the mood for something smoky, poolly, loud, and local. The **Last Dollar Saloon,** 100 E. Colorado, is it. Put your quarter down on the table, order a draft, and soak in the local flavor. During the summer the talk is of softball—aging adolescents' tales of catches almost made and hard grounders almost run out—and during the winter it's of skiing—how much snow'll fall tonight, the awesome bumps under Number 9, the new Rossi slalom ski. Just know that you'll have to wash the Marlboro out of your sweater (and hair) in the morning.

For live rock and rhythm and blues, check out **Fly Me To The Moon Saloon,** 132 E. Colo-

The New Sheridan Hotel in downtown Telluride dates from the early 1890s.

rado, tel. (970) 728-6666. You can also sometimes hear live tunes at the bar at **One World
Cafe,** (970) 728-5530.

CALENDAR

In addition to Telluride's better-known events—
the bluegrass, jazz, and film festivals—the community offers dozens of other intriguing workshops, conferences, bike and foot races, and
other festivals. In early June, you can attend
the simultaneous **Wine Festival** and **Balloon
Rally.** Taste fine wines or sip champagne as
the skies fill with colorful hot-air balloons. The
world-famous **Telluride Bluegrass and Country Music Festival** is the highlight of the summer. Hotels and campgrounds fill up, and music
fills the valley from the stages at Town Park.
Wednesday through Friday, lesser-known acts
take the stage, while Friday night through Sunday afternoon, players such as Bill Monroe,
James Taylor, John Prine, the Nitty Gritty Dirt
Band, Bela Fleck, and Wolfstone entertain the
crowds. **Fourth of July** has always been a time
of festivities and fireworks in Telluride, with much
of the action in Town Park.

The **Telluride Jazz Festival** in early August
began in the late 1970s and has featured mainstream and experimental artists from around
the world, including Herbie Hancock, Branford
and Wynton Marsalis, Etta James, and the
Neville Brothers. **Wild Mushrooms Telluride** is
a three-day celebration of the edible fungus. Included in the late August festival are lectures,
workshops, identification hikes, and cooking
and tasting events.

Over Labor Day weekend, the **Telluride Film
Festival** attracts big- and not-so-big-name directors, writers, and other scholars to retro-
spectives and national and world premieres.
Seminars, featuring directors and actors, take
place in Town Park and are free. **Talking
Gourds** in September is an annual gathering
of poets, storytellers, and performance artists
for workshops, readings, and shows. Finally,
the weeklong **Telluride Airmen's Rendezvous**
in June is the longest-running and largest hang-
gliding affair in the world. Top flyers sponsor
lectures and workshops and compete in the
World Hang Gliding Championships.

For festival tickets and information, phone
(800) 525-3455.

SHOPPING

Although no Aspen, Telluride does claim a number of moderately fancy specialty shops, galleries, and boutiques where without a movie-
star income you're not going to be able to do
much more than look and hope. In addition,
some of the ski shops display duds that are far
more flash than function. Still, isn't that partly
what vacation shopping's all about?

Whether you're looking to buy or simply to
ogle, Telluride's galleries are a kick to poke
around in. With primarily Native American- and
Southwestern-flavored artwork, the shops sell
pottery, jewelry, rugs, paintings, prints, and
sculpture. Check out **Golden West,** 101 W.
Colorado, tel. (970) 728-3664; **Telluride Gallery
of Fine Art,** 130 E. Colorado, tel. (970) 728-
4242; **Brody Art Gallery,** 575 W. Colorado,
tel. (970) 728-3734

If you're looking for souvenirs, you'll find plenty of T-shirt and cap stores on Colorado Avenue.

SERVICES

The offices of the **Telluride Police Department**
are in the town hall building at 113 W. Columbia,
tel. (970) 728-3071. The **Telluride Medical
Center** is at 500 W. Pacific, tel. (970) 728-3848.
The **post office** is at 101 E. Colorado.

Recycling
Drop off most recyclables at the transfer station for **United Waste and Recycle,** 330 Colorado Avenue.

INFORMATION

Telluride's **Telluride Visitor Services** operates a 24-hour automated **visitor information
center** at 666 W. Colorado (on the west side of
town, on your right as you approach). This is an
excellent place to pick up brochures and other
information on accommodations and things to
do in the area. Before your visit, write Box 653,

Telluride, CO 81435, or phone (800) 525-3455. For lodging and airline information and reservations, phone (800) 525-3455, or fax (970) 728-6475.

Telluride has two excellent newspapers, the daily *Telluride Times-Journal* and the weekly *Daily Planet*. Check both (25 cents each) for word on local events as well as on matters of interest to the community and visitors alike. Peter Shelton, of nearby Ridgway, named America's Ski Writer of the Year three times, has a regular column in the *Times-Journal*.

Telluride Magazine, published twice a year (summer and winter editions), is rife with information on things to do, and where to eat, stay, and play; it also profiles local celebrities, developers, and developments. Though this is a very commercial and slick publication, heavy on promotional fluff, reading between the lines will teach you a lot about Telluride. It's available at the Telluride Visitor Center and at most real estate offices in town.

Between The Covers Books And Music, 224 W. Colorado, tel. (970) 728-4504, carries an excellent selection of travel- and Colorado-related publications, with a lot of books of local interest. The **Wilkinson Public Library,** tel. (970) 728-4519 or 728-6613, is located at 134 S. Spruce—closed Sunday and Monday.

For **road and weather conditions,** phone (970) 728-3330.

Virtual Telluride

You can also access Telluride's visitor information center electronically. The address is **http://infozone.Telluride.CO.US/TVG.html**.

TRANSPORTATION

Considering its remote, box-canyon location, Telluride's remarkably easy to get into and out of, thanks (or curses, depending on your perspective) largely to the jet airport in town. **United Express,** tel. (800) 241-6522, **Continental Connection,** tel. (800) 525-0280, and **America West Express,** tel. (800) 235-9292, offer passenger service to **Telluride Regional Airport.** And once in town, you'll have no trouble at all getting around. You can walk in five minutes from one end of Telluride to the other, and free shuttles run regularly to Telluride Village and the base of the lifts (or you can ski directly from town, with two of the resort's lifts beginning two blocks from the main drag).

Taxis and Local Transportation

Mountain Limo, tel. (970) 728-9606, **Skip's Taxi,** tel. (970) 278-6667, and **Telluride Transit,** tel. (970) 728-6000, provide local get-around transportation and will meet all flights at the Telluride airport (with 24-hour advance notice). You can also get information on ground transportation by phoning the Central Reservations at (800) 525-3455.

HIGHWAY 145 SOUTH TO CORTEZ

One of the most scenic legs of the **San Juan Scenic Byway,** this 80-mile stretch of state highway cuts across San Juan National Forest and drops out of the San Juan Mountains toward the Four Corners area and the Ute Mountain Indian Reservation. About 10 miles out of Telluride, you'll pass through the tiny town of **Ophir,** a silver camp named for the location of the mines of mythical King Solomon. During the 1870s, the little community boasted some 500 people. Today, it's the starting point for the Ophir Pass road to Silverton.

Lizard Head Pass (elev. 10,222 feet), just a few miles south of Ophir, is named for the 400-foot-high monolith northwest of the highway. Apparently, the needle more closely resembled the head of a lizard before a slab of rock broke off.

Along this route, you'll drive along the east fork of the Dolores River, and pass by several high mountain lakes. The highway also parallels the west fork of the Dolores, a few miles to the west. About five miles north of Rico, you can catch a Forest Service-maintained dirt road that will take you over to and down the west fork, before rejoining CO 145 near the confluence of the two forks, just west of Stoner. From here south, the Dolores runs alongside the highway for 15 miles, past the town of the same name, before feeding into McPhee Reservoir. There are several campgrounds along the river, including **Priest Gulch Campground and RV Park,** at 26750 US 145, tel. (970) 562-3810, where you can also pick up fishing tackle and licenses.

CORTEZ AND VICINITY

Seat of Montezuma County, Cortez (pop. 9,000; elev. 6,200 feet) is the closest large town to Mesa Verde National Park. Situated in the heart of the Four Corners area, the community is surrounded by scrubby mesas and canyonlands once home to tens of thousands of Anasazis. Between about A.D. 550 and 1300, the Anasazi farmed this area, living in elaborate "cities" of stone pueblos, some clinging to cliffsides, some freestanding. The most well known, of course, are the cliff dwellings at Mesa Verde, but this entire area is full of ruins, and the region is remote enough that some of them will probably remain undiscovered forever. In addition, the area is so thick with ruins that even many of those that have been discovered—the smaller ones, that is—are considered no big deal. In fact, in the summer of 1995, a private developer offered to sell 35 acres of land just a couple miles north of Cortez, with at least one ruin guaranteed to exist on each parcel.

Cortez was first settled by nonnatives in 1885, when a group of farmers arrived in the area with plans to irrigate crops with water from the Dolores River. Within a year, the Mitchell Springs Project was pumping water from the river into nearby fields, and in 1887 the town of Cortez was officially founded. The town has served throughout the 20th century as a trading and supply center for local farmers and sheep and cattle ranchers—Ute, Navajo, Hispanic, and white. Recently, tourism has become of more importance, as Cortez capitalizes not only on its proximity to Four Corners-area ruins but to prime recreation areas as well.

SIGHTS

Anasazi Heritage Center

Ten miles north of Cortez and three miles west of Dolores, this BLM-operated research and display center includes laboratories, collection areas, a library, theater, museum, and gift shop, as well as a reproduction of an Anasazi dwelling. The center houses nearly two million artifacts and documents—some of which were recov-

ered from the 12th-century Anasazi site where the center was built—from yucca sandals to blankets and embroidery, and the museum is highlighted by several hands-on displays: grind corn like the Anasazi did or examine other seeds, pieces of bone, flint, or pottery shards under a microscope. In addition, the museum explains dig strategies and lab analyses, portrays the prehistoric Southwest on an Anasazi timeline, and includes a photograpic and textual explanation of the Dolores Valley Water Project and McPhee Dam. There's also an excellent gift-and-book store.

The Anasazi Heritage Center, 27501 CO 184 just west of downtown Dolores, is open daily in the summer 9 a.m.-5 p.m., and 9 a.m.-4 p.m. in the winter. For more information, phone (970) 882-4811. Admission is free; donations accepted.

The Cortez Center/ University of Colorado Museum

This small museum in downtown Cortez emphasizes pre- and post-Columbian Native American cultures of the Southwest. Included are explanations of cliff-dwelliing construction, examples of Anasazi pottery and basketry, and Ute and Navajo pottery and embroidery. Artifacts have been collected from throughout the Four Corners area. In addition, there are traveling exhibits; summer of 1995 boasted an extremely moving collection of Edward Curtis photographs of Native Americans taken during the 1920s (on loan from the CU museum in Boulder). There's also a small gift shop.

Summer evenings at 7:30, Native American dances are held on the grounds next door to the museum. Sometimes Native American storytellers recount ancient tales. Admission to the museum, dances, and storytelling is free, donations accepted. The museums is at 25 N. Market (a half block north of Main/US 160). Call (719) 565-1151 for more information.

A cautious word about scheduling and dependability: Native American dances are absolutely riveting, linked as they are to ancient mythologies and stories and ways of viewing life on Earth. However, due to various conflicts, scheduled Native American dances don't always occur, well, on schedule. In fact, sometimes scheduled Native American dances don't occur at all. I would definitely *not* plan my vacation around a scheduled performance, nor go too awfully far out of my way to attend one, without confirmation first. Call ahead, and then keep in mind that if they say it will happen, the pageant will *probably* happen. Probably.

Crow Canyon Archaeological Center

If you've ever wanted to take part in a dig, actually to visit and work at a legitimate archaeological site, here's your chance. Crow Canyon Archaeological Canyon is a serious research center, with library, laboratories, and computer tie-ins to other centers, all with an emphasis on the prehistoric cultures of the Southwest. In addition, the center offers an innovative program by which visitors can join in the research. A variety of programs are offered, from daylong to weeklong, as well as workshops designed especially for teachers. Cost for the daylong program—offered twice or thrice midweek, June through mid-October—is $30 for adults ($20 for ages 12-18, $15 for under 12), which includes lunch. Reservations are required at least a day in advance. To get to Crow Canyon, take US 666 four miles north from Cortez, turn left on Rd. L, and follow the signs. Note: the road is not paved the last couple of miles. For reservations, or more information on the programs available, call (970) 565-8975 or (800) 422-8975.

Lowry Pueblo Ruins

Occupied by some 100 Anasazis between A.D. 800 and 1000, Lowry was restored in the mid-1960s. Lowry Ruins are nine miles west of Pleasant View off US 666. Pick up a brochure detailing the self-guiding tour.

Dove Creek

Still farther north on US 666 is Dove Creek, seat of Dolores County, where many Dust Bowl farmers ended up after fleeing Oklahoma in the 1930s. Zane Grey lived here for a brief period, and his *Riders of the Purple Sage* is supposedly set here.

In the summer of 1990, two University of Colorado hikers who were tracking bighorn sheep in the Dove Creek area stumbled on the virtually untouched ruins of a 1,100-year-old Anasazi village. Mountain Sheep Village, as the site was named, is significant to archaeologists for several reasons, not the least of which is that it is one of the northernmost Anasazi sites ever discovered. The village, which dates from around A.D. 800, probably consisted of around 200 rooms on six acres and housed between 150 and 200 people.

Not much more populated than the abandoned Anasazi site, Dove Creek consists of several small businesses, a couple of gas station/minimarts, the **Budget Motel,** tel. (970) 667-2234, and the **Country RV Campground and Store,** tel. (970) 677-2850.

Ute Mountain Casino

Feelin' lucky? Want to see what the one-armed-bandits have in store? Think you can draw to beat the dealer's nineteen? Ute Mountain Casinos offers limited-stakes gambling ($5 max), with blackjack tables, video poker, keno, and over 300 slot machines. The casino is open daily 8 a.m.-4 a.m. To get there, take US 160 south from Cortez for 11 miles. You can't miss it.

PARKS AND RECREATION

Cortez City Park

Located next to the Cortez Visitor and Colorado Welcome centers, this grassy hillside park has very good picnic facilities—plenty of shade—as well as a kids' playground, basketball hoops, and a public swimming pool. Directly adjacent to the park (behind and to the north), **Centennial Park** sprawls for several city blocks, offering more picnic tables, large lawns, and a lake/pond where you can feed the resident ducks and geese.

McPhee Reservoir

In 1987, when McPhee Dam was completed and McPhee Reservoir filled in, the world lost some of its most gorgeous river and canyon country, as well as some of its most valuable archaeological treasures. Hundreds of ancient Anasazi ruins, and probably hundreds of thousands of artifacts, now lie deep beneath the surface of the lake, one of the largest in Colorado. Perhaps, though, that is a better place for them. Leaving them undisturbed at the bottom of a reservoir is certainly better than destroying them to build roadways, and maybe more ethical than transplanting them to museum storage rooms. At any rate, as you look out across the water, think about the people who lived in the river valley some 1,100-1,300 years ago, farming beans, corn, and squash, and building intricate stone pueblos. Think about nature's *true* course.

McPhee Reservoir is about 12 miles north of Cortez via US 160, CO 145, and a short access road—also via CO 184. The lake offers boating, waterskiing, camping, and fishing (for rainbow trout as well as warm-water fish such as bass and bluegill). Two Forest Service campgrounds, **McPhee** and **House Creek,** offer a combined 133 sites (no showers at either). For information, phone (970) 882-7296; for reservations, phone (800) 283-CAMP.

River Running

The Dolores River is one of western Colorado's premier streams, though McPhee Dam has impacted it in still-untold ways. Stretches are still runable, however, with several Four-Corners-area outfitters offering trips. Among them: **Durango Rivertrippers,** 720 Main, Durango, tel. (970) 259-0289; **Peregrine Outfitters,** also in Durango, tel. (970) 385-7600; and **Wilderness Aware,** tel. (719) 395-2112 (Buena Vista).

Fishing

The Dolores is also one of the Southwest's premier trout streams, and Cortez is a good point at which to begin an exploration of the river's upper stretches or the 11-mile stretch below McPhee Reservoir. The reservoir itself offers good fishing for trout, as well as warm-water fish. For licenses, supplies, and information, stop by **The Tackle Shack,** 11290 CO 145, tel. (970) 565-6090.

PRACTICALITIES

Accommodations

A junction town and base for folks exploring Mesa Verde National Park, Cortez offers plenty of relatively inexpensive lodging, with numerous motels along the main routes through town (Main St. and Broadway). Among the least expensive digs in the town are the rooms at the **Bel Rau Lodge,** 2040 E. Main, tel. (970) 565-3738.

Doubles run about $30-50. The Cortez **Super 8 Motel,** 505 E. Main, tel. (970) 565-8888, also has rooms for two starting at about $40.

The **Anasazi Motor Inn,** 666 S. Broadway, tel. (970) 565-3773, is one of the nicer lodges in Cortez and has doubles running $40-65. At the **Best Western Sands,** 1120 E. Main, tel. (970) 565-3761, doubles start at $45, and at the **Best Western Turquoise Motor Inn,** 535 E. Main, tel. (970) 565-3778, rooms for two go for $55-85. There's also a *huge* **Comfort Inn,** 2321 E. Main, tel. (970) 565-3400 ($45-90), and, next door, a **Holiday Inn Express,** 2121 Main, tel. (970) 565-3764 ($70-95).

You'll also find several RV campgrounds in the Cortez area, including the **Cortez-Mesa Verde KOA,** east of downtown on US 160, tel. (970) 565-9301, and the **Lazy-G Campground and Motel,** at the US 160-CO 145 junction, tel. (970) 565-8577 or (800) 628-2183.

Food

Cortez offers lots of fast-food restaurants and trucker-style cafes. In addition, several long-time favorites have been feeding locals and passers-through for years. **Stromsted's,** 1020 S. Broadway, tel. (970) 565-1257, is highly regarded for its standard American fare (beef, chicken, seafood), as well as its views from the patio of Mesa Verde; entrees run about $10-18. **Francisca's,** 125 E. Main, tel. (970) 565-4093, is a long-standing local favorite for Mexican food. For Italian, try **Nero's,** 303 W. Main, tel. (970) 565-7366, where dinner entrees run $10-15, with excellent pasta dinners in the $8 range. The **M and M Truckstop and Family Restaurant,** 7006 US 160, tel. (970) 565-6511, is a classic roadhouse, specializing in green chili, Navajo tacos (like a tostada, but on fry bread instead of a tortilla), and Mexican food—open 24 hours a day.

If you've been out in the backcountry living off freeze-dried campfood and just feel like binging, try the **Warsaw Inn Restaurant,** US 160 E, at the junction with CO 145, tel. (970) 565-8585, where a full-service, all-you-can-eat smorgasbord awaits empty tummies.

Shopping

In the heart of Native American country, Cortez has more than a sampling of Native American gift shops and "trading posts." If you're looking

IN CORTEZ "NOTAH-DINEH"

for authentic art—jewelry, sculpture, kachina dolls, etc.—expect to pay for it. The work has gotten very popular in recent years, and gone are the days when you could get a Navajo rug for $50. You'll also find that the prices don't vary a whole lot from one store to the next, though you still should shop and compare. Also, don't fall for the ubiquitous "50% off sale." Seems jewelry is *always* 50% off.

One store worth checking out is **Mesa Verde Pottery and Gallery Southwest,** 27601 US 160 E., tel. (970) 565-4492. Even if you're not interested in buying, poke your head in and take a look around—in addition to quality art, you'll also find inexpensive souvenirs.

Services

The offices of the **Cortez Police Department,** tel. (970) 565-8441, and the **Montezuma County Sheriff,** tel. (970) 565-8444 (or 565-8441 in emergencies), are at 601 N. Mildred. **Southwest Memorial Hospital** is at 1311 N. Mildred, tel. (970) 565-6666. The Cortez **post office** is at 35 S. Beech, tel. (970) 565-3181.

Information

The **Cortez Visitor Center** and a **Colorado Welcome Center** are housed in an adobe-style building at City Park on Main Street. Stop in for information on lodging, dining, recreation, and sightseeing in Cortez, the Four Corners area, and the rest of Colorado. For information before your visit, write **Cortez Area Chamber of Commerce,** Box 968, Cortez, CO 81321, or phone (970) 565-3414 or (800) 346-6526.

For **road and weather information,** phone (970) 565-4511.

FOUR CORNERS AREA

Four Corners is the only place in the United States where the borders of four different states meet. Colorado, New Mexico, Arizona, and Utah all touch here, and the spot is commemorated by an inlaid slab of concrete and a small visitor center.

This is the heart of Native American country. The Navajo, Ute, and Hopi tribes all lay claim to land nearby—the Navajo and Ute reservations abut here, and the Navajos, particularly, count the country around the Four Corners area among its most sacred. As you drive through, you can see why: It's a haunting and strangely beautiful land, miles and miles of barren plains marked by sudden mesas, red rock, and bizarre sandstone cliffs crumbling and melting away like alien landscapes. The hills, dotted with juniper and piñon, roll away like the soft waves of an ocean current to meet the deep sky on a far horizon.

FOUR CORNERS MONUMENT

A stone slab marks the spot where all four states' borders meet, and tourists gather for the requisite photo opportunity (pose on all fours—a foot in Arizona, a foot in Utah, a hand in Colorado, and a hand in New Mexico, and bring a slide of *that* back to show your friends . . .). Native Americans, all of whom are licensed, have booths set up near the parking lot and sell jewelry, pottery, sand paintings, and snacks and refreshments. Maps, brochures, and drinking water are available at the small visitor center, and there are portable toilets in the parking lot. To get to the monument from Cortez, continue south on US 160 for about 38 miles and watch for the signs. The monument is open 7 a.m.-8 p.m., and entrance is $1 per vehicle.

HOVENWEEP NATIONAL MONUMENT

Straddling the Colorado-Utah state line, Hovenweep National Monument consists of six individual ruins, although only one of them, Square Tower, is easily and commonly visited. Built by the Anasazi between A.D. 1000 and 1200, the pueblos, like those at Mesa Verde and Chaco Canyon, were abandoned by 1300. The buildings are characterized by tall square, circular, oval, and D-shaped towers, some of them appearing almost medieval.

The ruins at Hovenweep (a Ute word meaning "Deserted Valley") were first photographed in

1874 by William Henry Jackson. The site was explored in 1917-18 by the Smithsonian Institution, which lobbied for its designation as a national monument; it was given that status in 1923.

The headquarters of Hovenweep are at Square Tower Pueblos, across the border in Utah, though you can approach the monument from the Colorado side; neither road in is paved, and though they're well maintained they can get pretty nasty during summer's regular afternoon storms. At headquarters, you can get maps and advice for exploring the other ruins: Holly, Cutthroat Castle, Cajon, Horseshoe, and Hackberry (none of which you can drive to). To get to Hovenweep National Monument from Cortez, go south for three miles on US 160, and turn west on McElmo Canyon Road. From there, it's 39 miles to the monument (you'll turn north again just over the Utah state line). You can also get there from Pleasant View and Lowry Ruins (see "Sights" under "Cortez and Vicinity," above"). From Pleasant View (20 miles north of Cortez on US 666), go west 27 miles. The turnoff is well marked.

Hovenweep Campground, operated year-round by the National Park Service, has 31 sites and is open on a first-come, first-served basis ($4). For more information on the campground or the monument, write Mesa Verde National Park, CO 81330, or phone (970) 529-4465.

UTE MOUNTAIN TRIBAL PARK

Encompassing 125,000 acres of the Ute Mountain Indian Reservation south of Cortez, this is a sanctuary set aside to preserve the Anasazi ruins of the region. Native Americans lead day-hikes and backcountry overnighters into a gamut of ruins and remains of the ancient culture: cliff dwellings, freestanding pueblos, and petroglyphs.

Be forewarned, though: This may be the most natural and authentic way to see the ruins (no German tour buses), but it's not for lightweights. You'll travel by your own rig over 40 miles of dirt road, hike narrow trails into remote parts of the park, and scramble up primitive ladders to secluded kivas.

Tours usually begin around 8 a.m. June-Oct. and meet at the **Ute Mountain Pottery Plant** 15 miles south of Cortez on US 666. Be sure to call ahead. Tours are often delayed. For reservations and information, write Ute Mountain Tribal Park, Towaoc, CO 81334, or phone (970) 565-3751, ext. 282, or 565-8548.

MESA VERDE NATIONAL PARK AND VICINITY

Mesa Verde ("Green Table") is an 80-square-mile plateau rising 1,600 feet from the surrounding desert and river valley. As early as A.D. 550, Anasazi were living on the plateau, mainly in the shelter of the many narrow canyons that cleave its top. By 1200, their crude shelters had developed into lavish communities, and multistory pueblos were being built into the cliffsides. By the middle of the 13th century, as many as 5,000 people were living in pueblos scattered about the mesa, and the site was a bustling trade center for other pueblos and communities throughout the Four Corners area. Today, the ruins at Mesa Verde National Park are some of the world's largest and best-preserved testaments to ancient civilization.

The first whites to see the cliff dwellings at Mesa Verde were probably members of an 1874 U.S. Geological and Geographic Survey party. Among them was photographer William Henry Jackson, who took the first photos of the ruins.

The mesa's main ruins were discovered quite by accident, however. On December 18, 1888, Mancos Valley ranchers Richard Wetherill and Charlie Mason were riding across the mesa in search of stray cattle. As they peered over a canyon rim, they were shocked to see the ruins of Cliff Palace—several stories high with 200 rooms and 23 kivas. They scrambled down into the canyon and explored the ruin, taking with them bits of pottery and other artifacts, then returned to the top of the mesa, where they split up to look for more ruins. Wetherill soon discovered Spruce Tree House near where the museum now stands. The next day they stumbled upon Square Tower House.

Wetherill eventually became so fascinated with the Mesa Verde ruins he devoted his life to them. He and his family collected thousands of artifacts, most of which they sold to the Colorado State Historical Society and the C.D. Hazard and Jay Smith Exploring Company, which displayed them at the 1893 World's Fair in Chicago.

By the turn of the century, Mesa Verde was being deluged with treasure hunters, and the ruins were in danger of being destroyed. In June 1906, Theodore Roosevelt signed a bill creating Mesa Verde National Park.

The Anasazi

Two thousand years ago, Native Americans were farming along the banks of the Rio Grande south of present-day Albuquerque. Using techniques that had spread north from Mexico and Central America, the Rio Grande tribes farmed corn, beans, and squash, made baskets, and lived in primitive shelters along the river's shores. So fertile was this land and so successful were these early farmers that scientists believe the area actually experienced overcrowding.

Eventually, some of the people left the river area. By A.D. 550, splinter groups had begun to build pit houses and establish small communities on both sides of the Rio Grande, and others had begun to move north toward the Four Corners area.

Although anthropologists refer also to the early Rio Grande civilizations as Anasazi (Basketmaker period, A.D. 1-750), the term is most often used to describe the people who thrived in the Four Corners area from about A.D. 800-1300. The Anasazi (actually a Navajo word that has various translations, including "Enemies of our Ancestors" and "Ancient Foreigners") were a peaceful people—farmers and potters—and highly religious. Their huge adobe and stone pueblos are thought today to have been culture and trade centers, and evidence suggests they traded with other tribes as far west as the Pacific Ocean and as far south as what is now southern Mexico. Their pueblos, three- and four-story apartment-style buildings—both built into cliffs and freestanding—often contained up to 400 rooms, some of which were living quarters, some of which were used to store grain. Also characteristic of the pueblos were kivas, ceremonial meeting places, built partially underground and round—perhaps symbolic of the womb of Mother Earth. The largest of these Anasazi "cities" exist in ruins at Chaco Canyon

National Historic Park about midway between Gallup and Farmington, New Mexico, and at Mesa Verde National Park.

The first evidence of occupation of the Mesa Verde plateau is from the Modified Basketmaker Period (A.D. 550-750). Ruins of their pit houses, as well as their baskets and primitive pottery, have been found in the area. During the Developmental Pueblo Period (A.D. 750-1100) the Anasazi began to reach their full stride. Pit houses were replaced by larger, family-based dwellings, the classic black-on-white Anasazi pottery was being produced, and there is speculation that water-management systems were being developed. It wasn't until the middle of the Great Pueblo Period (A.D. 1100-1300), though, that they began moving into the alcoves formed by the overhanging cliffs. After living on mesas and in river valleys for some 1200 years, they suddenly began work on the cliff dwellings. For years the commonly held anthropological theory was that the dwellings had been built for protection from enemies. Recent research questions that, however. The Athapascan peoples (Navajos and Apaches) weren't to arrive in the area until later, and the Utes probably after them. The Anasazi don't seem to have *had* any enemies. It could be, too, that they moved into the alcoves to more easily control the temperature of their dwellings. For whatever reason the cliff dwellings at Mesa Verde were built, and by the middle of the 13th century, they were home to 5,000 people.

And then they left. Perhaps within the span of a single generation, the pueblos were abandoned.

And just as anthropologists debate the reasons for the dwellings' construction, so do they debate the reasons for their abandonment. One theory holds, however, that the Native Americans simply overfarmed their land and had to seek arable land elsewhere. Other contributing factors may have included a very long drought, as well as, according to former Park Superintendent Robert Heyder, a "mini-ice age." These factors and perhaps others, including the possible arrival of other native peoples, combined with dwindling resources in the late 1200s and possibly the problems that typically attend a city bursting at the seams—overcrowding, disease, unrest, internecine hostilities—most likely led to Mesa Verde's downfall. And yet another theory holds that it wasn't a "downfall" at all. In fact, some modern Pueblos claim that Mesa Verde was just a "stepping stone" for the Anasazi and that they weren't moving away from problems so much as moving on to new homes, perhaps inspired by their trade with other Anasazi in Arizona and New Mexico. At any rate, by 1300, they were gone.

But where'd they go?

As the Anasazi abandoned their large communities, they dispersed, living in small groups and ending up in different parts of the Southwest. Most likely the pueblo people living in northern New Mexico and Arizona—the Hopi, Zuni, Taos, Acoma, and others—are descendants of the people who once lived at Mesa Verde.

Visiting the Park

A visit to Mesa Verde is a highlight of any trip to the Southwest or to Colorado. Ideally, you'd spend several days here, exploring the ruins and the museum, and hiking about the mesa to get a sense of how its early inhabitants lived. But even if you've got half a day, you can still enjoy and benefit from the park. A couple of the ruins are very easy to get to, and even if you're not up for the short hikes to them, there are viewing platforms (wheelchair-accessible) from which you can see the impressive ruins under 100 yards away. In addition, a short visit to the museum and visitor center offers a fascinating lesson in the archaeology of the area and especially of the culture of the Mesa Verde Anasazi. On display are pottery, baskets, cradle boards, fetishes, and countless other artifacts, as well as exquisitely detailed dioramas suggesting how things at the cliff dwellings must have looked when they were thriving—when hunters were returning with game, farmers were harvesting crops, potters were making jars, and children were playing by the water. Other displays explain in great detail the construction and restoration of the pueblos, as well as the various stages of Anasazi culture.

Ruins Road takes motorists along Chapin Mesa to several of the major sites on two six-mile loops. Along the way are viewing platforms or trailheads to over 40 different pueblo ruins. A separate road leads to Weatherill Mesa, where you'll find other sites.

One of the largest, best-preserved, and most accessible cliff dwellings is **Spruce Tree House,** just behind the museum at park headquarters. A short walk on a paved pathway will take you down to the canyon floor and the base of the pueblo. The best-known ruin is **Cliff Palace,** on the east wall of Cliff Canyon. A little tougher, the hike to Cliff Palace requires some scrambling over and between huge boulders. Self-guided Spruce Tree House tours are offered in the summer, and in the winter you can join ranger-led tours. Cliff Palace is open only to guided tours. Another popular ruin is **Balcony House,** which is open during the summer for ranger-guided tours. The tours to Balcony House and Cliff Palace cost $1 per person; purchase tickets and make reservations at the Far View Visitor Center.

As you enter the park, you'll get a detailed map of the mesa, with ruins, turnouts, and other points of interest identified. Just beyond the park entrance is a special parking area for trailers—this will save you from hauling your rig up onto the mesa and trying to find a parking place—in addition, trailers are not allowed past Morefield Campground (see below), located six miles past the park entrance. In addition to the campground, **Morefield Village** has a small store, gas station, and ranger station. At **Far View Terrace,** another 10 miles in, there's a lodge (see below), gift shop, cafeteria, and gas station.

Mesa Verde National Park is open year-round, although lodging and gasoline are available in summer only. In addition, some of the ruins are closed in the winter, when snow and wet weather make the trails dangerous. Admission is $5 per vehicle; the pass is good for seven days.

Accommodations

To really appreciate Mesa Verde National Park, you need to spend a night here. You need to remain after the tour buses depart and the museum doors close. You need to watch the sun go down, and to listen to wind whispering through the piñons and canyons and ruins; you need to sense the magic and the spirit of the mesa, intensified by the eerie quiet of the night.

Morefield Campground is a huge area inside the park with 477 sites on 92 acres. The campground is open mid-April through mid-October and has showers, laundry, a grocery store and gift shop, and evening ranger-led campfire talks. For information or reservations, phone (970) 529-4474 (summer) or 529-4421 (winter).

The **Far View Lodge** is a scattering of single-story multiunit structures nestled in the juniper and piñons of the mesa. With private viewing porches offering stunning panoramas across the mesa and the southwest (clear to New Mexico's Shiprock), the Far View offers one of the state's most unique lodging experiences, with doubles running $75-90. The upscale dining room at the lodge serves chicken, seafood, veal, venison, and Mexican specialties (accompanied by Anasazi salad) for $12-18. For information or reservations, phone (970) 529-4421.

Information

For more information on the ruins, the museum, special group programs, etc., write Mesa Verde National Park, CO 81330, or phone (970) 529-4465 or 529-4475.

MANCOS

Mancos (pop. 870; elev. 6,993 feet) is a small ranching and shipping town about eight miles east of Mesa Verde and 30 miles west of Durango. Situated in a lush valley on the Mancos River, this is a laid-back and quiet little town in some of the prettiest country in Colorado. You'll find a very nice visitor center just off the highway at Railroad Avenue. In addition to literature on where to stay and what to do nearby, the center has a small museum, mostly displaying pioneer history. **Free camping** for tenters and RVers is available at **Boyle Park/Mancos Wayside Park** (two-week limit), where there's also a shady playground for kids. The **Old Mancos Inn,** an old-west-style hotel right downtown and dating from the late 19th century, has rooms for rent as well as a small restaurant. The inn specializes in arranging three-, four-, and seven-day adventure tours of the area—mountain biking, rafting, hunting, fishing, and gold panning. For rates and information, phone (970) 533-9019 or write Box 988, Mancos, CO 81328.

Echo Basin Dude Ranch and RV Park

Perched on a hillside overlooking the Mancos River Valley, this lodge and recreational paradise offers just about everything you could imagine in an absolutely beautiful setting. Stay in a log cabin, haul your RV in, or set up your tent beside one of the property's two lakes. Fish, ride horses, play tennis, croquet, and basketball; in the winter, go cross-country skiing, snowmobiling, sledding, or ice fishing.

Rates are quite reasonable: Cabins are about $120 a night for two, with three meals included, and RV sites are $8. For information or reservations, write 11033 N. 23rd Ave., Phoenix, AZ.

Mancos-Area Information

There's a very nice visitor information center in Mancos at the corner of N. Main and Railroad (frontage road through town). Pick up brochures on lodging, dining, and activities in the area, and talk to staff about the area's highlights. In addition, there's a small museum in back, with historical photos, pioneer clothing, branding irons, etc. Write for Mancos information at Box 494, Mancos, CO 81328, or phone (970) 533-7434.

1-800-449-2288

DURANGO

The largest town in the Four Corners area of Colorado, Durango (pop. 13,560; elev. 6,512 feet) offers excellent access to the area's many attractions—historical, cultural, and recreational. Situated between the southern border of the two-million-acre San Juan National Forest and the northern reaches of the Southwest's stark canyon country, the little community reflects all the vitality, contrast, and diversity of the surrounding geography.

Durango is a youthful and outdoor-oriented town, graced with a wonderful climate and crisp mountain sunshine. During the summer, the otherwise slow-paced town swells with tourists, many of whom come to ride the famous Durango and Silverton Narrow Gauge Railroad and to visit the Anasazi cliff dwellings at nearby Mesa Verde National Park. On those afternoons, motor homes line the streets; droves of shoppers pack into the gift shops, boutiques, and Native American galleries; and locals and passers-through cram the town's many restaurants and taverns, all enjoying a good time in this fun-loving little community.

History

In the mid-1870s, Animas City, two miles north of present-day Durango, was a thriving town with some 2,000 people and its own newspaper. When the Denver and Rio Grande Railroad pushed through, in 1880, it bypassed Animas City and built its own town. Almost immediately, most Animas City residents transplanted themselves south to the new community, Durango, named by a railroad stockholder who had recently returned from Mexico. By late 1880, Durango was home to about 2,500 people, and 500 buildings had been erected.

With a reputation for being a rowdy, shoot-'em-up town in its early days, Durango and the surrounding area was frequented by ranchers and rustlers, miners and claim jumpers, as well as railroad workers and vigilantes attempting to maintain some semblance of order. Between 1880 and the turn of the century, Durango served as a supply center for the mines in the region and also as an ore-processing center.

By the early 20th century, though, as the mining industry throughout the state began to see the full and long-term effects of the silver crash of 1893, Durango followed suit. Its boom days over, Durango became a quiet little shipping center for farmers and ranchers in the Animas River Valley and in the mesa country to the west.

Then things began to pick up again. As more and more people became interested in the cliff dwellings at Mesa Verde National Park and other Four Corners-area sites, and as roads made getting to them easier, Durango became a natural base camp for tourists. In addition, more and more travelers began to take advantage of Southwestern Colorado's myriad recreation activities, from fishing to snow skiing. Finally, in the early 1980s, the Durango and Silverton Narrow Gauge Railroad began to attract railroad buffs and other tourists from around the country.

So today Durango is experiencing another boom. During the summer, the little town's streets are overrun with motor homes, its sidewalks bustling with shoppers looking for Native American jewelry and railroad memorabilia, and outdoor enthusiasts waiting for their shuttles to the river.

ATTRACTIONS

Durango and Silverton Narrow Gauge Railroad

In continuous operation since 1882, the 45-mile railway was for many years the main connection between Durango and Silverton, supplying miners and transporting ore down out of the high country. Today, coal-burning trains take 200,000 people per season (May-Oct.) through the lush Animas River Valley and the gorgeous San Juan National Forest to Silverton. The trip takes eight hours roundtrip (three each way, plus a two-hour layover), although you can also arrange overnight lodging in Silverton or go one direction by bus (six hours is a *long* time to be on a loud, slow-moving, ash-spewing train no matter how

A Durango and Silverton Narrow Gauge Railroad train heads out of town.

gorgeous the scenery or authentic the experience).

Trains depart four times daily from the depot at 479 Main Ave. in downtown Durango (8:30 a.m. and 9:30 a.m.) and return about 5:15 p.m. and 6:15 p.m. Fares in 1995 were $42.50 for adults ($18.50 for kids five to 11; no charge for a kid under five sitting on an adult's lap).

This is Durango's primary summer draw, and reservations are very highly recommended (the main office suggests booking your trip at least 30 days in advance). However, if you're lucky, you can sometimes get last-minute tickets. For reservations and information, write Durango and Silverton Narrow Gauge Railroad Company, 479 Main Ave., Durango, CO 81310, or phone (970) 247-2733.

Animas Museum

This small museum at Durango's north end displays a wide array of historical artifacts from the area, from Anasazi pottery to early ranching gear to domestic items, as well as historical photos. The museum also has a small gift store.

The Animas Museum, at 31st St. and W. 2nd Ave., is open weekdays 10 a.m.-6 p.m. and weekends 11 a.m.-4 p.m., May to September. For more information, phone (970) 259-2402.

Southern Ute Indian Cultural Center

On the Southern Ute Reservation in Ignacio, about 25 miles southeast of Durango, this museum emphasizes the history and culture of the Utes and also displays a variety of Anasazi artifacts, including pottery from nearby ruins. Among the highlights of the museum's exhibits are elaborate 19th-century Ute bead leatherwork. An adjoining gift shop sells authentic arts and crafts. The museum is open Mon.-Sat. 9 a.m.-6 p.m. and Sunday 10 a.m.-3 p.m. For more information, phone (970) 563-9583.

PARKS AND RECREATION

City Park

You'll find a very nice city park on the Animas River, where you can picnic and let the kids play on the swings and slides while river rafters go by just yards away on the other side of the cottonwoods. Go west from US 550 at the Holiday Inn, and turn right when you get across the river. Kayakers can also put in here. There's also a very nice city park beside the visitor information center on the east side of town (US 160 coming in from Pagosa Springs), with more lawns, playground equipment, and picnic tables.

Vallecito Reservoir

About 20 miles northeast of Durango, this reservoir, originally built to store irrigation water, offers a wide range of recreational pursuits. A favorite among local lake anglers, the reservoir has over 22 miles of accessible shoreline, as well as five marinas, where you can rent fishing boats, sailboats, and canoes. The waters hold brown, rainbow, and cutthroat trout, plus kokanee salmon, northern pike, and walleye.

Vallecito Reservoir also offers excellent hiking, with trailheads leading into the Weminuche Wilderness Area. In addition, there are several Forest Service and private campgrounds. **The Wit's End Guest Ranch and Resort** at the lake offers lodging in "luxury log cabins" and a main lodge built in 1870. In addition, there's a dining room and tavern, with mirrors from the 1853 World Exposition. Summer guests can fish, hike, swim, and go horseback riding; winter guests can go snowmobiling, cross-country skiing, ice fishing, and showshoeing. Rates start at $2,670/week per person, plus a 15% service charge. For reservations or information, write The Wit's End, 254 County Rd. 500, Vallecito Lake, CO 81122, or phone (970) 884-4113.

For more information on Vallecito Reservoir, phone the **Vallecito Lake Chamber of Commerce** at (970) 884-9782, or write Box 804, Bayfield, CO 81122.

Hot Springs

Looking for a place to soak away the aches after a day of skiing, mountain biking, or scrambling around the ruins at Mesa Verde? Try **Trimble Hot Springs,** where you can relax in a private tub, swim laps in the Olympic-size swimming pool, or, if you're really hurtin', treat yourself to a massage. There's also a picnic area.

Trimble Hot Springs is six miles north of Durango on US 550. For information, phone (970) 247-0111.

River Running

Next to the narrow-gauge railroad, this is probably Durango's main tourist attraction, with numerous companies offering trips on the Animas and other nearby rivers. Booking a trip is easy. You'll find temporary booths set up along Main Avenue near the train depot, as well as flyers and posters tacked to telephone poles and taped to windows. You can also book river trips through most of the local sporting-goods stores.

The following companies offer a wide range of trips—half day and full day, in canoes, kayaks, and rafts, on the Animas, Piedras, and Dolores

rivers: **Durango Rivertrippers,** tel. (970) 259-0289; **Flexible Flyers Rafting,** tel. (970) 247-4628; **Mountain Waters Rafting, Inc.,** tel. (970) 259-4191; **Peregrine River Outfitters,** tel. (970) 385-7600; and **Rivers West Adventures,** tel. (970) 259-5077.

Cycling

Both touring and mountain biking are very big in Durango, as you'll quickly notice: Lycra-thighed riders pump lightweight racing bikes along roadsides, and it seems every porch has a muddy mountain bike locked to its railing. In fact, as one of Colorado's mountain-biking meccas, Durango is second only to Crested Butte. In addition, Durango is home to Ned Overend, one of the country's premier riders/racers.

Among the trails locals recommend are the **Colorado Trail, Hermosa Creek Trail,** and **La Plata Canyon Road.** The truly adventurous can drive 28 miles north to **Purgatory Ski Area,** tel. (970) 247-9000, haul their bikes to the top of the mountain via chairlift, and ride down on the ski trails.

For maps and information on mountain biking in the surrounding San Juan National Forest, stop by the **Animas Ranger District Office,** 710 Camino Del Rio no. 301, or phone (970) 247-4874. You can also get maps, information, and expert advice from most Durango-area cycling shops, including **Durango Cyclery,** 143 E. 13th St., tel. (970) 247-0747; the **Mountain Bike Specialist,** 949 Main Ave., tel. (970) 247-4066; and **Hassle Free Sports,** 2615 Main Ave., tel. (970) 259-3874—Hassle Free and Mountain Bike Specialist both rent bikes.

To arrange tours, contact **Mountain Bike Specialists.**

Hiking

From Durango you can head out into the woods for a full gamut of hiking experiences. Wander along the river for a couple of miles, taking in the scenery and the mountain air; hike up into the La Plata Mountains and the San Juan National Forest; or tackle part of the 469-mile Colorado Trail, whose southwestern trailhead is just outside town. A good mid-range hike is the six-mile **Red Creek Trail,** which winds through aspens to the top of Missionary Ridge and affords excellent views of the valley below. To get to the trailhead, go northeast on E. 3rd Ave. for 10 miles, turn left at the sign for Colvig Silver Camps, and continue for two more miles. You'll also find excellent hiking trails at Vallecito Reservoir, including several into the Weminuche Wilderness Area.

For more information on hiking and backpacking in the Durango area, stop by **Backcountry Experience,** 780 Main, tel. (970) 247-5830, where you'll find an excellent selection of maps and books, as well as equipment and clothing (rentals available). You can also get maps and information from the **Animas Ranger District Office** of San Juan National Forest, 701 Camino Del Rio, tel. (970) 247-4874.

Fishing

One of the most popular Durango-area fishing spots is **Vallecito Reservoir,** 18 miles northeast of town. Fish along the 22 accessible miles of shoreline or take a boat out into deeper waters and troll for lunker rainbow, brown, cutthroat trout, northern pike, walleye, and kokanee salmon. Boat rentals are available at the lake.

Stream anglers can work the Animas River. Though you can catch trout within the city limits, you're better off heading north or south where there's less traffic. Locals recommend the **Devils Falls** area near the Takoma Power Plant, about 20 miles north of town via US 550.

For gear, licenses, and information, stop by **Duranglers Flies and Supplies,** 801-B Main, tel. (970) 385-4081, or **Gardenswartz,** 863 Main, tel. (970) 247-2660.

Camping

With San Juan National Forest sprawling to the north, Durango offers plenty of camping possibilities. The largest concentration of campgrounds is in the Vallecito Reservoir area, about 20 miles northeast of town. You'll find over a half-dozen different areas with over 200 sites. The largest is **Vallecito Camgpground,** with 88 sites (pit toilets, no showers). The smaller and more private **Pine Point Campground,** also at Vallecito Reservoir, has 30 sites (pit toilets, no showers). For information on these and other Vallecito Reservoir campgrounds, phone the **Pine Ranger District Office** in Bayfield at (970) 884-2512. For campsite reservations, phone (800) 283-CAMP.

You'll also find several Forest Service campgrounds at the Haviland Lake area about 20 miles north of Durango on US 550. **Haviland Lake Campground** has 45 sites on 20 acres (pit toilets, no showers). In addition, there are several Forest Service campgrounds just off US 160 between Durango and Mancos, including **Target Tree,** where you'll find over 40 nicely secluded sites. Phone the **Animas Ranger District Office** at (970) 247-4874 for more information.

Golf

Durango's public course is the 18-hole **Hillcrest Golf Course** on the Fort Lewis College Mesa overlooking town. Phone (970) 247-1499 for information and tee times. The public can also play the private **Tamarron Resort Golf Course,** though Tamarron guests are given priority. Phone (970) 259-2000, ext. 2000.

WINTER SPORTS

Downhill Skiing

Though not the best-known resort in the Rockies, **Purgatory Ski Area,** 25 miles north of Durango on US 550, has its devoted fans—folks who care more about amount and quality of snow than about flash and fashion. With nine lifts on 720 acres and a vertical drop of 2,200 feet, Purgatory offers good skiing for all ability levels; its terrain is ideally diversified, rated 23% beginner, 51% intermediate, and 26% advanced.

Though Purgatory is primarily a day-use area, in recent years the resort has developed its base facilities. There's a shopping area, several restaurants, and on-site accommodations. Shuttles run regularly between Durango and the lifts; phone (970) 259-5438 for rates and schedule. If you're driving, note that the last few miles can get a bit icy during and after storms. Call ahead for road conditions. Ski rentals and instruction are available. You can also rent equipment at many of the sporting-goods shops in town, including **The Ski Barn,** 3533 Main, tel. (970) 247-1923, where you'll find a wide range of gear and accessories.

For more information on Purgatory Ski Area, phone (970) 247-9000 or (800) 525-0892.

Cross-Country Skiing

The lush valleys and deep forests of San Juan National Forest north of Durango offer some of the best Nordic skiing in Colorado. Check out the trails in the **Haviland Lake** area (beginning at Haviland Campground, about 18 miles north of Durango) and at **Molas Pass,** about 35 miles north of town. Both afford perfect opportunities for heading off into the quiet white backcountry—the views in the Molas Pass area are particularly exquisite. There are plenty of places to pull off the road and park.

For groomed trails, check out **Purgatory Ski Touring Center,** at the Purgatory Ski Area 30 miles north of Durango on US 550. The center offers 15 km of trails, as well as rentals and instruction (in Telemarking and touring). For more information on the Purgatory Ski Touring Center, phone (970) 247-9000.

For more information on cross-country skiing in the area, as well as for rentals, contact **Hassle Free Sports,** 2615 Main Ave., Durango, tel. (970) 259-3874. You can also get information from the Animas Ranger District Office of the Forest Service, 701 Camino Del Rio no. 310, Durango, CO 81301, tel. (970) 247-4874.

TOUR

San Juan Skyway

Durango is an ideal starting point for the 236-mile San Juan Skyway, mile by mile one of the most scenic drives in the country. From Durango, the route heads due north on US 550, winds up over Molas Pass (elev. 10,910 feet), drops down into Silverton, rises on the Million Dollar Highway again over Red Mountain Pass (elev. 11,008 feet), then falls dramatically down a series of switchbacks into Ouray. From Ouray, continue north to Ridgway, where you turn west on CO 62, which lifts gently over Dallas Divide (elev. 8,970 feet) and provides excellent views of the Mt. Sneffels Range. On the back side of Dallas Divide, CO 62 tees into CO 145; here, turn southeast for Telluride. From Telluride, continue south over Lizard Head Pass (elev. 10,222 feet), and then head toward the Four Corners area and Cortez. In Cortez, catch US 160 east back to Durango.

Note: The entire loop can be driven in a day— a long day—when the weather's good. However, there are enough interesting diversions along the way that you could easily take three or more days. (All the points of interest on the San Juan Skyway are covered in detail elsewhere in this book.)

ACCOMMODATIONS

Durango's got tons of places to hole up, from private RV parks and budget motels to condos, bed and breakfasts, guest ranches and private cabins, as well as a number of restored historic hotels. In fact, if you drive in from the north on US 550, you'll probably think Durango is nothing *but* lodging: It seems two of every three buildings along this route are motels. Be forewarned, though: Durango fills up during the high season (July and August), and if you show up without reservations you may find yourself scrambling to get a room. In addition, though many of the motels advertise budget rates, you might be surprised at what they are. In Durango in summer, "budget" generally means starting at around $50 for a double.

You've even got a range of choices (read *prices*) should you want to set up camp as close as possible to the train depot. Four accommodation options are within one block: the Durango Youth Hostel, the Durango Lodge, the Rio Grande Inn Best Western, and the General Palmer Hotel.

Prices below reflect the range you'll find for each property. Generally high seasons are summer (June, July, and August) and Christmas holiday (Dec. 24-Jan. 1). You'll find lower prices the rest of the year.

For more information on lodging in Durango, or for assistance booking a room, phone **Durango Area Chamber Resort Association** at (800) 525-8855.

Historic Hotels

The elegant **General Palmer Hotel,** tel. (970) 523-3358 or (800) 247-4747, offers convenience (one block from the train depot) and class, with doubles ranging about $65-145. A few blocks north, the **Strater Hotel,** tel. (970) 247-4431 or (800) 247-4431, has doubles running about $70-180. A couple of bonuses here: The **Diamond Circle Theater** and the **Diamond Belle Saloon** adjoining the lobby, where the bartender and waitresses dress in Gay Nineties garb, garters and all, and you can drink a draft by the window or bellied up to the bar and imagine you're a miner or railroad worker from Durango's early days.

Just south of the Strater and adjacent to the train depot, is the **General Palmer Hotel,** 567 N. Main, tel. (970) 247-4747, where, like at the Strater, the decor and architecture time-travel you back to the 19th century—the hotel was built in 1890. Continental breakfast is included in the rates, which run $70-185.

The **Jarvis Suite Hotel,** tel. (970) 259-6190, was built in the early 1890s and housed a variety of businesses, including a cobbler, a printer,

and a tailor. From 1910 to 1915, Durango's first theater operated on the first floor of the building. The building was remodeled in 1984, and today features 22 suites, each with a fully equipped kitchen. Doubles run about $70-145; ski packages are available in winter.

Other Lodging near the Train Depot

Several other hotels and motels are within a couple of minutes' walk of the train depot, including the **Durango Lodge,** 150 E. 5th St., tel. (970) 247-0955; the **Red Lion Inn,** 501 Camino del Rio, tel. (970) 259-6580; and the **Holiday Inn,** 800 Camino del Rio, tel. (970) 247-5393.

Motel Row

Highway 550 on the north end of town is virtually lined with motels, and rates don't vary a whole lot, generally running $40-60 for doubles. Among the best bets on the strip are the **Alpine Motel,** 3515 N. Main, tel. (970) 247-4042, where doubles run about $40-75; the **Rodeway Inn,** 2701 N. Main, tel. (970) 259-2540, $50-90; and the **Best Western Mountain Shadows,** 3255 N. Main, tel. (970) 247-5200, $50-90. The **Comfort Inn,** 2930 N. Main, tel. (970) 259-5373, has rooms for two starting at about $50.

North of Town

A couple miles north of the last streetlight in town lie a handful of motels that still offer convenience (they're on the trolley route) yet a bit more peace and quiet than those right downtown. The **Iron Horse Inn,** 5800 N. Main, tel. (970) 259-1010, is a sprawling complex with everything from small motel rooms to rooms with lofts and kitchenettes, and also offers horseback riding. Rates run $70-110 for two. Nearby are the **Comfort Inn,** tel. (970) 259-1430, where doubles run $50-90, and the **Hampton Inn,** tel. (970) 247-2600, $55-95.

Youth Hostel

The least expensive rooms in town are probably at the **Durango Youth Hostel,** 543 E. 2nd Ave., right across from the train depot, tel. (970) 247-9905. For $12, you can get a bunk in a shared room.

Camping and RVing

At the southern border of San Juan National Forest, Durango offers lots of good Forest Service camping. In addition, there are dozens of private campgrounds in the area, many of which flank the highway between Cortez and Durango. Durango's **East Piñon Acres KOA,** tel. (970) 247-0783, is just east of town on US 160 heading toward Pagosa Springs. North of town (15 miles) is **Ponderosa KOA,** tel. (970) 247-4499.

FOOD

Start Me Up

A very reasonably priced and popular breakfast spot is **Mr. Rosewaters,** 522 Main (across from the train depot), tel. (970) 247-8788, specializing in healthful meals for folks heading out adventuring (they also sell excellent lunches, including box lunches for train customers). A couple of blocks north is the **Durango Coffee Company,** 730 Main, tel. (970) 259-2059, where you can get excellent lattes and other espresso drinks, as well as muffins, pastries, and desserts, while you peruse the morning paper or plan your day. The little shop also stocks an interesting selection of kitchen accessories, from garlic presses to cookbooks to espresso makers, and also carries homebrew equipment and ingredients. The **Durango Bagel,** across from the train depot at 106 E. 5th, tel. (970) 385-7927, carries a zillion different kinds of bagels (cinnamon raison, strawberry) and cream-cheese spreads (maple walnut, Mexican spice).

North of downtown, where you'll find the majority of the motels, **Lori's Family Dining,** 2653 Main, tel. (970) 247-1224, has earned a solid reputation for its breakfast specials and friendly atmosphere. Lori's is also open for lunch and dinner, the salad bar a favorite.

Farquahrts, downtown at 725 Main, tel. (970) 247-9861, serves Bloody Marys for $1 on Saturday mornings.

Other Durango Restaurants

Another restaurant specializing in healthful meals, including bread (and beer) baked (and brewed) on-site, is **Carver's Bakery and Brew Pub,** 1022 Main, tel. (970) 259-2545, offering veggie specials (salads, stews, and stir-fry), with delicious black-bean dishes, as well as beef and chicken plates. Dinners run $3-7.

Carver's is also open for breakfast, featuring espresso drinks and fresh, home-baked 100% organic whole-wheat bread. Local musicians play informal live music.

If your tastes, or mood, run more toward pizza, try **Farquahrts Pizza Mia,** 725 Main, tel. (970) 247-5442, a local favorite for a variety of pizzas and Italian dishes, as well as Mexican food. A classic, saloon-style restaurant, the place is loud, smoky, and full of local color. Dinners run $6-9, and the restaurant regularly features live music (blues and rock 'n' roll), with open-stage jams every Sunday night. For Mexican food served in a large, cantina-style restaurant, try **Francisco's,** 619 Main, tel. (970) 247-4098, a Durango tradition since the late 1960s. In addition to Mexican food, Francisco's also serves steaks, seafood, and pastas. Dinners run $8-14. Another longtime favorite is the **Red Snapper,** 144 E. 9th St., tel. (970) 259-3417, where in addition to seafood, you can get steaks, beef, and pastas, plus an excellent salad bar; entrees average about $16.

If you step off the train feeling famished and flush, try **The Palace Grill,** tel. (970) 247-2018, one of Durango's best and best-known high-end restaurants. Beef, seafood, and poultry are grilled over mesquite and hardwoods; entrees run $12-18.

The Waiting is the Funnest Part

Downstairs in the Century Mall, 640 N. Main, **Lady Falconburgh's Barely Exchange,** tel. (970) 382-9664, stocks over 125 microbrews and import beers, from all corners of the earth . . . well, at least most corners of the U.S. and Europe. With a large rectangular bar in the center of the restaurant and tables situated around it, as well as high ceilings and skylights, the place has a wonderfully casual feel about it, with picnic tables as well as smaller tables tucked into corners. Wash down your beer with appetizers (fries, pretzels, etc.), or have dinner; salads, burgers, and pita sandwiches run $5-8.

Next door, at 635 Main, **Father Murphy's Pub and Garden,** tel. (970) 259-0334, is another way happenin' place, where locals and tourists sit side by side at the bar or table by table on the patio out back. Dinners—sandwiches, burgers, fish and chips, Mexican specials, prime rib—run $5-12. If the Rockies or

Broncos are playing, the TV above the bar will be tuned to the game.

ENTERTAINMENT

Durango's a hopping little town, especially during the summer when its motels swell with railroaders and river rats, and locals look for places to unwind after a day on their mountain bikes. A continually popular tourist attraction, the **Bar-D Wranglers** offer up a combo plate of live country-and-western music and chuckwagon suppers Memorial Day through Labor Day. A Durango institution for nearly a quarter century, the Wranglers serve a dinner of barbecued beef, baked pototoes, beans, and biscuits nightly at 7:30, "rain or shine." Get there early and explore the Wranglers' "spread"—blacksmith shop, record store (buy Wranglers' records, tapes, and CDs), and other gift shops. Tickets are $12 for adults, $8 for kids 16 and younger (dinner and show). Reservations required. Phone (970) 247-5753. To get there, go north about seven miles from downtown to Trimble Ln./County Rd. 252, where you'll turn right. Cross the railroad tracks and the Animas River, and then continue north on County Rd. 250.

If you're looking for live music in Durango, you don't have to look far, with several local watering holes offering up a variety of music. The **Pelican's Nest,** 656 Main, tel. (970) 247-4431, features live rock 'n' roll, blues, and other music, most evenings. **Farquahrts,** 725 Main, tel. (970) 247-5440, regularly books live rock and blues bands; check out Sunday nights' live jams. **Carver's,** 1022 Main, tel. (970) 259-2545, hosts very informal concerts beginning in the early evenings. For live rock and country-western, try the **Sundance Saloon,** 6th St. and 2nd Ave., tel. (970) 247-8821; Sunday is "family night," with all ages welcome 4 p.m.-11 p.m.

Watch the Durango *Herald* for current listings of who's playing where and what else is going on around town.

SHOPPING

Be sure to allow yourself at least a couple of hours to wander around the shops of Duran-go's downtown area, where you'll find a variety of galleries and gift shops, many of which specialize in Native American jewelry, pottery, sculpture, and prints. Among the galleries worth checking out are **Toh-Atin,** 145 W. 9th St., tel. (970) 247-8277, where you'll find an excellent selection of Navajo rugs, and **Gallery Ultima,** specializing in contemporary Southwestern art. The **Thompson River Trade Company,** 140 W. 8th St., tel. (970) 247-5681, specializes in pre-1940 Native American baskets, weavings, pottery, and other artifacts.

You'll find several sporting-goods stores—whose emphases are on adventure and backcountry outings—as well as a couple of dozen factory outlet stores, including London Fog and Benetton. In addition, there are several boutiques, emphasizing upscale Southwestern styles, and souvenir shops, including several at the train depot, as well as the requisite T-shirt emporiums.

East of town on US 160, the Durango Mall has a JCPenney, Sears, and other standard mall shops.

CALENDAR

Durango's calendar is practically fully booked, especially during the summer when the town's packed with tourists. Your best sources for details on upcoming events are *Durango Magazine* and *Southwest Summer,* both of which are promotional publications with complete listings. Pick up copies at the Resort Chamber office. In addition, watch the Durango *Herald* and its regular supplements.

Among the highlights of Durango's annual events: the **Iron Horse Bicycle Classic,** which attracts some 1,500 riders in a Memorial Day weekend race against a Durango and Silverton Narrow Gauge locomotive to Silverton (47 miles); **Whitewater Races,** a series of races and seminars on the Animas River, attracting some of the country's best-known river runners (early June); **Fiesta Days,** three days celebrating Durango's heritage, with a parade, music, and rodeo (late June); the **Durango Cowboy Gathering,** a three-day festival with musicians, storytellers, and cowboy poets (early October); and **Colorfest,** a multi-event "celebration of color, culture, and adventure" (Sept.-Oct.).

Since 1976, a highlight of Durango's winter has been the annual **Snowdown,** in late January. This five-day celebration includes over 60 different events, from snowsculpting to ski golf and softball, with lots of live music and good eats for competitors and spectators alike. For information on these and other events, contact the **Durango Chamber Resort Association** at (970) 247-0312 or (800) 525-8855.

SERVICES

The offices of the **Durango Police Department** are at 990 E. 2nd Ave., tel. (970) 247-3232. The **La Plata County Sheriff** is at 742 Turner, tel. (970) 247-1155. Phone the **State Patrol** at (970) 247-4722. Durango's **Mercy Medical Center** is at 375 E. Park Ave., tel. (970) 247-4311. The main **post office** is at 222 W. 8th, tel. (970) 247-3434.

Recycling

The City of Durango has its own recycling program, with several drop-off sites where you can leave aluminum, glass, newspaper, and tin cans. The most convenient are at the **City Markets,** 3130 N. Main and 6 Town Plaza (near the train depot). For information on recycling in Durango, or for a listing of other drop-off sites, phone (970) 247-5622.

INFORMATION

The office of the **Durango Chamber Resort Association** is an excellent source for brochures, dining and lodging guides, and complete lists of Durango-area services. Stop by 111 S. Camino Del Rio. In the same building is a National Forest visitor center, where you can get information on hiking, mountain biking, and backcountry skiing in the area. Before your visit, write Box 2587, Durango, CO 81302, or phone (970) 247-0312 or (800) 525-8855. The Durango **public library** is at 1188 E. 2nd Ave., tel. (970) 247-2492.

The independently published **Durango Herald** is published daily and is available in racks around town for 35 cents.

Electronic Information

You can get information on lodging, dining, and outdoor activities through their e-mail address: **durango@frontier.net**.

Bookstores

Durango has three exceptional bookstores always well stocked with books on the Southwest. **The Bookcase,** 601 E. 2nd. Ave., tel. (970) 247-3776, features collectors' and first editions, including some rare enough to be locked away in glass cases. The shop also carries used paperbacks and new books on Colorado and the Southwest, particularly the Four Corners area. **The Southwest Book Trader,** 175 E. 5th., tel. (970) 247-8479, has an excellent selection of books on Colorado and the Southwest, though you might have to dig around, as the little shop is wonderfully cluttered, with books piled on the floor, in every corner, and spilling out into aisles. **Maria's Bookshop,** 928 Main, tel. (970) 247-1438, specializes in books on the Southwest and Native Americana and also sells Navajo rugs and topographical maps of the area. There's also a **Waldenbooks** next to the train depot.

TRANSPORTATION

The **Durango-La Plata County Airport,** 14 miles east of Durango off CO 172, provides passenger service by **America West, United Express, Continental Express,** and **Mesa Airlines.** Durango's **Greyhound-Trailways bus depot** is at 275 E. 8th Ave., tel. (970) 247-2755.

The **Durango Lift** is the town's public transportation system. Buses run regularly through town year-round, as well as to Purgatory Ski Area during the ski season. For routes and information, phone (970) 247-5438. For 24-hour taxi service in Durango, phone **Durango Transportation, Inc.** at (970) 259-4818.

PAGOSA SPRINGS

Pagosa Springs is a combination Old West town and soon-to-be booming resort town. You'll probably be surprised at the huge number of real estate and land-sale offices, particularly on the west side of town. The **Fairfield Pagosa Resort,** also on the west side, is a deluxe spread, with gorgeous executive-style homes right on the golf course.

Named for the nearby hot mineral springs (Pagosa is Ute for "Healing Waters"), which average 153°, Pagosa Springs was the focus of a centuries-long dispute between Navajos and Utes. According to the WPA guide to Colorado, in 1866 the two tribes agreed to a final one-on-one duel over the springs' rightful ownership. The Utes chose as their representative Albert Henry Pfeiffer, a Scotsman who had worked alongside Kit Carson and who had served as a U.S. Indian agent in New Mexico, where Pfeiffer's Spanish wife had been killed by natives. Pfeiffer chose those Bowie knives for the duel. Apparently, the two men rushed at each other, and Pfeiffer flung his knife at his Navajo rival, killing him, and the Utes took undisputed possession of the springs.

Of course, Native American possession of anything of value was not part of the Great European Plan, and Pagosa Springs was no exception. By 1880, a one-square-mile area surrounding the springs had been claimed by the U.S. government, and a townsite was plotted that year.

Throughout the early 20th century, local boosters tried to promote Pagosa Springs as a resort spa, although they were largely unsuccessful. Only in the last decade or so has the area begun to see growth and development to any significant degree.

ATTRACTIONS

Chimney Rock Anasazi Ruins

An "outlier" community of the Chaco Canyon pueblos and cultural center, the Chimney Rock site is a fascinating thread in the Anasazi tapestry of the Southwest—a tapestry that includes not only Chaco, but Aztec, Bandelier (all three in New Mexico), Mesa Verde, and literally thousands of other ruins.

Chimney Rock was named for the twin spires that stand guard over the ruins, which during the 11th century were home to as many as 2,000 people. Recent archaeological research suggests the Chimney Rock site was very likely of great religious significance, and one theory is that the inhabitants of this remote outpost were priests sent north from Chaco. Other anthropologists suggest the community was a trading and shipping center, and timbers from the northern forests may have been harvested here, shipped south for pueblo construction in the barren area around Chaco.

Encompassing six square miles, the Chimney Rock site includes dozens of structures, many of which have been partially restored. Homes, ceremonial kivas, and storage rooms are scattered about the pueblo. Walking among these isolated ruins is a powerful spiritual experience that may help you ask questions to better understand your earth, your self, your ancestors, and your gods.

Touring Chimney Rock is possible only with Forest Service guides, May 15-Sept. 15, at 9:30 and 10:30 a.m. and at 1 and 2 p.m. Groups of 30 leave from the Chimney Rock entrance 17 miles west of Pagosa Springs via US 160 and and three miles south on CO 151. The two-hour tours are $3 for adults, $2 for kids five to 11; reservations for groups of 10 or more are required. For information or reservations, contact the **Pagosa Springs Ranger District** of San Juan National Forest, Box 310, Pagosa Springs, CO 81147, tel. (970) 264-2268, or the **Pagosa Springs Chamber of Commerce,** tel. (970) 246-2360.

San Juan Historical Museum

This small museum features most of the requisite historical-society-type displays, focusing on the Pagosa Springs area's Anglo settlement. Lots of ranching and farming artifacts are featured, as well as early domestic items: a horsehide coat, a turn-of-the-century loom, and early dentists' equipment. Admission is $1 for adults and 50 cents for kids.

The museum, on the east side of town at Pagosa and 1st, is open Mon.-Fri. 9 a.m.-5 p.m., Memorial Day through Labor Day. For more information, phone (970) 264-4424.

PARKS AND RECREATION

City Park

You'll find a very nice city park along the San Juan River next to Pagosa Springs visitor center. In addition to the recently built (1995) riverwalk, there's a lawn, playground equipment, picnic tables, and restrooms. On the other side of the parking lot is the Pagosa Springs Visitor Center.

Hot Springs

The mineral-water tubs at the **Best Western Oak Ridge Mineral Spring Inn,** tel. (970) 264-4173, and at the **Spa Motel,** tel. (970) 264-5910, are open to the public (small fees for nonguests). Both are right down on the river near the Pagosa Springs visitor center.

Golf

The **Fairfield Pagosa Resort** has both a nine- and an 18-hole course. The wide-open terrain offers excellent views of the mountains to the north and east, and of rolling hills and canyons to the south and west. For information, phone (970) 731-4141 or (800) 523-7704.

Fishing

Good fishing opportunities abound in the Pagosa Springs area, whether you like to stalk native rainbows with #18 flies or prefer to sit in a lawn chair and tip brews with a bell on your rod. Stream anglers can pull decent rainbows out of both the east and west forks of the **San Juan River;** the confluence of the two forks is 10 miles north of Pagosa Springs. From town, the San Juan flows southwest, eventually dumping into **Navajo Reservoir,** which straddles the Colorado-New Mexico state line. Another popular trout stream is the **Piedra River,** which drops down out of the Weminuche Wilderness Area about 20 miles west of Pagosa Springs.

Lake anglers often do well at **Capote Lake,** 16 miles west of Pagosa Springs at the junction of US 160 and CO 151 (boat rentals available), and at **Echo Lake,** five miles south of town via US 84. For more information on fishing in the area, stop by **Duranglers Flies and Supplies,** 801-B Main Ave., Durango, tel. (970) 385-4081, or **Gardenswartz Sporting Goods,** 863 Main Ave., Durango, tel. (970) 247-2660.

Arrange guided river trips from Pagosa Springs through **Colorado Fishing Adventures** at Fairfield Pagosa Resort, tel. (970) 731-4141, ext. 2086, or **Sundowner Outfitters,** (970) 264-2869.

Cycling

Biking's a natural here, and though some hardy road warriors attack these high passes, off-road cycling is much more popular. A moderate ride that will introduce you to the area is the 16-mile Willow Draw Loop. Go east on US 160 to US 84, and turn south. At Mill Creek Rd./Co. Rd. 302, turn left, and continue for four miles. The double-track dirt road will be on your left after you pass the third cattle guard. Other rides include several in the Turkey Springs and Chris Mountain areas. For maps and information, stop by any of Pagosa Springs' bike and sporting-goods stores, including **Juan's Mountain Sports,** 155 Hot Springs Blvd., tel. (970) 264-4730, and **Pedal the Peaks,** in the River Center, tel. (970) 264-4110.

Jeep Tours

Pagosa Springs is a popular jumping-off point for folks 4WD-ing up into the high country. A favorite trip is out East Fork Road to Elwood Pass and the Summitville Historic Mining District, a gold-mining camp dating from the early 1870s. **Pedal the Peaks** offers Jeep tours to Summitville, and, if you're so inclined, staffers will haul your mountain bike up for you so you can ride back down. Phone (970) 264-4110.

Camping

Pagosa Springs is literally surrounded by San Juan National Forest, so the camping opportunities in the area are virtually limitless. In addition to the primitive camping allowed by the Forest Service, you can head out in just about any direction and arrive at a designated Forest Service campground. To the northeast lie **Wolf Creek** and **West Fork** campgrounds (75 sites total); take US 160 13 miles to Forest Service Rd. 684. To the south is **Blanco Campground** (18 sites on eight acres, no water); take US 84 13 miles to Forest Service Rd. 656. To the west is **Cimarrona Campground** (21 sites on six acres); take US 160 two miles to Forest Service Rd. 631, and then follow 631 for 22 miles to Forest Service Rd. 640.

For more information on these and other Pagosa Springs-area Forest Service campgrounds, contact the **Pagosa Springs Ranger District** office, Box 310, Pagosa Springs, CO 81147, or phone (970) 264-2268.

Skiing

Wolf Creek Pass Ski Area is one of Colorado's little-known gems. Averaging well over 400 annual inches (!) of the Rockies' finest powder, Wolf Creek is a favorite of some of the sport's most discriminating connoisseurs.

Wolf Creek's six lifts service 700 acres and a nearly 1,500-foot vertical drop, and the area's terrain is about as well divided as you could hope for—20% beginner, 50% intermediate, and 30% advanced. The 10,350-foot base guarantees that all that snow will be nothing but the lightest, fluffiest, most skiable *powder* imaginable.

There are no overnight facilities at Wolf Creek, though there is a restaurant, cafeteria, and the proverbial bar for that post-ski nip. For more information, phone (970) 731-5605.

Cross-Country Skiing

Pagosa Pines Touring Center is west of town at the Fairfield Pagosa Resort. With 12 km of groomed trails winding about the resort's two golf courses, the area offers instruction and rental equipment. For information on rates and hours of operation, phone (970) 731-4755.

The Wolf Creek Pass area is very popular among Nordic skiers who prefer to cut their own trails through the fluff; the views from up here are exceptional. For maps and information on cross-country skiing in the San Juan National Forest, phone the **Pagosa Ranger District Office** at (970) 264-2268. You can also get information and maps, as well as rental equipment, from **The Ski and Bow Rack,** at the east end of Pagosa Springs, tel. (970) 264-2370.

PRACTICALITIES

Accommodations

If you plan to stay here, you might as well take advantage of the hot springs. The **Spa Motel,** tel. (970) 264-5910, and the **Best Western Oak Ridge Mineral Spring Inn,** tel. (970) 264-4173, both offer free mineral-water hot tubbing for guests, and rooms are reasonably priced (about $40 for two at the Spa, $55 at the Oak Ridge). Both are conveniently located right in town across from the visitor center.

The **First Inn,** 260 E. Pagosa, tel. (970) 264-4161, is on the east side of town and has rooms for two starting at about $40.

Food

A Pagosa Springs tradition, the **Elkhorn Cafe,** 438 Main, tel. (970) 264-2146, has a reputation for some of the best Mexican food in the area, as well as hearty American fare—located in the center of the downtown area. For a carb fix, try **Amore's House of Pasta,** 121 Pagosa St., tel. (970) 264-2822, offering standard choices plus vegetarian and low-cholesterol dishes. For beef, try the **Branding Iron Barbecue,** three miles east of town on US 160, tel. (970) 264-4268, which specializes in ribs, links, and chicken. For Chinese food, try **Hunan Restaurant,** 180 E. Pagosa, tel. (970) 264-5922, where lunch entrees run $4-7 and dinners $5-9. An excellent deal is the Sunday all-you-can-eat buffet for $6.50.

Information

Pagosa Springs' brand new **visitor center** building is in the center of town on the river (watch for the signs). You'll find lots of brochures and maps, particularly on recreation in southern Colorado, as well as information on lodging and real estate. To have information on the area sent to you, phone the chamber at (970) 264-2360 or (800) 252-2204.

Moonlight Books, located right downtown, tel. (970) 264-5666, stocks a good selection of books of local and regional interest.

NORTH OF PAGOSA SPRINGS

US Highway 160 lifts northeast out of Pagosa Springs into San Juan National Forest, crosses the Continental Divide into Rio Grande National Forest at Wolf Creek Pass (elev. 10,850 feet) and then drops down west of Del Norte Peak (elev. 12,400 feet) on its way toward the San Luis Valley. Without doubt one of the prettiest 45-mile stretches of highway in the country, the route offers views guaranteed to take your breath. Along the way are a dozen or so forest service campgrounds, as well as trailheads into the backcountry. The first time I drove along here I was returning to California after spending a summer in New Mexico. The lush green forests, the massive peaks, the sprawling lonesomeness of the countryside had me convinced I'd found paradise on earth. I'm not sure I hadn't.

Near the eastern base of the pass lies the little town of **South Fork,** a jumping-off spot for hikers, campers, fishers, and skiers. The **Wolf Creek Ski Lodge** in South Fork, tel. (970) 873-5547, has nice clean rooms (doubles run about $55) and a restaurant. The **Hungry Logger Restaurant,** tel. (970) 873-5504, is a popular refueling stop for locals and passers-through alike. Six miles west of South Fork is **Moon Valley Campground,** tel. (970) 873-5216, with RV sites, as well as guided fishing trips, horseback rides, evening campfires, and a "Sunday devotional."

DEL NORTE

Situated on the far west side of the San Luis Valley, Del Norte (pop. 1,700; elev. 7,874 feet) is the seat of Rio Grande County. Founded in 1860, it was a supply center in its early days for miners working the San Juan district to the west. Apparently those early days were rowdy ones, and a vigilante group was organized to try to bring peace to the community. A ragtag group, the vigilantes succeeded in doing more harm than good, one night shooting up much of the town, including each other—vigilante activity decreased substantially thereafter.

Rio Grande County Museum

Devoted to the multicultural heritage of the area, this small museum features exhibits highlighting the contributions of prehistoric peoples, early Spanish explorers, and Anglo trappers, miners, and farmers. The museum, at 580 Oak St., is open daily 10 a.m.-5 p.m. June-Aug., and 11 a.m.-4 p.m. Sept.-mid-Dec. and Feb.-May. Small admission fee. For more information, phone (719) 697-2847.

HIGHWAY 149 NORTH

Colorado 149 tees into US 160 about 15 miles west of Del Norte, winds north through Creede, crosses the Continental Divide at Spring Creek Pass (elev. 10,901 feet), rises again over Slumgullion Pass (elev. 11,361 feet), drops down into Lake City, and then connects up with US 50 about 10 miles west of Gunnison. Hardly one of the better-traveled routes in Colorado, it nonetheless offers the adventurous traveler a unique perspective on the state, including glimpses of one of the strangest chapters in western history. Also, the route provides a gateway to some of Colorado's most scenic recreation areas. Side trips to excellent fishing, skiing, and 4WD areas begin along here.

In addition, the scenery along here is downright gorgeous. In fact, the 75-mile stretch from South Fork to Lake City has been designated the "Silver Thread Scenic Byway" by the Forest Service. From the upper Rio Grande that parallels the roadside to waterfalls in distant canyons, from high mountain lakes to ghost towns, the scenery here is ever changing and uniquely Colorado.

CREEDE

Seat of Mineral County, Creede (pop. 610; elev. 8,852 feet) dates from 1890, when Nicholas C. Creede discovered silver and staked out the Holy Moses mine. In 1893, the population of Creede was 8,000, and the community had earned a reputation as one of Colorado's rowdiest mining camps. Gunfights were commonplace, and saloons, gambling houses, and brothels operated round the clock. One of Creede's early entrepreneurs was Bob Ford, who killed Jesse James (shot him in the back); Ford was murdered in Creede in 1892.

Creede's first newspaper, *The Candle,* was published by Cy Warman, whose versified description of the town became as well known in the mining camps and as oft recited as the poetry of Robert Service:

. . . the cliffs are solid silver, With wond'rous wealth untold, And the beds of running rivers Are lined with the purest gold While the world is filled with sorrow, And hearts must break and bleed—It's day all day in daytime, And there is no night in Creede.

Creede has faced more than its share of setbacks over the years. In addition to being pummeled by the crash of the silver market in 1893, Creede has four times been all or nearly destroyed by fire, most recently in 1936. The small number of folks who make their home here today, though, are a hardy lot, with much in common with the miners who first settled the town. They appreciate the rugged scenery and the independence guaranteed by their remote location.

Visitors to Creede will find shops and restaurants along the several-block main drag, Creede Avenue, which dates from the town's glory days. Creede's tourism, though, is oriented almost entirely toward summer, when folks flock to town to see the famous Creede Repertory Theater, and many of the town's businesses shut down for the winter.

Creede Repertory Theater

Featuring talented and well-known actors each summer in one of the Rocky Mountains' prettiest pockets, this little theater group presents highly polished productions that have been favorably reviewed by newspapers throughout the country. Established in 1966, the nonprofit company has been steadily growing in quality and repu-

tation for over a quarter century, and many playgoers are longtime "regulars." Plays, a different one each night of the week, are performed downtown in the Creede Opera House. They range from modern classics (Synge's *Playboy of the Western World*) to adaptations for kids. Tickets are about $10. Advance reservations highly recommended.

For tickets and information, write Creede Repertory Theater, Box 269, Creede, CO 81130, or phone (719) 658-2540.

Creede Underground Mining Museum

Operated in 23,000 square feet of tunnels, rooms, and bays, this museum displays artifacts and historical photos from the mining camp's heyday. On exhibit are the town's first fire truck (hand pulled), a horse-drawn hearse, and mining tools and equipment. The museum, at 6th and San Luis, is open daily, with tour times varying according to season. For information, write Box 608, Creede, CO 81130, or phone (719) 658-0811 or (800) 327-2102 (chamber of commerce).

Practicalities

Lodging is available in Creede at the rustic **Creede Hotel** (built in 1890), tel. (719) 658-2608, as are breakfast, lunch, and dinner (rotating dinner menu). Rooms for two are $70 (lower in winter). About 20 miles south of Creede on CO 149 is the **Bristol Inn,** tel. (719) 658-2455, which locals recommend for dinner and Sunday brunch (the restaurant's closed in the winter).

Information

For more information on the Creede area, write the **Creede-Mineral County Chamber of Commerce,** Box 580, Creede, CO 81130, or phone (719) 658-2374 or (800) 327-2102. For information on Rio Grande National Forest, phone the **Creede Ranger District Office** at (719) 658-2556.

LAKE CITY

Sandwiched between Uncompahgre and Rio Grande national forests, Lake City (pop. 250; elev. 8,671 feet) is an 1870s-era mining town with a unique history. First of all, the community seems to have been fortunate enough to avoid the traditional trappings of the other mountain mining camps—brothels, gunfights, gambling, and other assorted manifestations of lawlessness. In fact, by 1877, the town was defined largely by its healthy religious community, with its flocks divided into four churches—Presbyterian, Baptist, Episcopalian, and Catholic. Susan B. Anthony passed through the area on September 20, 1887, speaking for two hours on the suffrage movement.

History remembers lurid excess more than righteousness, though, malevolence more than virtue. And Lake City remembers Alferd Packer, cannibal.

Though Packer's tale has been mythologized over the last century, and historians will probably never fully untangle fact from fiction, a basic story has emerged. Packer had been part of a party of prospectors that stopped at a Ute camp near present-day Delta as the winter of 1874 set in. Chief Ouray, sensing the risk of heading into the mountains, encouraged them to turn back. But men are often blinded by the glare of gold and silver, and Packer and five others didn't listen to the chief. Instead they continued into the mountains. Come spring, Packer alone came down out of the mountains; he claimed he had gone lame and his fellows had deserted him. He had, he said, survived on roots and small game. When offered food, he turned it down; he wanted whiskey instead. He also claimed he was broke, but days later appeared drunk at a gambling hall; some say he was taking money out of several different wallets.

Shortly after a Ute stumbled upon strips of human flesh about five miles from Lake City, a photographer from *Harper's Weekly* discovered in the same area the remains of five men. Their skulls had been crushed and strips of flesh had been torn from their bodies.

Packer maintained his innocence, claiming the men had gone insane and that he had killed one of them, but in self defense. He was arrested, but escaped shortly thereafter and evaded the law for nine years—until 1883, when he was captured in Wyoming. On April 13, Packer was tried in Lake City and sentenced to hang. However, he got off on a technicality and was instead convicted of manslaughter. He was

paroled in 1906 and died of natural causes a year later.

The site where the bodies were found, on the northeast side of Lake San Cristobal, is now known as Cannibal Plateau. Colorado remembers Packer himself in strange ways: Lake City hosts an annual Alferd Packer Jeep Tour and Barbecue, and the cafeteria in the student union at the University of Colorado (Boulder) is the Alferd Packer Memorial Grill.

Lake City, meanwhile, has seen a recent rise in tourism. Though too remote to attract many winter visitors, summer sees the little town swell with passers-through, many of whom take advantage of the great recreational opportunities the area affords.

Summer Activities

Fishing is one of the Lake City area's primary draws, with nearby **Lake San Cristobal,** the state's second-largest natural body of water, known for its rainbow and brown trout. Try a Mepps, Kastmaster, or a red-and-white spoon for rainbows; browns, typically voracious and greedy, can often be taken with Rapalas and other lures that look like small bait fish. Of course, some diehards never give up their salmon eggs. Just below the lake, the **Lake Fork** of the Gunnison River offers good dry-fly fishing, with some decent holes right in town. Both the lake and the river are stocked regularly.

Another popular diversion in the area is four-wheeling, with one of the state's best loops beginning just outside town. The 49-mile **Engineer Pass/Cinnamon Pass Loop** takes you west from Lake City through Henson Creek Canyon and over Engineer Pass (elev. 12,810 feet). Once over the pass, you can either continue on to Silverton or Ouray or circle back to Lake City via Cinnamon Pass (elev. 12,620 feet). Between Lake City and Engineer Pass, you'll travel through several ghost towns, including **Capital City, Engineer City,** and **Rose's Cabin.**

The Lake City area also offers excellent **hiking and climbing** opportunities. **Uncompahgre Peak** is the state's sixth-highest mountain and one of the least technical "14ers." The day-long roundtrip hike gains 5,000 feet in elevation. In addition, the surrounding San Juan National Forest offers unlimited backcountry hikes.

Forest Service camping is available at **Slumgullion Pass Campground,** about nine miles south on CO 149 (21 sites on seven acres, no showers). **River Fork Camper Park,** tel. (970) 944-2389, offers RV and tent camping along the Lake Fork of the Gunnison River. Located right in town.

Winter Activities

Though winter doesn't see the tourists in the Lake City area that summer does, some still like to get out and explore the area. Cross-country skiers can head out in virtually any direction and find the soft peace and winter quiet that a

snowfall in the Rockies ensures. Those who prefer thrills and speed over peace and quiet take to the old 4WD roads on snowmobiles.

Information

For more information on Lake City, write the **Lake City Chamber of Commerce,** Box 430, Lake City, CO 81235, or phone (970) 944-2527 or (800) 569-1874.

For tips and information on recreation, stop by **The Sportsman,** in town on CO 149 S, tel. (719) 944-2526. You can get information on camping in San Juan National Forest from the **Creede Ranger District Office,** tel. (719) 658-2556.

Mesa Verde

Dillon Reservoir

SUMMIT COUNTY

This is one of Colorado's best and most popular year-round playgrounds. Just 70 miles west of Denver via I-70, Summit County—80% of which is within the borders of Arapaho National Forest—offers more recreational opportunities per square foot than any other area in the state, perhaps the country. Skiing, cycling, hiking, off-road touring, and water sports from fishing to windsurfing draw some three million visitors a year.

Situated just west of the Continental Divide in the high mountains of the Gore and Tenmile ranges, Summit County is an outdoor lover's Garden of Eden, with the Snake and Blue rivers, as well as Tenmile Creek, all tumbling through steep canyons and lush mountain valleys; Dillon Reservoir sprawls as the county's centerpiece. With many of the surrounding peaks topping 13,000 feet, and the towns themselves nestled in 9,000-foot-high valleys, this is about as close to the Rockies' soul as one can get.

During the winter, Summit County, whose full-time population is about 8,000, swells with winter sports enthusiasts from around the world. Skiers flock to the slopes of four of the state's best ski areas: Arapahoe Basin, Breckenridge, Copper Mountain, and Keystone. The funky little streets of Frisco and Breckenridge—mining towns rich in history—are full of shoppers and

SUMMIT COUNTY HIGHLIGHTS

skiing: Arapahoe Basin, Keystone, Copper Mountain, Breckenridge

fishing: Dillon Reservoir, Green Mountain Reservoir, Blue River, Tenmile Creek

whitewater rafting: Blue River, plus access to nearby Arkansas and Colorado rivers

bicycling: Blue River Bikeway, Tenmile Canyon National Recreation Trail, Vail Pass Bikeway

also: summer chairlift rides at Breckenridge and Copper Mountain, sleigh rides, snow tubing, museums, golf, hiking, horseback riding, jeep tours, historical tours, ballooning in Dillon, shopping, Breckenridge's Ullr Fest, Copper Mountain's West Fest après-skiers, bundled up against the cold, their ski boots crunching the dry snow. More skiers visit Summit County per year than Aspen and Vail combined.

When the snow disappears from the mountainsides and the ski lifts shut down, Summit County turns its attention to warm-weather recreation. Sails appear on Dillon Reservoir. Bicycles come out of storage, then are tuned and readied for the nearly 50 miles of paved bike paths and hundreds of miles of backcountry trails. Golf clubs are dusted off, tennis nets unfurled and strung across courts, softball gloves oiled for another season.

All of which means you won't have any trouble occupying yourself during your visit to Summit County. And on the off chance that occupying yourself isn't what you had in mind, this is one of the best places in Colorado to simply relax. The mountain sunshine, the scent of pines, the sound of water gently lapping against the shore—Summit County is the best prescription you'll find for urban anxiety, whether you're just passing through or you're here for the long haul.

INTRODUCTION

HISTORY

Summit County's history dates from summer 1859, when prospectors discovered gold on the Blue River and built a blockhouse near what is now **Breckenridge** as protection from the Utes, who had long claimed this land for their own. Word of the strike soon got out, and when the snows melted the following year, hordes of miners descended on the valley from Denver. Before long, a substantial mining camp had sprung up, with several other smaller ones in the surrounding area. Because the camps were so isolated, the miners sought to be assigned their own post office, and in a political move named their community for Vice President John C. Breckinridge. The town was then granted mail service. When the Civil War broke out and Breckinridge sided with the South, angry citizens changed the spelling of the town's name to Breckenridge.

Silverthorne was founded in 1881, when Judge Marshal Silverthorne purchased 160 acres of land from the U.S. government. Within a couple of years, the savvy Silverthorne, who ran the Silverthorne Hotel in Breckenridge, had discovered an efficient way to extract gold from the Blue River. He eventually got a patent for the Silverthorne Placer.

Dillon was founded around the same time as Silverthorne, although the present-day town is actually Dillon number three. The town was originally built east of the Snake River; when the railroad arrived, it was moved across the Blue River to be closer to the depot. The new little town did quite well, supporting two newspapers, four saloons, and a couple of general stores. In the early 20th century, local skiers built a ski run above the town, which in 1919 was the site of a world-record-setting ski jump: 213 feet.

In the late 1950s, though, in response to Denver's water shortage, the Blue River was dammed to form Dillon Reservoir. Old Dillon and the ski hill were submerged deep beneath the lake. Dillon was moved to its present site in 1961.

Though miners had used snow skis to get around as early as the 1880s, and turn-of-the-century Summit County residents had begun to use skis for recreation, it wasn't until the late 1940s that skiing really began to take off in the area. That was the year Arapahoe Basin opened, and a number of lodges and inns were built in the Dillon-Keystone area, turning the county into a prototypical ski resort. By the mid-1960s, the nation had caught "ski fever," and Summit County was in the perfect position to take advantage of it. By the winter of 1972-73, all four of Summit County's ski areas were open for business and attracting skiers from all over the world. That winter also saw the completion of the first bore of Eisenhower Tunnel through Loveland Pass, making for a safer and faster drive from Denver. See the "Eisenhower Memorial Tunnel" special topic.

The 1970s and '80s witnessed huge improvements at the ski areas, not only in additional acres and increased numbers of lifts, but in technology (better, faster, and safer lifts), in-structional methods, shuttle services, lodging facilities, and on-mountain amenities. Also during the '70s and '80s, Summit County began to develop into a four-season resort area, with summer visitors flocking to the area to golf, mountain bike, whitewater raft, and hike the back trails of Arapaho National Forest.

And as more came to play, more came and stayed. In the mid-1990s, Summit County began to show the unpleasant signs of growth. New housing developments crept toward Lake Dillon, and forested hillsides were laid bare to make way for shopping centers and condominium complexes. Traffic snarled at intersections, and folks began to resent newcomers, whom they blamed for the problems. So Summit County, like many of Colorado's wonderfully desirable destinations, will have some choices to make; if it is to remain the Eden it is, planning will have to be intelligent, sensitive, and far-sighted.

Meanwhile, Summit County today offers many chances to view its history, offering sometimes startling comparisons between past and present. The Summit County Historical Society sponsors walking tours of Breckenridge Historical District, as well as tours to mining towns; Frisco Historic Park displays buildings from that town's heyday. And if that's not enough, just take a gander at the tailings along the Blue River between Frisco and Breckenridge. Unfortunately, mining leaves ugly scars, and the county hasn't wholly escaped the fate that has befallen so many other Colorado mining regions.

SILVERTHORNE

Silverthorne lies at the junction of I-70, US 6, and CO 9, and though it dates from the 1860s, the town has the feel of the popular tourist stop that it is. Silverthorne sees millions of travelers annually, many of whom stop to take advantage of the chain motels and hotels, fast-food outlets, gas stations, recreation-equipment-rental outfits, and the huge Silverthorne Factory Stores mall. Get a sense of less-traveled Silverthorne, and take a drive north on CO 9; this is the gateway to the Blue River Valley and Eagles Nest Wilderness Area. Hidden in the pines directly west of the central shopping areas, on the hillside overlooking I-70 and the lake, are a number of condominium complexes and deluxe vacation homes.

DILLON

On the shore of Summit County's centerpiece, Dillon Reservoir, Dillon is a blend of backwoods cabins, modern vacation homes, and deluxe hotels and condo complexes. Its streets winding through the pines and down by the lake, Dillon is without a real "downtown," though the Dillon Mall is home to several restaurants, business offices, ski shops, and other retailers.

Dillon has been a popular resort community since the 1940s, when Arapahoe Basin skiers built log cabins in the area and the first restaurants and lodges opened. Today, the community offers some of the most upscale lodging in the county. During the summer, Dillon is very popular with sailors, anglers, and other water-sports enthusiasts, who can lodge within yards of the lakeshore.

KEYSTONE

Like Copper, Keystone is a self-contained vacation resort area devoted largely to skiing. Found in the lush Snake River Valley above Dillon Reservoir, Keystone is surrounded by massive mountains rising to over 13,000 feet. Keystone first opened for skiing in the winter of 1969-70.

Tucked away among thick pine forests, Keystone comprises condominium complexes, the Keystone Conference Center, and a small village with ski stores, gift shops, and restaurants. To keep the cash flow at least moderate between ski seasons, Keystone offers a wide range of summer activities, including gondola rides, horseback riding, and golf. The resort also hosts the annual Keystone Music Festival with classical and pop concerts by the National Repertory Theater and the Summit Brass.

MONTEZUMA

The highest occupied community in the United States (elev. 10,268 feet), Montezuma is a tiny town isolated just off the Continental Divide five miles east of Keystone; the main street through town is still unpaved. Dating from the late 1800s, Montezuma has yet to be taken over by T-shirt and souvenir shops, unlike other 19th-century silver-mining towns like Cripple Creek and Central City, although you will find a small grocery-and-supplies store in town. A small handful of hardy Summit Countians call Montezuma home. To get there take Montezuma Rd. off US 6 just east of Keystone.

HEENEY

Heeney is the northernmost community in Summit County. Established on Green Mountain Reservoir off CO 9, the town is small enough and far enough away from the ski resorts that it doesn't take itself too seriously. To wit: Each June, the town sponsors the Heeney Tick Festival, which, according to one story, began when a popular Heeneyite recovered from a tick-bite related sick spell. The highlight of the festival, which also features a dance and kids' programs, is the parade down Main St., with "tick-sized floats."

FRISCO

At the junction of I-70 and CO 9 in the center of Summit County, Frisco (pop. 1,320; elev. 9,000 feet) offers excellent access to the county's skiing and other recreational sports. A late-19th-century mining town, Frisco today is an unpretentious little community defined by friendly people who seem somehow less caught up in the glamour of the ski industry, though the town's economy is still largely dependent on winter tourists.

The town's quiet main drag has a handful of restaurants, older motels, and sports and gift stores. The back streets south of Main are lined with old homes and cabins, some converted to bed and breakfasts; larger vacation-type homes and complexes are scattered in the woods just north of Main. Not far from the downtown area, Frisco loses some of its intimacy and charm, the highway both north and south lined with fast-food restaurants, gas stations, and malls (with a Wal-Mart, a Safeway, and other modern conveniences).

BRECKENRIDGE

Breckenridge, the county seat (pop. 1,200; elev. 9,500 feet), is both the oldest and the largest community in Summit County. Located in the Blue River Valley at the base of the massive Tenmile range, Breckenridge is a ski town in the truest sense of the term, with the three-mountain Breckenridge Ski Resort dropping nearly down to the little town's ski-shop-lined Main Street.

Dating from the mid-19th century, when it was a roaring mining camp, Breckenridge is a National Historic District, and many of its Victorians have been gorgeously restored, today housing bed and breakfasts, restaurants, and retail shops. In contrast, several deluxe hotels, convention centers, and condominium complexes are scattered on the hills between Main Street and the ski area.

One of the oldest continually occupied mining towns in the state, Breckenridge still has a bit of a frontier feel to it. It's a young and vital town that can still get awfully rowdy on Saturday nights when the bars are packed with ski resort employees, grunged-out snowboarders, and miners down out of the mountains spending their paychecks.

During the summer, downtown Breckenridge becomes a shopping mecca, its sidewalks packed with visitors exploring the scores of gift and souvenir stores, boutiques, and T-shirt shops. Many of the restaurants feature patio seating, and you can sit and enjoy a salad and a lemonade, or a burger and a beer, in the crisp thin-air sunshine.

COPPER MOUNTAIN

Copper Mountain is a self-contained resort community, with several high-rise condominium complexes and lodges, as well as a central plaza area where you'll find a conference center, ski shops, boutiques, and restaurants. Many Copper employees live in on-site resort-owned housing.

Copper Mountain first opened in the winter of 1972-73 and revolves primarily around snow skiing. During the winter, the place bustles with skiers in for the day from Denver as well as Texans, New Yorkers, and Europeans here to hit the slopes for a week or more. In the summer, things die down considerably, though the resort also offers a variety of recreation, including golf at Copper Creek Golf Club, as well as tennis, fishing, and whitewater rafting.

MUSEUMS

Summit County is much richer in history than it is in museums, although the Summit Historical Society, with local dynamo Rebecca Waugh at the helm, has recently increased efforts to bring history

to the public. The **Dillon Schoolhouse Museum,** a 19th-century one-room schoolhouse, displays early educational supplies, desks, readers, and musical instruments. The museum is located at 403 La Bonte St., Dillon, and is open late May to early September, Wed.-Sat. 11 a.m.-4 p.m.

Also administered by the Summit Historical Society is the **Montezuma Schoolhouse Museum,** isolated in the deep woods east of Keystone at the old Montezuma mining camp. A visit here is an excellent way to learn about mining and the early settling of Summit County. The Montezuma Schoolhouse Museum is open

BRECKENRIDGE

CITY MARKET / SHOPPING CENTER

9 TO FRISCO

BLUE RIVER BIKE PATH

NORDIC SKI CENTER

SKI HILL RD.

WATSON

BRIAR ROSE LN.

FRENCH ST.

TO PEAK 8 SKILIFT BASE

SAWMILL RD.

BLUE RIVER

LINCOLN AVE.

SUMMIT COUNTY LIBRARY

WASHINGTON ST.

FOUR O'CLOCK RD.

PARK AVE.

MAIN ST.

ADAMS AVE.

KINGS CROWN RD.

PRIMROSE PATH

JEFFERSON AVE.

NOT TO SCALE

= SUMMIT STAGE STOP

P = PUBLIC PARKING

VILLAGE RD.

PEAK 9 SKILIFT BASE

TO FAIRPLAY

BOREAS PASS RD.

9

© MOON PUBLICATIONS, INC.

DILLON RESERVOIR AREA

EAGLES NEST

9

TO GREEN MOUNTAIN RESERVOIR

TO DENVER

70

DILLON

SILVERTHORNE

TOURIST INFORMATION CENTER

DAM RD.

6

TO ARAPAHOE BASIN & LOVELAND PASS

WILDERNEST

DILLON RESERVOIR

KEYSTONE

6

SNAKE RIVER

HEATON BAY

FRISCO

PINE GROVE

9

SUMMIT MEDICAL CENTER

FRISCO NORDIC CENTER

MAIN ST.

TOURIST INFORMATION CENTER

SWAN MOUNTAIN RD.

BLUE RIVER

TO VAIL

70 6

MOON

COPPER MOUNTAIN

91

TO LEADVILLE

TO BRECKENRIDGE

9

NOT TO SCALE

© MOON PUBLICATIONS, INC.

Saturday only early July through mid-August. To get there, take US 6 past Keystone to Montezuma Rd., and continue about five miles to the town of Montezuma. Admission to both museums is by donation. For more information on either, phone (970) 453-9022.

Frisco Historic Park

This collection of seven buildings from late-19th-century Frisco will give you a good idea of what the town was like as a logging and mining center. Included are a one-room schoolhouse, a jail, a ranch house, and a chapel. The museum also displays historical photos, clothing, and other artifacts from the period.

Frisco Historic Park, at the corner of Main and 2nd, is open Tues.-Sat. 11 a.m.-4 p.m. (through Sunday, Memorial Day through Labor Day). Admission is free. For more information, phone (970) 668-3428.

PARKS AND RECREATION

Okay, museums are all fine and well, but you can't fool me. You didn't come to Summit County to brush up on your history. You came to play. Though one of the side benefits of this playground is its marvelous sense of history, its main draw is recreation. And though Summit County's begun to sell itself this past decade as a year-round resort, the area's really about skiing. When the first downy flakes of the white stuff begin to swirl from a dark autumn sky, Summit County turns its attention to the slopes.

For complete information on the wide range of recreational possibilities in Summit County, contact the Forest Service office at 135 CO 9 in Silverthorne, tel. (970) 468-5400, and ask for their *Recreation Opportunity Guide*.

SKIING

Four of Colorado's best ski areas are concentrated within the borders of relatively tiny Summit County. No matter what your level—whether you're a first-time beginner or a retiring weideler, bump basher, powderhound, or chute shredder—you're bound to find something in Summit County to your liking. With a total of nearly 60 lifts servicing almost 300 marked trails on 4,000 acres of skiable terrain, Arapahoe Basin, Breckenridge, Copper Mountain, and Keystone combine to offer some of the finest skiing in the country.

Avoiding the Crowds

And, unfortunately, sometimes it seems as though *everyone* is here. Not only are these some of the best ski areas in the state, but they're also about the most accessible—just 70 miles from Denver, with shuttles running back and forth about every 10 minutes. So the slopes can get crowded.

And so can the roads.

Not only does I-70 bottleneck between the resorts and Denver on Friday and Sunday afternoons, but some of the smaller access roads can also grind to standstills. Hints to avoid crowds: unfortunately, no profound secrets here. In fact, most folks know exactly how to avoid crowded slopes—it's just that their jobs won't let them. If yours does, try this: don't ski weekends, especially long ones; don't ski during Christmas vacation (approximately Dec. 26-Jan. 2 or 3). If you have no choice but to ski during those crowded times, get up early, get to the parking lot early, buy your ticket early, start skiing early, break for lunch early, quit early. Then get to bed early and do it again.

Skiers pause to take in the view at Keystone.

Also, don't forget about late-season skiing. Arapahoe Basin regularly stays open until June, and then it might only close due to lack of customers. Just because your friends are calling you to play tennis or to chase trout, don't think the ski season's over. Indeed, you could very easily head up to the Basin one fine spring day and look around you and find that you *are* the lift line, that you're the only one on the entire lift, or that you've got a whole mile-and-a-half run all to your lonesome. Ain't nobody but you and the mountain, one of the greatest feelings in the world.

Lift Tickets

As lift-ticket prices surpass the $45 mark, a day's skiing takes a bigger and bigger chunk of your life's savings. And unless you're Donald Trump or Michael Jackson, you'll probably want to keep an eye out for ways to trim the cost. You won't be able to save a whole lot, but if you play your cards right, you will find breaks here and there. First of all, most of the resorts offer multiday discounts, and you can buy tickets good at all four resorts. Second, many of the retailers in the area—from grocery stores to ski-rental outlets—offer discounts. Watch the local papers, coupon booklets, and advertising. Three bucks saved on a lift ticket will almost buy you a beer at the end of the day.

Arapahoe Basin

A look at these terrain statistics: 40% advanced, 50% intermediate, 10% beginner tells you A-Basin is one demanding ski area. Steep, challenging, unforgiving—where some of the toughest skiers in the area fine-tune their chops. Skiers who don't care this is the smallest ski area in Summit County know it's the best, and a lot of them wouldn't ski anywhere else. Not only that, it's also the one with the longest season. Its high base ensures a late snowpack, and the resort regularly stays open until June. In fact, in 1995, A-Basin was open for skiing on July 4th (it got seven new inches of snow that day), with plans to stay open at least until Labor Day.

Arapahoe Basin first opened shortly after WW II, when members of the U.S. Army's 10th Mountain Division improvised a cable ski lift using old mining equipment. The resort stayed small and low-key, even as many of the state's

EISENHOWER MEMORIAL TUNNEL

First open to traffic in the spring of 1973 and completed in 1979, when the second bore was punched through, Eisenhower Memorial Tunnel cost just under $300 million and tremendously increased the accessibility of Colorado's ski resorts. The new route cut as much as an hour off the drive from Denver to the lifts at Vail, Copper Mountain, Breckenridge, and the others. In fact, the new tunnel so dramatically opened up the mountain resorts to motorists (its first year 4.6 million cars passed through) that within 10 years of its completion it was already being viewed as inadequate, and the highway department was bemoaning that the tunnel's four lanes weren't six. State highway officials estimate that by the turn of the century the tunnel will see some 10 million cars a year, far more than it was designed to, or is able to, accommodate.

In addition to the snags on the back sides of the two major summer holidays (Memorial and Labor days), Eisenhower and I-70 also get snarled on winter weekends, especially the three- and four-day presidents' celebrations in February.

For road conditions in the Eisenhower Tunnel area, phone (303) 639-1111.

other ski areas were being developed into major destination resorts. In the late 1970s, A-Basin was bought by Keystone, whose owners invested money in upgrading the Basin; still, it remains refreshingly unglitzy. This is in part because it's the least accessible of the four Summit County ski areas. Sitting high on the west side of Loveland Pass, Denver skiers must get there either by driving through Eisenhower Tunnel to Dillon and then turning around and going east again via US 6, or they must drive over the top of the pass, a harrowing if awesomely scenic road, and drop down to the base of the lifts.

Today, A-Basin has five lifts servicing 30 trails on 350 mostly above-timberline acres. Its 360-inch average snowfall, coupled with its 10,780-foot *base,* ensures a season through June, oftentimes longer. The same lift ticket is good at both Keystone and A-Basin, and shuttles run every 20 minutes between the two (there are no accommodations at Arapahoe), though again beginners would be better off heading elsewhere and mastering at least a decent christy turn before risking frustration here. Those whose goal is to sample the range of American skiing owe it to themselves to try the Basin, where you're as close to the top of the world as any chairlift will take you.

For more information on Arapahoe Basin, phone the resort at (970) 468-0718 or (800) 222-0188, or write Keystone Resort, Box 38, Keystone, CO 80435, tel. (970) 468-2316.

Keystone

In contrast to Arapahoe Basin, Keystone is an area ideally suited to beginners and intermediate skiers. Excluding the North Peak area (see below), Keystone's terrain is 20% beginner, 65% intermediate, and 15% advanced.

Keystone is the epitome of a user-friendly resort. Among its attractions: well-groomed slopes ideal for effortless cruising, high-tech lifts and equipment, exceptional instructional programs, convenient accommodations and facilities, and night skiing—lifts run for 13 hours.

The addition of Keystone's back side, the North Peak/Outback area, significantly increased the resort's advanced skiing; the Outback is 29% intermediate and 71% advanced. Combined, the two areas' 19 lifts service a 2,340-foot vertical drop (snowmaking on 849 acres). The longest run is over three miles.

To get there, take US 6 east from Dillon and watch for the signs.

For more information on skiing Keystone, contact the resort at Box 38, Keystone, CO 80435, tel. (970) 468-2316.

Copper Mountain

Privately owned Copper Mountain (the other three resorts are owned by Ralston-Purina) first opened in the winter of 1972-73 as a completely self-contained resort community. The second-largest ski resort in Summit County, Copper Mountain leases from the Forest Service three separate mountains, which naturally divide the resort's terrain fairly evenly among ski abilities (22% beginner, 27% intermediate, 35% advanced, 16% expert). Expansion in the late summer of 1995 added 700 more acres skiable terrain, bringing the total to 2,070 acres, serviced by 20 lifts, including two quad chairs and six triple chairs.

Because of the wide range of excellent skiing, as well as the resort's wonderful accessibility (it's just yards from I-70 on the east side of Vail Pass), it's a favorite of Denver day-trippers. Its range of fine skiing also attracts families and other groups within which ability levels vary. Groups can ski together awhile, then head off for terrain suited to their individual abilities, then meet again for lunch or to show off for each other before retiring at day's end.

Another one of Copper's advantages is its self-containment. There's plenty of on-site lodging, shopping, and dining, and it's a great place to hole up for a week doing nothing but skiing—you can be out your door and on the slopes in minutes.

For more information on skiing or accommodations at Copper Mountain, write Copper Mountain Resort Association, Box 3001, Copper Mountain, CO 80433, tel. (970) 968-2882 or (800) I-LUV-FUN.

Breckenridge

With over 2,000 skiable acres, Breckenridge is Summit County's largest ski area. Sixteen lifts service 112 designated trails, the longest of which is three miles. Like Copper Mountain, Breckenridge offers a roughly even mix of beginning, intermediate, and advanced skiing, though recent expansion has made the area increasingly attractive to advanced skiers (the actual breakdown is 17% beginner, 26% intermediate, and 57% advanced). Also like Copper, Breckenridge sprawls over three separate mountains—Peaks 8, 9, and 10. Beginning and low-intermediate skiers have the lower parts of Peaks 8 and 9 to roam, while advanced skiers claim the back sides of peaks 8 and 10, which are also good places to avoid crowds. The two base areas provide access to all three mountains.

One of Breckenridge's real pluses are its open-mindedness and the resulting on-mountain eclecticness. One of the first ski areas in the state to okay snowboarding—skiing's Eddie Haskell of a little cousin—then actively to court the wild snow surfers, Breckenridge has hosted the World Snowboard Championships. The resort is also popular with Telemarkers.

Something else distinguishing Breckenridge from Copper, Keystone, and A-Basin is both a town and the ski resort—in fact, the town and the ski area are virtually one and the same. Much like Telluride and Aspen, Breckenridge is a ski town in the truest and most aesthetically pleasing sense. Though Breckenridge claims its share of condos and fancy modern motels, the town is much more defined by its Victorian-lined main streets, its tiny shops, and its laid-back locals—young, unpretentious, and completely ski oriented. After a good dump, the little town's streets are all but deserted, as just about everyone's "gone skiin'."

For more information on skiing and accommodations in Breckenridge, contact **Breckenridge Ski Corporation,** Box 1058, Breckenridge, CO 80424, tel. (970) 453-2368, or **Breckenridge Resort Chamber,** Box 1909, Breckenridge, CO 80424, tel. (800) 221-1091 or (800) 822-5381 (in Colorado).

Cross-Country Skiing

Take a look at the racks atop cars coming into Summit County from Denver, as well as those on local rigs, and you'll see that cross-country skiing is, if not as popular as downhill, certainly the passion of *many* people. In fact, Summit County skinny skiers have even more to choose from than Alpiners do: everything from quiet, ungroomed lakeside trails to groomed skating tracks to the lift-serviced runs of the resorts themselves, where three-pinners practice Tele turns on the same slopes as downhillers.

Frisco Nordic Center, 1121 N. Summit Blvd., Frisco, tel. (970) 668-0866, offers nearly 40 km of trails (one-way loops) in the woods near Dillon Reservoir. Lessons and rentals are available. **Copper Mountain Nordic Center,** Box 3001, Copper Mountain, CO 80443, tel. (970) 968-2882, ext. 6342, has 25 km of groomed track and skate lanes. A favorite among intermediate and advanced Nordic skiers, this center also provides access to Copper Mountain's lifts, as well as a variety of special programs, including races, moonlight tours, and Telemark, waxing, and snow-safety workshops. **Breckenridge Nordic Ski Center,** Box 1200, Breckenridge, CO 80424, tel. (970) 453-6855, has 30 km, rentals, and lessons (located a mile west of town on Ski Hill Road). Cruise the Keystone area at **Keystone Cross-Country Center,** Box 38, Keystone, CO 80435, tel. (970) 468-4275, where 30 km of trails meander along the back-country lodges, creek, and valley.

In addition, the county has many easily accessible trails ideally suited to cross-country skiers, including some of the bike paths and areas around Dillon Reservoir. Parts of the 15-mile bike path paralleling CO 9 between Frisco and Breckenridge are perfect for easy-access sliding, as are some of the Forest Service campgrounds on the lake (roads and weather permitting).

For further information on Nordic skiing, contact the Dillon District office of **Arapaho Na-**

*base of lifts
at Copper Mountain*

tional Forest, 135 CO 9, Silverthorne, CO 80498, tel. (970) 468-5400. You can also get information from the retail ski shops in the area, including **Peak Performance,** 309 S. Main, Breckenridge, tel. (970) 453-4463, and **Breckenridge Ski Shop,** 211 N. Main, tel. (970) 453-7039. In Silverthorne, stop in at **Wildernest Sports,** 171 Blue River Parkway, tel. (970) 468-8519, and in Frisco, try **Antler's Ski and Sport Shop,** 908 N. Summit, tel. (970) 668-3152.

Helicopter Skiing

Helicopters provide expensive but quick and effortless access to untracked bowls high on backcountry mountainsides, offering advanced and expert skiers the experience of a lifetime. Dillon-based **Colorado Heli-Ski** offers a range of guided tours, including single-run flights and full-day multirun excursions that include lunch. Rates run from about $75 (one run, allow two hours) to $400 (six hours of runs, with lunch and instruction). The company also offers scenic flights and charters. For more information or to make reservations, phone (970) 468-1551.

OTHER WINTER ACTIVITIES

Snowmobiling

Though controversial by definition (the machines are loud, exhausty, and fossil-fuel gobbling), this sport has its fans, with several outfits in the county providing a range of services and activities. **Tiger Run Resort,** Box 1418, Breckenridge, CO 80424, tel. (970) 453-2231, has 150 snowmobiles for rent (as well as boots and snowsuits). Tiger Run is located four miles north of Breckenridge on CO 9. You can also rent snowmobiles at **Summit Adventure Park** at Farmers Korner between Frisco and Breckenridge, tel. (970) 453-0353. **White Mountain Snowmobile Tours,** tel. (970) 668-5323 or (800) 247-7238, offers hourly and half-day tours, with discounts available to groups.

Ice Skating

Summit County probably has more ice-skating rinks than any similar-size area west of New York and south of the Canadian border. One of the most popular is **Keystone Lake** in Keystone

Village, open daily 10 a.m.-10 p.m. Rental skates available. Phone Keystone Resort at (970) 468-2316 for more information.

Ice skating is also available on Maggie Pond in Breckenridge (next to the Bell Tower Mall) and on West Lake at Copper Mountain.

Over the River and through the Woods

A number of Summit County outfits offer day and evening sleigh rides, from short jaunts to dinner rides that might include buffalo soup or baked salmon. Copper Mountain's **Dining in the Woods** sleigh leaves the central plaza Wed.-Sun. evenings at 6 p.m. for an elegant meal in a miners' tent. Fixed price (about $40); menu changes nightly. Phone (970) 968-2882, ext. 6320 for reservations. **Alpine Adventures, Inc.** has 16-passenger "Dinner on the Trail" sleighs leaving twice nightly from **Summit Adventure Park** at Farmers Korner. Write Box 2620-B, Breckenridge, CO 80424, or phone (970) 453-0111.

Snowcat Tours

Still another way to experience the wintry backcountry, and to access some fine backcountry skiing, is by snowcat. Several companies offer tours. At **Copper Mountain** you can take a snowcat into the newly expanded part of the mountain; phone (970) 968-2318. You can also arrange snowcat tours through **Montezuma Snowcat Tours,** tel. (970) 468-0979.

Totally Tubular

In this world of high-tech, high-cost diversions and "adventure travel," it's often easy to forget the simple pleasures: snow tubing, for example. Simply speaking, tubing can be a *gas.* Bundle up, find yourself an inner tube and a hill, and let yourself be nine years old again. Guaranteed to cure what ails you; there's no room for depression, domestic squabbling, or existential angst sliding down a hill. And nothing tastes quite so good as a hot chocolate or brandy afterward.

If you truly can't find a tubing hill on your own, check out **Summit Adventure Park,** at Farmers Korner between Frisco and Breckenridge, tel. (970) 453-0353. Rentals available.

WHEN THE SNOW MELTS

Though Summit boosters have been very successful changing the area's image from that of a cluster of ski towns to a year-round resort, Summit County remains predominantly winter oriented. So far. But each summer, more and more tourists are drawn to the area for its myriad recreational opportunities—from cycling to windsurfing, fishing to horseback riding to just plain sightseeing.

Cycling

Anyone skeptical that this is the sport of the '90s, and that Summit County is one of the premier biking areas in the country, need only take a look around. Miles and miles of bicycle paths connect the various communities; not only are they ideal for exploring, but they make commuting easy for locals. Come spring, don't be surprised to see a mountain biker on Main Street in Breckenridge with a pair of skis under his arm or bungie-corded to his top bar. In fact, many of the ski shops serve double duty by turning to cycling—sales, rentals—in the spring, summer, and fall.

Among the excellent paved bike paths in the area are the **Blue River Bikeway,** which connects Breckenridge and Frisco and winds in and out of meadows and forests of sweet-smelling pines; **Tenmile Canyon National Recreation Trail** between Copper Mountain and Frisco; and **Vail Pass Bikeway,** a 20-mile route up over the 10,600-foot pass that drops down into Vail Village—excellent scenery en route.

For more serious touring, you can head off in just about any direction, though traffic will of course be heavier on some routes. Colorado 9 north along the Blue River is a moderate ride, with rises but no significant hills. At the other end of the range, US 6 east passes A-Basin and climbs over the grueling **Loveland Pass** (11,990 feet). Even Ah-nold or Bo might huff and puff a bit.

The county is also rife with mountain-bike trails, with several designated paths over nearby mountain passes, including **Boreas, Georgia,** and **Webster** passes. Your best source for

information on mountain biking in the area is the Dillon District Office of **Arapaho National Forest,** 135 US 9, Silverthorne, tel. (970) 468-5400. The Forest Service, in conjunction with the county, has published an excellent map showing the various trails in the area, which provides mileage, difficulty ratings, safety and camping information, and recommended tours. The maps are available free at the Forest Service office and at most bike shops in the area.

If you'd like guided tours of the area, contact **Kodi Mountain Bike Rentals,** Box 1215, Breckenridge, CO 80424, tel. (970) 453-2194 or (800) 525-9624, which has a variety of trips available.

Golf

Golf is another exceptionally popular summer activity in Summit County, and some of the ski resorts, specifically Keystone and Copper Mountain, promote golf-and-lodging packages with the same enthusiasm with which they promote skiing plans during the winter. The public **Breckenridge Golf Course** is owned and operated by the town of Breckenridge. Designed by Jack Nicklaus, the 18-hole course, located at 200 Clubhouse Dr., offers a wonderful natural setting in the Blue River Valley just north of town. Phone (970) 453-5544 for tee times and information. **Copper Creek Golf Club** at Copper Mountain, another lush 18-hole course with excellent views, claims to be the highest-elevation PGA course in the country. Phone (970) 968-2339.

Keystone Ranch Golf Course at Keystone Resort offers a blend of the old and the new: the 18-hole course is not yet a teenager, but the clubhouse dates from the 1930s. It's reserved for Keystone guests, except on a space-available basis. Phone the golf course at (970) 468-4250 or Keystone Resort at (970) 468-2316. The nine-hole **Eagles Nest Golf Course** is located in north Silverthorne off US 9, tel. (970) 468-0681.

Hiking

Summit County abounds in hiking trails, from half-mile walks to scenic overlooks to 10-mile (and longer), full-day wilderness excursions. The Forest Service, in conjunction with several local businesses, publishes an excellent *Summer Trailhead Guide,* which discusses a dozen trails of varying lengths and difficulty levels. The guide also includes recommendations for specific topo maps and provides a day-pack checklist and suggestions for environmental responsibility.

Here is a small sampling of Forest Service-suggested hikes: **Tenderfoot Mountain** is an easy mile-and-a-quarter hike offering views of Dillon Reservoir and the Gore and Tenmile mountain ranges. Turn north from the stoplight on US 6 in Dillon, and turn immediately right onto the frontage road, which you'll follow to the trailhead. **Gold Hill Trail** is a popular three-mile hike beginning five miles south of Frisco on CO 9. Ranked "more difficult," Gold Hill is part of the Colorado Trail and joins up with **Peaks Trail** three miles south of Frisco. **Wheeler National Recreation Trail** is an 11-mile hike, also ranked "more difficult," linking Breckenridge and Copper Mountain. The trail crosses the Tenmile Range through Breckenridge ski area, and offers views of the Tenmile, Gore, Sawatch, and Flat Top ranges. There are also lots of excellent hiking trails in the **Eagles Nest Wilderness Area** north of Silverthorne. The Forest Service can provide complete information.

Fishing

There's a lot of water in Summit County, most obviously the sprawling arms and main body of Dillon Reservoir. In addition, there are many streams and rivers, with lots of accessible shoreline. Also, Green Mountain Reservoir north of Dillon midway to Kremmling offers lots of fishing opportunities for both the shore and boat angler. Among the fish you'll find in the county's various waters are brook, brown, rainbow, and lake trout, and kokanee salmon.

Summit County waters are so accessible, they see an awful lot of traffic, and you've got to be pretty persistent and trout-savvy to hook into big fish. Remember, too, some of the streams have special restrictions; make sure you read and understand all regulations before making that first cast.

Dillon Reservoir offers decent fishing year-round (ice fishing in the winter) for trout and kokanee salmon. Boats are ideal, though fishing from the shore can be successful as well. **Green Mountain Reservoir** is also open year-round, with the narrower Blue River Channel stretches,

as well as the area between the town of Heeney and the dam, offering the best bets.

The **Blue River** north of Silverthorne is a Gold Medal Water-designated trout stream with some excellent catch-and-release-only sections (fly-fishing only). **Tenmile Creek** between Frisco and Copper Mountain can also be good.

An excellent source of information is *Fish The Summit,* a map and guide that discusses the Summit's various streams and lakes in detail, offering a season-by-season series of tips on lures, bait, and hot spots. The guide also identifies the individual species of fish (with both drawings and text), discusses stream restrictions, and provides a list of fishing-license agents. The map and guide is available at most tourist and chamber of commerce offices or by contacting New Sensations, Box 36203, Denver, CO 80236, tel. (970) 987-9330.

A number of outfitters in the county provide guided fishing trips. The following companies offer half- and full-day trips, as well as instructions and rental equipment: **Columbine Outfitters,** 502 Main St., Frisco, tel. (970) 668-3704; **Mountain Angler,** 311 Main St., Breckenridge, tel. (970) 453-HOOK—specializing in catch-and-release fly-fishing on private waters; and **Summit Guides,** 110 Ski Hill Rd., Breckenridge, tel. (970) 453-1430.

The Gore Range Anglers chapter of Trout Unlimited meets the last Thursday of each month at the Best Western Inn in Frisco.

Whitewater Rafting

Though there's not a whole lot of raftable whitewater in Summit County, there's plenty nearby, and a number of companies offer half- and full-day trips on the county's Blue River, as well as on the Arkansas and Colorado. Contact **Performance Tours Rafting,** tel. (970) 343-0661 or (800) 328-7238; **Tiger Run Resort,** 128 S. Main St., Breckenridge, tel. (970) 453-2231; or **Kodi Whitewater Rafting Tours,** Box 1215, Breckenridge, CO 80424, tel. (970) 453-2194.

Boating, Sailing, and Windsurfing

Dillon Reservoir and Green Mountain Reservoir are exceptionally popular for most water sports (though the water's *awfully* cold for swimming). There are several public boat launches around Dillon Reservoir, and the shore is generally gently sloped for easy put-ins. In addition, a handful of marinas rent sailboats, paddleboats, and fishing boats. In Dillon, check out Dillon Yacht Basin, on E. Lodgepole, tel. (970) 468-2396. In Frisco, you can rent canoes and motorboats at Osprey Adventures, 810 Main St., tel. (970) 668-5573, which also offers guided canoe tours.

Ballooning

To see Summit County from the basket of a hot-air balloon, contact the Dillon office of **Balloon America,** tel. (970) 468-2473, or **Aero-Cruise Balloon Adventures, Ltd.,** tel. (970) 845-9907 or (800) 373-1243.

Horseback Rides

This is superb country to explore by horseback, and a number of pack companies in the area offer a range of trips. **Alpine Adventures,** Box 2620-B, Breckenridge, CO 80424, tel. (970) 468-9297, offers short trail rides as well as overnight pack trips to the Montezuma Mining District and into Arapaho National Forest; meals and a sleeping bag provided. **Eagles Nest Equestrian Center,** Box 495, Silverthorne, CO 80498, tel. (970) 468-0677, also offers a full range of trips, specializing in extended backcountry tours and fall hunts. You can also arrange rides, from one hour to a full day, through **Keystone Stables,** tel. (970) 468-4156, and **Breckenridge Stables,** Box 1816, Breckenridge, CO 80424, tel. (970) 453-4438, both of which welcome large groups and offer rides that include meals.

Chairlift Rides

Breckenridge and Copper Mountain both offer off-season chairlift rides for sightseers, while you can ride Keystone's gondola. At the top, grab something to eat while you take in the panoramas, and then either ride or hike back down. Lifts are usually open from late spring through September. For more information, phone **Breckenridge Ski Area,** tel. (970) 453-2368; **Copper Mountain Resort,** tel. (970) 968-2318; or **Keystone Resort,** tel. (970) 468-2316.

Jeep Tours

The old mining roads and high mountain passes in Summit County make the area a natural for exploring with an off-road vehicle. From ghosts of old mining towns to high lakes, some of Summit's most interesting areas are accessible only by 4WD. For maps and information, stop by the Forest Service, 135 US 9 in Silverthorne. **Tiger Run Resort,** tel. (970) 453-2231, and **Tenderfoot Tours,** tel. (970) 468-5000, can arrange jeep tours of the backcountry.

Historical Tours

The Summit County Historical Society has designed a number of guided and self-guided tours of the area, including Breckenridge and local ghost and mining towns. Guided tours of the Breckenridge Historic District are offered Wed.-Sat. mornings (summers only)—a ghost is said to haunt the bathroom of the Brown Hotel. The society also sponsors tours to Washington Gold Mine and the Edwin Carter Museum. A separate tour to the Lomax Placer Gulch includes mining demonstrations, gold panning, and a slide show. For starting times and more information on the tours, stop by the Breckenridge Actvities Center, 201 S. Main St., or phone (970) 453-9022.

Take Me out to the Ball Game

One of the most relaxing ways to spend a summer evening or Saturday afternoon is by watching a local slow-pitch softball game. Spirits are high as teams representing local pizza parlors, construction companies, and ski shops vie for Summit County trophies. Watch excellent athletes (many of the best skiers in the area) drive ground balls up the middle or line deep ropes into the gaps. The Breckenridge fields are located just north of town; turn down behind the City Market and continue north.

Indoor Recreation

In addition to the health clubs at many of the larger hotels and condo complexes, the **Silverthorne Recreation Center** is a brand new public facility with racketball courts, cardiovascular machines, free weights, indoor basketball, and swimming pools with a water slide, as well as classes in yoga, tumbling, marshall arts, etc. Drop-in fee is $5 a day. The rec center is located in Silverthorne behind the factory stores. Phone (970) 468-0711.

PRACTICALITIES

You'll find a huge range of accommodations in Summit County, from small mom-and-pop motels to luxurious condominium complexes and convention centers—each year fewer and fewer of the former and more and more of the latter. You can also rent individual homes, some sprawling and estatelike, others smaller and more budget oriented. Generally, if you're looking for cheap digs, you'll be least disappointed in Frisco and Silverthorne, both virtually lakeside to Dillon Reservoir, whereas if you're more interested in being pampered, you might want to check out the condos and hotels in Breckenridge, Dillon, Keystone, or Copper Mountain. Between the two extremes are a handful of highway-side franchise inns both in Frisco and Dillon. Most of the lodges offer free shuttle service to the ski areas, as well as package deals that include lift tickets, equipment rentals, and transportation.

When it comes to lodging (and what you'll pay), though, the main consideration, as in most resort towns, is season: most places adjust their rates to the ol' law of supply and demand—when the snow comes down, prices go up. High-season prices generally revolve around the ski resorts and holidays. Rates will be highest between Christmas and the end of New Year's weekend. They'll also be high in February, around the time of Washington's and Lincoln's birthdays (often shoved together and celebrated jointly in ski country to allow schoolkids a whole week off). Predictably, rates will be lower once the snow melts, especially in late spring before the weather warms up enough to allow for swimming, sailing, and shirt-sleeved bike riding and hiking, and in the fall, when it cools off again and before the clearcuts on the mountainsides are snow covered and the engines of the chairlifts get fired up again.

The other thing to keep in mind is even though rates go up significantly when the skiing gets good, people still clamor to pay them. Don't even think of trying without reservations to find a room in this part of the country when the skiing's good. Book a room at least a month before you plan to come. Or better yet, two months.

Or six. A year if you can. The only way you might find a room at the last minute during high season is by calling to see if there have been any cancellations.

Summit County Lodging Information

For complete information on accommodations in Summit County, write the **Summit County Chamber of Commerce,** Box 214, Frisco, CO 80443, or phone (970) 668-5800. You can also get lodging information from the following ski resorts: **Breckenridge,** tel. (800) 822-5381 in Colorado, or (800) 221-1091 outside Colorado; **Copper Mountain,** tel. (800) I-LUV-FUN; and **Keystone,** tel. (800) 222-0188 for condos, (800) 541-0346 for the lodge. You can also book vacation rentals, summer or winter, through **Summit County Central Reservations,** Box 446, Dillon, CO 80435, tel. (800) 365-6365; or **High Country Travel And Tours,** tel. (970) 468-1080, (800) 999-0823 in Colorado, or (800) 367-1654.

MOTELS AND HOTELS

Most of the smaller motels and hotels are in Frisco and Silverthorne, each within a short drive of all of the Summit County ski areas, as well as Vail and Beaver Creek. They're also right in the heart of most of the summer resort activity—sailing, cycling, hiking, rafting, and golfing.

Frisco

Rooms at the **Holiday Inn,** tel. (970) 668-5000 or (800) 782-7669, start at about $60. The indoor jacuzzi and pool, shuttle service, on-site ski shop (rentals, repairs, and sales), and convenient location (just off I-70 at Exit 203) make this a natural for skiers. The **Frisco Lodge,** 321 Main St., tel. (970) 668-0195, probably has the cheapest rooms in town, bare-boned but comfortable. At the **Snowshoe Motel,** 521 Main, tel. (970) 668-3444, doubles run about $35-60. The **Sky-Vue Motel** is at 305 S. Second, tel. (970) 668-3311; rooms for two are $40-70. The new **Alpine Inn,** 105 Lusher Ct. (behind the Safeway), tel. (970) 668-3122, and the **Summit Inn,** 1205 N. Summit Blvd., tel. (970) 668-3220, also have nice rooms in the $60-80 range, while doubles at the **Best Western Lake Dillon Lodge,** 1202 N. Summit Blvd., tel. (970) 668-5094, start at about $75.

Silverthorne

In Silverthorne, you can get doubles at the **Wildernest,** 204 Wildernest Rd., tel. (970) 468-6291, for $50-100 (condos for two at the Wildernest run $70-150). The **Summit Inn and Conference Center,** tel. (970) 468-6200, has rooms running $60-150, and at the **Days Inn,** tel. (970) 468-8661, doubles are $60-110—both are right off I-70 on Silverthorne Lane.

Dillon

Dillon couldn't stay forever young, and the community's growth over the last decade or so has been phenomenal—the times they have a-changed. Most of its lodging is in condominiums and luxury hotels, though there are in fact a few relatively inexpensive inns. The **Super 8 Motel,** 808 Little Beaver Trail, tel. (970) 468-8888 or (800) 843-1991, has rooms for $50-75. At the **Best Western Ptarmigan Lodge,** tel. (970) 468-2341 or (800) 727-0607, you can get doubles for about $90-160.

CONDOMINIUMS AND MORE EXPENSIVE HOTELS

Breckenridge

The Village at Breckenridge Resort is a sprawling complex (actually encompassing three separate lodges) with over 400 rooms, ranging from studios to penthouse suites. Though prices range as well, this is generally for the expense-account crowd, those who've saved for the Big Splurge, and the fortunate (?) few who never have to ask, "How much?" Amenities include the standard exercise room, spa, and pool, as well as kitchens. Base, I mean *base,* prices start at about $80 for a double in low season, but you should expect to pay a lot more—like maybe $150. Cream-of-the-crop suites are over $400 a night for two. Phone (970) 453-2000 or (800) 321-8552.

Among other Breckenridge luxury accommodations: the **Breckenridge Hilton,** tel. (970) 453-4500 or (800) 321-8444, $80-200; the **Beaver Run Resort,** tel. (970) 453-6000 or (800) 525-2253, $70-300; and the **River Mountain Lodge,** tel. (970) 453-4711, $60-450.

Copper Mountain

The base of Copper Mountain is dotted with condominiums and lodges, many of which offer to-your-doorstep skiing, and all of which are steps away from a shuttle-bus stop. Copper's **Club Med** (the first in the United States), tel. (970) 968-2121, is near the central plaza right at the base of the lifts. For rates and a full listing of accommodations and ski and summer-vacation packages, write **Copper Mountain Resort Lodging Services,** Box 3001, Copper Mountain, CO 80443; or phone (800) 458-8386, ext. 1; locally, phone (970) 968-2882. Summer rates at Copper start as low $50 a night and include chairlift rides, fly-fishing, and other bonuses.

Dillon

Dillon offers about two dozen hotels and condominium complexes, many of which are right on or overlook the lake. Among them: **Summit Yacht Club,** tel. (970) 468-2703; **Lake Dillon Condotel,** tel. (970) 468-2409 or (800) 323-7892; and **The Spinnaker at Lake Dillon,** tel. (970) 468-8001. For more information on lodging in Dillon, write Town of Dillon, Box 8, Dillon, CO 80435, or phone (970) 468-2403, or 629-6342 from Denver.

Keystone

Like Copper Mountain, Keystone is a small village of condominium complexes, restaurants, ski shops, and boutiques built to accommodate the ski crowd but which in recent years has begun (successfully) to woo summer vacationers as well. Three basic options here: the lodge at the resort, the Ski Tip Lodge (see below), or one of the many condo complexes (some 800 suites total). Either way you can book rooms by the night or buy full-bore ski-golf-ride-sail-fish-bike-eat-drink-and-be-merry packages. Five-night ski packages at the **Keystone Lodge** or a nearby condo begin at around $300 per person, and include four days' skiing at Keystone and/or Arapahoe Basin. One-night's-lodging/one-day's-skiing packages start at about $60. For more information, write **Keystone Resort,** Box 38, Keystone, CO 80435, or phone (800) 541-0346 (the lodge) or (800) 222-0188 (condos); from Denver phone (970) 534-4806 (the lodge) or 534-7712 (condos).

BED AND BREAKFASTS

Gaining in popularity recently, bed and breakfasts offer a wider range of prices (and comfort levels) than one might imagine. The **Summit County Bed and Breakfast Association** includes some 20 members in the area. For a complete listing, write the Summit County Chamber of Commerce (Box 214, Frisco, CO 80443).

Of the two dozen bed and breakfasts in the county, one of the most comfortable and down to earth is the **Twilight Inn,** 308 Main St., Frisco, tel. (970) 668-5009, which owes its charm partly to its father-and-son team of innkeepers, Bjorn and Eric (two of the mellowest and most lovable Labrador retrievers in snow country). The Twilight has 12 rooms, some with private baths, some with shared baths (not to worry: the bathrooms for those rooms are huge). The Twilight allows dogs on all first-floor rooms (1-5), and during May and October offers two-nights-for-the-price-of-one promotional packages. Rates start at about $65.

The recently opened **Galena Street Mountain Inn,** 106 Galena St., tel. (970) 668-3224, has earned a solid reputation for catering to skiers and summer visitors alike. Rooms run about $80-170.

If you're looking to get away from the hustle and bustle of the Frisco-Dillon-Silverthorne-Keystone area, a couple of wonderful lodges back in the woods offer the perfect escape.

Keystone's **Ski Tip Ranch** (nee Ski Tip Lodge) was built in the 1940s as Colorado's first ski lodge. Set back among the pines, the inn was sold to Keystone in the early 1980s, and it's still a far cry from the more conventional condos at the resort. Fourteen rustic rooms are decorated with antiques and have neither phones nor televisions, and the old stone fireplace and relative isolation (shuttles to Keystone every half-hour in winter) provide the sense that you're an original guest with your baggy wool ski pants

drying by the fireside for tomorrows's weideling at Arapahoe Basin. For reservations and more information, phone (970) 468-4202.

About three miles deeper into the woods, the **Paradox Lodge,** tel. (970) 468-9445, offers rooms in the main inn or in one of the self-contained cabins on the property. The seclusion of the Paradox (its original owners were two doctors . . .), and the fact that the rooms don't have phones, makes it the perfect place to lose yourself after a particularly grueling project at the office or semester of school. For more information, write Paradox Lodge, 35 Montezuma Rd., Dillon, CO 80435.

In Breckenridge, the **Williams House,** tel. (970) 453-2975, is a much smaller bed and breakfast, the owners having just completed a third room. With an excellent location, especially in winter, when you're just a few blocks from Breckenridge skiing, this inn also offers a real sense of history (the house was built in the mid-1880s). Rooms start at about $65 a night, though they go up to over $100 during the ski season.

VACATION HOMES

Generally at the high end of vacation accommodations options, individual homes offer privacy and oftentimes the size needed to accommodate large groups, and they sometimes offer better long-term rates. To rent from owners, look in the "Vacation Homes" section of the *Denver Post*'s classified ads. In addition, **Americana Resort Properties,** tel. (800) 367-0458 or (970) 468-0485, **Columbine Rentals,** tel. (800) 289-7666 or (970) 468-0611, **Executive Resorts Rentals,** tel. (800) 662-5368 or (970) 453-4422, and **White Cloud Lodging Co.,** tel. (800) 345-0593 or (970) 453-1018, can all arrange lodging at individual homes in Summit County.

CAMPING AND RVING

Summit County is entirely contained within the borders of Arapaho National Forest, so summer visitors will find a variety of Forest Service-maintained campgrounds within short drives of

Breckenridge, Copper Mountain, Dillon, and Keystone, including several at Dillon Reservoir. Be forewarned, though: those on the lake (Heaton Bay, Peak One, Pine Grove, and Prospector campgrounds—over 300 sites total), though very nice, fill up quickly when the weather's warm. Don't expect to get a site without reservations. Some areas are designated hike-in and bike-in only.

Several campgrounds in the north arm of Summit County offer less developed but also somewhat less crowded facilities. Take CO 9 north from Silverthorne. The road winds through the beautiful Blue River Valley past Green Mountain Reservoir to Kremmling, with several campgrounds on the way. **Blue River Campground** is about five miles north of Silverthorne on CO 9 (well water and pit toilets only).

Cow Creek Campground offers free camping on the east shore of Green Mountain Reservoir just off CO 9. Another fairly primitive area (pit toilets), this campground has zippo in terms of shade, but the lack of trees makes for good winds, and the spot is very popular with sailboarders. Not much shade at **Prairie Point Campground,** either, at the south end of Green Mountain Reservoir, though the views, particularly of the massive Gore Range, make for a fair trade.

For information on camping in the area, or to make reservations, stop in at the Forest Service district office at 191 Blue River Parkway, Silverthorne, tel. (970) 468-5400.

Tiger Run RV Resort, tel. (970) 453-9690, on the Blue River between Frisco and Breckenridge, is the only RV park in the county, and, in true Summit County style, it's actually a full-fledged resort, with tennis courts, pool, hot tub, etc. Write Box 815, Breckenridge, CO 80424.

FOOD

Start Me Up

A veritable Summit County institution, established in the early 1940s when skiers would stop en route to a day at Arapahoe Basin, the **Arapahoe Cafe and Pub** in Dillon at the corner of Chief Colorow and La Bonte, tel. (970) 468-0873, serves a breakfast guaranteed to kick your morning in the backside. Try the "Hans

and Franz (we-just-want-to-pump-you-up) Power Breakfast" of steak, eggs, home fries, and toast ($6.95). The Arapahoe is also open for lunch and dinner, serving burgers, soups, salads, and other hearty fare.

Another favorite breakfast-and-lunch spot is the tiny, dinerlike (only a half dozen tables and the counter) **Alice's Restaurant,** 109 Dillon Mall, tel. (970) 468-9608. Opening at 6 a.m., Alice's serves standard American breakfasts, and sandwiches, burgers, burritos (excellent!), homemade soup, and salads for lunch ($4-6).

In Breckenridge, try the hearty ante-ski breakfasts at the **Prospector,** 130 S. Main, and the **Gold Pan,** 105 N. Main (see below). For espressos and pastries, try **Rocky Mountain Coffee Roasters,** 258 Main St., Frisco, tel. (970) 668-3470 or (800) 642-BEAN, or **The Stage Door Cafe,** 203 S. Main, Breckenridge, tel. (970) 453-6964.

Inexpensive to Moderate

The **Moose Jaw,** in downtown Frisco at 208 Main, tel. (970) 668-3931, is a classic little diner and bar for the pool/softball/country-music, just-finished-framing-a-house-up-in-Breck set. Originally built in the '50s as a bunkhouse for Dillon Dam workers, the structure was cut in half in 1961 and moved to its present site, where it initially served as a grocery store. Today, a burger with a basket of fries will run you $4-6, or you can get a fish sandwich or a bowl of chili and fries for about the same price.

Down the street from the Moose Jaw is **Barkley's Margaritagrille,** 680 Main, tel. (970) 668-3694, a small basement restaurant featuring excellent Mexican food (and margaritas!). Dinners run $6-8, but you can also order a la carte tacos, enchiladas, etc. for $2-4. Also available are pool, TV sports, and lotsa microbrews.

One of Summit County's better and more reasonably priced Chinese restaurants is **Szechuan Taste,** 310 Main St., Frisco, tel. (970) 668-5685. Specials (duck and seafood) run $11-13, but you can also get good-sized vegetable, beef, and noodle dishes for $6-9.

One of the best places to go for a hot lunch on a cold day is **The Prospector Restaurant,** 130 S. Main St., Breckenridge, tel. (970) 453-6858. Hide yourself in a cozy booth and enjoy a burger, omelette, or bowl of hot soup for $4-6. The

Prospector also serves excellent breakfasts and dinners.

Another Summit County institution is the **Gold Pan Restaurant and Bar,** 103 N. Main St., Breckenridge, tel. (970) 453-5499. In a building dating from the 1880s that has housed over the years a dry goods store, a bowling alley, and a gas station, the Gold Pan claims to hold the longest continually operating liquor license west of the Mississippi. The Gold Pan Bar is a longtime favorite of locals of all stripes, from Glen Plake wannabes to miners who look more like Hank Williams Jr. than ol' Hank does himself. The restaurant tends to cater to a slightly more civil crowd, après-skiers who munch on Mexican food (try the nachos) or the famous Gold Pan burgers. Dinners run $3-7.

A newcomer to Breckenridge, but an immediately successful one, is the **Breckenridge Brewery and Pub** at the south end of town at 600 Main St., tel. (970) 453-1550. Offering a half dozen or so different house beers (ranging from their Avalanche Ale—"it can overtake you before you know it"—to an oatmeal stout), the pub also serves a variety of traditional pub grub—shepherd's pie, fish and chips, burgers, sandwiches, and salads. Lunches run about $6-11, and pints of beer are $2. Home-brewed ginger ale and root beer are also available. Look for Breckenridge beer in local liquor stores. Also new, good, and in Breckenridge is **Breckenridge Barbecue,** 301 S. Main, tel. (970) 453-7313, where you can get links, briskets, chicken, etc. and sample from the 20 microbrews on tap.

In Dillon, try the **Arapahoe Cafe and Pub,** tel. (970) 468-0873, or **Alice's Restaurant and Pub,** 109 Dillon Mall, tel. tel. (970) 468-9808. **O'Shea's Restaurant and Bar** at the Copper Mountain Plaza, tel. (970) 968-2882, has good Mexican food, burgers, and steaks, and is a lively after-ski hangout.

Expensive

Summit County's not hurting for high-end white-linen-and-silver restaurants, and if you're looking to relax with a good meal and a special bottle of wine, you've got lots of choices. A consistently strong contender for local favorite is the **Blue Spruce Inn,** 120 W. Main, Frisco, tel. (970) 668-5900, which serves beef, veal, and seafood

dishes ranging from $14 to $25 (steak and lobster). For Italian food, it's hard to beat **Ristorante Al Lago,** 240 Chief Colorow, Dillon, tel. (970) 468-6111. Veal, chicken, seafood, and pasta dinners run $12-20. Another Dillon favorite is **Pug Ryan's Prime Rib and Seafood House,** 101 Dillon Mall, tel. (970) 453-0063, where steaks, prime rib, chicken, and fish dinners run $12-25 (there's also a Pug Ryan's in Breckenridge at 208 N. Main).

Among the better upscale Breckenridge restaurants are the **Briar Rose,** 109 E. Lincoln, tel. (970) 453-9948, specializing in exotic game dishes (elk, venison), beef, and seafood; **The Wellington Inn,** 200 N. Main, tel. (970) 453-9464, serving authentic German dinners and desserts; and the **Whale's Tail,** 323 S. Main, tel. (970) 453-2221, for seafood.

ENTERTAINMENT

When ski season's in full swing and Summit County's swollen with skiers of every hue—honeymooners from Houston, families from Fargo, and countless college students here between (or instead of) semesters—there's a lot going on, and you'd be hard-pressed not to find something to do when you pull your ski boots off. Most of the ski-area bars feature live music, and there's a huge range of clubs and nighteries around the county. Summer's a bit slower, though, and spring and fall slower still.

For current information on what's happening where, check out the local papers. The *Summit County Journal* and the *Summit Daily News* provide up-to-date information on everything from reggae concerts to dinner theater, gallery openings to pool tournaments. Both papers are available in racks around town.

Though you'll find live music and other entertainment throughout the county, the largest cluster is in Breckenridge, and come nightfall, locals as well as visiting skiers often head into "Breck" where a dozen or so clubs are within walking distance of each other. **Downstairs at Eric's,** in the Georgian Square, tel. (970) 543-0999, **Shamus O'Toole's,** 115 S. Ridge St., tel. (970) 453-2004, and **JohSha's,** 500 Park Ave., tel. (970) 453-4146, regularly feature dance music—from reggae to Cajun to experimental and progressive rock. The **Alligator Lounge,** 318 S. Main, tel. (970) 453-7782, features jazz and blues, with open mike Tuesday nights. **The Gold Pan,** 105 N. Main St., tel. (970) 453-5499, books live music "when we feel like it," generally softer rock, in the Kenny Rankin-James Taylor-Jackson Browne mode. **Alice's Restaurant and Pub,** 109 Dillon Mall, tel. (970) 468-9808, has live music most nights, with cowboy-line-dancing Thursday.

Other Summit County Entertainment

In Keystone, several clubs offer live and dance music, including the **Snake River Saloon,** 23074 US 6 in Keystone, tel. (970) 468-2788 (ski movies in the winter), and **Bandito's,** 22869 US 6 in Keystone, tel. (970) 468-0404, and, in Keystone Village, the **Last Chance Saloon,** tel. (970) 468-9501.

A tradition in Summit County, the **Old Dillon Inn,** 321 Blue River Parkway in Silverthorne, tel. (970) 468-2791, books country and country rock, for those whose tastes run to Merle Haggard and Marshall Tucker. Up in Dillon, **Pug Ryan's,** tel. (970) 468-2145, also books live music.

Theater

Breckenridge's **Backstage Theater** is a local favorite and has been putting up a range of productions for over 20 years. Seasons are July through August and mid-December through April. Tickets are $10 for adults ($5 for kids under 12). For information and reservations, phone (970) 463-0199.

CALENDAR

Summit County's annual events range from ice sculpture and snowboard competition to sailing regattas, horse and bike races, and a wide range of concerts. The winter biggie is Breckenridge's **Ullr Fest** in mid-January, honoring the Norse god Ullr, Thor's son. According to a slightly revisionist version of the legend, the mighty Thor and his gorgeous wife Sif had no time for Ullr, and so out of boredom, the kid hit the road. And where do you think he ended up? Why, Breckenridge, of course, where he fell in love with the beautiful Blue River Valley.

The weeklong party commences with the International Snow Sculpting Competition (in town on Main Street), and includes a variety of skiing competitions (aerials, moguls, ballet), a parade, and the "Mr. and Mrs. Ullr Beauty Pageant and Dance." In March, Breckenridge hosts the increasingly popular **Snowboard Race Series.** Also in Breckenridge is the **Alamo Freestyle Classic,** in mid-January, where you can watch the country's best freestylers compete in ballet, moguls, and aerials.

At the other end of the scale is the **Bach, Beethoven, and Breckenridge** concert series in July. Not limited to the two Big B's of classical music, performances also include the works of other major and minor composers, from Copland to Wagner. The monthlong season also features workshops—on music theory, education, and individual instruments. For more information, write Box 1254, Breckenridge, CO 80424, or phone (970) 453-9142.

A variety of festivities and events punctuate the Fourth of July weekend throughout Summit County, including fireworks, food booths, and concerts. The route of mid-July's **Montezuma's Revenge Mountain Bike Race** crosses the Continental Divide seven times in the course of 200 miles. Over Labor Day weekend, Copper Mountain hosts the **West-Fest,** which focuses on the art and culture of the western and southwestern United States. Lots of Native American art and jewelry, as well as music and food. Phone (800) 458-8386 for more information. Also in September is Breckenridge's **Fall Classic Mountain Bike Race,** which attracts the best riders in the country.

For complete listings of the county's myriad events, contact the Summit County Chamber of Commerce. Also, watch the *Summit Daily News* and the *Summit County Journal* available in racks all over town.

SHOPPING

A favorite recreational activity among visitors to Summit County, shopping knows no bounds here in what would seem to be an unlikely place to find everything from Native American pottery to bargains on lingerie, from Christmas ornaments to T-shirts (Breckenridge must have the highest number of T-shirt shops per capita in the country). In Frisco, be sure to check out **Peddlar's Barn,** on Main St. across from the Twilight Inn. This place carries a bizarre collection of odds and ends, from first-edition Hardy Boys books to vintage snow skis (from the 1920s and '30s). Look for the locomotive in the window.

Silverthorne Factory Outlets
A seemingly unlikely spot for a factory outlet mall, the Silverthorne site is nonetheless extremely popular. For those who'd rather shop than ski or mountain bike, there's Van Heusen, Bass shoes, Evan-Picone, American Tourister, Liz Claiborne, London Fog, Nike, plus socks, underwear, ribbons, toys, wallets, fragrances and bath oils, and jewelry (there's even a real estate office)—81 stores in all. Take the Silverthorne exit from I-70 and follow the signs; keep a leash on your credit card.

SERVICES

The **Breckenridge Police Department** is located at 150 Ski Hill Rd., tel. (970) 453-2941. Reach the **Dillon Police** at (970) 468-6078. The offices of the **Summit County Sheriff** are in Breckenridge at 501 N. Park, tel. (970) 453-2232.

Provenant Medical Center in Frisco is open weekdays 9 a.m.-5 p.m (plus 24-hour emergency care). The clinic is at the corner of CO 9 and School Rd., tel. (970) 668-3300 or (800) 843-0953. The **Breckenridge Medical Center** is located at 535 S. Park St., tel. (970) 453-9000.

Post offices are found at the following addresses: Breckenridge, 300 S. Ridge Rd., tel. (970) 453-2310; Dillon, 224 Dillon Mall, tel. (970) 468-2501; Frisco, 400 Granite, tel. (970) 668-5505; and Silverthorne, 390 N. Brian Ave., tel. (970) 468-8112.

Recycling
The **Summit Recycling Project** has two drop-off spots, both of which will take most recyclables: 301 8th Ave., Frisco, and on Summit Ln., Breckenridge.

Child Care
Breckenridge, Copper Mountain, and Keystone ski areas all have children's centers, providing day care for kids two months to five years old, with snow and ski programs for kids three and older. Reservations are required at all three. Phone Copper Mountain's **Belly Button Bakery** at (800) 458-8386, ext. 5; **Breckenridge Children's Center** at (970) 453-2368; and **Keystone's Children's Center** at (970) 468-4182.

INFORMATION

One of the best places to begin your visit to the area is the **Summit County Chamber of Commerce** in Frisco at the east end of Main St. between Dillon Reservoir and CO 9. Pick up maps, brochures, and tips on everything from lodging to cycling, fishing, rafting, and after-hours entertainment. Write the chamber at Box 214, Frisco, CO 80443, or phone (970) 668-2051, 668-5800, or (800) 530-3099, fax 668-1515.

The chamber also operates a tourist information center just off US 6 between Silverthorne and Dillon with lots of information on places to stay and eat, and things to do and buy, tel. (970) 262-0817. Watch for the road signs. The Breckenridge Resort Chamber operates the **Breckenridge Information Center** out of their offices at 309 N. Main.

The toll-free number for **Summit County Reservations** is (800) 365-6365. For **ski information** (transportation, lodging, ski school, lift tickets, etc.) in Summit County, write **Ski the Summit,** Box 267, Dillon, CO 80435, or phone (970) 468-6607. You can make lodging reservations by calling the following numbers: (800) 221-1091 (Breckenridge); (800) 458-8386 (Copper Mountain); and (800) 222-0188 (Keystone/Arapahoe Basin).

You can also get more information from the **Breckenridge Resort Chamber,** Box 1909, Breckenridge, CO 80424, tel. (970) 453-6018, and the **Town of Dillon,** Box 8, Dillon, CO 80435, tel. (970) 468-2403.

Libraries and Bookstores
The main branch of the Summit County **public library** is in Frisco at 43 Mt. Royal Dr., tel. (970) 668-5555. The north branch is at the town

hall in Silverthorne, tel. (970) 468-5887, and the south branch is in Breckenridge at 103 S. Harris, tel. (970) 453-6098.

Write the **Summit County Historical Society** at Box 747, Dillon, CO 80435, tel. (970) 468-6079. Offices are located at 104 N. Harris, Breckenridge, tel. (970) 453-9022, and 403 La Bonte, Dillon.

The **Book Nook,** 120 Dillon Mall, tel. (970) 468-5446, is a cozy little store whose friendly owners are full of tips on the area. In Frisco, stop in at **Daily Planet,** 308 Main, tel. (970) 668-5015, or at **Frisco Books, Ltd.,** 220 Main, tel. (970) 668-5399. In Breckenridge, both **Morris' Books,** 216 Lincoln (at Main), tel. (970) 453-0085, and **Weber's Books,** in the Lincoln West Mall, tel. (970) 453-4723, both carry excellent selections of history, recreation, and other local interest.

Electronic Information
You can get information on lodging, dining, skiing, and many other activities through Summit County's Internet address: **http://www.colo.com//summit/.**

Forest Service Information
For maps and information on camping, hiking, mountain biking, jeep touring, and backcountry skiing in Summit County, contact the Silverthorne district office of **Arapaho National Forest,** 191 Blue River Parkway, tel. (970) 468-5400.

Ski Reports and Weather Conditions
Remember when calling ski resorts for their snow conditions that they're in business to make money, and their reports are often optimistic and overly enthusiastic. Sometimes you're better off stopping by a local ski shop.

For information from the resorts, phone (970) 345-6118 (Breckenridge), 968-2100 (Copper Mountain), and 468-4111 (Keystone and Arapahoe Basin). For the latest in **road and weather conditions** in Summit County, phone (970) 453-1090.

Newspapers
In addition to the several locally published commercial guides to Summit County, check out the *Summit County Journal* and the *Summit Daily News,* available in racks throughout the area. Both list upcoming events and run stories spotlighting local celebrities, as well as pieces on local political maneuvering.

Further Reading
Janet Marie Clawson's *Echoes of the Past: Copper Mountain Colorado* (published by Copper Mountain Resort, 1986) is a thoroughly researched narrative history of the old mining-camp-turned-resort, and except for the last few pages is mostly free of PR-type promotion for the ski area.

An excellent account of the history of Frisco and the area is *Frisco! A Colorful Colorado Community* (it's livelier than the title would suggest!), by local writer Mary Ellen Gilliland and published by the Frisco Historical Society. After a brief discussion of the area's natives (the Utes), Gilliland chronicles the town's development and discusses its major players.

TRANSPORTATION

Summit County's very easy to get to and around in. Only 70 miles from Denver via the I-70 autostrada, the area is serviced by a number of independent shuttle services, and many of the hotels offer free transportation from Denver's International Airport (serviced by most major domestic airlines). You can also fly into DIA and rent a car for the short drive up over Loveland Pass.

Buses and Shuttles
The **Resort Express,** Denver's airport shuttle, offers buses hourly during the ski season and every hour and a half the rest of the year. Cost is about $60 (roundtrip), and reservations are required. Phone (970) 468-7600 or (800) 334-7433, or write Box 1429, Silverthorne, CO 80498. The main office is at 273 Warren Ave. in Silverthorne. Denver-to-Summit County shuttle service is also provided by **The Skiers' Connection,** tel. (970) 668-0200 or (800) 824-1104. During the ski season, buses leave on the hour from DIA 8 a.m.-11 p.m. and from Breckenridge 5 a.m.-8 p.m. (during the summer, buses run every other hour). Roundtrip fare is about $45.

In addition, free shuttle service is offered within the county by the **Summit Stage.** Bus routes link Breckenridge, Frisco, Copper Mountain, Dillon, Silverthorne, and Keystone (no service to Arapahoe Basin). For route schedules and more information, phone (970) 453-1241 or 453-1339. The **Breckenridge Free Shuttle and Town Trolley** provides service through town and up to the ski resort (both base areas). For schedule information, phone (970) 453-2368. The **Frisco Flyer** has routes throughout Frisco, from the Safeway at I-70 and CO 9 up into town on Main and back through into the condos and vacation homes. Phone (970) 668-5276 for a map and schedule. Keystone offers regular shuttle service between Keystone Ski Area and Arapahoe Basin.

Greyhound-Trailways, tel. (970) 668-5703, offers passenger service to Summit County, with a local depot at 1202 N. Summit Blvd. in Frisco.

Rental Cars

If you're coming into Summit County via Denver International Airport, you can either rent a car in Denver, where you'll find all the major franchises plus a couple of independents, or take a shuttle to Summit County and rent a car there. All rental agencies in this neck of the woods provide mountain-ready cars, with snow tires, ski racks, etc., as well as lots of 4WD rigs (significantly more expensive). See the Denver chapter following for rentals at Denver International.

In Summit County, you can rent from **American International Rent-a-Car,** tel. (970) 968-6719, at the junction of I-70 and CO 9, and from Copper Mountain Resort, tel. (970) 968-6311. You can also rent cars in Frisco from **Alpine Rent-a-Car,** 857 N. Summit Blvd., Frisco, tel. (970) 668-3785, and from **Summit Car Rental,** 325 S. Main, Frisco, tel. (970) 453-4600.

Taxis

Breckenridge-based **Around Town Taxi,** tel. (970) 453-6425, offers 24-hour 4WD taxi service.

bison

Denver city and county building

THE DENVER AREA

DENVER

The only Word I had was "Wow!". . . Here I was in Denver . . . I stumbled along with the most wicked grin of joy in the world, among the bums and beat cowboys of Larimer Street.

—Jack Kerouac, On the Road

INTRODUCTION

Situated at the far western edge of North America's Great Plains, and sprawling north, south, east, and west almost up into the foothills of the massive blue Rocky Mountains, Denver (pop. 480,000, with some two million in the metro area; elev. 5,280 feet) is the focal point of Colorado's commerce, government, and transportation. It's also a major tourism center, offering not only abundant attractions within the city limits, but also easy access to some of the state's premier playgrounds and historical sites.

A bona fide urban center, with high-rise office buildings lifting steep and glassy off the plain, and downtown professionals marching gray-suited and power-tied through the day, Denver is the American Rockies' largest and busiest city. As testimony, consider the major additions Denver witnessed in the mid-1990s alone: Denver International Airport; the Colorado Rockies, a National League Baseball expansion team; a beautiful downtown baseball stadium; and, as of summer 1995, a hockey team and new indoor sports pavilion for not only the ice arena but for a new home court for the Denver Nuggets, the city's NBA basketball team.

All of which runs contrary to the image many people have of Denver: Some still mislabel it a glorified cow town, or simply a cold, wintry stepping-stone to the world-class ski resorts fewer than 100 miles west. And Denverites seem unduly self-conscious of their image, going out of their way to teach outsiders the truth—which is that it's not a cow town at all (save for a couple of weeks each January, when the world's biggest

DENVER AREA HIGHLIGHTS

Denver: state capitol, historic and art museums, botanical gardens, Denver Zoo, recreation areas, hiking, biking, and skiing along the Colorado Urban Trail System, dining, nightlife, Tattered Cover Bookstore, 16th Street Mall, Capitol Hill People's Fair, LoDo (transformed and rejuvenated) lower-downtown area, Coors Stadium and Colorado Rockies baseball games

Boulder: climbing, cycling, and virtually all forms of recreation, people-watching, shopping, nightlife, bookstores and cafes, Colorado Music Festival, Kinetic Sculpture Challenge, Colorado Indian Market

Golden: Coors Brewery, Colorado School of Mines, hiking and biking in Golden Gate Canyon State Park, museums, International Heritage Festival of Folk Arts

Georgetown/Idaho Springs: museums, historic districts, the Georgetown Loop Railroad, skiing, hiking, and camping in Arapaho National Forest, Indian Springs Resort

Central City/Black Hawk: museums, mine tours, shopping, gambling, festivals, Central City Opera

rodeo comes to town), and it's hardly as cold and wintry as many people think.

To get an idea of how Denver's grown up since the turn of the century when it *was* very much a stock and agriculture center, just take a walk downtown. Many of the high-rises you see (though deplored by many locals because historical buildings were razed to build them) are as contemporary in design and as elegant as anything you'll see in any other major North American city. And take a look at the people going to work in them. They're young—young and, on the average, very highly educated: 35% of Denver's residents are between the ages of 18 and 35, and the city claims its downtown workforce is the highest educated in the country, and that the city overall has the country's fourth-highest number of college graduates (behind Washington, D.C., San Francisco, and Boston). In addition, Denver claims to lead the nation in movie attendance—though I've seen no figures distinguishing between films by Sylvester Stallone and, say, Martin Scorsese or Woody Allen.

And as far as Denver's being cold and wintry—and only a necessary obstacle en route to the ski slopes—consider: According to city statistics, the sun shines on Denver an average of 300 days a year, and less than 15 inches of precipitation fall. Of course, cold winter winds can and do sweep across the plains, whipping icy particles of snow against unprotected cheeks (as anyone who's watched a Broncos' home game knows . . .). And anyone visiting town between October and April would be well advised to bring hat, scarf, gloves, thermal underwear, and down jacket (Denver's annual average minimum temperature is 37.2°). But even when it's cold, it's dry, and, as the figures show, it's often sunny (in fact, the U.S. Weather Bureau claims Denver gets "more hours of annual sun than San Diego or Miami Beach"). And when it's dry, cold temperatures are a *lot* easier to take than when the barometer falls and there's moisture in the air.

A lot's changed in Denver since Jack Kerouac and Neal Cassady and the gang were raising hell on Larimer Street and trying their damnedest to live life on the stark edges of experience, and most of the old pool halls and flophouses are long gone (much to the chagrin of purists, who deplore the city's gentrification). But it's still a wonderful place, very much tied to the psyche of the American West and its vision of itself. And modern travelers looking for the heart of America must not overlook Denver, a city sprawling at the confluence of two of the country's greatest geological features and offering a history rich with the deepest textures of the American experience.

HISTORY

Though Denver is Colorado's capital, as well as its largest city, its history is more recent than many of the other cities and towns in the state. And it's much younger, historically, than other parts of the West—particularly the coast and New Mexico, where Spaniards explored and began to colonize as early as the late 16th century. The first outpost in the Denver area was built in 1832 by fur trader Louis Vasquez, though there were no permanent settlers in the region until 1858. That year William Green Russell discovered small amounts of gold along the South

Platte River. When word of his strike spread southeast to Pikes Peak, which wasn't living up to its promises, a handful of hopefuls packed up in search of better prospects. Along what is now W. Evans Ave., the new arrivals built several cabins, which they named Montana City. The gold there soon played out, however, and the group, led by Charles Nichols, moved downstream to the confluence of the Platte and Cherry Creek, where in the fall of 1858 they drew up plans for their new town, St. Charles City.

Meanwhile, word of gold in the Cherry Creek-South Platte area reached the East Coast, and optimistic miners soon rushed west to try to

make their fortunes. Also, members of William Russell's party, who had moved back into the mountains, learned that their original find may have been more significant than they first thought; they returned to the Cherry Creek area and built a small settlement, which they named Auraria, across the stream from St. Charles City. Shortly afterward, General William Larimer arrived from Kansas and established next door to St. Charles City the area's third townsite, which he named Denver City, after General James W. Denver, a former governor of Kansas Territory (of which Colorado was still part). Almost immediately, though, Larimer's party "in-

The Brown Palace is still one of the state's grand hotels.

COLORADO HISTORICAL SOCIETY

corporated" Nichols' camp (some say by force), and once again there were just the two towns, Denver City and Auraria.

Denver's Silver Lining

For the next several years, the two towns grew in size, with saloons, hotels, schools, and churches springing up along the creek. The first edition of the *Rocky Mountain News* was published from its "office" on mid-stream pilings between the camps on April 23, 1859. Meanwhile, more gold strikes occurred in the area—some highly exaggerated—many of which played out almost as soon as word of their existence reached the public. Still, prospectors continued to flock to the area, and on April 3, 1860, Denver and Auraria were consolidated; in January 1861, when the new town held its first election, the population was approximately 6,000.

Over the next 20 years, gold fell off in Denver, and with it so did the infant city's economy. Prices fell, and discouraged miners left for greener pastures. In the early 1880s, however, focus on Colorado's ore changed from gold to silver. Prospectors in the mountains west of Denver discovered immensely lucrative lodes, particularly at Cripple Creek, Leadville, Aspen, and Georgetown. Almost overnight, Denver's future again looked bright. Between 1880 and 1890, Denver's population tripled; banks, machine shops, smelters, and other businesses sprouted up downtown; and boutiques and other retail shops opened on Lawrence Street. By the end of the decade, Denver was producing more mining machinery than any other city in the world. In addition, Denver was becoming somewhat of a social hub, as miners who had made their fortunes in the nearby mountains moved to the city and built elaborate houses and threw lavish parties. Among the silver barons who brought their prosperity and high living to Denver was Horace Tabor, who opened the Tabor Opera House (located on 16th St. where the Tabor Center now stands) in 1881 and soon afterward built a magnificent mansion whose grounds covered an entire city block on Capitol Hill (see "History" under "Leadville" in the Southwestern Colorado chapter).

The 1890s saw a depression in Denver's economy, brought on by a sudden drop in silver prices, although by the turn of the century the city was already well on the road to recovery. Throughout the early 1900s, Denver continued to grow, with great improvements in roadways, schools, and parks, although the massive Rocky Mountains pretty much kept the city isolated from the rapidly developing cities on the West Coast, Los Angeles and San Francisco in particular. In 1928, however, Moffat Tunnel was blasted through the Rockies, providing a direct railway to the coast, and Denver was finally a part of the burgeoning national village.

Modern Times

Still, though, Denver retained its image as a Wild West frontier town. Its location in America's heartland, as well as the fact that it had become a veritable hub for an expanding national highway and railway system, ensured lots of short- and long-term visitors—from the upper crust to the down and out. In fact, until the city's "urbanization" in the late 1970s and early '80s, Denver still boasted (or bemoaned, depending on your perspective) many of the things that attracted the Kerouac gang in the '50s: pool halls, saloons, flophouses, and more than its share of folks who had slipped through the cracks in the American Dream.

In the early 1980s, natural resources again changed the face of Denver—this time in the form of oil and coal, which brought new revenues to the city. Although preservationists argued for the restoration of Denver's historic buildings, many—including the Tabor Opera House, of course—were razed and replaced with shopping centers, office buildings, and hotels. Though costing Denver much of its unique architectural heritage, this resulted in a very attractive and contemporary city, thoroughly modern in every sense of the word.

National League Baseball And an International Airport

Still more and bigger changes were in store, beginning in 1992, when the people of the state voted to build Coors Stadium on the west side of the downtown area near the train station. Though the stadium wasn't ready for play until the 1995 season, as soon as it was under way, the area, which came to be known as LoDo (for Lower Downtown District), began a true transformation: long-empty machine shops and warehouses were converted to brew pubs, antiques stores, coffee shops, and art galleries; live music filled the streets on summer evenings; and, of course, rents skyrocketed. Today, no visit to Denver is complete without a trip to LoDo. Sip a latte at a sidewalk table beside local businessfolk poring over blueprints for more restoration. Sample a local ale or stout from one of the microbreweries. And, if they're in town, go see the Colorado Rockies play, and marvel at one of the nation's finest baseball stadiums.

Like Colorado baseball, a new Denver airport had been a long time coming. The city's old airport, Stapleton, had long since outlived its design and small size, and passengers frequently complained of delays, traffic jams (both auto and airplane), and of generally outdated facilities. Denver International Airport (DIA), which opened for business in early 1995, was the solution. Though not without problems itself—not least among them the technical problems that delayed its opening, sparking a legal nightmare—DIA is an efficient and attractive airport that should make getting in and out of town and the mountains a whole lot easier.

MUSEUMS AND OTHER SIGHTS

A United States mint, a children's museum, and museums of history, art, natural history, transportation, and firefighting—many of which are

mid-19th-century storekeepers

The capitol building is a short walk from downtown.

right downtown—will keep museophiles entertained for days. Spend a morning learning about the history of the state; break for lunch; then take in prehistoric, Native American, modern, and postmodern art in the afternoon. Or head out to the transportation museum, and (appropriately enough) take a trolley along the Platte River to Denver's Children's Museum.

Colorado History Museum

Without doubt one of the best places to begin your exploration of Denver, particularly if your knowledge of the state's and city's history is at all sketchy, this beautifully designed and impressively laid-out museum provides the opportunity to wander among a huge assortment of exhibits. Start at the Colorado time line, a multidimensional and multimedia display that explains the history of the state from just before the Louisiana Purchase of 1803. You'll also want to check out the re-created machine shop, the displays of the various mining techniques used in Colorado's past, and the beautiful textile exhibit with Native American rugs, mostly from the Rio Grande Valley, from the mid-19th through the late-20th century. The museum also features lots of Plains and Ute Native American clothing (take a look at the beaded leggings), a Conestoga-style wagon built in 1824, and a 100-Mile Fritchle Electric Car (which could go 100 miles between battery chargings) built in 1910—displayed with the car are the original owner's manual, the pur-

chase deed, and various advertisements for the early autos, manufactured in Denver between 1904 and 1917. The museum is located downtown at the corner of 13th and Broadway and is open Mon.-Sat. 10 a.m.-4:30 p.m. and Sunday noon-4:30 p.m. Admission is $3 for adults, with discounts for kids and seniors. For more information, phone (303) 866-3682.

State Capitol

On July 5, 1886, almost 10 years after Colorado achieved statehood, and after the territorial government had been moved first from Colorado City and then from Golden City, excavation began on the state capitol building. Built on 10 acres of land donated by Henry C. Brown—who retained much of the surrounding property and grew rich by developing it for settlers and merchants who wanted to be near the state's new headquarters—the capitol took 22 years to complete, though 160 rooms were in use for the last 12 years of construction. In an attempt to represent Colorado in the building, designers worked primarily with materials from the state: The outer walls are of granite from the Gunnison area; the marble floors are from Marble; and the interior walls are wainscoted with rose onyx from Buelah (whose resources were exhausted by the shipments to Denver).

Particularly impressive are the building's gold-plated outer dome, the gorgeous stained-glass and hand-carved white oak throughout the building, and the monstrous chandeliers—

the one in the original Supreme Court chambers weighs a ton and was originally lighted with gas, as the engineers didn't trust the newly discovered electricity.

The Colorado State Capitol is at Colfax and Broadway. Free 30-minute tours, which end at the rotunda and provide wonderful views of both downtown and the distant mountains, are offered weekdays 9 a.m.-3:30 p.m. (on the half-hour). For more information, phone (303) 866-2604.

Denver Museum of Natural History

Ideally, you'd allow yourself at least an entire day to wander around this place and see everything, and one could easily spend more than that here. The seventh-largest museum in the United States, this is a beautifully and intelligently designed multistory complex of exhibits that will delight visitors of all ages. A sampling: Dinosaur fossils and skeletons (including the stegosaurus, Colorado's state fossil), skeletons from La Brea Tar Pits (a saber-toothed tiger, dire wolf, and ground sloth); a display of the world's minerals; a small Egyptology exhibit, with a mummy, a casket, and an illustrated explanation of the mummification process; a "Development of Man" display, beginning with a facsimile of the remains of "Lucy," who, named for the Beatles' song *Lucy in the Sky with Diamonds,* is probably 3.2 million years old; and exhibits of whales of the world, fishes of Colorado, and, well, you get the picture.

Don't miss the museum's IMAX Theater, the world's largest motion picture system. Films are projected onto a four-story-tall screen, and the wide-angle photography is absolutely stunning. Shows are also regularly offered at the musuem's Charles C. Gates Planetarium. Separate admission prices: museum, $4.50; theater, $5; and planetarium, $3.50 (all with discounts for kids and seniors). An excellent gift shop is in the museum's lobby. The Denver Historical Museum is located at 2001 Colorado Blvd.; phone (303) 322-7009 for more information.

United States Mint

Free guided tours of this penny-printing press explain the history of the mint (next to Fort Knox, the second-largest gold depository in the U.S.) and the process of making coins. During the height of the tourist season in summer, you'll want to get here early to beat the crowds; otherwise, expect to stand in line for up to a half-hour (sometimes more). Avoid the crowd (and the tour) by going to the gift store entrance around back—pick up freshly minted commemorative coins for your collection. The mint is open Mon.-Fri. 8 a.m.-3 p.m. (8:30 a.m.-2:45 p.m. in winter). It's directly behind the city and county building at W. Colfax and Cherokee, tel. (303) 844-3582.

Children's Museum of Denver

My friend Kristin, who knows kids as well as anyone I know, gives this museum a big A+. "Fantastic," she says. "A *perfect* place to take kids." With regularly changing exhibits, the museum offers dozens of hands-on experiences. Kristin continues: "A media display allows kids to videotape each other in a miniature newscasting room complete with weather station, news desk, viewing booth, and kid-size video recorders and monitors." In an Indians of the American North-

west display, kids can also create their own totem poles, and there are "classes" on such things as recycling and candy making, as well as "Kidslope," an artificial ski hill where kids can practice their technique and take lessons from professional ski instructors. And if that's not enough to wear them out, there's a park outside with all kinds of equipment to climb around on *and* a trolley that'll take the clan two miles along the South Platte to the Transportation Museum (the trolley costs $2 for adults and $1 for seniors and kids and takes about 25 minutes). Special days at the museum include Cinco de Mayo (May 5, Mexican Independence Day), Disney Days (late June), Young People's Mini Prix (mid-August), Big Shoes to Fill Career Day (late September), and Trick or Treat Street (you guessed it, late October).

The Denver Children's Museum is just off I-25 (take Exit 211) across from Mile-High Stadium at 2121 Crescent Drive. Admission is $4 kids, $3 adults, age two and under free. Hours are Tues.-Sat. 10 a.m.-5 p.m. and Sunday noon-5. Friday the museum is also open 5:30-8 p.m. for "Friday Night Live" (free). For more information, phone (303) 433-7444.

Denver Firefighters Museum

An unassuming little building at 1326 Tremont houses Denver's original firehouse, dating to the mid-19th century. Though the old uniforms, fire carts and trucks, nets (used in drills only, never in real fires), switchboards, and bells are all interesting, the bonus of this museum is tour guide Mary Felix, whose animated storytelling turns the little museum into theater. With a wink and an "I-don't-tell-everyone-this-Honey," the grandmotherly woman launches into the story of Chief Healy, who held the reins from just after the turn of the century until 1945. "The story goes that Ol' Chief Healy had but two questions for new recruits, and a yes answer to either one disqualified him. The first was 'Would you take a drink?' and the second was 'Would you step out on your wife?' If a potential firefighter answered yes to either question, why the chief felt he wasn't man enough to be a firefighter." Mary pauses, grins, and winks again. "Good thing times have changed, isn't it, Honey?"

Mary also delights in telling about how dalmatians came to be used—to keep the horses clipping along en route to the fire, the dogs nipped at their hooves; then once they got there, the dogs led them away from the fire and kept them waiting until it was time to return to the stables, located in the back of the firehouse. Mary also encourages kids to try on the old fire-fighting uniforms at the end of the tour.

Today, the museum is on the first floor, where the carts (and later, trucks) were kept, and a restaurant (see "Food," following) is on the second, formerly the men's living quarters. The Denver Firefighters Museum is open Mon.-Fri. 10 a.m.-2 p.m. Admission is $2. Phone (303) 892-1100 for more information.

Molly Brown House and Museum

Though most people remember Debbie Reynolds' character and the 1960s MGM movie when they hear of "The Unsinkable Molly Brown," there really was such a woman. And what a woman she was—part redheaded Irish-Catholic pioneer, part early women's rights activist, rabble-rouser, and all-around bon vivant. Born in 1867 in Hannibal, Missouri, Molly (née Margaret Tobin), moved to Leadville at age 18 and married J.J. Brown there on September 1, 1886. After their two children were born (Larry in 1887 and Helen in 1889), the family moved to Denver, where in 1909, as a result of the conflict between Molly's love of traveling and J.J.'s commitment to Colorado business, the couple legally separated.

In 1912, the world learned of Molly. Traveling on the "maiden" voyage of the Titanic, Molly, with her knowledge of seven languages, helped save many of the immigrants and later went on to help the survivors chart new courses for their lives—by organizing them and donating money to them.

The Molly Brown House and Museum is an ornate Victorian mansion built in 1889 and purchased by the Browns in 1894. It has been completely restored (having been used for many purposes over the years, including a men's boardinghouse), and the furniture is either original (such as the horsehair sofa) or replicated (such as the piano). Particularly impressive is the gilt-relief wallpaper throughout the house, lending the walls a look that's part European parlor, part Las Vegas brothel.

The Molly Brown House can be found at 1340 Pennsylvania (between 13th and 14th streets). Note: No off-street parking is available, and you're probably better off walking from downtown than driving the few blocks and trying to park. Tours (by docents dressed in Victorian garb) are offered year-round; admission is $3.50 for adults, $2.50 for seniors over 65, and $1.50 for ages six to 12. Museum hours are: June-Aug., Mon.-Sat. 10 a.m.-4 p.m. and Sunday noon-4 p.m.; Sept.-May, Tues.-Sat. 10 a.m.-4 p.m. and noon-4 p.m. For more information, phone (303) 832-4092.

the Molly Brown House and Museum

Black American West
Museum and Heritage Center

Though naturally overlooked in the white-washed histories of the country, blacks played an important role opening up the West. In fact, according to documentation at this unique museum, roughly a third of the West's cowboys were black, as were many pioneer doctors, politicians, and teachers. Fortunately, historians are beginning to realize their vast contributions to American history, and textbooks are slowly beginning to reflect the truth. Maybe someday, museums like this one won't seem such anomalies, and the history of black America will be fully integrated into our museums, books, and consciousnesses.

The museum is at 3091 California St., right on the city's new light-rail system. Hours are Wed.-Fri. 10 a.m.-2 p.m., Saturday 10 a.m.-5 p.m., and Sunday 2-5 p.m. Admission is $2 for adults, discounts for kids and seniors. Phone (303) 292-2566.

Museo de las Americas

This museum, which recently opened on Santa Fe Avenue after moving from several different directors' homes, aims to reach out to the Hispanic community in the Denver area by focusing on the art, culture, and history of Latino Americans. In addition to the regular displays, the museum offers a range of educational programs and works with local schools. The museum is located at 861 Santa Fe and is open Tues.-Sat. 10 a.m.-5 p.m. Admission is $2 for adults, $1 for seniors and students; phone (303) 571-4401 for more information.

Forney Transportation Museum

Housed in an old brick warehouse on the Platte River west of downtown, this museum features a gigantic array of vintage automobiles, railroad cars, sleighs, carriages, and just about anything else that once carried human beings (or cargo) from one place to another. Among the cars are an 1898 Renault Opera Coupe, a 1915 Hudson, 1919 Fiat limousine, and 1924 Moon sedan (built between 1906 and 1929), and scores more—from 1930s roadsters to a 1970 limited-edition Ford Mustang. An eccentric and eclectic museum, the Forney offers a chance to wander around—even to get lost—in the maze of half-completed exhibits, storerooms, and the weedy, overgrown yard full of rusted train engines, passenger cars, and careening sailing ships, their paint faded and chipped; one room, and I'm not sure how it fits into the general theme, is full of mounted game fish in glass cases, all of apparently near-record size. A small gift shop sells posters, postcards, model airplanes, and other souvenirs. The Forney Transportation Museum is located at 1416 Platte. From downtown, take 15th St. west, and turn left on Platte. The museum is open Mon.-Sat. 10 a.m.-5 p.m. and Sunday 11 a.m.-5 p.m. Admission is $4 for adults, discounts for kids and seniors, tel. (303) 433-3643.

Mizel Museum of Judaica

This museum features permanent and changing exhibits demonstrating Jewish heritage and cultural contributions throughout the world. Included in the free admission are films, tours, and lectures. The museum is at 560 S. Monaco Parkway. Hours are Mon.-Thurs. 10 a.m.-4 p.m. and Sunday 10 a.m.-noon. Phone (303) 333-4156.

ART MUSEUMS

Denver Art Museum

This modern six-story downtown facility offers visitors a mind-boggling array of art and information about the countries and societies where the works originated. One of the true beauties of this museum is that the exhibits are arranged to demonstrate the distinct links between the various cultures and societies. Just a preview of what you'll find: African masks, sculpture, and beaded belts and necklaces, along with Northwest Native American totems, gigantic carved masks, and rattles, and South Pacific ceremonial staffs, masks, and clothing (pieces range from prehistoric to mid-20th century); Spanish colonial paintings and sculpture, including a beautiful collection of Santos (carved cottonwood or pine figures, usually of Christ on the cross or the Madonna), a recreated 17th-century New Mexican church; European and Mediterranean art, Egyptian caskets, Greek statues, and Roman urns; modern pieces by Picasso, Juan Gris, Georges Braque, Matisse, and Breton; and art

DENVER
DOWNTOWN

EXIT 212C

PARKING

COORS FIELD PARKING

COORS FIELD

COORS FIELD PARKING

PEDESTRIAN WALK

BROADWAY

22nd ST.

PARK AVE.

COORS FIELD PARKING

UNION STATION

HISTORIC

20th ST.

21st ST.

STOUT ST.

SOUTH PLATTE RIVER

OXFORD HOTEL

WYNKOOP BREWERY

BLAKE ST.

MARKET ST.

19th ST.

LARIMER ST.

LOWER

CALIFORNIA ST.

RTD LIGHT RAIL

WYNKOOP ST.

WAZEE ST.

16TH STREET MALL

DOWNTOWN

LAWRENCE ST.

ARAPAHOE ST.

CURTIS ST.

CHAMPA ST.

QUEEN ANNE INN

SPEER BLVD.

TABOR CENTER

18th ST.

STATION

AURARIA PKWY.

CHERRY CREEK

LARIMER SQUARE

BUS STATION

STATION

STATION

20th AVE.

TO I-25

14th ST.

15th ST.

STATION

17th ST.

STATION

19th AVE.

18th AVE.

DENVER CENTER FOR THE PERFORMING ARTS

WELTON ST.

16TH STREET MALL

BROWN PALACE HOTEL

SHERMAN ST.

17th AVE.

WARWICK HOTEL

13th ST.

STATION

GLENARM PL.

TREMONT PL.

COURT PL.

CLEVELAND PL.

16th AVE.

LOGAN ST.

SPEER BLVD.

RTD LIGHT RAIL

13th ST.

DENVER FIREFIGHTERS MUSEUM

TRIANON ART MUSEUM

CHAMBER OF COMMERCE VISITOR INFORMATION CENTER

COLFAX AVE.

12th ST.

STATION

UNITED STATES MINT

CIVIC CENTER

BROADWAY

STATE CAPITOL

14th AVE.

MOON PUBLICATIONS, INC.

KALAMATH ST.

SANTA FE DR.

INCA ST.

FOX ST.

ELATI ST.

DELAWARE ST.

CHEROKEE ST.

BANNOCK ST.

ACOMA ST.

DENVER ART MUSEUM

DENVER PUBLIC LIBRARY

COLORADO HISTORY MUSEUM

LINCOLN ST.

MOLLY BROWN HOUSE

GRANT ST.

13th AVE.

12th AVE.

SPEER BLVD.

NOT TO SCALE

from the United States and the American West, with pieces by Frederic Remington, Winslow Homer, Thomas Hart Benton, and E. Irving Crouse and Joseph Sharp, two of the founders of the early-20th-century Taos artists' colony.

The Denver Art Museum is at 100 W. 14th Ave. (near the corner of Broadway), and is open Tues.-Sat. 10 a.m.-5 p.m. and Sunday noon-5 p.m. Admission is $3 for adults, seniors and students $1.50—free admission on Saturday. The museum also has a classy gift shop, with an especially fine selection of books. For more information, phone (303) 640-2793.

Museum of Western Art

Located downtown right across from the Brown Palace, this small museum features three stories of the art of western America. Included are bronzes and paintings by Frederic Remington (one of the most remarkable is the sculpture *Coming Through the Rye,* four wild horsemen, pistols waving madly), Charles Russell oils, Georgia O'Keeffe's *Cow Skull on Red* (1931), Grant Wood's *Spring Flowers* (1932), and Norman Rockwell's *Gary Cooper as Texan* (1930). The museum also shows works by Ernest L. Blumenschein and E. Irving Crouse (for information on these Taos painters, please refer to Moon Publications' wonderfully illuminating *New Mexico Handbook),* and also offers an interesting perspective on westward expansion and the death of the frontier. A highlight is a letter from Charles Russell, dated May 4, 1914, which is illustrated with a cartoon of people at an art gallery. Russell writes: "Was shure good to here from you London is a sisobol camp."

The museum also has a small gift shop with jewelry, rugs, pottery, and postcards, as well as a bookstore with coffee-table-size art books and books on the American West, including some rare books and some signed by the authors.

The Museum of Western Art is located at 1727 Tremont Place and is open Tues.-Sat. 10 a.m.-4:30 p.m. Admission is $3, $2 for students and seniors. For more information, phone (303) 296-1880.

Trianon Museum and Art Gallery

Half a block from the Denver Firefighters Museum is this classic example of the adage, "Don't judge a book by its cover." From the outside this little place looks all but abandoned, save for the small awning out front. But step inside, and you're in a world of stunningly beautiful antique vases, furniture, silver, china, Oriental screens, and much more, all arranged—some might say cluttered—into two small rooms. Betty Metzger (no direct relation) gives tours as minutely detailed as the pieces she shows. Among the works are Louis XVI service plates, a silver tray once owned by Czar Peter the Great, and a 60-key Steinway piano from the early 18th century. In addition, there's an antique gun collection dating to the 16th century, as well as a late-19th-century Gatling gun and a 12-pound mountain howitzer. Visit the Trianon is at the corner of 14th St. and Tremont; it's open Mon.-Sat. 10 a.m. to 4 p.m. Admission is $1. Some art, antiques, and prints for sale. For more information, phone (303) 623-0739.

PARKS AND RECREATION AREAS

With Denver's youthful and outdoor-oriented population, an abundance of parks should come as no surprise. In fact, there's more than an abundance: There are over 200 parks in the metro area, and Denverites take full advantage of them—for cycling, picnicking, swimming, tennis, or just sprawling on a lawn and napping. For a complete listing of city parks, contact the Denver Parks and Recreation Department, (303) 575-3043.

City Park

When this park was first established in 1881, it was a good horse-and-buggy day-trip from Denver out to the lawns and lakes. Since then, the city has grown up around it, and though still a bit of a drive from downtown, the facility is a city park in the truest sense of the word. In addition to the spacious lawns perfect for picnicking, the small lakes where you can rent rowboats, and the rose gardens (the place makes you feel like you're living in a Matisse painting), the park also contains the **Denver Zoo,** the **Natural History Museum,** and a golf course (see below). You could spend an entire day here, maybe even a weekend, and still not see everything. To get to the park from downtown, take Colorado Blvd. to 17th Street.

Denver Zoo

Now I'll admit to being somewhat of a cynic when it comes to zoos—the sight of sickly looking animals baking under a too-hot sun in too-small cages doesn't do a whole lot for me. But some zoos seem to respect the animals more than others, and as zoos go, Denver's is all right. In fact, it's a participant in the North American Species Survival Program, which attempts to keep the bloodlines of different species thriving and to educate the public about the plight of animals other than the human type. The Denver Zoo draws special attention to endangered species (officially recognized and otherwise), and among the gift shop's more popular T-shirts are the ones with the logo "Extinction is Forever."

If you're not up for wandering footloose around the 76-acre compound, viewing the lions, and tigers, and bears (oh, my!), hop on the "Zooliner," a nonstop-train through the zoo complete with a "safari lecture." Interested in pinnipeds? Stop by the seal and sea lion exhibit, where regular feedings and shows are scheduled.

Snack huts are scattered around the complex, though the many lawns make ideal picnic areas, as do the lawns at the City Park, just outside the gate. (By the way, full literary pun awards go to the snack shack "Ice Cream Station Zebra.")

The Denver Zoo is located at E. 23rd and Steel streets (on weekends, a shuttle runs between the zoo and the Natural History Museum, and concerts are scheduled throughout the summer). Admission is $6 for adults, $4 for students and seniors. For more information, phone (303) 331-4110.

Denver Botanic Gardens

If you've been pounding the pavement of downtown Denver, taking in the sights and sounds of the city, chances are you're starting to feel the effects: The noise and crowds have gone from attractive novelties to overbearing encroachments on your senses. If this is the case, one of the best places in town to restore your sanity is the Botanic Gardens, where you'll find acres of gardens, from gorgeous spreads of wildflowers and native grasses to plots of domesticated perennials, vegetables, and a water garden with a dozen or more different types of water lilies. With paved sidewalks wandering among the

various gardens, benches, and gazebos, and arboretums for shade, the Botanic Gardens—still in the heart of the city—is one of the best places to come for a change of pace. (In addition, people planning to do a little landscaping of their own might want to wander around simply gathering ideas and inspiration; pamphlets and fliers explaining the different plants are available in racks throughout.) There's also a gift shop and huge library. In the summer, the gardens feature a series of evening concerts.

Denver's Botanic Gardens, 1005 York, are open daily 9 a.m.-5 p.m. Admission is $4. To get there from downtown, take 14th St. to York. For general information, phone (303) 331-4010, or 744-9999 for concert series updates.

Bear Creek Lake State Park

Operated by the City of Lakewood Parks and Recreation Department, this small park (just short of 3,000 acres) also contains the two smaller Soda Lakes and offers many different recreation opportunities—from windsurfing and fishing to picnicking, overnight camping, horseback riding, and birdwatching (waterfowl and birds of prey). You can rent sailboards, paddleboats, canoes, and sailboats. The best way to get there is to take Kipling Ave. to Morrison Rd. and go west. Entrance fee is $2 per car. For more information, phone (303) 987-7880 or 987-7800.

Cherry Creek Lake State Recreation Area

Offering easy-access relief from the strip malls, townhouses, and high-rise office buildings of surrounding Aurora, this multi-purpose recreation area is popular among Denverites looking to cool off on hot summer days. Lately, the lake has become especially popular with jet-skiers, who jam around the lake, much to the chagrin of some of the other folks—waterskiers, windsurfers, fishermen, picnickers, cyclists, and campers. In the winter, the lake opens for ice fishing, skating, and boating, as well as cross-country skiing and snowmobiling (over 1.5 million visitors a year).

Built between 1946 and 1950 as a flood-control project, Cherry Creek Dam is nearly 1,500 feet long and 150 feet high; the lake is 3.5 miles long. Public recreation facilities include bicycle and jet-ski rental, campgrounds and picnic areas, a golf course, riding stables, nature trails, and fishing areas, with some especially designated for use by people with disabilities.

For general information on Cherry Creek Lake State Recreation Area, phone (303) 690-1166, or write 4201 S. Parker Rd., Aurora, CO 80014. For information on horseback riding, phone (303) 690-8235; for information on nature walks, picnicking (to reserve sites), and special events, phone (303) 690-1211.

To get to the lake from downtown, take Leetsdale to Parker Rd.; from I-225, take the Parker Rd. Exit. The gates are well marked.

Chatfield Lake State Recreation Area

Quite a bit nicer than Cherry Creek Lake (you can't see high-rises from the shores), Chatfield isn't quite as accessible from downtown. But it's worth the drive, especially for nature lovers. In addition to a blue heron reserve at the lake, the area has a nicely presented visitors center with the skull of a mammoth found during dam excavation, a United States Army Corps of Engineers exhibit of rivers, flooding, and damming, and includes excellent historical photos of 19th-century floods. The lake has several marinas and campgrounds, as well as riding stables, bike trails, and hiking paths. In the winter, Denverites go with the floe (sorry . . .) and head to Chatfield for ice fishing and cross-country skiing.

The Army Corps of Engineers offers free hour-and-a-half tours of Chatfield Dam on Saturday mornings from late May through August. Call (303) 979-4120 for information about tours, or 791-7276 for information about the recreation area.

SPORTS AND OUTDOOR ACTIVITIES

Skiing

Skiing, of course, is the sport most people associate with Denver. And with good reason—the city's gateway to a concentration of ski resorts offering some of the finest runs, conditions, and facilities the sport has to offer. Not only are there huge destination resort complexes—Vail, Aspen, Breckenridge, and others—within easy drives of Denver International Airport, but several other smaller resorts—Arapahoe Basin, for example—offer world-class skiing in less crowded (as well as less pretentious) areas, also within easy reach of the metropolitan area.

From Denver, it's very easy to get to the slopes. Whether your destination is Winter Park, Copper Mountain, or Vail, you can drive your own car, rent one, or take a shuttle, and be buckling your boots in under two hours (weather permitting). For more information on the ski areas, as well as on transportation to them, refer to the specific destination chapters. **People's Choice Transportation,** based at Denver International Aiport, offers rides to the ski areas; phone (303) 289-2222 or (800) 777-2388.

For an only-in-Denver ski experience, take a ride on the **Ski Train.** Departing from Union Station on weekends at 7:15 a.m., Dec.-April, the train takes you out of the city, northwest into the mountains, through Moffat Tunnel (completed in 1928), and eventually deposits you at the base of **Winter Park Ski Resort.** The train leaves the ski area in late afternoon, and will have you back at Union Station (conveniently located across the street from the Wynkoop Brewery) by early evening (it's a two-hour trip). Coach tickets are $25 roundtrip; first-class tickets are $40.

For more information on the Ski Train, write 555 17th St. no. 2400, Denver, CO 80202, or phone (303) 296-I-SKI.

Cycling

Bicycling is so popular in Denver that speed limits are enforced in the city parks. In addition, the city offers a huge network of bike paths that can take the adventurous cyclist into most areas of the metro Denver area. From downtown, a bike path follows Speer out to Cherry Creek Shopping Center. The outlying areas offer limitless cycling, and some Colorado bikers "collect" passes: Berthoud (elev. 11,315 feet), Loveland (elev. 11,992 feet), Independence (elev. 12,095 feet), and others.

The **Denver Bicycle Touring Club** offers regular rides at all levels of interest and ability, and also publishes maps and a newsletter (with complete listings of events and rides). For information, write Box 8973, Denver, CO 80201, or phone (303) 798-3713 to learn more about current ride schedules and meeting places, as well as for names and numbers of ride leaders.

Golf

There are so many public golf courses in the Denver metro area that you could almost play a different course every day for a month without walking (or driving) the same fairway. Ranging from plain and pleby to elaborate and aristocratic, Denver's courses offer something for just about every level of skill and dedication.

One of the area's most popular courses is **Arrowhead Golf Club,** in Roxborough State Park, 45 minutes southwest of Denver (south of Chatfield Dam). Designed by Robert Trent Jones Jr. Arrowhead is famous for its views and setting, as well as the challenge it provides golfers of all abilities. For information and tee times, phone (303) 973-9614.

City Park Golf Course, E. 25th Ave. and York, is an ideal family course, especially for the family whose members don't all share the same enthusiasm for the sport—also located at the park are tennis courts, the Denver Zoo, the Museum of Natural History, and 134 acres of sprawling lawns. For more information, phone (303) 295-2095.

Other popular Denver-area courses: **Hyland Hills** in Westminster, tel. (303) 428-6526; **Meadow Hills** in Aurora, tel. (303) 690-2500; **Riverdale** in Brighton, tel. (303) 659-6700; and **Welshire** in Denver at the corner of Hampden and Colorado boulevards, tel. (303) 757-1352.

The **Colorado Golf Resort Association,** at 1407 Larimer Square, has golf-oriented visitor and convention information and can arrange accommodations-and-greens-fees packages. Phone (303) 973-4076.

For information on the courses owned and operated by the Denver Parks and Recreation Department, phone (303) 575-3155.

Colorado Urban Trail System

The Colorado State Trails Program, a division of the state Parks and Outdoor Recreation Department, organizes a series of nearly 100 hiking, cycling, horseback riding, and cross-country ski trails throughout the Denver metro area, from Golden to Aurora to Roxborough State Park. You can get maps, which designate degrees of difficulty and list facilities (restrooms, picnic tables, shelters, etc.), by writing the Colorado Division of Parks and Outdoor Recreation, 1313 Sherman St. no. 618, Denver, CO 80203, or by phoning (303) 866-3437.

Kayak Course

Unbeknownst even to many Denverites, the city has its own kayak course, at the confluence of Cherry Creek and the South Platte near the Forney Transportation Museum.

Amusement Centers and Parks

Denver offers a handful of amusement parks, for those whose diversions need direction. The **Celebrity Sports Center,** 888 S. Colorado Blvd., is a 150,000-square-foot facility featuring everything from bowling, swimming, and water slides to video arcades, bumper cars, and pinball machines. The complex is open weekdays till midnight and Friday and Saturday till 2 a.m. Free child care. Phone (303) 757-3321.

Elitch Gardens and Amusement Park is sort of a Rocky Mountain version of Coney Island, with over 32 rides, including whitewater rafting and a huge roller coaster, plus miniature golf, musical revues, and islands of flowers, as well as fast food at every turn. Dating to the early part of the century, Elitch's was home for years to one of the country's original summer stock theaters. In the spring of 1995, Elitch's moved (and expanded) from its location west of town to a more central downtown site near Coors Stadium. The park is open daily June through Labor Day (and weekends in May). Unlimited ride admission is about $20 for adults and $15 for folks 52 inches tall and shorter. Phone (303) 455-4771.

If you drove into Denver from the west, chances are you noticed **Lakeside Amusement Park** just before you got into town. Like Elitch's, Lakeside is a classic amusement park, evoking a simpler and more innocent America. Get your thrills on the roller coaster, speedboat rides on the lake, or any number of other rides; there are also rides for the less adventurous, and those whose stomachs insist they stay in tamer territory (see you there . . .). Located at I-70 and Sheridan, tel. (303) 477-1621.

Take Me out to the Ball Game

On July 5, 1991, less than a year after Colorado voters approved the construction of a new baseball stadium, Denver was awarded a National League Baseball team. The Colorado Rockies began playing on April 9, 1993, in Mile High Stadium, home of the Denver Broncos,

*downtown Denver
from the capitol
building*

and in spring of 1995 moved to the gorgeous new Coors Stadium in lower downtown Denver. This stadium has been instrumental in transforming that area from a warehousy district to an upscale one of antique stores, brew pubs, nightclubs, and coffee shops.

Admission to Colorado Rockies' games ranges from $1 to $16, and the season runs from early April through late September. For tickets or more information, phone (303) ROCKIES. You can also arrange ticket-hotel-rentalcar packages through the Denver Metro Convention and Visitors Bureau, tel. (303) 892-1112.

TOURS

Best Mountain Tours by The Mountain Men, tel. (303) 750-5200, offers half- and full-day historic and scenic tours, as well as ski charters. Write to 3003 S. Macon Circle, Aurora, CO 80014. **Discover Colorado Tours,** tel. (303) 277-0129, also offers scenic and historic tours, specializing in off-road trips, with full-day, half-day, and campfire tours. Write to Box 205, Golden, CO 80402. **Gray Line of Denver,** tel. (303) 289-2841, offers sightseeing tours of the city and the area, and can arrange tours of other areas outside the city. **British Double Decker,** tel. (303) 892-1800, has a fleet of 10 buses available for sporting events, conventions, etc.

ACCOMMODATIONS

Although you can find motels throughout the Denver metropolitan area, particularly at major artery junctions and interstate offramps, the city's accommodations are primarily concentrated in the downtown area and in the southeastern region. If you can afford to, the best area to stay is downtown, where a good number of Denver's main attractions lie within walking distance—the 16th Street Mall, the capitol building, several excellent museums and historical landmarks, and some of the city's best restaurants are concentrated within an area not much bigger than a couple of square miles. And the best way to see them is by walking tour.

Downtown
Denver's oldest and most elegant downtown hotel is the **Brown Palace,** 321 17th St. between Tremont and Broadway, tel. (303) 297-3111, (800) 321-2599, or (800) 228-2917 in Denver. Completed in 1892 and designed in Italian Renaissance style, this grande dame of Denver's hotels is worth a visit just to have a look around—even if you're staying somewhere a bit less ostentatious. Management actually printed up a descriptive walking-tour guide (available at the registration desk) providing information on design, construction materials, former guests, and furnishings. Rooms start at about $160 a night and go up to over $675.

Another of downtown's nicer and more elegant hotels is the **Oxford Hotel,** tel. (303) 628-5400. This European-style hotel at the corner of 17th St. and Wazee offers luxurious rooms and all the pampering you can take—including a health club, complimentary limousine service downtown, and hosts who take the time to know their guests almost as family. Plus, it's the closest hotel to Coors Field. Rates start at $120 for a double.

The **Warwick,** tel. (303) 861-2000, at the corner of 17th and Grant, is a classically styled high-rise offering complimentary downtown transportation, athletic facilities, and a rooftop pool looking out over the modern, glassy high-rises of the city. Rooms start at about $135. Just three blocks away, at 401 17th St., the **Comfort Inn,** tel. (303) 296-0400, has high-rise rooms overlooking the city—the corner rooms are especially impressive, with wraparound floor-to-ceiling windows for excellent views of the downtown area. Doubles run about $70.

Downtown on Curtis between 18th and 19th is the **Embassy Suites Hotel,** 1881 Curtis, tel. (303) 297-8888, where large rooms afford privacy and easy access to LoDo and Coors Stadium. Doubles start at about $100.

The new **Adam's Mark** (née Radisson), tel. (303) 893-3333, at 1550 Court, offers first-class digs and easy access to downtown. Doubles run $70-100.

Other conveniently located downtown hotels include the **Westin,** tel. (303) 572-9100 or (800) 228-3000, and the **Holiday Inn,** tel. (303) 573-1450 or (800) 423-5128.

The South End

You'll see it from a distance—the black tower standing apart from the other muted southern Denver high-rises, penetrating the sky with an almost otherworldly feel to it. But step inside **Loews Giorgio Hotel,** tel. (303) 782-9300, and the change seems as dramatic as the tower itself. Suddenly you feel like you're in Milan and that La Scala or DaVinci's *Last Supper* is just a short cab ride away. Indeed, this Italian-style hotel is one of Denver's real luxuries, and though located a bit south of downtown still affords easy access to most of the city's attractions. An added bonus is you don't have to pay for parking here—unless you opt for valet—which you usually do down-

town, where parking alone can add a sizable sum to your bill. Rooms at the Giorgio start at about $90. To get there, take the Colorado Blvd. Exit from I-25, go south to Mississippi, and turn left.

Other, more moderate lodging at the south end of town (still at the junction of Colorado and I-25) includes the **Belcaro Motel,** tel. (303) 756-3671, **Days Inn,** tel. (303) 691-2223 or (800) 325-2525, the **Landmark Best Western,** tel. (303) 388-5561, and **La Quinta,** tel. (303) 578-8886 or (800) 531-9500.

Also on the south side of town (in Englewood, near the junction of I-25 and US 88) are **Days Inn,** tel. (303) 790-8220 or (800) 325-2525, **Hampton Inn,** tel. (303) 792-9999 or (800) 426-7866, and **Radisson,** tel. (303) 799-6200.

West of Town

As you head into Denver on I-70 from the west, you'll find another cluster of motels and hotels to choose from. Among them: a **Regal 8,** tel. (303) 455-8888 or (800) 851-8888; a **Howard Johnson,** tel. (303) 433-8441, I-70 at Exit 272/Federal north; and a **Motel 6,** tel. (303) 232-4924, at Exit 266.

Bed and Breakfasts

The **Queen Anne Inn,** tel. (303) 296-6666, is just east of downtown at 2147 Tremont. Constructed in 1879, the building is on the National Register of Historic Places and was beautifully restored and decorated by proprietors Chuck and Anne Hillestad, who court honeymooners and often hold weddings on the premises. The Queen Anne has been touted in dozens of national publications and was recently named Denver's best bed and breakfast by the local weekly, *Westword.* Its residential neighborhood is within easy walking distance of most downtown attractions and restaurants. Rooms run $75-125, suites $135-165. To get to the Queen Anne from I-25, take the Colfax Exit, and follow Colfax past the capitol to Logan; go left on Logan until it tees into a small park (you'll be looking straight across at the Queen Anne); go left, and then veer right onto Tremont.

The **Capitol Hill Mansion Bed and Breakfast,** 1207 Pennsylvania, tel. (303) 839-5221, is just a couple of blocks from the state capitol building and within walking distance to most of Denver's downtown attractions.

Hostels

Generally the least expensive way to travel, and one of the best ways to meet fellow travelers, hosteling can be a real adventure, though it's not for everyone. The typical dorm-style accommodations, the chore(s) you'll be asked to do to offset the exceptionally low rates, and the socializing demanded by the lack of privacy can either suit your needs and moods or not. If this is the kind of digs you prefer, or one that your budget insists upon, the city offers the **Hostel of the Rocky Mountains,** 1530 Downing St., tel. (303) 861-7777, where shared and private rooms run $20-40. For more information on hosteling in the Rocky Mountain area, write **American Youth Hostels, Inc.,** Rocky Mountain Division, Box 2730, Boulder, CO 80306.

The downtown **YMCA,** tel. (303) 861-8300, at 25 E. 16th St., a block from the capitol, also offers inexpensive rooms.

Camping and RVing

Of course the mountains west of Denver are full of campgrounds, both privately owned and government run, and hundreds of thousands of acres of national forest and wilderness areas lie within a short drive of the city (see specific destination chapters). If you're heading into Denver and just need a place to pull off the road, you've got several options, including **Chief Hosa Campground,** tel. (303) 526-0364, west of town just off I-70 at Exit 253, and **Denver-North Campground,** tel. (303) 452-4120, north of town at Exit 229 (Broomfield) off I-25.

FOOD

Start Me Up

One of the best places to face the morning in Denver is at **The Market,** in LoDo on Larimer Square at 1445 Larimer, tel. (303) 534-5140. Grab a newspaper and get in line at the espresso bar for a latte, cappuccino, or house coffee and a croissant or fresh-baked muffin. Open at 6:45 weekday mornings (8:30 on Saturday) and till midnight on Friday and Saturday. The Market also sells gourmet groceries, deli sandwiches, and desserts (try a creampuff or truffle). Seating available both inside and on the sidewalk outside, weather permitting. Just down the street at

1480 Larimer is a **Starbucks,** and many other coffee shops are scattered around the LoDo area, including at the Tabor Center Writer Square, and Larimer Square. At the other end of the 16th Street Mall is the **Rockies Cafe,** 535 16th St., tel. (303) 892-5802, a deli and coffee shop popular with the downtown business set, who come in for espressos and bagels on their way to work or for a deli sandwich at lunch.

If you're in the mood for something heartier, you might try the **Delectable Egg,** 1642 Market (between 16th and 17th streets in LoDo), tel. (303) 572-8146. Open at 6:30 weekday mornings and 7 a.m. on Saturday, the Egg serves daily specials for around $5 in a large airy, woody, and ceiling-fanned dining room. There's also a Delectable Egg at the other end of the 16th Street Mall at 1625 Court Pl., tel. (303) 892-5720. Both also serve very good lunches, including croissant and pita sandwiches, salads, and fritatas; lunch will run you $5-8.

Dozens, 236 W. 13th, tel. (303) 572-0066, is a veritable downtown institution. Housed in a restored Victorian, the restaurant is walking distance from downtown businesses and many of the local tourist attractions. That fact, along with its reputation for excellent food at reasonable prices, ensures its popularity with locals and out-of-towners alike. Another downtown tradition is **Duffy's Shamrock Restaurant and Bar,** 1635 Court Pl., tel. (303) 534-4935, where you can get reasonably priced steak and eggs, omelettes, and waffles, as well as bloody Marys to wash it all down with (full bar service begins at 7 a.m.). Duffy's also serves lunch (burgers, prime rib, salads: $4-7) and dinner (burgers, steaks, seafood, spaghetti: $4-12).

Mexican

One local favorite—regularly recognized by *Westword's* "Best of Denver"—is the **Blue Bonnet Café,** at 457 S. Broadway, tel. (303) 778-0147. Nothing fancy here—in fact the rather tacky decor goes hand in hand with the run-down look of the building's exterior, not to mention the boarded-up buildings nearby—but if it's good cheap food you're after, look no further. Be prepared to wait, though: The Blue Bonnet's no secret. But even the wait is part of the picture—try one of the half dozen or so types of margaritas, by the glass or by the pitcher, on which the

Blue Bonnet prides itself. Dinner combos run $4-6, specials $6-8; a la carte tacos, burritos, enchiladas, and tamales are $1.50-3.

Right up there with the Blue Bonnet, and even more authentic (no Anglo "hosts" here), is **Las Delicias,** tel. (303) 839-5675, at the corner of E. 19th and Pennsylvania. With the television in the lobby tuned to a Spanish-language station and the waitresses, busboys, and cooks rarely breaking into English, this is the *cosa real* (real thing). And the prices are unbeatable: Dinners run $3-8, with most right around $4. The tamale plate (three tamales), for example, is $3.30, the three-chicken-enchilada dinner is $3.50, and a bowl of *menudo* is $3.75. All of Las Delicias' food is available for carryout (including the green chile stew, at $2.90 a pint). In addition to the restaurant on 19th, **Las Delicias II** is located at 50 E. Del Norte, tel. (303) 430-0422, and a new store, Las Delicias III, has recently opened up in LoDo at 1530 Blake, tel. (303) 629-5051. Hours at Las Delicias are Mon.-Sat. 8 a.m.-9 p.m. and Sunday 9 a.m.-9 p.m.

The recently opened **Croc's Cafe,** in LoDo at 1630 Market, tel. (303) 436-1144, caters to a younger crowd and is an excellent place to sip a margarita or microbrew before a Rockies' game. Mexican-style pastas, seafood, chili, and burrito dinners run $6-12.

Brew Pubs

The flagship of Colorado's microbrewery fleet **Wynkoop Brewing Company,** tel. (303) 297-2700, is at the corner of 18th and Wynkoop, just a couple of blocks from Coors Stadium. Whether you stop in to taste the half dozen or so beers the day presents, or you're more interested in pub chow, this place is a must. The brews vary from week to week, and, particularly, from season to season, but they usually range from a light ale to a dark stout or porter. Lunch specials include salads, soups (including the Gorgonzola Ale, made with cheese and beer, natch!), sandwiches, the Ploughman's Platter (buffalo and veal bratwurst, cheeses, eggs, onions, beer mustard, and fresh fruit chutney), as well as Shepherd's Pie, bangers and mashers, bockwurst, and Italian sausage—all lunches range $5-7. For dinner, try grilled game hen, curried coconut chicken, trout or shark—running from about $8 to $12.

Whatever your preference, whether it's bangers or bratwurst, be sure to wash it down with a Wynkoop's beer (assuming you're of age). It'd be sacrilege to drink anything else—I actually witnessed an otherwise intelligent-appearing gentleman order a Miller Lite, *and drink it.* Wynkoop's also has 40 deluxe pool tables upstairs and a cabaret theater downstairs, as well as meeting and banquet rooms rooms adjoining the main bar and restaurant.

The Rock Bottom Brewery, 1001 16th St. (16th St. Mall at Curtis), tel. (303) 534-7616, is another brew pub, especially popular with the downtown business set. We stopped by on a Friday for a late lunch to find it packed with suited businesspeople who, judging by the amount of beer being quaffed, were apparently planning to take the afternoon off. Food is excellent here, too. Try the brew burger, the Taos chicken sandwich, pesto Genovese, or buffalo fajitas. Lunch entrees run $6-9, and dinner $6-14.

Asian Food

Denver has scores of excellent Asian restaurants, offering everything from authentic cuisine direct from Saigon to excellent Mandarin, Hunan, and Mongolian dishes. And many of these restaurants are perfect for the budget traveler, because you often get a *lot* of food for your buck. One of the best deals in town is at LoDo's **Lim's Mongolian Barbecue,** 1530 Blake St., tel. (303) 893-1158, where you can either pack your own bowl for a stir fry ($5, with wonton, egg roll, rice, and drink) or order from the menu, which includes Kung Pao chicken, hot tofu and vegetables, sesame chicken, etc. ($4-7). You can also get takeout or have the food delivered.

Other favorite Chinese restaurants in Denver include **Imperial,** 431 S. Broadway, tel. (303) 698-2800; **The Empress,** 2825 W. Alameda, tel. (303) 922-2822; the **Panda Café,** 1098 S. Federal, tel. (303) 936-2500. Among the city's favorite Japanese/sushi restaurants are **Mori,** 2019 Market, tel. (303) 298-1864, and **Sushi Heights,** 2301 E. Colfax, tel. (303) 355-2777.

For Thai food, try **Taste of Thailand,** 504 E. Hampden Ave. (Englewood), tel. (303) 762-9122. A perennial favorite for Vietnamese food is **New Saigon,** 630 S. Federal, tel. (303) 936-4954.

Other Downtown Restaurants
One of the best places downtown to see and be seen, as well as to get decent grub at reasonable prices, is the **Paramount Café,** tel. (303) 893-2000. This little bar and cafe, with plenty of outside tables for watching 16th Street strollers, serves fajitas, cajun chicken, meatloaf or albacore sandwiches, Tex-Mex specialties ($5-8), and a variety of appetizers, ranging from wontons to potato skins ($3-4). Daily specials are $4-6.

For authentic Russian food, try the **Little Russian Café,** tel. (303) 595-8600, in Larimer Square. Dinners run $10-16 and include a complimentary shot of vodka. Indoor and patio seating available. A favorite for fish and other seafood is **McCormick's,** tel. (303) 825-1107, a classic fish house and oyster bar on the corner of 17th and Wazee (right next door to the Oxford Hotel).

A long-standing west-Denver tradition, McCormick's is these days enjoying its location near Coors Field: before and after ballgames the place is packed with Rockies' fans powering microbrews and scarfing everything from burgers and fries to fresh swordfish, salmon, and crab, as well as bouillabaisse and Bluepoint oysters.

Although a chain/franchise restaurant, **The Old Spaghetti Factory,** corner of 18th and Lawrence, tel. (303) 295-1864, offers excellent food at bargain prices. Spaghetti, fettuccine, and tortellini dinners (with salad and French bread) run $4-7, and the atmosphere is great to boot—crowded and rowdy, with Victorian-style velvet couches (in the waiting lobby) and fringed chandeliers. Spumoni is included in the price. The Spaghetti Factory is open for lunch Mon.-Fri. 11:30 a.m.-2 p.m., and for dinner Mon.-Thurs. 5-

WHERE TO FIND LIVE MUSIC IN THE DENVER AREA

As a breeding ground for new music, Denver has yet to, well, really score. The city has its share of rock 'n' roll interlopers, but most have just flitted through Denver stopping only long enough to pick up their bags at the airport before heading to the mountains.

When it comes to music, Denver is no New York or Los Angeles—or even a Minneapolis, Austin, or Nashville. Local musicians, however, have a one-word reply to that statement: yet.

First, those that perform take little for granted. They work hard. Second, the clubs fill up, depending on the act, but are rarely packed. Even touring national club acts can be studied from close range. And third, the cover charges are nominal—$5 or so on the weekends for local favorites, less earlier in the week. Even better, many shows start by 9:30 p.m. or so, which means it's possible to take in a couple of bands before midnight (which also means that Denver is not a late-night town . . .).

At a host of fun and funky clubs you'll discover a wonderful assortment of people out absorbing a wide range of live music. And new clubs pop up out of nowhere every month or so and can just as easily disappear into the twilight zone. There are, however, two methods for finding what's on tap each week.

Method #1: Look for a telephone or light pole along E. 13th Ave. on Capitol Hill. That's the sprawling central neighborhood east of the capitol. Hardworking bands wanting to publicize a gig

decorate the poles with announcements on a weekly basis. Of course, the flyers will give you no idea of what the bands might sound like.

Which leads to Method #2: Walk into the mecca known as **Wax Trax** (the music store on the corner of E. 13th Ave. and Washington), and try to get the attention of the friendly clerks behind the counter. As you point astutely to the stack of flyers on the counter in front of you, ask for a recommendation and casually mention what kind of music you like. Chances are good at least one band playing is worth a listen.

As a backstop, check the pages of *Westword*, which is distributed on Tuesday and widely available in restaurants, clubs, bookstores, and record shops. Just about every local show is listed. Again, the question comes: But what do they sound like? If you're intent on knowing beforehand, none of the major club operators will refuse a few questions over the phone. And beyond that, there's always that one far-out rock 'n' roll possibility: Take a chance.

The new favorite in Denver is **The Bluebird,** 3317 E. Colfax, tel. (303) 322-2308, a former X-rated movie theater (the adjacent X-rated book-and-video store still stands) that showcases local and national talent six nights a week. The Bluebird offers a host of microbrews on tap, quality coffee, and a sweet sound system. The theater has been carefully remodeled and includes a spot down front for

10 p.m., Friday and Saturday 5-11 p.m., and Sunday 4-10 p.m.

High-End Denver Classics

Cliff Young's, 700 E. 17th Ave., tel. (303) 831-8900, is one of those institutions that regularly surpasses even the mile-high expectations it engenders—perfect for no-holds-barred special occasions. Of course, the place ain't cheap, but that's not what you go here for. Try the rack of lamb (about $30). Reservations recommended.

Another Denver restaurant with a reputation for excellent food and atmosphere (very modern, with lots of chrome and glass), is the **Zenith, an American Grill,** 1750 Lawrence, tel. (303) 820-2800. Duck, seafood, lamb, and buffalo dinners run $14-23. All pastas, breads, and ice creams are homemade.

Claiming to be Denver's oldest restaurant, and having served countless luminaries over the years—from Teddy Roosevelt to Ernest Hemingway, many of whose photos adorn the walls—**The Buckhorn Exchange,** 10th Ave. and Osage, tel. (303) 534-9505, is yet another Denver tradition. Specialties include buffalo, elk, alligator, rattlesnake, and Rocky Mountain oysters. A word of caution: If the sight of animal trophies makes you at all uncomfortable, you won't enjoy the Buckhorn. Heads of elk, reindeer, bison, deer, and antelope, as well as mounted ducks, foxes, and other critters, fill every square inch of wall space and stare down at the tables; we happened to be sitting directly below a coyote with a pheasant in its mouth—Betsy ordered the salmon. . . Dinner for two will run you a minimum of $60, easily more if you

---

dancing. There's something about the warm atmosphere here that invites regulars down to listen to acts they know nothing about. Another good place to see live music is the slightly larger is **TheOgden,** 935 E. Colfax, tel. (303) 830-2525, which hosts a bit rowdier rock shows.

Herman's Hideaway, 1578 St. on Broadway, tel. (303) 778-9916, started as a funky neighborhood bar, and though it's expanded twice in recent years, the atmosphere is still down-home casual and friendly. Watch for special showcase nights when bands are whisked off after only 45 minutes or so, providing the kind of evening when boredom doesn't stand a chance. Herman's is located a couple of miles south of where Broadway passes under I-25.

Back downtown, **The Mercury Cafe,** 2199 California, tel. (303) 294-9281, is a multipurpose facility with a main music room, restaurant, and theater. It's possible to eat an exquisite and healthful meal, watch some drama, and then head upstairs for some music, which, slightly more eclectic than at Herman's, often includes acoustic sets, jazz, experimental music, and a lot of rock 'n' roll.

In nearby Boulder, check out **The Fox Theater,** 1135 13th St., tel. (303) 447-0095, for consistent, near nightly output, while for jazz, don't overlook the tiny club in lower downtown known as **El Chapultapec,** 1962 Market, tel. (303) 295-9126, no cover charge. This spot used to involve a sometimes-iffy trek into lower downtown. Now it sits kitty-corner to Coors Field and almost gets swallowed up in the

rush of new-fangled restaurants that have swamped the area. (On Friday and Saturday nights, it's often standing room only, but you can have Mexican food delivered to wherever you're standing . . .) A real bonus is big-name talents playing other venues in town often drop in unannounced to jam.

If you're coming into town from the mountains, always keep in mind the **Little Bear,** 28075 CO 74, tel. (303) 674-9991. Smack in downtown Evergreen in the foothills south of Denver, the Little Bear offers a true roadhouse feel and romps with friendly enthusiasm on Sunday afternoons, not to mention Friday nights—check out the bra collection on the wall. The emphasis here is on blues and rock, and the last time somebody whispered alternative music he was thrown out on his ear and accused of being a communist.

And if you're in Denver during the summer, don't miss a chance to watch an outdoor show at **Red Rocks,** tel. (303) 694-1234 or 595-INFO, a natural amphitheater in the rust-red cliff outcroppings just west of downtown Denver. When the moon rises over the city lights, and you're listening to a band and gazing up at the giant rocks, everybody's a music fan. And it doesn't matter where you're from.

—Mark Stevens

Mark Stevens has been a reporter for 20 years, including stints at the Denver Post, MacNeil/Lehrer News Hour, Rocky Mountain News, *and the* Christian Science Monitor. *He's now director of public information for Denver Public Schools.*

THEATER IN THE DENVER AREA

It's not necessary to hop on a plane to New York or L.A. to find good live theater in Colorado. While obviously not as big as these two king-of-the-hill cities, Denver has some excellent theater to offer. There are three professional theaters in the Denver/Metro area, The Denver Center for the Performing Arts, The Country Dinner Playhouse, and the Arvada Center for the Performing Arts. They are defined as professional because they all work under contract with the Actor's Equity Association.

The Denver Center for the Performing Arts, or DCPA, makes its home in the county-owned Denver Performing Arts Complex, a grand structure with eight auditoriums, which range in capacity from 193 to 2,880 seats. Some of the auditoriums are in the round, some are in three-quarters round, and others are prosceniums. The DCPA shares the entire facility with the Colorado Symphony, the Ballet, and others.

The largest theater company between Chicago and Los Angeles, the DCPA has a reputation for doing Broadway-caliber shows. In fact, some of the shows presented are Broadway shows. When a New York show finishes its run, it may go on tour and stop in Denver. A Broadway show is easy to recognize because it is advertised under Robert Garner Center Attractions, the branch of the DCPA specializing in touring shows. According to Beki Pineda of Colorado Alliance for Stage Theatre, "They have elevated Denver to an accepted and welcomed stop on the Broadway circuit."

The DCPA produces a wide variety of material—classics such as Shakespeare, George Bernard Shaw, and Moliäre, as well as American classic dramas and comedies. Sometimes they're willing to risk new material. They recently scored a major hit with the world premiere of *Ain't Nothin' But the Blues,* and plan more shows by the same authors. The DCPA has two acting schools, The National Theatre Conservatory and the Denver Center Theatre Academy. The former is the only congressionally chartered acting school in the country and admits just eight students per year on full scholarships. The latter is open to the general public.

The Arvada Center for the Performing Arts is both a theater and an art gallery. Established in 1976, The Center produces well-established popular theater such as Neil Simon and children's plays in either the three-quarters-round 502-seat indoor auditorium or in the 1200-seat outdoor amphitheater. They offer classes in the arts and humanities for children and adults.

In addition to these equity houses, Denver is blessed with scores of small non-equity theaters, many of which seat fewer than 100. These theaters generally have much smaller budgets than equity theaters, but often manage to do outstanding work for which they charge modest prices.

Many are specialized. For instance, the Changing Scene Theatre does exclusively brand-new unpublished plays, while the Playback Theatre West invites the audience to share an emotional experience, either a serious or a funny one, after which the actors improvise a scene based on an audience member's experience. Kidskits, Inc., specializes in original musical theater for children performed by children. Kidskit's goal is to provide educational entertainment for children in a fun way. The Germinal Stage Denver does revisited classics, especially George Bernard Shaw and Eugene O'Neil. Other theaters specialize in ethnic issues. Eulipions, Inc., does African American shows while El Centro Su Teatro does Hispanic plays in a mixture of Spanish and English.

Each of these small theaters has its own charms. The Theatre At Muddy's is an alternative coffeehouse/restaurant at ground level with a theater and used bookstore in the basement. You can buy a dusty old tome at a ridiculously low price and read it while sipping your favorite herbal tea, then proceed downstairs for the show. Currently Cattlecall Productions works out of Muddy's. They don't shy away from the avant-garde; their goal is to provide engaging entertainment that makes people think. A theater with a similar goal is Theatre On Broadway. Like Cattlecall, they're not afraid to do risqué shows with complex themes.

The Denver Victorian Theatre is probably the only theater in the country to have produced every Shakespeare play ever written. Prescribed Shakespearean acting by his doctor to improve his asthmatic lung capacity, George Schwartz founded the 72-seat theater in 1912. He therefore built a proscenium theater in the basement of his bungalow home. While the theater has changed ownership many times, it has remained in business all these years. Today the theater performs a wide variety of contemporary work, and does not rule out doing more Shakespeare.

Every Friday the *Denver Post* and *Rocky Mountain News* publish special entertainment sections which list virtually every live theater performance in the Denver area and some outlying areas. The Post's section is called Weekend, while the News' section is named Spotlight.

If you're a real theater fiend, consult a current issue of *Curtain Up!*, published five times a year by Colorado Alliance for Stage Theatre (CAST). While many Colorado Theaters carry free copies of this impressive statewide theater guide, you can also get a free sample copy by contacting CAST, 702 Speer Blvd., Denver, CO 80203, tel. (303) 698-2216. For audition and show information, phone (303) 615-5898 (metro Denver) or (800) 20STAGE (statewide).

CHANGING SCENE THEATRE

If you go see a show at the Changing Scene, you will see a play you have never seen before. The theater does world premieres exclusively. The Changing Scene has been defying conventional wisdom for over 25 years, risking new scripts for almost 300 productions. "We've managed to survive by the harness because people are still reluctant to gamble an evening on something they haven't heard about," says theater owner/founder Al Brooks.

The 76-seat theater has managed not only to survive since 1968, but it has won several awards including both the Governor's and Mayor's Awards for Excellence, as well as the Larry Tjiri Award and the Downtown Denver Award. It has enjoyed national recognition with grants from the Rockefeller Foundation and the National Endowment for the Arts. Some of the plays that premiered at the Changing Scene have gone on to be published and produced professionally in New York, Los Angeles, and even Europe.

Brooks believes "talent is the most important natural resource we have," which is why he's willing to give new playwrights a chance. In Changing Scene productions, the author becomes a part of the inherently collaborative process of theater, while the director and the actors get input from the author, which certainly is not the case when small theaters perform standard theater fare. ". . . the satisfaction is doing new work and seeing that artist develop," says Brooks.

Because of his willingness to consider new scripts, he gets manuscripts from all over the United States, Canada, and Europe. He not only considers new authors, but new actors and directors as well, and he

is not a member of the Actor's Equity Association.

Some shows are written in straight-forward dramatic form, others are avant garde or experimental. While the theater takes a risk presenting new material, you as an audience member take a risk as well, but for generally well under $10 a ticket.

The Changing Scene Theatre schedules shows Thursday and Sunday evenings 7 p.m. and Friday and Saturday evenings at 8. The theater is in downtown Denver at 1527 Champa. For more information, phone the box office at (303) 893-5775.

COUNTRY DINNER PLAYHOUSE

Looking for a little different kind of evening entertainment? Feel like getting in on a local tradition? How about the Country Dinner Playhouse, where you can kick back and enjoy an evening of fine food and top-notch theater?

Since 1970, the Country Dinner Playhouse (CDP), recent winner of the *Rocky Mountain News*' Reader's Choice Award for Best Local Theatre Group, has been producing some of the finest theatrical work in Colorado. The 470-seat theater, in a cozy barn-like structure, gives the feeling of being in an old-fashioned country restaurant. In this homey atmosphere, the CDP does productions suitable for the family. Many, but not all, of their shows are musicals. Producer/Director Bill McHale "has a way with musical acting companies that seems to grow richer and more perceptive with time," writes *Rocky Mountain News* theater critic Jackie Campbell. The Playhouse performs standard dinner theater fare such as *The Sound of Music, Oklahoma,* or *The Music Man.* "We don't do any of the more risqué or vulgar shows that you might see or read about today," says General Manager David Lovinggood. While risqué is out, moderate violence is sometimes acceptable, if the story line warrants it. For instance, the Playhouse did Kopit and Yestin's *Phantom,* in which, according to McHale, the main character is a violent man, but the play contains a beautiful love story. "This was very beautiful and heart-warming and [the audience] understood it. And I'll guarantee you, there were very few dry eyes in the house at the end of the play. And that's what theater is about," says McHale.

The CDP is a theater in the round, equipped with an ascending hydraulic stage. Actor Marcus

(continues on next page)

THEATER IN THE DENVER AREA
(continued)

Waterman says he likes the Playhouse's round format because it allows a "naturalism of movement on stage." McHale says he and his fellow co-founders chose the round format because it makes the shows more intimate. "If this were a proscenium with 470 [seats], those last 150 people would be way in the back somewhere," says McHale. The way the theater is set up, the farthest seat from the stage is only 33 feet away. Because the performers sometimes enter and exit through the aisles, an actor might stride past your table so close you'll feel the air rushing by.

No curtains are used at the Country Dinner Playhouse. Instead, the actors and their props descend from the ceiling on the hydraulic stage, the only one of its kind in Colorado. The visual effect is quite dramatic.

The all-you-can-eat dinner buffet starts two hours before the show and consists of beef, chicken, and fish entrees, as well as assorted vegetables, salads and deserts. Cocktails are served by the Barnstormers, a charming crew of about nine singer/musicians who provide the pre-show entertainment. A half hour before the main show, they welcome their customers to the Country Dinner Playhouse by singing and playing and, in a humorous way, going over the rules of the house.

The CDP is a professional theater, a member of The Actor's Equity Association. The shows produced are consistently outstanding while the food is tasty. If you're looking for quality family or business entertainment, your chances of disappointment are slim indeed. At less than $30 for dinner and show, your entertainment dollar goes a long way. Reservations are strongly recommended. Shows are scheduled throughout the year Tues.-Sun. at 8 p.m. (buffet 6-7:15, pre-show at 7:30), with matinees Saturday and Sunday at 1:45 p.m. (buffet noon-1:15, pre-show at 1:15). Free parking.

For more information, phone the Country Dinner Playhouse Box Office at (303) 799-1410, or write 6875 S. Clinton, Englewood, CO 80112. For group rates contact Joanie Buffington at (303) 790-9311

—Thomas Owen Meinen

Thomas Meinen is a freelance writer in Denver. He studied acting and playwriting at California State University, Chico. He has both acted in and written plays for small theater.

have drinks and/or appetizers. Live folk music Friday and Saturday nights.

Another Denver-area tradition is **The Fort,** 19192 Route 8, in Morrison, tel. (303) 697-4771, which was built in 1962 as a full-size replica of Bent's fort. The restaurant specializes in "old-west" favorites, such as Rocky Mountain oysters, buffalo heart and tongue, rattlesnake, and elk, and has been written up in *Esquire, Bon Appetit, Gourmet,* and the *New York Times.* Entrees run $14-28. The Fort is 22 miles from Denver. Take I-70 west to Hampden (US 285), and go south to the junction with CO 8.

Farmers Market
Each Saturday morning from late June through late October, farmers back their pickups against the curb at 17th and Market streets and sell fresh produce. There's usually live music and an array of T-shirt booths as well. Open from 7 a.m. to 1 p.m.

ENTERTAINMENT

Again, with the transformation of lower downtown from a run-down warehouse district to LoDo, where clubs and pubs are two, three, and four to a block, entertainment in Denver has taken a giant leap forward. In fact, it can be downright entertaining just wandering through the area, especially before and after Rockies' games, when the streets fill with folks sharing their love of the city and their team with a vibrant energy that's unusually infectious. There's also lots of music, comedy, and dance. The best way to find out what's going on where is to check the *Weekend* magazine supplement to the *Denver Post* and *Westword,* the free weekly distributed in racks and in cafes and restaurants around town.

According to *Westword's* "Best of Denver," 1995, the best place to hear blues is **Brendan's**

Pub, 1624 Market, tel. (303) 595-0609. Just walking by in the evening you'll hear wonderful riffs snaking out of the basement club.

If you feel like kickin' up your heels and doin' some two-steppin', check out the **Grizzly Rose,** 5450 N. Valley US, tel. (303) 295-1330, regularly named best country-and-western club by *Westword*. Big-name performers—from Willie Nelson to Stephen Stills—stop in here and there's always something country going on.

An only-in-Denver opportunity is "jazz at the art museum" on Wednesday afternoons. Described by one local as "art, jazz, and yuppies," it's been a popular singles scene, particularly among the young downtown set. See "Denver Art Museum," under "Art Museums" above.

The **Comedy Works,** tel. (303) 595-3637, also right downtown at 1226 15th St., in Larimer Square, features local and comedy-circuit comedians most nights of the week. Two shows Friday and Saturday nights. A recorded message will give you showtimes and prices.

Concert Venues

Among Denver's places to see acts big enough to draw huge crowds is **Red Rocks,** tel. (303) 640-7300, a gorgeous natural amphitheater in the hills on the city's west side. Recent acts include Rickie Lee Jones, Lyle Lovett, and Jimmy Cliff. **Fiddler's Green,** tel. (303) 741-5000, also features outdoor concerts ranging from country (the Judds) and folk (Peter, Paul, and Mary, Garrison Keillor) to rock (Joe Cocker, Santana), jazz (Kenny G), and classical (local and national orchestras and symphonies).

The renovated **Paramount Theatre,** downtown at Glenarm and 16th, tel. (303) 623-0106, is historical, plush, and evocative of the early 20th century; the Paramount books a wide range of acts and activities—from rock to theater to bodybuilding contests. **Elitch's Gardens and Amusement Park,** tel. (303) 455-4771, also known for its roller coaster and other rides, as well as its perennial county-fair atmosphere, books live music throughout the summer. Often

THE CAPITOL HILL PEOPLE'S FAIR

In the first weekend of June over 275,000 people swarm through scores of colorful booths at Civic Center Park, the stretch of lawn between the gold-domed capitol and the majestic Greco-Roman-style courthouse in downtown Denver. An arts-and-crafts fair on a grand and multicultural scale, the Capitol Hill People's Fair offers a perfect opportunity to examine everything from ceramics and paintings to bamboo art and African masks. In addition, you can find a booth representing almost any political, philosophical, or religious viewpoint. You can have your fortune told by tarot-card readers, then walk a few feet to Rocky Mountain Skeptics and learn that it's all bunk anyway. From the Caleb Campaign learn that Jesus loves you, and then talk to the Freedom From Religion Foundation and find He doesn't even exist. You can talk to right-wingers and socialists, yoga teachers and chess experts.

If all that philosophical discussion makes you weary, you might want to relax and enjoy some entertainment. A variety of music, from heavy metal and modern jazz to country and classical, is offered on the six different stages. In addition, there are dance performances, ballet to break dancing, while clowns juggle machetes, torches, and even watermelons.

And then there are the food booths, where you'll find every imaginable food type and cuisine—Chinese, Japanese, Greek, Turkish, Mexican, Indonesian, and more, not to mention good old-fashioned hamburgers, hot dogs, and popcorn.

Attending the People's Fair is an act of bravery because you never know what Colorado's temperamental Mother Nature might do—despite the meteorologist's predictions. You might enjoy several hours of sunshine, only to be bombarded by rain, hail, and gusty winds. In anticipation of such outbursts, the booths are all covered by canopies, and it's not uncommon to make new friends while weathering a storm. If bad weather's expected, the event's organizers move the fair to the second weekend in June. The fair opens at 10 a.m. and closes at 7 p.m. on Saturday and 6 p.m. on Sunday.

For more information on the Capitol Hill People's Fair, contact CHUN (Capitol Hill United Neighborhoods) at (303) 830-1651 or 1490 Lafayette, Denver, CO 80218.

—Thomas Owen Meinen

country-flavored, acts have included Emmylou Harris, Riders in the Sky, and Air Supply.

Denver Performing Arts Complex

This center, downtown at 14th and Curtis, is home to many of Denver's entertainment and cultural events, shows, and troupes, including the Denver Symphony Orchestra, the Colorado Ballet, and the Denver Theater Company, which produces 12 plays each season on the center's four stages. For tickets, phone (303) 893-4100; for information, free tours, and season brochures, phone (303) 893-4000.

CALENDAR

Denver's a big city, the biggest for over 600 miles in any direction, and there's something going on almost every day, evening, and weekend—from arts-and-crafts fairs to auto races, from music festivals (*lots* of music in this town) to golf tournaments. The new year kicks off in mid-January with the two-week **National Western Stock Show and Rodeo,** the largest such show on the planet. In addition to pro and amateur rodeos and livestock competitions, you can watch the city transmogrify into a shit-kickin' cow town with Ralph Lauren and Obsession stepping aside for Wrangler and *eau de chevaux.* If you plan to be in Denver during the festivities, whether you're ridin' and ropin' or just watching from the rails, be sure to make hotel reservations well in advance. For schedule and ticket information, phone (303) 297-1166.

Denver's annual two-day **Cinco de Mayo** party takes place on the 16th Street Mall and features music, dancing, arts and crafts, and food—in a salute to Denver's Chicano heritage and to Mexican independence. For more information, phone (303) 534-6161.

Also in May, things get crazy for a couple of days at the Civic Center Park during the annual **Capitol Hill People's Fair.** Join the more than 100,000 revelers, politicos, and New-Agers, and check out everything from the latest in low-impact high technology to noncompetitive games, from herbal teas to current political agendas. Virtually nonstop live music. Phone (303) 388-2716. (See accompanying special topic.)

Another folky favorite is the **Colorado Renaissance Festival,** in Larkspur, south of Denver, on weekends in June and early July. Paint your face, don a beret and plume, or squeeze into your favorite pair of tights, and get thee to the funnery. Once inside the grounds, situated on a hillside amid pine and scrub oak, you can forget the travails that the centuries since Elizabeth I hath wrought. Listen to buxom wenches tell bawdy tales; toss overripe fruit at shackled heads; gnaw on a fresh-fired turkey drumstick and wash it down with a pint of mead; listen to the sweet melodies of zithers and lutes; and sample the wares—glassware, hats, and jewelry of local artisans. Phone (303) 756-1501 for exact dates and more information.

In late June/early July, the **Cherry Creek Arts Festival,** a huge juried event at the Cherry Creek Mall, attracts folks from throughout the Denver area with quality art and crafts, as well as music, food, and first-class people-watching.

As is true throughout the state, the Fourth of July offers a wide array of activities, highlighted by the fireworks at Coors Field. Take in the evening's Rockies' game, and stick around for the fireworks afterward. For ticket information, phone (303) 762-5437.

For current information on annual events in Denver, contact the **Denver Metro Convention and Visitors Bureau** at (303) 892-1112. The staff publishes an exhaustive Denver events guide, which they'll gladly send you. Watch also the entertainment sections of the *Denver Post,* the *Rocky Mountain News,* and *Westword.*

SHOPPING

Downtown Denver is rife with shopping malls, plazas, squares, and "centers." In fact, there are so many so close to one another that sometimes you don't realize you've passed from one to the next.

16th Street Mall

Even if you're the type whose blood runs cold at the very sound of the word "mall" and you find yourself looking for a tavern to duck into whenever shops and boutiques have the nerve to enter your line of vision, you won't mind Denver's 16th Street Mall. In fact, you'll probably enjoy it. Here, strolling, people-watching, win-

mural at 14th
and Champa,
downtown Denver

dow-shopping, or stopping for junk food or a cup of coffee is much more important than *buying things.* You'll be endlessly entertained by street vendors ("Get your ice cold lemonade"), jugglers, flirting teenagers, and local business-people talking about the Rockies' or stocks and commodities. And if you do want to do some shopping, there's every kind of store imaginable—from Walgreen's and Eddie Bauer, to bookstores, T-shirt shops, and jewelers.

The **Tabor Center** at the mall's north end is where you'll find most of the upscale stores, including Brooks Brothers (suits and menswear), Crabtree and Evelyn (soaps, lotions, and cosmetics), Johnston and Murphy (shoes), Keep-sakes (fou-fou throw rugs, scents, lamps, etc.), and Pollyanna (fine lingerie). In addition, check out the Lawrence Street Bridge Market on the third floor (be sure to take the glass elevator near the fountain). This is an almost European-style potpourri of assorted cart vendors and booths—selling everything from hats and jewelry to kites and rubber stamps. On the bottom floor of Tabor Center, you'll find The Sharper Image— an amazing array of high-tech toys and equipment, much of it on working display for passersby. A few shops toward 17th Street is Watson's Soda Fountain, open long after most everything else around closes (till 11 p.m. Mon.-Thurs., till midnight Friday and Saturday, and till 9 p.m. Sunday), and in addition to grabbing a malt, a hot dog, or a bag of popcorn, you can pick up convenience items, soft drinks, liquor, prescrip-

tions (the pharmacy is open Mon.-Fri. 9 a.m.-5 p.m.), and snacks.

Free shuttle buses run every few minutes from one end of the mall to the other with stops at each block.

Still More Downtown Shopping
In addition to the 16th Street Mall, **Larimer Square** and **Writer Square,** at Larimer and 14th and 15th, have a number of shops and boutiques, including **Overland Outfitters** and **Williams and Sonoma.** If you're looking to send word of your travels to folks back home, be sure to check out **Avant-Card,** which, as its name suggests, stocks an excellent selection of greeting cards—innovative and provocative (postcards, as well).

Cherry Creek Mall
This is Denver's most upscale shopping complex. Stores include Abercrombie and Fitch, Liz Claiborne, Sak's Fifth Avenue, and Neiman-Marcus, as well as the other mall-standard shoe, jewelry, cookie, and frozen-yogurt shops (over 100 stores in all). The Cherry Creek Mall is located at 3000 1st Avenue.

Tattered Cover Bookstore
Bibliophiles go nuts here, for this is one of the west's truly great bookstores: three stories of floor-to-ceiling books on everything you can imagine, as well as chairs and tables and a wonderfully friendly and knowledgeable staff who

DENVER'S BEST BOOK AND RECORD STORES

If you want to go shopping and feel like you're right at home—if home is just about anywhere in the U.S.—head for the mall. Denver has an ample supply, and they're all in the obvious locations—stuck by interstates or in the heart of suburbia. There's even one mini-version (the Tabor Center) smack downtown, where the outside is beautiful, the atrium stunning, and the products la-de-da.

But if you've got records or books on the mind, a couple of Denver landmarks ought to be on your itinerary. Both pass a few simple tests of retail success: They stock everything (or try to); they don't let on that they stock everything; and they'll help you find anything if that anything is available.

For music, it's **Twist and Shout.**

For books, it's the **Tattered Cover.**

Gaping up at the volume of books in "TC" is the equivalent of staring up at the skyscrapers in New York. You may as well tattoo "tourist" on your forehead.

The Tattered Cover is a retail curiosity, breathtaking for sheer size yet still somehow understated. There are 400,000 volumes (150,000 titles) tucked into dozens of nooks and crannies throughout the four-floor building. The local mall bookstore might have one book on woodworking, but how about choosing from among fifteen? Need a mystery? How 'bout a mystery bookstore within a bookstore?

In 1974, three people managed the Tattered Cover, then located a few blocks from its present site in the Cherry Creek shopping district. One of those people was Joyce Meskis, who owns the operation and can still be found digging in the stacks, unassumingly helping customers. Denver book lovers quickly spread the word about the endless racks of books, friendly service, and low-key, almost library-like style. Comfy chairs? You mean you can actually sit down and read a book? For an hour or so and nobody will bother you? Come on . . .

After an interim stop in a nearby space to accommodate the burgeoning racks, the Tattered Cover is now in its third location. The exterior is cool and indifferent, smack across the street from Denver's snobbiest mall, the Cherry Creek Mall. The interior is warm, inviting. But again, it's about to burst at the seams. The store now has 300 employees. That's not customers per day. That's employees.

But this isn't a warehouse—it's a group of bookstores within one. You walk in for a cookbook or a magazine and find yourself browsing through the computer manuals and travel guides, suddenly thinking about a new hobby, wondering about climbing a mountain, or thinking about what modern American literature has really managed to say about modern American life.

The Tattered Cover is located at 2955 E. 1st Avenue. Hours are Mon.-Fri. 9:30 a.m.-9 p.m., Saturday 9:30 a.m.-6 p.m., and Sunday noon-5 p.m. For more information, phone (303) 322-7727. **Note:** The Tattered Cover has recently opened a second, and very comprehensive, store in LoDo (next to the Wynkoop Brewery) at 1828 16th St., tel. (303) 436-1070.

Like the Tattered Cover, **Twist and Shout** is several stores in one. What makes this store special, like the Tattered Cover, is a friendly and helpful staff. No record is too obscure to track down and order. No question too beneath their expertise. A chalkboard tracks new releases and those coming up. There are magazines, videos, and huge stock of used CDs. The strength of the store is rock and roll, but the reggae, international, rap, and country sections aren't given short shrift. The store is due to move from an old, cramped neighborhood location on South Pearl St. to a renovated grocery store at Alameda Blvd. and S. Logan St. so call ahead at (303) 722-1943.

As another alternative closer to downtown, look for **Wax Trax,** which is actually four stores strung out on two sides of E. 13th Ave. (at Washington). One store features CDs, another T-shirts and and videos, another reissued CDs and albums, and the final used albums and used CDs. It can take hours to do justice to all four stores. The stock here is solid, but the service in the main store just doesn't cut it. They won't offer to order anything if they're out, but urge you to come back. However, the "reissue" store really has no parallel; the staff here is very friendly and quite helpful.

Wax Trax is located on the 600 block of E. 13th Avenue. Hours are Mon.-Sat. 10 a.m. to 8 p.m. and Sunday 11 a.m.-5 p.m. For more information, phone (303) 831-7246.

Note: If you really want to blow the afternoon, Wax Trax and the Tattered Cover are just a few miles apart. You might waste 15 minutes getting from one to the other. And then you could count on a couple of weeks at home where all you'd do is sit around, listen to music . . . and read.

—Mark Stevens

encourage you to hang around and read. A bonus: The Tattered Cover validates your parking in the adjacent garage for up to an hour and a half. You can find the Tattered Cover at 2955 E. 1st Ave., tel. (303) 322-7727 or (800) 833-9327; with a second location now in LoDo at 1828 16th St. and Wynkoop, tel. (303) 436-1070, the new store though not as sprawling as the original, is both huge and cozy in its own right.

Gart Brothers

Denver has more sporting goods stores per capita than any other city in the world, thanks in large part to Gart Brothers. With stores throughout the Denver area, Gart's offers multistory sports emporiums with gigantic equipment selections in golf, skiing, bow hunting, roller blading, and everything else you can imagine. With entire floors and rooms devoted to single sports, some Gart stores are so huge directional signs are provided to help you find your way around. Anyone with even the slightest interest in sports owes it to herself to stop by a Gart's. The Gart's closest to downtown is at 10th and Broadway.

SERVICES

The central information number for the Denver **Police Department** is (303) 575-3127 (in emergencies dial 9-1-1). The number for the **sheriff's office** is (303) 375-3451. For general information at the City and County of Denver, phone (303) 575-2790. To report accidents and emergencies to the **Colorado State Patrol,** or for non-emergencies, phone (303) 239-4501.

In emergency medical situations, dial 9-1-1. Denver's **University Hospital** is located at 4200 E. 9th Ave. at the corner of Colorado, tel. (303) 270-8901 in emergencies or (303) 399-1211 for general information. **AMI St. Luke's Hospital** is at 601 E. 19th; phone (303) 629-2111 in emergencies or (303) 839-1000 for general information.

The main branch of the Denver **post office** is located at 1823 Stout, tel. (303) 297-6168. Two **post offices** are located downtown. One is in the basement of the May D and F Building at the corner of 16th and Tremont, and the other is on the first floor of Tabor Center underneath the Westin Hotel at 16th and Lawrence. For zip code information, phone (303) 297-6000.

Recycling

The best places to drop off recyclables in Denver are the **King Soopers** grocery stores, which all take aluminum, glass, newspapers, and plastic bottles. There are over two dozen stores in the Denver metropolitan area. **Albertsons** and **Safeway** stores will take aluminum.

For information, phone the **City of Denver Recycling Hotline,** (303) 640-1675.

Child Care

Summer Fun Day Camp, tel. (303) 232-9191, provides entertainment for visiting kids, including trips to Elitch's amusement park and other kids' favorites. **Mile High Child Care Association,** tel. (303) 388-5700, has locations throughout the metro Denver area, with its main office at 1510 High Street. **Mile High United Way Child Care Resource and Referral Service** can provide information on thousands of day-care centers in the Denver area; phone (303) 433-8900.

INFORMATION

Downtown and within a few blocks of each other are several good sources of different kinds of information. On the triangle formed by Colfax, Court, and 14th streets is the **Denver Metro Convention and Visitors Bureau,** where you'll find an office staffed with helpful and knowledgeable people, as well as brochures on everything from the city's museums and accommodations to parks, events, and galleries. Their mailing address is 225 W. Colfax, Denver, CO 80202; reach the bureau by phone at (303) 892-1112. Hours are Mon.-Fri. 8:30 a.m.-5 p.m. and Saturday 9 a.m.-5 p.m. (winter hours are Mon.-Fri. 8 a.m.-5 p.m. and Saturday 9 a.m.-1 p.m.).

Two blocks south of the convention and visitors bureau, at the corner of Broadway and 13th Ave., you'll find the downtown branch of the **Denver Public Library,** open Mon.-Wed. 10 a.m.-9 p.m., Thurs.-Sat. 10 a.m.-5:30 p.m., and Sunday 1-5 p.m. For more information, phone the library at (303) 640-8845; the number for the children's library is 640-8820. There are over 20 branches of the Denver public library; the downtown branch can provide addresses, phone numbers, and hours of the others.

DRIVING DISTANCES TO DENVER

SEATTLE

MINNEAPOLIS

NEW YORK

1300 mi.

925 mi.

CHICAGO

CHICO

SALT LAKE
CITY

1050 mi.

1800 mi.

WASHINGTON
D. C.

1200 mi.

507 mi.

1700 mi.

1275 mi.

DENVER

SAN
FRANCISCO

1050 mi.

650 mi.

800 mi.

LOS
ANGELES

825 mi.

ALBUQUERQUE

PHOENIX

DALLAS

1250 mi.

2050 mi.

HOUSTON

MIAMI

© MOON PUBLICATIONS, INC.

For **road conditions,** phone (303) 639-1111 (Denver and the west) or (303) 639-1234 (I-25).

To find out what's happening where, check out the *Weekend* magazine supplement to the *Denver Post* or pick up a copy of *Westword,* the free weekly, found in racks, cafes, and restaurants all over town.

Bookstores

The best source for books and other publications on Denver and Colorado is **The Tattered Cover,** with two locations. The original store (four floors with 500,000 books in stock!) is near the Cherry Creek Mall at 2955 E. Cherry Creek, tel. (303) 322-7727; the newer store, smaller than the original but still huge by most standards, is in LoDo at 16th St. and Wynkoop, tel. (303) 436-1070. In addition, on the 16th Street Mall, you'll find several chain stores (B. Dalton, Waldenbooks), as well as a handful of small newsstands with tourist publications, Denver and Colorado magazines, and guidebooks.

TRANSPORTATION

Getting There

Finally, after countless delays and problems, **Denver International Airport** opened in early 1995. The new airport, which replaced Stapleton International, is a still a major controversy in the region, due in part to its *long* distance from downtown (allow at least 30-40 minutes from downtown), as well as the many low and loud flights over areas in the mountains (Boulder, Ward, Golden), where folks had moved to avoid the trappings of the city. But it's a user-friendly airport and visually arresting—the "peaks" of the main building represent the Rocky Mountains—and it should make travel into and out of Colorado much more convenient. Accessed by I-70, there are several shuttle services including The Airporter (303) 333-5833, (800) 355-5833 or the Denver Airport Shuttle (DASH) (303) 342-5454, (800) 525-3177.

The John Maddens and Erica Jongs among us don't have to fly to get to Denver. The city's

Union Station, downtown at the west end of 17th St., is a stop on **Amtrak**'s major east-west route (between Chicago and Los Angeles). For information, phone (303) 893-3911.

Getting Around

Several shuttle and taxi companies offer transportation to and from the airport, as well as to the nearby towns and ski areas. Phone **The Airporter** at (303) 333-5833, **Denver Airport Shuttle** at (303) 342-5454 or (800) 525-3177, or **People's Choice Transportation,** tel. (800) 777-2388.

For taxi service in the Denver area, phone **Yellow Cab,** tel. (303) 777-7777, **Metro Taxi Company,** tel. (303) 333-3333, or **Zone Cab,** tel. (303) 444-8888.

You can rent cars in Denver from all the major chain agencies, as well as from **VAMS 4x4 Express Rent-A-Car,** tel. (800) 669-8267, specializing in 4WD vehicles, and **Resort Rent-A-Car,**

tel. (800) 289-5343. Denver also has an elaborate and much-used bus system (RTD—Regional Transportation District), with service throughout the metro area and to some of the smaller nearby towns, including Boulder. For route and schedule information, phone (303) 778-6000.

Once here, you'll find Denver is amazingly easy to get around in. First, you can walk from one end of downtown to the other in about a half-hour—and that includes window-shopping along the way. And if you're not up for walking—if your arms are too loaded with packages or the day has taken its toll on your feet—there's always the **Mall Ride,** a free bus that runs from one end of 16th Street Mall to the other. With buses running every few minutes and taking on and letting off passengers at every block, the system will take you from the capitol to the Tabor Center in a matter of minutes (though you'll have to hoof it a block or so from the capitol to the east end of the mall).

AROUND DENVER

Heading South

After slicing south through downtown Denver, rising up over railroad tracks and waterways, scooting under overpasses, and passing within yards of the Broncos' Mile-High Stadium, I-25 (which at peak hours is often commuter-crowded) routes down through the city's sprawling southern suburbs and finally out onto the rocky plains, always paralleling the massive Front Range, looming just to the west. The 70 miles between Denver and Colorado Springs don't offer a whole lot in terms of scenery and diversions—save for the Rockies' forested shoulders and towering peaks to the west—although the trip is quick and easy; it's not unusual for folks in Colorado Springs to run up to Denver for a day of shopping, or even to meet friends for lunch.

Just south of Denver proper, Littleton, seat of Arapahoe County and once a thriving farming community, shows the effects of urban sprawl, with little to distinguish it from southern Denver—strip malls, office buildings, and quiet, whitewashed suburban housing developments, with nice lawns and fences. Nearly halfway to Colorado Springs is the little town of Castle Rock (pop. 3,900; elev. 6,000 feet), named for the stone outcropping appearing very much like some medieval European castle. Over the centuries, the "castle" served as a landmark for travelers—Native Americans, traders, miners, pioneers, and early settlers. Modern travelers now have another landmark, the recently opened **Larkspur Factory Shops.** Take the Meadows Parkway Exchange from I-25.

About 10 miles south of Castle Rock is the turnoff to Larkspur, a tiny little community where the plains begin to green and gently roll as they rise up to meet the steep eastern wall of the Rockies. Although not a year-round tourist destination, for a month or so every summer Larkspur is extremely popular among faire travelers and pilgrims, who don leotards and feathered caps and spend the day here (see "Colorado Renaissance Festival" under "Calendar" above).

You'll find a **KOA** campground between Castle Rock and Larkspur—open May through October. Take Exit 174/Tomah Road.

Heading West

As you head west out of Denver on I-70 toward Dillon and Summit County, a number of interesting stops could stretch the 70-mile drive into a full-day (or longer) excursion. From the museums and brewery tour in Golden to the old mining towns of Idaho Springs and Georgetown, from Buffalo Bill's grave and museum to the handful of National Forest picnic areas, there are seemingly countless diversions. In fact, one of the best and most fascinating is the pure and simple scenic wonder: As you barrel out of the Denver flats and into the high country of the western slope—where pine and fir encircle mountain meadows and aspen and spruce mingle on ridgetops—the vistas and panoramas get downright *serious.* Take the time to pull over at the turnouts along the way: Geology buffs will appreciate the little exhibit at Exit 258, where you can examine closely the layers of rock cut away to build the interstate; near Genesee, you might get lucky and see a herd of buffalo; and if you look really closely, up on the hill to the south just west of Exit 256, you can see the futuristic house that Woody Allen used in *Sleeper* (don't get too excited: The orgasmatron's long gone . . .).

Just off the freeway, at Exit 253, **Chief Hosa,** tel. (303) 526-0364, is a pleasant little campground with RV and tent sites nestled in the pines. Not the type of place you'd want to spend your two-week vacation, but ideal for short-term, we'll-be-moving-on-in-the-morning camping.

GOLDEN

Probably best known for the massive Coors brewery, which attracts nearly 400,000 visitors a year, Golden (pop. 15,000, elev. 5,680 feet) is a compact and isolated little town in Clear Creek Canyon in the rocky foothills about a half-hour drive west of Denver. Seat of Jefferson County, Golden is also home to the Colorado School of Mines, the Colorado Railroad Museum, the Buffalo Bill Museum and gravesite, and several other small museums and parks. Central Golden is an Old-Westy little downtown area, with gift shops, taverns, and western-wear stores.

HISTORY

Though officially founded in the summer of 1859 by a group of Bostonians in search of gold, the little camp on Clear Creek had been a popular stopover for miners heading west for some time, and at least one settler, farmer David Wall, called the place home for over a year. In fact, during the spring of '59, Wall made over $2,000 selling produce to the hordes of miners flocking to the canyon to make their fortunes off the area's fabulous lodes.

On June 12 of that year, Bostonian George West and crew, calling themselves the Boston Company, built the area's first frame house and dubbed the then-thriving camp Golden City, apparently after miner-cum-merchant Thomas Golden. The group also built a bridge across Clear Creek (at what is now Washington St.), charging tolls to the increasing numbers—from the nearby towns of Black Hawk, Central City, Silver Plume, and Georgetown—dependent on Golden for trade. About this time, journalist Horace Greeley rode a rented mule up into Clear Creek Canyon. Mightily impressed by the mines and bustling enterprises, he returned to the east coast to write, "Go West, young man, and grow with the country."

By the early 1860s, Golden City could claim some 800 year-round residents, as well as saloons, stores, hotels, and a school, and from 1862 to 1867, the town served as the capital of Colorado Territory. In 1872, the word "City" officially dropped from the town's name.

The 1870s saw the arrival of three important contributors to the development of Golden: the Colorado School of Mines, the railroad, and the Coors-Schueler Brewery. Though originally founded in 1869, the Colorado School of Mines, first called Jarvis College and headed by a missionary bishop of the Church of Colorado, opened its doors to students in 1871, offering degrees in assaying and chemical ore testing. With a 25 acre campus, the school is still home to three of the town's earliest buildings, constructed between 1880 and 1890. Colorado's first railroad—the Colorado Central—began operation in late 1870, and by the early part of the decade had a line to Golden. In fact, within a few short years, Golden became the site of the company's headquarters as well as its western terminus, supplying other nearby camps and towns. Golden's heyday as a railroad center was short-lived, however, as the headquarters moved to Denver in the early 1880s.

The Coors-Schueler brewery was built in 1873 by Adolph Herman Joseph Coors and by the turn of the century produced 500,000 barrels of beer a year. Prohibition (1919-1933) definitely put a damper on the outfit, although management was savvy enough to move into the production of non-alcoholic commodities—"near beer," malted milk, and other milk by-products. By Prohibition's end, the brewery was able to again produce beer, unlike the vast majority of the nation's breweries permanently shut down by the Constitution's ill-fated 18th Amendment.

ATTRACTIONS

Coors Brewery

Tours of the Coors brewery—the largest single brewery in the world—are the reason most visitors come to Golden, and indeed, summer days the town is packed with people who've come to pay their respects to the great "Colorado Kool-Aid" and to see how it's made. The tour's free, too. And at the end—assuming you're of age—you can even sample a couple of glasses of Coors' products: Coors, Coors Lite, the "Silver Bullet," etc. And then there's the gift shop (it's no accident that the gift shop is *after* the free sampling), where you can buy Coors T-shirts, steins, Frisbees, and all kinds of other knickknacks with the Coors logo.

In addition to tours of the brewery, Coors offers brief tours of Golden, with buses routing their ways through town, picking up tourists from parking lots, while drivers point out important historical landmarks before delivering passengers to the brewery's doors.

Note: It'll come as no surprise that Coors has had its share of PR problems over the years, from labor and race issues to unfortunate alliances (James Watt and the Sagebrush Rebellion in the 1970s). However, within the past ten years, Coors has become known as one of the most progressive large companies in the country in several areas, most notably in terms of employee relations. A company-sanctioned Diversity Council, which includes Women at Coors, African-Americans at Coors, Hispanics at Coors, and other groups, including LAGER (Lesbian and Gay Employee Resources), meets regularly to make recommendations to top management regarding employee relations. In the summer of 1995, at the suggestion of the Diversity Council, Coors wrote into company policy a Domestic Partners Benefits package, which guarantees the same benefits to same-sex partners of employees that it guarantees to spouses.

Tours of the Coors brewery are offered Mon.-Sat. 10 a.m.-4 p.m. (June-Aug.) and 10 a.m.-4 p.m. (Sept.-May). To get to Golden from Denver, take US 70 west and then CO 58 north; you can also take US 6 (6th Ave.) directly west out of Denver. A shuttle bus will take you to the brewery from the parking lot at 13th and Ford. For more information, phone (303) 277-BEER.

*Welcome to
Coors Country.*

locomotive in the yard of the Colorado Railroad Museum

Colorado Railroad Museum

This is an absolute must for train buffs, from old-timers who recall the train in its glory days to those whose childhoods were spent assembling model trains and villages. Nothing fancy or high-tech here (as it should be—in fact, the yard is overgrown with weeds and truly invokes ghosts of a bygone era), but the museum does display plenty to recall the railroad and to teach about its past. From historical photos and original ledgers and records to a model train with an impeccably detailed miniature town of Golden (cars, people, the courthouse, even a baseball game in progress); from switch lamps, uniforms, and silver, from dining cars to the cars and locomotives themselves, this is a wonderful testament to the railroad, as well as a lesson in Colorado's (and the west's) history. The gift shop, in addition to selling mugs and other souvenirs, carries an excellent selection of books on the railroad and on Colorado history, as well as authentic historical papers (original schedules, announcements, records, etc.).

The Colorado Railroad Museum is open daily 9 a.m.-5 p.m. (till 6 p.m. during the summer). To get there from Denver, take I-70 west to US 58, and follow the signs (take Exit 265). If you're heading east on I-70, take Exit 266. For more information, phone (303) 279-4591.

Colorado School of Mines

First open to students in 1871, this is the largest and most important school of mineral engineering in the United States. The college's **Geology Museum,** open daily 8:30 a.m.-4:30 p.m., displays gems, ore, and minerals from around the world, including pieces from Golden's 19th-century mining boom. Located at the corner of 16th and Maple, tel. (303) 273-3823.

The School of Mines is also home to the **National Earthquake Information Center,** recording continental drift and other geological activity around the world. The center's 24-hour-a-day Earthquake Early Alerting Service determines the location and magnitude of temblers around the world (roughly 12,000 a year) and disseminates relevant information to authorities. The center is also responsible for publishing data on seismic activity. Free 30- to 45-minute tours available by appointment (weekdays 9-11 a.m. and 1-3 p.m.); phone (303) 236-1500.

For general information on the Colorado School of Mines, phone (303) 273-3300.

DAR Pioneer Museum

Exhibiting local pioneer artifacts from the mid-19th century to the 1930s, this small museum at 911 10th St. displays a wide variety of local and American historical artifacts—in addition to individual rooms (kid's nursery, lady's boudoir, etc.), you'll see an eclectic collection of domestic items and historical military gear (Civil War bayonets and uniforms). For hours and information, phone (303) 278-7151.

Astor House Hotel Museum

Built in 1867 of local stone, this hotel at the corner of 12th and Arapahoe has been restored and decorated with authentic Victorian furnishings and is now on the National Register of Historic Places. For information, phone (303) 278-3557.

Rocky Mountain Quilt Museum

Located at 1111 Washington Ave. in Golden (temporarily—the board of directors is looking for a larger space), this museum displays over 100 antique and contemporary quilts and attempts to keep alive this American tradition. Nonagenarian Eugiana Mitchell, the museum's primary donor, has taught quilting in the Rockies for over 30 years and continues teaching classes at the museum.

For hours or more information, call (303) 277-0377.

Buffalo Bill's Grave and Museum

Even those not particularly interested in Buffalo Bill, or who feel the hunter, guide, and entrepreneur did as much to make a circus of the West as he did to open it up, will enjoy the drive up Lookout Mountain to his grave and the memorial museum. First of all, just the drive up is quite impressive, with a view from the top of Golden and of Denver in the distance. Second, you'll be surprised how quickly you'll have risen up out of the scrubby foothill fauna and into the fresh-smelling pines.

The grave itself is small and unimposing, though the location is spectacular, and you can easily understand why the outdoorsman would want to be buried here—especially before the view was dominated by the gigantic Coors brewery, only partially obstructed by electrical wires and radio antennae. A small museum displays Cody's saddle, western rifles, Sitting Bull's bows and arrows, supposedly from the Battle of the Little Big Horn, lots of Plains Native American clothing and gear, and, appropriately enough, barbed wire (one of the great contributors to the conquering of the West) from throughout the area.

In addition, there's a small souvenir and curio shop and a snack bar, with homemade fudge. A picnic area, with barbecue pits and restrooms, is located near the parking lot. The museum is open daily 9 a.m.-5 p.m. (May-Oct.) and 9 a.m.-4 p.m. (Nov.-April). To get there, take 19th Ave. out of Golden, or Exit 256 from I-70. For more information on the Buffalo Bill Museum, phone (303) 526-0747.

PARKS AND RECREATION

Golden Gate Canyon State Park

This 8,500-acre park about 15 minutes northwest of Golden offers hiking, fishing, horseback riding, camping (both backcountry and in campgrounds), cross-country skiing, and year-round sightseeing—from fields of wildflowers to deep, pine-forested hillsides and steep, rocky cliffs. Orient yourself at the visitor center, where you'll find exhibits of the park's flora and fauna, as well as naturalists and rangers to answer your questions and suggest the best ways to enjoy the park.

To get to the Golden Gate Canyon State Park, take Washington Ave. north to Golden Gate Canyon Rd. and turn left (west). From there it's about a 15-mile drive to the park's entrance. For more information, write Route 6, Box 280, Golden, CO 80403, or phone (303) 592-1502.

Golf

Golden's **Applewood Golf Course** is an 18-hole public facility located just east of town at 14001 W. 32nd Ave.; phone (303) 279-3003 for tee times and information.

Hiking

In addition to the 50-plus miles of marked trails meandering through Golden Gate Canyon State Park, **Jefferson County Open Space** also has its own 14,000-acre park system, with nearly 100 city-, county-, and recreation-district-managed parks, many with excellent hiking and sightseeing possibilities. Check out **Apex Trail,** which takes hikers from Heritage Square in Golden to the **Jefferson County Nature Center** on Lookout Mountain, and from there to **Beaver Brook Trail.** You can also get to Beaver Brook Trail from a trailhead and parking lot a few miles up 19th Ave. en route to the Buffalo Bill Museum (watch for the sign and small parking lot). Up there, chances are good you'll get to see a hang glider or two, as this is a popular launching site for these crazy sky pilots.

For maps and more information on hiking in the Golden area, phone the administrative offices of Jefferson County Open Space at (303) 278-5925.

TOURS

In addition to the tours of the Coors Brewery (see above), the Historical Preservation Board of Golden designed a self-guided walking tour of historic Golden, specifically the town's Twelfth Street District, which is on the National Register of Historic Places. Included on the tour are the Astor House Hotel Museum (see above) and many residences dating from the 1860s, as well as Colorado's original National Guard Armory (1913), the largest cobblestone building in the country (made from 3,300 wagonloads of stone from Clear Creek).

ACCOMMODATIONS

Golden's accommodations range from state park campgrounds to mom-and-pop-type motels and chain hotels. The recently opened **Table Mountain Inn,** tel. (303) 277-9898, is located in downtown Golden and offers comfortable accommodations in a Southwestern setting. Also downtown is the **Williamsburg Inn,** tel. (303) 279-7673. For bed-and-breakfast accommodations, try the **Jameson Inn,** tel. (303) 278-0351, in a historic Golden home. The **Golden Motel,** tel. (303) 279-5581, 24th and Ford, also has reasonably priced rooms, some with kitchenettes. All of the above are within walking distance of the Coors Brewery and the Colorado School of Mines. You'll also find in Golden a **Ramada Inn,** tel. (303) 279-7611, **Days Inn,** tel. (303) 277-0200, **La Quinta Motor Inn,** tel. (303) 279-5565, and the **Denver Marriott West,** tel. (303) 279-9100.

Golden Gate Canyon State Park (see above), tel. (303) 592-1502, about 20 minutes from downtown Golden, offers RV and tent sites, with laundry facilities and showers. **Clear Creek**

Campground, tel. (303) 278-1437, just west of town (take 10th St. from Washington), also has tent and RV sites, showers, and a dump station. Showers at the campground are open to the public (at $1.50 per person). **Scenic Rock RV Park** is an upscale campground located five minutes west of Golden at 17700 W. Colfax, tel. (303) 279-1625.

FOOD

From Old-West saloon-style diners to Mexican restaurants to fast-food franchises, Golden's got something for just about every appetite and budget. **Kenrow's,** 718 12th St., tel. (303) 279-5164, is a great place to grab lunch after a morning of poking around Golden. The restaurant serves deli and hot sandwiches, salads, Mexican food, pizzas, burgers, and for the hungrier, steaks and seafood dinners. Or check out the **Briarwood Inn,** tel. tel. (303) 279-3121, for fine dining and the **Mesa Bar and Grill,** tel. (303) 277-9898, at the Table Mountain Inn for Southwestern fare. The **Golden Ram** above Foss Drug, tel. (303) 279-6011, is a local favorite for a casual breakfast or lunch. Fast-food freaks can satisfy their cravings at Wendy's, Dairy Queen, and others.

The Observatory, 29259 US 40, tel. (303) 526-1988, is an aptly named cafe, whose distinguishing features are its retractable roof and eight-inch telescope, which allow diners to view the heavens, weather permitting. Try a Moon Dog or an Observa Burger and wash it down with a Milky Way.

ENTERTAINMENT

Visitors to the **Heritage Square Music House** can see post-Civil War musicals and comedies performed by local actors and musicians. The Victorian setting adds authenticity to the experience. For information and reservations, phone (303) 279-7800. If cummerbunds and melodrama aren't your style, then the **Buffalo Rose,** tel. (303) 279-5190, might be. Located downtown at 1119 Washington, this little bar features live music Thurs.-Sat. nights (sometimes other nights), with local and touring acts, some surprisingly well known: Rick Derringer, Edgar Winter, Charlie Musselwhite, and Delbert McClinton have all played the Rose. Across the street, **Kenrow's,** tel. (303) 279-5164, also features live music on weekend nights and pool tournaments on Monday.

Foothills Art Center, at 15th and Washington in downtown Golden, features art galleries with rotating exhibits, an artisans' showcase for local artists, and a gift shop. In addition, the center offers workshops, demonstrations, lectures, poetry readings, and concerts, and each year from late November to Christmas the center is the site of the Holiday Art Market.

For current information on Golden entertainment, check the *Rocky Mountain News,* the *Denver Post,* and the local paper, the *Golden Transcript.*

CALENDAR

Golden's annual events calendar is virtually booked solid with a variety of things for both visitors and locals to see and do—from free concerts in the downtown park to fireworks displays, parades, bike races, and car, gun, flower, and art shows. Among the highlights: **International Heritage Festival of Folk Arts** (mid-June), **Fourth of July fireworks, Buffalo Bill Days** (late July), and the **GoldenFest** (mid-September). For more information on these and other Golden events and activities, phone the Golden Chamber of Commerce at (303) 279-3113. Also be sure to check the local newspaper, the *Golden Transcript,* for current goings-on.

SHOPPING

Golden is particularly proud of its **Heritage Square,** a re-created late-19th-century Western village with boutiques, gift shops, restaurants, and even an Alpine slide and other rides for the kids. Open daily 10 a.m.-6 p.m. (till 9 p.m. Memorial Day through Labor Day). Phone (303) 279-2789.

In the downtown you'll find a variety of boutiques, galleries, and specialty shops.

SERVICES

The **Golden Police Department** is located at 911 10th St., tel. (303) 279-3331. Contact the **Jefferson County Sheriff** at (303) 277-0211 and the local offices of the Colorado **State Patrol** at (303) 273-1616. Jefferson County's general hospital, **Lutheran Medical Center,** is located at 8300 W. 38th St., Wheatridge (between Golden and west Denver—take the Wadsworth Blvd. exit from I-70); phone the hospital at (303) 425-4500 (425-2089 in emergencies).

Golden's main **post office** is located at 619 12th St., tel. 278-8537.

Recycling

Drop off aluminum, glass, newspaper, and plastics at **Evergreen Disposal,** 15969 S. Golden Rd., tel. (303) 278-6000.

INFORMATION

For more information on Golden and Jefferson County, write the Golden **Chamber of Commerce,** Box 1035, Golden, CO 80402, tel. (303) 279-3113, or stop by their offices at 507 14th Street. The Jefferson County **public library,** tel. (303) 279-4585, is located at 923 10th St., and the **Arthur Lakes Library** (largest map collection in the area), tel. (303) 273-3690 is on the campus of the Colorado School of Mines.

For **road conditions** in the Golden area, phone (303) 639-1111 (westbound) or 639-1234 (eastbound).

TRANSPORTATION

Golden is about a half-hour by car from Denver. Get there by heading west on either I-70 or US 6 (W. 6th Ave.). Turnoffs are well marked. You can also get to Golden from Denver by bus (Golden's part of the Denver metro Regional Transportation District); phone (303) 778-6000. **Golden West Shuttle,** tel. (303) 422-1277 provides limousine, taxi, and shuttle service throughout the Golden area.

IDAHO SPRINGS, GEORGETOWN, AND SILVER PLUME

Interstate 70 barrels west past the turnoff to Golden then begins to lift slightly into the sorrel foothills of the Front Range before winding dramatically up into the Rockies' steep and forested canyons, finally rising entirely above the timberline just east of Loveland Pass. From the junction with US 6 (to Golden) to the east side of Eisenhower Tunnel, the road snakes its way through Clear Creek Canyon, where the water, particularly during late-spring runoff, roars riotously toward the plains.

Had you found yourself in this part of Colorado between the early 1870s and 1893, when the silver market crashed, you would have witnessed a canyon teeming with miners, merchants, and railroad workers, and your ears would have buzzed with sounds of men building cabins, mills, and smelters, which they either squeezed into the canyon floor or hung hopefully from cliffsides. Three communities grew out of this mad rush (which eventually produced more than $90 million in silver, gold, copper, and zinc): Georgetown, Idaho Springs, and Silver Plume, which today provide both entertaining and educational tableaux of Colorado's past.

HISTORY

Though a handful of small gold claims were staked in Upper Clear Creek Canyon in the late 1850s, by the mid-'60s silver became the area's most abundant, lucrative, and sought-after ore. Idaho Springs (originally called Jackson's Diggin's, after an early gold miner) was named for the nearby hot springs, which attracted aching and arthritic pioneers. Georgetown was named after George Griffith, another early Clear Creek miner, who came down from Central City around 1860.

Placer mining was the first method of extracting ore from the canyon, and it wasn't long before the few mines played out. By the 1870s, however, lode mining had been developed, and by the middle of the decade Georgetown, home to some 5,000 people, was the third-largest city in Colorado; until silver was discovered in Leadville in 1878, Georgetown was the most important silver camp in the state.

The Colorado Central Railroad reached Georgetown in 1877. With the completion a few years later of the Georgetown Loop Railroad, which connected Georgetown and Silver Plume, two miles upstream, silver could be much more easily transported out of the canyon. When silver fell off in 1893, though, many of Clear Creek Canyon's residents left for towns whose economies were not strictly dependent on mining. Many of Georgetown's and Idaho Springs' homes and businesses were abandoned.

Still, a few persistent miners stayed, working away in a labyrinth of tunnels beneath the earth's rocky crust, and in 1910 the Argo Tunnel, connecting Idaho Springs and Central City, was completed. In the 1930s, when gold and silver began once again to command high prices, some of Clear Creek Canyon's mines reopened. Today, Georgetown, Idaho Springs, and Silver Plume rely heavily on tourism to keep their economies stable, as well as on the abundance of nearby recreational opportunities—particularly skiing, cycling, camping, fishing, and hiking.

ATTRACTIONS

Georgetown Historic District

Even if you're just passing through and don't have time for the railroad and mine tours, you'll enjoy a few hours poking around the restored Victorians and gift shops in downtown Georgetown.

Of particular interest in Georgetown are the **Hotel de Paris Museum** and the **Hamill House Museum**. At one time one of the best-known hotels west of the Mississippi—for its elegant design and cuisine, as well as for its controversial builder/owner/proprietor—the Hotel de Paris has been restored with original furnishings that suggest the building's, and area's, colorful past.

Louis du Puy, born in Alençon, France, in 1844, as the wealthy and titled Adolphus Francis Gerard, came to Georgetown in 1869. Injured in a mining accident in 1873, he later bought Georgetown's Delmonico Bakery in 1875 and immediately set about converting it to a hotel to rival those he remembered from his homeland. Known as a fine cook, philosopher, misogynist, and all-around crank, albeit an intelligent and well-educated one, du Puy was rumored to have been a deserter from the French army. As a hotel proprietor, du Puy constantly angered and amused the residents of Clear Creek Canyon, for most of whom he had little or no respect. Nor did du Puy care much for his guests—only those who met his capricious demands were permitted to stay, while others, upon earning his disfavor, would be ordered to leave mid-stay. When du Puy died in 1900, he willed the hotel to Sophie Galet, about whom history seems to know little, except that she was the widow of a French cabinet maker, worked for du Puy at the hotel, survived him a scant four months, and was buried beside him as she had requested.

The Hotel de Paris Museum is located at 409 6th St. in Georgetown and is open to visitors daily Memorial Day through Labor Day 10 a.m.-5 p.m. Admission is $2.50 for adults, $1.50 for seniors over 60, and 50 cents for ages six to 12. For more information phone (303) 569-2840.

The Hamill House, built in 1869 by silver baron and politician William Hamill, is a restored Victorian home, once one of the most elegant in Colorado Territory. With an interior rich with marble, walnut, and glass, as well as gas lighting and central heating, the house is testament to the wealth the Rockies' mines (and miners) brought to their owners.

The Hamill House, in Georgetown at 305 Argentine St., is open 10 a.m.-5 p.m. Memorial Day through Labor Day, and noon-4 weekends (and by appointment) the rest of the year. Admission is $2.50 for adults, with discounts for kids and seniors. Phone the Georgetown Society at (303) 569-2840 for more information.

Georgetown Loop Railroad

This six-mile tour takes passengers from Georgetown to Silver Plume (and back) via a narrow-gauge steam train that winds through Clear Creek Canyon, up Devil's Gate High Bridge (100 feet high, 300 feet long). Included on the trip is a stop at the Lebanon Mine and Mill, with an optional added tour.

World famous as an engineering marvel when completed in 1884, the railroad was all but forgotten—in fact, the tracks were completely torn up in 1939—from the turn of the century until a hundred years after its inauguration, when the route was restored. Today, roundtrip tours begin from either Silver Plume (9:20 a.m.-4 p.m.) or Georgetown (10 a.m.-3:20 p.m.), with a slide show at the Georgetown depot and a gift shop in Silver Plume. Trains run daily late May through October, departing every hour and twenty minutes (allow two and a half hours for the loop and mine tour; an hour and ten minutes for just the train ride). Adult rates are around $12 ($4 more for the mine tour), with discounts for children four to 15. Reservations recommended.

Note: The Lebanon Mine tour, led by guides from the Colorado Historical Society, takes you 600 feet underground, and it gets cold (44° F) and wet. If you plan to include the mine on your trip, bring warm clothes. Also, wear comfort-

Kristin would rather pet horses than sightsee, downtown Georgetown.

able shoes, as the tour includes a quarter-mile hike. Mine tours are offered Memorial Day through Labor Day only.

To get to the depots, take I-70 Exit 226 (Silver Plume) or 228 (Georgetown). You can also buy tickets at the Old Georgetown Station Visitor Information Center, 1106 Rose St., Georgetown. For more information, phone (303) 670-1686, 569-2403 (locally), or (800) 691-4FUN. You can also send away for brochures by writing Box 217, Georgetown, CO 80444.

Georgetown Walking Tours

Guided walking tours of Georgetown's historic district are offered twice a day (10:30 a.m. and 1:30 p.m.) on weekends Memorial Day through Labor Day. The 90-minute tours include the Hamill House, the Hotel de Paris, old firehouses, churches, and private residences (no entry). Tours, sponsored by the nonprofit Historic Georgetown, Inc., cost $4.50 per person and begin at the Georgetown Community Center, 613 6th Street. You can also arrange private and weekday tours by appointment. For information, phone (800) 472-8230.

Georgetown Carriage Tours

You can also tour Georgetown by horse-drawn carriage. Rutherford Carriage is a private company offering 45-minute jaunts through historic Georgetown, customizing trips for groups, weddings, and other private parties. For more information and rates, phone (303) 569-2675.

George Rowe Museum

One of the most prominent buildings in Silver Plume (it's the big boxy number nestled against the hillside, visible from the freeway), the museum was once a schoolhouse built just before the turn of the century. In addition to displaying sundry artifacts from Clear Creek's past and a restored school room, the museum sells books about and maps of the area. The museum, at 95 Main St., Silver Plume, is open daily 10 a.m.-4 p.m., Memorial Day through Labor Day, and weekends into September. For more information, phone (303) 569-2562.

Argo Gold Mill

Idaho Springs' Argo Gold Mill, built in 1913, served as a processing plant for much of the area's ore, primarily brought down from Central City via the 22,000-foot Argo Tunnel. In 1943, the Argo Mine flooded and the mill shut down; today it is on the National Register of Historic Places and is open to the public for self-guided tours from late May through mid-October, 10 a.m.-7 p.m. It's at 2350 Riverside Dr.; admission is adults $10, ages six to 12 $7, and six and under $5. For more information, phone (303) 567-2421.

Phoenix Mine

A small, family-owned mine first worked in the early 1870s, the Phoenix offers guided public tours during which you can experiment with 19th-century mining tools as well as pan for gold (keep what you find). Open Wed.-Mon. 10

a.m.-6 p.m; group tours by appointment, tel. (303) 567-0422. Admission: adults $7, children under 12, $4.

Take Exit 239 at Idaho Springs, go one mile west on the frontage road, and take Trail Creek Road.

Mt. Evans Road/CO 103

The highest paved road in the country, this breathtaking and sometimes unnerving route climbs out of Clear Creek Canyon, winding through spruce, fir, and pine to Echo Lake. At Echo Lake, the road quickly leaves timber behind and nearly reaches cloud level, clinging to rocky hillsides of glacial moraine and offering stunning views of the Front Range, as well as the dozens of Rockies sub-ranges sprawling to the north, west, and south. Eventually, the road rises to 14,260 feet, where a small lookout station affords one of the most awesome views on the planet.

At the small, alpine Echo Lake, you'll find a picnic area, a forest service campground, and the **Echo Lake Lodge,** a restaurant (buffalo burgers, pastas) and gift shop. You can also stop below Echo Lake at two picnic areas: sit streamside at **Chicago Forks** or enjoy great views at **Ponder Point.**

Note: This road is neither for the faint of heart nor large RVs, and weather sometimes keeps it closed anyway. It's 28 miles to Mt. Evans; allow one hour each way. For road conditions, check at the Arapaho National Forest Information Center. (See following.)

PARKS AND RECREATION

Georgetown, Idaho Springs, and Silver Plume are surrounded by Roosevelt and Arapaho national forests, whose lands abound with campgrounds, hiking trails, and streams for fishing. Whether you're a cross-country skier, ice climber, mountain biker, or mule trainer, you'll find lots of area to explore.

An excellent source for maps, advice, and general information is the **Arapaho National Forest Information Center** (Clear Creek Ranger Station), at the west end of town at the junction of US 103 and I-70 (take Exit 240), tel. (303) 567-2901 or 893-1474.

If you're just passing through and looking for a nice place to pull off the road, check out the quiet little creekside picnic area in downtown Idaho Springs at the corner of Colorado Blvd. and 23rd St.—no overnight camping. There's also a very nice city park in Georgetown, about a quarter-mile east of the central historic district, with picnic benches and a playground. In Silver Plume, directly across the street from the George Rowe Museum, you'll find a small playground.

Downhill Skiing

Whoever coined the term "centrally located" could certainly have been referring to the Clear Creek Canyon area and its relation to Colorado's ski areas. Within an easy hour's drive (weather permitting) lie some of the finest slopes in the country: Winter Park, Arapahoe Basin, Copper Mountain, Vail, and several others. In addition, the mountain roads provide access to some of the state's finest expert-only off-piste skiing. A favorite is **Loveland Pass,** where you can drive up, hoist your skis ashoulder, hike along the ridge-top, and ski down to a waiting car. When all that's left of the snow are a few scattered patches and the resorts are closed (as late as June for Arapahoe Basin), downhill diehards head to **St. Mary's Glacier,** where you can ski year-round. Take the Fall River Rd. exit from I-70 (two miles west of Idaho Springs). For more information, phone (303) 567-2191.

The nearest lift-serviced downhill skiing is at **Loveland Basin,** a small family-oriented resort 12 miles west of Georgetown near the east entrance to Eisenhower Tunnel. Loveland offers over 800 acres of skiable terrain, equipment rental and sales, a restaurant, and day-care facilities. For more information on Loveland, write Box 899, Georgetown, CO 80444; or phone (303) 569-3203 (from Denver, phone 303-571-5580).

Cross-Country Skiing

Arapaho National Forest provides virtually unlimited cross-country skiing opportunities within a few short miles of these little towns and the interstate connecting them. Again, the ranger station (at I-70 Exit 240) is an excellent source for maps and general information. Write Box 3307, Idaho Springs, CO 80452, or phone (303) 567-2901 or 893-1474.

Cycling

The steep roads leading into the high country above Clear Creek Canyon are excellent for in-shape riders, and they get surprisingly little auto traffic, considering their proximity to the busy interstate. Colorado touring clubs hold a number of races and rides in the area.

Colorado 103, winding south from Idaho Springs (Exit 240), offers a gently rising ride alongside the rippling waters of Chicago Creek. If you turn onto CO 5 (Mt. Evans Rd.) at the junction (about 14 miles south of Idaho Springs), you'll be in for one doozy of a ride—the road now rises suddenly up toward the treeline, over it, and twists up nearly to the 14,264-foot summit of Mt. Evans. At Summit Lake, you'll find a small picnic area with tables and restrooms.

For information on mountain biking in the area, stop by the Clear Creek ranger station or **Chickenhead Mountain Sports** in Idaho Springs. See "Information" following.

Hiking

The Clear Creek area is surrounded by miles and miles of excellent hiking trails and back-packing wonderlands, much of it within the borders of Arapaho National Forest. Among the better designated trails are **Chicago Lakes Trail,** south of Idaho Springs off CO 5, **Summit Lake Trail,** a 12-mile walk-that-turns-to-climb from Echo Lake Campground to the summit of Mt. Evans, and the **Griffin Monument Trail,** a two-mile hike from downtown Silver Plume to a hillside monument erected to honor a 19th-century English miner.

For more information on hiking in the area, stop in at the Clear Creek Ranger Station or Chickenhead Sports in Idaho Springs. See "Information," following.

Fishing

Though Clear Creek looks awfully trouty from the road, fishing has been all but ruined by the century and a half of mining in the area. Locals like to work Chicago Creek, south of Idaho Springs along CO 103 (respect private property), and the lawnchair crowd competes for the rainbows regularly stocked in the easily accessible Georgetown Lake, at the east end of town.

ACCOMMODATIONS

You'll find a handful of relatively inexpensive motels along Colorado Blvd. on the east end of Idaho Springs. Among the newest and nicest are the **Argo Motor Inn,** tel. (303) 567-4473, and the **H and H Motor Lodge,** tel. (303) 567-2838; doubles at both start at about $50. Just before Colorado Blvd. feeds back onto the freeway, you'll find a couple of other motels. The **Peoriana Motel,** tel. (303) 567-2021, has doubles in the $30-40 range.

Indian Springs Resort, tel. (303) 567-2191, is a hot springs with a long history (claiming visitors including Teddy Roosevelt). Today the spa and resort offers mineral baths, vapor caves, a swimming pool, and the "Club Mud" (a mud puddle supposedly capable of cleansing the skin and soul . . .). You can get a room in either the main lodge (125 years old and quite rundown; no private baths) or in the motel across the street.

In Georgetown, $50-60 should get you a double at the **Georgetown Super 8,** tel. (303) 569-3211, or the **Georgetown Motor Inn,** tel. (303) 569-3201. The **Hardy House Bed and Breakfast,** tel. (303) 569-3388, has rooms in an 1880 Victorian for about $75.

In nearby Empire, you can stay at the **Peck House,** 83 Sunny Ave., tel. (303) 569-9870, built in 1862 as a stage stop. Claiming to be Colorado's oldest hotel, the Peck House has been wonderfully restored, and its hillside location (and dirt-road entrance) truly make the visitor feel like a time traveler. The Peck House dining room has won many awards, and is especially a popular Sunday-brunch spot. Rooms run $45 (no private bath) to $100. Oh, and the Peck House is said to be haunted . . .

Camping and RVing

In the heart of Arapaho National Forest, the Georgetown-Idaho Springs-Silver Plume area is naturally very near to some excellent campgrounds. One particularly nice one is **West Chicago Creek Campground** about nine miles from the west of town just off CO 103 (take Exit 240 from I-70). Go south on CO 103 for six miles, then follow the signs up a short dirt road to Chicago Creek. Sites are $8 a night.

You'll also find several campgrounds just west of Idaho Springs near the junction of I-70 and US 40. At Exit 232, take US 40 three miles toward Winter Park to the privately owned **Mountain Meadow Campground.** If you'd rather be in the national forest, continue on US 40 for another couple of miles, and almost as soon as you cross back into Arapaho National Forest, you'll find **Mizpah Campground,** where nice shaded sites lie right on Clear Creek, with well water and pit toilets; fee is $8 a night. There are also two Forest Service picnic areas nearby (well marked from the highway): **Clear Creek** and **Big Bend,** both piney, shaded, and cool.

FOOD

Start Me Up

On Colorado Blvd. at the east end of Idaho Springs, **Marion's of the Rockies** serves breakfast specials daily, as well as biscuits and gravy, eggs, pancakes, and waffles, from 6 a.m.—this is where local contractors scarf down big breakfasts before heading out to their job sites. **Mainstreet, A Restaurant,** at 1518 Miner Street, Idaho Springs, is a popular local hangout and down-home kind of place, where waitresses call everyone "Hon." Lots of pancake dishes, including the "Skier's Special" (blueberry), as well as other standard American breakfast fare— prices range $2-4.50. Mainstreet also serves lunch—sandwiches, burgers, etc.—for $3-6.

Other Restaurants

The newest restaurant in the area, **Tommyknocker Brewery,** 1401 Miner St., tel. (303) 567-2688, once served as a lunch stop on the Colorado Central Railroad, as well a bowling alley dating from 1929. Typical brew-pub fare— homemade pastas and sausages, miners' stew, Cornish pasties, etc.—runs $6-12. Some of the best pizza in the Denver area can be devoured at **Beaujo's Pizza,** just down the street at 1517 Miner, tel. (303) 567-4376. A favorite among Denver-area pizza aficionados, Beaujo's regularly wins rave reviews from local media and readers' polls. Idaho Springs is also home to an excellent and unpretentious little Chinese restaurant, **Szechwan Fu,** located at 1744 Miner St. toward the middle of town, tel. (303) 567-

9378. Though prices here top out at $16-18 for dinner specials and seafood (lobster with hot Szechwan sauce), you can order off the south end of the menu and get a huge and satisfying meal for $5-7. The chow and lo mein noodles are excellent, as are the moo shu vegetables.

In Georgetown, try the **Red Ram Restaurant and Saloon,** 606 6th St., tel. (303) 569-3263. Part Old-West saloon and part family restaurant, the Ram serves good food (burgers, salads, pastas) at very reasonable rates. For Southwestern and Rocky Mountain fare in Georgetown, check out the **Silver Queen Restaurant and Wine Cellar,** also on 6th St. in Old Georgetown, tel. (303) 568-2961. Lunch specials include burritos, buffalo burgers, and pita-bread sandwiches. The Silver Queen also serves upscale dinner entrees, including shrimp, veal, and pasta specials. Dinners run $8-14. The **Happy Cooker,** corner of 6th and Taos (across from the Hotel de Paris Museum), tel. (303) 569-3166, is a good choice for a hearty breakfast, lunch, or dinner. Daily specials include waffles, soups, lasagna, and homemade bread.

ENTERTAINMENT

A favorite night spot among locals as well as for tipped-off passers-through (particularly skiers heading home to Denver) is Idaho Springs' **Buffalo Bar,** 1617 Miner, tel. (303) 567-2729. In Georgetown, check out **Marti's Crazy Horse Saloon,** 1211 Argentine Street, tel. (303) 659-2475.

INFORMATION

The **Town of Georgetown Visitor Center** is at 404 6th Street. Stop in for more information on dining, lodging, and exploring the area. Before your visit, write Box 426, Georgetown, CO 80444, or phone (303) 569-2555. You can also get information from the **Georgetown Society,** Box 667, Georgetown, CO 80444, tel. (303) 569-2840, and the **Idaho Springs Visitors Information Center,** Box 97, Idaho Springs, CO 80452, tel. (303) 567-4382 or (800) 658-7785. You can also stop by the center at the intersection of Colorado Blvd. and Miner Street.

WEST OF GEORGETOWN

Loveland Pass

Once featured in *National Geographic* magazine as one of America's most harrowing passes for interstate truckers, Loveland is a twisting, turning, switchbacking climb to well above the treeline (11,992 feet, that's over *two miles* high). In the late spring of 1973, Eisenhower Tunnel was opened, so motorists traveling between Denver and Summit County no longer had to go up and over the pass, which of course is especially nasty in winter. And, naturally, the tunnel is still the wisest way to go if your main objective is to get where you're going as quickly (and as safely) as possible. But if you've got an extra half-hour or so (when the road's clear), and if your brakes are good, take the drive up over the pass. The views are astounding, and it's one of the best ways to get a real sense of the Rockies. When snow lingers on the mountainsides, watch for skiers, who drive up the pass, hike along the ridgetop, and ski down (recommended for experts only!). Also see the special topic on Eisenhower Tunnel in the Summit County chapter.

BOULDER

The Berkeley of Colorado? The Chamonix of the Rockies? A bastion of upscale fitness freaks, politically progressive intellectuals, New Age tofu heads, and the last remnants of 1960s hippiedom?

Perhaps. Of course it's easy to resort to reductionism when trying to capture the essence of a town and its people in a few words. And it's neither possible nor fair to classify Boulder and Boulderites. Sure, in the early 1990s *Outside* magazine named it the number-one town in the country for outdoor sports, and the city has a disproportionate amount of open-space-designated land. Granted, the state's number-one academic institution is one of the town's major influences. Yes, you do see more Saab Turbos, BMWs, Jeep Wagoneers, and other Yuppie rigs here than you do anywhere east of Marin County, California. True, you're likely to find in your motel-room nightstand—competing for space with *Gideon's Bible*—a copy of *The Teachings of Buddha*. And, okay, long-haired, barefooted street musicians still strum Dylan tunes on street corners, their guitar cases open for coins, and the city is relatively tolerant of transients, who hit up passers-by for spare change, while the occasional space case floats by talking to himself, or maybe conducting an orchestra only he can hear.

But still, Boulder is its own town, completely defying classification—in fact, the only generalization one can safely make about the city is that it's diverse, and, for a relatively small town a *long* way from either coast and the cosmopolitan influences there, it's a remarkably tolerant one. Tolerant, that is, of just about everything but outsiders. Unfortunately, as the town has grown—housing blanketing once-green pastures, traffic snarled at dozens of intersections—so has an anti-newcomer attitude. Of course, you can't blame Boulderites for wanting

BOULDER, DOWNTOWN

TO ESTES PARK AND ROCKY MOUNTAIN NAT'L PARK

BROADWAY

FOLSOM AVE.

28th ST.

119

TO LONGMONT

VALMONT RD.

BOULDER BREWERY

SUNSHINE CANYON

7

MAPLETON AVE.

PEARL ST.

TO GOLD HILL

PEARL ST. MALL

CHAMBER OF COMMERCE VISITOR INFORMATION CENTER

BOULDER CANYON

119

CANYON BLVD.

ARAPAHOE AVE.

TO NEDERLAND AND GOLD HILL

7

36

FLAGSTAFF MT.

THE HILL

UNIVERSITY OF COLORADO

BASELINE

TO LOUISVILLE AND LAFAYETTE

CHAUTAUQUA PARK AND AUDITORIUM

BOULDER TURNPIKE

THE FLATIRONS

TO DENVER

TABLE MESA DR.

NOT TO SCALE

NOTE: ONLY MAIN ROADS SHOWN

93

TO GOLDEN AND DENVER

NCAR

© MOON PUBLICATIONS, INC.

to preserve their little Eden—but on the other hand, they need to remember it was someone else's paradise long before they came.

HISTORY

In part because the Boulder area was once sacred to several different Native American tribes (predominantly Arapahoe), the line between mythology and history often blurs, creating a folklore that both defines and reflects the town's rare blend of whimsy and stubborn intellectualism. Among the legends of the region is Chief Niwot's (Chief Left Hand) curse, profoundly proximate to the hearts of thousands of transplanted Boulderites who originally came with no intentions to stay but just to vacation or attend the university. According to the curse, anyone who sets eyes on the area will be so drawn to it that she will be unable to leave, leading eventually to the area's overcrowding and self-destruction (some claim the curse has already proved itself prophetic).

White Settlement

Evidently, Chief Niwot's curse is grounded in history and is linked with his first encounter with white settlers.

In 1858, Captain Thomas Aikens led a small group of settlers up the South Platte River and, after spotting the area through a telescope from the walls of Fort St. Vrain, described it as "right for gold and the valleys . . . rich for grazing." Shortly thereafter, Aikens led a splinter group from the main wagon train and set up camp at what is today Boulder. Also camped in the area was a group of Southern Arapahoe, led by Chief Niwot. According to the WPA guide to Colorado, when the two men first met, Niwot asked Aikens if he remembered when the stars fell. Aikens responded that it was 1832, and Niwot told him he was correct, and that that was the year the whites first came. Then Niwot pointed to a comet in the sky and said its tail pointed "back to when the stars fell as thick as the tears of our women shall fall when you come to drive us away." Three days later, Niwot, after asking the whites to leave (and being rebuffed), came alone to Aikens's camp and told of a dream he had had: Boulder Creek had over-flowed, the Arapahoe had been washed away, and the whites were saved. From then on, the natives in the area pretty much left the white settlers to their own devices, watching from woods as the newcomers planted crops, dug irrigation ditches, carved roads, and built structures with corners.

Boulder City

As early as 1859, Boulder City, then part of Nebraska Territory, was being laid out, with the first 4,044 lots selling for $1000 each. By 1860, the town claimed 324 residents; in 1861, a federal bill put the town officially in Colorado Territory.

During the 1860s, Boulder's survival depended largely on its proximity to both the plains and the mountains, with crops as well as gold contributing to its economy. Still, though, Boulder was more a trading center for goods than a supply source, and the 1860s weren't really the best of times for the town; eventually many of the area's early settlers became discouraged and left. Things began to look up in the early 1870s, however, when the town began to build schools and the tracks of a couple of railroads (Colorado Central and Boulder Valley) reached town. In 1871, Boulder was incorporated (and "City" dropped from the name), and in 1874, the state legislature approved $15,000 for the construction of the University of Colorado, on the condition that the community match the funds, and work was begun on Old Main, which still stands tall, like the campus patriarch that it is. The first class of freshmen consisted of just 12 students, yet by 1880 the university population was over 3,000.

With the establishment of the university, the school's and the town's history and development became complexly intertwined. At the turn of the century, the campus claimed over 6,000 students, and the university "Hill" began to develop into the colorful blend of small businesses, university-affiliated buildings, and student housing found there today.

It was also around the turn of the century that Boulder was first targeted for its tourism potential. In 1898, the Colorado Chautauqua was built at the base of the Flatirons by a group of Texans looking for a place to escape the heat of the summer lowlands. Included were an auditorium, dining hall, community center, and over 100 cottages. Chautauqua is still used today for music festivals, conferences, and retreats, and cabins can still be rented by individual parties—see "Accommodations," following.

Postmodern Boulder

At the end of WW II, Boulder's population took a significant leap, as the university attracted students on GI loans. By the late 1960s, Boulder began to establish a reputation as one of the counterculture's strongholds, a sort of geographical, political, and spiritual link between Madison and Berkeley—the town was known locally as "the People's Republic of Boulder"—and the area nightclubs were hosting some of the best rock and folk bands in the country, thanks primarily to the students. Susan Berman, author of the 1971 book *The Underground Guide to the College of Your Choice*, wrote, "For the most part it looks like Berkeley—heavy hip types, mostly freaks. Lots and lots of hair and beards and fringed leather jackets and old jeans, chicks without bras wearing all kinds of good stuff . . . Chicks are very liberated . . . Entertainment is balling . . . Survival is easy. Plenty of drugs, cohabitation, and smiles."

"I Don't Know Why, They Call Someplace Paradise, Kiss It Good-bye"

Well, the times they have a-changed. There are still plenty of "freaks," but so too are there lots of Porche-driving babyboomers seemingly oblivious to the problems outside their city. Indeed, a local joke defines Boulder as "twenty square miles surrounded by reality." In addition, the area's desirability and the large number of students who'll work for peanuts keeps wages low. The number of homeless is shocking and sad, yet ironically, new homes sprawl hugely and homogenously on hillsides north and east of town.

All of which pisses people off. How to control the inevitable growth? Can you just keep buying open space, and not allowing folks to move in? According to Mayor Leslie Durgin, quoted in *Boulder Magazine*, in the early 1990s growth was limited to "two percent a year, measured in residential terms by building permits." But in 1993, the Boulder city council cut that in half and targeted for development 1,600 acres north of town on which 3,000 new homes would be built. Yet predictions are that by the year 2020,

900,000 more people will live in the area than do now.

These figures ask tough questions, and there are no easy answers. But Boulderites should keep in mind they do have a little bit of paradise here, and it would be awfully easy to lose it.

ATTRACTIONS

Face it. You don't go to Boulder to go to museums. *But,* if you need some time off from mountain biking, hiking, and outdoor sightseeing, or if the afternoon brings with it a storm that makes doing indoor activities more sensible, the town does offer a handful of museums and other attractions worth checking out.

University of Colorado Museum

With three stories of small rooms—some with revolving exhibits—the CU museum features a good display of Southwestern cultures, with Anasazi pottery, and Clovis and Sandia points; one wing is devoted to prehistory, with dinosaur fossils and bones, including the skull of a triceratops, and a display of the evolution of the horse, with the hooves and skull of the tiny Eohippus. Kids will love Discovery Corner ("Please Touch"), which teaches them about X-rays, seashells, and starfish. There's also a gigantic bird exhibit. Hours are Mon.-Fri. 9 a.m.-5 p.m., Saturday 9 a.m.-4 p.m., and Sunday 10 a.m.-4 p.m. Admission is free. Phone (303) 492-6892 for information. The museum is located on the main CU campus just off Broadway. Look for the signs.

Harbeck House

This museum, which occupies an 1899-vintage Victorian home just west of the university, displays items from the town's past—quilts, dolls, china, a huge dollhouse, and other domestic artifacts. On the second floor is a small gift store specializing in books on Boulder's and the state's history. Hours are Tues.-Sat. noon-4 p.m.; group tours offered by appointment. Admission is $2. The museum is at the corner of 12th and Euclid streets. Adjacent to the museum is Beach Park, lawny, shady, and perfect for picnicking. Phone (303) 449-3464 for more information.

the University of Colorado's ivy-covered museum

University of Colorado Heritage Center
Located in "Old Main," the University of Colorado's first building, this museum contains a variety of artifacts from the area's past, as well as historical photos and photos of well-known CU alumni. Open Tues.-Fri. 10 a.m.-4 p.m. Phone (303) 492-6329 for more information.

National Center for Atmospheric Research
Situated on a gorgeous 360-acre site in the Boulder foothills just southeast of the Flatirons Mountains, the National Center for Atmospheric Research (NCAR) is the world's foremost research center for scientists studying weather—"from the tiniest snowflake to the cataclysm of droughts and hurricanes." Known as Mesa Laboratories, the facility is open to visitors Mon.-Fri. 8 a.m.-5 p.m. and weekends and holidays 9 a.m.-3 p.m. Both guided and self-guided tours are offered (a highly detailed map, with explanatory text, makes the self-guided tour informative and rewarding). View the massive supercomputer system and the 30-foot-high portable automated mesonet (PAM), a weather station that measures wind speed and direction, temperature, humidity, and air pressure. Check out the display of some absolutely stunning photographs of lightning.

To get to NCAR, take Table Mesa Rd. west from Broadway and follow the signs to the parking lot. Tours are Mon.-Sat. at 12 p.m. in the summer. Admission is free. For more informa-tion, phone (303) 497-1174 (recorded tour information) or 497-1000 (main office).

PARKS AND RECREATION

This is what Boulder's all about. Named the country's number-one sports town by *Outside* Magazine, Boulder at times looks like an amusement park for outdoor lovers. No sooner do you cross over into the city limits than the whole landscape comes alive with runners (*not* joggers), cyclists, and overall the most active, healthy-looking people you've seen this side of an Olympic training camp. In fact, many world-class athletes live and train in Boulder. Among them are Norway native Ingrid Kristiansen, who won the 1989 New York Marathon and holds the record for the women's 10,000 meters; and Christian Griffith, a Boulder native and former member of the United States Rock Climbing Team.

And it's not only the people who'll tell you this is one outdoor-oriented town. Pull into any parking lot, or take a look at the cars on the street: skis, bikes, kayaks, sailboards, climbing gear, and every kind of outdoor equipment imaginable is strapped, bungie-corded, or racked atop and stuffed into the backs of 4WD Jeeps, Subarus, and other rigs built for the mountains.

Hiking
Boulderites claim that one of the true beauties of living in the area is the easy access to so many

wonderful hiking areas. In fact, many homes in town literally lie within a few yards of trailheads leading into some magnificent country.

Boulder's prime close-to-town hiking is in and around **Chautauqua Park** on the southwest side of town. Newcomers to town will be amazed to find such a place exists within the city limits. Located at the base of the Flatirons and reached by taking Baseline Rd. west from town, Chautauqua begins as a sloping meadow, then quickly (within a few hundred yards) gets into some steep, rocky, and piney backcountry that feels miles from nowhere—with several different trails webbing up into the woods. If you'd rather start a bit higher, continue up Baseline (it turns into Flagstaff Mountain Rd.) into the **Boulder Mountain Parks,** where you'll find over 33,000 acres of city open space and 100 miles of trails. In fact, it seems a trailhead awaits around every bend in the road—and there are *lots* of those, as the road switchbacks steeply up the mountainside. In addition to the trailheads, picnic tables are scattered along the road, especially at the top, where you'll find 20 or so, along with grills and a shelter (groups can reserve the facility by calling the city **Parks and Recreation Department** at 303-441-3400). A bonus of hiking on Flagstaff Mountain is the views—you look directly down on Boulder, offering a great way to orient yourself to the city.

There's also a plethora of hiking trails in the lower reaches of **Sunshine Canyon** at the west end of Mapleton, as well as farther up the road on Bald Mountain. Good hiking trails also begin at NCAR. (See "National Center for Atmospheric Research," above).

Another hike, albeit a much shorter one than most of those in the Chautauqua or Sunshine Canyon area, is one that begins not far above the Pearl Street Mall. Just west of the mall, where Pearl St. joins Canyon Rd., is a small parking lot and trailhead. From there, a short hike takes you up the side of the hill to some redrock outcroppings and an excellent view of Denver and the valley.

When you're ready to head out of town a ways, one of the best places to hike is up by the **Eldora Ski Area.** Take Canyon Rd. to Nederland, turn south on CO 119, and turn off at the ski area; follow the paved road to the trailhead. Several great hikes wander into the moun-

tains. You can follow the creek, hike up to **Lost Lake,** or let your soul get lost in the high peaks; whether you just want to get outside and sniff the mountain air or get into serious hiking, this area offers excellent opportunities.

Golden Gate Canyon State Park also offers excellent hiking, as well as fishing and camping. A sprawling park off CO 119 between Nederland and Blackhawk, Golden Gate Canyon offers a wide range of trails—from simple roadside walks, or strolls to nearby lakes, to serious backcountry challenges, with close to 30 campsites accessible only by foot. For more information, phone the park at (303) 592-1502.

This is just a small sampling of available hiking near Boulder; it would take a book-length guide to list everything. Besides, you want to do some exploring on your own, don't you? For some excellent guides to the area see the Booklist.

For maps and more information on hiking in and around Boulder, stop by the **Boulder Mountain Parks Ranger Cottage** at Chautauqua Park (south end of parking lot by main entrance at Grant and Baseline), or phone (303) 441-3408. Boulder Mountain Park Trail Maps are $3. You can get information from the **City of Boulder Open Space Operations/Ranger Services** at 1405 S. Foothills Hwy., tel. (303) 494-0436. Open Space Trail maps are $5.

Cycling

One of the first things you'll notice about Boulder is that just about everyone rides—mountain bikes, touring bikes, racing bikes. In fact, according to a recent *Colorado Daily* article, seven out of every 10 Boulderites own cycles. And so of course the area's got miles and miles of bike trails, including a wonderful trail system that will take you just about anywhere and everywhere in the city you want to go. Commuters, students, weekend cyclists and out-of-towners make sure the Boulder Bike Path gets lots of use.

More serious riders head out of town, though—into the canyons or up the switchback roads like the one up Flagstaff Mountain. Following are just a few basic suggestions. For more information, contact the **University of Colorado Bike Office,** tel. (303) 492-7384, the **Bike Touring Group of the Colorado Mountain Club,** tel. (303) 449-1135, or most any bike shop in town. The City of Boulder Bicycle Program also has more information on routes, and can provide you with maps, brochures, and safety manuals; phone (303) 441-3216.

East Boulder Trail: This is the longest of the city's off-road trails. Pick it up at the Teller Farm Trailhead on Arapahoe Rd. between 75th and 95th streets.

Flagstaff Mountain: If you're really in shape and want to give your legs the ultimate workout, head up Flagstaff Mountain (from Baseline). This is one rude ride as the road rises up by a series of serious switchbacks, but the rewards should be great—not only the knowledge you did it, but the views of Boulder you'll get along the way (assuming you can keep the sweat from your eyes). The four-mile ride rises 900 feet.

Gold Hill-Nederland Loop: Another serious ride is the loop (or any part thereof) winding up out of town via Mapleton Rd., up over Bald Mountain, through Gold Hill, down into Nederland, and back to town through Boulder Creek Canyon. (Note: A good portion of this road is not paved—in fact, it's downright rutty—and you'll need fat tires, not to mention legs of iron, to make it the entire way.)

You can also do this loop the opposite direction; many riders head up Boulder Creek Canyon, where a not-so-steep paved path follows CO 119 and the creek out of town. After a few miles, the pavement ends, then continues as dirt for a bit longer before joining the highway; if you continue on the curvy road, you need not only be in good shape but constantly vigilant for cars, which are known to drive this road faster than they ought.

Boulder-to-Jamestown Loop: This 34-mile roundtrip ride begins at the corner of Broadway and Canyon. Take Broadway eight miles east to Left Hand Canyon Drive. After about six miles, watch for James Canyon Dr., a four-mile stretch that takes you to Jamestown.

Rollins Pass: Originally a section of the Northwestern and Pacific Railway, this route took passengers—en route between Denver and Winter Park—over the Continental Divide from 1903 to 1927, when the Moffat Tunnel was completed. Eventually the tracks were torn out, and today the road is a popular 4WD vehicle pass and one of the premier mountain-bike routes in the state. You can catch the pass at a

number of different places (get a map), but the main road runs from Rollins, on CO 72 south of Nederland, over to Winter Park.

For a complete guide to mountain-bike riding in the Boulder area, stop by any bike shop and pick up **Boulder Mountain Biking Map.** Also, watch the *Colorado Daily* (CU's newspaper) for regular articles about mountain biking and recommended trails.

If your derailleur, brakes, or cones need adjusting, stop in at **High Wheeler Bicycles,** tel. (303) 442-5588, on Pearl a half block up from the Pearl Street Mall, where the friendly and helpful crew will loan you tools for repair.

Bikes, Rentals, and Equipment: Among Boulder's shops that rent bikes are **The High Wheeler,** 1015 Pearl St., tel. (303) 442-5588; **Full Cycle,** 1205 13th St., tel. (303) 440-7771; **Morgul Bismark,** 1221 Pennsylvania, tel. 447-1338; **University Bicycles,** 839 Pearl, tel. (303) 444-4196; **Wheels of Boulder,** 1538 28th St., tel. (303) 444-2415; and **Doc's Ski and Sport** at Table Mesa Center, Table Mesa and Broadway, tel. (303) 499-0963.

Further Reading: If you're serious about biking in the Boulder area and throughout the state, you ought to pick up a copy of Jean and Hartley Alley's *Colorado Cycling Guide* (Pruett Publishing Company, Boulder, 1990). This exhaustive book examines back-road and main-route tours around Colorado for both weekend cyclists and serious tourers. Included are over 30 different trips, with several variations on each one. Learn how to get from Denver's International Airport to Boulder, as well as where to ride in Telluride. The authors also include maps, photos, discussions of difficulty, brief histories of several of the towns along the way, suggestions for accommodations, and contact listings of interest to Colorado cyclists.

River Running

With Boulder's penchant for outdoor sports, coupled with the many rivers and streams in the area, it should come as no surprise this town is big on kayaking, rafting, and canoeing. One of the best places to get your feet wet, so to speak, is at the **Boulder Outdoor Center,** tel. (303) 444-8420, at 2510 N. 47th St., between Pearl and Valmont. Offering classes and clinics for all abilities, as well as a variety of trips (including to the Cache La Poudre, the Arkansas, Clear Creek, and Royal Gorge), the Outdoor Center is a highly professional outfit dedicated to river preservation and environmental awareness. The Boulder Outdoor Center also rents and sells equipment.

Acquired Taste, tel. (303) 443-4120, and **Boulder Outdoor Center,** tel. (303) 444-8420 are two of Boulder's best-regarded whitewater guide services, offering half-, full-, and multiday trips down the Arkansas, Colorado, and other rivers in the area.

Fishing

The lakes and streams around Boulder, including many operated by the city, offer good fishing for both warm- and cold-water species. **Boulder, Viele,** and **Lagerman** reservoirs are popular for boat and shore fishing, as are **Wonderland** and **Thunderbird** lakes, **Walden** and **Sawhill** ponds, and **Barker Meadow Reservoir** in Nederland. Among the streams attracting trout fishermen are the Middle and South forks of **St. Vrain Creek, Left Hand Creek** between Left Hand Reservoir and Buckingham Park, **North Boulder Creek** between CO 72 and Boulder Falls, **Middle Boulder Creek** from its headwaters to 28th St. (special restrictions within city limits), and **South Boulder Creek** from its headwaters to Baseline Rd. (special restrictions between Walker Ranch and South Boulder Rd.).

You'll also find excellent trout fishing in the streams and lakes of the high country west of town. For more information on fishing in Boulder, phone the Colorado Division of Wildlife, tel. (303) 297-1192, City of Boulder Open Space, tel. (303) 441-3440, or County of Boulder Open Space, tel. (303) 441-3950.

Golf

Boulder's 18-hole **Flatirons Golf Course,** at 5706 Arapahoe Ave., is among the more popular public links in the area; phone (303) 442-7851 for information and tee times. Five miles north of town on Neva Rd., **Lake Valley Golf Club** is another 18-hole course open to the public; phone (303) 444-2114.

Other courses in the area: in Golden, **Applewood Golf Course,** tel. (303) 279-3003; in Broomfield, **Eagle Golf Club,** tel. (303) 466-

3322; and in Longmont, **Haystack Mountain Golf Course,** tel. (303) 530-1400, **Sunset Municipal Golf Course,** tel. (303) 776-3122, and **Twin Peaks Municipal Golf Course** (where you still won't find out who killed Laura Palmer), tel. (303) 772-1722.

COMMERCIAL ATTRACTIONS

Claiming to be the oldest microbrewery in the United States, the **Boulder Brewing Company** began in 1979 as a 1,000-square-foot shed near Longmont. By the early '80s, the beer had achieved an excellent local reputation, and in 1984, the company moved to its present location; with increased capacity and efficiency, the beer could be better marketed and distributed. In 1987, Boulder Beer's porter won a silver medal at the Great American Beer Festival, and its stout took home the gold.

Free tours of the brewery (which include a sampling) are offered Mon.-Sat. at 2 p.m. The brewery also operates a restaurant, open till 10 p.m. for food, midnight for brews. Take Valmont to 2880 Wilderness Place. For more information, phone (303) 444-8448.

Celestial Seasonings tea makers, 1780 55th St., tel. (303) 581-1202, is based in Boulder and offers free tours of the production and packaging plants, as well as of the research-and-development lab. Tours are on the hour Mon.-Sat. 10 a.m.-2 p.m.

TOURS

From historical walking tours through specific areas of downtown to Jeep, mining, railroad, brewery, and national park tours, you needn't look far in Boulder.

Boulder Historical Tours

Every Sunday from early June through September, groups meet at the Hotel Boulderado at 10 a.m. and 1 p.m. for tours of Boulder's historical districts. The three different areas (the downtown commercial area, the Whittier neighborhood, and Mapleton Hill) are visited on a rotating basis; tours last about 90 minutes and cost $3 per person (groups of 10 or more should make reservations). Wear good, comfortable walking shoes. Phone (303) 444-5192 for more information.

Scenic Drives from Boulder

If you want to see the Boulder area without having to worry about driving and parking, it may help to have a guide, yet being your own guide can be far more rewarding. And since the area abounds in stunning scenery, with scenic drives lasting from 20 minutes to several days in length, you really owe it to yourself to get out and do a little exploring. Following are but a few of the many routes providing fascinating history and stunning scenery.

One of the more popular day-trips is the loop into Estes Park via the north part of the Peak to Peak Highway. Start by heading out Canyon Rd. through Boulder Creek Canyon. At Nederland, turn north on CO 72. This road takes you past the old mining town of Ward, along the eastern side of Rocky Mountain National Park (with several access roads to picnic areas and campgrounds along the way), through Allenspark and Ferncliff, Meeker Park, and into Estes Park. In Estes Park, you can either catch US 34 west into Rocky Mountain National Park, or you can loop back through Lyons and into Boulder via US 36 east.

A shorter, but more demanding (at least on your car) tour is a mostly dirt road up through the mining town of Gold Hill and back into Boulder via Nederland and Boulder Creek Canyon. Take Mapleton Ave. west out of town into some of Boulder Open Space lands (you'll pass several trailheads leading up into the hills), and follow it to Bald Mountain and then down into Gold Hill; just west of Gold Hill, you'll come back onto CO 7 (where you'll turn south), which will take you back down to Nederland. Allow at least an hour and a half—more if you want to get out and hike, or wander around Gold Hill or Nederland.

Another popular day excursion is the 80-mile round trip southwest to Black Hawk and Central City. The scenery is stunning along the way, although by the time you get to Central City you'll have met up with hordes of other visitors—mostly tourists taking day jaunts from Denver—and if the point of your trip was to get out and "away from it all," you're probably better off heading elsewhere (on weekends in the summer, traffic can be backed up bumper to bumper a half-mile *outside* Central City, while motorists wait to park). If, on the other hand, you're in the mood for wandering through casinos or going on mine tours, then an afternoon in Central City might be just the ticket.

ACCOMMODATIONS

As you'd figure, Boulder offers a full range of lodging options, from bare-bones budget to

Sunday brunches at the Chautauqua Dining Hall

outrageous opulence. You can camp, stay in a hostel, check into a motel, or go first class by staying in one of the city's luxury hotels.

Boulder Chautauqua

For no-frills yet uniquely Boulder accommodations, consider a room or cottage at Boulder Chautauqua. Rent by the day, week, month, or season in a quiet, self-contained mini-community at the base of the Flatirons. The two lodges (13 and 15 rooms) and the 61 cottages are throwbacks to the turn of the century when the Chautauqua was founded. Maintained by the City of Boulder, the complex features a gorgeous old dining hall, an auditorium, and spacious lawns and hiking areas. Ideal for a quiet getaway or isolated retreat.

Lodge rooms at the Boulder Chautauqua start at about $40 for two, and cottages start at $43 a night (minimum of four consecutive nights for the cottages). For a complete brochure, write Colorado Chautauqua Association, Chautauqua Park, Boulder, CO 80302, or phone (303) 442-3282.

Hotels

Boulder's most elegant hotel is the **Hotel Boulderado,** tel. (303) 442-4344 or (800) 433-4344, made famous in song and story (John Prine sings about the prerestoration days, "at the dark end of the hall"). Built just after the turn of the century and first open for business on New Year's Day, 1909, the hotel underwent renovations in the 1980s and today has over 100 rooms, plus restaurants and convention facilities, while still retaining its early-20th-century feel. Centrally located, the hotel is within easy walking distance of the Pearl Street Mall, The Hill, and the University of Colorado neighborhoods. Doubles start at about $115.

If you're the *Accidental Tourist* type, and would prefer something a little more conventional and less "Boulder-like," you can go with either of the two Marriotts (the **Residence Inn,** tel. 303-449-5545, or the **Courtyard,** tel. 303-440-4700); a **Holiday Inn,** tel. (303) 443-3322 or (800) HOLIDAY; a **Days Inn,** tel. (303) 499-4422 or (800) 325-2525; or the **Clarion Harvest House,** tel. (303) 443-3850 or (800) 252-7466.

Motels

Boulder hosts a large number of motels, some located right along the highways, some tucked up in canyons and hidden in trees, others right downtown. The **Silver Saddle Motel,** tel. (303) 442-8022, claims one of the choicest lodging sites in Boulder. Located on the city's west end, right at the entrance to Boulder Creek Canyon, this unassuming little motel features 32 units, some with kitchenettes; fall asleep to the sound of Boulder Creek tumbling by. Rooms for two start at about $40. A few bends downstream, the **Foot of the Mountain Motel,** tel. (303) 442-5688, also offers quiet, perfectly located rooms starting at about $40.

Another lodge with an ideal location is the **Boulder Mountain Lodge,** tel. (303) 444-0882, located in Four-Mile Canyon just north of Boulder Creek Canyon. Offering motel rooms, kitchenettes, bunkhouse rooms, and campsites, with rates ranging from $50 to $85, Boulder Mountain probably claims the widest range of accommodation options in the area. The motto of **University Inn,** tel. (303) 442-3830 or (800) 258-7917, is "in the center of things," and that's a pretty decent description of its location. With the university directly to the south and the Pearl Street Mall three blocks to the north, this lodge offers excellent access to libraries, shopping, biking, as well as mingling with locals in their own milieu.

In 1985, a classic downtown Boulder Victorian was restored, and the result is the **Pearl Street Inn,** tel. (303) 444-5584. Located at 1820 Pearl, this elegant inn offers private rooms, a restaurant, and full bar, as well as meeting rooms for up to 30 and banquet facilities for 150. The **Arapahoe Lodge,** 2020 Arapahoe, tel. (303) 449-7550, is one of the most centrally located inns in town—between the university and the Pearl Street Mall. Rooms are nice and reasonably priced.

If you're just passing through and you don't want to get off the beaten track, you've got several options right on US 36 (28th St. through town). The **Super 8,** 970 28th St., tel. (303) 443-7800 or (800) 525-2149, offers rooms starting at $50. Doubles at the **Golden Buff Best Western,** 1725 28th St., tel. (303) 442-7450 or (800) 999-BUFF, start at about $60.

Hostels

The **Boulder International Youth Hostel,** tel. (303) 442-0522, is at 1107 12th St. on The Hill just a couple blocks west of campus. The office for **American Youth Hostels, Inc.** is in Boulder at 1058 13th St., tel. (303) 442-1166.

Bed and Breakfast

Downtown at 2151 Arapahoe, near both the university and the Pearl Street Mall, the **Briar Rose Bed and Breakfast,** tel. (303) 442-3007, has 11 rooms in a secluded old home, and you can either lose yourself in privacy or join other guests around the fire or on the sunporch. Rooms run $100-145.

Camping and RVing

Boulder is virtually surrounded by campgrounds—or at least national forest lands where you can camp anywhere anyway. In addition, two state parks, **Eldorado Canyon** and **Golden Gate Canyon,** are within short drives of town. And, perhaps most spectacular of all, **Rocky Mountain National Park** is only about 45 minutes away.

Kelly-Dahl Campground is one of many in the nearby Roosevelt National Forest. With 46 units, running water and pit toilets, trailheads leading up onto the Continental Divide, as well as some of the most stunning vistas on the Front Range, this is a choice little campground. You'll find it three miles south of Nederland on CO 119—$7 per night. Other Roosevelt National Forest campgrounds include **Camp Dick,** in the Middle St. Vrain Recreation Area; **Olive Ridge,** about 15 miles south of Estes Park on North St. Vrain Creek next to Rocky Mountain National Park; **Peaceful Valley,** on CO 72 southwest of Lyon; and **Rainbow Lakes** and **Pawnee,** north on CO 72 just north of Nederland. For more information on camping in Roosevelt National Forest, stop by the district ranger station in Boulder at 2995 Baseline Rd., Room 16, or phone (303) 444-6001.

Golden Gate Canyon State Park, just off CO 119 south of Nederland, offers camping for all tastes. **Reverend Ridge** touts over 100 sites with hookups; **Aspen Meadows** has nearly three dozen tent-only sites, with some 30 backcountry sites scattered throughout the park (which features over 50 miles of hiking trails). In addition, the park offers stream and lake fishing (check out the rainbows in the pond near the visitor center—sorry, no fishing allowed there), and stunning Front-Range scenery. For maps and information, phone Golden Gate Canyon State Park at (303) 592-1502.

Rocky Mountain National Park offers thousands of square miles of camping, hiking, and backpacking, with entrances on both the west (Grand Lake) and east (Estes Park) sides. See the section on the park in the North Central Colorado chapter.

Closer to town (five miles up Boulder Creek Canyon), **Boulder Mountain Lodge,** tel. (303) 444-0882, offers creek-side tent and RV sites (in addition to the motel—see above).

FOOD

Start Me Up

Dot's, tel. (303) 449-1323, at 799 Pearl St. in an old gas station just west of the mall, has the look and feel of a classic greasy-spoon-type dive, yet true to Boulder form, this little place offers its own interpretation of tradition: It specializes in soy and other vegetarian products, including tofu, and the chai tea is as popular as the coffee. An excellent place to see who crawls out of the woodwork on Saturday and Sunday mornings, Dot's serves omelettes, eggs and grits, huevos rancheros, cinnamon rolls, and muffins; for lunch try the burrito, stir-fry, or black-bean chili.

Another Boulder breakfast restaurant with an atmosphere all its own is the **Last American Diner,** tel. (303) 447-1997, also known as the LA Diner. With the hostess and waitresses on roller skates, and the jukebox pumping out songs like "Blueberry Hill" and "In the Still of the Night" this retro-diner on US 36 (28th St.) just north of the corner of Canyon serves standard American fare (you were expecting maybe couscous?) at very reasonable rates. Hours are Mon.-Thurs. 6:30 a.m.-10 p.m., Friday 6:30 a.m.-3 a.m., Saturday 8 a.m.-3 a.m., and Sunday 8 a.m.-10 p.m.

For a good morning espresso jolt, try **Buchanan's Coffee Pub,** 1301 Pennsylvania (on the hill just across Broadway from the university), tel. (303) 440-5905, or **Espresso Roma,** up the street at 1101 13th, tel. (303) 442-5011.

You'll also find plenty of cafes and coffee shops on the Pearl Street Mall. A personal favorite is **Trident Booksellers and Cafe,** 940 Pearl St., tel. (303) 443-3133, which, as the name would suggest, is bookstore and coffee shop under one roof. The **New York Delicatessen,** 1117 Pearl, tel. (303) 449-5161, serves everything from potato latkes to lox and bagels to matzo brie. The deli also serves lunch—sandwiches, calzone, and tofu stir fry.

Inexpensive to Moderate

Visitors who truly want a taste of Boulder need to hit the **Chautauqua Dining Hall,** tel. (303) 440-3776, in the shadows of the Flatirons at Chautauqua Park. Eat inside in the high-ceilinged dining room, as light slants in onto the polished hardwood floors, or, if you prefer, dine on the porch overlooking the park's lawns, wildflowered meadows, and rocky cliffs. As if that weren't enough, the food perfectly reflects much that is Boulder: For breakfast ($3-7), try a hearty helping of pancakes (blueberry or buttermilk), French toast, or an omelette (yolkless eggs, tofu, and non-dairy soy cheese are available as substitutions); if you prefer something lighter, try the fresh fruit bowl or yogurt and granola. For lunch, the Chautauqua specializes in healthful variations of old favorites—turkey burgers, spinach and pasta salads, quiches, and soups; lunches run $4-7. To get there, take Baseline Rd. toward the Flatirons and watch for the signs to the park. Expect to wait a bit, as the place is popular, but it's difficult to imagine a more pleasant spot to wait for a good meal.

Another place that captures much of the Boulder mystique—and is an extremely popular gathering for locals as well—is **Walnut Brewery,** tel. (303) 447-1345, at 1123 Walnut. Boulder's first brew pub, the Walnut serves beer made on the premises, as well as a wide range of meals, from typical pub fare (fish and chips, bratwurst, burgers) to full-course dinner entrees, pastas, soups, and salads—a favorite is the duck enchiladas. To wash down with the various beers, the Walnut also serves a variety of appetizers, including beer-shrimp boil and crab cakes. Of course the real attraction here is the beer. Ranging from light ales and wheat beers to porters and stouts, the brew ranks right up there with the best from other microbreweries. Try a

pint of Buffalo Gold; or get a sampler: Taste six beers for about $5.

Speaking of beer, Boulder is home not only to a brewpub but a microbrewery as well. The **Boulder Beer** tasting room and small restaurant, tel. (303) 444-8448, serves beer-cheese soup, salads, sandwiches, and burgers, Mon.-Fri. 11 a.m.-11 p.m. Take Valmont Rd. to Wilderness Place and go south; you can't miss the brewery.

The James Pub and Grille, 1922 13th St., tel. (303) 449-1922, is as close as you're going to get to a traditional Irish pub on the Rockies' Front Range. Specializing in corned beef and cabbage, but serving a variety of other Irish dishes as well, The James, just off the Pearl Street Mall, also features an outstanding selection of British-Isles beers on tap. Dinners run $5-14. Friday and Saturday nights, The James hosts live music, usually in the acoustic/folk vein and with an Irish bent, and on Tuesday nights there's an all-out traditional Irish jam, when anywhere from 12 to 45 musicians circle up their chairs and play whatever moves them—if you've got an instrument, join in, or just keep time by tapping a spoon on your glass. Music generally starts around 9 p.m.

Pasta fans swear the best pasta in town can be found at **Pasta Jay's,** tel. (303) 444-5800, at 925 Pearl. Pizzas, pastas, and other Italian specialties (eggplant parmigiana, for example) run $5-8; sandwiches are about $4. When weather permits, sit outside on the patio.

If Jay's is too crowded, try **Old Chicago,** 1102 Pearl on the Pearl Street Mall, tel. (303) 443-5031, which also serves good Italian food—pastas, pizzas, and sandwiches. Old Chicago is especially popular among the younger crowd, who appreciate the restaurant's huge beer selection. Also on Pearl Street Mall is the **Boulder Cafe,** tel. (303) 444-4884, an unpretentious little restaurant and bar where you can get everything from burgers to pizzas to entrees such as prime rib and shrimp. Excellent homemade soups, and lots of microbrews and espresso drinks. Dinner can run $4-14.

For health and vegetarian food, try **The Harvest Restaurant and Bakery,** 1738 Pearl, tel. (303) 449-6223. This place has Boulder written all over it, from the fried brown rice (it's a main dish) to broccoli and walnut casseroles, scrambled tofu, vegetarian enchiladas, and tempeh burgers. Dinners run about $4-8.

From its modest beginnings as a hamburger stand on The Hill in 1972, **Nancy's,** 825 Walnut, tel. (303) 449-8402, has grown into a full-fledged restaurant with an extremely loyal following. Breakfast (omelettes, eggs Benedict, blintzes, etc.) run $3.50-6; lunch (salads, homemade soups, pastas, and vegetable dishes), $6-7; and dinners (steaks, veal, fowl—including quail—pastas, and salads), $7-18.

Another popular restaurant is **Rudi's,** 4720 Table Mesa Dr., tel. (303) 494-5858, which serves a variety of international vegetarian dishes made with local organic produce and range-fed chicken. There doesn't seem to be too much debate about where the best hamburgers in town are. **Tom's Tavern,** 1047 Pearl, tel. (303) 442-9363, serves a variety of burgers and sandwiches ($4-6), with excellent people-watching window booths and tables.

When the Boss is Buying

The **Flagstaff House,** tel. (303) 442-4640, on Flagstaff Mountain overlooking town, is one of the most famous and elegant restaurants in the entire Boulder-Denver area, popular for high-class special occasions. In addition to the over three dozen main courses offered (including elk, Maine lobster, and pheasant breast), the Flagstaff goes above and beyond the call of duty in presenting a huge array of gourmet side dishes and other treats, from the rattlesnake appetizers to the cappuccino-chocolate-mousse dessert; entrees run $20-35. Those on special diets can call ahead to have the staff cook up custom gourmet meals. Reservations requested. Take Baseline Rd. up past Chautauqua, and watch for the sign on your right.

For excellent Italian food, try **Antica Roma,** on the Pearl Street Mall at 1308 Pearl, tel. (303) 442-0378. Not only is the food excellent here, but the owners go to great lengths to create a true Roman ambience: It truly feels like a converted farmhouse, with a tile floor, faux-brick-and-plaster walls, and Italian graffiti visible through the dim light. Veal, chicken, and pasta dishes run $9-18.

Mexican Food

Two places seem regularly to vie for most votes for Boulder's favorite Mexican food. The **Rio Grande Mexican Restaurant,** tel. (303) 444-3690, just east of the mall at 1709 Pearl St., offers excellent food and service at reasonable prices—dinner plates and combinations run $6-8, and lunch specials are $4-6. A bonus: 99-cent lunch-special margaritas. Note: A second Rio Grande Mexican Restaurant is in Fort Collins, at 150 North College Ave.

The Rio Grande's competition is just up the street at 1043 Pearl. **Juanita's,** tel. (303) 449-5273, also offers excellent food and service in the same price range, in the same low-key atmosphere. Differences? The Rio Grande doesn't serve chimichangas; Juanita's does. Juanita's doesn't serve 99-cent margaritas; the Rio Grande does. Hell, try them both.

Still another excellent Mexican restaurant is **Pablo's,** tel. (303) 442-7512, combining Mexican and Central American cooking with the Boulder health consciousness (including what they claim is the only no-smoking bar in town). Pablo's uses black instead of the conventional pinto for their refried beans, and strict vegetarians will delight in the soy cheese. Entrees run $6-10. The restaurant is at the corner of Baseline and 28th streets.

For good Mexican food in a more cantina-style setting, try **Jose Muldoon's,** 38th and Arapahoe, tel. (303) 449-4543. Serving Mexican and Southwestern food, Muldoon's prides itself on its chimichangas, cilantro chicken, and fajitas, as well as its happy hours and margaritas (enjoyed during nice weather on the patio). The restaurant is also open for Sunday brunch.

Outside Town, but Worth the Drive

A half-hour out of Boulder in Nederland, **Neapolitan's,** tel. (303) 258-7313, is a small unassuming Italian restaurant. From the homemade rolls and salad dressings to the huge portions of lasagna, vegetarian combos, and other pasta specials, this fare is guaranteed not to disappoint. Complete dinners and pizzas are $5-11. All food can be ordered to go.

Just a few miles up Boulder Creek Canyon is one of Boulder's more popular and, well, unique restaurants. **The Red Lion Inn,** tel. (303) 442-9368, specializes in wild game (elk, caribou, buffalo, pheasant, and others), as well as in presentation (many of the dishes are prepared table-side). Dinners run $10-25, but early-bird (of course, pun intended) specials ($7.95) are offered Mon.-Fri. 5-6:15 p.m., Saturday 4:30-5:45 p.m., and Sunday 4-6:15 p.m.

In Gold Hill about 10 miles west of and 3,200 feet above town is the **Gold Hill Inn,** tel. (303) 443-6461, which is somewhat of an institution. It's been written up in several national magazines and has achieved a reputation for huge and delicious dinners. The menu changes nightly, but entrees may include roast duck, paella, or venison; the price is fixed at $21.

Farmers Market
In the summer (through October) on Saturday mornings 8 a.m.-1 p.m., 35-40 local farmers set up stands in Boulder City Park, at 13th and Canyon, and sell their wares directly to the consuming public. Whether it's apples or apricots, pears or peaches, honey or honeydew, these fruits, vegetables, and other products are fresh and pesticide-free, and this is the place to stock up. Growers are required to display explanations of their farming methods, and most will gladly discuss their theories with you.

Grocery Stores
Alfalfa's, at the corner of Arapahoe and Broadway, tel. (303) 442-0082, is an organic-new-age grocery store and deli that carries everything: organically grown fruits and vegetables, pet health food, biodegradable paper towels, dairy-less bakery items, and "cruelty-free" cosmetics. Alfalfa's also has a fish market and deli, yogurt-and-smoothie bar, flower shop, bookstore, the town's best selection of mineral waters, spritzers, and juices. It's open 8 a.m.-10 p.m. Mon.-Sat. and 8 a.m.-9 p.m. Sunday. Alfafa's offers a five percent discount to seniors.

ENTERTAINMENT

Boulder's a college town, which means it's a young town, which means there's usually a lot going on—from poetry readings to head-banging rock 'n' roll, from gallery openings to outdoor jazz. The best sources for what's happening are *The Colorado Daily,* the newspaper of the University of Colorado (available free around town); *Friday,* the supplement to Friday's *Daily Camera* (Boulder's daily newspaper; available in

racks around town); *Westword,* Denver's free weekly alternative paper; as well as the Denver dailies, the *Post* and the *Rocky Mountain News.*

You can count on many clubs in Boulder booking quality acts regularly, and there's certain to be music to suit just about every taste. A favorite is **Tulagi,** on The Hill at 1129 13th St., tel. (303) 442-1369. This Boulder institution, having survived since the '60s, has featured hundreds of big-name acts and can always be relied on for a distinctly Boulder evening, even if it's just a lineup of local college bands. Other clubs and theaters regularly booking live music are **The Catacombs,** 2115 13th St. in the Hotel Boulderado, tel. (303) 443-0486; and the **Boulder Theater,** 2030 14th Street, tel. (303) 444-3600.

If you have something a little tamer in mind, check out the Mezzanine at the **Hotel Boulderado,** tel. (303) 442-4344, an elegant place to dig some cool jazz—located at 13th and Spruce. **The James Pub and Grille,** 1922 13th St., tel. (303) 449-1922, regularly features live Irish music (to go with the Guinness on draft and the specialty—corned beef and cabbage). Tuesday night, local folk musicians descend on The James, circle up their chairs, and jam—as many as 45 musicians at a time.

Another classic Boulder bar is the **West End Tavern,** tel. (303) 444-3535. Now, even if the West End hadn't been named "best neighborhood bar" by both the Boulder *Daily Camera* and the Denver *Post,* this would still be one of the best spots in town to go sip a cold one. On a warm afternoon, it doesn't get much better than sitting up on the roof, with one of Boulder's best views of the Flatirons, and listening to some live music with friends while you work through a Boulder Pale. Located just above the Pearl Street Mall, between 9th and 10th streets, **Buchanan's Coffee Pub,** 1301 Pennsylvania on the Hill, features live folk, jazz, and blues most nights of the week.

For those who like to kill two birds with one stone—eat and be entertained at the same time—there's the **Boulder Dinner Theater,** tel. (303) 449-6000. Summer stock actors, based around the country, perform well-known and lesser-known plays and musicals. Tickets run $22-28.

Other typically Boulder ways to spend the evening include attending the **Shakespeare Festival** (see "Calendar," following), poetry readings, public lectures and workshops, film festivals, and even open-mike nights. Even a simple evening stroll down the Pearl Street Mall guarantees surprises and no small amount of entertainment (see "Shopping," following).

CALENDAR

Boulder's annual events—much like the town itself—are incredibly diverse, from steeply serious to downright silly, and some of them offer a little bit of both.

Kinetic Sculpture Challenge

Another only-in-Boulder attraction, this parade and "race" on Boulder Reservoir in early May combines equal parts competitiveness, engineering savvy, and silliness. A bizarre array of human-powered vehicles tread and float (and often stall and sink) 'cross land and water before thousands of cheering spectators, many of whom have taken advantage of the bountiful food and drink booths available both at the pre-event parade at the Pearl Street Mall and the race at the lake. For more information, phone (303) 444-5600.

Fourth of July

From fireworks to Frisbee, Boulder's Fourth of July events offer something for every taste and mood. One of the country's largest "Ultimate Frisbee" competitions (a non-contact team sport combining a bit of basketball, football, and soccer), usually runs three days around the Fourth; phone (303) 443-6343 for more information. Over 50 years old, the annual Independence Day Celebration at Folsom Field features the Boulder Summer Concert Band, a sing-along, and fireworks. You can also see fireworks over Barker Meadow Reservoir in Nederland. **Note:** Fireworks in the mountains, particularly in the forested areas, are always subject to fire conditions. Recent drought years have seen the cancellations of many Colorado fireworks displays.

Shakespeare Festival

Founded in 1957, Boulder's Shakespeare Festival generally runs from late June through mid-August and tackles the full range of the bard's work—comedy, history, tragedy—with varying degrees of success. The summer production of *As You Like It* (1990) was particularly well received, as was a recent *King Lear* and *Richard III*. Part of what makes this festival so special is the theater itself: the Mary Rippon Outdoor Theater on the University of Colorado campus. Surrounded by ivy-covered stone buildings, the amphitheater and stage send even the most cynical play-goer back to 17th-century Stratford-on-Avon. Tickets to the festival range about $12-25. For information and reservations, phone (303) 492-8181.

Colorado Music Festival

Very highly regarded—both locally and outside the area—Boulder's classical music festival runs for six weeks, from mid-June to early August. Attracting some of the biggest names in the profession—musicians and conductors—the festival typically includes some two dozen concerts, with music by everyone from Bach, Beethoven, and Shostakovich, to Ravel, Bernstein, and Gershwin.

As if the music weren't enough, the concerts are performed in Chautauqua Auditorium, where the shadow-of-the-Flatirons setting, combined with the turn-of-the-century structures, makes for the ideal concert locale.

For information on the Colorado Music Festival, phone (303) 449-1397. See also the accompanying special topic.

Gilbert and Sullivan Festival

For music lovers whose tastes run a little less *profundo* than the classical music of the Colorado Music Festival, Boulder also offers Gilbert and Sullivan. Begun in 1980, the fest runs matinees and evening shows through July. For information, phone (303) 492-4205.

Colorado Indian Market

Taking place in early or mid-July each year, the Colorado Indian Market draws artists, dancers, storytellers, and other craftspeople from tribes throughout the United States, as well as South

THE COLORADO MUSIC FESTIVAL

Every summer for about seven weeks, the Colorado Music Festival (CMF) fills Chautauqua Auditorium in Boulder with fine music and other artistic projects. Inside this century-old, barnlike structure with bare cement floors, one can hear the rich tones of Mozart, Beethoven, Vivaldi, Mahler, and others. The bare wooden walls inside Chautauqua make for excellent acoustics because, according to conductor Giora Bernstein, the wood is a "live material" and "resonates the sound." As *New York* magazine put it, "Boulder, by any standard, is a fulfilling place, but Giora Bernstein and his brilliantly planned festival make the place extraordinary."

On Thursday and Friday nights, the Colorado Festival Orchestra (CFO) plays; on Sunday nights the Festival Chamber Orchestra plays. World-renowned guest artists are often featured with both the philharmonic and chamber orchestras. Tuesday nights are for the Celebrity Series, solo and ensemble performances by CFO musicians and guest artists.

The Colorado Music Festival also offers a special humanities project each year: a series of concerts, lectures, and films focused on a central theme. Projects have included La Belle Epoche—Paris 1885-1914; Stravinsky—The Late Works; WW II through McCarthyism; Music of the Sixties; and Celebration: The Arts of Yamagata, Japan. A recent series included a tribute to the 50th anniversary of the founding of the United Naitons.

The Chautauqua Auditorium sits at the base of a mountain and is elevated just high enough to provide a panoramic view of the town. In front of the hall is a long, lush, sloping lawn, perfect for enjoying the fresh air and sunshine, and maybe even a picnic, before a concert. In addition to the auditorium concerts, the CMF sponsors several free outdoor events, including a Young People's Concert and a Fourth of July Pops Concert.

The CMF is strictly a summer orchestra made up of musicians from all over the world chosen by Bernstein. "This is a very intensive program," says Bernstein. "There's music going on all the time—mornings, afternoons, evenings. It's a pace that would be difficult to keep on a year-round basis. In a concentrated summer, it's very exciting."

Maestro Bernstein's intensity has delivered results. His orchestra has won two awards from the American Society of Composers, Authors, and Publishers, as well as the 1988 Governor's Award for Excellence in the Arts. In 1994, they won *Westword's* "Best Classical Festival Award." CFO music has also been featured on National Public Radio and on European radio.

Chautauqua Auditorium is located at Baseline and 9th. For schedule and ticket information, write 1525 Spruce St., Suite 101, Boulder, CO 80302, or phone (303) 449-1397.

—Thomas Owen Meinen

and Central America. Jan Esty, the original organizer of the event—which first came to Boulder in 1982—feels since there were no borders in the Americas before it was colonized, all New World natives should be allowed to participate. The inside scoop: If you're looking for art—from sand paintings and sculpture to jewelry and basketry—you'll get better deals on the show's last day, usually a Sunday. The selection won't be as good, but artisans, not excited about packing up their work and moving it, will be more inclined to bargain.

For current information on the Indian Market, phone (303) 447-9967.

SHOPPING

Pearl Street Mall

Boulder's famous Pearl Street Mall is certainly as much an attraction as it is a place to go shopping, for here's where you can see Boulder at its most crazy, colorful, and cosmopolitan, hip, happy, and unhomogenous. Join the parade of street musicians and jugglers, tourists from Tennessee, kids, families, and local students—everyone's having a good time. And if you get tired of strolling the five-block area, there are several cafes, restaurants, bars, and snack shops—many with sidewalk seating—where you can rest and refuel while the mall continues to buzz around you. Even in the evening after the shops close, street activities continue and the strollers keep strolling.

Among the more interesting shops are **Old Tibet** at 948 Pearl, a small import store with authentic clothing, jewelry, and other items from Tibet and Nepal. In the same building, **Narayan's Gateway to Nepal,** tel. (303) 440-0331, specializes in treks and tours to Nepal, Tibet, and India—run by native Nepali.

State of the Arts, a large import and craft store, stocks everything from Grateful Dead T-shirts to African and South American jewelry and clothing. **El Loro Jewelry and Clog Company** is the closest thing I've seen in a long time to a late '60s "head shop" (a true remembrance of things passed), selling incense, jewelry, T-shirts, and, yes, clogs; my only question is, Where're the black-light posters? Across the street, **Ecology House,** much more than a faddy I-heart-baby-seals, limousine-liberal store, carries *good* books on survival (personal and environmental), posters, T-shirts, jewelry, bumper stickers, and lots of stuff for kids, with 10% of each sale going to environmental organizations. **Boulder Arts and Crafts Cooperative** is a large shop with jewelry, pottery, woodcarvings, weavings, stained glass, etc. by local artisans. A couple of fun novelty shops include **Golden Oldies,** which carries a fine selection of funky vintage men's and women's clothing, from ties and hats to vests and dresses; and **Into the Wind,** which specializes in, well, wind toys—kites, wind chimes, weather vanes, Frisbees. Be sure to check out **Peppercorn,** too, which carries a huge array of gourmet kitchenware, as well as zillions of cookbooks and a huge selection of coffee beans. **The Page** sells great children's books, carrying everything from Dr. Seuss to international mythology retold for kids.

Rue Morgue Mystery Bookshop carries *only* mystery/murder/detective novels (the name is from a story by Edgar Alan Poe, the grandfather of the mystery novel). Not only does the little shop carry books by mainstream authors (Raymond Chandler, Tony Hillerman, Robert Parker, etc.), but it stocks hundreds of titles by lesser-known writers as well—both new and used books.

If you're looking for food on the mall, you don't have to look far, but you do have to be able to make decisions—because there's a *lot* from which to choose, from Mexican to Chinese, pasta to popcorn. There's also a crepe cart, a vegetarian takeout place, and a pizza-by-the-slice shop. The **Trident Cafe,** just west of the mall, is an Old-World-style coffeehouse, serving espressos and other coffees, as well as pastries. Adjoining the Trident is **Bookseller Used Books** (you can walk between the two without stepping out onto the sidewalk), lending the place a legitimate literary air. **Public restrooms** are located about mid-mall, at the corner of Pearl and 13th.

The Hill

At 13th and College just west of the campus, the Hill is a collage of cafes, taverns, boutiques, and used-book and record stores. Bordering one of the city's densest concentrations of student housing, The Hill is a way hip hangout:

the Boulder courthouse, just off Pearl Street Mall

Coeds pierced and tatooed linger solo over cappuccinos and Camus; Lycra-shorted frat studs pound beers and trade insider information on papers in their fraternity files; transients hit up passers-by for spare change; freshmen, always walking a few steps ahead, give their parents the grand tour; and the music, incense, and even patchouli oil waft from open doorways. A must for anyone visiting Boulder.

Particularly impressive are the book and record stores (three of each lie within a few hundred yards). Check out **Albums on the Hill,** 1128 13th St., specializing in rare albums; when you see some of the price tags you'll wish you hadn't donated your Herman's Hermits records to your little sister. While you're at it, wander into **Rock and Roll Posters,** 1091 13th St., or **Art to Go,** 1118 13th, for excellent full-sized rock, film, and celebrity posters and prints. For books of all kinds, as well as University of Colorado mementos, be sure to hit the university bookstore at the corner of College and Broadway.

If the youthful nature of The Hill gets to be too much, take time out at **Kinsley & Co.,** 1155 13th Street—not only does this shop sell upscale men's and women's clothing, but they also have a fly-fishing department with Orvis gear and other equipment up-nose from the bait plunker. On the corner of 13th and Broadway, **Buchanan's Coffee Pub** is one of the best places in town to cop a cappuccino and read the morning news, while eavesdropping on what the local students are up to (and were the night before). Around the corner, at 1322 College, **Brillig Works Café and Bakery** also serves cappuccino and other gourmet coffees, as well as dynamite baked goods and vegetarian specials—with background music from the Dead to Miles Davis to Brahms.

SERVICES

The **Boulder Police Department** can be reached by calling (303) 441-4444 (911 in emergencies). The offices of the **Boulder County Sheriff** are at 1777 6th St., tel. (303) 441-4444. **Boulder Community Hospital** is at 1100 Balsam (corner of N. Broadway), tel. (303) 440-

2037 (emergency care) or 440-2273 (hospital switchboard). The central **post office** is at 1905 15th, tel. (303) 938-1100.

Recycling

Drop off aluminum, glass, newspaper, and plastic at the three **King Soopers** (6550 Lookout Rd., 3600 Table Mesa Rd., and 1650 30th St.) and at both **Safeways** (4800 E. Baseline and 2798 Arapahoe). For information, phone **Recycle Boulder** at (303) 441-4234.

INFORMATION

If you drive into Boulder from Denver, you'll notice the Boulder information kiosk on the hill south of town. Stop in for maps, brochures, current papers and newsletters, directions to many of the area's highlights, and listings of events. The central office of the **Boulder Convention and Visitors Bureau** is at 2440 Pearl (corner of Folsom),tel. (303) 442-2911.

The Boulder **public library** can be found at 1000 Canyon Dr.; phone (303) 441-3111 for hours and information. The historical library is at 1125 Pine, tel. (303) 441-3110.

For **road and weather information,** phone (303) 639-1234 (I-25 and east) or 639-1111 (Denver and west). Tune to Boulder's public radio station, KGNU, at 88.5 FM.

Virtual Boulder

Electronic information on Boulder (via the Boulder Chamber of Commerce), including restaurant menus and lodging specs, may be accessed at bcn.boulder.co.us

Bookstores

With one of the highest per-capita number of bookstores in the West (the phone book lists over 30), Boulder could, and does, entertain bibliophiles for days on end—it would take you that long to make the rounds from the usual chains, Waldenbooks and B. Dalton, to shops specializing in rare books or politics. **Stage House Books and Prints** would be an excellent place to start. This two-story shop on Pearl, a block above the mall, is a used-book lover's dream. Not only will you find every kind of book imaginable, but there are chairs for plunking down and actually *reading,* while books are literally *everywhere*—strewn on the stairs, cluttered on the countertops, lined and piled up on the floor. Stage House features a special section of first editions and signed books.

Almost directly across the street you'll find the **Rue Morgue Mystery Bookshop** and **The Bookseller** (adjacent to the Trident Café). On The Hill, **Aion Bookshop** stocks used and out-of-print books on most subjects, with a focus on literature, science, and the humanities. The **Boulder Bookstore,** with stores in both the Pearl Street Mall and the Village Shopping Center, carries a wide range of books, with lots on Colorado and the West. **Left Hand Books and Records,** 1200 Pearl, carries books of political interest, specializing in feminism and other progressive issues.

Naropa Institute

Offering an educational and intellectual environment alternative to traditional universities, Naropa is a fully accredited undergraduate and graduate school inspired by a 5th-12th century Buddhist university in India. Though the general tenor and underlying philosophy of the school reflects its Buddhist model, the courses are non-sectarian and wide ranging, with a general emphasis in arts, humanities, and social sciences. In addition to the classes and seminars available to students, many programs and events—from poetry readings to deep-ecology workshops—open their doors to the public. Semi-regular faculty members include Gary Snyder and Allen Ginsberg.

For more information, phone (303) 444-0202.

Boulder Graduate School

This is a small nonprofit institution offering a variety of workshops and seminars, most of which focus on holistic living and peaceful coexistence—with lovers, neighbors, the environment, and the Earth. Catalogs are available free in racks around town. For more information, phone (303) 444-1946.

Boulder Peace Institute

Offering a rotating series of lectures, seminars, and concentrated one- and two-week workshops, the Boulder Peace Institute is dedicated to resolving conflict in all aspects of our lives—

from personal to global levels. Phone (303) 444-4150 for more information.

Further Reading

Anyone who's poked around in any one of Boulder's many bookstores can tell you there's a lot written about the town and area. For starters, check out *A Look at Boulder, From Settlement to City,* a thorough and illustrated history by Phyllis Smith (Pruett Publishing Company).

TRANSPORTATION

If you're coming into Boulder via Denver International Airport, you can get here quite easily. **Boulder Airporter** offers door-to-door service for $14 each way; phone (303) 321-3222.

Getting around in Boulder is quite easy, what with the excellent public transportation system, the fine network of bike trails, and the straightforward way in which the town's laid out. For starters, remember the numbered streets run parallel to the mountains—north to south—as do Broadway, which runs along the west end of Boulder between town and the mountains, and Folsom, running pretty much through the center of town. (US 36 through town is 28th Street.) The main drags running east to west, crossing the numbered streets, are Baseline, Arapahoe, Canyon, Pearl, and Valmont. Iris Avenue, which runs east from Broadway, becomes the Diagonal Hwy., CO 119, to Niwot.

In addition, **The Ride!,** Denver's bus system, offers regular service to Boulder (60 cents, 50 cents for seniors) as well as a depot at 14th and Walnut; phone (303) 299-6000 for route and schedule information. The **HOP,** Boulder's shuttle service that connects downtown, the university, and the Hill, runs weekdays 7 a.m.-7 p.m. with buses every 10 minutes. Rides are 25 cents. For information, phone (303) 447-8282.

For 24-hour taxi service, phone **Boulder Yellow Cab** at (303) 442-2277.

NEDERLAND

Colorado 119 winds west out of Boulder into Boulder Creek Canyon. Just a few miles out of town, you enter Roosevelt National Forest, and at Nederland, 17 miles out of Boulder, the road tees into CO 72. From there, you can either turn north toward Estes Park and Rocky Mountain National Park or turn south to Central City and Black Hawk.

Nederland (pop. 1,200; elev. 8,236 feet) is a quirky little town in three parts: the funky, one-block old town, with a natural-foods store, gift shop, and a couple of cafes; the restored old town, with restaurants and liquor stores; and a new shopping center with large grocery store, video store, and Mail Boxes, Etc.

Barker Meadow Reservoir is a stone's throw from town and is a favorite fishing lake (stocked regularly). No camping or boating allowed. Public parking and restrooms can be found in the center of town at the junction of CO 119 and CO 72. **Chipeta Park** behind the shopping center has a nice playground and picnic area. Next to the lodge, in an old railroad car, is **Happy Trails Bicycle Shop,** where you can rent and buy mountain bikes and get information and maps on cycling in the area.

Nederland Practicalities

You can stay in Nederland at the **Lodge at Nederland,** tel. (303) 258-9463 or (800) 279-9463, a brand new log inn right off the highway. Doubles run about $85. The **Nederland International Hostel,** tel. (303) 258-9231, offers inexpensive dorm-style accommodations; call for rates and reservations. For a great place to get your morning going, stop in at **Acoustic Coffee,** tel. (303) 258-3209, a "community coffeehouse" right downtown on First St., the only coffee shop I've seen where you can also pick up a new set of banjo or mandolin strings. Live acoustic (of course!) music most evenings at 8. **Neopolitan's Italian Restaurant,** tel. (303) 258-7313, 1 W. First St., serves excellent lasagna, pizzas, and sandwiches.

South of Nederland, at Rollinsville, the **Stage Stop Inn Restaurant,** tel. (303) 258-3270, is a classic roadhouse catering mostly to locals. Stop in for a burger, chicken sandwich, or homemade soup ($4-8). Play a game of shuffleboard, and check out one of the best jukeboxes around, with everything from Jimi Hendrix to Flatt and Scruggs.

CENTRAL CITY AND BLACK HAWK

Long known as the home of the Central City Opera, attracting well-known performers and discriminating fans since 1932, Central City and Black Hawk recently underwent a serious makeover that has greatly affected the area's complexion as it enters its third century: Legalized gambling came to the two communities in October of 1991. Though maximum bets stand at only $5, and gaming is limited to blackjack, poker, and slots, the new diversion has already divided locals and thrown a bizarre variable at real estate. Property values skyrocketed as soon as the measure passed (summer, 1990), casinos went up seemingly overnight (as of April 1993, there were 17 casinos in Central City and 21 in Black Hawk), and the atmosphere of the area became one of excitement mixed with general chaos.

Whatever the result, gambling is guaranteed to draw even greater numbers of travelers to the region, and the two communities, situated in a narrow gulch where traffic posed a problem

well before legal betting showed up, will be forced to rethink local transportation, as well as housing and other sundry business concerns.

HISTORY

When gold was first discovered in Gregory Gulch in 1859, word spread quickly to the gold camps of Auraria and Denver City, where disgruntled miners cursed the "Pikes Peak Hoax." Many of them immediately headed for the hills, and soon the Central City area was teeming with newly hopeful prospectors. Horace Greeley, the New York *Tribune* editor, researching a piece on the West's goldfields, visited the camp and was given a tour by a group of miners. Unbeknownst to Greeley, the men had "salted" a placer mine by shooting gold dust into it with a shotgun. Greeley's subsequent report dramatically increased East Coast interest in the area, and soon even more miners poured into the gulch.

*downtown
Central City*

Originally, Gregory Gulch was dotted with a number of small camps, including Gregory Point, Mountain City, Black Hawk, and Nevadaville. Soon, though, Central City, named for its location about midway up the gulch, became the hub of the area's action, informally incorporating some of the other camps. Greeley, in addition to writing about the easily extractable gold, described the camps and the miners themselves: "I doubt there is as yet a table or chair in these diggings . . . the entire population sleep in tents or under pine boughs."

Between 1859 and 1867, the gulch produced $9 million in gold, earning it the nickname, "The richest square mile on earth." During this time, engineers perfected mining techniques, smelters were built in Central City and Black Hawk, and more and more prospectors arrived in the gulch hoping to strike it rich. Central City's mid-1860s population hit 15,000.

From its very beginnings, Central City earned a reputation for being more "cultured" and sophisticated than some of the other mountain mining camps, and its diverse group of miners—Russians, Welshmen, French, Germans, Italians, blacks, among others—lent the little community a cosmopolitan air. In 1861, the Central City Opera House hosted its first production, *Camille,* and throughout the decade the town was well known for its Vaudeville and minstrel shows.

The railroad came to Black Hawk in 1872 and extended to Central shortly thereafter, making the community much more accessible. In 1874, a fire swept through Central City, destroying many buildings, including the opera house, although the theater was rebuilt four years later—with four-foot-thick stone walls—and by the late '70s was attracting some of the biggest names in American theater, including Sarah Bernhardt, Lillian Russell, and Edwin Booth.

Like most other Colorado mining towns, Central City and Black Hawk were all but abandoned by the early 20th century once silver was devalued and production in the gold mines had slowed to almost nothing. The opera house was boarded up. Then in 1932, the newly formed Central City Opera Association pulled down the boards, restored the seats and interior, and reopened the opera house. In honor of the old building's history, the first show put on was, again, *Camille.* The Central City Opera remains one of the town's primary draws.

During the 1950s, Central City was known as a wild and woolly anything-goes outpost town, with more than its share of colorful characters. Among those who showed up to raise hell here were Jack Kerouac and gang. In *On the Road,* Kerouac describes his adventures: "It was a wonderful night. Central City is two miles high; at first you get drunk on the altitude, then you get tired, and there's a fever in your soul. We approached the lights around the opera house down the narrow dark street; then we took a sharp right and hit some old saloons with swinging doors. . . . Beyond the back door was a view of the mountainsides in the moonlight. I let out a yahoo. The night was on."

Through the '60s, '70s, and '80s, Central City continued to draw tourists. In addition to the opera, boosters bragged about the museums, mine tours, and the century-old buildings. And with its proximity to Denver, Central City attracted large numbers of travelers. In fact, during this time, traffic was often bumper to bumper through town in the summer, and on particularly busy days (weekends), cars were often backed up well below town. The little streets and sidewalks, meanwhile, swelled with tourists; the gift and souvenir shops, T-shirt shops, and restaurants packing in camera-toting visitors.

And now, with legalized gambling and increased tourism, the little towns are changing even more. Precisely how and to what degree remains to be seen.

ATTRACTIONS

Gilpin County Historical Museum
Displaying a huge array of authentic items and artifacts from the area's fascinating history, this museum is one of Central City's less touristy attractions. Its rooms represent various eras and themes, including early travel, education, fashion, business, and medicine. In addition, historical photos and miniature reproductions of a Victorian-era mining town combine to give the visitor a very real sense of life in the rough-and-tumble Colorado of the late 19th century.

The museum, at 228 E. High St. (a half block east of Eureka), is open daily 10 a.m.-4 p.m., Memorial Day through Labor Day. Admission is $3. For more information, write Box 244, Central City, CO 80427, or phone (303) 582-5283.

Teller House and Opera House Tour
Tours of the Central City Opera House and adjoining Teller House, at one time one of the West's most luxurious hotels, are offered June through August from late morning to early evening for a small fee. In the bar of the Teller House, you'll see the famous **Face on the Barroom Floor,** painted in 1936 by a Denver journalist.

The tours begin at 120 Eureka St. and take about a half-hour. For exact times, phone (303) 582-3200.

Central City Cemeteries
One way to escape Central City's shameless appeal to tourism is to continue driving straight through town—Lawrence to Eureka to the dirt road—to the pioneer cemeteries that sprawl over the hilltops west of town. Park and wander among the hundreds of plots. Mostly overgrown, and with some of the headstones broken and/or lying on the ground, the plots offer poignant insights into the area's past; note the young ages at which people died here in the late 19th century. Chances are that even if the city sidewalks are packed, you'll be alone up here.

ACCOMMODATIONS

Lodging in Central City and Black Hawk includes the **Golden Gate Casino Bed and Breakfast** (five rooms available), tel. (303) 582-1650, where rates start at about $55; the **Winfield Scott Bed and Breakfast,** tel. (303) 582-3433, doubles starting at about $80 (with a one-bedroom suite available); and the **Carriage House Inn,** tel. (303) 642-3636. The **Gold Dust Lodge,** tel. (303) 582-5415, two miles off US 119, offers doubles for about $45 (including free shuttle service to casinos).

Camping and RVing
A **KOA** campground can be found four miles north of Black Hawk on CO 72; phone (303)

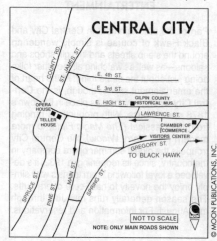

CENTRAL CITY

COUNTY RD
ST. JAMES ST.

E. 4th ST.
E. 3rd ST.

GILPIN COUNTY
E. HIGH ST. HISTORICAL MUS.

OPERA
HOUSE
TELLER
HOUSE

LAWRENCE ST.

CHAMBER OF
COMMERCE
VISITORS CENTER

GREGORY ST.

TO BLACK HAWK

SPRUCE ST.
PINE ST.
MAIN ST.
SPRING ST.

NOT TO SCALE
NOTE: ONLY MAIN ROADS SHOWN

© MOON PUBLICATIONS, INC.

582-9979. There's also camping at **Golden Gate Canyon State Park,** also just north of Black Hawk on CO 72. In addition, the 8,500-acre park offers hiking, horseback riding, and cross-country skiing. For information, phone (303) 592-1502. Also see "Parks and Recreation" under "Boulder," above.

FOOD

The dining scene in Central City and Black Hawk changed considerably when the casinos arrived—essentially, all independent restaurants were offered big bucks to hit the road and make room for the casinos. These days, dining is pretty limited to restaurants in the casinos, many of which offer excellent deals (prime-rib dinner at the Glory Hole for $3.95). A note of caution, though. Most of the deals are offered simply to get you in the door, and few are those who eat and leave without making a few bets on the way in or out; your $3.95 dinner can wind up costing you $15 or $20 before you can say "craps."

One of the restaurants that has managed to escape much of touristy trappings of the area is the **Black Forest Inn,** 260 Gregory St., tel. (303) 279-3333, specializing in Bavarian food and wild game, and which locals regularly cite as the "best in town." Dinners run $8-18.

ENTERTAINMENT

Part of the entertainment in Central City and Black Hawk of course is simply wandering around the steep streets and into gift shops and saloons—as well as watching all the other folks doing just about the same thing. At the heart of the entertainment scene, though, is the **Central City Opera,** which takes place in the town's 1878 opera house. With productions ranging from the classical *(The Magic Flute)* to more modern *(The Merry Widow)*, the Central City troupe is the oldest summer opera company in the country; since its reopening in 1932, it's developed a loyal following, from tourists who simply enjoy the novelty to hard-core opera buffs. The season generally runs mid-July through mid-August. For information and reservations,

face on the barroom floor

write Central City Opera House Association, 621 7th St., Suite 1601, Denver, CO 80293, or phone (303) 292-6500.

CALENDAR

The highlight of Central City's tourist season is the opera, which runs mid-July to mid-August (see above). In addition, there are a number of other festivals of note, some serious, some silly. The **Jazz Festival** takes place in mid-August, while early June marks the **Lou Bunch Days** "Bed Races" (contestants feel like sheet afterwards . . .). For information on annual events in Central City and Black Hawk, contact the Gilpin County Chamber of Commerce, tel. (303) 582-5077.

SERVICES

Phone the **Central City Police** at (303) 582-5411 and the **Gilpin County Sheriff** at (303) 582-5511. The **post office** is on Gregory just east of Spring Street.

Recycling

The closest recycling centers are in **Nederland,** about 25 miles north on CO 72. The **Boulder County Transfer Station** on County Rd. 128 E, tel. (303) 258-7878, takes aluminum, glass, and newspaper, and the **BF Super Foods,** 60 Lakewood Dr., tel. (303) 258-3105, takes aluminum.

INFORMATION

Be sure to stop in at the offices of the **Gilpin County Chamber of Commerce,** located at the east end of town. For information before your visit, write Box 343, Black Hawk, CO 80422, tel. (303) 582-5077, or phone the **Central City Public Relations Office** at (303) 582-

5251. You can also get information about the area by phoning **Central City Public Information** toll-free at (800) 542-2999.

TRANSPORTATION

Central City and Black Hawk are close to the metro Denver area and easily accessible. From Denver, take I-70 or US 6 about 45 miles west and turn north on CO 119 (the turnoff is well marked), and continue for about eight miles; allow 45 minutes to one hour. You can also get there from Boulder by going west on CO 119 and continuing south through Nederland, a distance of about 35 miles; allow 30-45 minutes.

BOOKLIST

In 1989, when I first started seriously researching this book, there weren't all that many others to recommend. The last few years, however, have seen an explosion of books about the state, nearly all of them interesting and valuable to at least some degree. Shelves in Colorado bookstores are packed with books on the state's history, culture, ecology, economy, and everything else imaginable, from hiking and mountain biking to cooking and bed-and-breakfasting. It would be impossible to list them all. I'd suggest, then, taking a look at the list I have assembled here—these are all top-notch publications—but allowing yourself plenty of time to browse in the bookstores you come across on your trip. I also must add that far and away the best place to find books on Colorado and the west, as well as just about every subject that interests you, is the Tattered Cover in Denver. There are two locations: at the Cherry Creek Mall (2955 E. Cherry Creek) and at 16th and Wynkoop in LoDo (see also "Information" under Denver). Caution: Bibliophiles have been known to enter into these stores virtually to disappear, only to reappear at some later date, their arms laden with books, to find their kids grown and their marriages collapsed.

HISTORY

Buchholtz, C.W. *Rocky Mountain National Park: A History.* Boulder: Colorado Associated University Press, 1983. Exhaustive story of the park area, from the Native Americans who once called this region of the Rockies home to National Park designation in 1915 and the problems of overcrowding in the 1970s and '80s. A refreshing blend of academic research and pleasantly readable writing—full of details, anecdotes, and colorful characters.

Bueler, William M. *Roof of the Rockies: A History of Colorado Mountaineering.* Evergreen: Cordillera Press, Inc., 1986. Bueler, who had climbed all of Colorado's "14ers" by 1952, divides Colorado climbing into two periods: exploration and modern mountaineering. Very well written and thorough, with maps, charts, and photos.

Burroughs, John Rolfe. *Steamboat in the Rockies.* Fort Collins: The Old Army Press, 1974. The story of Steamboat Springs, from the discovery of the springs in 1839 to the development of the ski resort in the 1970s—as seen through the loving eyes of a 50-year resident of the Steamboat area. Burroughs, who has written extensively on the west—fiction, nonfiction, and poetry—has won several prestigious awards for his writing and draws on both local lore and published reports in the Routt County Sentinel; the result is a pleasant blend of homespun folksiness and footnotey history.

Conlin, Joseph H. *Bacon, Beans, and Galatines.* Reno: University of Nevada Press, 1988. A well-researched and witty account of "chow" on the western frontier.

Dodds, Joane West, photography by Edwin Lloyd Dodds. *Pueblo: A Pictorial History.* Norfolk, VA: Donning Company, 1982. A coffee table-style book on the history of Pueblo, with excellently detailed text accompanying the photos.

Gilliland, Mary Ellen. *Frisco! A Colorful Colorado Community.* Silverthorne: Alpenrose Press, 1984. A history of Frisco and Summit County, with profiles of major players, contributors, and characters.

Henderson, Junious, ed. *Colorado: Short Studies of its Past and Present.* New York: AMS Press, 1969. A series of academic essays on Colorado—from prehistoric peoples through the gold rush to 20th-century education. Particularly interesting, if only because the subject is otherwise so scantily written about, is Irene Pettit McKeehan's "Colorado in Literature." McKeehan's piece is a scholarly examination of the state's well-known as well as lesser-known writers and writings—from Whitman and Parkman to obscure poets whose works have only recently been rediscovered.

Lee, Mabel Barbee, foreword by Lowell Thomas. *Cripple Creek Days*. Lincoln: University of Nebraska Press, 1984. Well-written and personal narrative account of Cripple Creek, from first word of gold to the early 1900s, and the author's return in mid-century (her father had been one of Cripple Creek's original miners).

Lister, Florence, and Robert Lister. *Those Who Came Before*. Tucson: University of Arizona Press, 1983. A fascinating study of the Native Americans who lived in and/or passed through the Southwest, including Arizona, Colorado, New Mexico, and Utah. The Anasazi, Mogollon, and Hohokam cultures are examined in depth, as are the later Pueblo peoples. Beautiful color and black-and-white photos.

Marks, Paula Mitchell. *And Die in the West*. New York: William Morrow and Company, Inc., 1989. An exhaustive socio-historical examination of the famous gunfight at the OK Corral. Though not specifically about Colorado (the shootout took place in Tombstone, Arizona), this book will be of interest to any fan of the American West (besides, Doc Holliday, one of the fight's participants, is buried in Glenwood Springs, Colorado). Combining the scholar's eye for detail and passion for accuracy with a lively writing style, Marks debunks many of the fictionalized accounts of the gunfight, putting it into a larger context and looking at the conflicting loyalties that led to the showdown.

Marshall, Muriel. *Red Hole in Time*. College Station, TX: A and M University Press, 1988. A poetic and heartfelt study of the geology and history of the remote Escalante Canyon, a sharp crease in the Uncompahgre Plateau. Treated as a microcosm of the settling of the west itself, the story of Escalante is rich in its people, landscapes, and folklore.

McTighe, James. *Roadside History of Colorado*. Boulder: Johnson Publishing Company, 1984. Route-by-route (milepost-by-milepost!) look at the state's history.

Riley, Glenda. *Women and Indians on the Frontier, 1825-1915*. Albuquerque: University of New Mexico Press, 1985. In a refreshingly unique look at the settling of the West, Riley argues

that women were less likely to prejudge the natives than were men, and that women both greatly contributed to and were significantly liberated by westward expansion.

Rohrbough, Malcolm J. *Aspen: The History of a Silver Mining Town, 1879-1893*. New York: Oxford University Press, 1986. Detailed and scholarly look at the influences of both mining and the railroad, ending with the collapse of the silver market.

Smith, Duane A. *Silver Saga*. Boulder: Pruett Publishing Company, 1974. A close-up, historical examination of the mining town of Caribou, discovered in 1869, with special emphasis on the characters who populated it and the reason "a generation's struggle to plant a lasting settlement failed."

Smith, Duane A. *Rocky Mountain Boom Town: A History of Durango, Colorado*. Boulder: Pruett Publishing Company, 1986. Very thorough and well-written account of Durango's history, with tables, charts, historical photos, etc.

Smith, Phyllis. *A Look at Boulder, From Settlement to City*. Boulder: Pruett Publishing Company, 1981. Meticulously researched and detailed history of Boulder, with excellent historical photos.

Sprague, Marshall. *Money Mountain*. New York: Ballantine Books, 1971. A detailed and highly readable history of Cripple Creek, from the discovery of gold to the early days of reconstruction.

Ubbelohde, Carl, Maxine Benson, and Duane A. Smith. *A Colorado History*. Boulder: Pruett Publishing Company, 1972 (third edition). A nicely readable narrative of the state, from the first cliff dwellers through 20th-century economic challenges. Particularly interesting and well written is the section on frontier Colorado and the Pikes Peak gold rush.

DESCRIPTION AND TRAVEL

Abbey, Edward. *Desert Solitaire: A Season in the Wilderness*. New York: Ballantine Books (through arrangement with McGraw-Hill Book

Co.), 1968. Abbey's notes and observations as a May-to-September Park Service ranger, spent in virtual solitude in the Southwest desert (actually Arches National Monument in southeastern Utah). Some of the most poetic, emotional, and inspiring writing to come out of the Southwest.

Casewit, Curtis. *Colorado Off the Beaten Path.* Chester, CT: Globe Pequot Press, 1987. A selective guide to Colorado's less-traveled roads and places. A quirky book with lots of oddball tips and information, it's a good companion to other available guides.

Caughey, Bruce, and Dean Winstanley. *The Colorado Guide.* Golden: Fulcrum Press, 1989. An exceptional general guide to Colorado with an emphasis on recreation. Excellent discussions and descriptions of backcountry hiking trails and tips on out-of-the-way lodges and restaurants.

Chronic, Halka. *Roadside Geology of Colorado.* Missoula, MT: Mountain Press Publishing Company, 1980. Part of the popular series, this is an immensely informative book detailing Colorado's fascinating geology along the state's major and minor roads and highways.

Eberhart, Perry. *Guide to the Colorado Ghost Towns and Mining Camps.* Denver: Sage Books, 1959. Another difficult-to-find but fascinating and useful book, Perry's guide is fraught with maps, historical photos, and descriptions of the old towns, camps, and characters.

Genres, Eleanor M., Sandra Dallas, Maxine Benson, and Stanley Cuba, eds. *The Colorado Book.* Golden, Colorado: Fulcrum Publishing, 1993. A huge compendium of histories, essays, memoirs, poetry, and odds and ends about Colorado. Contributers range from Walt Whitman and Horace Greeley to John Denver, Stephen King, and Congresswoman Pat Schroeder. An excellent book to "read around" in.

Gregory, Lee. *Colorado Scenic Guide, Northern Region.* Boulder: Johnson Books, 1990. Full of facts, maps, and advice for hikers, jeepers, cross-country skiers, and anyone else who wants to explore Colorado's outdoors. Focuses on areas north of Cañon City, particularly on Colorado Springs and Front Range areas.

Gregory, Lee. *Colorado Scenic Guide, Southern Region.* Boulder: Johnson Books, 1990. Same as above, with most sites concentrated south and west of Cañon City, particularly in the Telluride-Creede-Pagosa Springs areas.

Hillestadt, Charles, and Toni Knapp. *Absolutely Every Bed and Breakfast in Colorado.* Colorado Springs: Rockrimmon Press, Inc., 1991. A just-the-facts-ma'am guide to the state's bed and breakfasts, with locations, prices, and amenities—written by the co-owner (Hillestadt) of Denver's Queen Anne Inn.

Houk, Rose. *A Guide to the Rimrock Drive of Colorado National Monument.* Fruita: Colorado National Monument Association, 1987. Photos, history, anecdotes, and suggestions for tours.

Layton, Marie T. *Colorado Bed and Breakfast Guide.* Boulder: Fulcrum Publishing, 1990. Insider's guide to over 50 bed and breakfasts throughout the state. Detailed descriptions of inns, individual rooms, and specific highlights.

Robbins, Michael, photos by Paul Chesley. *High Country Trails Along the Continental Divide.* Washington, D.C.: National Geographic Society, 1981. Excellent photos and exhilarating narrative/descriptive text discussing Continental Divide Trail from New Mexico to Canada—profiles of people, examinations of history, etc.

Smith, Duane A. *Mesa Verde National Park.* Lawrence: University Press of Kansas, 1988. The story of one of Colorado's most visited tourist attractions. Includes descriptions of the life of the Anasazi, who dwelled in the cliffside palaces from about A.D. 1000 to 1300, as well as a look at contemporary park policies and problems.

Work Projects Administration. *The WPA Guide to 1930s Colorado.* Lawrence: University Press of Kansas, 1987 (originally published in 1941 as *Colorado: A Guide to the Highest State*). Reprint from the classic WPA guidebook series, the book is most useful when discussing the state's history (pre-1940). The original, now long out of print, is a wonderful way to get a sense of what Colorado (and traveling) was like between the world wars. Exceptionally thorough discussions of back roads, as well as sites and incidents of relatively minor historical consequence.

RECREATION

Alley, Jean, and Hartley Alley. *Colorado Cycling Guide.* Boulder: Pruett Publishing Company, 1990. A thorough look at back-road and main-route tours in Colorado. Photos, maps, degrees of difficulty, brief histories of some towns, and listings of campgrounds, motels, and restaurants.

Boddie, Caryn, and Peter Boddie. *A Hiker's Guide to Colorado.* Billings and Helena, MT: Falcon Press, 1984. Seventy-five hikes with descriptions, maps, and advice.

Borneman, Walter R., and Lyndon J. Lampert. *A Climbing Guide to Colorado's Fourteeners.* Boulder: Pruett Publishing Company, 1988. Peak-by-peak discussions of routes, dangers, what to bring. With maps and photos.

Cahill, Rick. *Colorado Hot Springs Guide.* Boulder: Pruett Publishing Company, 1986. Dozens of springs around the state are covered, with maps, photos, history, and technicalities, such as water flow.

Coello, Dennis. *Bicycle Touring Colorado.* Flagstaff, AZ: Northland Publishing Company, 1989. A look at longer rides around the state, full of suggestions and tips. Lots of first-person anecdotes, lively writing.

de Haan, Vici. *Bike Rides of the Colorado Front Range.* Boulder: Pruett Publishing Company, 1989. Nicely detailed discussions of dozens of rides in and out of the Boulder, Golden, Lyon, and Estes Park areas, with maps, photos, difficulty ratings, etc.

de Haan, Vici. *Hiking Trails of the Boulder Mountain Parks and Plains.* Boulder: Pruett Publishing Company, 1989. Excellent descriptions of scores of hikes in the Boulder area, with photos, maps, difficulty ratings, etc.

Fielder, John, and M. John Fayhee. *Along the Colorado Trail.* Englewood, Colorado: West-cliffe Publishing, 1992. A guide to hiking the Colorado Trail.

Kelly, Tim. *Tim Kelly's Colorado Hunting, Fishing, and Outdoor Guide.* Denver: Don Hart Publishing, 1990. Wonderfully detailed maps, photos, charts, and textual discussions of Colorado's streams, lakes, hiking trails, and backcountry. Full of expert advice.

Lund, Morten, Bob Gillen, and Michael Bartlett, eds. *The Ski Book.* New York: Arbor House, 1982. With a foreword by winter Olympic gold medalist Jean-Claude Killy, this is an anthology of some of the best ski writing of the century. Essays and articles from *Skiing, Ski, Powder,* and *Sports Illustrated,* as well as from many fine books on the subject, with pieces by Percy Bysshe Shelley, Robert Frost, Ernest Hemingway, Gay Talese, Thomas Mann, John Updike, Art Buchwald, and other writers who have written over the years for ski magazines.

Martin, Bob. *Hiking the Highest Passes of Colorado.* Boulder: Pruett Publishing Company, 1988. Based on the premise that hiking Colorado's high passes (the author includes 60) is more rewarding than "bagging peaks," this book offers road directions, hiking routes, advice, and suggests other points of interest en route. Includes maps, charts, and photos.

Mays, Buddy. *Guide to Western Wildlife.* San Francisco: Chronicle Books, 1988. Pocket-sized guide to the huge variety of the West's critters.

Muller, Dave. *Colorado Mountain Hikes For Everyone.* Denver: Quality Press, 1987. A very accessible book with over 100 hikes throughout Colorado, with maps, charts, photos, advice, directions, etc.

Ohlrich, Warren. *Aspen/Snowmass Guide to Outdoor Activities.* Aspen: Warren H. Ohlrich, 1994. An exhaustive guide to winter and summer activities in the Aspen area, from hiking and ballooning to telemark skiing and dogsledding. Tons of useful references (guide and equipment shops, etc.).

Ormes, Robert M. *Guide to the Colorado Mountains.* Colorado Springs: 1986. Amazingly detailed climber's guide, with maps, photos, suggested routes and trails.

Pixler, Paul. *Hiking Trails of Southwestern Colorado*. Boulder: Pruett Publishing Company, 1981. Maps, charts, text descriptions, degrees of difficulty, and time allowances for trails in some of the state's finest and most scenic hiking areas.

Schmidt, Jeremy. *Adventuring in the Rockies: The Sierra Club Travel Guide to the Rocky Mountain Regions of the United States and Canada*. San Francisico: Sierra Club Books, 1986. Guide to hiking, camping, and sightseeing in the Rockies, with an emphasis on low-impact exploration.

Stienstra, Tom. *Rocky Mountain Camping*. San Francisco: Foghorn Press, 1989. Campground-by-campground guide to over 1,200 spots in Colorado, Wyoming, and Montana, with number of sites, fees, other activities in the area, etc., as well as whom to contact.

Stoehr, William L. *Bicycling the Back Country: A Mountain Bike Guide to Colorado*. Boulder: Pruett Publishing Company, 1987. Maps, charts, descriptions of a huge range of rides in just about every imaginable corner of the state. A must for the serious off-road rider.

Wheat, Doug. *The Floater's Guide to Colorado*. Billings and Helena, MT: Falcon Press Publishing Company, 1983. An immeasurably detailed and well-written book exhaustively discussing the state's rivers—fit for kayak, canoe, or raft. Wheat is a biologist and geologist who pioneered many of the rivers covered in the book. The *Denver Post* called it "the American Express card for river running. Don't leave home without it."

POLITICS AND GOVERNMENT

Prucha, Francis Paul. *The Great Father: The United States Government and the American Indian*. Lincoln: University of Nebraska Press, 1984. This huge (1,300 pages) two-volume set is one of the definitive reference works on the delicate and often stormy relationship between Native Americans and those who subdued and govern them.

Wright, James Edward. *The Politics of Populism: Dissent in Colorado*. New Haven: Yale University Press, 1974. Tracing the beginnings of Colorado's progressive politics from the gold rush of the late 1850s through the Populist revolution of the latter part of the century, Wright, a history professor at Dartmouth, argues the state's mining origins were largely what led to its strident support of unionism and other movements that defined 20th-century labor and politics.

BIOGRAPHY, AUTOBIOGRAPHY, AND MEMOIR

Conner, Daniel Ellis. *A Confederate in the Colorado Gold Fields*. Norman: University of Oklahoma Press, 1970. Reworked by editors Donald J. Berthong and Odessa Davenport from a manuscript written in the late 1860s, this book tells the story of a gold seeker who during the Civil War sympathizes and becomes involved with a group of Colorado Confederates hiding out near Pueblo. Especially interesting are Conner's descriptions of modes of travel (using a gold pan for a snow sled, for example) and of other Colorado pioneers.

French, Emily, edited by Janet Lecompte. *Emily: The Diary of a Hard-Worked Woman*. Lincoln: University of Nebraska Press, 1987. An extraordinary collection of diary entries of a 47-year-old laundress, cleaning woman, and nurse, who wrote daily of her life on the Colorado plains and in Denver from January 1 to December 31, 1890. "I got up so early, thinking of the one that now seems to fill all my cravings for a companion, will he be all to me," she writes on June 17, and on November 8: "Another day, oh when will I have my time all to rest, will it ever come, I try to be kind, it does no good."

Hamil, Harold. *Colorado Without Mountains: A High Plains Memoir*. Kansas City, MO: The Lowell Press, 1976. A story of growing up in the "other" Colorado, the cattle ranches east of the Rockies, at a time when the West had been won and the way it was being run was changing dramatically. The author, a former AP reporter and journalism professor, tells his story in short, chatty chapters—one particularly intriguing as well as disturbing anecdote is about the appearance of the Ku Klux Klan at Hamil's high school graduation in 1924.

Townshend, Robert T. *A Tenderfoot in Colorado*. Norman: University of Oklahoma Press, 1968 (originally published in 1923). "In 1869 I found myself five thousand miles to the westward of Old England, in a car on the newly opened Union Pacific Railroad, with a good hope of being safely landed by it in the part of the Far West known as Wyoming Territory, U.S.A. I was a tenderfoot, though the title was strange to me; but I was out to learn." Thus begins Townshend's first-person account of his exploration of the central Rockies. Though the prose is rather archaic and some of his observations seem racist ("He was an Indian with brains"), the book does exude a certain charm. And if we can assume that Townshend's rendering of Old-West dialogue is accurate, we get a good idea of how folks spoke in them days.

ENVIRONMENT/ECOLOGY

Clow, Deborah, and Donald Snow, eds. *Northern Lights: A Selection of New Writing from the American West*. New York: Vintage Books, 1994. Widely ranging essays, fiction, poetry, and memoirs on the West and its relation to the individual. Pieces by David Quamman, Gretel Ehrlich, Edward Abbey, Simon J. Ortiz, Doug Peacock, and two stunning pieces by Leslie Ryan. Forward by Louise Erdrich. Highly recommended.

Devall, Bill, and John Sessions. *Deep Ecology: Living as If Nature Mattered*. Salt Lake City: Peregrine Smith Books, 1985. A mind-bogglingly important tome that instructs us in how to live in a world that is falling victim to "progress"—that is, the book asks us literally to reconstruct our thinking about our relationship to Nature and the Earth: "The nature of deep ecology is to keep asking more searching questions about human life, society, and Nature as in the Western philosophical tradition of Socrates. . . . Deep ecology goes beyond the so-called factual level to the level of self and Earth wisdom."

Seed, John, et al. *Thinking Like a Mountain: Toward a Council of All Beings*. Philadelphia and Santa Cruz: New Society Publishers, 1988. An anthology of writings, prose and poetry, most dealing to some degree with the *gaia* concept, of the earth as a spiritual life-force. Includes pieces by Robinson Jeffers, Chief Seattle, Gary Snyder, and others.

ETHNIC COLORADO

de Onis, Jose, ed. *The Hispanic Contribution to the State of Colorado*. Boulder: Westview Press, 1976. A collection of essays looking at the many facets making up Hispanic Colorado, from early Spanish contacts and original Spanish and Mexican land grants to Hispanic folklore and close-up examinations of specific regions—including the San Luis Valley, where the Spanish language is more alive than perhaps anywhere else in the state.

NATIVE AMERICANA

Bruchas, Joseph. *Survival This Way: Interviews With American Indian Poets*. Tucson: University of Arizona Press, 1988. Interviews with Joy Harjo, N. Scott Momaday, Simon Ortíz, and 18 others.

Dodge, Robert K., and Joseph B. McCullough, eds. *Voices from Wah'Kon-Tah*. New York: International Publishers, Inc., 1976. A widely varied collection of Native American poetry, uneven in quality, but always evocative, stirring, and often disturbing. Contributors include such well-known Native American writers as Paula Gunn-Allen, N. Scott Momaday, Simon Ortíz, Marnie Walsh, and James Welch. Excellent introduction by Vine Deloria, Jr.

Eagle/Walking Turtle. *Indian America: A Traveler's Companion*. Santa Fe: John Muir Publications, 1989. A state-by-state guide to many of the country's Native American tribes, reservations, visitor information centers, art forms, museums, and public festivals. Although there's not a whole lot on Colorado, the book suggests the variety and scope of the hundreds of tribes and their involvements.

Marriot, Alice, and Carol K. Rachlin, eds. *American Indian Mythology*. New York: New American Library, 1968. One of the best available collections of Native American myths, including many from Southwestern tribes. Meet Coyote, Spider Woman, the War Twins, and many others, and watch for the huge difference and fascinating parallels between Native American and Judeo-Christian mythology. Introduction alone is worth the price of admission.

Murphy, James E., and Sharon M. Murphy, eds. *Let My People Know.* Norman: University of Oklahoma Press, 1981. Scholarly study of Native American journalism, from confiscated presses of the mid-19th-century to modern journals and newspapers.

Neihardt, John G. *Black Elk Speaks.* New York: Washington Square Press, 1959. Told to Neihardt by the Sioux warrior and medicine man, the story recounts Black Elk's youth on the plains, his Vision, the coming of the white man, and the battle of Wounded Knee. Though not specifically about Colorado, the book offers a unique insight into Native American life in the late 19th century. A painful yet important book.

Olson, James S., and Raymond Wilson. *Native Americans in the 20th Century.* Chicago: University of Illinois Press, 1984. A somewhat academic but highly readable account of the forces working against the 20th-century Native American. The authors look at past government attempts at "helping" the natives, from Compensation to Termination and Relocation, as well as Native American responses—from passive resistance to militancy. Excellent historical and contemporary photographs.

Witt, Shirley Hill, and Stan Steiner, eds. *The Way, An Anthology of Native American Literature.* New York: Alfred A. Knopf, Inc., 1972. Wonderfully eclectic collection of songs, poetry, oratory, mythology, and contemporary journalism by Native Americans. Includes poetry by Simon Ortíz and N. Scott Momaday, oratory by TecumsEh, and Geronimo's surrender speech to General Cook.

ART AND PHOTOGRAPHY

Dallas, Sandra. *Yesterday's Denver.* Miami: E.A. Seemann Publishing Company, 1974. Collection of historical photographs of Denver, from 1859 through WW II. Excellent shots of pioneers, transportation, and architecture, as well as of visiting celebrities, including Billy Sunday, Dwight Eisenhower, and Gary Cooper.

Muench, David, text by David Sumner. *Colorado.* Portland, OR: Graphic Arts Center Publishing Company, 1978. Most readers are familiar with Muench's work—some of the most glorious nature photography of the century—so suffice it to say this is Muench at his best, working one of the most gorgeous spots on the planet. Accompanying text, as always, is as informative, eloquent, and inspiring as the photos.

Shapiro, Michael Edward, and Peter H. Hassrick (with other contributors). *Frederick Remington: The Masterworks.* New York: Harry N. Abrams Press, Inc. 1988. An impressively large study of both the work and the man who helped define western art and gave many Americans their only view of late-19th-century cowboys, soldiers, Indians, and mountain men.

LANGUAGE

Cobos, Ruben. *A Dictionary of New Mexican and Southern Colorado Spanish.* Santa Fe: Museum of New Mexico Press, 1983. Like the remote pockets in rural Appalachia where small, linguistically incestuous groups, isolated from outside influences, still speak an English very much like 17th and 18th century "King's English," some areas of the Southwest are so similarly isolated that the people living there speak a Spanish much like that of 16th and 17th century Spaniards. This fascinating dictionary gives the background of the phenomenon and translates Spanish words unlikely to be encountered outside small rural pockets of New Mexico and southern Colorado.

Smith, Cornelius C. *A Southwestern Vocabulary: The Words They Used.* Glendale, CA: Arthur H. Clark Co., 1984. Over 500 words brought to the southwest by its various settlers and passers-through: Spanish, Anglo, Native American, and U.S. military.

FICTION

Abbey, Edward. *The Monkey Wrench Gang.* New York: Avon Books, 1976. The founding father of modern environmentalism tackles the money-hungry bureaucrats wrecking the Southwest's deserts and rivers.

Hillerman, Tony. *Dance Hall of the Dead; Skinwalker; People of Darkness; The Ghostway; Listening Woman; The Fly on the Wall; The Blessing Way; Thief of Time; Talking God, Coyote Waits.* Most available in Avon paperback. Hillerman's murder mysteries, most of which take place on the Navajo reservation in the Four Corners area, are universally acclaimed for their authenticity and brilliant depictions of the Southwest. Readers trying to unravel the crimes along with Detective Jim Chee and Lieutenant Joe Leaphorn learn intimate and fascinating details about Indian culture.

Michener, James. *Centennial.* New York: Random House, 1974. A typically Michenerian (that is, l-o-n-g) historical novel of the Colorado plains. Follow professor Lewis Vernor to Greeley and the surrounding area as he researches the geology, prehistory, Native American history, and settlement of the region while on assignment for a major magazine. Meet a colorful cast of characters—some real, some invented—as you absorb the story of this fascinating area.

Momaday, N. Scott. *House Made of Dawn.* New York: Perennial Library, 1977. A young Native American attempts to return to the traditions of his pueblo after fighting in WW II. Beautifully written by one of our great American novelists and poets, the story draws on the mythology, vision, and spirit of the Pueblo peoples.

Shuler, Linda Lay. *She Who Remembers.* New York: William Morrow and Company, 1988. (Also available in paperback from New American Library.) Imagine *Clan of the Cave Bear* in a Four Corners setting. A historical bodice-ripper (with a strong heroine who's not above a little loincloth-ripping herself). The story of Kwani and her attraction to the Anasazi stud, Kokopelli. Very well researched, providing good background reading on Mesa Verde and the Anasazi people. Ideal vacation reading.

Silko, Leslie Marmon. *Ceremony.* New York: Viking Press, 1977. Powerful story of the spiritual healing of a Navajo veteran of WW II. Blends Native American mythology and storytelling with conventional fictional devices. A must for anyone interested in southwestern tribes, and especially their literature.

COOKBOOKS

Junior League of Denver. *Creme de Colorado Cookbook.* Three hundred pages of Colorado cooking, from the relatively tame (Creamy Banana Coffee Cake) to wild (Minted Grouse Breasts and Gunnison Trapper Game Pie).

Volunteers of the State Historical Society of Colorado. *Pioneer Potluck: Stories and Recipes of Early Colorado.* Boulder, 1963. Though difficult to find (check libraries and used bookstores), this little loose-bound paperback is a western bouillabaisse of characters, cooks, and recipes of pioneer Colorado. Each contributor is described briefly (oftentimes by a daughter or granddaughter), and then some of his or her specialties are described. Learn how to make pickled peaches, beaver tail, vinegar pie, squatter's soup, posole, Rocky Mountain oysters, and son-of-a-bitch stew ("From a freshly killed beef take the following: liver, heart, brains, sweetbreads, kidneys, and marrow-gut. Wash them carefully, then cut them up into pieces a little bit bigger than the wrapped cubes of sugar you find in a restaurant . . .").

ODDS AND ENDS

Stegner, Wallace. *The American West as Living Space.* Ann Arbor: University of Michigan Press, 1987. Stegner shares his insights and offers intriguing analyses of why folks are drawn to, live in, and love the West.

Godfrey, Peggy. *Write 'em, Cowboy.* Lake City, Colorado: Peter Carlyle Elliott Publishing, 1993. A collection of "cowboy poetry" that captures in light verse the ranchin', wranglin', cowpokin' life on a western ranch.

MAGAZINES

Backpacker. Subtitled "The Magazine of Wilderness Travel," this publication mixes hard-hitting stories on environmental issues with destination pieces spotlighting backcountry areas around the world. The magazine also reviews equipment and runs stories on health and safety in the woods. Excellent photo essays, too. Available at most newsracks. For subscription information, write 33 East Minor Street, Emmaus, PA 18098.

Colorado Woman News. A monthly news magazine focusing on women's issues, with regular departments, feature stories, and a broad editorial slant—ranging from black feminism to health and day care problems to softball coverage. Available in newsstands around the state.

Denver Magazine. Standard metropolitan production, with a variety of well-written and entertaining pieces, from profiles of local artists to looks at successful Denver businesses—also dining guides and suggested trips around Colorado. $2/copy around the state. Subscription information: Box 1673, Inglewood, CO 80150, or phone (303) 322-6400.

Icon. Billing itself the "arts alternative," this little monthly newspaper/magazine is actually being quite modest. With intelligently written art, music, film, and drama reviews, as well as features on the arts in the Denver area, *Icon* is a must for anyone interested at all in any of the various art media. If the reviews and features aren't enough for you, the schedules of events, concerts, gallery openings, and club bookings should convince you. Available free throughout the Denver and Boulder areas. For subscription and other information, write 2548 15th St., Denver, CO 80211, or phone (303) 455-4643.

Powder. A monthly ski magazine for chute-shredders, powderhounds, and cornice-jumpers (including pinheads and snowboarders). Never taking itself too seriously, *Powder* is an excellent blend of intelligent writing, humor, and just the right amount of smugness. Tons of outrageous photos, lots of expert advice. Published seven

times a year. Box 1028, Dana Point, CA 92629; tel. (714) 496-5922.

Rocky Mountain Sports Fitness. Monthly oversized newsprint magazine crammed with information on competitive and noncompetitive sports events of all kinds. Find out where the next 100-mile mountain run is, or when the next five-km walk/jog/wheelchair competition around Lake Dillon is. *Sports Fitness* also profiles local athletes and runs stories on fishing, sailboarding, mountain biking, hiking, kayaking, skiing, triathlons, and just about every other outdoor sport. Distributed free around the mountain area. For information, write 1919 14th St., Boulder, CO 80302, or phone (303) 440-5111.

Ski and Skiing. The two biggest and most widely read ski magazines in the country, both are Times Mirror publications and run many of the same types of pieces—from annual equipment reviews and instructional articles to exotic travel (from Heavenly Valley to the Himalayas), as well as profiles and reader surveys. Watch *Ski* and *Skiing* for pieces by the country's best ski writers, including Peter Shelton, Andrew Slough, Lito Tejada-Flores. *Ski* and *Skiing* are available at newsstands, grocery stores, and ski shops around the U.S.

Snow Country. Upscale guide to year-round resort living and vacationing, aimed at the traveler with the bucks to consider investing in properties he finds to his liking. Very well edited and written, and with a sometimes paradoxical social attitude: It's pro-development yet gives its writers free reign to explore environmentally sensitive issues. Also includes profiles of "snow country" celebrities. Ten issues a year; costs $1.95 at newsstands. Executive and editorial offices are at 5520 Park Ave., Trumbull, CT 06611-0395; tel. (203) 373-7000.

Trail And Timberline. Monthly publication of the venerable Colorado Mountain Club featuring stories on all aspects of Colorado mountaineering, plus pieces on hiking and climbing around the world. Regular departments include "Book Reviews" and "Outings," which lists upcoming hikes and other CMC-sponsored events. For information, write the club at 2530 W. Alameda Ave., Denver, CO 80219, or phone (303) 922-8315.

Vail Magazine. Nicely packaged blend of views on Vail real estate, architecture, and history, as well as photo essays, promotional pieces, ads for galleries, and a monthly calendar. $3.25/copy at bookstores and newsracks throughout the state. Subscription information: Box 368, Vail, CO 81658, or phone (303) 476-6600.

NEWSPAPERS

The Aspen Times. Weekly paper focusing on Aspen's development, real estate, politics, and sports, with a big emphasis on skiing (not surprisingly). Ranges in tone from light-hearted and tongue-in-cheek to stern editorializing. Also includes dining and lodging supplements. Published every Thursday and available throughout the Aspen area at 35 cents a copy. For subscriptions, write Box E, Aspen, CO 81612.

Colorado Daily. University of Colorado (Boulder) paper, emphasizing local and campus news but also with short pieces of national and international interest. Good entertainment listings and reviews, also provocative editorial and oped pages. "Colorado Daily Trail Guide" column examines riding and hiking trails in the area, and offers advice on what to see and do along the way, as well as what to take along for a safe and enjoyable trip. Available free in newsracks throughout Boulder. Phone (303) 443-6272 for subscription information.

Daily Camera. Boulder's daily, with large national and international news and sports sections, and editorials of local and worldwide interest. Good source for what's happenin' in Boulder. Phone (303) 442-1202, or write Box 591, Boulder, CO 80306.

Denver Post. The best paper in Colorado, in fact one of the best in the west. Progressive editorial slant, in-depth reporting (longer stories than those in the *Rocky Mountain News),* excellent columnists. Printed on recycled paper. Pick one up daily while you're visiting the state for local, national, and international news.

Gazette Telegraph. Daily newspaper of Colorado Springs and Pikes Peak area. For subscription, phone (719) 632-5511.

The Parent. This small monthly more than makes up for its lack of size with its excellent articles and listings of interest to Colorado parents, as well as those passing through. Regular features focusing on kids and their folks include the calendar of events, profiles of local teachers and other educators, lists of classes and workshops, as well as a regular Q-and-A column, where readers' questions about their kids are answered. Free throughout the Denver area, though not as easy to find as some publications. For information, write Denver Parent, Inc., 818 E. 19th Ave., Denver, CO 80218, or phone (303) 832-7822.

Rocky Mountain News. Founded on April 23, 1859 by William N. Byers, the *News* is Colorado's oldest paper and with the *Denver Post* one of the two largest. Stories shorter and less developed than the *Post*'s, and the editorial slant a bit more conservative.

Summit Daily News. The refreshingly brazen regional paper of Summit County, with a wide range of stories on international and national politics, as well as the standard local fare: sports, dining guides, real estate. Write 120 3rd Ave., Frisco, CO 80443, or phone (303) 668-3998.

Westword. This is Denver's controversial news and arts weekly, irreverently written by committed journalists whose aim is to "comfort the afflicted and afflict the comfortable." Particularly good—and eagerly awaited by the entire city—is the annual "Best of Denver" edition, which comes out in late June. Here you'll find the editors' recommendations—as well as those of their readers—for everything from best neighborhood bar and best Mexican restaurant to "Best Ethnic Selection in a Megamarket," and "Best Massage for Those Who Are Embarrassed About Their Bodies" to "Best Gay Rodeo." *Westword* is also one of the best sources for entertainment in and around the Denver area—from comedy clubs to jazz concerts to gallery openings. For information, phone (303) 296-7744, or write Box 5970, Denver, CO 80217.

INDEX

Page numbers in **boldface** indicate the primary reference. *Italicized* page numbers indicate information in captions, charts, illustrations, maps, or special topics.

ACKNOWLEDGMENTS

This book is now in its third edition, and a lot of good people have helped me get it this far. I'm indebted to all of you. Any strengths herein are due your assistance; faults, errors, and oversights are my own.

Specifically, thanks to Blake and Kristin; Karl Kumli; Jane and Rich at the Twilight Inn in Frisco; Barb Bowman and Char Shoffner in Grand Junction; Barb Loken in Telluride; Shelly Gill in Aspen; Patti Zink in Durango; Kris Bricker in Colorado Springs; Joan Christensen and Julie Klein in Winter Park; Carolyn Deall in Boulder; Jean Anderson, Kathleen Brown, and Carolyn Livingtstone in Denver; Raili Mood with the Colorado Rockies; Kristin Kopplin at Copper Mountain; Gina Croft in Crested Butte; Cindy Montañez in Pueblo; Stacey Kramer in Steamboat Springs; and Becky Brown at the Ute Mountain Tribal Park. A special thanks to Mike Talcott in Cortez for listening to me and helping put in perspective the most difficult and potentially dangerous experience I've ever had on the road.

I'm also grateful to Rebecca Lintz at the Denver Historical Museum, Kathy Swan of the Denver Public Library, and Anne Marie Vellar of the Colorado Department of Corrections for helping to locate and arrange for permission to publish the wonderful historical photos herein.

To Tom Meinen, Mark Stevens, and Lito Tejada-Flores: Thanks for the special topics you contributed to *Colorado Handbook*—and to Mark, especially, for those afternoons at the Wynkoop Brewery, the evening of music, champagne, and salmon, and the friendship (and road tapes) in otherwise lonely summers on the road.

For help on the third edition, thanks to Matt Orendorff, for your phone calls, mailings, and proofreadings. I am also grateful for the criticism and suggestions from Dave Fishell, who straightened me out on the history of Grand Junction; Robert C. Heyder, former Superintendent of Mesa Verde National Park, who pointed out several errors in my section on the park; to Tom Vaughan of the Anasazi Heritage Center in Cortez; and David D. Roberts, Chief Ranger at Black Canyon of the Gunnison.

Thanks, too, to all the readers of the first and second editions of the book who took the time to point out misteaks, tyops, and omis ions, as well as to the staffs at the chambers of commerce, convention and visitors bureaus, and national park and monument visitors centers that took the time to read the text I sent and to make the appropriate corrections. Thanks, too, to the many friends, old and new, who suggested a backroad, offered a couch to crash on, let me pick their brains over espressos or microbrews, or feigned interest as I passed around photos of my family back in California.

Finally, thanks and love to my family: Betsy, Hannah Rose, and Gina. "Twenty-thousand roads, I went down, down, down, and they all led me straight back home to you."

ABOUT THE AUTHOR

Stephen Metzger lives in Northern California with his wife Betsy, daughters Hannah and Gina, and golden retrievers Murphy and Patrick. He has written for the San Francisco *Chronicle* and *Examiner,* for several national and international skiing, health and fitness, and in-flight magazines, and is the author of *California Downhill* and *New Mexico Handbook* (Moon Publications). He has also published poetry and short fiction in literary journals and is a member of the English Department at California State University, Chico. When not writing, traveling, or teaching, Steve enjoys reading, playing basketball and softball, running, bicycling, gardening, brewing beer, and playing guitar.

MOON TRAVEL HANDBOOKS
THE IDEAL TRAVELING COMPANIONS

Moon Travel Handbooks provide focused, comprehensive coverage of distinct destinations all over the world. Our goal is to give travelers all the background and practical information they'll need for an extraordinary travel experience.

Every Handbook begins with an in-depth essay about the land, the people, their history, art, politics, and social concerns—an entire bookcase of cultural insight and introductory information in one portable volume. We also provide accurate, up-to-date coverage of all the practicalities: language, currency, transportation, accommodations, food, and entertainment. And Moon's maps are legendary, covering not only cities and highways, but parks and trails that are often difficult to find in other sources.

Below are highlights of Moon's North America and Hawaii Travel Handbook series. Our complete list of Handbooks covering North America and Hawaii, Mexico, Central America and the Caribbean, and Asia and the Pacific, are listed on the order form on the accompanying pages. To purchase Moon Travel Handbooks, please check your local bookstore or order by phone: (800) 345-5473 Monday-Friday 8 a.m.-5 p.m. PST.

MOON OVER NORTH AMERICA
THE NORTH AMERICA AND HAWAII TRAVEL HANDBOOK SERIES

> "Moon's greatest achievements may be the individual state books
> they offer. . . . Moon not only digs up little-discovered attractions,
> but also offers thumbnail sketches of the culture and state politics
> of regions that rarely make national headlines."
> —*The Millennium Whole Earth Catalog*

ALASKA-YUKON HANDBOOK
by Deke Castleman and Don Pitcher, 460 pages, **$14.95**
"Exceptionally rich in local culture, history, and reviews of natural attractions. . . . One of the most extensive pocket references. . . . An essential guide!" — *The Midwest Book Review*

ALBERTA AND THE NORTHWEST TERRITORIES
by Nadina Purdon and Andrew Hempstead, 466 pages, **$17.95**
"Alberta and the Northwest Territories Handbook provides strong coverage of one of the most rugged territories in Canada."
— *The Bookwatch*

ALASKA~YUKON HANDBOOK

DEKE CASTLEMAN & DON PITCHER

ARIZONA TRAVELER'S HANDBOOK
by Bill Weir and Robert Blake, 445 pages, **$16.95**
"This is the best book ever published with practical travel
information about the state." —*Arizona Republic*

ATLANTIC CANADA HANDBOOK
by Nan Drosdick and Mark Morris, 436 pages, **$17.95**
Like a corner of Europe, Canada's eastern seacoast provinces
boast Irish brogue, Scottish kilts, Highland flings, and a rich
heritage of British influence. *Atlantic Canada Handbook* provides extensive coverage of this region, including New
Brunswick, Nova Scotia, Newfoundland, and Prince Edward
Island. While there are many guides to Canada, none offers
the detailed regional coverage of this comprehensive handbook.

BIG ISLAND OF HAWAII HANDBOOK
by J.D. Bisignani, 347 pages, **$13.95**
"The best general guidebooks available" —*Hawaii Magazine*

BRITISH COLUMBIA HANDBOOK
by Jane King, 375 pages, **$15.95**
"Deftly balances the conventional and the unconventional, for both
city lovers and nature lovers."
—*Reference and Research Book News*

COLORADO HANDBOOK
by Stephen Metzger, 447 pages, **$18.95**
"Hotel rooms in the Aspen area, in the height of winter sports
season, for $20-$30? . . . who but a relentless researcher from
Moon could find it?" —*The New York Daily News*

GEORGIA HANDBOOK by Kap Stann, 350 pages, **$17.95**
". . . everything you need to know to enjoy a journey through
Georgia." —*Southern Book Trade*

HAWAII HANDBOOK by J.D. Bisignani, 1004 pages, **$19.95**
Winner: Grand Excellence and Best Guidebook Awards,
Hawaii Visitors' Bureau
"No one since Michener has told us so much about our 50th
state." —*Playboy*

HONOLULU-WAIKIKI HANDBOOK by J.D. Bisignani,
365 pages, **$14.95**
"The best general guidebooks available." —*Hawaii Magazine*

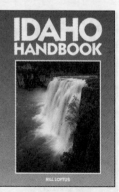

IDAHO HANDBOOK by Bill Loftus, 282 pages, **$14.95**
"Well-organized, engagingly written, tightly edited, and chock-full
of interesting facts about localities, backcountry destinations,
traveler accommodations, and cultural and natural history."
—*Sierra Magazine*

KAUAI HANDBOOK by J.D. Bisignani, 274 pages, **$13.95**
"This slender guide is tightly crammed. . . . The information
provided is staggering." —*Hawaii Magazine*

MAUI HANDBOOK by J.D. Bisignani, 393 pages, **$14.95**
Winner: Best Guidebook Award, Hawaii Visitors' Bureau
"*Maui Handbook* should be in every couple's suitcase. It
intelligently discusses Maui's history and culture, and you can
trust the author's recommendations for best beaches, restaurants,
and excursions." —*Bride's Magazine*

MONTANA HANDBOOK
by W.C. McRae and Judy Jewell, 450 pages, **$17.95**
"Well-organized, engagingly written, tightly edited, and chock-full
of interesting facts about localities, backcountry destinations,
traveler accommodations, and cultural and natural history."
—*Sierra Magazine*

NEVADA HANDBOOK by Deke Castleman, 473 pages, **$16.95**
"Veteran travel writer Deke Castleman says he covered more
than 10,000 miles in his research for this book and it shows."
—*Nevada Magazine*

NEW MEXICO HANDBOOK
by Stephen Metzger, 322 pages, **$14.95**
"The best current guide and travel book to all of New Mexico"
—New Mexico Book League

NORTHERN CALIFORNIA HANDBOOK
by Kim Weir, 779 pages, **$19.95**
"That rarest of travel books—both a practical guide to the region
and a map of its soul." —*San Francisco Chronicle*

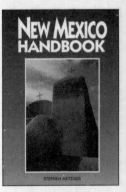

OREGON HANDBOOK by Stuart Warren and
Ted Long Ishikawa, 520 pages, **$16.95**
". . . perhaps the most definitive tourist guide to the state ever
published." —*The Oregonian*

ROAD TRIP USA by Jamie Jensen, 800 pages, **$22.50**
Road Trip USA is a comprehensive travel guide to the "blue
highways" that crisscross America between and beyond the
interstates. This guide provides 11 cross-country, non-interstate
routes, many of which intersect, allowing travelers to create their
own driving adventure.

TEXAS HANDBOOK by Joe Cummings, 598 pages, **$17.95**
"Reveals a Texas with a diversity of people and culture that is as breathtaking as
that of the land itself." —*Planet Newspaper,* Australia

"I've read a bunch of Texas guidebooks, and this is the best one." —Joe Bob Briggs

UTAH HANDBOOK by Bill Weir and Robert Blake, 458 pages, **$16.95**
"What Moon Publications has given us—at long last—is a one-volume, easy to
digest, up-to-date, practical, factual guide to all things Utahan. . . . This is the best
handbook of its kind I've yet encountered." —*The Salt Lake Tribune*

WASHINGTON HANDBOOK by Don Pitcher, 630 pages, **$18.95**
"Departs from the general guidebook format by offering information on how to cope
with the rainy days and where to take the children. . . . This is a great little book,
informational, fun to read, and a good one to keep." —*Travel Publishing News*

WYOMING HANDBOOK by Don Pitcher, 495 pages, **$14.95**
"Wanna know the real dirt on Calamity Jane, white Indians, and the tacky Cheyenne
gunslingers? All here. And all fun." —*The New York Daily News*

MOONBELT

A new concept in moneybelts. Made of heavy-duty Cordura nylon, the Moonbelt offers maximum protection for your money and important papers. This pouch, designed for all-weather comfort, slips under your shirt or waistband, rendering it virtually undetectable and inaccessible to pickpockets. It features a one-inch high-test quick-release buckle so there's no more fumbling around for the strap or repeated adjustments. This handy plastic buckle opens and closes with a touch, but won't come undone until you want it to. Moonbelts accommodate traveler's checks, passports, cash, photos, etc. Size 5 x 9 inches. Available in black only. **$8.95**

Visit Moon Online

In 1994, Moon Publications created a World Wide Web (WWW) travel information center featuring current and back issues of Moon's quarterly newsletter, *Travel Matters,* and an extended excerpt from Moon's *Staying Healthy in Asia, Africa, and Latin America.* Special features of Moon's Web site include: a sophisticated multimedia adaptation of Moon's *Big Island of Hawaii Handbook,* by J.D. Bisignani, with point-and-click imagemaps and dozens of pictures, sound files, and hypertext links. Also included on the site is *Road Trip USA,* a travel guide to the "blue highways" that crisscross America between and beyond the interstates. The *Road Trip* exhibit includes a map with hundreds of original entries and links to local Internet sites. WWW explorers are encouraged to participate in the exhibit by contributing their own travel tips on small towns, roadside attractions, regional foods, and interesting places to stay. The center is located at:

http://www.moon.com

Travel Matters

Travel Matters is Moon Publications' free quarterly newsletter, loaded with specially commissioned travel articles and essays that get at the heart of the travel experience. Every issue includes:

Feature Stories covering a wide array of travel and cultural topics about destinations on and off the beaten path. Past feature stories in *Travel Matters* include Mexican professional wrestling, traveling to the Moon, and why Germans get six weeks off and Americans don't.

Transportation tips covering all forms of transportation by land, sea, and air. Transportation topics covered recently have included driving through Baja California, new Eurail passes, trekking in Tibet, and biking through Asia.

Health Matters, by Dirk Schroeder, author of *Staying Healthy in Asia, Africa, and Latin America,* focusing on the most recent medical findings that affect travelers. Learn about hepatitis A and B, critical travel supplies, and how to avoid common ailments.

Book and Multimedia Reviews providing informed assessments of the latest travel titles, series, and support materials. Recent reviews include The Rough Guide to *World Music, Passage to Vietnam* CD-ROM, and *I Should Have Stayed Home: The Worst Trips of Great Writers.*

The Internet page, which provides updates on Moon's WWW site, online discussions, and other travel resources available in cyberspace. A wide range of topics have been covered in this column including how to go online without going crazy, the Great Burma Debate, and details on Moon's *Road Trip USA* project.

Fellow Traveler, a reader question and answer column for travelers written by an international travel agent and world traveler.

To receive a free subscription to *Travel Matters,* call (800) 345-5473, e-mail us at travel@moon.com, or write to us at:

Moon Publications

P.O. Box 3040

Chico, CA 95927-3040

Please note: subscribers who live outside of the United States will be charged $7.00 per year for shipping and handling.

MOON TRAVEL HANDBOOKS

NORTH AMERICA AND HAWAII

Alaska-Yukon Handbook (0161). $14.95
Alberta and the Northwest Territories Handbook (0676) . . . $17.95
Arizona Traveler's Handbook (0536) $16.95
Atlantic Canada Handbook (0072) $17.95
Big Island of Hawaii Handbook (0064) $13.95
British Columbia Handbook (0145). $15.95
Colorado Handbook (0447). $18.95
Georgia Handbook (0390) $17.95
Hawaii Handbook (0005) $19.95
Honolulu-Waikiki Handbook (0587). $14.95
Idaho Handbook (0617). $14.95
Kauai Handbook (0013). $13.95
Maui Handbook (0579) $14.95
*Montana Handbook (0498) $17.95
Nevada Handbook (0641). $16.95
New Mexico Handbook (0153) $14.95
Northern California Handbook (3840) $19.95
Oregon Handbook (0102). $16.95
*Road Trip USA (0366) $22.50
Texas Handbook (0633). $17.95
Utah Handbook (0684) $16.95
*Washington Handbook (0455) $18.95
Wyoming Handbook (3980) $14.95

ASIA AND THE PACIFIC

Bali Handbook (3379) $12.95
Bangkok Handbook (0595). $13.95
Fiji Islands Handbook (0382). $13.95
Hong Kong Handbook (0560) $15.95
Indonesia Handbook (0625) $25.00
Japan Handbook (3700). $22.50
Micronesia Handbook (3808) $11.95
*Nepal Handbook (0412) $18.95
*New Zealand Handbook (0331) $19.95
*Outback Australia Handbook (0471). $18.95
*Pakistan Handbook (0692) $19.95
Philippines Handbook (0048) $17.95

Southeast Asia Handbook (0021) $21.95
South Korea Handbook (3204) $14.95
*South Pacific Handbook (0404) $22.95
Tahiti-Polynesia Handbook (0374) $13.95
Thailand Handbook (0420) $19.95
Tibet Handbook (3905) $30.00
*Vietnam, Cambodia & Laos Handbook (0293) $18.95

MEXICO

Baja Handbook (0528) $15.95
Cabo Handbook (0285) $14.95
Cancún Handbook (0501) $13.95
Central Mexico Handbook (0234) $15.95
*Mexico Handbook (0315) $21.95
Northern Mexico Handbook (0226) $16.95
Pacific Mexico Handbook (0323) $16.95
Puerto Vallarta Handbook (0250) $14.95
Yucatán Peninsula Handbook (0242) $15.95

CENTRAL AMERICA AND THE CARIBBEAN

Belize Handbook (0307) $15.95
Caribbean Handbook (0277) $16.95
Costa Rica Handbook (0358) $18.95
Jamaica Handbook (0129) $14.95

INTERNATIONAL

Egypt Handbook (3891) $18.95
Moon Handbook (0668) $10.00
Moscow-St. Petersburg Handbook (3913) $13.95
Staying Healthy in Asia, Africa, and Latin America (0269) . . $11.95

* New title or edition, please call for availability

PERIPLUS TRAVEL MAPS

All maps $7.95 each

Bali	Cambodia	Penang
Bandung/W. Java	Hong Kong	Phuket/S. Thailand
Bangkok/C. Thailand	Java	Singapore
Batam/Bintan	Ko Samui/S. Thailand	Vietnam

WHERE TO BUY MOON TRAVEL HANDBOOKS

BOOKSTORES AND LIBRARIES: Moon Travel Handbooks are sold worldwide. Please write to our sales manager for a list of wholesalers and distributors in your area.

TRAVELERS: We would like to have Moon Travel Handbooks available throughout the world. Please ask your bookstore to write or call us for ordering information. If your bookstore will not order our guides for you, please contact us for a free title listing.

> Moon Publications, Inc.
> P.O. Box 3040
> Chico, CA 95927-3040 U.S.A.
> Tel: (800) 345-5473
> Fax: (916) 345-6751
> E-mail: travel@moon.com

IMPORTANT ORDERING INFORMATION

PRICES: All prices are subject to change. We always ship the most current edition. We will let you know if there is a price increase on the book you order.

SHIPPING AND HANDLING OPTIONS: Domestic UPS or USPS first class (allow 10 working days for delivery): $3.50 for the first item, 50 cents for each additional item.

EXCEPTIONS:

Tibet Handbook, Indonesia Handbook, and *Mexico Handbook* shipping $4.50; $1.00 for each additional *Tibet Handbook, Indonesia Handbook,* or *Mexico Handbook.*

Moonbelt shipping is $1.50 for one, 50 cents for each additional belt.

Add $2.00 for same-day handling.

UPS 2nd Day Air or Printed Airmail requires a special quote.

International Surface Bookrate 8-12 weeks delivery: $3.00 for the first item, $1.00 for each additional item. Note: Moon Publications cannot guarantee international surface bookrate shipping. Moon recommends sending international orders via air mail, which requires a special quote.

FOREIGN ORDERS: Orders that originate outside the U.S.A. must be paid for with either an international money order or a check in U.S. currency drawn on a major U.S. bank based in the U.S.A.

TELEPHONE ORDERS: We accept Visa or MasterCard payments. Minimum order is US$15.00. Call in your order: (800) 345-5473, 8 a.m.-5 p.m. Pacific Standard Time.

ORDER FORM

Be sure to call (800) 345-5473 for current prices and editions or for the name of the bookstore nearest you that carries Moon Travel Handbooks • 8 a.m.–5 p.m. PST.
(See important ordering information on preceding page.)

Name: _____Date: _____

Street: _____

City: _____Daytime Phone: _____

State or Country: _____Zip Code: _____

QUANTITY	TITLE	PRICE

Taxable Total _____

Sales Tax (7.25%) for California Residents _____

Shipping & Handling _____

TOTAL _____

Ship: ☐ UPS (no P.O. Boxes) ☐ 1st class ☐ International surface mail

Ship to: ☐ address above ☐ other _____

Make checks payable to: **MOON PUBLICATIONS, INC.** P.O. Box 3040, Chico, CA 95927-3040 U.S.A. We accept Visa and MasterCard. **To Order**: Call in your Visa or MasterCard number, or send a written order with your Visa or MasterCard number and expiration date clearly written.

Card Number: ☐ **Visa** ☐ **MasterCard**

☐ ☐ ☐ ☐ ☐ ☐ ☐ ☐ ☐ ☐ ☐ ☐ ☐ ☐ ☐ ☐

Exact Name on Card: _____

Expiration date: _____

Signature: _____

THE METRIC SYSTEM

1 inch = 2.54 centimeters (cm)
1 foot = .304 meters (m)
1 mile = 1.6093 kilometers (km)
1 km = .6124 miles
1 fathom = 1.8288 m
1 chain = 20.1168 m
1 furlong = 201.168 m
1 acre = .4047 hectares
1 sq km = 100 hectares
1 sq mile = 2.59 square km
1 ounce = 28.35 grams
1 pound = .4536 kilograms
1 short ton = .90718 metric ton
1 short ton = 2000 pounds
1 long ton = 1.016 metric tons
1 long ton = 2240 pounds
1 metric ton = 1000 kilograms
1 quart = .94635 liters
1 US gallon = 3.7854 liters
1 Imperial gallon = 4.5459 liters
1 nautical mile = 1.852 km

To compute celsius temperatures, subtract 32 from Fahrenheit and divide by 1.8. To go the other way, multiply celsius by 1.8 and add 32.

